P9-CNH-473

DAY-HIKING
California's
NATIONAL PARKS

Exploring Mountains, Deserts,
Volcanos, Islands, & Redwood Forests

ANN MARIE BROWN

Foghorn Press
BOOKS BUILDING COMMUNITY™

1-57354-055-2

9 781573 540551   51895

Library of Congress ISSN Data:
March 1999
Day-Hiking California's National Parks:
Exploring Mountains, Deserts, Volcanos, Islands, & Redwood Forests
1st Edition
ISSN: 1523-8830

CREDITS

Managing Editor	*Kyle Morgan*
Editors	*Sherry McInroy, Lisa Burke*
Production Assistant	*Monte Morgan*
Maps	*Kirk McInroy*
Photos	*Ann Marie Brown*
Cover Photo	*Cathedral Lakes, Yosemite*

Printed in the United States of America

DAY-HIKING
California's
NATIONAL PARKS

Exploring Mountains, Deserts, Volcanos, Islands, & Redwood Forests

ANN MARIE BROWN

Foghorn
Press
BOOKS BUILDING COMMUNITY™

CONTENTS

DAY-HIKING CALIFORNIA'S NATIONAL PARKS

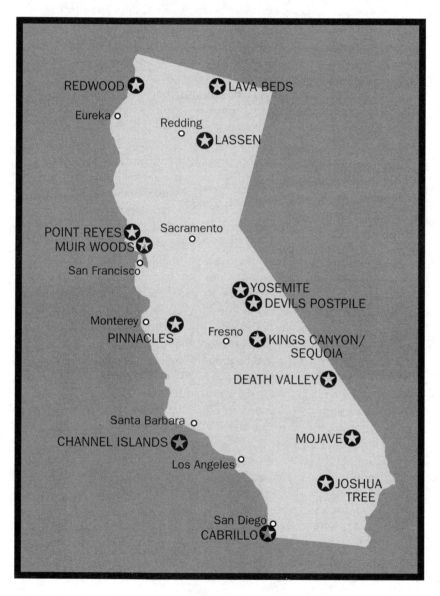

Maps of each park are located at the front of each chapter

INTRODUCTION

A wise person once said that a culture can be measured by the resources it chooses to preserve. It's a credit to our culture that we have the National Park system and our 54 American national parks, plus 322 other park units including national monuments, preserves, recreation areas, seashores, lakeshores, and so on.

Of all the 50 states, California in particular is blessed with an abundance of national parks. California boasts 15 federally designated parks, monuments, preserves, and seashores—more than any other state in the country except Arizona—plus three national recreation areas, four national historic sites, and one national historical park.

The great variation in California's landscape has provided us with three national parks in the desert (Death Valley, Mojave, and Joshua Tree), four national parks in the Sierra Nevada Mountains (Yosemite, Kings Canyon, Sequoia, and Devils Postpile), and three national parks that were formed by volcanoes (Lassen, Lava Beds, and Pinnacles).

In addition, California has three national parks situated on its spectacular coastline (Redwood, Point Reyes, and Cabrillo), and one that encompasses five islands in the Pacific Ocean (Channel Islands). Plus we have parks that celebrate and protect the world's tallest living things, the towering coast redwoods (Muir Woods and Redwood); and those that honor the world's largest living things by volume, the giant Sequoias (Yosemite and Sequoia). One of our national parks has the highest peak in the contiguous United States—Mount Whitney in Kings Canyon at 14,495 feet. Another has the lowest point in the western hemisphere—Badwater in Death Valley at 282 feet below sea level. Quite simply, we live in a land of superlatives.

These parks are some of my favorite places on earth. With this book, I hope to share some of the best trails in California's 15 national parks, monuments, preserves, and seashores, because I believe that everyone should go to these places and witness their wonders. But this wish comes with a caveat attached: We must tread lightly and gently on our parks, with great respect and care for the land. And we should do whatever is required to ensure the protection of these beautiful lands for future generations.

I wish you many inspiring days on the trail....

Ann Marie Brown

HOW TO USE THIS BOOK

This book is divided into 14 chapters, each covering one of California's national parks, preserves, monuments, or seashores. Use the table of contents or index to find the park you want to read about. The first pages of each chapter include basic information on each park, including where to stay, when to go, weather conditions, driving directions, and how to get more information. Following these pages are the trail listings for each park. Use the park map at the front of each chapter to determine the location of the trails.

Each trail listing includes the following information:

DISTANCE—Distance is provided in round-trip mileage. Also listed under "distance" is an estimation of time required for hiking. Note that this is trail time only; it does not account for time spent driving to the trailhead or lingering at a destination. I've given a fairly conservative estimate of hiking time, assuming that you will stop for photographs, snacks, and rests, and not just proceed on a forced march.

LEVEL—The following difficulty designations are assigned to each trail: easy, easy/moderate, moderate, strenuous, and very strenuous. The designation takes into account the steepness of the trail, the condition of the trail surface, and the total length of the trail. In the terms of this book, families with small children will find all "easy" and some "easy/moderate" trails suitable. Most adults and older children can manage "moderate" trails. Only fit hikers should attempt trails rated as "strenuous," and only extremely fit hikers should attempt trails rated as "very strenuous."

Keep in mind that variables such as hot weather can make a big difference in the difficulty of a trail. If you hike on a sunny slope at midday, it feels much harder than it would on a cloudy early morning. Strong winds or a rough trail surface can also make a trail more difficult than expected.

ELEVATION—Trailhead elevation is noted for each trail in the book, so you can see at a glance whether you'll be hiking near sea level or high in the mountains. "Total change" is also listed. This is the approximate elevation change for the entire round-trip trail. On many out-and-back trails, all the elevation is gained in one direction and lost in the other. But some trails have an undulating pattern: they may climb 500 feet, lose 200 feet, then climb 300 feet to reach their destination. The pattern gets reversed on the return trip. Under "total change," I have listed the amount of total climbing involved, whether it's on the way in, on the way out, or as you circle around a loop. For example, a trail that climbs 500 feet, loses 200 feet, then climbs 300 feet to reach its destination would have "total change" listed as 1,000 feet—800 feet on the way in, and 200 feet on the way out.

CROWDS—The following crowd ratings are assigned to each trail: minimal, moderate, or heavy. This denotes typical usage on an average day during the park's main season. You should use this rating as an indication of whether you need to time your trip carefully to avoid the crowds. For instance, the crowds on the trail to Upper Yosemite Fall are rated as "heavy," but if you hike it at 7 A.M. on a Tuesday in April, you'll miss a lot of the foot traffic. On that particular morning, the crowds might be only "moderate."

Note that the ratings are specific to each park. "Heavy" crowds in Lassen or Death Valley are not the same thing as "heavy" crowds in Yosemite.

BEST SEASON—For mountain parks, like Lassen, Sequoia, Kings Canyon, and Yosemite, I have listed the months in which the trails (and roads to the trailheads) are most likely to be open. Note that this varies somewhat from year to year depending on snowfall and snowmelt. If you have your heart set on hiking a specific trail, always check with the park before visiting to make sure the trail is accessible.

For parks in the desert, at the coast, or anywhere else where trails and roads are open year-round, I have listed the best months for hiking. Although technically you could hike in Joshua Tree or Death Valley in August, I don't recommend it. Some parks, like Point Reyes, Redwood, and Channel Islands, are excellent for hiking year-round, but specific trails may have features (wildflowers, waterfalls, views, wildlife) that are best seen at certain times of the year. Wherever possible, I have noted these months.

RATING—Trails are rated on a scale of 1 through 5 stars (★). The rating is based on the overall beauty of the area and quality of the experience. The trail ratings are subjective, but I tried to balance out my own opinions with those of other hikers.

DIRECTIONS—Directions to trailheads are given from a main entrance point in the park. In cases where it seemed more useful, I provided directions from the most logical town or city in the area. General directions to each park from major California highways are given in the introduction to each chapter.

WHY DAY-HIKE?

Day-hikers are in on a great secret. They see more and experience more than most park visitors, including many backpackers. During their vacations, they can hike every day from a different trailhead and cover a tremendous amount of territory. They've learned that if they want to get to know a park, they should camp in a campground or stay overnight in a local lodge, then set out every morning and hike all day.

Carrying only a couple pounds of water and some lunch, day-hikers can cover a lot more miles at a much faster rate than fully loaded backpackers. Frequently I've observed the envious glances of heavily burdened backpackers as day-hikers sail by them on uphill switchbacks, carrying only their lightweight day-packs. In a completely unscientific survey on trails all over California, I've seen that day-hikers have more smiles per trail mile than anybody else, and they put in the most miles.

TIPS FOR AVOIDING THE CROWDS

National parks are notorious for crowds. But there's no reason to subject yourself to packed parking lots, uninterrupted lines of people snaking up and down switchbacks, and ostensibly peaceful trail destinations that look like Times Square on New Year's Eve. If you take a few simple steps, you can avoid the crowds almost anywhere, including the most popular national parks like Yosemite:

• First, whenever possible, visit in the off-season. For most parks, that's any time when school is in session. Late September through mid-May are excellent times to travel, except for the week between Christmas and New Years, and Easter week. Beware of periods like the week immediately following Labor Day or the week just before Memorial Day. Lots of people try to beat the crowds by traveling right before or after a holiday, and the result is more crowds.

• Second, whenever possible, time your trip for midweek. Tuesday, Wednesday, and Thursday are the quietest days of the week in the national parks. They're my favorite days to hike.

• Third, get up early. Even Yosemite Valley is often serene until 8 or 9 in the morning. In most parks, if you arrive at the trailhead before 9 A.M., you'll have the first few hours on the trail all to yourself. As an insurance policy, I'm usually at the trailhead around 7:30 A.M.

• Fourth, if you can't get up early, stay out late. When the days are long in summer, you can hike shorter trails from 4 P.M. until 7:30 P.M. You may see other hikers in the first hour or so, but they'll soon disappear. I often drive by crowded trailhead parking lots at 1 P.M., then pass by again at 5 P.M. and see only a few cars.

But note that if you hike in the late afternoon or evening, you should always take a flashlight with you (one per person), just in case it gets dark sooner than you planned.

DAY-HIKING ESSENTIALS

(carry these items without fail on every day hike)

• a good map
• compass
• warm clothing
• food
• water
• boxes of matches in Ziploc bags
• first-aid kit, including supplies for blister repairs
• pocket knife
• small flashlight with fresh batteries
• whistle
• rain gear

DAY-HIKING NON-ESSENTIALS

(but they'll make your trip a whole lot more enjoyable)

• camera, film, extra battery
• sunglasses
• sunscreen and lip balm
• sun hat
• insect repellent
• wildflower and/or bird identification book
• small binoculars
• fishing license and lightweight fishing equipment
• extra pair of socks

REDWOOD NATIONAL PARK

and adjoining state parks

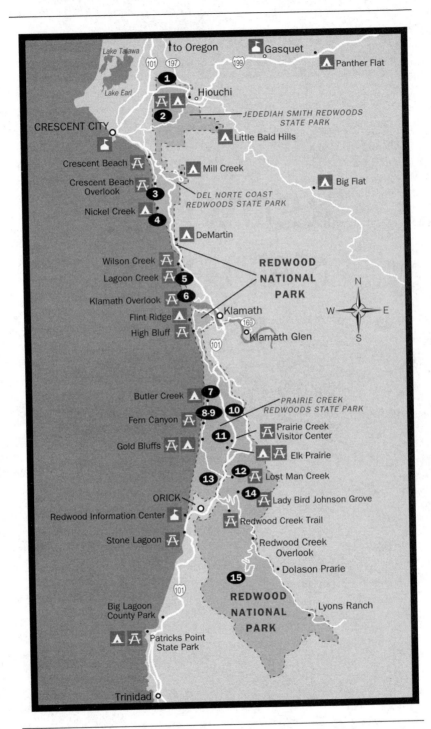

Lake Talawa

↑to Oregon

Gasquet

Lake Earl

Panther Flat

1

Hiouchi

CRESCENT CITY

JEDEDIAH SMITH REDWOODS STATE PARK

2

Little Bald Hills

Crescent Beach

Mill Creek

Big Flat

Crescent Beach Overlook

3

DEL NORTE COAST REDWOODS STATE PARK

Nickel Creek

4

DeMartin

Wilson Creek

REDWOOD NATIONAL PARK

Lagoon Creek

5

N

Klamath Overlook

6

W   E

Flint Ridge

Klamath

S

High Bluff

Klamath Glen

Butler Creek

7

PRAIRIE CREEK REDWOODS STATE PARK

8-9   **10**

Fern Canyon

Prairie Creek Visitor Center

11

Gold Bluffs

Elk Prairie

12   Lost Man Creek

13

14   Lady Bird Johnson Grove

ORICK

Redwood Creek Trail

Redwood Information Center

Redwood Creek Overlook

Stone Lagoon

• Dolason Prarie

15

REDWOOD NATIONAL PARK

Big Lagoon County Park

Lyons Ranch

Patricks Point State Park

Trinidad

REDWOOD NATIONAL PARK
TRAILS AT A GLANCE

Map Number/Trail Name	Page	Mileage	Difficulty
1. Simpson-Reed & Peterson Trails	16	0.7	Easy
2. Boy Scout Tree Trail	17	6.0	Easy/moderate
3. Enderts Beach Trail	19	1.8	Easy
4. Damnation Creek Trail	20	4.4	Moderate
5. Yurok Loop/Coastal Trail	22	2.2	Easy
6. Klamath Overlook to Hidden Beach/Coastal Trail	23	6.0-8.0	Easy/moderate
7. Ossagon Trail	25	4.0	Easy/moderate
8. Coastal Trail/Gold Bluffs Beach	27	6.0	Easy
9. Fern Canyon Loop	30	0.7	Easy
10. Brown Creek, Rhododendron, & South Fork Loop	32	3.6	Easy
11. James Irvine & Miner's Ridge Loop	34	6.0-9.0	Moderate
12. Lost Man Creek Trail	36	3.0	Easy
13. Skunk Cabbage/Coastal Trail	37	6.0	Easy/moderate
14. Lady Bird Johnson Grove	39	1.0	Easy
15. Tall Trees Grove	41	3.0	Easy/moderate

THE TOP 6, DON'T-MISS DAY HIKES:

Map Number/Trail Name	Page	Features
2. Boy Scout Tree Trail	17	redwoods, waterfall
6. Klamath Overlook to Hidden Beach/Coastal Trail	23	wildflowers, beach
8. Coastal Trail/Gold Bluffs Beach	27	elk, waterfalls, beach
9. Fern Canyon Loop	30	ferns, stream
11. James Irvine & Miner's Ridge Loop	34	redwoods, spruce
15. Tall Trees Grove	41	champion redwoods

TRAIL SUGGESTIONS FOR IF YOU ONLY HAVE ONE DAY:

Map Number/Trail Name	Page	Features
1. Simpson-Reed & Peterson Trails	16	redwoods
9. Fern Canyon Loop	30	ferns, stream
14. Lady Bird Johnson Grove	39	redwoods

REDWOOD NATIONAL PARK

ABOUT THE PARK

Redwood National Park and its adjoining state parks are monuments to the coast redwood tree, the world's tallest living thing. The park's magnificent trees are as much as 370 feet high. Redwood National Park also boasts miles of pristine, rocky beaches and a resident herd of Roosevelt elk. The park covers a narrow strip of land that runs 40 miles up the coast and is interspersed with private lands and towns. Three state parks are within the area of Redwood National Park; the national and state parks are cooperatively managed.

ADDRESS, PHONE, & WEBSITE

Redwood National Park Headquarters, 1111 Second Street, Crescent City, CA 95531; (707) 464-6101.
Website: www.nps.gov/redw

VISITOR CENTERS

The Redwood Information Center is located off U.S. 101 near the town of Orick. Park headquarters is located at 1111 Second Street in Crescent City. Both offices offer visitor information and maps. Prairie Creek Redwoods State Park also has an excellent visitor center.

HOW TO GET THERE

• By air: The closest major airports are in Eureka or Crescent City.
• By car: The park is located 40 miles north of Eureka on U.S. 101, and extends 40 miles to the north, all the way to Crescent City. U.S. 101 accesses the entire park. If you are coming from central or eastern California, take Highway 299 from Redding. Highway 299 joins U.S. 101 south of the park.

DRIVE TIME

• Drive time from Los Angeles: approximately 12 hours.
• Drive time from San Francisco: approximately 6 hours.

ENTRANCE FEES

There is no entrance fee at Redwood National Park, although an entrance fee is charged at adjoining state parks. The day-use fee at Jedediah Smith Redwoods State Park, Del Norte Coast Redwoods State Park, and Prairie Creek Redwoods State Park is $5. Payment is good for one day at all three state parks.

WHEN TO GO

Redwood National Park is accessible year-round for hiking. Avoid the crowded summer vacation season if possible. Winter is the least crowded, but it gets the most rain. Spring and fall are good bets.

WEATHER CONDITIONS

Redwood National Park has cool, mild weather most of the year, but receives heavy rainfall between November and April. Fog is common in every season; the sunniest days are usually in spring and fall. Temperatures year-round are generally in the 50s and low 60s during the day, and in the 40s at night. Plan on the weather being cool and damp. The general rule for hiking in the park: Carry rain gear in every season. Wear a warm jacket and bring a variety of clothes for layering.

WHERE TO STAY

Redwood National Park has six hike-in campgrounds requiring a hike of at least a quarter mile. These are Little Bald Hills, Nickel Creek, DeMartin, Flint Ridge, Butler Creek, and Redwood Creek Gravel Bar. Only Redwood Creek requires a permit.

Drive-in camping is available at neighboring state park campgrounds, including Mill Creek Campground at Del Norte Coast Redwoods State Park, Jedediah Smith Campground at Jedediah Smith Redwoods State Park, and Elk Prairie or Gold Bluffs Beach Campground at Prairie Creek Redwoods State Park. Reservations for state park campgrounds can be made by phoning (800) 444-7275.

The only lodging within the park is the Redwood Hostel run by American Youth Hostels (AYH); phone (707) 482-8265 for information. However, the nearby towns of Klamath, Orick, and Crescent City provide many lodging options. Phone the Crescent City Chamber of Commerce at (800) 343-8300 or (707) 464-3174.

FOOD & SUPPLIES

Restaurants and stores can be found in the towns of Eureka, Klamath, Orick, and Crescent City.

SUGGESTED MAPS

Park maps are available at visitor centers or by contacting Redwood National Park at the address on page 14. The Redwood National Park Trail Guide (with a map) is available for a fee from the Redwood Natural History Association at (707) 464-9150. A detailed map is available for a fee from Trails Illustrated at (800) 962-1643.

1. SIMPSON-REED & PETERSON TRAILS

Jedediah Smith Redwoods State Park
A beautiful redwood trail with a nature lesson

DISTANCE: 0.7 mile round-trip; 30 minutes   **LEVEL:** Easy

ELEVATION: Start at 100 feet; total change 20 feet   **CROWDS:** Moderate

BEST SEASON: Year-round; summer is more crowded   **RATING:** ★ ★ ★

DIRECTIONS: From Crescent City, drive three miles north on U.S. 101, then turn east on U.S. 199. Drive just under three miles to mile marker 2.84. The Simpson-Reed Trailhead is on the left. Park in the gravel pullout alongside the road.

OTHER: An interpretive brochure is available at the trailhead.

If you haven't had much exposure to coast redwoods and their ecosystem, hiking in the forests of northwestern California can raise a lot of questions. The Simpson-Reed and Peterson trails can answer them, and provide a half hour of pleasant walking in the process. The Simpson-Reed Trail serves as an excellent introduction to the redwoods; the connecting Peterson Trail extends the trip by making a figure-eight loop.

Get out your notebooks and your number two pencils. Here's the kind of information you'll gather on the Simpson-Reed Trail: California has two species of native redwoods—the coast redwood and the Sierra redwood or Sequoia. Sequoias grow wider and bulkier, but coast redwoods grow taller—as tall as 360 feet. They are the tallest living things on earth. Coast redwoods like fog and rain, and grow best at less than 2,000 feet in elevation. These giants can live for more than 2,000 years.

A redwood forest is often considered to be a monosystem, but in fact many other plants live alongside the big trees, including ferns of all kinds, vine maples, huckleberries, salmonberries, and redwood sorrel. (Sorrel has distinctive, clover-like leaves with purple undersides, and pink flowers.) You'll notice these neighbors of the redwoods as you walk the Simpson-Reed Trail, and learn how to identify them.

Other trees may grow in a redwood forest, including Douglas firs and maples. One of the redwood's most interesting cohabitants can be seen on this trail; it's a special type of tree nicknamed the "octopus tree." These are western hemlocks that have sprouted on the tops of redwood stumps, then grown over and around them, clutching the stumps in their roots or "legs." When the fallen redwood has finally rotted away, the hemlock remains standing on its long, thick roots.

An old-growth forest doesn't support much wildlife, because there is little for animals to eat. But the huge stumps of redwoods make perfect nesting grounds for the spotted owl. I was lucky enough to see one in midday as I drove down the road to this trailhead. You'll also hear the sounds of busy woodpeckers, drilling holes in trees with the precision of miniature jackhammers.

The Simpson-Reed Trail shows visitors how redwood trees reproduce and grow. Unlike other conifers, redwoods can sprout additional trunks as well as reproduce by seed. Often you'll see a circle of baby redwoods, called "cathedral trees," surrounding an old redwood that has been fire-scarred or felled. The sprouts begin as dormant buds that are stored in burls, the large bumpy growths you see near the base of the redwood. The dormant buds, or sprout seeds, are released during forest fires or through the gradual decay of the tree.

As you loop around to the east side of the Simpson-Reed Trail, be sure to take the connecting loop to the Peterson Trail. This quarter-mile path shows off a riparian area with impressive big-leaf maples, skunk cabbage, and many charming footbridges over cascading streams.

2. BOY SCOUT TREE TRAIL

Jedediah Smith Redwoods State Park
An old-growth redwood forest and a waterfall

DISTANCE: 6.0 miles round-trip; 3 hours **LEVEL:** Easy/moderate
ELEVATION: Start at 250 feet; total change 300 feet **CROWDS:** Minimal
BEST SEASON: Year-round; summer is more crowded **RATING:** ★ ★ ★ ★ ★

DIRECTIONS: From U.S. 101 at Crescent City, turn east on Elk Valley Road and drive 1.1 miles to Howland Hill Road on the right. Turn right and drive 3.5 miles to the Boy Scout Tree Trailhead on the left.

The Boy Scout Tree Trail is three continuous miles of old-growth redwood trees, giant sword ferns, and clover-like sorrel, ending with a visit to a pretty waterfall aptly named Fern Falls. If you like the feeling of being surrounded by 300-foot-tall trees with trunks large enough to build a room in, you'll like this trail. On one trip, we passed a hiker who had just completed the trail as we were starting out. He grinned at us and said, "Go back! We're outnumbered by the trees!" In a few footsteps, we knew exactly how he felt. It is downright humbling to walk among these giants.

The trail is in Jedediah Smith Redwoods State Park, one of the

Fern Falls on the Boy Scout Tree Trail

three state parks that is located amid Redwood National Park lands, a part of the rather nebulous political boundary known as Redwood National and State Parks. As is the case in the national park proper, you don't need to pay a day-use fee to hike here. Just drive up, park, and start walking.

The Boy Scout Tree Trail is simple to follow, with no trail junctions to worry about. It's a gentle up-and-down route that never gains or loses much elevation. Despite the minimal grade, hiking on it tends to be slow because there's so much to see, photograph, and remark on. The sword ferns, wood ferns, and sorrel at your feet are as oversized and remarkable as the redwoods that tower overhead. This forest is about as close as you'll come to a true rainforest in California.

Nearing two miles out, the trail comes close to a creek, and the redwoods increase in size. One particular monster-sized tree appears on your right, just inches from the trail. Creekside foliage includes huckleberry, salmonberry, and vine maples. Greenery seems to spring out of every available millimeter of space.

At 2.3 miles, you'll pass an unsigned junction on your right. Take the spur trail a short distance to see the largest tree on this trail—the Boy Scout Tree. It was named by its discoverer, who also founded the local Boy Scout troop. The tree has one huge base that splits into two trunks. It appears so large and commanding that we thought it should be called the Eagle Scout Tree.

In another mile, you'll reach the trail's end at Fern Falls, a pretty 35-foot cascade on a feeder stream into Jordan Creek. The waterfall makes a sharp S-curve down the hillside—it's a twisting rope of refreshing white set amid deep green ferns and redwoods. Admire it for a while, then turn around and follow this same lovely path right back to your car.

3. ENDERTS BEACH TRAIL

Crescent City area, Redwood National Park
A beach for swimming, fishing, or playing in the sand

DISTANCE: 1.8 miles round-trip; 1 hour   **LEVEL:** Easy
ELEVATION: Start at 300 feet; total change 300 feet   **CROWDS:** Moderate
BEST SEASON: Year-round; summer is more crowded   **RATING:** ★ ★ ★

DIRECTIONS: From Crescent City, drive three miles south on U.S. 101 and turn right (south) on Enderts Beach Road. Drive 2.2 miles to the end of road. The trailhead parking lot is just beyond the Crescent Beach Overlook.

The Enderts Beach Trail may be too short to be considered much of a hike, but it leads to a terrific stretch of beach with pristine sand and good tidepooling opportunities. A bonus is that the trail goes right past Nickel Creek Campground, an easy-to-reach backpacking camp that makes a great first-time overnight trip for families or couples.

The trail begins where Enderts Road ends near Crescent Beach Overlook, just a few miles south of Crescent City. It follows an old abandoned road that has partly collapsed into the sea. Just to show you that Mother Nature isn't finished yet, the trail passes by an impressive landslide, just a few yards from the parking area.

Licorice ferns near Enderts Beach

Most of the route is wide enough for hand-holding, and it's just a simple downhill walk of six-tenths of a mile to a three-way trail junction. To the left is a short nature trail along Nickel Creek, straight ahead is the Coastal Trail heading south, and to the right is the path to Nickel Creek Campground and Enderts Beach. Before you make a beeline for the beach, walk the quarter-mile Nickel Creek Nature Trail to your left. In its short stretch it leads to some truly remarkable fern-covered trees. The ferns are the licorice variety, which grow high off the ground on tree branches and trunks. Along Nickel Creek, they hang off tree limbs from every possible angle and look like massive, leafy burls on the trees.

The nature trail ends abruptly at a viewing bench by the creek. Have a seat and remind yourself that you're in the northwest corner of California; this short stretch of trail is like a walk in the Florida Everglades.

After exploring Nickel Creek, return to the junction and follow the opposite trail into Nickel Creek Campground. Check out its five campsites and make a plan for a future overnight trip, then take the right fork that leads uphill above the rest room. In a matter of minutes you reach a grassy bluff above a long, crescent-shaped beach. You can easily descend to the beach, or pick a high perch on the bluffs to survey the scene. Enderts Beach is rocky and driftwood-strewn, but it also has large sandy stretches where you can lay out your towels. We saw two families sprawled out on the sand, complete with beach umbrellas, coolers, and the like. One father and son were earnestly fishing for surf perch and sea trout.

If you like exploring tide pools, check your tide chart before you visit. During low tides, Enderts Beach has some excellent pools at its southern end. At certain times of the year, park rangers lead visitors on guided tidepool walks. Check with the ranger station in Crescent City for information on current dates and times.

4. DAMNATION CREEK TRAIL
Del Norte Coast Redwoods State Park
Old-growth redwoods and a remote, hidden beach

DISTANCE: 4.4 miles round-trip; 2.5 hours   **LEVEL:** Moderate
ELEVATION: Start at 1,100 feet; total change 1,100 feet   **CROWDS:** Minimal
BEST SEASON: Year-round; summer is more crowded   **RATING:** ★ ★ ★ ★

DIRECTIONS: From Crescent City, drive eight miles south on U.S. 101 to the Damnation Creek trailhead at the wide turnout on the west side of the highway by milepost 16.0. (It is four miles south of the Mill Creek Campground turnoff and 3.3 miles north of the Wilson Creek Bridge.)

Many trails in Redwood National Park and its adjoining state parks are level, or nearly so. Not the Damnation Creek Trail. If your heart and lungs are hungering for an aerobic workout, the Damnation Creek Trail will provide it. As part of the bargain, the trail also offers plenty of redwood scenery and a rocky beach overlook. Plus, because of the climbing involved, you'll have fewer companions on this trail than on many in the redwood parks.

The trail starts with a steep, quarter-mile ascent northward to the top of a redwood-lined ridge. Never mind the noise from U.S. 101 behind you; soon you will leave it far behind. Instead, focus on the beauty of the old-growth redwood forest and the ferns and rhododendron that accent the big trees.

When you reach the ridgetop—surprise!—you discover that the trail heads downhill, to the west. The

Redwoods on the Damnation Creek Trail

majority of the work on this trip is on the way home, when you must gain 1,000 feet in elevation. It's easier than it looks because the trail is completely shaded, and the lovely forest gives you many reasons to pause and catch your breath. For now, it's a downhill cruise.

Start descending through the giant redwoods and Douglas firs. In springtime, you'll find a profusion of white fairybells and false lily of the valley bordering the trail. At six-tenths of a mile, you'll cross a stretch of old pavement; this road was once U.S. 101 and is now a part of the 40-mile Coastal Trail. On the far side of it you'll move into tight switchbacks for a more serious descent to the beach.

By 1.5 miles, the redwoods begin to thin out and are replaced by Douglas fir and Sitka spruce trees. Through their branches you'll catch glimpses of the ocean. You'll near the steep canyon of Damnation Creek on your right, then cross two of its tributary streams on sturdy wooden bridges. Just a short distance farther puts you on a blufftop overlooking the ocean and the rocky, hidden cove below.

A right spur trail leads directly to the beach, but the steep, 50-foot descent down the cliffs may be too treacherous to attempt, depending on how muddy it is. You be the judge. (If you want to visit the beach, make sure you time your trip for a low tide, or else there won't be much beach available.) If you choose not to descend, the view from the blufftop offers plenty to satisfy: the mouth of Damnation Creek as it empties into the sea; wild surf crashing against multitudinous offshore sea stacks; and the secluded, rocky cove.

5. YUROK LOOP/COASTAL TRAIL

Klamath area, Redwood National Park
A protected lagoon, Native American history, and Hidden Beach

DISTANCE: 2.2 miles round-trip; 1 hour
ELEVATION: Start at 150 feet; total change 150 feet
BEST SEASON: Year-round; summer is more crowded

LEVEL: Easy
CROWDS: Moderate
RATING: ★ ★ ★

DIRECTIONS: From Klamath, drive north on U.S. 101 for six miles. Turn left at the sign for Lagoon Creek Fishing Access. The trail begins on the west (ocean) side of the parking lot. (Coming from the north, the trailhead is located 14 miles south of Crescent City.)

Everybody likes to walk along the ocean at the end of the day, and watch the waves come in and the sun dip into the water. But few people enjoy facing the gale-force winds that attack the coast on most clear days in Northern California. That's what makes the semi-protected Yurok Loop a great little trail, especially when combined with a one-mile section of the Coastal Trail that leads to spectacular Hidden Beach.

Begin hiking at the northwest end of the Lagoon Creek parking lot. You'll cross a bridge and then head out toward the ocean to the north. The Yurok Loop is an interpretive trail with numbered posts keyed to its brochure, which is usually available from a box at the bridge. If you pick up a brochure, you'll learn about Yurok Indian culture and their many uses of the land in this area. The trail itself is an ancient Yurok pathway leading south along the sea bluffs, which alternates through an oak and alder forest and open, grassy areas. What captures your attention are the views of driftwood-laden False Klamath Cove to the north and massive False Klamath Rock to the west. At 209 feet tall, this huge rocky outcrop dwarfs all the other sea stacks in the area. The Yurok Indians used to dig for the bulbs of brodiaea plants (called "Indian potatoes") by this rock.

Stay to the right when the trail forks at the sign for the Coastal Trail, saving the second part of the Yurok Loop for your return. Ramble along the Coastal Trail, a forested, fern-lined route. In a half mile of

Hidden Beach, accessible from the Yurok Loop/Coastal Trail

mostly level walking, you'll meet up with the spur trail to Hidden Beach. Follow it to the right for 100 yards to reach a classic Northern California stretch of sand, complete with jagged rocks, mighty waves, and driftwood of all shapes and sizes. The beach is prime for sunset-watching. Bring a flashlight in case it gets dark sooner than you expect.

After visiting Hidden Beach, head back the way you came on the Coastal Trail. This time turn right and walk the other side of the Yurok Loop, descending through a tunnel-like canopy of alders.

When you return to the parking lot, be sure to explore around the freshwater pond on Lagoon Creek. It's covered with big yellow pond lilies and happy water birds, including ducks, egrets, and herons. The pond is also popular with trout fishermen.

6. KLAMATH OVERLOOK to HIDDEN BEACH/COASTAL TRAIL

Klamath area, Redwood National Park
Ocean views, spring wildflowers, and Hidden Beach

DISTANCE: 6.0 or 8.0 miles round-trip; 3 or 4 hours   **LEVEL:** Easy/moderate
ELEVATION: Start at 600 feet; total change 600 feet   **CROWDS:** Minimal
BEST SEASON: April to June; good year-round   **RATING:** ★ ★ ★ ★

DIRECTIONS: From the town of Klamath, drive north on U.S. 101 for two miles, then turn left (west) on Requa Road. Drive 2.3 miles to the end of the road at Klamath Overlook. (Requa Road changes names to Patrick J. Murphy Memorial Highway.) Begin hiking on the Coastal Trail heading north.

There are easier ways to access Hidden Beach than starting from the Klamath Overlook. The easiest route of all begins at the Trees of Mystery parking lot; from there, it's only a half-mile hike to Hidden Beach. But shorter doesn't always mean better. In the case of the three-mile-long route from Klamath Overlook to Hidden Beach, the journey is as good as the destination. The six-mile round-trip is an excellent hike filled with wildflowers, ocean views, and a thick alder and spruce forest. Hidden Beach, as beautiful as it is, is only one small part of this trip's splendor.

The route follows a portion of the 40-mile Coastal Trail, beginning at the drive-to overlook just north of where the Klamath River empties into the Pacific Ocean. The overlook parking area is a fine destination by itself, with picnic tables and spectacular coastal views. Consider taking the quarter-mile paved path that leads to a second, lower overlook featuring more views of the mighty Klamath and the tremendous rock outcrop that guards its mouth.

If you like the vistas at the trailhead, start hiking. Take the Coastal Trail north from the parking lot, closely paralleling the coast. The trail

Spring wildflowers along the Coastal Trail near Klamath Overlook

undulates up and down, alternating between grassy bluffs with ocean views and thick forest cover. If you are fortunate enough to visit in springtime, you will be wowed by the variety and profusion of wild-flowers in the sunny, grassy areas of the trail. Nurtured by the ocean fog and mild climate, the flowers explode with color from March to May. Tall, elegant foxgloves bloom in myriad colors. They are accompanied by daisies, bleeding hearts, white and blue irises, cow parsnip, lupine, and many more. This trail has one of the best wildflower displays in the redwood parks.

For 2.9 miles, the trail alternates ocean views and flowery extrava-gance with deep, shaded woods filled with ferns, berries, and vines. Watch for abundant banana slugs in the wooded sections. You will probably hear the sound of sea lions barking, although only rarely can you see down to their rocky shoreline perches.

Where the trail junctions with the Hidden Beach Trail coming in from Trees of Mystery, turn left and descend 100 yards to the beach. This is a spectacular strip of sand and sea, with crashing waves, freezing cold water, brayed tan sand, and a multitude of small crabs crawling over rocks. You can explore the cove, examine the driftwood and wave-smoothed stones, and search for treasures tossed up from the sea.

Hidden Beach is your destination for a six-mile round-trip. If you wish, you can continue another mile north on the Coastal Trail to reach a spectacular vista of False Klamath Cove near the Lagoon Creek Picnic Area. Hikers who can arrange shuttle transportation can hike this trail four miles one-way by scheduling a pickup at Lagoon Creek. (This is the trailhead for the Yurok Loop Trail; see page 22.)

7. OSSAGON TRAIL

Prairie Creek Redwoods State Park
A forested descent to the beach at Ossagon Rocks

DISTANCE: 4.0 miles round-trip; 2 hours   **LEVEL:** Easy/moderate
ELEVATION: Start at 700 feet; total change 700 feet   **CROWDS:** Minimal
BEST SEASON: Year-round; summer is more crowded   **RATING:** ★ ★ ★ ★

DIRECTIONS: From Eureka, drive north on U.S. 101 for 41 miles to Orick. Continue north for approximately five more miles, then take the Newton B. Drury Scenic Parkway exit and turn left. Drive 6.5 miles to the parking pullout near mileage marker 132.7, the Hope Creek Trailhead. Walk north along the highway (use caution!) for about 150 yards to access the Ossagon Trail on the west side of the road. (You can also try to park right at the Ossagon Trailhead, but there is very little room to pull off the road.)

The Ossagon Trail is one of the few "nearly secret" trails of the Redwood National Park area. The only reason the whole world doesn't know about it is because the trailhead is practically invisible, and it has no parking lot. If you can find the trailhead and a place to safely park your car, you're in for a good time on the trail.

I should mention that while the Ossagon Trail is not well known to hikers, it is better known to mountain bikers, who ride this trail as part of a spectacular 19-mile loop through Prairie Creek Redwoods State Park. Hiker and biker conflicts are rare on this trail, but do keep on the lookout for riders, especially on summer weekends. The trail follows an old road and is quite wide in places; there should be plenty of room for all trail users.

Like many of the highway-to-ocean hiking trails in the redwood parks, the Ossagon Trail is an upside-down hike: Downhill on the way in, and uphill on the way back. That means you must save some energy for the 700-foot elevation gain on your return. Just so you know before you go, the elevation change is not neatly spread out; most of it occurs in the space of less than a mile.

The trail's scenery is first-class, beginning in a tree-filled canyon abundant with redwoods, Douglas fir, huckleberry, sorrel, and salal. The trail's first quarter mile climbs, then the path begins its long descent. The redwoods diminish as you hike closer to the coast; they are replaced by Sitka spruce and alders. A great bonus on this trail is that you may see some of Prairie Creek Redwoods State Park's resident herd of Roosevelt elk. Most likely you will notice their tracks along the trail, especially as you near the ocean. (For more information on the elk, see pages 28 and 30.)

The trail keeps a steady downhill course, then levels at one mile out, just before it crosses Ossagon Creek on a footbridge. A brief climb up railroad-tie stairsteps leads to another downhill stretch. Vistas begin to open wide here, as the forest alternates with grassy meadows. Soon the beach is in sight. Just before the trail reaches the mouth of Ossagon Creek, you pass the site of an old homestead on the left.

The steep canyon of Ossagon Creek meets the Pacific Ocean at Ossagon Rocks, a group of large boulders (or small sea stacks) that are almost, but not quite, attached to the shore. The Ossagon Trail leads right down to the creek mouth, where it meets up with the Coastal Trail coming in from the south, across the stream. (While fording Ossagon Creek is usually easy during the summer months, it can be dangerous during the rainy season. Use your judgment.) A lovely alder thicket is situated along the creek.

If the creek level is low, you can ford across and follow the Coastal Trail to the right (north). Shortly, you'll have to ford the creek again. From this second crossing you can leave the trail and head for the beach to get a close-up look at Ossagon Rocks. Travel is a bit tricky; you must negotiate your way through a marshy area and then over low sand dunes and grasses. At low tide, some hikers choose to scale the westernmost of Ossagon Rocks—a worthy endeavor.

Less ambitious hikers will be satisfied with the grassy flat and alder forest at the mouth of Ossagon Creek. Here, protected from the coastal wind, is a fine place for a picnic and a rest before you begin the climb back uphill.

8. COASTAL TRAIL/GOLD BLUFFS BEACH

Prairie Creek Redwoods State Park
Roosevelt elk, waterfalls, and a walk on an oceanside prairie

DISTANCE: 6.0 miles round-trip; 3 hours   **LEVEL:** Easy
ELEVATION: Start at 90 feet; total change 0 feet   **CROWDS:** Minimal
BEST SEASON: Year-round; summer is more crowded   **RATING:** ★ ★ ★ ★ ★

DIRECTIONS: From Eureka, drive north on U.S. 101 for 41 miles to Orick. Continue north for 2.5 more miles to Davison Road, then turn left (west) and drive seven miles to the Fern Canyon Trailhead. No trailers or RVs are permitted on unpaved Davison Road.

OTHER: A $5 state park day-use fee is charged per vehicle at the entrance kiosk on Davison Road. A park map is available at the entrance kiosk.

Imagine a trail that runs parallel to the ocean, framed by coastal bluffs and a mossy spruce forest. Imagine that wildlife abounds, and that the animals are fearless enough to stand still and let you take photographs. Imagine three waterfalls tucked into the forest, one after another as you pass by, like secret treasures you can discover.

Very good. You just imagined the Coastal Trail in Prairie Creek Redwoods State Park, from Fern Canyon to the start of the Ossagon Trail. With its oceanside grasslands, waterfalls, and giant Roosevelt elk, the trail is bound to satisfy even the most discriminating hiker. I rate this as one of the finest coastal hikes in all of California.

Getting there may require some effort. The route to the trailhead is a seven-mile stint on unpaved Davison Road, which may or may not be graded, depending on recent weather. Sometimes the road is full of potholes and mudholes; other times it is as smooth as asphalt.

Sometimes the streams that cross the road are only two inches deep; sometimes they are more substantial. You never can be sure, especially during the winter months.

Along the drive you may spot some of the huge Roosevelt elk that roam this coastal prairie. If you don't see them near the road, you'll probably see them along the trail, munching on grasses to feed their 700- to 1,000-pound bulk. The elk usually travel in herds of a few dozen or so. Usually the males and females are in separate groups, but during the autumn rutting season, you may see them together.

Start your hike from the Fern Canyon parking lot by negotiating the sometimes tricky crossing of Home Creek. The Coastal Trail begins due north of the lot at a signpost on the far side of the creek. In the wet season you may need to make a mighty leap to cross. (You'll probably see other hikers heading east along Home Creek into Fern Canyon; that trip is detailed on page 30.) Beyond the stream crossing, the rest of the trail is incredibly easy, dry, and level.

After a brief stint in the forest, you walk on open grasslands with the ocean to your left and tall vertical bluffs to your right. The sound of the ocean is always with you, but the waves are as much as 150 yards away. You are separated from the coast by a plain of dune grass and wetlands.

At 1.1 miles, start listening for the sound of falling water on your

Roosevelt elk along Davison Road on the way to Gold Bluffs Beach

right, and look for an unmarked spur trail leading into the alder and spruce forest. Follow the short spur and you'll find the trail's first waterfall, a tall, narrow cascade surrounded by prolific ferns. On one visit here, we saw hundreds of three-inch-wide mushrooms growing on a log near the waterfall's base, forming a thick forest of fungus.

Walk a quarter-mile farther on the main trail, listen for the sound of water, seek out another spur trail, and you'll find yourself holding court with Gold Dust Falls. This waterfall is 80 feet high and very narrow. A bench is placed near its base for waterfall-watching, but it's often soaking wet and covered with moss.

Gold Dust is the only waterfall of the three on this trail that is named. Its moniker is a reference to the short-lived 1850s gold rush along Gold Bluffs Beach, when five prospectors discovered gold dust in the sand and staked a claim. Thousands of people came to this beach and set up a tent city, but alas, extracting the gold turned out to be hard work that produced little profit. The boom ended almost as quickly as it began.

The third waterfall is very close to Gold Dust Falls. Another few hundred feet on the Coastal Trail brings you to its spur trail. Like the others, it's a tall, narrow cataract, hidden in the deep shade of forest and ferns. Pay a visit, then continue hiking on the Coastal Trail. You'll soon move inland, away from the oceanside prairie and into a narrow strip of forest. At 2.2 miles, you arrive at the backpacker's camp at Butler Creek. Cross the creek, then hike back into the grasslands again for the last half-mile to Coastal Trail's junction with Ossagon Trail. Pick a spot near Ossagon Creek with the best view of near-shore Ossagon Rocks. The wave-smoothed rocks are a geologic oddity; they're

Gold Dust Falls

similar to offshore sea stacks but they are connected to the beach.

You'll probably want to call it a day here; beyond Ossagon Rocks, the Coastal Trail is often impassable except at low tide. Many people choose to experience the magic of this trail all over again by hiking back the way they came. But another excellent option is to make a 7.2-mile loop by turning east at a trail junction at Butler Creek Campground. The Butler Creek/West Ridge Trail connects to the Friendship Ridge Trail in 1.2 miles. The Friendship Ridge Trail leads 2.5 miles back to the James Irvine Trail, which you follow west to Fern Canyon and the trailhead parking area.

9. FERN CANYON LOOP

Prairie Creek Redwoods State Park
A steep-walled, fern-covered stream canyon

DISTANCE: 0.7 mile round-trip; 30 minutes   **LEVEL:** Easy
ELEVATION: Start at 20 feet; total change 250 feet   **CROWDS:** Heavy
BEST SEASON: Year-round; summer is more crowded   **RATING:** ★ ★ ★ ★

DIRECTIONS: From Eureka, drive north on U.S. 101 for 41 miles to Orick. Continue north for 2.5 more miles to Davison Road, then turn left (west) and drive seven miles to the Fern Canyon Trailhead. No trailers or RVs are permitted on unpaved Davison Road.

OTHER: A $5 state park day-use fee is charged per vehicle at the entrance kiosk on Davison Road. A park map is available at the entrance kiosk.

When you hike the Fern Canyon Loop, the drive to the trailhead is part of the day's adventure. Unpaved Davison Road runs through the middle of the Elk Prairie section of Prairie Creek Redwoods State Park, home to a large herd of Roosevelt elk. You'll have several chances to see these enormous creatures, which have the distinction of being California's largest land animals. Some weigh nearly 1,000 pounds. Large groups of elk will frequently stand just a few feet from Davison Road, grazing on the roadside grasses. For the most part, they ignore park visitors. The elk are extremely docile, although you shouldn't mess with the bulls, especially during mating season.

But the wildlife is not the only excitement on a trip to Fern Canyon. Your destination is a secluded fern grotto—a hidden paradise of giant ferns growing on 50-foot-high rock walls on both sides of a forest stream. After driving the length of Davison Road, park at the Fern Canyon Trailhead, just steps away from beautiful Gold Bluffs Beach.

Hiking amid 50-foot-high canyon walls covered with ferns

Put on your waterproof hiking boots and start walking to your right, heading up the gravel streambed of Home Creek. You may or may not have to do some rockhopping to get across the stream. From late spring through fall, park rangers make the hiking easy by installing small footbridges. In the rainy season, the creek runs with a fury, so the bridges are removed.

Hike up the streambed, observing as the canyon walls grow taller and squeeze tighter. The going may be slow, but you won't mind in the slightest. Dense ferns line the canyon walls like wallpaper. Home Creek gushes near your feet. Miniature waterfalls pour down the rock walls. Moss grows everywhere, and combined with the multitude of ferns, the canyon feels like a rainforest. Green is the color of the day.

Look for the many frogs, salamanders, and newts that make their home in the canyon, including the rare Pacific giant salamander. If you're very lucky, you might spot the coastal cutthroat trout, which travels from the ocean in spring to lay its eggs in the gravel streambed. You can practice your fern identification as you walk. An interpretive sign at the trailhead explains the identifying characteristics of various fern varieties, including sword, lady, five-finger, chain, and bracken ferns—up to eight different species, all waving delicately in the breeze.

Continue up the canyon for a half mile until you reach a signed trail on the left that climbs out of the canyon on wooden stairsteps and loops back through the forest to the parking lot. (This is a short section of the James Irvine Trail.) When you finish out the loop, you have the option of continuing your hike by crossing the access road near the parking area and walking down to pristine, windswept Gold Bluffs Beach, then wandering as far as you please. Another way to extend the trip is to turn right on the James Irvine Trail after you climb out of Fern Canyon. A mile or two out-and-back on this densely forested trail can only be a fine addition to your day. (See the story on page 34 for more details on the James Irvine Trail.)

10. BROWN CREEK, RHODODENDRON, & SOUTH FORK LOOP

Prairie Creek Redwoods State Park
Ancient redwood forests and wildflowers

DISTANCE: 3.6 miles round-trip; 2 hours   **LEVEL:** Easy
ELEVATION: Start at 250 feet; total change 600 feet   **CROWDS:** Moderate
BEST SEASON: Year-round; summer is more crowded   **RATING:** ★ ★ ★ ★

DIRECTIONS: From Eureka, drive north on U.S. 101 for 41 miles to Orick. Continue north for approximately five more miles, then take the Newton B. Drury Scenic Parkway exit and turn left. Drive 2.7 miles to the parking pullout near mileage marker 129. The trail is signed "South Fork Trail."

This loop trail through the redwoods may give you a neck ache. It leads through a colossal old-growth forest in which you will walk with your head raised, neck craned, and eyes gazing toward the sky. You won't be checking for rain or gawking at skyscrapers—just looking at big trees.

The loop is a combination of three trails: Brown Creek, Rhododendron, and South Fork. Start walking from the South Fork trail sign, following the South Fork Trail for two-tenths of a mile. Turn left on the Brown Creek Trail, and prepare your neck for a workout. The path leads through prime redwood forest, complete with virgin groves and lots of old growth. It meanders along a perfectly charming stream, which serves as the lifeblood for the towering trees. You simply follow the creek, crossing it on a footbridge at a half-mile out. Be sure to take one or more of the short spur trails that lead to memorial groves and trees.

The size of the redwoods is truly inspiring. Try as you may, it's impossible to see their tops, which are as much as 300 feet off the ground. Often the trees that make the greatest impression are the fallen giants lying on the ground, toppled by centuries of weather. Their huge root balls look like intricate sculpted knots, and their horizontal trunks serve as natural planters for entire microcosms of ferns, moss, mushrooms, and sorrel. Some of these tree trunks make such perfect garden boxes that you'll wonder if Mother Nature hasn't hired elfin landscape architects to help her do her work.

Big redwoods on the Brown Creek Trail

The Brown Creek Trail junctions with the Rhododendron Trail at 1.3 miles from the start. Turn right to continue the loop. The trail climbs a bit steeply, then curves across the hillside, with views back down into the canyon. True to the trail's name, bright pink rhododendrons are plentiful, adding splashes of vibrant color to the forest's myriad shades of green. The giant redwoods continue, although the forest gets drier and less dense as you climb.

At 2.5 miles, you'll meet up with the South Fork Trail. Turn right and finish out the loop with a switchbacking descent. Look for orange leopard lilies in the spring, growing as tall as five feet. They are mixed in with redwoods, huckleberries, and rhododendrons. As you lose elevation, you'll get a wider perspective on the big trees with views across the wooded slopes. When you reach the Brown Creek Trail again, turn left and follow the South Fork Trail for two-tenths of a mile back to your car. Now, how does your neck feel?

11. JAMES IRVINE & MINER'S RIDGE LOOP

Prairie Creek Redwoods State Park
A world-class redwood & spruce forest

DISTANCE: 6.0 or 9.0 miles round-trip; 3 or 5 hours   **LEVEL:** Moderate
ELEVATION: Start at 100 feet; total change 800 feet   **CROWDS:** Moderate
BEST SEASON: Year-round; summer is more crowded   **RATING:** ★ ★ ★ ★ ★

DIRECTIONS: From Eureka, drive north on U.S. 101 for 41 miles to Orick. Continue north for approximately five more miles, then take the Newton B. Drury Scenic Parkway exit and turn left, following the signs for one mile toward the Visitor Center. Turn left at the sign for Elk Prairie Campground and Visitor Center. The trail begins at the northeast corner of the visitor center parking lot; it is signed as "Nature Trail."

OTHER: A $5 state park day-use fee is charged per vehicle at the entrance kiosk. A park map is available at the entrance kiosk.

The lush foliage is the star of the show on this loop trail in Prairie Creek Redwoods State Park. The nine-mile round-trip features huge redwood trees, Sitka spruce, Douglas fir, hemlocks, alders, ferns, and moss—in more shades and shapes of green than you can possibly imagine. Hikers who don't have time for the full loop can simply hike out-and-back on the James Irvine Trail, going as far as their schedules afford. Even if you only have one hour to spare, a walk on this trail shouldn't be missed.

Begin hiking on the Nature Trail at the park visitor center, crossing the bridge over Prairie Creek. Pass some mammoth redwoods in the first quarter-mile, then turn right on the James Irvine Trail, heading northwest. You'll meet up with several trail junctions at first, but simply stay your course and you'll soon leave the other paths behind. The James Irvine Trail climbs gently, following Godwood Creek amid huge, ancient redwoods. The trail levels out and keeps crossing the stream back and forth on sturdy footbridges. You'll start to notice more and more fallen redwoods, many of which cross the trail. The farther you go, the more primeval the forest looks and feels, as if untouched by humans. This is a dark and dense forest, filled with moss and ferns. The towering trees block most of the sunlight, creating a dreamy, shadowy effect.

At 2.4 miles, you'll reach an intersection with the Clintonia Trail. A left turn here will bring you to Miner's Ridge Trail for the return of this loop; for now, continue straight. (If you wish, you can cut your trip short here and loop back, making a six-mile round-trip.)

The James Irvine Trail
starts to descend, and at
2.8 miles it reaches a bridge
over the start of Home
Creek. Now the trail crosses
and recrosses Home Creek,
heading through amazingly
dense foliage. You'll enter a
lush mixed forest of Sitka
spruce, redwoods, alders,
ferns, and vines, and see
some very large and old
examples of "octopus" trees:
Western hemlocks that have
sprouted on the tops of
redwood stumps, then
grown over and around
them, clutching the stumps
in their roots or "legs."

At 3.6 miles, the trail
crosses a bridge marked
with two small benches,

Redwoods and ferns on the James Irvine Trail

where a 25-foot-tall, delicate waterfall drops into a remarkably narrow
and deep canyon, eventually flowing to Home Creek. A sign denotes
that the bridge and benches are dedicated to John Baldwin, and bears
this lovely verse: "You shall walk where only the wind has walked
before, and when all music is stilled, you shall hear the singing of the
stream, and enter the living shelter of the forest."

Another half mile of travel will bring you to spectacular Fern
Canyon. Follow the Fern Canyon Loop in either direction (see the
story on page 30 for details), then retrace your steps on the James
Irvine Trail back to the junction with Clintonia Trail, 1.6 miles away.
Turn onto Clintonia Trail and climb steeply to Miner's Ridge. In
springtime, you will be compensated for your climb by the sight
of the trail's namesake—blooming pink-red Andrews' clintonia, a
member of the lily family. Take breaks from the steady ascent by
following the short spur trails to memorial groves.

After one mile, you'll meet up with Miner's Ridge Trail and turn
left. Climb steeply again for a quarter mile, then begin a long, mellow
descent, dropping 450 feet over two miles. Take advantage of the
benches placed at random intervals along the trail; each provides a

place to sit and listen to the silence of the forest. The redwoods along Miner's Ridge Trail rival those of the James Irvine Trail; each tree you pass leaves you feeling like the tiny Lilliputians in *Gulliver's Travels.*

Too soon, you meet up with the Nature Trail near the visitor center. Turn left and cross a fork of Godwood Creek to finish the trip.

12. LOST MAN CREEK TRAIL

Orick area, Redwood National Park
Stream, alders, and redwoods

DISTANCE: 3.0 miles round-trip; 1.5 hours   **LEVEL:** Easy
ELEVATION: Start at 100 feet; total change 200 feet   **CROWDS:** Moderate
BEST SEASON: Year-round; summer is more crowded   **RATING:** ★

DIRECTIONS: From Eureka, drive north on U.S. 101 for 41 miles to Orick, then continue north for three more miles to the turnoff for Lost Man Road on the right. Drive nine-tenths of a mile to the end of the paved portion of the road, where the trailhead is located. Begin hiking by walking through the picnic area.

No matter what the weather is like in Redwood National Park, the Lost Man Creek Trail is a fine route to hike. Along its wide path, tall redwoods spread their branches to the sky, moss dangles gently from alder branches, and ferns grow to huge sizes. These sights are the essence of a trip to the redwoods, the reason hikers flock to this park every year to be awed and humbled by the majestic forests.

The first 1.5 miles of the Lost Man Creek Trail are nearly level and closely parallel gurgling (or sometimes surging) Lost Man Creek. The next 2.5 miles leave the stream's edge to make a much steeper climb to Holter Ridge, gaining 1,300 feet in elevation. Those who want an easy and pretty hike through first- and second-growth redwoods can hike 1.5 miles out, then turn around when the trail starts to climb like a son-of-a-gun. (This is a perfect trip for families with small kids.) More serious hikers can tackle the ridge, heading uphill as far as they like.

Hikers who are addicted to single-track trails should be fore-warned: This trail is an old gravel roadbed. It's so wide, you could hike the trail with 10 people shoulder to shoulder. To its credit, the road is covered with fallen leaves and redwood needles, which make it seem more trail-like. It is also covered, to a lesser extent, with bright yellow and green banana slugs, the most charming member of the slug family. Keep your eyes peeled to avoid stepping on them as they slug across the road. (Where are they going? we wondered.)

The first stretch of road follows closely along Lost Man Creek. Two bridge crossings in the first quarter mile of trail offer eye-opening peeks into the beautiful, rock-lined creek canyon. Aside from the clear stream, the big attraction of the hike is the trees. In addition to huge redwoods, you'll find thick stands of alders along the creek, which put on a color show in the fall. In winter, after the alders lose their leaves, heavy moss completely covers every inch of their trunks and branches like a thick fur coat.

13. SKUNK CABBAGE/COASTAL TRAIL

Orick area, Redwood National Park
Spruce and alder forest, skunk cabbage, and a secret beach

DISTANCE: 6.0 miles round-trip; 3 hours   **LEVEL:** Easy/moderate
ELEVATION: Start at 50 feet; total change 500 feet   **CROWDS:** Minimal
BEST SEASON: March to July; good year-round   **RATING:** ★ ★ ★ ★

DIRECTIONS: From Eureka, drive north on U.S. 101 for 41 miles to Orick, then continue north for 1.1 miles. Just past the right turnoff for Bald Hills Road, take the left turnoff that is signed for the Skunk Cabbage Section of the Coastal Trail. Drive a half mile down the road to the parking area and trailhead.

Sometimes it takes a while for the obvious to become apparent. My hiking partner and I were walking on the Skunk Cabbage Trail, marveling at the dense forest and especially the huge, leafy plants that were growing on the ground near every stream or spring. But we kept shaking our heads, puzzled by the plants' identification. Neither one of us had a clue about what the large-leafed foliage could be. It took almost three miles of hiking before the light bulb in my brain turned on. "Hey! I bet these big leafy plants are the trail's namesake—skunk cabbages!"

Indeed they were. The Skunk Cabbage Trail is a section of the Coastal Trail in Redwood National Park. It leads deep into a lush, jungle-like alder and spruce forest—so dense with foliage that you may think you've walked onto the set of *Jurassic Park*. Then, without any advance notice, the trail suddenly opens out to a wide stretch of coast at Gold Bluffs Beach.

The out-and-back trail is three miles each way, but with very little elevation change. The scenery will capture your imagination, particularly from about a half-mile in where the trail closely follows Skunk Cabbage Creek. Here you'll find the largest numbers of skunk cabbages

Among the skunk cabbages

growing near the stream. They are vibrant green and as large as five feet across, with individual leaves growing a foot wide. The plants look something like cabbage heads on steroids, although they are actually a relative of the corn lily.

The skunk cabbages grow in dense clusters under a canopy of alders, Sitka spruce, and occasional big redwoods. The white bark of the alders shines bright white in the dimly lit forest. Where you don't see skunk cabbages, you see massive clumps of sword ferns and redwood sorrel. Your trail weaves among all this foliage, crossing and recrossing Skunk Cabbage Creek on wooden footbridges.

After two delightful miles like this, the trail ceases its mostly level meandering and suddenly starts to climb. Leaving the creek behind, you continue up a ridge through a dense alder forest. (We saw probable bear evidence here in one stand of trees, where the bark on several alders had been torn to shreds as high as eight feet off the ground.)

At 2.7 miles out, you round a curve in the trail, and—surprise— you're high on a bluff overlooking the ocean. It's quite startling to see the dense, terrarium-like forest end so abruptly at a broad expanse of open coastline.

Here, at a trail junction, you must make a choice: right is the continuation of the Coastal Trail that eventually leads to Gold Bluffs Beach, and left is a spur trail that beckons you to the beach directly below. And just a few yards west of this junction is a fine view of the coast, and perhaps a spot to sit and have lunch. Take your pick. If you want to hike farther, left is the best option (and the only choice for a six-mile round-trip). A descent of about 300 feet over a quarter-mile of moderate switchbacks will take you to the dune-like stretch of sand below. Once there, what are you likely to find? Mussel Point, a rocky outcrop, lies about three-quarters of a mile to the south. Other than that, there's plenty of driftwood, sand verbena, and precious solitude.

14. LADY BIRD JOHNSON GROVE

Orick area, Redwood National Park
Interpretive trail in a virgin redwood forest

DISTANCE: 1.0 mile round-trip; 30 minutes   **LEVEL:** Easy
ELEVATION: Start at 1,250 feet; total change 20 feet   **CROWDS:** Moderate
BEST SEASON: Year-round; summer is more crowded   **RATING:** ★ ★ ★

DIRECTIONS: From Eureka, drive north on U.S. 101 for 41 miles to Orick, then continue north for one mile. Turn right on Bald Hills Road and drive 2.7 miles to the trailhead parking area on the right.

OTHER: An interpretive brochure is available at the trailhead.

It was on the Lady Bird Johnson Grove that I first had "The Redwood Experience." In case you've never felt it, it happens something like this: You are wandering among ancient redwood trees that are hundreds of feet tall. Perhaps the fog has moved in, casting eerie filtered shadows in the forest. Your footsteps begin to slow. You find yourself noticing the most minute details, like the dewdrops on the pink petals of a rhododendron, or the bark pattern on one square inch of a 300-foot-tall redwood tree. Your voice drops to a whisper; you walk very softly, almost on tiptoe. The redwood forest has wrapped you in its embrace, and you may never want to leave.

That's "The Redwood Experience." It has happened to many hikers on many trails in Redwood National Park. It's this kind of feeling that makes visitors return to the redwoods, year after year. The Lady Bird Johnson Grove is one of the easiest places to get a taste of it.

From the trailhead parking area, cross the sturdy bridge over Bald Hills Road to access the trail. The 300-acre Lady Bird Johnson Grove was named for President Lyndon Johnson's wife, who dedicated the park in 1969. President Johnson signed the bill that created Redwood National Park in 1968, protecting these trees for generations to come.

The trail through the redwoods is only one mile round-trip, but you may find it takes you a while to hike it. You'll want to stop to read the interpretive signs, which explain about the history of white men in the redwood region. Jedediah Smith first explored this area in 1828, and Josiah Greg took the first recorded measurements of the redwood trees in 1849. Not surprisingly, the logging industry moved in next, although the loggers did not touch this particular grove.

In the understory of the redwoods, you'll see salmonberry, huckleberry, salal, and rhododendron. Sword ferns and sorrel grace the forest floor. If you picked up an interpretive brochure at the trailhead, you'll learn to identify "goose pens" (hollowed out redwood trunks that early settlers used for keeping poultry) and "sprout trees" or "cathedral trees" (redwoods that have sprouted additional trunks instead of reproducing by seed).

On the return half of the loop, you'll see more Douglas fir and western hemlock trees in addition to the coast redwoods. The trail is short and simple, but it's likely to leave you feeling different from when you started.

Lady Bird Johnson Grove

In the words of Lady Bird Johnson: "One of my most unforgettable memories of the past years is walking through the redwoods last November, seeing the lovely shafts of light filtering through the trees so far above, feeling the majesty and silence of that forest, and watching a salmon rise in one of those swift streams. All our problems seemed to fall into perspective and I think every one of us walked out more serene and happier."

15. TALL TREES GROVE

Orick area, Redwood National Park
The tallest trees in the world

DISTANCE: 3.0 miles round-trip; 1.5 hours   **LEVEL:** Easy/moderate
ELEVATION: Start at 650 feet; total change 650 feet   **CROWDS:** Moderate
BEST SEASON: Year-round; summer is more crowded   **RATING:** ★ ★ ★ ★

DIRECTIONS: From Eureka, drive north on U.S. 101 for 40 miles to the Redwood Information Center on the west side of the highway. (It's two miles south of the town of Orick.) At the visitor center, pick up a Tall Trees Grove permit and the gate combination for the access road. Then drive north on U.S. 101 for three miles and turn right on Bald Hills Road. Drive seven miles on Bald Hills Road to the Tall Trees Access Road on the right (just past Redwood Creek Overlook). Turn right, stop at the gate, use your combination to open it, then drive through. Close and lock the gate behind you. Drive six miles on the Tall Trees Access Road (also called C-Line Road) to the trailhead parking lot.

OTHER: An interpretive brochure is available at the trailhead.

It might sound like too much trouble to go to the Redwood Information Center, pick up a permit and a gate combination for the Tall Trees Access Road, then drive 16 miles to the trailhead—just to hike a trail that features big redwoods. After all, there are plenty of other redwood trails in the area that don't require a permit. But these aren't your average big redwoods; the Tall Trees Grove features the world's tallest tree at 367 feet high, as well as the third and sixth tallest trees in the world.

Of course, if there weren't plaques on the ground identifying the first, third, and sixth tallest tree, you'd never know which was which. Every redwood in this grove is immense. It's impossible to see all the way to their skyscraping summits.

The permit system is necessary because the Tall Trees Access Road (also called C-Line Road) is narrow and winding; too many cars at once would surely result in accidents. But the side benefit of the permit system is that it limits the number of hikers in the grove and adds to the serenity of the experience. (Only 50 cars are given a permit each day, but that limit is rarely reached except on peak summer weekends. If you are concerned about getting a permit on a particular day, just show up at the visitor center when it opens in the morning—don't wait until later in the day.)

At the Tall Trees Trailhead, pick up an interpretive brochure at the kiosk and head downhill. You'll pass a junction with the Emerald Ridge

---

Tall Trees Grove

Trail in the first 100 yards; stay right. The first stretch of trail leads gently downhill through a mixed forest with myriad rhododendrons—no big redwoods yet. At 1.2 miles, you pass a rest room, which seems oddly out of place with the natural beauty of the forest. Just beyond it, the trail bottoms out and you reach the start of the loop trail through the grove. Follow the trail clockwise (to the left). Take the left spur trail to see Redwood Creek; in summer a bridge spans the creek to connect hikers to the Redwood Creek Trail. (If the bridge is in place, walk across it. The best view of the world's tallest tree is from the far side of the creek.) In winter and spring the creek is wide and powerful—more on the order of a river. The rich soils from its streambed, combined with the coastal climate, cause the redwoods here to grow to their enormous size.

Back on the main trail, you reach the base of the world's tallest tree in short order. But don't turn around there, because this trail isn't about numbers, or about any one specific tree. The entire grove is remarkable. There are so many mammoth-sized trees in such close proximity that humans feel ant-sized in comparison. Even the rhododendrons grow extra large—as tall as 15 feet. They display flashy pink blooms among the dark shadows of the redwoods.

The trail continues past more huge redwoods to the north end of the loop, where you walk through a quarter-mile stretch of big leaf maples and California bays—a distinct contrast to the giant redwoods. This area is beautiful in its own way, especially in autumn when the maples turn colors. Then the loop heads back into the big trees, passing the sixth tallest and third tallest trees in the world. Finally, the loop rejoins the main trail to head back uphill. Linger a while among the giants before you go.

LAVA BEDS NATIONAL MONUMENT

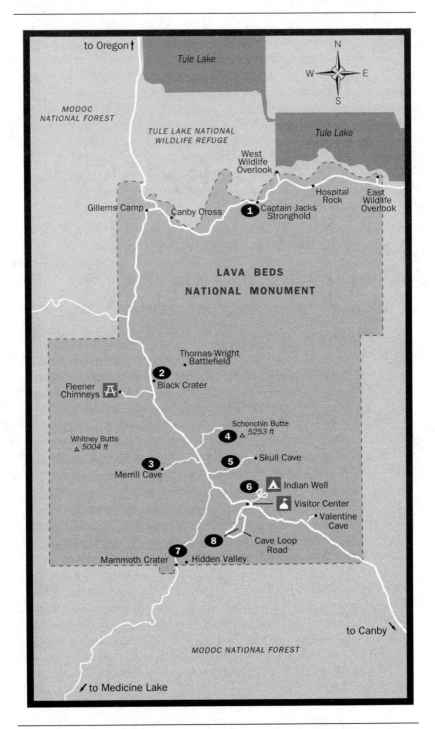

to Oregon↑

Tule Lake

N
W · E
S

MODOC
NATIONAL FOREST

TULE LAKE NATIONAL
WILDLIFE REFUGE

Tule Lake

West
Wildlife
Overlook

Hospital
Rock

East
Wildlife
Overlook

Gillems Camp

Canby Cross

1 Captain Jacks
Stronghold

LAVA BEDS

NATIONAL MONUMENT

Thomas-Wright
Battlefield

Fleener
Chimneys

2 Black Crater

Schonchin Butte
4 △ 5253 ft

Whitney Butte
△ 5004 ft

5 Skull Cave

3 Merrill Cave

6 Indian Well

Visitor Center

Valentine
Cave

8 Cave Loop
Road

7 Mammoth Crater Hidden Valley

to Canby↘

MODOC NATIONAL FOREST

↗to Medicine Lake

LAVA BEDS NATIONAL MONUMENT
TRAILS AT A GLANCE

Map Number/Trail Name	Page	Mileage	Difficulty
1. Captain Jack's Stronghold	48	2.0	Easy
2. Thomas-Wright Battlefield	50	2.4	Easy
3. Merrill Cave & Whitney Butte	51	6.8	Moderate
4. Schonchin Butte	52	1.5	Easy
5. Symbol Bridge & Big Painted Cave	54	1.6	Easy
6. Bunchgrass Trail	56	2.0	Easy
7. Heppe Ice Cave, Hidden Valley, & Mammoth Crater	57	1.0	Easy
8. Cave Trails at Lava Beds	59	Various	Various

THE TOP 3, DON'T-MISS DAY HIKES:

Map Number/Trail Name	Page	Features
3. Merrill Cave & Whitney Butte	51	ice cave, vistas
4. Schonchin Butte	52	fire lookout, vistas
8. Cave Trails at Lava Beds	59	cave explorations

TRAIL SUGGESTIONS FOR IF YOU ONLY HAVE ONE DAY:

Map Number/Trail Name	Page	Features
4. Schonchin Butte	52	fire lookout, vistas
5. Symbol Bridge & Big Painted Cave	54	ancient pictographs
8. Cave Trails at Lava Beds	59	cave explorations

LAVA BEDS NATIONAL MONUMENT

ABOUT THE PARK

Lava Beds National Monument was created to protect the unique volcanic features of its landscape, including more than 300 lava tube caves, and rugged lava beds punctuated by cinder cones, craters, and spatter cones. Its terrain is mostly flat, sagebrush covered plains, dotted with mountain mahogany and western junipers.

ADDRESS, PHONE, & WEBSITE

Lava Beds National Monument, Box 867, Tulelake, CA 96134; (530) 667-2282.
Website: www.nps.gov/labe

HOW TO GET THERE

- By air: The closest major airport is in Klamath Falls, Oregon.
- By car: The park is located in northern California, 60 miles south of Klamath Falls, Oregon. Several roads access it:

  From Highway 97 at Klamath Falls, take Highway 97 south for 20 miles to Highway 161. Turn east on Highway 161 and drive 17 miles to Hill Road. Turn south on Hill Road and drive 15 miles to the north entrance to the monument.

  From Interstate 5 at Weed, take Highway 97 north for 54 miles to Highway 161. Turn east on Highway 161 and drive 17 miles to Hill Road. Turn south on Hill Road and drive 15 miles to the north entrance to the monument.

  From Interstate 5 at Redding, drive east on Highway 299 for 56 miles to the junction of highways 299 and 89. Continue east on Highway 299 for 34 miles, past Fall River Mills and Nubieber. Watch for the turnoff for Lookout Road on the left. Turn left and drive 32 miles north on Lookout Road to its junction with Highway 139. Turn left (north) on Highway 139 and drive 11 miles to the turnoff for Lava Beds National Monument on the left (Tionesta Road). Turn left and drive three miles, then turn right and drive 10 miles to Lava Beds National Monument.

DRIVE TIME

- Drive time from Los Angeles: approximately 13 hours.
- Drive time from San Francisco: approximately 7 hours.

ENTRANCE FEES

There is a $4 entrance fee per vehicle at Lava Beds National Monument, good for seven days. A Lava Beds annual pass is available for $10. A Golden Eagle Passport, an annual pass for all 375 national park units, is available for $50. A Golden Age Passport, a lifetime pass for all 375 national park units, is available to U.S. citizens and residents aged 62 and over for a one-time $10 fee. You can purchase these passes at the monument's visitor center.

WHEN TO GO

Lava Beds National Monument is open year-round, but snow often covers the park's trails in winter. The monument's main hiking season is April to November. Wildflowers are best in the spring; wildlife viewing is best in the autumn. Summer can be quite hot in this shadeless park.

WEATHER CONDITIONS

Lava Beds National Monument has variable weather year-round. The park is usually snow-covered in winter, and low-lying fog is common. Winter daytime temperatures range between 25 and 40 degrees. Late spring, summer, and early fall daytime temperatures range between 60 and 90 degrees; rain and thunderstorms may occur. There is very little shade in the monument, so bring your sun hat. If you are planning to explore the park's caves, you should wear long pants and carry a jacket or sweater—even on warm summer days.

WHERE TO STAY

Lava Beds National Monument has a 40-site campground that is available on a first-come, first-served basis. Modoc National Forest, which surrounds the monument, has several campgrounds. Phone the Tule Lake Ranger District for more information about camping in Modoc National Forest; (530) 667-2246.

There is no lodging within the park; the closest motels are located in Tulelake, 25 miles away, and Klamath Falls, 60 miles away.

FOOD & SUPPLIES

No food or supplies are available within the monument. The nearest stores and restaurants are found in Tulelake and Klamath Falls.

SUGGESTED MAPS

Park maps are available at the visitor center or by contacting Lava Beds National Monument at the address on page 46.

1. CAPTAIN JACK'S STRONGHOLD

Lava Beds National Monument
Fascinating history of the 1870s Modoc War

DISTANCE: 2.0 miles round-trip; 1 hour

ELEVATION: Start at 4,000 feet; total change 50 feet

BEST SEASON: April to November

LEVEL: Easy

CROWDS: Minimal

RATING: ★ ★ ★

DIRECTIONS: From the Lava Beds Visitor Center, drive north and then east on Lava Beds National Monument Road for 13.4 miles to the parking area on the right for Captain Jack's Stronghold.

NOTE: An interpretive brochure is available at the trailhead.

History lovers shouldn't miss the easy hike around Captain Jack's Stronghold in the northern part of Lava Beds National Monument. The interpretive walk tells the sad tale of Modoc Indians fighting to maintain their homeland around Tule Lake in the 1870s, which resulted in the only major Indian war fought in California.

The story begins in the late 1860s, when the Modoc Indians were forced off their native land and sent to a reservation in southern Oregon. White settlers in the Tule Lake area felt anxious having the Modocs as neighbors and insisted that the government remove them. Naturally, the Modocs were unhappy with this arrangement. Not only was the government reservation unfamiliar territory, but the Modocs also had to share it with Klamath and Snake Indians, who were the Modocs' traditional enemies.

In April 1869, the Modoc leader Kientpoos, nicknamed "Captain Jack," led 371 Modoc people off the reservation and back to their native land. Because they repeatedly had been refused a reservation of their own, they decided they would no longer try to negotiate with the white settlers' government.

Finally, in November of 1872, troops were sent to force the Modocs to return to the reservation, and fighting broke out. Fifty-two Modoc Indian men, plus their wives and children, fled to this "stronghold" on the south shore of Tule Lake. Here, amid a landscape of ancient lava flows, the Modocs were able to hold off some 600 government troops for nearly five months until April 1873.

The Modocs' secret weapon was their knowledge of their homeland—the rather hostile landscape of the lava beds. Today, as you walk the interpretive trail at Captain Jack's Stronghold, you see how the lava beds created a natural fortress for the Modocs, with deep trenches and

Mount Shasta from Captain Jack's Stronghold Trail

small caves. Despite the cold winter, the Modocs were able to make camps inside these caves and under overhanging ledges. The families slept on tule mats and blankets to soften the harshness of the lava surfaces. The men fired their guns and fought their battles from rocky outposts and wide natural trenches. The lava beds made it possible to perform military maneuvers without being seen by the enemy.

The interpretive trail is two separate but connected trails—an inner and an outer loop. Hiking both trails results in a two-mile round-trip; hiking the inner loop only is a half-mile round-trip. At the junction of the two trails, you'll find a "prayer tree" colorfully hung with ribbons and other small offerings from people who have visited this battlefield and felt moved by its story.

In addition to the trail's historical interest, the views from its surrounding lava beds of Mount Shasta and Tule Lake are excellent. But be prepared for hot weather in summer; there is no shade along the route and the hard, volcanic surfaces reflect heat and make the temperature hotter. Also, watch the trail for rattlesnakes. On our trip, I spotted one ahead of me just a millisecond before I put my foot down on it, and had to do the "rattlesnake two-step" to avoid a confrontation. The snake shook his rattle in reproach, and slithered away.

2. THOMAS-WRIGHT BATTLEFIELD

Lava Beds National Monument
Volcanism, Modoc history, spring wildflowers

DISTANCE: 2.4 miles round-trip; 1.5 hours   **LEVEL:** Easy
ELEVATION: Start at 4,200 feet; total change 120 feet   **CROWDS:** Minimal
BEST SEASON: April to November   **RATING:** ★ ★

DIRECTIONS: From the Lava Beds Visitor Center, drive north on Lava Beds National Monument Road for 4.8 miles to the Black Crater parking area on the right.

Human history and geological history are combined on this trail to the Thomas-Wright Battlefield, which makes it a great educational experience as well as a fine hike on a cool spring or fall day. The trail starts from the Black Crater parking area along the main park road. The flora here is typical of much of the park—low-growing rabbitbrush, sagebrush, and bunchgrass, with western junipers making up the sparse tree population.

In only 100 yards, you reach a trail fork and turn right for Black Crater. A slight climb leads to the crater, which is really a spatter cone, created when globs of molten lava burst through a vent in the earth's surface, then fell to the ground and landed on top of each other. (Another interesting example of a spatter cone can be seen at the picnic area at Fleener Chimneys, across the park road and just south of this trailhead. At Fleener Chimneys, the spatter cone has a 50-foot-deep hole, or chimney, in its center.)

Black Crater also supports a fine view of Mount Shasta and various park landmarks. The slight ascent you make to get to it provides you with a view that encompasses much of the park. This is a fine place for sunsets, without having to worry about a long, dark walk back.

From Black Crater, return to the main trail and bear right for the Thomas-Wright Battlefield. Walk along the edge of Black Crater's lava flow, and head gently downhill. In minutes, you reach an interpretive sign at a "tree mold." This is not the kind of mold that you find on aging leftovers, but rather a form or frame left from liquid lava that long ago flowed around a tree trunk, then hardened. You may find other examples of tree molds in the park.

Continue past more interpretive signs to the trail's end at the historic battlefield. Here, in 1872, Modoc Indians were able to hide and attack U.S. troops who were camped in the low area below. Forty of the 68 U.S. soldiers were wounded or killed in the surprise attack.

3. MERRILL CAVE & WHITNEY BUTTE

Lava Beds National Monument
Longest day-hiking trail in the park to a high cinder cone

DISTANCE: 6.8 miles round-trip; 3.5 hours   **LEVEL:** Moderate

ELEVATION: Start at 4,600 feet; total change 500 feet   **CROWDS:** Minimal

BEST SEASON: April to November   **RATING:** ★ ★ ★ ★

DIRECTIONS: From the Lava Beds Visitor Center, drive north on Lava Beds National Monument Road for two miles to the left turnoff for Merrill Cave. Turn left and drive one mile to the cave and trailhead for Whitney Butte.

The Whitney Butte Trail qualifies as the longest day hike in Lava Beds National Monument. On a cool day, it's the perfect trail for a half-day excursion and a picnic with a view. The path curves around Whitney Butte to the western boundary of the monument and offers excellent vistas of the park and much of Northern California. On a hot day, however, you might be better off exploring an underground cave.

Conveniently, there's one right at the trailhead. The Whitney Butte Trail begins at the parking area by Merrill Ice Cave; pay a visit to the cave before or after your hike. Make sure you have a few sources of light per person and proper clothing—long pants and a sweater or jacket.

Merrill Ice Cave is a remnant of two lava tubes, one piled on top of the other. They were formed by two separate eruptions. A stairway takes you down to the first lava tube; a ladder takes you farther down to the second, older lava tube. Inside, you'll find a small pond with permanent ice. Not surprisingly, it's very cold inside the lower cave.

Back above ground, the Whitney Butte Trail leads northwest through a typical Lava Beds landscape of sagebrush, rabbitbrush,

View of Mount Shasta from Whitney Butte

antelopebrush, and mountain mahogany. The elevation is just high enough to support a few ponderosa pines in addition to the hardy western junipers. You may spy a snowy mountain to the north—that's Mount McLoughlin in Oregon. Mount Dome and Schonchin Butte are the most prominent park features. After the first two miles of hiking, Mount Shasta also comes into view. When you look at its immense size, it's hard to believe that it's 45 miles away.

Nearing three miles out, you'll reach the edge of Whitney Butte. At 5,004 feet in elevation, the butte is a cinder cone like Schonchin Butte—a type of volcano that is composed of layers of volcanic ash and cinders. Hike around the base of Whitney Butte to the trail's end at the monument boundary and the edge of the Callahan Lava Flow. Take a close-up look at the black basalt of the lava flow, then retrace your steps to one of the various paths that lead up Whitney Butte. You'll have to pick your own route to the summit, but it's obvious that many others have gone before you. The view from the top is nearly as good as from the fire lookout tower on top of Schonchin Butte. (The difference is that here, the view is most likely to be yours alone.) Pull out your park map and identify all the volcanic features in your scope. Not surprisingly, massive Mount Shasta steals the show.

4. SCHONCHIN BUTTE

Lava Beds National Monument
Fire lookout tower on the monument's highest peak

DISTANCE: 1.5 miles round-trip; 45 minutes **LEVEL:** Easy
ELEVATION: Start at 4,700 feet; total change 600 feet **CROWDS:** Moderate
BEST SEASON: April to November **RATING:** ★ ★ ★

DIRECTIONS: From the Lava Beds Visitor Center, drive north on Lava Beds National Monument Road for 2.2 miles to the right turnoff for Schonchin Butte. Turn right and drive one mile on a graded dirt road to the trailhead.

Lava Beds National Monument is a tiny part of a giant volcanic plateau that encompasses Lassen Volcanic National Park to the south and Crater Lake National Park to the north. Nowhere is this geological fact quite so clear as from the top of Schonchin Butte, elevation 5,302 feet, where you can see for miles in every direction over the vast volcanic tableland. Here and there, the flatness is punctuated by isolated volcanic peaks and cinder cones, which accentuate the drama of the landscape.

Schonchin Butte's fire lookout tower

There's no reason not to go see for yourself. The trail to Schonchin Butte, with only a 600-foot climb, is short and easy enough for families. If anyone in your party tires out, there are benches in place along the trail to give weary legs a rest. It's unlikely you'll need them, though; the trail is well built and moderately graded.

From the trailhead, a few long, sweeping switchbacks take you uphill on a pumice-lined path. Your destination—the fire lookout tower on top of Schonchin Butte—is easily spotted. The foliage on the slopes of the butte is mostly chaparral: Sagebrush, rabbitbrush, and the like. Shrubby mountain mahogany makes an appearance, as well as a few western junipers, but nothing is tall or plentiful enough to obscure the vistas as you climb. Spring wildflowers are excellent along this trail. If you hike between April and early June, look for yellow violets and larkspur. Later in the summer, you'll find blooming sage and buckwheat. Both have yellow to white flower clusters.

Near the top of the butte, you'll reach a trail fork with two options for reaching the summit: The longer, flatter route to the right; or the shorter, steeper route to the left. Take your pick. Both will bring you to Schonchin Butte's summit and the lookout tower.

Head up to the tower's perimeter deck and enjoy the panorama. The lookout was built in 1939 by the Civilian Conservation Corps, who carried all the lumber and building materials on their backs. The tower is usually staffed from June through September, and if the lookout person is not busy, he or she may invite you inside.

A map on each corner of the square tower names the various landmarks in each direction. To the north is Tule Lake and the Schonchin Lava Flow, and far off in the northeast is Mount McLoughlin in Oregon, which is snow-covered in early summer. To the southwest is mighty Mount Shasta. (Many Californians will find it strange see Mount Shasta to the south, because we are most often south of *it*.) On the clearest days of the year, if you have very good eyesight, you can see the south rim of Crater Lake. Within the park's borders, you'll spot several cinder cones, including Cinder Butte and Whitney Butte. Cinder Butte is a cinder cone that may have formed in the last 500 years. In contrast, Schonchin Butte (on which you stand) formed over 30,000 years ago. You can also see Mammoth Crater, the volcano that produced most of the lava that created the park's lava tube caves, as well as numerous other volcanic features.

5. SYMBOL BRIDGE & BIG PAINTED CAVE

Lava Beds National Monument
Collapsed lava tubes bearing Native American pictographs

DISTANCE: 1.6 miles round-trip; 1 hour   **LEVEL:** Easy
ELEVATION: Start at 4,600 feet; total change 80 feet   **CROWDS:** Minimal
BEST SEASON: April to November   **RATING:** ★ ★ ★

DIRECTIONS: From the Lava Beds Visitor Center, drive north on Lava Beds National Monument Road for 1.5 miles to the right turnoff for Skull Cave. Turn right and drive one mile to the trailhead on the left for Symbol Bridge and Big Painted Cave.

Unlike many of the lava tube caves in Lava Beds National Monument, which are located right alongside the park road, Symbol Bridge and Big Painted Cave require a short hike to access them. This serves to increase the anticipation of their hidden treasures and makes the experience more rewarding. Because of the walk required, and because these caves are not located with the large group of caves near the visitor center, solitude can often be found at these two special places.

Symbol Bridge and Big Painted Cave lie just south of Schonchin Butte, accessible via Skull Cave Road. The trail to reach them heads northwest through bunchgrass, rabbitbrush, sagebrush, and junipers. Wildflowers in late April or May include blue gentians; the delicate mariposa lily blooms a month or so later.

Along the path, you pass over and alongside volcanic rock- and boulder-strewn trenches, the remains of collapsed lava tubes. Many of the park's 350 lava tubes, which are available for you to explore, have collapsed walls and roofs. Often the collapsed area is the opening that allows you into the cave. Seeing all the rubble alongside this trail can make you wary of going caving inside the lava tubes, but it's good to know that most of them collapsed at the time their lava was cooling, which was thousands of years ago. Their scattered remains have been resting here, untouched, for eons.

Pictographs at Symbol Bridge

A half-mile from the trailhead, you'll find a spur trail to Big Painted Cave on your left. Take it and walk 100 feet to the cave. If you brought flashlights, turn them on and use them to look for the faint pictographs on boulders at the entrance of the cave. Hundreds or maybe thousands of years ago this lava tube cave was discovered and used by the ancient Native Americans. This may have been a place where they held ceremonies or rites of some kind.

If you can't find the weathered pictographs at Big Painted Cave or see them well, just continue back to the main trail and walk the remaining short distance to Symbol Bridge. Here, under a collapsed lava tube "bridge," the pictographs are much more self-evident. Very little of this lava tube is still intact, so plenty of daylight penetrates it. It's shaped like an amphitheater, and light enters inside to illuminate drawings on both sides of its entrance. An interpretive sign reminds visitors that this is a sacred site and that you should enter it as you would a church.

Have a seat on a rock and admire the drawings at Symbol Bridge.

If you are quiet, you may see birds flying around the cave entrance, or a pika peeking up among the rocks. Pikas look like small guinea pigs with small, rounded ears and no visible tail. They make their homes in the piles of lava rubble.

6. BUNCHGRASS TRAIL

Lava Beds National Monument
Easy walk through native flora, wildlife viewing

DISTANCE: 2.0 miles round-trip; 1 hour   **LEVEL:** Easy
ELEVATION: Start at 4,600 feet; total change 150 feet   **CROWDS:** Minimal
BEST SEASON: April to November   **RATING:** ★ ★

DIRECTIONS: From the Lava Beds Visitor Center, cross the main park road to access Indian Well Campground. From the camp entrance, drive four-tenths of a mile down the hill and turn left for B Loop. The Bunchgrass Trail begins by site B-7; park your car near the B Loop rest rooms (not in any campsite).

Okay, so the Bunchgrass Trail may not be the most glamorous trail in Lava Beds National Monument. But you won't need your flashlights or headlamps to hike it—this path is most decidedly above ground. And if you're hungering for an easy nature walk, the Bunchgrass Trail fits the bill.

The trail begins at Lava Beds' only campground and follows an old road around the northeast side of Crescent Butte. Many campers hike this trail after dinner or early in the morning, when the chance of seeing wildlife is good. Most prevalent are jackrabbits, sage grouse, and ground squirrels. In summer, it's unlikely you would hike here at midday; temperatures can soar and the wide road has no shade.

The trail is named for the grassy, tuft-like native shrub that grows in profusion alongside it. Park rangers are proud of the monument's fine display of bunchgrass; just outside the park borders, you won't see much of this shrub because of decades of unrestricted livestock grazing. In addition to the bunchgrass, you'll see plenty of Lava Beds' chaparral-type plants: sagebrush, rabbitbrush, antelope brush, and mountain mahogany. (The latter is more like a small, shrubby tree.) At least one true species of tree is represented: the western juniper, which bears blue berries enjoyed by birds.

Watch for birds as you hike: We spotted a bright blue mountain bluebird here and saw two flashy meadowlarks singing from the top of a juniper tree. You may see larger birds as well: Lava Beds National

Monument is home to 24 species of hawk, falcon, owl, and other birds of prey. It is not uncommon to see an eagle.

The dirt road begins a gentle climb, then eventually narrows to single-track trail as it nears the main park road. The flat terrain of Lava Beds lends itself to far-reaching views. Schonchin Butte is easily identified with its tinker-toy lookout tower on top. The trail ends at an overlook point, 150 feet higher than where you started. Bring your park map so you'll be able to point out Mount Dome, Gillem Bluff, the Schonchin Lava Flow, Tule Lake, Crescent Butte, Whitney Butte, and the Callahan Lava Flow.

7. HEPPE ICE CAVE, HIDDEN VALLEY, & MAMMOTH CRATER

Lava Beds National Monument
Three short walks with big rewards

DISTANCE: 1.0 mile round-trip; 30 minutes   **LEVEL:** Easy
ELEVATION: Start at 4,600 feet; total change 100 feet   **CROWDS:** Minimal
BEST SEASON: April to November   **RATING:** ★ ★

DIRECTIONS: From the Lava Beds Visitor Center, drive north on Lava Beds National Monument Road for one mile to the left turnoff for Medicine Lake Road (a graded dirt road). Turn left and drive 2.3 miles to the trailhead for Heppe Ice Cave. After visiting the cave, drive (or walk) another half mile to the Mammoth Crater parking area, on the right side of the road. Hidden Valley is directly across the road.

Lava Beds National Monument: It's one park above ground, and another park below. To get a good sense of the divided nature of Lava Beds, drive north from the visitor center on the main park road, then turn left on the dirt road leading to Medicine Lake. In just three miles, you'll reach three trailheads for three short walks, two above and one below ground. If you walk all three trails, you cover only about a mile in distance, but you get the complete Lava Beds experience.

First stop is one of the monument's fascinating lava tubes—Heppe Ice Cave, accessible via a quarter-mile walk. Unlike many of the caves in the park, this one is open to the light, so you don't need to carry flashlights. The trail begins in the semi-shade of tall pines, then climbs gently for a quarter-mile. At the trail's high point, you can see the collapsed remains of a lava tube, with Heppe Bridge at the far end. The trail passes Heppe Chimney, where various sun-loving wildflowers grow among the rocks, exposed to the light by the "chimney" or hole.

As you drop down into Heppe Cave, you'll notice the sudden chill in the air, which can be most welcome on a summer day in Lava Beds. Ferns grow in the cool shade near the cave's mouth, and swallows and other birds fly around the entrance. Various colorful lichens line the cave walls where light can penetrate.

The trail winds down through piles of rocks and rubble to a pool of water. The water lies on top of a bed of ice that was formed when rain collected inside the cave at freezing temperatures. Because lava is an excellent insulator, even in summer when the outside air temperature rises above 100 degrees the inner cave temperature stays below freezing. Although other year-round ice pools are found in caves in Lava Beds, most require a long cave crawl to reach. Because its lava tube is collapsed and open to daylight, the Heppe Ice Cave is the most accessible of the park's ice caves.

A trail register can be found near the pool, safely enclosed in a plastic tube. If it's not too cold and damp, take a seat on a rock and read the comments of other ice cave explorers, or write a few notes of your own.

Return to your car when you're ready, then drive another half-mile farther south on the road (or walk, if you're in the mood) to the trailhead on the right for Mammoth Crater and Hidden Valley. There are more trees in this part of the park than you see elsewhere; the elevations

Entering a lava tube cave at Lava Beds

are just high enough to support a ponderosa pine forest. Take the short walk across the road to Hidden Valley, where you will find a surprising number of these pines. The trail edges along the south rim of the valley, then peters out after about a quarter-mile. You can descend to the floor of the valley and explore on your own if you wish, or return to the trailhead and walk the trail on the other side of the road to Mammoth Crater.

Mammoth Crater was the volcano that produced most of the lava that formed the park's lava tube caves, as well as numerous other volcanic features. Today, when you visit the rocky crater, it seems like little more than an immense hole in the ground, filled with and surrounded by volcanic rocks. As you look around, try to imagine what occurred here 30,000 years ago, when the crater erupted.

8. CAVE TRAILS at LAVA BEDS

Lava Beds National Monument
Exploring lava tubes on feet, hands, and knees

DISTANCE: Various   **LEVEL:** Moderate
ELEVATION: Various   **CROWDS:** Minimal
BEST SEASON: April to November   **RATING:** ★ ★ ★

DIRECTIONS: There are lava tube caves located throughout the monument, but the largest concentration of them is along Cave Loop Road. From the Lava Beds Visitor Center, drive west (don't get on the main park road) to access the Cave Loop Road. It's a one-way, paved road.

Lava Beds National Monument isn't famous for its hiking trails, it's famous for its caves. Calling them "caves" is a bit misleading, though; they're not limestone caverns like we have in many parts of California. These caves are hardened lava tubes, which were formed during a volcanic eruption. As the lava flowed, its outer edges cooled and formed a shell-like crust, while the inside remained liquid. When the eruption ended and all the lava had drained out, the outside crust of hard lava remained standing in the shape of a tube or tunnel.

Even people who have never considered themselves spelunkers will enjoy exploring some of these fascinating lava-tube caves. You don't need any experience to explore the smaller caves, and you don't have to go with a guide or a ranger. The park visitor center loans out flashlights and sells hard hats; all you need are a comfortable pair of pants, sturdy shoes, and a sweater for the cool cave temperatures. Then, you're on your own.

Some of the caves are "developed," which means that a ladder has been installed to make entering and exiting the caves easier. Once inside, you'll find that most of the caves are pitch black. In many, you'll reach forks in the tube where you don't know if you should turn right or left. The answer is often that you should explore both avenues until they squeeze smaller and smaller and travel becomes impossible. Even though it seems like it would be easy to get lost, it's actually fairly difficult—all you need to do is backtrack to find your way out.

The caves are categorized according to level of difficulty. The Catacombs Cave is one of the longest and most complex caves, with a total length of 6,903 feet and numerous forks, twists, and turns. Beginners would do better to start at one of the smaller, easier caves, like the Hopkins Chocolate Cave (1,405 feet) or Blue Grotto Cave (1,541 feet). Before you start exploring, talk to a ranger at the visitor center to determine which caves are suitable for your level of ability. Many of the caves are located on the Cave Loop Road near the visitor center, so you can go from one cave to the next in a matter of a few minutes. You won't do much driving in this park.

If the length of the caves, or lava tubes, sounds like too short a distance to be considered hiking, you'll be surprised at how tired you are after exploring three or four caves. That's because much of the time you won't walk. Instead, you'll crawl on your hands and knees, or duck your head and shoulders, or stumble over the rough, boulder-lined floors of the caves. It takes a certain amount of agility to travel through the lava tubes. Carrying plenty of light makes your exploration a lot easier, and a lot prettier. Your light will illuminate the walls and ceilings of the lava tubes and reveal minerals that shine like diamonds, year-round ice, colorful lichens, and cave features such as pillars, benches, falls, and cascades. A headlamp is much better than a regular flashlight, because your hands remain free. You'll have to bring your own headlamp; the park only loans out hand-held flashlights. Rangers recommend that you carry two or three sources of light per person (just in case your batteries die), and they caution that you shouldn't explore the caves alone.

The Lava Beds caves appeal strongly to your imagination and sense of adventure. What makes this park special is that the cave experience is not spoon-fed. Each visitor gets to enter each lava tube as if he or she were the first human being to come upon it. It's a rare and unique opportunity—one you'll remember for a long time.

LASSEN VOLCANIC NATIONAL PARK

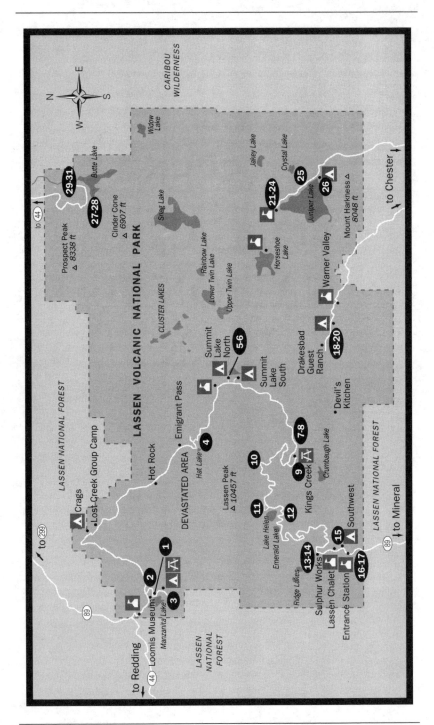

CARIBOU WILDERNESS

Widow Lake

Butte Lake

29-31

27-28

Cinder Cone
△ 6907 ft

Prospect Peak
△ 8338 ft

Snag Lake

Jakey Lake

Crystal Lake

25

21-24

26

Juniper Lake

Mount Harkness △
8048 ft

to Chester

Rainbow Lake

Lower Twin Lake

Upper Twin Lake

Horseshoe Lake

Warner Valley

CLUSTER LAKES

LASSEN VOLCANIC NATIONAL PARK

18-20

Summit Lake North

5-6

Summit Lake South

Drakesbad Guest Ranch

Devil's Kitchen

LASSEN NATIONAL FOREST

Lost Creek Group Camp

Emigrant Pass

Crags

Hot Rock

DEVASTATED AREA

Hat Lake

4

7-8

Crumbaugh Lake

10

Lassen Peak
△ 10457 ft

9

Kings Creek

LASSEN NATIONAL FOREST

11

12

15

Southwest

to Mineral

Lake Helen

Emerald Lake

13-14

Sulphur Works

Lassen Chalet

16-17

Entrance Station

Ridge Lakes

to 299

to 44

1

2

3

Loomis Museum

Manzanita Lake

LASSEN NATIONAL FOREST

to Redding

44

LASSEN VOLCANIC NATIONAL PARK
TRAILS AT A GLANCE

Map Number/Trail Name	Page	Mileage	Difficulty
1. Manzanita Lake	68	1.6	Easy
2. Chaos Crags & Crags Lake	69	3.6	Easy/moderate
3. Manzanita Creek Trail	71	7.0	Moderate
4. Paradise Meadows Trail	72	2.8	Easy/moderate
5. Summit Lake to Echo & Twin Lakes	73	8.0	Moderate
6. Cluster & Twin Lakes Loop	75	11.0	Moderate
7. Kings Creek Falls	77	2.4	Easy/moderate
8. Kings Creek Falls & Sifford Lakes Loop	79	5.2	Moderate
9. Cold Boiling Lake, Crumbaugh Lake, & Conard Meadows	81	4.0	Easy
10. Terrace, Shadow, & Cliff Lakes	82	3.4	Easy/moderate
11. Lassen Peak	84	5.0	Strenuous
12. Bumpass Hell	87	3.0	Easy/moderate
13. Sulphur Works	89	0.2	Easy
14. Ridge Lakes	91	2.0	Moderate
15. Mill Creek Falls	93	3.2	Easy
16. Brokeoff Mountain	94	7.4	Strenuous
17. Forest Lake	96	3.0	Easy/moderate
18. Boiling Springs Lake	98	3.0	Easy
19. Devils Kitchen	100	4.8	Easy/moderate
20. Drake Lake	101	5.0	Moderate
21. Juniper Lakeshore Circle	103	5.8	Easy/moderate
22. Juniper, Snag, & Horseshoe Lakes Loop	105	7.5	Moderate
23. Jakey Lake	107	6.0	Moderate
24. Inspiration Point	108	1.4	Easy/moderate
25. Crystal Lake	109	0.8	Easy/moderate
26. Mount Harkness Lookout	111	3.8-5.6	Moderate
27. Cinder Cone	113	4.0	Strenuous
28. Prospect Peak	115	7.0	Strenuous
29. Butte Lake to Snag Lake	117	7.0-10.0	Moderate
30. Widow Lake	119	7.2	Moderate
31. Bathtub Lakes	121	1.0	Easy

THE TOP 10, DON'T-MISS DAY HIKES:

TRAIL SUGGESTIONS FOR IF YOU ONLY HAVE ONE DAY:

LASSEN VOLCANIC NATIONAL PARK

ABOUT THE PARK
Before the 1980 eruption of Mount Saint Helens in Washington, Lassen Peak was the most recently erupted volcano in the contiguous United States. It first blew its top in May 1914, and major volcanic outbursts continued for seven years. The park has many examples of active geothermal activity, including steaming sulphur vents, mudpots, and boiling springs. Lassen's terrain is mostly forested, with many lakes and mountain peaks.

ADDRESS, PHONE, & WEBSITE
Lassen Volcanic National Park, P.O. Box 100, Mineral, CA 96063; (530) 595-4444.
Website: www.nps.gov/lavo

VISITOR CENTERS
The main park visitor center is the Loomis Museum, located near the northwest entrance to the park by Manzanita Lake. A smaller visitor center is located at the Lassen Chalet, near the southwest entrance station.

HOW TO GET THERE
- By air: The closest major airport is in Redding.
- By car: The park has several entrances. One main road (Highway 89) cuts through the entire west side of the park, but no roads go through the east side of the park. The east side has three different entrances, each requiring long out-and-back drives: Butte Lake, Warner Valley, and Juniper Lake.

Northwest Entrance at Manzanita Lake—Take Interstate 5 to Redding. From Redding, drive east on Highway 44 for 46 miles. Turn right on Highway 89 and drive a half-mile to the park's northwest entrance station at Manzanita Lake.

Southwest Entrance—Take Interstate 5 to Red Bluff. From Red Bluff, drive east on Highway 36 for 45 miles. Turn north on Highway 89 and drive 4.5 miles to the park's Southwest entrance station.

Butte Lake Entrance—Take Interstate 5 to Redding. From Redding, drive east on Highway 44 for 46 miles. At the turnoff for Lassen Park, bear left to stay on Highway 44/89 (don't turn into the park). From this junction, drive 24 miles farther on Highway 44 (turn right at Old Station to stay on Highway 44). Turn right at the signed turnoff for Butte Lake, and drive six miles to the ranger station and trailhead parking lot.

Juniper Lake Entrance—Take Interstate 5 to Red Bluff. From Red Bluff, drive east on Highway 36 for 70 miles to Chester. Turn left on Feather River Drive. In seven-tenths of a mile, bear right for Juniper Lake. Drive 5.5 miles, then take the right fork signed for Juniper Lake. The road turns to dirt and gravel and continues for another 7.4 miles to the lake. Continue straight, past the campground turnoff. Park in the lot near the ranger station signed "Trailhead Parking." Most trails begin at the ranger station.

Warner Valley Entrance—Follow the Juniper Lake directions to Feather River Drive. In seven-tenths of a mile, bear left for Warner Valley and Drakesbad. Drive six miles, then turn right on Warner Valley Road. Drive 11 miles to Warner Valley Campground, then continue past it for a quarter-mile to the trailhead parking area.

DRIVE TIME
• Drive time from Los Angeles: approximately 10.5 hours.
• Drive time from San Francisco: approximately 4.5 hours.

ENTRANCE FEES
There is a $10 entrance fee per vehicle at Lassen Volcanic National Park, good for seven days. A Lassen annual pass is available for $20. A Golden Eagle Passport, an annual pass for all 375 national park units, is available for $50. A Golden Age Passport, a lifetime pass for all 375 national park units, is available to U.S. citizens and residents aged 62 and over for a one-time $10 fee. You can purchase these passes at the park entrance stations.

WHEN TO GO
Lassen's hiking season is quite short; most park trails are free of snow only from July to September. The Butte Lake area and Manzanita Lake area are usually the first park regions to be snow-free. The Lassen Park Road is closed by snow each winter, usually from late October to mid-June. As the timing of snowfall and snowmelt varies greatly from year to year, always phone the park for a road and trail update before planning your trip.

WEATHER CONDITIONS

Lassen Volcanic National Park has lovely but brief summer weather. Summer days are often warm and clear with temperatures in the 70s and 80s. Nights are cooler with temperatures in the 40s and 50s. Rain is not uncommon in summer; afternoon thunderstorms sometimes occur. Stay off mountain peaks if a thunderstorm is threatening. The general rule for summer in the park: Bring warm clothes for evenings (especially if you're camping) and a variety of layers for hiking.

WHERE TO STAY

Lassen has seven campgrounds that are available on a first-come, first-served basis: Manzanita Lake, Southwest, Summit Lake North and South, Crags, Warner Valley, and Juniper Lake. Campgrounds are usually open from late June to mid-September. More campgrounds can be found in neighboring Lassen National Forest.

Only one lodge exists within the park: Drakesbad Guest Ranch, open June to September; (530) 529-9820. Just outside the park borders are several lodging choices of varying styles and prices:

- **Near the Southwest Entrance:**
  Lassen Mineral Lodge, Mineral, (530) 595-4422
  McGovern's Mount Lassen Chalets, Mineral, (530) 595-3241
  Black Forest Lodge, Mill Creek, (530) 258-2941
  Mill Creek Resort, Mill Creek, (530) 595-4449
  St. Bernard Lodge, Mill Creek, (530) 258-3382

- **Near the Northwest Entrance at Manzanita Lake:**
  Rim Rock Ranch, Old Station, (530) 335-7114
  Rippling Waters Resort, Hat Creek, (530) 335-7400
  Adam's Hat Creek Resort, Hat Creek, (530) 335-7121

FOOD & SUPPLIES

The Lassen Chalet by the Southwest Entrance serves breakfast and lunch. A small store with food and camping supplies is located by Manzanita Lake Campground. Other supplies are available in Mineral, 10 miles south of the park, and Old Station, 15 miles north of the park. A few restaurants are found in Mineral and Mill Creek.

SUGGESTED MAPS

Park maps are available at park entrance stations or by contacting Lassen National Park at the address on page 65. A detailed map is available for a fee from the Loomis Museum; phone (530) 595-4444.

1. MANZANITA LAKE

Manzanita Lake area, Lassen Volcanic National Park
Plentiful wildlife and lakeside views of Mount Lassen

DISTANCE: 1.6 miles round-trip; 45 minutes
ELEVATION: Start at 5,900 feet; total change 0 feet
BEST SEASON: May to October

LEVEL: Easy
CROWDS: Moderate
RATING: ★ ★ ★

DIRECTIONS: From the northwest entrance station at Manzanita Lake, drive southeast on Highway 89 for a half mile to the right turnoff for Manzanita Lake Campground (just beyond the Loomis Museum). Turn right and drive a half mile to the boat ramp and picnic area parking lot at Manzanita Lake. Begin hiking from the right side of the parking lot.

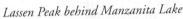

The hike around Manzanita Lake isn't really a hike, it's more like a saunter or a wander. But whatever you want to call it, make sure you do it, particularly either early in the morning or right at sunset. Although at midday Manzanita Lake can be crowded with swimmers and picnickers, at the edges of the day it's a tranquil place where you're likely to see plenty of wildlife.

Beginning from the boat ramp area on the north side of the lake, hike to the right and make a counterclockwise circle around the lake's perimeter. Your first few minutes of walking will suffer somewhat from

Lassen Peak behind Manzanita Lake

Lassen Volcanic National Park—map page 62

noise from the nearby park road, but you will be compensated by fine views of Mount Lassen looming over the lake's far side, appearing close enough to swim to. The north and west sides of Manzanita Lake provide many excellent vantage points for photographers, and the big snowy volcano makes a perfect backdrop for the lake.

The trail moves away from the park road in a quarter mile, continually hugging the lake's shoreline. Enjoy the views of Mount Lassen and the Chaos Crags while you have them; soon the big mountain will be at your back. As you travel around to the south side of the lake, watch for ducks and geese. In spring and early summer you will often see entire waterfowl families parading by, with the proud parents leading a flotilla of ducklings.

Keep your eyes trained on the water's edge and you may see some very large trout lurking in the shallows. The reason they're so big is because the fishing regulations are strict at Manzanita Lake: It's catch-and-release only with artificial lures, and all fishing is prohibited where Manzanita Creek empties into the lake. Some anglers try their luck from kayaks and canoes; all power boats are prohibited.

2. CHAOS CRAGS & CRAGS LAKE

Manzanita Lake area, Lassen Volcanic National Park
Early-season lake for swimming; recent volcanic activity

DISTANCE: 3.6 miles round-trip; 2 hours
ELEVATION: Start at 5,900 feet; total change 800 feet
BEST SEASON: June to September

LEVEL: Easy/moderate
CROWDS: Minimal
RATING: ★ ★ ★ ★

DIRECTIONS: From the northwest entrance station at Manzanita Lake, drive southeast on Highway 89 for a half mile to the right turnoff for Manzanita Lake Campground (just beyond the Loomis Museum). Turn right and drive 100 yards to the Chaos Crags Trailhead on the left.

When most of Lassen Volcanic National Park is still buried in snow, it can feel like summer in the Manzanita Lake area of the park. This early season is an excellent time to hike uphill to Crags Lake, and perhaps take a bracing swim before the long days of sunshine dry up the snow-fed lake. Crags Lake is a beauty, and the trail to reach it is an easy ascent of only 1.7 miles, followed by a short but steep drop to the water's edge.

Initially, the path climbs very gently through pine and fir forest. Many of the trees are stunted from the poor volcanic soil they grow in;

Crags Lake at the base of Chaos Crags

some have a healthy quantity of bright green staghorn lichen coloring their trunks. The forest is situated along the edge of Chaos Jumbles—a two-mile-square rockslide caused by volcanic activity sometime around the year 1700 or so.

The trees hide much of your view of the rockslide, but as you climb, you'll see other evidence of volcanism. A group of six plug domes called the Chaos Crags rise above the upper reaches of the trail. The Chaos Crags were formed by thick, viscous lava. The lava was so thick that it didn't flow outward; rather it squeezed upward through vents in the earth and then hardened in place. The Crags are estimated to be about 1,000 years old—much older than the Chaos Jumbles. A depression or small crater at the base of the Crags is what forms Crags Lake each year as the snow melts.

As you proceed uphill, the forest cover starts to thin and your views get wider. A few switchbacks take you up to the crest of a ridge—the high point on this trail. You are rewarded with a dramatic view of the Chaos Crags towering hundreds of feet above you. Below you is the steep bowl in which blue-green Crags Lake lies, and far off in the distance are the Chaos Jumbles and forested Hat Creek Valley.

Many people turn around at this point, but it's only a short descent of about 100 yards down to the lake's edge. If you go swimming, you'll find that the water temperature is comfortable near the shore, but it drops dramatically the deeper you go. If you don't want to swim, you can find a spot along the water's edge and have a picnic, admiring the ephemeral lake. By about September, its snow-fed waters will have dried up under the Lassen sun.

3. MANZANITA CREEK TRAIL

Manzanita Lake area, Lassen Volcanic National Park
Flower-filled meadows and mountain views

DISTANCE: 7.0 miles round-trip; 3.5 hours   **LEVEL:** Moderate
ELEVATION: Start at 5,900 feet; total change 1,200 feet   **CROWDS:** Minimal
BEST SEASON: June to October   **RATING:** ★ ★ ★

DIRECTIONS: From the northwest entrance station at Manzanita Lake, drive southeast on Highway 89 for a half-mile to the right turnoff for Manzanita Lake Campground (just beyond the Loomis Museum). Turn right and drive a half-mile to the Manzanita Lake Store. Park in the lot (or park in the lot by the boat ramp and picnic area), then walk uphill to the F Loop of Manzanita Lake Campground. The trailhead is on the left (upper) side of the loop.

Don't be turned away by the fact that the Manzanita Creek Trail is a wide dirt road instead of a narrow single-track path. Its flower-filled meadow destination makes the hike worthwhile, and its trailhead location in Manzanita Lake Campground makes it easily accessible to park visitors.

But trail connoisseurs, be forewarned that the trail itself is somewhat ordinary. For the first three-quarters of a mile, you hike through thick pine forest and manzanita on a moderately ascending dirt road, with little indication that any highlight or destination is forthcoming. There are no trail junctions, no spurs, nothing to pique your interest. Of course, during a snow-bound spring or early summer, this can be a bonus: Because the trail is so wide, there is no possibility of losing your way, even if there is still snow on the ground.

In about 20 minutes of hiking, the forest thins out to more mature stands of red and white fir. You start to catch glimpses of Chaos Crags, Loomis Peak, and Mount Lassen through the trees. If you're hiking in the proper season, you'll also get a sneak preview of the wildflower display to come. The predominant flowers here are lupine and paintbrush; once you reach the meadows, there will be many others. The road keeps climbing moderately, with only two brief sections where it levels out. Just beyond two miles, you'll cross Manzanita Creek; this is the sign that you're nearing the reward for your efforts.

At 2.8 miles you'll reach the first large meadow clearing, where not only the wildflowers, but also the mountain vistas, are magnificent. Take your eyes off the surrounding cliffs and look for wandering daisies, fireweed, purple monkshood, pennyroyal, paintbrush, and monkeyflower. Cross the stream, then continue another half mile to a second, larger meadow. Manzanita Creek winds through its center, and flowers bloom in profusion all summer. If you are fortunate enough to miss the few weeks of the mosquito hatch, you'll want to spend some time beside the meandering stream, counting the blooms among the meadow grasses. Was it worth the trip? You betcha.

4. PARADISE MEADOWS TRAIL

Manzanita Lake area, Lassen Volcanic National Park
Glorious wildflowers and Hat Creek cascades

DISTANCE: 2.8 miles round-trip; 1.5 hours   **LEVEL:** Easy/moderate
ELEVATION: Start at 6,300 feet; total change 600 feet   **CROWDS:** Minimal
BEST SEASON: June to September   **RATING:** ★ ★ ★ ★

DIRECTIONS: From the northwest entrance station at Manzanita Lake, drive southeast on Highway 89 for 9.6 miles to the Paradise Meadows trailhead on the right (south) side of the road. Park near the sign for Hat Lake.

Spring comes to Lassen Volcanic National Park whenever it feels like it. Some years it comes as early as June, but other years it can be as late as August. One thing is for certain: Spring comes later to Lassen than just about any other place in California.

When spring finally arrives, one of the first places it visits is Paradise Meadows, in the northern part of the park. The elevation is a bit lower in this area, so the snow melts a few weeks earlier, the trails clear, and the wildflowers push up through the ground and bloom. This is the perfect opportunity for a hike to the meadows.

From the trailhead, the path leads uphill along Hat Creek. It's only a 1.4-mile walk to the meadow, but with a sturdy grade and a 6,300-foot elevation, your heart will beat in a quick, steady rhythm. No matter; plentiful shade from pine and fir trees will keep you cool. Plus, many beautiful sights will inspire you to pause along the route, particularly the boisterous whitewater cascades along Hat Creek and the wildflowers blooming along its streambanks. We saw both blue and yellow lupine, shooting stars, corn lilies, columbine, scarlet gilia, gentian, and wallflowers.

The last 100 yards of trail level out, then bring you gently to the edge of Paradise Meadows. The meadows are a huge green expanse— the size of a couple of football fields—and strewn with lavender wandering daisies. Upon reaching the meadow, hikers stand respectfully at its edge, gazing out at the wonder of Paradise, too awe-inspired to tread on even one precious blade of grass. If the meadow area is wet, it's wise to stay off—this is a fragile and delicate ecosystem. But use your eyes to hunt for penstemon, columbine, and corn lilies among the grasses.

If you want to hike more, you can continue beyond the meadow to Terrace and Shadow Lakes, another two miles farther.

And if you need one more reason to make the trip to Paradise Meadows, the area's abundant views of glistening, snow-capped Mount Lassen should do the trick.

Paradise Meadows

5. SUMMIT LAKE to ECHO & TWIN LAKES

Summit Lake area, Lassen Volcanic National Park
Large swimming lakes and beautiful forest

DISTANCE: 8.0 miles round-trip; 4 hours   **LEVEL:** Moderate
ELEVATION: Start at 6,700 feet; total change 1,100 feet   **CROWDS:** Moderate
BEST SEASON: June to October   **RATING:** ★ ★ ★ ★

DIRECTIONS: From the northwest entrance station at Manzanita Lake, drive southeast on Highway 89 for 12 miles to the left turnoff for Summit Lake North Campground. (From the Southwest entrance station, drive north on Highway 89 for 16 miles to the right turnoff for Summit Lake North Campground.) Turn into the campground and park near the lake in the spots designated for day-use. Walk along the camp road, paralleling the lake, following signs toward the amphitheater.

Many people rave about the beauty of Echo Lake, but two much larger and deeper lakes lie only 1.5 miles beyond it: Upper and Lower Twin Lakes. As with many lakes in Lassen Volcanic National Park, all three lakes lack a distinct shoreline, with the surrounding forest running right down to their edges. But the Twin Lakes and Echo Lake are so pretty that this missing element won't disturb you. You'll just sit yourself down on a fallen log and watch the ripples on the water.

On warm days, you'll also find plenty of spots to wade in. Lower Twin Lake is the deepest of the three lakes and the best for swimming. (The choicest area is on the northwest side.) Upper Twin Lake runs a close second, both for swimming and for overall beauty. Echo Lake is lovely early in the year, but loses much of its depth as summer progresses. By August the lake may be too shallow for swimming, although you could certainly stick your feet in.

The trail to reach the lakes begins at Summit Lake North Campground. After you wander on pavement along the north edge of Summit Lake, follow signs to the camp amphitheater and turn right on the dirt path along the lake's edge. In about 150 yards, before you reach the amphitheater, you'll see a trail sign for Echo Lake and Upper and Lower Twin Lakes, as well as several other destinations. Bear left at the trail sign.

The path, which has been level up to this point, will climb steadily for nearly a mile to the top of a ridge. There's a 500-foot gain to reach the top, but the slope is thickly forested with big firs and pines and low-growing manzanita. As you climb, turn around occasionally for good views of Lassen Peak, Reading Peak, and Chaos Crags. At the ridge's crest, you'll enjoy another short, level stretch, then reach another trail fork. Bear right for Echo Lake and Twin Lakes. Hikers making a full 11-mile loop trip to Cluster Lakes and then back around to Lower and Upper Twin Lakes will bear left here (see the following story).

The trail soon starts to descend to Echo Lake, losing most of the 500 feet

Lower Twin Lake

just gained in a mere half-mile. Echo Lake is the smallest of the three lakes you'll visit, more like a large pond, and the trail curves around its north side. Stop here for a while if you please, or continue onward. A slight climb and then more descent follows. Pass a couple of small ponds, and then travel through another level, forested stretch. A couple of switchbacks bring you down the trail to Upper Twin Lake, a broad, blue body of water that could be large enough for motor boats. The trail is almost completely flat as it winds around the north edge of Upper Twin; then it continues a quarter-mile to the edge of Lower Twin. At Lower Twin Lake, you reach a trail junction. Go either way, and make a long, pleasant circle around the big lake. If you wish to head directly to the best swimming spots, stay to the left and hike to the northwest side.

Hikers with enough energy to add another mile to their trip might consider taking the trail from the northeast side of Lower Twin Lake that leads a half-mile to Rainbow Lake. Situated at the base of Fairfield Peak, Rainbow Lake has good swimming potential and bountiful scenic beauty.

Wherever you wander and however you spend your day at the lakes, remember to save some energy for the uphill climb home. You have a brief climb and then a level stretch back to Echo Lake, followed by a steep ascent from Echo Lake back to the top of the ridge above Summit Lake Campground. The final mile, thankfully, is all downhill.

6. CLUSTER & TWIN LAKES LOOP

Summit Lake area, Lassen Volcanic National Park
An all-day loop trip to nearly a dozen lakes

DISTANCE: 11.0 miles round-trip; 6 hours   **LEVEL:** Moderate
ELEVATION: Start at 6,700 feet; total change 1,300 feet   **CROWDS:** Moderate
BEST SEASON: June to October   **RATING:** ★ ★ ★

DIRECTIONS: From the northwest entrance station at Manzanita Lake, drive southeast on Highway 89 for 12 miles to the left turnoff for Summit Lake North Campground. (From the Southwest entrance station, drive north on Highway 89 for 16 miles to the right turnoff for Summit Lake North Campground.) Turn into the campground and park near the lake in the spots designated for day-use. Walk along the camp road, paralleling the lake, following signs toward the amphitheater.

This trail is an extended version of the hike to Echo and Twin Lakes, detailed in the previous story. It adds more miles and adventure for people who want a longer day in the woods. You'll visit nearly a dozen lakes over the course of the 11-mile loop, plus enjoy a long meander through a pine and fir forest. But first, an insider's tip: You should know that the best of the dozen lakes are Echo and Twin Lakes. You might want to simply hike out-and-back to them instead. If not, this tip should help you decide in which direction to hike the loop—counterclockwise, so the best lakes come first, or clockwise, so you save the best for last. Decisions, decisions.

To reach the start of this hike, walk along the edge of Summit Lake Campground on pavement, heading for the amphitheater. Before you reach it, you'll see a trail sign for numerous lake destinations; bear left. The path climbs a forested ridge for eight-tenths of a mile. At the top, you'll find another trail sign and the start of this loop. Here you must choose which lakes you want to visit first. We chose the Cluster Lakes, saving Echo Lake and the Twin Lakes for last. If you do the same, you'll bear left and set off on a mostly level stretch, followed by a long, rather uninspiring descent through the forest. The descent is so long—covering almost two miles—that you may start to feel concerned about how much elevation you're losing, and at what point you'll have to gain it back. Fear not; it's not as bad as it seems.

At two miles from the trailhead, you'll pass your first lake, which is actually an unnamed large pond. One mile farther, Little Bear Lake is on the left, then in another quarter-mile, Big Bear Lake also appears on the left. Neither lake is particularly handsome, especially by late summer when the water level drops, but at least you've arrived in lake country. If you don't like these lakes, there are plenty more to follow.

From Big Bear Lake onward, the trail finally ends its long downward trend and levels out. A half-mile of easy hiking brings you to the left turnoff for the Cluster Lakes, two long, narrow lakes with lodgepole pines ringing their edges. The Cluster Lakes are just five minutes off your loop, so take a jaunt to the left to see them if you wish, then return to the main trail.

Back on the loop, you'll find that Silver Lake is only a quarter-mile from the Cluster Lakes junction. It's the first lake that's worthy of a lengthy stop. Its shallow waters have a silvery cast, and you'll find a few grassy shoreline spots between the trees, where you can set down your day-pack and pull out your lunch. Silver Lake, like its neighbor Feather Lake, is considered to be part of the Cluster Lakes' chain of six lakes.

When you're ready, continue on to Feather Lake, a quarter-mile farther. It's just as pretty as Silver Lake, but its deeper waters make for better swimming. As at the other lakes, the trail runs right along its shoreline. At Feather Lake, you're about halfway through the loop.

It comes as a surprise when you reach a lakeless stretch between Feather Lake and Lower Twin Lake that lasts for 1.6 miles. Instead of looking for lakes, you can focus on the quiet of the forest. Enjoy the fact that the trail has not yet begun its final climb, and you still have three more gorgeous lakes to visit. At the first of these, Lower Twin Lake, you have the choice of circling the lake if you wish. Most people just bear right and follow the trail along the lake's western end; this is the shortest route and provides plenty of opportunities for swimming or admiring the wind-rippled, watery expanse. Lower Twin Lake is my favorite on this lake-filled loop, but its neighbor, Upper Twin, wins a close second. The trail runs a mere five feet from the edge of Lower and Upper Twin Lakes, providing continual water views.

The return climb begins between Lower and Upper Twin Lakes, but there are good rest spots at both Upper Twin Lake and Echo Lake. The final half-mile climb from Echo Lake to the top of the ridge above Summit Lake Campground will make you thankful that the mile after it—the final mile of this trip—is all downhill.

7. KINGS CREEK FALLS

Southwest area, Lassen Volcanic National Park
Waterfall, forest, and meadows

DISTANCE: 2.4 miles round-trip; 1.5 hours
ELEVATION: Start at 7,260 feet; total change 700 feet
BEST SEASON: June to September
LEVEL: Easy/moderate
CROWDS: Heavy
RATING: ★ ★ ★ ★

DIRECTIONS: From the Southwest entrance station, drive north on Highway 89 for 12 miles to the Kings Creek Falls pullout area on both sides of the road. The trail begins on the right side of the road. (From the northwest entrance station at Manzanita Lake, drive south for 17 miles.)

The waterfall on Kings Creek is pretty, not spectacular, but the beauty of the trail to reach it makes Kings Creek Falls one of the most visited attractions in Lassen Volcanic National Park. The hike is a downhill trek along Kings Creek, starting from a nondescript pullout along the park road. On weekdays, a yellow school bus is often parked in this pullout; Kings Creek Falls is a popular destination for visiting school classes.

The first part of the trail meanders under the shade of big fir trees, but at a quarter mile out, the trail leaves the forest for a pleasant

Kings Creek near Lower Meadow

traverse along the edge of Lower Meadow. The meadow is dark green and teeming with ebullient corn lilies in spring and early summer. It makes a perfect place to rest on the uphill hike back.

Beyond the meadow, you reach a fork and have two options: the Foot Trail or the Horse Trail. The Foot Trail is the most scenic choice. It leads steeply downhill for a half-mile on stair-steps cut into the rock, just inches away from an area of Kings Creek called The Cascades. Hikers who have trekked the world-famous Mist Trail in Yosemite will find a kinship between that trail and the granite walkway to Kings Creek Falls, although the latter has much less of a grade.

Just before you step down the granite staircase, take a look ahead at the far-off valley vista. Once you're on the stair-steps, you must keep your eyes on your feet and their placement, because you're hiking only a few inches from the rushing cascade of white water. Some hikers mistake these cascades for Kings Creek Falls, and they unknowingly turn around before they reach the real thing. Keep going until you come to a fenced overlook area.

Kings Creek Falls are about 50 feet high and split by a rock out-crop into two main cascades, which make a steep and narrow drop into the canyon. The fence surrounding the waterfall keeps hikers out of trouble on the unstable canyon slopes. If you want to take pictures, arrive here in the morning, when the cataract is evenly lit.

For your return trip, you can retrace your steps on the spectacular Foot Trail back uphill along Kings Creek, or you can take the easier Horse Trail, which connects back with the main trail near Lower Meadow.

8. KINGS CREEK FALLS & SIFFORD LAKES LOOP

Southwest area, Lassen Volcanic National Park
Waterfall, lakes, and views on a loop hike

DISTANCE: 5.2 miles round-trip; 2.5 hours   **LEVEL:** Moderate
ELEVATION: Start at 7,260 feet; total change 900 feet   **CROWDS:** Moderate
BEST SEASON: June to September   **RATING:** ★ ★ ★ ★

DIRECTIONS: From the Southwest entrance station, drive north on Highway 89 for 12 miles to the Kings Creek Falls pullout area on both sides of the road. The trail begins on the right side of the road. (From the northwest entrance station at Manzanita Lake, drive south for 17 miles.)

Hikers seeking either a longer walk or a chance to get away from the throngs on the Kings Creek Falls Trail will enjoy this loop hike to the Sifford Lakes. By following this route, you get to pay a visit to Kings Creek Falls (see the previous story for details), but instead of returning via the same trail, you'll circle around on the Sifford Lakes Trail, where you can stop at one of the Sifford Lakes for lunch or perhaps a swim.

To make the trip, follow the trail directions in the previous story to Kings Creek Falls, but watch for the Sifford Lakes Trail junction on your right, about 100 yards before you reach the falls. After admiring the waterfall, return to this junction and cross Kings Creek on a log footbridge. The trail climbs quite steeply uphill, but only for about 200 yards. You'll gain the top of a ridge, located at the base of a fascinating volcanic wall.

Hike along the base of this wall, getting many looks at the crags and caves in its rock, then descend until you reach tiny, nondescript Bench Lake. The "lake" is only a small pond, which nearly dries up by the end of summer.

Next comes a long downhill stretch of more than a half-mile in an open, sunny forest. Watch for a trail junction, then make a sharp right turn and—surprise!—climb back uphill to Sifford Lake in seven-tenths of a mile. Along the way you'll pass a junction on the right for the Kings Creek Falls Trailhead at Lassen Park Road. Take note; this is the return of your loop. For now, go left and head for the lake.

The first Sifford Lake, at elevation 7,200 feet, has many fallen snags in it, but you can wade in on the far (west) side. However, if this lake doesn't suit your fancy, you can head for the second Sifford Lake via a faint use trail. From the far end of the first lake, pick up the use

The first Sifford Lake

trail and follow it northwest for three quarters of a mile. Reaching the second Sifford Lake requires covering some distance and a bit of an ascent, but a third and a fourth lake are located close to the second one. Once you make it to the second lake, you might as well visit the others.

Don't leave this area without checking out the great overlook just to the south of the first Sifford Lake. Next to Kings Creek Falls, it's the highlight of the trip. From where the trail deposited you at the first lake, walk to your left (south) for about 70 yards, passing a couple of campsites. You'll find yourself standing on the edge of a remarkably steep canyon. About a thousand feet below you are the steam vents and boiling springs of Devils Kitchen at Warner Valley.

The return leg of the loop is an easy 1.8 miles, first heading downhill from Sifford Lake to the previously noted trail junction, then continuing downhill for another mile to a crossing of Kings Creek. This crossing is located at a lovely, green expanse of Lower Meadow, where the glassy stream makes lazy S-turns through the lush grasses. Take a seat on the Kings Creek footbridge, remove your hiking boots, and dangle your feet in the icy cold water.

Finally, you have a blissful stroll across this meadow before you rejoin the busy Kings Creek Falls Trail. Turn left and finish out the last four-tenths of a mile back to the park road.

9. COLD BOILING LAKE, CRUMBAUGH LAKE, & CONARD MEADOWS

Southwest area, Lassen Volcanic National Park
Two lakes and meadows filled with wildflowers

DISTANCE: 4.0 miles round-trip; 2 hours   **LEVEL:** Easy
ELEVATION: Start at 7,500 feet; total change 300 feet **CROWDS:** Minimal
BEST SEASON: July to October   **RATING:** ★ ★ ★ ★

DIRECTIONS: From the Southwest entrance station, drive north on Highway 89 for 11 miles to the Kings Creek Picnic Area turnoff on the right. Turn right and drive one mile to the end of the road and the trail sign on the right.

As a trailhead, the Kings Creek Picnic Area gets overlooked by many park visitors, who tend to hike the trails located right along the main park road. Although some people make their way to Kings Creek Picnic Area for picnicking or fishing in Kings Creek, they usually aren't thinking about hiking. This leaves the area's trails to you.

At the end of the road in the picnic area, you'll find a trail marker on the right signed for Cold Boiling Lake in seven-tenths of a mile, Crumbaugh Lake in 1.2 miles, and other destinations. Begin your hike there. Make a brief climb uphill, then continue on a pleasant, level grade through sparse forest. A half-mile in, you'll see a trail fork for Twin Meadows, a worthy trip for another day (if the wildflowers are in bloom). In a few more minutes of walking, Cold Boiling Lake shows up just off the trail to the right. A sign points out the "boiling" feature of the small pond lined with grasses: Cold gases continually bubble up through the surface of the water.

The trail forks at Cold Boiling Lake; bear left to continue to much larger Crumbaugh Lake. You'll probably see plenty of deer prints from this point onward, and quite possibly the creatures who made them. The trail makes a shady descent through a lovely forest filled with dense red fir and mountain hemlock, until it arrives at the trail junction by Crumbaugh Lake.

Crumbaugh is a big, blue body of water, with Mount Conard looming behind it to the south at 8,204 feet. The lake is set at 7,204 feet, and a trail fork to the left will lead you around the lake's perimeter clockwise. (You may have to do a little trailblazing along the lake's north side, but the route is obvious.) The right fork leads directly to the west side of the lake (good swimming here), then onward to Conard Meadows and beyond to Mill Creek Falls. In the foreground of Crumbaugh Lake is a wide meadow, littered with corn lilies and

Crumbaugh Lake and Mount Conard

lupine. The best spot to sit and admire the scene is on the rocky hillside just to the left of the trail fork. Climb up the slope a few feet and find a good rock to perch on.

If you're visiting early in the year when the wildflowers are in bloom, I highly recommend continuing six-tenths of a mile from Crumbaugh Lake to Conard Meadows. The trail is basically flat, and in about 15 minutes of walking through a gorgeous red fir forest, you reach the meadow's edge. Look for pennyroyal, leopard lilies, lupine, asters, and mountain heather.

10. TERRACE, SHADOW, & CLIFF LAKES

Southwest area, Lassen Volcanic National Park
Three of Lassen's prettiest lakes

DISTANCE: 3.4 miles round-trip; 2 hours   **LEVEL:** Easy/moderate
ELEVATION: Start at 8,050 feet; total change 650 feet   **CROWDS:** Moderate
BEST SEASON: July to October   **RATING:** ★ ★ ★ ★

DIRECTIONS: From the Southwest entrance station, drive north on Highway 89 for 8.8 miles to the pullout area on the left. A small trail sign indicates the path to Terrace, Shadow, and Cliff Lakes.

There are many, many lakes in Lassen Volcanic National Park, and they spawn a fair amount of debate about which one is the best, the prettiest, and/or the most suitable for swimming. It's hard to make a definitive choice on the matter, but certainly this hike to Terrace, Shadow, and Cliff Lakes takes you to three lakes that qualify for the park's Top 10 list. Surprisingly, all three are remarkably different, although they lie only one mile apart.

Although some hikers trek to the lakes the long way, starting from Hat Lake in the north part of the park, the more common route is a short downhill hike from the park road two miles east of the Lassen Peak Trailhead. Following this path, you'll reach Terrace Lake in a half mile, Shadow Lake in eight-tenths of a mile, and Cliff Lake in 1.7 miles. Of the three lakes, Shadow Lake is the largest and is best for swimming. If you hike only to Shadow Lake, you'll have a mere 1.6-mile round-trip. Remember that no matter how far you go, it's downhill on the way in, and uphill on the return.

Although many lakes in Lassen are a disappointment for swimmers, due to shallow waters, forested or grassy shorelines, and too many tree snags in the water, these three lakes are exceptions. You'll reach the first lake, Terrace, in about 15 minutes of hiking. Terrace Lake is long and narrow, with a cliff forming its back wall and trees and rocks surrounding the rest of it. The trail leads closely along its south side. At the far end of the lake, you can look back and see the tip of Mount Lassen peeking up. Hike a few yards farther on the trail and you'll peer down on Shadow Lake, remarkably close by.

The trail drops to Shadow Lake, which is huge and round—at least double the size of Terrace Lake. Like Terrace, it has a rocky shoreline and some trees, but overall it is much more

Terrace Lake

open and exposed. Conveniently, the trail clings to the lake's southeast shore, so at any point, you can kick off your shoes and wade in. It takes another 10 minutes to hike to the far side of Shadow Lake, but when you get there, look back over your shoulder for a fine view of Mount Lassen in the background.

Shadow Lake makes a fine destination by itself, but it would be a shame to turn around here, because the trail just keeps getting more scenic. It descends again, then crosses a stream and passes a small pond in a meadow. Again, look over your shoulder for admirable views of Lassen Peak—the best of the entire trip. The trail then re-enters the forest. Watch for a fork and a spur leading to the right; this is the path to Cliff Lake. Hike through the trees to the small lake, which does indeed have a cliff, plus an impressive talus rockslide of white rocks on its southwest perimeter. Reading Peak rises to the south; the rockslide began on its slopes.

Cliff Lake's waters are shallow, clear, and green. The lake's most intriguing element is a small, tree-lined island on the west end. Walk to your right along the shoreline until you reach the lake's inlet, where you'll find an abundance of wildflowers, including wandering daisies, lupine, heather, and corn lilies.

11. LASSEN PEAK

Southwest area, Lassen Volcanic National Park
A climb to the summit of a giant volcano

DISTANCE: 5.0 miles round-trip; 2.5 hours **LEVEL:** Strenuous
ELEVATION: Start at 8,500 feet; total change 2,000 feet **CROWDS:** Heavy
BEST SEASON: July to October **RATING:** ★ ★ ★ ★

DIRECTIONS: From the Southwest entrance station, drive north on Highway 89 for 6.9 miles to the Lassen Peak Trailhead on the left.

NOTE: An interpretive brochure is available at the Loomis Museum.

Lassen Peak must be the most frequently hiked mountain in all of Northern California. The season that the trail is open is remarkably short—usually only three or four months between July and October. But in that brief time, the huge Lassen Peak parking lot is filled with cars every day of the week, and the Lassen Peak Trail is lined with people hiking slowly up and down the old volcano.

Why is this trail so popular? For starters, Lassen Peak is one of the largest volcanic domes in the world, topping out at elevation 10,457 feet. (Mount Shasta, 70 miles northeast, is nearly 4,000 feet higher, but its summit is far more difficult to attain.) In addition, the views from Lassen Peak are truly breathtaking. But the main reason this trail attracts so many hikers is that it's a surprisingly short hike to the top— only five miles round-trip.

The trek is not necessarily easy, however, and shouldn't be treated as if it's a ride at Disneyland. Many park visitors show up at the parking lot, see all the cars, and make the assumption that the hike is an easy cruise. Then, without carrying water or any other hiking essentials, they set off on the trail in whatever clothes and shoes they happen to be wearing. On one trip, I saw a woman hefting a bulging pocketbook over her shoulder, and two little kids wearing flimsy sandals. Park rangers say that many more people attempt the trail than actually make it to the top, simply because they aren't prepared.

That said, the Lassen Peak Trail isn't terribly difficult. It's a mostly moderate ascent of 2,000 feet spread out over 2.5 miles, with some short, steep sections. It is harder to hike on some days when variables such as lingering snow patches, occasional gale-force winds, or hot sun at midday make the trail more arduous. Another potential difficulty is that clouds can move in quickly and obscure the view. For safety reasons, thunderstorms must be avoided at all costs.

But you can plan your trip so that everything will go perfectly. First, wait to climb the trail until late July, August, or September when

Brokeoff Mountain from the summit of Lassen Peak

it is free of snow, or nearly so. Second, pick a clear, windless day, and start your trip early in the morning. (The crowds are nonexistent before 9 A.M., and you'll be off the mountain before the day gets too hot.) And finally, wear sunscreen and sunglasses, and bring plenty of water and a jacket for the summit. No matter how warm you get climbing up the trail, the wind on top will cool you down fast.

The trail starts out on an easy grade from the parking lot, and gets steeper as you climb. Occasional mountain hemlocks and whitebark pines grow alongside the volcanic rock outcrops on the mountain's slopes; you may see the bold Clark's nutcracker flitting among the tree branches. (It looks and behaves like a large blue jay, but it's grey and white instead of blue.)

The trail is wide and shadeless; there's no respite from the sun and little respite from the wind. Mileage markers give you a countdown on how far you have to go (not how far you've come.) Terrific views of Brokeoff Mountain, Lake Helen, Mount Conard, and Crumbaugh Lake are evident as you climb the south face of the peak. Lake Almanor is the big lake far to the south, outside of the park.

A few interpretive signs posted at switchback turns bring the now quiet volcano's history to life. The signs feature quotes from the *San Francisco Examiner* in May 1915, when the peak began spilling white hot lava. You'll find yourself staring at the barren, beautiful, silent mountain, trying to imagine the huge mudslides, towering gas clouds, and repeated violent eruptions that flattened trees and devastated the area for miles around. The peak's eruptions officially began in May 1914, but the real devastation didn't occur until May 1915. Minor eruptions of lava continued until 1917; steam eruptions continued until 1921.

Although your mind may be fixed on volcanoes, it's important to remember that Lassen was formed not just by volcanism but also by glacial action. The glacial evidence along Lassen's slopes gives away its age—about 11,500 years. An interpretive sign at an east-facing switch-back points out glacial features.

One of the most fascinating trail sections is between miles one and two, where the path curves through more than a dozen short switchbacks. This is an incredible feat of trail building on a very steep grade. On your return trip downhill over this section, you'll have many excellent opportunities to photograph the long line of peak hikers snaking their way uphill.

When at last you reach the summit, your view opens up to the north, all the way to Mount Shasta and beyond on clear days. Look carefully for Shasta, which often has a ring of clouds surrounding it. If you walk around the edge of the yawning crater to the highest rocky point on the summit, where the United States Geological Survey marker is, you can see down the east side of the volcano. On this slope, you can observe the furrowed lines left from mud, snow, and water flowing down to the Devastated Area during the 1915 eruptions.

Try to find a wind-sheltered spot among the summit's many boulders. You'll want to stay up here for a while, enjoying both the peak's fabulous vistas and also its remarkable history.

12. BUMPASS HELL

Southwest area, Lassen Volcanic National Park
Largest hydrothermal area in Lassen

DISTANCE: 3.0 miles round-trip; 1.5 hours   **LEVEL:** Easy/moderate
ELEVATION: Start at 8,200 feet; total change 700 feet   **CROWDS:** Heavy
BEST SEASON: July to October   **RATING:** ★ ★ ★ ★

DIRECTIONS: From the Southwest entrance station, drive north on Highway 89 for 5.8 miles to the Bumpass Hell Trailhead on the right.

NOTE: An interpretive brochure is available at the trailhead.

If you travel Lassen Volcanic National Park with children, you will quickly learn that Bumpass Hell is their favorite trail destination because it has the distinction of having not one but two foul words in its name. When you explain that "Bumpass" was the name of the man who discovered this strange geologic area, this distinction may be lessened somewhat, but then again, maybe not.

The "Hell" in Bumpass Hell is easy to recognize. Bumpass Hell is an active hydrothermal area, part of the Lassen Geothermal System, which encompasses Bumpass Hell, Sulphur Works, Boiling Springs Lake, Little Hot Springs Valley, Morgan Springs, and Terminal Geyser. Bumpass Hell is geology in action—16 acres of boiling springs, hissing steam vents, noisy fumaroles, and bubbling mud pots.

This geologic commotion is the result of crack-like fissures in the earth that penetrate deeply enough to tap into volcanic heat (or with a little imagination, into the searing hot landscape of Hades). Surface water from rain and snowmelt seeps into these fissures and travels downward until it touches volcanically heated rock. This creates steam, which rises back up to the surface. As a result, pools of water in the Bumpass Hell area can reach temperatures of 250 degrees. Kendall

Bumpass Hell Trail

Vonbook Bumpass, who discovered Bumpass Hell in the 1860s, lost one of his legs when he stepped into one of these boiling thermal pools.

Fortunately, today hikers have a trail to follow in Bumpass Hell, and a plethora of signs to remind us to stay on the boardwalk and off the unstable soil. The hike is an easy stroll with a gradual elevation change, and it's a popular route for families. Visitors seeking a longer walk can trek 1.5 miles to Bumpass Hell, then another 1.5 miles to Cold Boiling Lake. Most people simply explore Bumpass Hell and then return.

In addition to its fascinating geology, the Bumpass Hell Trail features wide views of surrounding peaks in its first mile. A half-mile in, between interpretive posts 10 and 11, is a short spur on the right leading to an overlook of Mount Conard, Diamond Peak, Brokeoff Mountain, Mount Diller, and Pilot Pinnacle. All of these mountains are a part of the ancient volcano Mount Tehama, which once stood on this spot. Long since collapsed and eroded, Mount Tehama once soared to an elevation of 11,500 feet. Lassen Peak was formed from lava that flowed from Mount Tehama.

As you round a curve and reach the highest point in the trail, you find an interpretive sign explaining the wonders of Bumpass Hell, which is now directly below you. You also hear the strange ruckus caused by all the hydrothermal activity—sounds variously described as steam engines, trucks speeding by, or turbine motors. The smell of sulphur is ubiquitous. A short descent takes you into the hydrothermal area, and boardwalks lead you over and around the various hot pools, steam vents, and mudpots. Even the stream that flows through Bumpass Hell is odd looking—its water is milky gray instead of clear. Most of the hot pools in the area are also gray, except for the large pool at the end of the boardwalk, which is a marvelous turquoise blue.

13. SULPHUR WORKS

Southwest area, Lassen Volcanic National Park
Easily accessible hydrothermal area

DISTANCE: 0.2 mile round-trip; 10 minutes   **LEVEL:** Easy
ELEVATION: Start at 6,900 feet; total change 25 feet   **CROWDS:** Heavy
BEST SEASON: June to October   **RATING:** ★ ★ ★

DIRECTIONS: From the Southwest entrance station, drive north on Highway 89 for nine-tenths of a mile to the Sulphur Works and Ridge Lakes Trailhead on the left.

NOTE: An interpretive brochure is available at the trailhead.

In 1865, two enterprising gentlemen got the bright idea to develop the sulphur and clay properties in the hydrothermal areas in today's Lassen National Park. They were unsuccessful in their business endeavors, but the name "Sulphur Works" was given to the main area they tried to commercialize, and it stuck.

Park visitors today know the Sulphur Works as an easy stop off the park road, a place where even non-hikers can get a close-up look at hydrothermal activity. Just by rolling down the car windows, you can smell the "rotten egg" smell of sulphurous gases, and see the giant plumes of billowing steam from fumaroles or steam vents. The Sulphur Works is a smaller hydrothermal area than either Bumpass Hell (see the previous story) or Devils Kitchen (see page 100), but it's worth a short walk-through nonetheless.

As you hike up wooden stair-steps and across the boardwalks that surround the various mudpots, fumaroles, and hot springs, try to imagine this area 10,000 years ago, when it was part of the ancient volcano, Mount Tehama. A predecessor to Mount Lassen, giant Mount Tehama peaked at 11,500 feet in elevation and measured four miles across. Eventually the huge volcano was weakened by faulting and by the activities of smaller volcanoes on its slope, which siphoned lava from Tehama's main vent. The volcano collapsed in on itself, and over time, glaciers removed most of its large remains. The Sulphur Works is believed to have been the central vent of Mount Tehama.

If you visit the Sulphur Works soon after snowmelt, when there is a lot of water in the ground, its mudpots will be visibly boiling. Large drops of the icky mud stuff pop up a few inches into the air, then plop back down into small pools. If you visit in late summer or fall, when

The Sulphur Works

the ground has dried up, you will see only puddles of still, clay-like mud. (Although these are far less dramatic looking, they are still far too hot to touch.) At any time of year, the Sulphur Works' mud and soils are vividly colored by a variety of minerals. Plus, the steam vents are always active, sending billowing gases high into the air and causing visitors to wrinkle up their noses at the sulphurous odor.

14. RIDGE LAKES

Southwest area, Lassen Volcanic National Park
Small, isolated lakes in a dramatic setting

DISTANCE: 2.0 miles round-trip; 1 hour   **LEVEL:** Moderate
ELEVATION: Start at 6,900 feet; total change 1,000 feet   **CROWDS:** Minimal
BEST SEASON: July to October   **RATING:** ★ ★ ★ ★

DIRECTIONS: From the Southwest entrance station, drive north on Highway 89 for nine-tenths of a mile to the Sulphur Works and Ridge Lakes Trailhead on the left.

Almost everybody at Lassen Park stops to see the Sulphur Works and walk the short interpretive trail around odoriferous steam vents, rumbling fumaroles, and bubbling mudpots. But hardly anybody notices the other trail that begins at the Sulphur Works parking lot, and few folks bother to hike it. That's the Ridge Lakes Trail, which leads one steep mile uphill to the Ridge Lakes (plural) or Ridge Lake (singular). They are two small lakes if you visit late in the summer, and one larger lake if you visit early in the summer, when snowmelt has joined the two basins with deep, cold water. The lake is prettier when it is one lake, not two, so try to time your hike for soon after snowmelt. A bonus is that the lake is not thickly forested around its edges—a welcome contrast to so many Lassen lakes—so it has an accessible shoreline for swimming and sunning. The water, of course, is cold.

You will have to earn a swim in Ridge Lake. The trail is a bit of a butt-kicker, with a nearly constant 20 percent grade over one mile. You'll be huffing and puffing for sure. Part of the route is forested, and the rest traverses open meadows with lovely wildflowers, especially lupine and pennyroyal (notice the minty smell). An interesting feature near the trail's beginning is a view over the boardwalks of the Sulphur Works. To see it, look to your right as you climb.

Make sure you wear good hiking boots. This trail has some rocky sections, although much of the path is on smooth forest floor. Also,

Ridge Lakes

don't forget your sunscreen—the open meadows and the lake itself have almost no shade. It might be wise to hike this trail early in the morning, so that the sun is at your back.

The path more or less follows West Sulphur Creek, the stream that pours into the Sulphur Works. As you climb, take breaks so that you can look back at the increasingly wide views to the south of the Mill Creek and Childs Meadow areas. When you finally ascend the Ridge Lakes' ridge, you'll find that the lakes are surrounded by three mountainous knobs on an even higher ridge above the lakes. They're part of the rim of ancient Mount Tehama. The "knobs" are Brokeoff Mountain, Mount Diller, and Diamond Peak.

Swimmers will find that the best place to wade in is right where the trail deposits you at the lake, or slightly to the right. If you visit when the two lakes are joined as one, look for the point that is lined with a stand of trees. This is the place where the lakes divide in late summer.

You can easily wander around the lakes, and you might choose to climb to the low saddle on the southwest side to check out the vistas. Some people attempt a more challenging ascent up a ravine on the northwest side of the lake. From the high point of this short but steep climb, you can see all the way to Mount Shasta.

15. MILL CREEK FALLS

Southwest area, Lassen Volcanic National Park
The park's tallest waterfall

DISTANCE: 3.2 miles round-trip; 1.5 hours   **LEVEL:** Easy
ELEVATION: Start at 6,700 feet; total change 300 feet   **CROWDS:** Minimal
BEST SEASON: June to October   **RATING:** ★ ★ ★ ★

DIRECTIONS: From the Southwest entrance station, drive north on Highway 89 for 100 yards to the parking area on the right side of the road, near the rest room by Southwest Campground (just south of Lassen Chalet.) Begin walking on the paved trail by the rest room, heading left through the camp to the signed trailhead.

Mill Creek Falls is the highest waterfall in Lassen Park, and it's arguably also the prettiest. Better still, the waterfall has an excellent hiking trail leading to it that is sheer pleasure to walk.

At only 3.2 miles round-trip and with an easy up-and-down undulation, the trail is suitable for hikers of almost any ability. You won't find yourself saddled with any long uphill stretches on either the way in or the way out. This hike is an easy cruise.

The trailhead is on the south side of Lassen Park, near Lassen Chalet and Southwest Campground. The Mill Creek Falls Trail begins on the left (north) side of the campground, then drops downhill to a log bridge over West Sulphur Creek. Here, only a quarter-mile in, is one of the most scenic spots of the whole trip. Acres and acres of mule's ears grow on the hillside on the far side of the bridge. It's the largest continuous patch of them I've ever seen. In summer, their leaf display is vibrant emerald green, sporting big yellow flowers. In fall, the mule's ears appear shriveled and brown, but they're still impressive in their numbers. To the north of this spot is a postcard-perfect view of Mount Lassen. More than a few photographs have been shot here.

The trail laterals across hillsides and over feeder streams for 1.6 miles. Mainly it travels under a canopy of red firs, white firs, and pines, but occasionally the path leads to small open meadows rife with corn lilies and grassy wildflowers. You'll head steadily eastward through the trees, climbing gently and descending gently, then repeating the pattern. Suddenly you hear the sound of falling water, and in moments you're standing at a clearing, peering across the canyon at plunging Mill Creek Falls.

At 75 feet high, the waterfall makes a lasting impression. Two creeks join together at its lip, then spill through a very steep and narrow

Mill Creek Falls

chute. Sulphur Creek contributes to Mill Creek Falls' greatness; the pairing and funneling of the two streams result in its tremendous water flow. The rock face over which the waterfall pours is layered with moss and lichens, ranging in colors from rust and orange to deep green. Big old-growth fir trees grow on the cliff above the falls, adding to the majesty.

Most people end their hike at this clearing, which is the best place to view Mill Creek Falls. But if you like, you can follow the trail another quarter mile to the waterfall's brink. Those who desire a longer hike can continue another mile to Conard Meadows, which sports excellent wildflowers in early summer. Yet another mile of trail leads to Crumbaugh Lake. (For details on Conard Meadows and Crumbaugh Lake, see the story on page 81.)

16. BROKEOFF MOUNTAIN

Southwest area, Lassen Volcanic National Park
The park's second highest summit

DISTANCE: 7.4 miles round-trip; 4 hours   **LEVEL:** Strenuous
ELEVATION: Start at 6,600 feet; total change 2,600 feet   **CROWDS:** Minimal
BEST SEASON: July to October   **RATING:** ★ ★ ★ ★ ★

DIRECTIONS: From the Southwest entrance station, drive south on Highway 89 for three-tenths of a mile to the trailhead parking pullout on the east side of the road. The trail begins on the west side of the road. (Even though this trail begins south of the entrance station, you are still expected to pay the park entrance fee at the station before hiking here.)

Serious day-hikers seeking a more substantial trek in Lassen Park shouldn't miss the ascent of Brokeoff Mountain. At 9,235 feet, Brokeoff is the highest peak in the park after Mount Lassen. But the trail to reach Brokeoff's summit is longer than the trail to Lassen's summit, which means you'll find far fewer people attempting the trip. Its views rival those from Mount Lassen; the difference is that from Brokeoff, Mount Lassen is the main feature in the panorama.

Frequent visitors to the park will tell you that Lassen Peak is for the tourists, whereas Brokeoff Mountain is for serious hikers. I say you shouldn't miss climbing either peak, as long as you are in good enough physical condition.

From the Brokeoff Mountain Trailhead, just south of the Southwest entrance station to the park, the trail begins climbing immediately, and keeps a steady grade throughout most of the hike. The first mile of trail and the last half-mile are the least steep. If you tire of the ascent, or if cloudy weather is obscuring the peak, a good alternate destination is Forest Lake, only 1.3 miles up the trail (see the following story).

Although the trail to Brokeoff Mountain is one of the last in the park to clear of snow, it's wise not to wait too late in the year to hike it. Brokeoff's trail has one of the finest wildflower displays of anywhere in Lassen, but if you show up after too many hot days of summer, the flowers will be shriveled and brown. Look for abundant silver leaf lupine, penstemon, and Indian paintbrush. Along with the flowers come an abundance of deer, who munch on the blooms and foliage and drink from the mountain's many streams.

As you ascend the mountain, you'll witness the forest changing from dense, thick stands of red firs and pines, to a more stunted, high-alpine forest of mountain hemlock. The higher

Lassen Peak from the summit of Brokeoff

you go, the more barren and volcanic the landscape appears. You have many views of Brokeoff Mountain in the first half of your climb, but the face you see is not the face you will hike. The trail leads around to the back (west) slope of Brokeoff, adding an extra mile as you circum-navigate the mountain.

The trail's last three-quarters of a mile is filled with views. The trees have all but disappeared at this elevation, and the barren ridgeline gives you ample opportunities for a new perspective every few minutes. The peak is really a ridge with three summits; each one is worth visiting and offers a slightly different view. Vistas to the south include Lake Almanor and Childs Meadows. Lake Helen and Mount Lassen appear to the north. All of the major peaks in the western region of the park are visible: Chaos Crags, Lassen, Diller, and Conard. On clear days, you can make out the San Joaquin Valley and the Coast Range beyond. If you hike early enough in the summer when bright white snow fields are still lingering in the park, the view appears even more dramatic.

A few hundred yards before the highest summit, a use trail leads off to the left, taking you along the ridgeline to the north. The view of Mount Shasta from this point (70 miles away!) is well worth a side trip.

17. FOREST LAKE

Southwest area, Lassen Volcanic National Park
Pretty lake below the summit of Brokeoff Mountain

DISTANCE: 3.0 miles round-trip; 1.5 hours   **LEVEL:** Easy/moderate
ELEVATION: Start at 6,600 feet; total change 700 feet   **CROWDS:** Minimal
BEST SEASON: July to October   **RATING:** ★ ★ ★

DIRECTIONS: From the Southwest entrance station, drive south on Highway 89 for three-tenths of a mile to the trailhead parking pullout on the east side of the road. The trail begins on the west side of the road. (Even though this trail begins south of the entrance station, you are still expected to pay the park entrance fee at the station before hiking here.)

Hikers heading for the summit of Brokeoff Mountain will some-times become dismayed by two factors: The trail is steep and tiring, and the summit can quickly become ensconced in clouds, which obscure the view.

If either of these factors affect your trip to Brokeoff Mountain, you still have an option: A visit to Forest Lake, scenically nestled below the base of Brokeoff. Even those who have no intention of hiking to Brokeoff's summit should consider this easy trail to Forest Lake, if only to see the early summer wildflowers in bloom alongside the trail.

The trail begins just south of the Southwest entrance station to Lassen. (Make sure you pay your park entrance fee, even though you may not have passed through the park entrance kiosk. Rangers do check car windshields for park receipts.) The trail begins to climb immediately and maintains that same pitch almost every step of the way. The vegetation is thick at the start, including tunnel-like willows and alders growing alongside a boisterous stream. Some sections can be wet and

Forest Lake below Brokeoff Mountain

muddy. In a few hundred yards, the trail enters pine and red fir forest, and then alternates between forest and meadows for the rest of the trip. Each time the forest thins, you get a good look at Brokeoff Mountain, and the ground becomes littered with wildflowers, such as Indian paintbrush, lupine, baby blue eyes, and purple penstemon. Mountain heather and pink bleeding hearts are also plentiful, especially near the stream. The wonderful minty smell in the meadows comes from pennyroyal.

You'll pass a couple of small ponds in marshy meadows along the trail, but these are not your destination. Forest Lake is hidden, a quarter-mile off the main trail. At 1.3 miles from the start, the trail bends left to cross the stream on two small log bridges, then continues up-slope through the forest. Don't cross here. Instead, look for a use trail that branches off to the right before the stream crossing, then continues uphill on the right side of the stream. This is the path to Forest Lake; it parallels the stream for a quarter-mile uphill to the lake.

You need to keep your eyes on the faint trail, but this is not so easy to do. You're distracted by the sound of a small waterfall dropping into a meadow, and the sight of many terrific volcanic boulders alongside the path, some the size of minivans. In 10 minutes of trailblazing you'll reach Forest Lake, which has a great view of Brokeoff and its surrounding mountainous walls. The lake's eastern edge has a few clearings where you can lay down your day-pack and admire the scene.

18. BOILING SPRINGS LAKE

Warner Valley area, Lassen Volcanic National Park
Hydrothermal theatrics and a lake of colored clay

DISTANCE: 3.0 miles round-trip; 1.5 hours   **LEVEL:** Easy
ELEVATION: Start at 5,600 feet; total change 250 feet   **CROWDS:** Minimal
BEST SEASON: June to October   **RATING:** ★ ★ ★ ★

DIRECTIONS: From the Southwest entrance station, drive four miles south on Highway 89, then turn left and drive east on Highway 36/89 for 25 miles to Chester. Turn left on Feather River Drive. In seven-tenths of a mile, bear left for Warner Valley and Drakesbad. Drive six miles, then turn right on Warner Valley Road. Drive 11 miles to Warner Valley Campground, then continue past it for a quarter-mile to the trailhead parking area on the left.

NOTE: An interpretive brochure is available at the trailhead.

Boiling Springs Lake may be the strangest-looking volcanic feature in Lassen Volcanic National Park—a place not lacking in strange-looking volcanic features. The lake is milky gray and tan, not clear blue or green, and it has a shoreline of colorful clay, not dirt. It looks more like a lake out of *Alice in Wonderland* than a real lake.

Interpretive brochures for Boiling Springs Lake are available at the trailhead in Warner Valley; they provide an excellent education on the flora and geology of the area. Begin hiking on the Pacific Crest Trail, heading southwest and crossing Hot Springs Creek almost immediately. You'll hike through a mixed conifer forest of lodgepole pine, red and white fir, incense cedar, and Jeffrey pine. If you're carrying the interpretive brochure, you'll be able to identify them all.

In four-tenths of a mile, the Pacific Crest Trail junctions with trails leading to Devils Kitchen and other points in Warner Valley. Bear left at two neighboring junctions, staying on the Pacific Crest Trail but now heading southeast, for another seven-tenths of a mile. After a gradual climb, you'll reach the start of the Boiling Springs Lake loop, where you turn right and exit the Pacific Crest Trail.

Immediately you know you are in hydrothermal country. The odorous scent of "rotten eggs"—hydrogen sulfide—gives it away.

Although water in the form of steam and carbon dioxide make up 95 percent of the materials billowing upward from the hydro-thermal steam vents, it's the traces of hydrogen sulfide that make themselves known.

Soon you will hear the heartbeat sound of the bubbling mudpots, and see the odd coloring of Boiling Springs Lake. A bit cooler than some thermal pools in the park, Boiling Springs Lake is heated to 125 degrees Fahrenheit. Its temperature is consistently maintained by steam vents located underneath the lake. The lake's strange color

Boiling Springs Lake

is caused by various elements in the water. Clay, opal, iron oxide, and sulphur mix to make the gray and tan colors; the turquoise and green near the lake's edges are caused by algae that have adapted to hot water.

On the far side of Boiling Springs Lake, you rejoin the Pacific Crest Trail. A right turn will take you 1.5 miles to Terminal Geyser, a small thermal area with more noisy steam vents. (One in particular emits an impressively large plume of steam; it's worth seeing if you don't mind hiking three more miles round-trip.) Turn left to stay on the Boiling Springs Lake Loop and you'll be rewarded with a fine view of Lassen Peak, followed by a close-up look at Boiling Springs Lake's mudpots. These mudpots are considered to be some of the most color-ful in the park, but their show is best seen early in the year when there is still plenty of ground water keeping them wet. Otherwise, they will look like caked, dried-up mud. The mudpots are colored by the same minerals that color the water of Boiling Springs Lake.

19. DEVILS KITCHEN

Warner Valley area, Lassen Volcanic National Park
Dramatic hydrothermal area without the crowds

DISTANCE: 4.8 miles round-trip; 2.5 hours   **LEVEL:** Easy/moderate
ELEVATION: Start at 5,600 feet; total change 400 feet   **CROWDS:** Minimal
BEST SEASON: June to October   **RATING:** ★ ★ ★ ★

DIRECTIONS: From the Southwest entrance station, drive four miles south on Highway 89, then turn left and drive east on Highway 36/89 for 25 miles to Chester. Turn left on Feather River Drive. In seven-tenths of a mile, bear left for Warner Valley and Drakesbad. Drive six miles, then turn right on Warner Valley Road. Drive 11 miles to Warner Valley Campground, then continue past it for a quarter-mile to the trailhead parking area on the left.

Devils Kitchen is not the largest hydrothermal area in Lassen Park; Bumpass Hell holds that title. But it is certainly the most remote hydrothermal area in the park, and the long drive plus the hike to reach it make it seem even more otherworldly than the rest.

The trail to Devils Kitchen begins in the Warner Valley area of Lassen Park, accessible only by a long drive out of the town of Chester. From the trailhead parking area on the south side of the road near Warner Valley Campground, start hiking on the Pacific Crest Trail (PCT), heading south. The PCT crosses Hot Springs Creek a few hundred yards from the parking area. The creek is fed by thermal water from Boiling Springs Lake, Devils Kitchen, and other hot springs areas, but surprisingly, the water is cold. At four-tenths of a mile, you'll reach a junction of trails; bear right for Devils Kitchen.

In short order you will cross Hot Springs Creek once again, directly across from the cabins and buildings that comprise Drakesbad Guest Ranch. The ranch is the only lodging service available in Lassen Park; it's a historic lodge with cabins, a hot springs pool, a restaurant, and horses for rent. Keep it in mind for next summer.

Prepare yourself for a visually stunning section of trail that cuts through the immense meadow west of the ranch. Turn left and walk right down the center of Drakesbad Meadow, watching for wildflowers and wildlife as you walk. We saw both deer and marmots here, munching on flowers, and a young bear in the nearby forest.

At the edge of the meadow you'll enter the forest and hike on a slight uphill grade to a trail junction at 1.2 miles. Continue straight for another mile to Devils Kitchen, a seven-acre hydrothermal area with boardwalks and bridges, just like at Bumpass Hell and Sulphur Works.

Follow the half-mile loop trail through Devils Kitchen. Interpretive signs are posted along the trail.

Devils Kitchen was aptly named for the mudpots and fumaroles running along Hot Springs Creek. It's not hard for anyone with imagination to picture the Prince of Darkness busy cooking dinner over those rumbling, steaming vents. As with the other hydrothermal areas at the park, your senses will get a workout here: You'll hear the *glub-glub* thumping sound of boiling mudpots, smell the odor of hydrogen sulfide, and see the dramatic sight of billowing fumaroles.

With steam vents hissing and thermal pools boiling all around you, it's obvious that Devils Kitchen qualifies as an active hydrothermal area. It's part of the Lassen Geothermal System, which encompasses Bumpass Hell, Sulphur Works, Boiling Springs Lake, Little Hot Springs Valley, Morgan Springs, and Terminal Geyser. The heart of all this hydrothermal activity—the major plume of magma-heated water—is at Bumpass Hell. But large amounts of this hot water flow laterally from Bumpass Hell to Devils Kitchen, and to nearby Boiling Springs Lake. (See the story on Boiling Springs Lake on page 98.)

20. DRAKE LAKE

Warner Valley area, Lassen Volcanic National Park
Out-of-the way lake accessible via a loop trail

DISTANCE: 5.0 miles round-trip; 2.5 hours   **LEVEL:** Moderate
ELEVATION: Start at 5,600 feet; total change 900 feet   **CROWDS:** Minimal
BEST SEASON: June to October   **RATING:** ★ ★

DIRECTIONS: From the Southwest entrance station, drive four miles south on Highway 89, then turn left and drive east on Highway 36/89 for 25 miles to Chester. Turn left on Feather River Drive. In seven-tenths of a mile, bear left for Warner Valley and Drakesbad. Drive six miles, then turn right on Warner Valley Road. Drive 11 miles to Warner Valley Campground, then continue past it for a quarter-mile to the trailhead parking area on the left.

You want a near-guarantee of solitude at Lassen Volcanic National Park? Place your bets on Drake Lake, a small, out-of-the-way body of water in the Warner Valley section of Lassen. To reach it, first you make the long drive to Warner Valley. Then you must hike, negotiating your way though a long series of route options and trail junctions. Finally, you make a long, gut-thumping climb up a shadeless ridge to the water's edge. After all that, there's a good chance that Drake Lake will be all yours. No wonder.

Drakesbad Meadow

Few people make a trip exclusively to Drake Lake; most combine it with either a hike to Devils Kitchen or a hike to Boiling Springs Lake. The intrepid can go see all of these Warner Valley features in one day, making a nine-mile loop trip. But no matter how you do it, keep in mind that the final stretch of trail to Drake Lake is a butt-kicker, especially on a hot day. And when you reach the lake, you may not want to swim: Mosquitoes are voracious in the early season, and the lake level drops substantially by late summer. If you time it perfectly, in between the mosquito hatch and the late-summer drought, you will be rewarded.

Begin hiking on the Pacific Crest Trail, heading southwest from the parking lot at Warner Valley. Cross Hot Springs Creek almost immediately, then at four-tenths of a mile, reach a trail junction. For the most direct route to Drake Lake, turn left here (this is also the trail to Boiling Springs Lake), then 40 yards farther, bear right. The trail leads through the forest for 1.2 miles to a junction with a trail to Devils Kitchen. Bear left for Drake Lake and in less than a quarter-mile, start a serious climb, gaining 700 feet in three-quarters of a mile. A half-dozen switchbacks carry you up the exposed, manzanita-covered slope; luckily, the views get more inspiring as you climb higher. You can see the Drakesbad Guest Ranch and meadow, plus miles of forested slopes and Lassen Peak.

At the top of the ridge you'll re-enter the forest; the shade here is a welcome relief. A short, level jaunt of a quarter-mile brings you to Drake Lake. The forest remains thick; trees and grass run right down to the waterline in early summer. It's difficult to find any shoreline at the shallow lake, but if you're hot enough, and if the mosquitoes aren't eating you alive, you'll swim anyway.

Note that on your return from Drake Lake, you have the option of following the trail fork toward Devils Kitchen. If you take it, you'll cross Hot Springs Creek, then have the choice of hiking one mile to Devils Kitchen or just turning right and hiking back to the trailhead. This alternate route is highly recommended, not just for the side trip to Devils Kitchen (see the previous story for details), but also for the lovely stretch of trail through Drakesbad Meadow on the way back to the trailhead. The alternate route won't add any extra miles to your round-trip; a visit to Devils Kitchen will add two miles.

21. JUNIPER LAKESHORE CIRCLE

Juniper Lake area, Lassen Volcanic National Park
Easy stroll around Lassen's largest lake

DISTANCE: 5.8 miles round-trip; 3 hours   **LEVEL:** Easy/moderate
ELEVATION: Start at 6,800 feet; total change 300 feet   **CROWDS:** Moderate
BEST SEASON: July to October   **RATING:** ★ ★ ★

DIRECTIONS: From the Southwest entrance station, drive four miles south on Highway 89, then turn left and drive east on Highway 36/89 for 25 miles to Chester. Turn left on Feather River Drive. In seven-tenths of a mile, bear right for Juniper Lake. Drive 5.5 miles, then take the right fork signed for Juniper Lake. The road turns to dirt and gravel and continues for another 7.4 miles to the lake. Continue straight, past the campground turnoff. Park in the lot near the ranger station signed "Trailhead Parking." Hike from here, following the dirt road past the ranger station and some private cabins. Alternatively, you can begin hiking from the Juniper Lake Campground or the hikers' parking lot by the campground.

At 575 surface acres and 235 feet deep, Juniper Lake is the largest and deepest body of water in Lassen Volcanic National Park. Is this a good reason to hike all the way around its perimeter? Yes indeed.

Most campers at Juniper Lake Campground take this simple hike around the edges of Juniper Lake because the trail runs right through their camp. If you're camping, you can start right from your tent door and head in either direction, although the trail is prettier to the south (left as you face the lake). If you aren't camping at Juniper Lake, begin hiking by the ranger station, following the dirt road past a mile-long row of private cabins along the northwest shore. The cabins, each with their own private boat dock, are nestled in the fir forest surrounding the lake.

After the last cabin, the dirt road becomes a narrow trail and continues south along the west shore of the lake. In short order, you'll reach a cove with excellent swimming areas. Many people only hike this far, then turn around. If you continue, at 2.3 miles from the start, you'll reach a trail junction with the path to Indian Lake and Horseshoe Lake. Take note: This is a fine trip for another day. For now, stay left and endure a short stretch of traveling away from the lake's edge, heading a good distance south and then reaching two forks, one shortly after the other. Turn left at both forks and head north again, regaining your proximity to the lake.

Now you're on the south shore of the lake, where occasional boulders or fallen trees make good spots for sunning or picnicking. This stretch of trail nears perfection: It undulates gently up and down along the lakeshore, rarely moving out of sight of the lake. Most of the route is shaded by big conifers. There are dozens of places where you can leave the trail, step down to the lake's edge, and wade in.

Four miles through your loop, you'll reach the edge of Juniper Lake Campground. This is an excellent camp for kayakers and canoers, where almost every site is within a few feet of the water's edge. Anglers won't necessarily like it, however: There are no fish in Juniper Lake. Rainbow trout are the only native fish in the park, and they require moving water in which to spawn. Juniper Lake, like many lakes in Lassen, has no moving water. The lake was created approximately 50,000 years ago, when the volcano Mount Harkness was formed. The volcano blocked the southern drainage for the large basin in which Juniper Lake sits. With no drainage, the basin filled with water and stayed that way. Today the lake water is replenished each year by snowmelt and rain.

Walk through the campground, then follow the camp road back to the main dirt road heading to the ranger station. These last two miles of trail are the dullest slice of the whole trip; you will have to tolerate occasional cars driving past, creating dust clouds. But it's a small price to pay for the other four miles. If walking on roads insults your hiking sensibilities, you can always make an out-and-back trip instead, skipping the dirt road portion. To go out and back, the best place to start is at the Juniper Lake Campground, heading south.

22. JUNIPER, SNAG, & HORSESHOE LAKES LOOP

Juniper Lake area, Lassen Volcanic National Park
Three-lake grand tour of the Juniper Lake region

DISTANCE: 7.5 miles round-trip; 4 hours   **LEVEL:** Moderate
ELEVATION: Start at 6,800 feet; total change 1,500 feet   **CROWDS:** Moderate
BEST SEASON: July to October   **RATING:** ★ ★ ★ ★

DIRECTIONS: From the Southwest entrance station, drive four miles south on Highway 89, then turn left and drive east on Highway 36/89 for 25 miles to Chester. Turn left on Feather River Drive. In seven-tenths of a mile, bear right for Juniper Lake. Drive 5.5 miles, then take the right fork signed for Juniper Lake. The road turns to dirt and gravel and continues for another 7.4 miles to the lake. Continue straight, past the campground turnoff. Park in the lot near the ranger station signed "Trailhead Parking." Begin hiking by the ranger station, following the signs to Snag Lake.

You could just hike out-and-back from Juniper Lake to Snag Lake, but then you'd see mostly forest and more forest. If you follow this loop trail from Juniper Lake to Snag Lake to Horseshoe Lake, then back to Juniper Lake, you'll see forest, three lakes, a gurgling stream, and verdant meadows. If you like a little variation on the trail, this hike is your ticket.

From the ranger station flagpole, take the trail to the right for Snag Lake (the left trail to Horseshoe Lake will be the return of your loop). The trip begins with a moderate half-mile climb through the forest to the top of a ridge, then a half-mile descent down the other side. Purple penstemon blooms at your ankles almost every step of the way. At 1.3 miles, you'll reach a trail junction with one path leading right for Jakey Lake; turn left for Snag Lake.

At 1.5 miles, you reach another trail junction; this one goes left for a shortcut to Horseshoe Lake. If anyone in your party is tiring out, this is a good option for a shorter loop (5.3 miles), although if you take it, you'll miss Snag Lake. The main trail continues gently downhill through the forest; you rarely leave the trees for the entire hike to Snag Lake. Only short stretches through tiny meadows provide a brief change. In spring, you'll find wildflowers in the meadows, including columbine, lupine, asters, and corn lilies. By late summer, you'll have missed the show.

The trail maintains a downhill or level grade for the rest of the route to Snag Lake. You can tell you are nearing it when the path begins to get sandy. At a trail junction just before the lake, your loop will turn left, but you should take a short jaunt to the right to visit Snag Lake. (The trail you're on bypasses the lake.) In a quarter-mile of walking, you'll be on Snag Lake's southeastern edge, staring out at its vast expanse. Snag Lake is the second largest lake in Lassen, after Juniper Lake. The dark-colored Fantastic Lava Beds and Cinder Cone rise up behind it, to the north. Numerous tree snags have fallen into the water, giving the lake its name and an eerie quality, especially in late summer after the water level has dropped.

After your visit to Snag Lake, backtrack to the previous junction and head first west, then south, for Horseshoe Lake. Cross the marshy bog around Grassy Swale Creek, then climb upward through a mixed conifer forest, moving away from the creek. Shortly, you'll join the creek again, and parallel it for a long and lovely stretch with a gentle uphill grade. This section from Snag Lake to Horseshoe Lake is the best of the hike.

The farther you go, the more placid the stream becomes. The trail eventually levels and you pass some lovely meadows. At their far end, you'll see a log cabin ranger station. Its setting is so perfect, you may find yourself wishing you were a park ranger. Before turning left and crossing the creek to head past the log cabin, bear right at the sign for Twin Lakes and walk 100 yards to the northeast shore of Horseshoe

Log cabin ranger station at Horseshoe Lake

Lake. (As at Snag Lake, you must make a short side trip off the loop trail in order to visit Horseshoe Lake.) Most would agree that Horseshoe Lake is prettier than either Snag or Juniper lakes, with a forested shoreline and mountainous backdrop to the west. Swimmers will enjoy the fact that Horseshoe Lake has a cinder and gravel bottom, which is very pleasant on the feet.

After visiting Horseshoe Lake, backtrack to the last junction, cross Grassy Swale Creek and walk past the ranger station. Continue straight ahead to close out the loop to Juniper Lake. The wide trail between Horseshoe and Juniper lakes presents you with a half-mile climb, then a three-quarter-mile descent, back to your starting point.

23. JAKEY LAKE

Juniper Lake area, Lassen Volcanic National Park
Meadows, forest, and small lake

DISTANCE: 6.0 miles round-trip; 3 hours   **LEVEL:** Moderate
ELEVATION: Start at 6,800 feet; total change 1,200 feet   **CROWDS:** Minimal
BEST SEASON: July to October   **RATING:** ★ ★ ★

DIRECTIONS: From the Southwest entrance station, drive four miles south on Highway 89, then turn left and drive east on Highway 36/89 for 25 miles to Chester. Turn left on Feather River Drive. In seven-tenths of a mile, bear right for Juniper Lake. Drive 5.5 miles, then take the right fork signed for Juniper Lake. The road turns to dirt and gravel and continues for another 7.4 miles to the lake. Continue straight, past the campground turnoff. Park in the lot near the ranger station signed "Trailhead Parking." Trails begin at the ranger station. Bear right for Snag Lake and Jakey Lake.

For a moderate hike to a small, secluded lake in the Juniper Lake area of Lassen Volcanic National Park, the trip to Jakey Lake fits the bill. The lake is surrounded by several smaller bodies of water, all of which attract birds, but only Jakey Lake is big enough for swimming. Compared to hiking to nearby Snag Lake or Horseshoe Lake, your chances of solitude are better at Jakey Lake. Jakey's small size and the climb required to reach it (and to return to the trailhead!) limit the number of people willing to make the trip.

The first half-mile is a good healthy ascent to the top of a ridge, followed by a long half-mile descent down its far side. You may see a few other hikers on this stretch; many use this path as a route to large Snag Lake to the north. At 1.3 miles, you'll reach a junction with a trail to the right for Jakey Lake. Take it, and enjoy a gentler uphill stretch

Meadow near Jakey Lake

through small meadows and past good-sized ponds for a half-mile. If you hike early in the summer, there will probably be water flowing in the ravine beside the trail; this is Jakey Lake's outlet.

The final half-mile to Jakey Lake climbs with a bit more fervor, but the closer you get, the more water you'll find—both in the stream and in tiny ponds. Wildflowers bloom in profusion, especially big bunches of lupine and corn lilies. Song birds and water birds are plentiful in this forested, wet area.

The trail skirts along the south edge of Jakey Lake. The grasses are dense and green around the lake edge, which can bring plenty of mosquitoes in the early season. Follow a use trail to the north side of the lake for the best swimming areas, which are a bit grassy and muddy, but serviceable. You may see campers setting up to spend the night on the lake's west side.

24. INSPIRATION POINT

Juniper Lake area, Lassen Volcanic National Park
Scenic views accessible by a short, easy hike

DISTANCE: 1.4 miles round-trip; 45 minutes   **LEVEL:** Easy/moderate
ELEVATION: Start at 6,800 feet; total change 400 feet   **CROWDS:** Minimal
BEST SEASON: July to October   **RATING:** ★ ★ ★

DIRECTIONS: From the Southwest entrance station, drive four miles south on Highway 89, then turn left and drive east on Highway 36/89 for 25 miles to Chester. Turn left on Feather River Drive. In seven-tenths of a mile, bear right for Juniper Lake. Drive 5.5 miles, then take the right fork signed for Juniper Lake. The road turns to dirt and gravel and continues for another 7.4 miles to the lake. Continue straight, past the campground turnoff. Park in the lot near the ranger station signed "Trailhead Parking," then walk back down the road about 100 feet (head away from the ranger station) to the Inspiration Point trailhead.

Hikers and campers who have been making the trip to Juniper Lake for many years will tell you that the vista at Inspiration Point is not what it used to be; the trees are slowly crowding out the view. But if you've never been to Inspiration Point before and have nothing to compare it to, you'll think the views are terrific and well worth the short walk from the trailhead. Perspective is everything.

Like the nearby trail to Crystal Lake (see the following story), the Inspiration Point Trail is short and steep. It's such a brief trek that it's ideal to save for the end of the day, when the light is getting low or your energy is running out. You can make the round-trip in less than an hour and still have plenty of time to enjoy the view. (However, don't expect to get good photographs at this time, because you will face the setting sun. Photographers should hike this trail in the morning.)

There's only one brief section of 100 yards or so where the trail runs flat; otherwise, you have a simple, steady, uphill grade. The route is mostly forested with pines and firs as it ascends to the top of a ridge. When you reach the ridgetop, walk along it for about 150 yards, and you'll see that it is lined with more of the view-obstructing pines and firs. Never mind: Look around and above the trees, and many of Lassen's best features are in focus. You can see East and West Prospect Peak, Cinder Cone, Butte Lake, and Snag Lake to the north; Lassen Peak, Chaos Crags, and Brokeoff Mountain to the west; and Mount Harkness and Juniper Lake to the south. On the clearest days, snow-capped Mount Shasta can be seen to the northwest, a remarkable 70 miles distant.

---

25. CRYSTAL LAKE

Juniper Lake area, Lassen Volcanic National Park
Great swimming in one of Lassen's most scenic lakes

DISTANCE: 0.8 mile round-trip; 30 minutes   **LEVEL:** Easy/moderate
ELEVATION: Start at 6,800 feet; total change 450 feet   **CROWDS:** Moderate
BEST SEASON: July to October   **RATING:** ★ ★ ★ ★

DIRECTIONS: From the Southwest entrance station, drive four miles south on Highway 89, then turn left and drive east on Highway 36/89 for 25 miles to Chester. Turn left on Feather River Drive. In seven-tenths of a mile, bear right for Juniper Lake. Drive 5.5 miles, then take the right fork signed for Juniper

Lake. The road turns to dirt and gravel and continues for six miles to the Juniper Lake Campground turnoff. Continue straight at the turnoff (don't bear left to the camp) for three-tenths of a mile. The Crystal Lake Trailhead is on the right; park off the road. (If you reach the Juniper Lake Ranger Station, you've gone one mile too far.)

Crystal Lake has what almost no other lake in Lassen Volcanic National Park has: shoreline. Not just any shoreline; I mean some very fine large granite rocks that are perfect to lay on and use as your own private swimming dock. This ranks Crystal Lake several cuts above many Lassen lakes, which are lined with trees, grass, and mud, and provide no place to sit down while you take off your hiking boots.

Not only is Crystal Lake a terrific swimming hole, but it also features an excellent ridgetop vista overlooking the Juniper Lake area that rivals the views from nearby Inspiration Point. Need more to convince you to take the hike? Okay, the Crystal Lake Trail is less than one mile round-trip.

It's a steep hike, however. You can park your car and be at the lake in about 15 minutes, but not without effort. From the trailhead, set off on the well-signed trail, which climbs immediately. The forest cover is mostly pines and firs; the trees' shade keeps the trail cool. Set your sights on the goal—the top of this ridge where Crystal Lake lies in a small cirque. On the right, just before you reach the lake, observant tree-lovers will spot a tiny stand of juniper trees on a rocky slope, the namesake of large Juniper Lake below. (Ironically, Juniper Lake has none of these trees near its edges.)

Granite-backed Crystal Lake

Crystal Lake is not large; it's only about 100 yards wide and long, but it's backed by the dramatic,

250-foot-high Crystal Cliffs to the north and east. You can and should hike all the way around the lake, enjoying the beauty of it from all perspectives. Glacially formed Crystal Lake is first-rate for swimming due to its clean, rocky edges. It's like a much smaller version of many lakes in Yosemite.

After thoroughly appreciating the lake, walk a few yards to the west of it on the rocky slabs facing back toward Juniper Lake. From those slabs, you get an awesome view of Juniper Lake with Mount Lassen in the background. (To reach this viewpoint as you come up the trail to Crystal Lake, cross the usually dry outlet creek and head to your left.) Vistas are also good from the high granite slabs on the south side of the lake (on your right as you ascend the trail).

26. MOUNT HARKNESS LOOKOUT

Juniper Lake area, Lassen Volcanic National Park
Fire lookout tower with far-reaching views

DISTANCE: 3.8 or 5.6 miles round-trip; 2 to 3 hours   **LEVEL:** Moderate
ELEVATION: Start at 6,800 feet; total change 1,300 feet   **CROWDS:** Moderate
BEST SEASON: July to October   **RATING:** ★ ★ ★ ★

DIRECTIONS: From the Southwest entrance station, drive four miles south on Highway 89, then turn left and drive east on Highway 36/89 for 25 miles to Chester. Turn left on Feather River Drive. In seven-tenths of a mile, bear right for Juniper Lake. Drive 5.5 miles, then take the right fork signed for Juniper Lake. The road turns to dirt and gravel and continues for six miles to the Juniper Lake Campground turnoff. Bear left at the turnoff and park in the lot signed "Trailhead Parking." Walk downhill, past the organizational campground and into the regular campground. The trail begins by campsite number 5 (on the left).

Without a doubt, Lassen Volcanic National Park's most famous peak is the old snowy volcano Mount Lassen. But hikers who aren't up for the strenuous ascent to its summit or those who don't like its crowded trail can find other Lassen mountains to climb. One of the best of these is found way over in the southeast corner of the park near Juniper Lake. It's Mount Harkness, elevation 8,048 feet, accessible via a 3.8-mile round-trip trail that also can be turned into a 5.6-mile loop hike.

Like many of Lassen Park's peaks, Mount Harkness is an old volcano. On its summit sits an operational fire lookout tower that was built in 1930. On most summer days, you can hike to the summit, sign

Ascending Mount Harkness

the tower register, and have a nice chat with the lookout person. If you prefer to keep to yourself, you'll find that Mount Harkness' summit is broad, allowing plenty of room for a private picnic with a view.

The view, as you might guess, is extraordinary. Not only is it one of the best views possible of Mount Lassen, but the scene extends to the north to Juniper Lake and to the south to Lake Almanor. Walk around Mount Harkness' wide summit and you have a 360-degree panorama. Throw in a few big puffy clouds and you may never want to leave.

Reaching Mount Harkness is surprisingly easy. The trail begins from the campground at Juniper Lake, near site number 5. It climbs moderately through a forest of lodgepole pines and red firs. The shade keeps the climb comfortable, even on hot days. In short order you top out on a ridge, where the forest clears away to a huge, grassy slope. You can see the trail switchbacking up the slope, but surprisingly, you can't see the summit or the lookout tower. What you can see is an incredible view of Mount Lassen to the west. That view just keeps getting better as you hike up a half-dozen long, sweeping switchbacks. Keep climbing, and watch for the appearance of Juniper Lake to the north. If the sun is shining, you may long for the shade you enjoyed on the first half of the trail, but the rapidly widening views will spur you on.

When you reach the top of Mount Harkness, you see it all: Juniper Lake and Mount Lassen are the most prominent landmarks, but to the south is Chester and Lake Almanor, to the east is Susanville and points beyond, and to the north is the astoundingly large Mount Shasta.

If you can tear yourself away from the view, take a close-up look at the Harkness Fire Lookout. It has a beautiful natural stone base, with an upper story of wood and glass. Although it was built in 1930, it has been refurbished several times since. The lookout is usually open and staffed from snowmelt until October 1, and if the lookout person isn't busy, he or she will probably invite you upstairs for an even better view.

For your return trip, simply retrace your steps to the trailhead for a 3.8-mile round-trip, or backtrack down the open, switchbacked slope to a trail junction signed for Warner Valley Road and Juniper Lake Outlet. The path heads steeply downhill for 1.7 miles, and it offers more views of Lassen Peak much of the way. The trail travels a bit too far to the west, but then it reaches a junction where you turn right and head east again. A quarter-mile from the junction, you reach the south shore of Juniper Lake. You have the pleasure of walking along the lake's shoreline for 1.8 miles, all the way back to the campground.

This return loop adds only 1.8 miles to your round-trip, and is highly recommended for its scenic beauty and variety.

27. CINDER CONE

Butte Lake area, Lassen Volcanic National Park
Steep climb up a young volcano

DISTANCE: 4.0 miles round-trip; 2 hours   **LEVEL:** Strenuous
ELEVATION: Start at 6,000 feet; total change 900 feet   **CROWDS:** Minimal
BEST SEASON: June to October   **RATING:** ★ ★ ★

DIRECTIONS: From the northwest entrance station at Manzanita Lake, drive west (out of the park) for a half-mile, then turn right (east) on Highway 44/89. Drive 24 miles east on Highway 44 (turn right at Old Station to stay on Highway 44). Turn right at the signed turnoff for Butte Lake, and drive six miles to the ranger station and trailhead parking lot. The trail begins by the boat ramp, on the west end of the parking lot.

NOTE: An interpretive brochure is available at the Loomis Museum.

This may be the hardest four-mile-long trail you'll ever hike. Simply put, the Cinder Cone Trail brings new meaning to the word "steep." Add in a hot, sunny day and a soft, cinder-and-gravel trail surface, and you may be swearing your way to the top of the Cinder Cone. No matter. Once you reach its summit and walk the level perimeter of its crater, you'll be glad you made the trip.

This also may be the most unusual four-mile-long trail you'll ever hike. The Cinder Cone is another of Lassen Volcanic National Park's many expressions of volcanism. It's a tephra cone volcano, composed of volcanic ash and cinders. (Lassen Peak, in contrast, is a plug dome volcano, formed from one giant plug of thick, viscous lava.) Scientists estimate that the Cinder Cone has erupted as many as five times, beginning around 1567. The most recent eruption was in 1851. When you climb to its summit, you'll be able to see that the cone's crater has two visible rims, indicating at least two separate eruptions. The unusual lava landscape you survey from the top of the Cinder Cone is the result of these eruptions.

But there's still another interesting dimension to this trip. The Cinder Cone Trail is a section of the Nobles Emigrant Trail, which was used by several thousand emigrants in the 1850s and 1860s as their travel route from Oregon and eastern states to the Sacramento Valley. Today, this section of the historic trail begins by the boat ramp at Butte Lake. It is wide enough for a wagon train and extremely sandy. Even the level, initial stretch of trail is more difficult than you would expect due to its loose soil surface. As you progress—making your way through a lodgepole and Jeffrey pine forest—the sandy soil changes to tiny pieces of gravel, or volcanic cinders. While you tromp through it, searching for the firmest areas for better footing, try to imagine pushing your overloaded pioneer wagon through the ash and cinders.

Mount Lassen from the Cinder Cone's rim

Less than a half mile out, you'll pass a junction with the trail to Prospect Peak, but continue straight for the Cinder Cone. You'll walk alongside the Fantastic Lava Beds— otherworldly piles of black basalt rubble, on your left as you hike. Not all of the lava from the Cinder Cone's eruptions spewed out from the top; these piles were formed by a lava flow that pushed out from the base of the cone.

At 1.5 miles, you reach the bottom of the Cinder Cone. Make sure your water bottle is at the ready before beginning your ascent. The Cinder Cone is almost perfectly symmetrical and rises 750 feet from its base. The trail to the top is a half-mile long, with nary a switchback, and not even one moment of shade relief. Plan to stop to catch your breath a few times, and perhaps to question why you're doing this. As you climb, watch for Lassen Peak peeking up over the right shoulder of the Cinder Cone. The slow ascent may seem like it goes on forever, but in fairly short order you'll reach the top.

An obvious trail makes a double circle around the crater, and you should walk every step to enjoy the awesome views you've earned. If you're following the park's interpretive brochure, walk to your right along the crater's outer rim, then walk the inner rim. If you aren't carrying the interpretive brochure, wander as you please. From the outer rim, within sight are Mount Lassen, the Fantastic Lava Beds, Snag Lake, Butte Lake, the Painted Dunes, the Red Cinder Cone, Fairfield Peak, Chaos Crags, and Prospect Peak. Perhaps most exciting of all is the far-off view of Mount Shasta.

Aside from the terrific view, one of the great surprises on top of the barren Cinder Cone is that a few trees have managed to take hold in the infertile cinders of the crater's rim. The white pines and lodgepole pines are dwarfed and thin, but as long as the volcano does not erupt again, they will thrive and multiply.

From the rim, you have two choices: Return the way you came, or take the trail down the south side of the crater (by interpretive post number 33), then head back around to the right.

28. PROSPECT PEAK

Butte Lake area, Lassen Volcanic National Park
A climb to the summit of a shield volcano

DISTANCE: 7.0 miles round-trip; 4 hours   **LEVEL:** Strenuous
ELEVATION: Start at 6,000 feet; total change 2,300 feet   **CROWDS:** Minimal
BEST SEASON: July to October   **RATING:** ★ ★ ★ ★

DIRECTIONS: From the northwest entrance station at Manzanita Lake, drive west (out of the park) for a half-mile, then turn right (east) on Highway 44/89. Drive 24 miles east on Highway 44 (turn right at Old Station to stay on Highway 44). Turn right at the signed turnoff for Butte Lake, and drive six miles to the ranger station and trailhead parking lot. The trail begins by the boat ramp, on the west end of the parking lot.

Here's your Lassen Park volcano lesson: Mount Lassen is a plug dome volcano, formed when one giant plug of thick lava was forced up from a vent in the earth. The Cinder Cone by Butte Lake is a tephra cone volcano, comprised of layer upon layer of cinders and ash. And Prospect Peak is a shield volcano, gradually built up from repeated small eruptions of very thin lava.

From a distance, a shield volcano looks less dramatic than either a plug dome or tephra cone volcano. It is rounded and smooth, like a Roman shield, not conical in shape, and its slopes are more gradual and less abrupt. Nonetheless, when you climb to the top of Prospect Peak, you'll find plenty of drama. With an elevation of 8,338 feet, its vista is one of the finest in the park, bringing into perspective major park landmarks to the south and west, the Warner Mountains to the east, and Mount Shasta to the north. On high visibility days, you can make out the northern Sierra Nevada to the south, plus the Central Valley and the Coast Range far to the west.

The trail is the same as the Cinder Cone Trail (see the previous story) for the first four-tenths of a mile. Turn right at the trail sign for Prospect Peak, and enjoy the promise of the trail surface becoming firmer as you climb. Slowly but surely, the ash and cinder surface gives way to hard dirt.

If you've climbed Brokeoff Mountain in the southern part of Lassen Park, you'll find the difficulty level of this trail to be similar. The

Deer on the trail to Prospect Peak

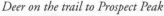

path makes a continual ascent on a moderate grade, never letting up until you reach the summit. You're frequently shaded by Jeffrey pine and fir forest, although the tree cover becomes thinner and more open the higher you go. You get occasional good views of the Cinder Cone over your left shoulder.

A few final switchbacks bring you to the summit. Technically, you're standing on East Prospect Peak; West Prospect Peak is the neighboring peak (to the west, of course). The building remains that you see are all that's left of the fire lookout tower that once stood atop this peak. It was removed in the early 1980s.

A surprising feature of the summit is that it is actually two summits, one on top of the other. In addition to the main shield volcano that created the major bulk of Prospect Peak, a small cinder cone was formed on top, probably much later. You can circle around the rim of the cinder cone, enjoying the tremendous views in all directions.

29. BUTTE LAKE to SNAG LAKE

Butte Lake area, Lassen Volcanic National Park
Two loops between two of Lassen's biggest lakes

DISTANCE: 7.0 to 10.0 miles round-trip; 3 to 5 hours   **LEVEL:** Moderate
ELEVATION: Start at 6,000 feet; total change 800 feet   **CROWDS:** Moderate
BEST SEASON: June to October   **RATING:** ★ ★ ★ ★

DIRECTIONS: From the northwest entrance station at Manzanita Lake, drive west (out of the park) for a half-mile, then turn right (east) on Highway 44/89. Drive 24 miles east on Highway 44 (turn right at Old Station to stay on Highway 44). Turn right at the signed turnoff for Butte Lake, and drive six miles to the ranger station and trailhead parking lot. If you want to hike to Snag Lake via the Cinder Cone, the trail begins by the boat ramp on the west end of the parking lot. If you want to hike to Snag Lake via the east shore of Butte Lake, the trail begins on the east end of the parking lot.

In the case of Butte Lake and Snag Lake, there is more than one way to get from here to there, so you need to make a choice.

Most people hike from Butte Lake to Snag Lake by way of the Cinder Cone. If you are visiting the Butte Lake area of Lassen Park for only one day, this is the best option, because it combines a visit to the volcanic Cinder Cone with a few hours at Snag Lake, where you can swim. However, this route requires hikers to put up with a loose, cinder-and-gravel trail surface for much of the hike, and precious little shade.

Snag Lake's southern end

If you have time to hike more than one trail in the Butte Lake area, you might do well to make a short trip to the Cinder Cone, then take a second hike in the opposite direction around Butte Lake to Snag Lake. This route to Snag Lake is one mile longer than the other route, but the trail surface is far superior. This trail also features lovely views of Butte Lake and the Fantastic Lava Beds and has plenty of shade for hot days.

Of course, intrepid hikers always have the option of making a 14-mile loop out of the trip, visiting Butte Lake, Snag Lake, and the Cinder Cone all in one long day.

The two routes to Snag Lake begin at opposite ends of the Butte Lake parking lot. Any way you go, Snag Lake is worth the trip, especially early in the summer when the lake level is at its highest. Snag Lake is the second largest lake in the park, after Juniper Lake. The lake's east shore has both the best swimming spots and the best views of the Cinder Cone and Fantastic Lava Beds. If you travel to Snag Lake via the east shore of Butte Lake, you will reach Snag Lake's east shore directly. This route includes a pretty walk along the shore of Butte Lake, a good climb through the forest from Butte Lake up to a ridge, and then a descent down to the edge of Snag Lake. You'll pass two lovely stands of aspens: One at the southern edge of Butte Lake, and a larger one on the east side of Snag Lake.

If you travel to Snag Lake via the Cinder Cone, you will reach the west shore of Snag Lake in 3.4 miles. In the last mile, the trail surface becomes much firmer (thank goodness). A spur trail leads to a small beach at the edge of the lava flow, where you can swim. Although many people stop here for a seven-mile round-trip hike, it's worth following the trail counterclockwise for a mile or more along the lake's west and south shores to reach its east shore. If you don't want to hike that far, choose your picnicking or swimming spot from those available on the west shore.

Snag Lake was formed when a lava flow from the Cinder Cone dammed the creek that flowed into Butte Lake. Water backed up from this dam and filled Snag Lake. The trees that were previously growing here died and eventually collapsed, leading to the name "Snag Lake." Today, overflow water from Snag Lake seeps through pores in the lava beds and continually refreshes the water in Butte Lake.

30. WIDOW LAKE

Butte Lake area, Lassen Volcanic National Park
From big Butte Lake to smaller, remote Widow Lake

DISTANCE: 7.2 miles round-trip; 3.5 hours
ELEVATION: Start at 6,000 feet; total change 1,000 feet
BEST SEASON: June to October

LEVEL: Moderate
CROWDS: Minimal
RATING: ★ ★ ★

DIRECTIONS: From the northwest entrance station at Manzanita Lake, drive west (out of the park) for a half-mile, then turn right (east) on Highway 44/89. Drive 24 miles east on Highway 44 (turn right at Old Station to stay on Highway 44). Turn right at the signed turnoff for Butte Lake, and drive six miles to the ranger station and trailhead parking lot. The trail begins on the east end of the parking lot.

You're unlikely to have much company at Widow Lake. Most people in the Butte Lake area of Lassen Park are occupied with hiking to the Cinder Cone or swimming at Snag Lake, so few bother with the jaunt to Widow Lake. It's a good place for hikers who don't want any neighbors.

One reason for the solitude is that the trail's final mile is a steep climb, far more difficult than the rest of the hike. The first 2.5 miles are comparatively easy and offer terrific views as you hike along the eastern edge of Butte Lake. You get to enjoy both the sparkling, blue-green water and the lake's backdrop: The odd-looking dark hills of the Fantastic Lava Beds. This imaginatively named lava flow is solid black and runs for several miles. As you walk along the edge of Butte Lake, you see that the lava flow not only frames the southwest side of the lake, but pieces of it also create unusual jet-black islands in the lake.

Except for one brief hill climb near the start of the trail, where you ascend and then descend a series of short switchbacks in a fire-scarred forest, most of the route along Butte Lake is within five feet of the water's edge. You'll spot numerous likely places for a swim, if you choose. (Or save this diversion for the return trip.) Views of the Cinder Cone, and occasionally, Lassen Peak, are excellent.

On the southern end of Butte Lake, you enter into a small, lovely aspen grove, and the trail remains pleasant and level. But at a junction with the right fork to Snag Lake, you bear left for Widow Lake, 1.4 miles away, and quickly start to climb. The ascending trail follows Widow Lake's often dry outlet stream. In the space of about a mile, you gain 1,000 feet. Most of the climb is fairly steady, but a few short sections will surely make your heart pound.

A final push over a ridge takes you out of the forest to a high point where the vistas behind you open wide. Make sure you turn around to look; otherwise you won't see the fine views of the Cinder Cone and other Lassen landmarks until your return trip.

When at last you reach Widow Lake, you arrive at the marshy western side, which looks like a grassy pond. Don't be disappointed;

Hiking along Butte Lake en route to Widow Lake

follow the path to the right to access the larger body of the lake, which is much deeper and dark blue in color. Along the southwest shore you'll find a rocky area, good for sunning or picnicking. The rest of the lakeshore is lined with trees and grasses.

One final note: You might want to check with the ranger station on the timing of the mosquito hatch before setting off for Widow Lake. When we arrived at the marshy west side of the lake in mid-July, we were nearly eaten alive. Even though we were covered head-to-toe with repellent, we couldn't stand still for one second without massive squadrons of mosquitoes landing on us. Fortunately, the mosquito hatch only lasts about two weeks. But those are two weeks when you definitely want to avoid Widow Lake.

31. BATHTUB LAKES

Butte Lake area, Lassen Volcanic National Park
Two easy-to-reach swimming lakes

DISTANCE: 1.0 mile round-trip; 30 minutes   **LEVEL:** Easy
ELEVATION: Start at 6,000 feet; total change 80 feet   **CROWDS:** Moderate
BEST SEASON: June to October   **RATING:** ★ ★ ★

DIRECTIONS: From the northwest entrance station at Manzanita Lake, drive west (out of the park) for a half-mile, then turn right (east) on Highway 44/89. Drive 24 miles east on Highway 44 (turn right at Old Station to stay on Highway 44). Turn right at the signed turnoff for Butte Lake, and drive six miles to the ranger station and trailhead parking lot. The trail begins on the northeast side of the parking lot.

Every year, the Butte Lake area of Lassen Volcanic National Park is one of the first areas of the park where the snow melts and trails are accessible. This is a blessing in June and early July, when visitors to the park may have few places to go without their snowshoes. But it also means that temperatures are typically higher around Butte Lake, the sun is hot, and even the shade can feel dry. That makes the Bathtub Lakes a perfect hiking destination, both for parents looking for an easy place to walk with their kids, and for hard-core hikers hoping to finish off a long day with a swim.

The hike to the Bathtub Lakes is remarkably easy. From the Butte Lake parking lot, it's only a quarter mile to the first lake, heading up and over a low ridge that is covered with Jeffrey and ponderosa pines. With a mere 10 minutes of walking, you can be seated on a rock, stripped down to your bathing suit for a swim. The second lake is slightly larger than the first, situated off to the left. It can be reached in another few minutes of walking. Both Bathtub Lakes have a smooth cinder bottom, making the swimming more pleasant than at some Lassen lakes, which have muddy bottoms and/or plenty of fallen snags. Both lakes are also shallow enough to be warm most of the summer.

On our trip, we saw a pair of osprey near the second lake, and after watching them for a few minutes, we spotted the location of their nest in a tall tree.

A new section of this trail continues beyond the lakes to Butte Creek, which it crosses on two sawed-off logs. This is a beautiful spot, with many wildflowers blooming along the edges of the stream.

POINT REYES NATIONAL SEASHORE

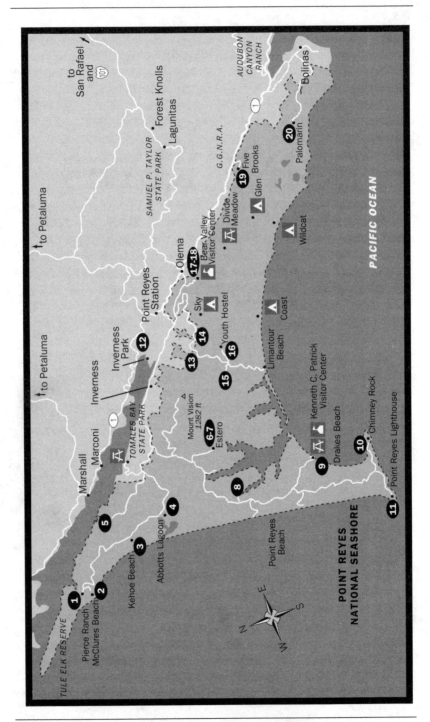

to San Rafael and 101

to Petaluma

Forest Knolls

Lagunitas

SAMUEL P. TAYLOR STATE PARK

AUDUBON CANYON RANCH

Bolinas

G.G.N.R.A.

20 Palomarin

19 Five Glen Brooks

Divide Meadow

Bear Valley Visitor Center

Olema

17-18

Sky

14

Youth Hostel

16

Coast

15

13

Point Reyes Station

Inverness Park

12

Inverness

to Petaluma

Marshall

Marconi

TOMALES BAY STATE PARK

Mount Vision 1282 ft

6-7 Estero

8

9 Kenneth C. Patrick Visitor Center

Drakes Beach

Limantour Beach

Wildcat

PACIFIC OCEAN

10 Chimney Rock

Point Reyes Lighthouse

11

Point Reyes Beach

POINT REYES NATIONAL SEASHORE

5

4

3

Abbotts Lagoon

Kehoe Beach

2

Pierce Ranch

McClures Beach

1

TULE ELK RESERVE

N E S W

124   *Point Reyes National Seashore—map page 124*

POINT REYES NATIONAL SEASHORE
TRAILS AT A GLANCE

Map Number/Trail Name	Page	Mileage	Difficulty
1. Tomales Point Trail	128	4.0-9.4	Easy/moderate
2. McClures Beach	130	1.0	Easy
3. Kehoe Beach	131	1.0-3.0	Easy
4. Abbotts Lagoon	133	2.4	Easy
5. Marshall Beach	135	2.4	Easy
6. Estero Trail to Sunset Beach	137	7.8	Moderate
7. Estero Trail to Drakes Head	139	8.8	Moderate
8. Bull Point	141	3.6	Easy
9. Drakes Beach	142	1.0-4.0	Easy
10. Chimney Rock	144	1.4	Easy
11. Point Reyes Lighthouse	147	0.8	Easy/moderate
12. Tomales Bay Trail	150	2.4	Easy
13. Inverness Ridge, Bucklin, & Bayview Loop	152	7.8	Moderate
14. Sky Trail to Mount Wittenberg Loop	153	4.5	Easy/moderate
15. Muddy Hollow Trail	155	3.6	Easy
16. Coast, Fire Lane, & Laguna Loop	157	5.0	Easy/moderate
17. Bear Valley Trail to Arch Rock	159	8.2	Easy/moderate
18. Bear Valley, Old Pine, Woodward Valley, & Coast Loop	161	12.0	Moderate
19. Stewart & Greenpicker Loop	163	7.0	Moderate
20. Bass Lake, Double Point, & Alamere Falls	164	8.4	Moderate

THE TOP 5, DON'T-MISS DAY HIKES:

Map Number/Trail Name	Page	Features
1. Tomales Point Trail	128	elk, coastal views
6. Estero Trail to Sunset Beach	137	bay, estero, ocean
14. Sky Trail to Mount Wittenberg	153	highest summit in park
18. Bear Valley, Old Pine, Woodward Valley, & Coast Loop	161	forest, meadow, ocean
20. Bass Lake, Double Point, & Alamere Falls	164	waterfall, coast

TRAIL SUGGESTIONS FOR IF YOU ONLY HAVE ONE DAY:

Map Number/Trail Name	Page	Features
9. Drakes Beach	142	protected beach
10. Chimney Rock	144	flowers, ocean views
11. Point Reyes Lighthouse	147	lighthouse, whales
17. Bear Valley Trail to Arch Rock	159	forest, meadow, ocean

POINT REYES NATIONAL SEASHORE

ABOUT THE PARK

Point Reyes National Seashore is a large triangular peninsula attached to the coast north of San Francisco. The seashore is known for its numerous sandy beaches, lagoons, estuaries, and ponds, as well as its thick forests of Bishop pines and Douglas firs. The park is also noted for its wildlife, including plentiful deer and elk on land and seals and sea lions at the shore. Birdwatching and whale watching are popular activities in the park.

ADDRESS, PHONE, & WEBSITE

Point Reyes National Seashore, Point Reyes Station, CA 94956; (415) 663-1092.
Website: www.nps.gov/pore

VISITOR CENTERS

The park's main visitor center is located at the Bear Valley trailhead on Bear Valley Road. Smaller visitor centers are located at Drakes Beach (the Ken Patrick Visitor Center) and the Point Reyes Lighthouse.

HOW TO GET THERE

• By air: The closest major airport is in San Francisco.
• By car: The park is located only 30 miles northwest of San Francisco, but it takes more than an hour to get there. From San Francisco, cross the Golden Gate Bridge and drive north on U.S. 101 for 7.5 miles. Take the Sir Francis Drake Boulevard exit west toward San Anselmo, and drive 20 miles to the town of Olema. At Olema, turn right (north) on Highway 1 for about 150 yards, then turn left on Bear Valley Road. Drive a half-mile to the left turnoff for the Bear Valley visitor center, signed as "Seashore Information."

DRIVE TIME

• Drive time from Los Angeles: approximately 8 hours.
• Drive time from San Francisco: approximately 1.5 hours.

ENTRANCE FEES

There is no entrance fee at Point Reyes National Seashore.

WHEN TO GO

Point Reyes National Seashore is accessible for hiking year-round. Spring and fall days often have the best weather.

WEATHER CONDITIONS

Expect any kind of weather in Point Reyes National Seashore. Fog and wind are frequent, especially in the summer months. Winter, spring, and fall often have the best weather, although winter months may bring rain. Daytime temperatures range between 50 and 70 degrees most of the year. The general rule for hiking in the park: Wear or carry a variety of layers. At Point Reyes, anything goes.

WHERE TO STAY

Point Reyes National Seashore has four hike-in campgrounds that are available on a reservations basis: Coast, Glen, Sky, and Wildcat. Each camp requires a hike of at least 1.7 miles. Reserve sites by phoning (415) 663-8054 or (415) 663-1092, or make reservations in person at the Bear Valley Visitor Center. The closest drive-in campgrounds are at Samuel P. Taylor State Park (415-488-9897) and at private Olema Ranch (415-663-8001).

The only lodging option in the seashore is the Point Reyes Hostel, which has dormitory-style accommodations. Phone (415) 663-8811. There are many lodging possibilities in the small towns neighboring the national seashore, including Olema, Point Reyes Station, and Inverness. Some suggestions:

> Bear Valley Inn, (415) 663-1777
> Manka's Inverness Lodge, (415) 669-1034
> Golden Hinde Inn, (415) 669-1389
> Point Reyes Seashore Lodge, (415) 663-9000
> Olema Inn, (415) 663-9559 or (800) 532-9252
> Holly Tree Inn, (415) 663-1554 or (800) 286-4655

FOOD & SUPPLIES

The only food available in the park is at the Drakes Beach Cafe, which is open most weekends and some days during the week, depending on weather. Stores and restaurants are found in the neighboring towns of Olema, Inverness, and Point Reyes Station.

SUGGESTED MAPS

Park maps are available at the Bear Valley Visitor Center on Bear Valley Road. A more detailed map is available for a fee from Tom Harrison Cartography at (415) 456-7940.

1. TOMALES POINT TRAIL

Pierce Point Road area, Point Reyes National Seashore
A herd of tule elk, bay and ocean views

DISTANCE: 4.0 to 9.4 miles round-trip; 2 to 5 hours   **LEVEL:** Easy/moderate
ELEVATION: Start at 320 feet; total change 900 feet   **CROWDS:** Moderate
BEST SEASON: Year-round; spring and fall are best   **RATING:** ★ ★ ★ ★

DIRECTIONS: From San Francisco, cross the Golden Gate Bridge and drive north on U.S. 101 for 7.5 miles. Take the Sir Francis Drake Boulevard exit west toward San Anselmo, and drive 20 miles to the town of Olema. At Olema, turn right (north) on Highway 1 for about 150 yards, then turn left on Bear Valley Road. Drive 2.2 miles on Bear Valley Road until it joins with Sir Francis Drake Highway. Bear left on Sir Francis Drake and drive 5.6 miles, then take the right fork onto Pierce Point Road. Drive nine miles to the Pierce Point Ranch parking area.

If seeing wildlife is one of the reasons you enjoy hiking, the Tomales Point Trail is sure to satisfy. You'll have a good chance at spotting big, furry animals before you even get out of your car (and not just the usual Point Reyes bovines).

The wildlife is plentiful because the Tomales Point Trail is located in Point Reyes National Seashore's tule elk preserve. Before 1860, thousands of native tule elk roamed Tomales Point. In the late nineteenth century, the animals were hunted out of existence. The tule elk reserve is part of the park service's effort to re-establish the elk in their native habitat. Today the herd is numbered at 200 and going strong.

Seeing the magnificent tule elk is almost a given. Frequently they're hanging out in large numbers near the trailhead parking lot, and often you can see them as you drive in on Pierce Point Road. Once you're out on the trail, you may see more elk, and you may also see other wildlife. If you hike early in the morning before a lot of other people have traipsed down the trail, check the dirt path for footprints. I've seen mountain lion tracks as well as the more common raccoon and elk prints. While hiking, I've encountered large jackrabbits, various harmless snakes, big fuzzy caterpillars, and more birds than I could possibly remember. Once my hiking partner and I had to make a wide circle off the path to avoid a big skunk who insisted on walking down the trail ahead of us. He was just moseying along, indifferent to our presence.

It's 4.7 miles to the trail's end at the tip of Tomales Point, but you don't have to walk that far to have a great trip. Only a mile or two of hiking will provide you with splendid coastal and Tomales Bay views, plus a probable wildlife encounter. Set your own trail distance; turn around when you please. Just make sure you pick a clear day to take this trip; although you may still see tule elk in the fog, you'll miss out on the trail's world-class views. And be sure to carry a few extra layers; if the weather is clear, the trail is likely to be windy.

The Tomales Point Trail begins at Pierce Point Ranch, one of the oldest dairies in Point Reyes. The ranch manufactured milk and butter for San Francisco dinner tables in the 1850s. Begin by hiking around the western perimeter of the ranch, or take a few minutes to inspect its buildings. Interpretive signs describe the history of the ranch and its dairy business. The trail curves uphill around the ranch, then heads northwest along the blufftops toward Tomales Point, the northernmost tip of Point Reyes. Wildflowers bloom profusely in the spring, particularly poppies, gold fields, tidy tips, and bush lupine.

The trail is wide, smooth, and easy to hike from beginning to end. At a half mile out, you reach your first climb, in which you gain about 100 feet. Turn around and look behind you as you ascend—you've got the ocean on one side, and Tomales Bay on the other. Views are spectacular in all directions. Look for forested Hog Island in Tomales Bay, a popular pull-up spot for kayakers.

At 1.8 miles, the trail starts to descend, and you get a good view

Female elk along the Tomales Point Trail

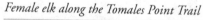

of Bird Rock out at sea, and the town and campground at Lawson's Landing across Tomales Bay. At 2.5 miles, you reach the trail's highest point. Views of Bodega Bay and the Sonoma Coast to the north are excellent. Many hikers make this high point their turnaround point for a five-mile round-trip; if you continue, you'll descend to the site of an outpost of Pierce Point Ranch, then pass by windswept Bird Rock, often covered with pelicans and cormorants.

In the final three-quarters of a mile beyond Bird Rock, the trail becomes more sketchy. Yellow bush lupine carpets the sandy soil in April and May. Amid a series of low dunes, the trail vanishes. But the route is obvious; just keep hiking until the land runs out. When it does, your views of Bodega Head and Tomales Bay are breathtaking. You can even make out little tiny boats in the harbor at Bodega Bay.

2. McCLURES BEACH

Pierce Point Road area, Point Reyes National Seashore
A remote, rocky cove

DISTANCE: 1.0 mile round-trip; 30 minutes
ELEVATION: Start at 250 feet; total change 250 feet
BEST SEASON: Year-round; spring and fall are best

LEVEL: Easy
CROWDS: Minimal
RATING: ★ ★ ★ ★

DIRECTIONS: Follow the directions on page 128 to the town of Olema in western Marin County. At Olema, turn right (north) on Highway 1 for about 150 yards, then turn left on Bear Valley Road. Drive 2.2 miles on Bear Valley Road until it joins with Sir Francis Drake Highway. Bear left on Sir Francis Drake and drive 5.6 miles, then take the right fork onto Pierce Point Road. Drive 8.9 miles to the left turnoff for McClures Beach, just before you reach Pierce Point Ranch. Turn left and park in the small lot.

If you've driven all the way out to the northern tip of Point Reyes National Seashore to visit the Pierce Point Ranch or hike the Tomales Point Trail (see the previous story), don't miss a visit to neighboring McClures Beach. Because of its remote location and relatively small size, the beach is not heavily visited. It often provides a chance for solitude along its rocky stretch of sand.

The trail from the parking lot leads steeply downhill to the beach in a half-mile. This same stretch will get you huffing and puffing on the way back up, but it's short enough so that anybody can handle it. The trail starts out as loose sand, but it gets firmer as it winds its way downhill. Buckwheat, ice plant, and morning-glories border the path. You'll walk parallel to the eroding streambed of a steep ravine, which can roar

McClures Beach

with water during winter storms, but is usually just a trickle in summer.

The rocky beach is a prime area for tidepools, especially if you are fortunate enough to time your visit for a minus tide. The south end of the beach has the best tidepool areas. Even at high tide, when sand and water have covered many of the pools, you'll find shards of abalone shells, mussels, and assorted body parts of crabs as you walk along the sand. You don't have to walk far to see all there is to see—McClures Beach is only about three-quarters of a mile long, and bounded by granite cliffs.

Swimming is definitely not recommended. McClures Beach is considered to be one of the most dangerous in Point Reyes, because of its rocky shores and crashing waves.

3. KEHOE BEACH

Pierce Point Road area, Point Reyes National Seashore
Marsh, dunes, and sandy beach

DISTANCE: 1.0 to 3.0 miles round-trip; 1 to 2 hours   **LEVEL:** Easy
ELEVATION: Start at 40 feet; total change 40 feet   **CROWDS:** Minimal
BEST SEASON: Year-round; spring and fall are best   **RATING:** ★ ★ ★ ★

DIRECTIONS: Follow the directions on page 128 to the town of Olema in western Marin County. At Olema, turn right (north) on Highway 1 for about

150 yards, then turn left on Bear Valley Road. Drive 2.2 miles on Bear Valley Road until it joins with Sir Francis Drake Highway. Bear left on Sir Francis Drake and drive 5.6 miles, then take the right fork onto Pierce Point Road. Drive 5.5 miles to the Kehoe Beach Trailhead on your left. Park along either side of the road in the pullouts.

At most beaches in California, you just drive up, park your car in the paved parking lot, and then walk a few feet and plop down in the sand. Kehoe Beach beats that by a mile. Exactly a mile, in fact, because that's how far it is to hike there and back. The distance is long enough for a pleasant, level walk, and it can be combined with another mile or so of sauntering along the wide strip of beach.

The trail proves that the journey can be as good as the destination. The fun starts right where you park your car. In late spring and summer you'll find a huge patch of blackberries growing just across the road from the trailhead. If you're wearing long sleeves and long pants, you can pick enough berries to sustain you as you hike.

The trail is gravel, almost completely level, and wide enough for hand-holding. You walk alongside Kehoe Marsh, which provides excellent habitat for birds and birdwatchers. Songbirds are nearly as abundant as the non-native iceplant that weaves thick cushions of matted foliage alongside the trail. Grasses and vines also grow in profusion, encouraged by the proximity of the marshy creek and its underground

Kehoe Beach

spring. As you get closer to the ocean, the marsh land transforms to sandy dunes, where you may see big jackrabbits hopping among the grasses.

Before you sprint down to Kehoe's brayed tan sands, take the spur trail that cuts off to the right and up the bluffs above the beach. In springtime, the bluffs are completely blue and gold with lupine and poppies—a glorious sight to behold. Once you've admired them, head to the beach for more walking or a picnic lunch. You'll return on the same trail.

Dogs are allowed on leash at Kehoe Beach, which is a great bonus for dog-lovers and their canine companions. There is little that makes a dog happier than going to a huge, wide open beach, and there are only a few beaches in Point Reyes where dogs are permitted. Keep your canine friend leashed, though. The strict leash rules protect harbor seals that occasionally haul out on Kehoe Beach. Take care not to disturb them—they need to rest for an average of seven hours per day, and they nurse pups on land from late March through June.

4. ABBOTTS LAGOON

Pierce Point Road area, Point Reyes National Seashore
A birdwatcher's paradise

DISTANCE: 2.4 miles round-trip; 1.5 hours
ELEVATION: Start at 60 feet; total change 60 feet
BEST SEASON: Winter or spring

LEVEL: Easy
CROWDS: Moderate
RATING: ★ ★ ★ ★

DIRECTIONS: Follow the directions on page 128 to the town of Olema in western Marin County. At Olema, turn right (north) on Highway 1 for about 150 yards, then turn left on Bear Valley Road. Drive 2.2 miles on Bear Valley Road until it joins with Sir Francis Drake Highway. Bear left on Sir Francis Drake and drive 5.6 miles, then take the right fork onto Pierce Point Road. Drive 3.3 miles on Pierce Point Road to the Abbotts Lagoon Trailhead on the left side of the road.

If the wind is howling and you've nearly been blown off the trail on other hikes at Point Reyes, drive over to the trailhead at Abbotts Lagoon for a trip through a sheltered watery paradise. The trail is not long, but it leads to Point Reyes Beach, where you can continue hiking along the sand in either direction. The result is a spectacular two-part trip: first, an easy 1.2-mile stroll through protected lagoons teeming with bird life; second, a windswept walk along wide-open coastline.

Abbotts Lagoon is huge—more than 200 acres—and joined by a

Abbotts Lagoon

spillway to two freshwater ponds. The lagoon is only rarely influenced by tides. This occurs when harsh winter storms break through its low sand bar and open the lagoon to the ocean. Eventually sand accumulates and seals off the lagoon, but these brief openings result in water that is continually brackish—a mix of saltwater and freshwater, and a haven for many species of birds, mammals and plants.

The trail is equally loved by birdwatchers and beach lovers. The latter are thrilled by the amount and diversity of bird habitat in a relatively small area; the former enjoy the level trail and easy access to Point Reyes Beach, also known as Ten-Mile Beach or the Great Beach. If you're a birding novice and want to give it a try, look for these easy-to-spot species: western grebes (large, gray and white diving birds with a long, swanlike neck and yellow bill); pie-billed grebes (similar to western grebes but with a short, rounded bill and no white patch); coots (dark grey/black hen-like birds that skitter across the water when they fly, dragging their feet); and caspian terns (like seagulls but more angular and elegant, with large red bills). The autumn migration season is the best time to birdwatch, although birds are present at the lagoon year-round.

The first half-mile of trail is level and hard-packed for wheelchair use, and the rest of the route is wide, level, and sandy. The scenery is pretty right away. You walk through coastal scrub and open grasslands that are gilded with wildflowers in the spring. A bucolic-looking white farmhouse, perched on a distant hillside over your right shoulder, keeps watch over the scene.

At 1.1 miles, you'll cross a small footbridge that separates the two parts of the lagoon. This is an excellent spot to pause and look for birds, or just to admire the beauty of the water. But the sound of the ocean draws you straight ahead. If you want to walk along Point Reyes Beach, pick up the spur trail that leads away from the lagoon and to the ocean in a quarter mile, or just hike across the dunes. As you walk, watch for seals and sea lions who sometimes haul out on the beach. You'll probably want to put on another layer of clothing; the beach is much windier than the protected lagoon.

Wildflower season from March through May brings spectacular shows of poppies and lupine along the Abbotts Lagoon Trail. Also look for cobweb thistle, a native thistle that is a brilliant red color. But perhaps the best time to visit is on a crystal-clear day in late fall or winter, when the fog has vanished and the rich, primary colors of water, sky, and grasslands are thoroughly saturated.

5. MARSHALL BEACH

Tomales Bay area, Point Reyes National Seashore
A wind-protected beach on Tomales Bay

DISTANCE: 2.4 miles round-trip; 1.5 hours   **LEVEL:** Easy
ELEVATION: Start at 300 feet; total change 300 feet   **CROWDS:** Minimal
BEST SEASON: Year-round; spring and fall are best   **RATING:** ★ ★ ★ ★

DIRECTIONS: Follow the directions on page 128 to the town of Olema in western Marin County. At Olema, turn right (north) on Highway 1 for about 150 yards, then turn left on Bear Valley Road. Drive 2.2 miles on Bear Valley Road until it joins with Sir Francis Drake Highway. Bear left on Sir Francis Drake and drive 5.6 miles, then take the right fork onto Pierce Point Road. In 1.2 miles you'll see the entrance road for Tomales Bay State Park. Drive just past it to Duck Cove/Marshall Beach Road; turn right and drive 2.6 miles. The road turns to gravel and dirt; stay to the left where it forks. Park in the gravel parking area, taking care not to block any of the dirt roads that connect here.

The Marshall Beach Trail is one of the best kept secrets in Point Reyes. Few visitors know about Marshall Beach, because the trailhead is situated on a dirt road to nowhere, at the northeastern tip of the Point Reyes peninsula. While thousands of visitors pour into neighboring Tomales Bay State Park for its protected bay waters and stunning white beaches, few realize that right next door is Marshall Beach, with all the same advantages but none of the crowds, and no entrance fee.

On your first trip to the trailhead, you'll constantly wonder if you are going the right way, because the road leads through cow country, with no beach in sight. The paved road turns to dirt, and you continue driving along flat coastal bluffs until you reach a nondescript trailhead sign. Then you start hiking through cow pastures. This is one trail where you have to keep a vigilant lookout for meadow muffins because the stuff can stay on your boot soles for days.

Cattle and dairy ranches have been operating in Point Reyes since the 1850s. The 1962 law that authorized Point Reyes National Seashore made allowances so that the original ranch owners could continue operating within the seashore boundaries. Ranching is considered to be part of the "cultural history" of the park. Currently, seven dairies operate within Point Reyes, milking about 3,200 cows and producing over five million gallons of milk each year. Just wave and smile at Bessie as you walk to the beach.

The hike is a simple out-and-back, with no trail junctions. Just amble down the wide ranch road, which curves around the hillside and descends to the water's edge. There is no shade along the way, except for at the edge of Marshall Beach's cove, where you'll find a grove of windswept cypress trees with thick lichen hanging from their branches.

Hiking to Marshall Beach

Marshall Beach is a nearly perfect beach, with coarse white sand and azure blue Tomales Bay water. It's a small slice of paradise over-looking the hamlet of Marshall on the other side of the bay. You can swim in the calm bay waters, which are protected from the wind by Inverness Ridge. The usual visitors to the beach are kayakers who have paddled over from the town of Marshall across the bay, or from Tomales Bay State Park to the south.

Essentials for this trip include a picnic, a bathing suit, a good book, and some binoculars for birdwatching. Settle in for a perfect afternoon, then drag yourself away—and back up the hill—when it's time to leave.

6. ESTERO TRAIL to SUNSET BEACH

Western area, Point Reyes National Seashore
A walk along waterways to a pristine beach

DISTANCE: 7.8 miles round-trip; 4 hours
ELEVATION: Start at 150 feet; total change 720 feet
BEST SEASON: Spring for wildflowers

LEVEL: Moderate
CROWDS: Moderate
RATING: ★ ★ ★ ★

DIRECTIONS: Follow the directions on page 128 to the town of Olema in western Marin County. At Olema, turn right (north) on Highway 1 for about 150 yards, then turn left on Bear Valley Road. Drive 2.2 miles on Bear Valley Road until it joins with Sir Francis Drake Highway. Bear left on Sir Francis Drake and drive 7.6 miles to the left turnoff for the Estero Trailhead. Turn left and drive one mile to the trailhead parking area.

NOTE: A large section of the Estero Trail was badly damaged in the El Niño storms of early 1998. As of February 1999, the Estero Trail is officially closed, as it will require extensive rerouting to steer clear of the eroded bluffs. However, the trail is still frequently hiked by park visitors, and park rangers do not object to this. Between 1.2 miles and 1.6 miles, you will need to do some scrambling to follow the washed-out trail. Except for this one section, the Estero Trail is in good shape. Until the trail is repaired or rerouted, only hike the trail in dry weather, when the eroded slopes won't be muddy and subject to further damage.

The Estero Trail to Sunset Beach is quintessential Point Reyes. It's full of good surprises, including an exemplary display of Douglas iris in spring, a thick forest of Monterey pines, nearly non-stop views of estuary, bay, and ocean, and access to pristine Sunset Beach. Plus, the 7.8-mile round-trip mileage is the perfect length for a day hike in Point Reyes.

The trail leads from the left side of the Estero parking lot and laterals across a grassy hillside, with little or no indication of what lies ahead. As you hike, take a look over your left shoulder to observe the regenerating hillsides of Inverness Ridge. After the Point Reyes wildfire of 1995, the ravaged slopes are slowly turning from black to green.

You'll round a corner and drop quickly into a stand of dense Monterey pines, the remainders of an old Christmas tree farm. About this time, you may start wondering where the water is, because you haven't seen any yet. Have patience; in another few minutes of walking, the trail opens out to blue, serene Home Bay, one mile from the trailhead. (This is the point where the park service has officially closed the trail; see the note above.)

Walk across the footbridge on the edge of the bay. You'll be surrounded by water, or mud flats if the tide is out. On the bridge's far side, you'll move into your first hill climb, as the trail rises above Home Bay, on its way to the point where Home Bay opens up to Drakes Estero. Water views are lovely as you ascend the short but steep hill, then descend down the other side. You'll cross another levee in another protected cove.

Continue hiking up and down the undulating trail, paralleling the edge of Drakes Estero and enjoying nonstop views and nonstop Douglas irises in spring. Their lavish, sky-blue blooms decorate the hillsides. If the tide is out when you hike, you'll see mostly mud flats and the oyster beds of nearby Johnson's Oyster Farm. If the tide is in, you'll see miles of azure blue water. You'll climb and descend a total of three hills on this trail; the third one has a lone eucalyptus tree growing on its summit.

Your chance of seeing wildlife along the route is excellent. Waterfowl and shorebirds can be seen close-up every time the trail dips down to one of Home Bay's many coves. On one trip, I saw the largest great blue heron of my life, slowly beating his wings and taking off from the ground like a huge, mythical creature. In addition to the many birds, herds of deer frequent this section of the park, including a small herd of white fallow deer that were brought here by a rancher a generation ago. (Before I knew that exotic white deer roamed in Point Reyes, I spotted a pure white buck early one morning on the hillside above the Estero Trail. I was sure that the fog was playing tricks on my eyes.) Many more common black-tail deer are also present. The males bear impressive racks in the winter.

At 2.4 miles out, you'll reach a trail sign for Drakes Head to the left, and Sunset Beach straight ahead. Continuing straight on the

Sunset Beach Trail, the route levels and becomes easier to walk. At 1.5 miles from the junction, you are within view of Sunset Beach. A large, quiet pond separates it from you. You can hear the ocean waves ahead, even though the water directly in sight is completely calm and still. Hike around the left side of the pond; the trail may become narrow and muddy, but just keep going. In another quarter mile you reach the place where Drakes Estero empties into the sea. Beautiful Sunset Beach is hikeable to your left. It's littered with fascinating rounded boulders of sculpted sandstone.

Sunset Beach

On many days, you can hear the barking of sea lions who have hauled out on Limantour Spit, just across from you.

7. ESTERO TRAIL to DRAKES HEAD

**Western area, Point Reyes National Seashore
A walk along waterways to a coastal overlook**

DISTANCE: 8.8 miles round-trip; 4.5 hours

ELEVATION: Start at 150 feet; total change 800 feet

BEST SEASON: Year-round; spring and fall are best

LEVEL: Moderate

CROWDS: Moderate

RATING: ★ ★ ★

DIRECTIONS: Follow the directions on page 128 to the town of Olema in western Marin County. At Olema, turn right (north) on Highway 1 for about 150 yards, then turn left on Bear Valley Road. Drive 2.2 miles on Bear Valley Road until it joins with Sir Francis Drake Highway. Bear left on Sir Francis Drake and drive 7.6 miles to the left turnoff for the Estero Trailhead. Turn left and drive one mile to the trailhead parking area.

NOTE: See the note on page 137 about the Estero Trail's condition.

The dictionary definition of an estero is a meeting of ocean saltwater and freshwater runoff, producing a rich habitat for waterfowl and shorebirds. Hiking the Estero and Drakes Head trails gives you a double dose of these rich estuarine wetlands, as the Estero Trail parallels Home Bay and Drakes Estero, and the Drakes Head Trail delivers you to the edge of Limantour Estero.

The trail begins on the same path as the Estero Trail to Sunset Beach for the first 2.4 miles. (Read the trail notes for the previous story.) At the junction with Sunset Beach Trail, turn left, hiking away from Drakes Estero and over a small ridge. A half mile later, you meet up with Drakes Head Trail at the intersection of a maze of cattle gates and fences.

This trip differs greatly from the previous hike to Sunset Beach. For starters, there is more climbing to be done, which results in excellent views at your destination and on your return trip downhill to the edge of Drakes Estero. Plus there is often more wind to contend with, as the bluffs at Drakes Head are completely exposed. The Drakes Head Trail cuts right down the middle of a coastal prairie, with Limantour Estero on the left and Limantour Spit—a long, narrow strip of sand separating the estero from the sea—straight ahead.

Rising above Home Bay on the Estero Trail

The trail to Drakes Head is also slightly more difficult to follow. After climbing up the ridge and away from Drakes Estero, you hike along a ranch road on top of the ridge. The road passes through a cattle gate, then continues to a fenced-in corral. The road parallels the fences, and it looks like you should follow it, but watch for posted blue and white directional arrows. They guide you to go through another cattle gate into the fenced area, then follow an indistinct trail inside the fence and along a cattle reservoir for about 150 yards. You exit out another cattle gate, where trail signs point you to the right along the bluffs for the Drakes Head Trail (signed as "not a through trail"). Finally you follow the Drakes Head Trail south (to the right), toward the ocean. Although it sounds complex, if you just watch for the blue and white arrows, you'll be fine.

The final 1.4 miles beyond the corral are easier going. Simply hike along the Drakes Head Trail all the way to its terminus at the edge of the bluffs over Limantour Estero. On a clear day, this is one of the best viewpoints in all of Point Reyes. Limantour Spit is straight ahead, usually covered with barking sea lions. Your vista expands over the entire length of Drakes Bay, from the headlands to Double Point.

Chances of seeing wildlife along this trail are excellent. Aside from the birds along Home Bay and Drakes Estero and the sea lions on Limantour Spit, deer are abundant around Drakes Head. I've seen herds of several dozen or more grazing along the bluffs. You may notice some exotic deer among them; non-native white fallow deer and spotted axis deer make their home in Point Reyes and graze alongside the native black-tailed deer. The best time to see the deer is in the fall, when the males bear impressive racks.

8. BULL POINT

Western area, Point Reyes National Seashore
A birdwatcher's hike to the edge of Drakes Estero

DISTANCE: 3.6 miles round-trip; 2 hours   **LEVEL:** Easy
ELEVATION: Start at 100 feet; total change 50 feet   **CROWDS:** Minimal
BEST SEASON: Year-round; spring and fall are best   **RATING:** ★ ★

DIRECTIONS: Follow the directions on page 128 to the town of Olema in western Marin County. At Olema, turn right (north) on Highway 1 for about 150 yards, then turn left on Bear Valley Road. Drive 2.2 miles on Bear Valley Road until it joins with Sir Francis Drake Highway. Bear left on Sir Francis Drake and drive 10.7 miles to the Bull Point parking area on the left side of the road. The trail leads from the left side of the parking area.

Bull Point is one of the forgotten Point Reyes trails, one that only the cows seem to know about. It's located far out on Sir Francis Drake Highway, where most visitors who pass by are on their way to more famous destinations like Drakes Beach or the Point Reyes Lighthouse.

Despite its lack of celebrity, the Bull Point Trail is an interesting hike. It leads through a coastal prairie on a wide strip of land between two arms of Drakes Estero: Creamery Bay and Schooner Bay. Schooner

Bay was once the launching areas for schooners carrying butter from Point Reyes dairies to dinner tables in San Francisco. (The bay was much deeper in those days.) Creamery and Schooner bays, as well as Barries and Home bays, are the four fingers of the hand that is Drakes Estero—the Spanish word for estuary, a place where saltwater and freshwater mix.

The trail begins on the left side of the parking lot, at a cattle gate that you must close behind you. You'll probably walk past some grazing bovines on the first section of the route. The footpath is an old ranch road, which is rather indistinct at the trailhead but gets more distinct as you travel. The pastoral landscape makes you feel like you're in a Merchant-Ivory film; backdrops of green, grassy hills are interwoven with vistas of wide blue water. No, this is not 19th-century England, but rather dawn-of-the-21st-century Point Reyes, although it's easy to confuse the two. The proper equipment for this trip is a thermos of Earl Gray tea, a pair of binoculars, and a collection of Wordsworth.

There are no trail intersections to confuse you; it's just a straight shot to the waterway across grassy coastal bluffs. The last 20 feet of trail, just before you reach the bluff's edge at Drakes Estero, are caved in. Be careful around the crumbling cliff edges.

Looking toward the water, Creamery Bay is on your right and Schooner Bay is on your left. When the tide is low, you can see poles sticking up out of Schooner Bay, and grey mesh bags lying in the shallows and along the shoreline. The bags are filled with oysters; they are the property of Johnson's Oyster Farm, located across the bay. The farm is accessible by a side road off Sir Francis Drake Highway; it's open to the public and worth a stop on your drive home.

As with all the bays, estuaries, and lagoons at watery Point Reyes, the coves here are host to thousands of resident and migratory birds. Great egrets are the most noteworthy; their grand white plumage provides a stark, elegant contrast to the greens and blues of the landscape.

---

9. DRAKES BEACH

Western area, Point Reyes National Seashore
A long and wide protected beach

DISTANCE: 1.0 to 4.0 miles round-trip; 1 to 2 hours   **LEVEL:** Easy
ELEVATION: Start at 10 feet; total change 10 feet   **CROWDS:** Heavy
BEST SEASON: Year-round; spring and fall are best   **RATING:** ★ ★ ★ ★

DIRECTIONS: Follow the directions on page 128 to the town of Olema in western Marin County. At Olema, turn right (north) on Highway 1 for about

150 yards, then turn left on Bear Valley Road. Drive 2.2 miles on Bear Valley Road until it joins with Sir Francis Drake Highway. Bear left on Sir Francis Drake and drive 13.4 miles to the left turnoff for Drakes Beach. Turn left and drive 1.5 miles to the large parking area.

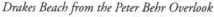

There used to be a fine trail at Drakes Beach that climbed up on the rugged headlands above the sea and curved around to the mouth of Drakes Estero, to the great meeting place of estero and ocean. But the forces of erosion and entropy took their toll on the bluffs that supported the trail; they caved into the sea and took the trail with them.

Still, that sad fact shouldn't stop you from hiking at Drakes Beach. On a calm, clear day (most common in fall, winter, or spring), the beach itself is an excellent place for a stroll. Drakes Beach faces south toward Drakes Bay and is more protected from the wind than Point Reyes' western beaches. Even if nearby Limantour Beach is windy, Drakes Beach may be fairly calm.

The popularity of Drakes Beach is clear from the size of the parking lot, the presence of a visitor center, and—most surprising of all—the existence of a cafe that serves decent food. This is the only food service in the entire park, unless you count Johnson's Oyster Farm, and it's open Friday through Monday each week, more often during the summer. It is housed with the visitor center in a terrific redwood build-

Drakes Beach from the Peter Behr Overlook

ing with an outside deck that faces the sea. The visitor center has excellent displays on the history of Drakes Bay.

It's best to start your trip with a walk up the paved overlook trail that leads to the right (south) along the oceanside bluffs. The quarter mile trail leads somewhat steeply uphill to the Peter Behr Overlook, where you can peer down at the length of Drakes Beach. Scan the beach, choose which direction you'd like to explore, then backtrack downhill and start walking. The beach to the southwest is accessible for at least two miles; the beach to the northeast is only accessible for a long stretch if the tide is low. When it is, you'll find interesting sandstone shelves jutting up from the sand, as much as three feet high. They're the remains of ancient marine terraces.

Drakes Beach is most remarkable for its tall white cliffs, which you will pass as you walk. A grand historical debate rages over whether or not Sir Francis Drake landed here at Drakes Bay, but those who argue in favor believe that these cliffs reminded Drake of the white cliffs of Dover. (Other experts say that Drake landed at what is now San Quentin Point in Marin County; some holdouts insist that it was actually San Francisco Bay, Tomales Bay, Bolinas Lagoon, or even Santa Barbara.) The pro-Drakes Bay theory holds that Drake sailed the *Golden Hinde* into the bay for repairs in 1579, and took possession of this beach in the name of Queen Elizabeth I.

10. CHIMNEY ROCK

Western area, Point Reyes National Seashore
Wildflowers, whales, elephant seals, and coastal views

DISTANCE: 1.4 miles round-trip; 45 minutes   **LEVEL:** Easy
ELEVATION: Start at 150 feet; total change 70 feet   **CROWDS:** Moderate
BEST SEASON: December to May   **RATING:** ★ ★ ★ ★

DIRECTIONS: Follow the directions on page 128 to the town of Olema in western Marin County. At Olema, turn right (north) on Highway 1 for about 150 yards, then turn left on Bear Valley Road. Drive 2.2 miles on Bear Valley Road until it joins with Sir Francis Drake Highway. Bear left on Sir Francis Drake and drive 17.6 miles to the left turnoff for Chimney Rock. Turn left and drive nine-tenths of a mile to the trailhead and parking area.

NOTE: During peak weekends, the park service may require visitors to ride a shuttle bus from Drakes Beach to the Chimney Rock Trailhead. Phone the Bear Valley Visitor Center at 415/663-1092 for updated information.

Hiking to Chimney Rock

If you like wildflowers and ocean views, there may be no better hike in Point Reyes than the Chimney Rock Trail. Each year from March to May, colorful wildflowers carpet the grassy hillsides along the trail. This is one of the best flower displays in all of Point Reyes. If you hike the trail earlier in the season—December to February—you're likely to see elephant seals on the beaches below Chimney Rock and the spouts of gray whales out at sea. Adding to the trail's attractions, a tidepooling area is found at a rocky beach near the trailhead, which offers a chance to inspect the contents of the sea during low tides.

The best trip on the Chimney Rock Trail is achieved with some planning. First, know that the wind can blow fiercely at Chimney Rock. Although the first half of the trail is on the sheltered side of the point that faces Drakes Bay, the second half extends onto the thin peninsula of land that separates Drakes Bay from the Pacific Ocean. At the point where the bay and ocean meet, you'll find Chimney Rock— and frequently, a howling wind. Make sure you dress for it. On the up side, this trail is usually not as windy as nearby Point Reyes Lighthouse (see the following story), if that's any consolation.

From the trailhead parking lot, you can head straight for the Chimney Rock Trail, or you can take a couple of short, worthwhile detours. The latter requires a brief descent on the paved road that continues beyond the parking lot. In a few hundred feet you'll see a dirt trail on the left signed for Elephant Seal Overlook. If you take it, you'll go through a cattle gate, walk about a quarter-mile, then come out to a fenced overlook with a view of the southern tip of Drakes Beach. This is where elephant seals haul out in the winter months. The cacophony of barking and snorting is tremendous. Although you are a few hundred feet above the seals, you can clearly see them brawling with each other, and watch their strange, jerking movements as they go from sand to sea and back.

Elephant seals started to colonize the beaches in Point Reyes in 1981, and the annual seal population has expanded to more than 1,000 individuals. (Elephant seals were almost extinct from hunting by the year 1900; their comeback in the last century has been extraordinary.) The huge male elephant seals arrive in late November to claim the best spots on the beaches; the pregnant females come to shore two to three weeks later to give birth and breed. In a few months they disappear back into the ocean and are usually not seen again until the following winter.

After you've watched the seals' antics, you can continue down the paved road to see the Point Reyes Lifesaving Station, which was built in 1889 and operated until 1968. Despite the proximity of the Point Reyes Lighthouse, many shipwrecks have occurred along the Point Reyes peninsula, and the crews at the lifeboat station had the daring job of rescuing survivors. Just beyond the lifeboat station is a rocky

Elephant seals on the southern tip of Drakes Beach

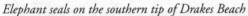

beach that offers good tidepooling at low tides. (You can find out the daily status of the tides at the Bear Valley, Lighthouse, or Drakes Beach visitor centers, or just by checking a local newspaper.)

With these detours completed, you're ready for the main event—the Chimney Rock Trail. The path is a narrow, dirt trail leading from alongside the rest rooms at the trailhead parking lot. The route crosses grassy headlands, at first on the sheltered Drakes Bay side, where you can see the tall white cliffs that mark Drakes Beach. Then the trail climbs slightly to the top of the narrow bluffs that divide Drakes Bay from the sea. If it's a windy day, you'll feel it here.

At four-tenths of a mile, you'll see a faint trail leading off to the right; this path travels one-tenth of a mile to an overlook of the Point Reyes Headlands Reserve and the Farallon Islands, 20 miles away. The main trail continues another three-tenths of a mile to a fenced overlook of multiple sea stacks, the largest of which is Chimney Rock. It's impossible to see the rock's "chimney" from here. However, you can see it from the south end of Drakes Beach.

On a clear day this is an excellent spot to look for passing gray whales. If there are none, you're still rewarded with stellar ocean views. A small beach just to the left of the trail's end is the temporary winter home of a group of elephant seals. You'll hear them barking and making a ruckus. Do not attempt to descend to any of the beaches near Chimney Rock; the cliffs are rugged and unstable.

Wildflower lovers, take note: in addition to the more common flowers such as poppies, owl's clover, lupine, Douglas iris, and footsteps-of-spring that you'll find along the trail in springtime, look for the more rare pussy's ears near the end of the Chimney Rock Trail. They're white and somewhat furry-looking, as you might expect.

---

11. POINT REYES LIGHTHOUSE

Western area, Point Reyes National Seashore
A lighthouse on the Pacific Coast's windiest point

DISTANCE: 0.8 mile round-trip; 45 minutes **LEVEL:** Easy/moderate
ELEVATION: Start at 480 feet; total change 260 feet **CROWDS:** Heavy
BEST SEASON: Year-round; spring and fall are best **RATING:** ★ ★ ★ ★

DIRECTIONS: Follow the directions on page 128 to the town of Olema in western Marin County. At Olema, turn right (north) on Highway 1 for about 150 yards, then turn left on Bear Valley Road. Drive 2.2 miles on Bear Valley Road until it joins with Sir Francis Drake Highway. Bear left on Sir Francis Drake and drive 18.7 miles to the lighthouse parking area at the road's end.

NOTE: The stairs to the lighthouse are open Thursday through Monday only from 10 A.M. to 4:30 P.M. The park service may close the trail in extreme weather. The lighthouse is always closed on Tuesdays and Wednesdays. Also, during peak weekends, the park service may require visitors to ride a shuttle bus from Drakes Beach to the lighthouse trailhead. Phone the Lighthouse Visitor Center at (415) 669-1534 or the Bear Valley Visitor Center at (415) 663-1092 for updated information.

All lighthouses have an air of romance about them, but the Point Reyes Lighthouse seems to have an abundance of that air. Dramatically perched on the windiest and foggiest point on the Pacific Coast, the Point Reyes Lighthouse steered ships away from this rocky, dangerous point from 1870 to 1975.

Today, the lighthouse offers a glimpse into our coastal history and is one of the best places in Point Reyes to look for passing gray whales. In spring, wildflowers bloom in profusion along the trail. Year-round, sea lions haul out on the offshore rocks surrounding the lighthouse. On most days, the wind blows forcefully at this westernmost tip of Point Reyes, making the lighthouse a fine place to snuggle close to your hiking partner while you gaze wistfully out to sea.

Despite all the scenic beauty, the lighthouse is a serious undertaking. Although the lighthouse building is no longer in operation (it was replaced in 1975 by an automated light on the cliffs below), its light was once visible for 24 nautical miles. At sunset each day for more than 100 years, a lightkeeper lit an oil lamp inside the lighthouse's first-order Fresnel lens, and thousands of prisms directed the light beam to the horizon. To fulfill his duty, the lightkeeper endured hard labor, extreme monotony, loneliness, and terrible weather conditions. (If this sounds anything like your job, you know how he felt.) The lightkeeper's log of September 21, 1885 bears this entry: "Fog, fog, and nothing but fog. Had no mail service since 9th. Getting short of provisions. Oh solitude, where are the charms that sages have such in thy face? Better dwell in the midst of alarms than reign in this horrible place."

If you are fortunate enough to choose a sunny day for your trip to the lighthouse, it may be hard to imagine the lighthouse keeper's great hardships. Although the wind will likely be howling, the extraordinary coastal views are generous compensation. Starting from the parking lot, you hike uphill on a paved road, getting fine views over your right shoulder of long and wide Point Reyes Beach. You'll stroll past grasslands, clumps of ice plant, and big boulders. In spring, colorful wildflowers pepper the grasses. Look carefully at the rock faces along the trail. They are covered with a red, furry-looking alga called rock violet, and a pale green lichen. Both of these plants can grow without any soil.

In a quarter mile, you'll pass a cluster of park residences on the right, then proceed a few more yards to the lighthouse visitor center. Be sure to stop in before or after your visit; the small center has fine displays on the natural history of Point Reyes. Also, look outside the visitor center for a sign posted with "Today's Whale Count." During the fall and spring grey whale migration, the number can be in the hundreds. The whales are best seen in December and January, when they migrate from their northern feeding grounds to the calving lagoons of Baja, Mexico. As you hike, look out to sea for their spouts. You may also see the whales in spring, when they are heading south to north, but then they are usually farther out to sea.

Just beyond the visitor center you'll pass a grey whale skull on exhibit, then reach a landing area just before the stairway that leads down to the lighthouse. Pause at the landing area to look where you're heading; the stairway has more than 300 steps and is the height of a 30-story building. It's quite easy to go down; coming back up is another matter. (The lighthouse was built far down the cliff in order to keep it below the level of the coastal fog.) From the landing area, you can look down at the rocks below and see large flocks of common murres, which are black and white and look like small penguins.

Point Reyes Lighthouse

When you're ready, make the descent down the stairs, then step inside either the small building next to the lighthouse, or the base of the lighthouse itself. Both rooms have interesting interpretive displays describing the building of the lighthouse and the workings of its original lens and light.

Explore all you like, then make the long climb back up the stairs. Traveling in the upward direction, you'll notice the stairs have numbers painted on them, so you can mark your progress as you ascend.

To make your lighthouse visit the best it can be, go on a clear day. (You can call the Lighthouse Visitor Center for weather information before making the long drive; phone 415/669-1534.) Also, bring a thick jacket even if it's sunny and warm elsewhere in Point Reyes. Fog is frequent at the lighthouse; the wind never ceases. Forty mile-per-hour winds are common; gusts of more than 100 miles-per-hour are not uncommon. The wind record for the California coast was set here with a gust recorded at 133 miles per hour.

Finally, remember that the lighthouse is always closed on Tuesdays and Wednesdays, and the park service may close the stairs to the light-house if the wind becomes excessive. The stairway is usually open between 10 A.M. and 4:30 P.M. every Thursday through Monday.

12. TOMALES BAY TRAIL

Point Reyes Station area, Point Reyes National Seashore
Tomales Bay views, an old railroad

DISTANCE: 2.4 miles round-trip; 1 hour   **LEVEL:** Easy
ELEVATION: Start at 80 feet; total change 80 feet   **CROWDS:** Minimal
BEST SEASON: Year-round; spring and fall are best   **RATING:** ★ ★

DIRECTIONS: Follow the directions on page 128 to the town of Olema in western Marin County. At Olema, turn right and drive north on Highway 1 for four miles, passing through the town of Point Reyes Station, to the Tomales Bay Trail parking area on the left. (It is 1.8 miles beyond Point Reyes Station.)

Now don't get the Tomales Bay Trail confused with the Tomales Point Trail, just because both are in Point Reyes. The Tomales Point Trail is the hike with the tule elk on the northern tip of Point Reyes (see page 128). The Tomales Bay Trail is one of the few paths on the east side of Tomales Bay—not actually on the Point Reyes peninsula—that's administered by the park service. It gives you a unique view of the far southern end of Tomales Bay, just before the bay transitions into marshland.

A side attraction is that the hike leads right across the San Andreas Fault line, where the North American Plate and the Pacific Plate divide and conquer. The waters of Tomales Bay cover the northern end of the fault.

From the trailhead at Highway 1, you hike along rolling hills to the edge of the bay. This is an easy hike, and a good path for a contemplative walk on a foggy day—the norm in summer in Point Reyes. In the fog, the green hillsides and meandering waterways of the bay have a brooding, moody look to them, making you feel like you're hiking in Scotland's moors or the diked farmlands of the Netherlands.

Head straight west from the parking area on the only possible trail. At a few points, narrower spur trails branch off the Tomales Bay Trail, but stay on the main path and keep heading for the water. You'll walk downhill first, then uphill again to the top of a ridge with a wide view of Tomales Bay and the town of Inverness across the water.

Just after topping the ridge, you'll descend again and skirt a couple of small ponds. They're surrounded by tall reeds and cattails. Red-winged blackbirds can be seen here, as well as coots and mallards.

Make a final drop down to the bay's edge, where you'll find an old lock system on a levee that's no longer in use. In the early 1900s, the North Pacific Coast Railroad cut through this marsh. Its tracks were built around levees that channeled the flooded wetlands. You'll see several fallen-down trestles that once supported the tracks. Walk to the north along the water's edge for a few hundred yards until you come to the trail's end at a fence. From this point, you can see how Tomales Bay divides into tiny shallow inlets here at its southern terminus, before draining into marshlands of willow, coyote brush, and grasslands.

Tomales Bay Trail

13. INVERNESS RIDGE, BUCKLIN, & BAYVIEW LOOP

Limantour Road area, Point Reyes National Seashore
Coastal views and a regenerating forest

DISTANCE: 7.8 miles round-trip; 4 hours   **LEVEL:** Moderate
ELEVATION: Start at 700 feet; total change 1,400 feet   **CROWDS:** Moderate
BEST SEASON: Spring for wildflowers   **RATING:** ★ ★ ★

DIRECTIONS: Follow the directions on page 128 to the town of Olema in western Marin County. At Olema, turn right (north) on Highway 1 for about 150 yards, then turn left on Bear Valley Road. Drive 1.7 miles on Bear Valley Road, then turn left on Limantour Road. Drive 4.4 miles on Limantour Road to the Bayview Trailhead on the right. Turn right and park in the lot. Begin hiking on the gated dirt road.

This loop trail begins at the Bayview Trailhead, in an area that was severely burned in the 1995 Point Reyes fire. The first stretch on the Inverness Ridge Trail leads through a scorched Bishop pine forest, with blackened trees still standing as reminders of what occurred. While this may sound like a depressing place for a hike, it's not. Rather, it's a fascinating place for a nature lesson, as you travel past young Bishop pines sprouting up among the skeletons, combined with a rash of huckleberry vines, coyote brush, and wildflowers.

Plus, on a clear day, the views of Tomales Bay and Drakes Bay don't get any better than from the high points on the Inverness Ridge Trail. For the best experience, hike this loop on a sunny spring day, when the wildflowers are out in force and the coastal vistas are crystal clear.

Start hiking on the wide dirt road at the parking lot, signed as Inverness Ridge Trail. The trail starts out with a short downhill and then ascends gently to the north for one mile to a junction with a road leading into the community of Inverness Park. You'll see several new homes on the ridge above you; these were rebuilt after the original houses were destroyed in the fire.

Continue on the dirt road past a junction with Drakes View Trail at 1.3 miles. Three-quarters of a mile farther you'll reach a saddle below Point Reyes Hill with an extensive view to the north of Tomales Bay. Admire it for a moment, then start climbing on the narrow trail to the top of the hill. Trailside foliage is low growing coastal scrub, allowing unobstructed views of the bay as you climb.

At 2.6 miles, you gain the broad, flat summit of Point Reyes Hill, elevation 1,336 feet, which is covered with FAA equipment. Never mind; just walk past the electronics (now on a paved road) for about 40 yards to a junction with the Bucklin Trail. Turn left. Here is the highest view of the day, looking to the southwest at Drakes Estero, Drakes Bay, and the ocean beyond. This might be a good spot for a picnic before you descend on the Bucklin Trail, which rolls down the open ridgeline to the southwest for 2.4 miles. Your views stay with you for most of this stretch.

At five miles out, the Bucklin Trail ends at Muddy Hollow Road, a wide dirt fire road. Turn left, hike east for three-quarters of a mile, then turn left again on the narrower Bayview Trail. You'll have a 2.2-mile climb back to your starting point at the Bayview Trailhead, but it's a mellow ascent of only 700 feet.

14. SKY TRAIL to MOUNT WITTENBERG LOOP
Limantour Road area, Point Reyes National Seashore
The highest summit in Point Reyes

DISTANCE: 4.5 miles round-trip; 2.5 hours   **LEVEL:** Easy/moderate
ELEVATION: Start at 650 feet; total change 750 feet   **CROWDS:** Moderate
BEST SEASON: Year-round; spring and fall are best   **RATING:** ★ ★ ★ ★

DIRECTIONS: Follow the directions on page 128 to the town of Olema in western Marin County. At Olema, turn right (north) on Highway 1 for about 150 yards, then turn left on Bear Valley Road. Drive 1.7 miles on Bear Valley Road, then turn left on Limantour Road. Drive 3.4 miles on Limantour Road to the Sky Trailhead on the left. Turn left and park in the lot. Begin hiking on the gated dirt road.

There's an easy way and a hard way to hike to Mount Wittenberg, the tallest summit in Point Reyes National Seashore. The route from Sky Trailhead is the easy way, a 4.5-mile semi-loop with a 750-foot elevation gain. The route from Bear Valley Trailhead is the hard way, a 4.6-mile loop or out-and-back with a 1,300-foot elevation gain. Both trails are excellent, so make your decision based on your energy level. Either way you go, your reward is the summit of Mount Wittenberg at 1,407 feet, where on a clear day you'll have panoramic views of the coast and Olema Valley.

Notice I said on a *clear* day. I've been on Wittenberg's summit more than half a dozen times, and only twice have I seen much in the way of a view. For the best experience, you need to hike to the summit on one of Point Reyes' rare cloudless, fogless days. These occur most

Sky Trail near Limantour Road

often in autumn, although you might get lucky in winter or spring.

For the Sky Trail route to the summit, begin hiking from the Sky Trailhead on Limantour Road. The path is a wide dirt fire road through a dense forest of Douglas firs, with a steady, moderate grade. Only once do the trees open up sufficiently to provide you with a clear view to the west of Limantour Beach and Drakes Bay. This occurs at an obvious curve in the road with a wooden railing on the right side. Consider it a brief preview of what's to come.

Keep steadily climbing until seven-tenths of a mile, where you'll crest a ridge and reach a junction of trails. Bear left on the narrow Horse Trail, which climbs some more through the fir trees for four-tenths of a mile to a junction with Z Ranch Trail. Turn right on Z Ranch Trail and follow its level path for seven-tenths of a mile past woods and meadows to a grassy saddle below the summit of Mount Wittenberg. Views of Drakes Bay are fine from here, but they'll be even better from the peak. Here, at a junction of trails, the Wittenberg Summit Trail makes a sharp left turn and heads up the mountain. Go for it—it's less than a quarter-mile to the top.

In contrast to the route you just walked, the summit of Wittenberg is mostly bald and grassy, with only a few trees. This turns out to be a good arrangement, because when you reach the top in a few minutes of climbing, you have a 360-degree view of the entire Point

Reyes peninsula. You can see Olema Valley and Bolinas Ridge to the east, Drakes Bay and the ocean to the west and south, and Tomales Bay to the north. Looking beyond the peninsula, you can make out Mount Tamalpais in Marin County, Mount Saint Helena in Napa County, and Mount Diablo on the East Bay, 50 miles distant. If it's a clear day and the view is this good, you probably won't be alone on the summit. But there's plenty of room for everybody. In spring, the mountain's grassy slopes are gilded with lupine, poppies, and tidy tips.

When you've seen enough, backtrack down the summit trail to the saddle, and turn right on Z Ranch Trail (don't go back the way you came). In four-tenths of a mile, you'll connect with Sky Trail's wide road, where you turn right and enjoy an easy jaunt to Sky Camp. Throughout this mostly level stretch, you'll enjoy more views of the coast through the trees. Once you reach the camp, you can find an unoccupied campsite and relax for a while. The best sites are at the far end of the camp near site number 10, where there are views over the fire-scarred forest to the ocean beyond. The 1995 Point Reyes fire stopped right at the edge of Sky Trail and Sky Camp, but severely burned the forests between Sky Trail and the coast.

From Sky Camp, you have a mostly downhill stroll on Sky Trail back to the trailhead and your car.

Note that you can nearly double the length of this trip by adding on a loop from Mount Wittenberg down to Bear Valley and back. After visiting the summit and returning to the junction of trails at the saddle, bear left on the Mount Wittenberg Trail and follow it downhill for 1.8 miles to the Bear Valley Trail. Turn right on Bear Valley Trail and hike six-tenths of a mile to Meadow Trail, then turn right on Meadow Trail and hike 1.5 miles back uphill to a junction with Sky Trail. Turn right on Sky Trail to finish out the loop via Sky Camp as described above. This makes an excellent 8.4-mile loop.

15. MUDDY HOLLOW TRAIL

Limantour Road area, Point Reyes National Seashore
A marsh and wetlands walk to Limantour Beach

DISTANCE: 3.6 miles round-trip; 2 hours   **LEVEL:** Easy
ELEVATION: Start at 100 feet; total change 100 feet   **CROWDS:** Moderate
BEST SEASON: Year-round; spring and fall are best   **RATING:** ★ ★ ★

DIRECTIONS: Follow the directions on page 128 to the town of Olema in western Marin County. At Olema, turn right (north) on Highway 1 for about 150 yards, then turn left on Bear Valley Road. Drive 1.7 miles on Bear Valley

Road, then turn left on Limantour Road. Drive 5.9 miles on Limantour Road to the right turnoff for the Muddy Hollow Trailhead. Turn right and drive a quarter mile to the parking area. Take the trail on the left signed as "Muddy Hollow Trail," not the upper trail that is signed "Muddy Hollow Road."

"Traveling on the Muddy Hollow Trail is like visiting the thickest woods of northern Canada, where trees and vines grow so densely alongside moist ravines that if it weren't for the trail, you'd have to cut your way through the thicket with a machete."

I wrote those words about the Muddy Hollow Trail in Point Reyes just one month before the great wildfire of October 1995. The fire, which was started accidently by an illegal campfire, burned for five days and destroyed more than 12,000 acres in the park. Muddy Hollow was dead center in the path of the blaze.

Only a handful of years have passed since that fire, and although Muddy Hollow Trail is not as lush as it used to be, it is rife with vegetation once again. Unlike other fire-scarred areas of the park, where tall, blackened Bishop pines stand as constant reminders of the fire, the vegetation in the Muddy Hollow area is the kind that heals quickly. It consists of smaller trees like willows and alders, and plenty of fast-growing vines and chaparral. For those who knew Muddy Hollow Trail in its previous incarnation, a walk here offers a tangible example of regeneration after devastation. New growth popped out of the charred earth as soon as six weeks after the fire, and after only a few rains, the hills started to turn green.

The Muddy Hollow Trail leads to the edge of Limantour Estero and eventually to Limantour Beach. It's the best possible route for accessing Limantour Beach—far better than driving there—because you can see the transition from forest to wetlands to ocean as you walk. The path begins in the trees, parallels a creek enroute to a small pond, meets the estero, and then ends at oceanside sand dunes.

A bonus is that the trail is completely level. You hike from the trailhead on a dirt road, passing a park service maintenance building a half-mile in. The trail narrows considerably and passes through a spring-fed marsh area. (In winter, the trail can be flooded here.) In another mile, you reach Muddy Hollow's large freshwater pond, surrounded by cattails, alders, and coastal scrub. Where you can see above the foliage, birdwatching is good. Often you'll spy literally hundreds of ducks and grebes on the pond's surface.

As you hike past the pond and the right turnoff for the Estero Trail, you'll meet up with the eastern tip of Limantour Estero. Here,

Egret on the edge of Limantour Estero

you're likely to see egrets and herons fishing in the mudflats. Finally, the trail veers to the left and meets a paved trail that leads from Limantour Beach's rest rooms to the beach. (The trail is paved to protect the nesting grounds of snowy plovers.) If you wish, you can continue your hike by exploring along the fine sands of Limantour. In spring, yellow bush lupine blooms along its dunes. The scent of lupine is so fragrant that you can smell it from 50 yards away.

16. COAST, FIRE LANE, & LAGUNA LOOP

Limantour Road area, Point Reyes National Seashore
An easy coastal walk with beach access

DISTANCE: 5.0 miles round-trip; 2.5 hours   **LEVEL:** Easy/moderate
ELEVATION: Start at 100 feet; total change 450 feet   **CROWDS:** Moderate
BEST SEASON: Year-round; spring and fall are best   **RATING:** ★ ★ ★

DIRECTIONS: Follow the directions on page 128 to the town of Olema in western Marin County. At Olema, turn right (north) on Highway 1 for about 150 yards, then turn left on Bear Valley Road. Drive 1.7 miles on Bear Valley Road, then turn left on Limantour Road. Drive 5.9 miles on Limantour Road to the left turnoff for the Point Reyes Youth Hostel. Turn left, drive a half mile (past the youth hostel) and park in the lot on the right. Then walk back up the road for three tenths of a mile, passing the hostel again. Begin hiking on the dirt fire road just west of (and across the road from) the youth hostel. The fire road is signed as Coast Trail to Coast Camp.

If you've ever wanted to take an easy hike to a windswept beach, then find a private spot to sit on the sand and look out to sea for an hour or so, the Coast Trail provides the chance.

Like neighboring Muddy Hollow Trail, Coast Trail was badly burned in the Point Reyes fire of 1995. And like the Muddy Hollow Trail, Coast Trail recovered quickly. Six months after the fire, the surrounding grasslands and hillsides were already green with millions of ferns, berry bushes, and vines poking out of the ground, and grasses covering much of the blackened earth. Now the coastal scrub has regained its place.

The Coast Trail is an L-shaped wide road, beginning at the Point Reyes Youth Hostel and making a beeline for the coast, then turning left (south) and running parallel to the beach for another mile to Coast Camp and beyond. An excellent loop trip is to follow the Coast Trail to Coast Camp (2.8 miles), explore the nearby beach, then return to the trailhead on Fire Lane and Laguna trails (1.8 miles).

The Coast Trail is sunny and open most of the way, except for a short section where you near a stream and its surrounding thicket of alders. In winter, the stream creates a few marshy areas, which are thick

Coast Trail

with cattails. Hiking is easy on the wide, dirt road, which has a slight downhill grade. When you reach the coast, you can head straight for the sand, but it's better to keep hiking to your left on Coast Trail for another 1.1 miles to Coast Camp. (This camp is a fine spot to keep in mind in case you ever want to take an easy backpacking trip. To reserve a spot at the 14-site camp, you must obtain a camping permit from Point Reyes headquarters.)

From Coast Camp, take the narrow foot trail by the camp rest rooms that leads to Santa Maria Beach. Once there, you can walk as far as you like in either direction, either right toward Limantour Beach or left toward Sculptured Beach, with miles of uninterrupted shoreline in between. Or, if you're tired of walking, just flop down in the sand.

For your return trip, take the Fire Lane Trail from Coast Camp for one mile to a junction with the Laguna Trail. You'll have to climb; keep turning around to check out the views as you gain elevation. At the junction, bear left on Laguna Trail and hike a final eight-tenths of a mile back to your parked car.

17. BEAR VALLEY TRAIL to ARCH ROCK

Bear Valley, Point Reyes National Seashore
Forest, streams, meadows, and a rocky ocean overlook

DISTANCE: 8.2 miles round-trip; 4 hours   **LEVEL:** Easy/moderate
ELEVATION: Start at 100 feet; total change 400 feet   **CROWDS:** Moderate
BEST SEASON: Year-round; spring and fall are best   **RATING:** ★ ★ ★ ★

DIRECTIONS: Follow the directions on page 128 to the town of Olema in western Marin County. At Olema, turn right (north) on Highway 1 for about 150 yards, then turn left on Bear Valley Road. Drive a half mile, then turn left at the sign for Seashore Headquarters Information. Drive a quarter mile and park in the large lot on the left, past the visitor center. Start hiking along the park road, heading for the signed Bear Valley Trail.

The Bear Valley Trail is hands-down the most famous trail in Point Reyes, and for that reason alone I avoided it for years. I feared the crowds at the trailhead, the noise of other chattering trail users, and the probable lack of peace in a place as sacred as Point Reyes.

But when I finally hiked it, I realized that bypassing the Bear Valley Trail had been a big mistake. The trail is incredibly beautiful, and easy enough to be a perfect family hiking trip. Best of all, arriving at the trailhead before 9 A.M. assures you of some solitude along the route, even on weekends. Winter is the best season for low crowds, and

Final steps to Arch Rock

the trail is prettiest then anyway, when the stream is running full and the ferns are in full leafy display.

The trail is simple to follow. It begins just past the Bear Valley Visitor Center and Morgan Horse Ranch. Several trails junction with Bear Valley Trail, but just stay on the wide, main road and meander your way through the mixed bay and Douglas fir forest, following the path of Bear Valley Creek. Ferns of many kinds adorn the creek's banks. You'll have a slight uphill in the first mile, but the entire route never gains or loses more than 200 feet in elevation.

At 1.5 miles from the trailhead, you reach the edge of large Divide Meadow. This is a lovely spot for a rest or a picnic on your return trip. At Divide Meadow, you leave Bear Valley Creek behind, but before long the trail starts to parallel Coast Creek, which it follows all the way to the ocean. More forest, ferns, and lush foliage along the stream keep you company as you walk. In spring, the buckeye trees along this stretch bloom with perfumy white flower clusters. Also in spring, the trail is bordered by a profusion of blue forget-me-nots and tasty miner's lettuce.

At 3.2 miles you reach a junction of trails. Glen Trail goes off to the left and Baldy Trail to the right, but you simply continue straight on the Bear Valley Trail to Arch Rock. Although you are deep in the forest, surrounded by alders, laurel, and Douglas fir trees, you will soon leave it. Without warning, a half mile farther the trail opens out to coastal marshlands, and you spot the ocean straight ahead.

Near the cliff's edge the trail splits off, meeting up with Coast Trail. You can take either trail to Arch Rock—continue straight ahead, or go right and then jog left 100 yards later. The junction is not well-signed, so keep in mind that you want to end up at the edge of the bluffs looking out over the ocean. (If you keep heading to the right on Coast Trail, you'll miss Arch Rock altogether and wind up at Kelham Beach in eight-tenths of a mile.)

The final steps of the hike are extremely dramatic as you walk along the top of Arch Rock's jagged, jade-green bluff that juts out over the sea. Coast Creek, the gentle stream that you've been following, now cuts a deep and eroded gorge on its way to the ocean. After the peaceful, sheltered forest, the frequent raging wind on top of Arch Rock can be a shock to your system.

A spur trail leads down the cliffs to the beach, worth hiking only during low tides when there is enough beach to explore. (Some people even crawl through Arch Rock's tunnel during very low tides.) Most hikers are content to stay on top of Arch Rock and enjoy the view, which includes numerous rock outcrops, the shoreline below, and the perpetually rolling surf.

18. BEAR VALLEY, OLD PINE, WOODWARD VALLEY, & COAST LOOP

Bear Valley, Point Reyes National Seashore
A grand tour of forests, meadows, and coast

DISTANCE: 12.0 miles round-trip; 7 hours   **LEVEL:** Moderate
ELEVATION: Start at 100 feet; total change 1,700 feet   **CROWDS:** Minimal
BEST SEASON: Year-round; spring and fall are best   **RATING:** ★ ★ ★ ★ ★

DIRECTIONS: Follow the directions on page 128 to the town of Olema in western Marin County. At Olema, turn right (north) on Highway 1 for about 150 yards, then turn left on Bear Valley Road. Drive a half mile, then turn left at the sign for Seashore Headquarters Information. Drive a quarter mile and park in the large lot on the left, past the visitor center. Start hiking along the park road, heading for the signed Bear Valley Trail.

You say you're looking for an epic day hike in Point Reyes National Seashore? Well here it is. If you like variety, this loop trail provides it. You'll hike past forest, meadows, and ocean over the course of 12 miles. Make sure you bring a map with you; there are numerous junctions to negotiate among the myriad trails of Point Reyes.

The loop begins just past the Bear Valley Visitor Center. Follow the Bear Valley Trail for 1.5 miles to Divide Meadow (see the previous story for details on this stretch). Leave the crowds behind at the scenic meadow and turn right on Old Pine Trail, which begins next to Divide

Meadow's rest rooms. In contrast to the wide Bear Valley Trail, Old Pine Trail is a narrow footpath closely bordered by dense Douglas fir forest and an undergrowth of elderberries and huckleberries. It is much less traveled than other nearby trails; you may have this peaceful forest all to yourself. You'll climb steadily for 1.5 miles through the trees, then descend for just under a half-mile. Here, at a trail junction, turn right on Sky Trail, and enjoy some limited views of the coast through the trees. In three-tenths of a mile, you'll meet up with Woodward Valley Trail, where you turn left.

Woodward Valley Trail has long been considered the most lush, greenery-filled trail in Point Reyes, a park not lacking in trails of this sort. When the Point Reyes fire burned in 1995, Woodward Valley Trail was largely spared, even though it was near the edge of the burned area. You'll see only a small amount of fire evidence along the trail. Follow Woodward Valley Trail for almost two lovely miles to the coast, passing through an assortment of grassy meadows and shady conifer forests. The path is downhill all the way, except for occasional short rises where you'll gain brief views of Drakes Bay and the ocean.

At a junction with Coast Trail, turn left and follow the bluffs along the shoreline. Every step of the way, spectacular ocean views are yours for the taking. There are two good places to cut off Coast Trail and follow spur trails to the beach: one is a half-mile in near Sculptured Beach, and the other is 2.7 miles in at Kelham Beach. Both spur trails are clearly marked; make sure you visit both beaches. Sculptured Beach features some fascinating eroded rock terraces, and good tidepools.

The 3.5-mile stretch on Coast Trail is followed by a left turn on to Bear Valley Trail, just north of Arch Rock. If you've never visited Arch Rock, take a short side trip and do so now. It's a spectacular ocean overlook on a jagged, grassy bluff. Then, with a deep sigh, wave a sorrowful good-bye to the coast; it's time to turn inland on the Bear Valley Trail. A 2.4-mile walk along Coast Creek brings you back to Divide Meadow; a final 1.5 miles on the trail returns you to your starting point.

Note that if you want to add in a visit to the summit of Mount Wittenberg to this loop, you can start your trip on the Mount Wittenberg Trail from Bear Valley, instead of Old Pine Trail from Divide Meadow. The Mount Wittenberg Trail climbs steeply for 1,300 feet to the tallest peak in the national seashore; take the short summit trail on the right to reach the top. (For more on Mount Wittenberg, read the story on page 153). From the base of the summit trail, follow Z Ranch Trail south to Sky Trail, then continue south on Sky Trail to pick up

Woodward Valley Trail. The rest of the loop is the same as outlined above. This loop is also 12 miles long, but it has a bit steeper climb. The Mount Wittenberg Trail is also likely to be more crowded than the Old Pine Trail.

---

19. STEWART & GREENPICKER LOOP

Five Brooks, Point Reyes National Seashore
Douglas fir forest and a high meadow

DISTANCE: 7.0 miles round-trip; 3.5 hours   **LEVEL:** Moderate
ELEVATION: Start at 250 feet; total change 1,300 feet   **CROWDS:** Minimal
BEST SEASON: Year-round; spring and fall are best   **RATING:** ★ ★ ★

DIRECTIONS: Follow the directions on page 128 to the town of Olema in western Marin County. At Olema, turn left (south) on Highway 1 and drive 3.5 miles to the Five Brooks Trailhead on the left. Turn left and drive a quarter-mile to the parking area. Begin hiking on the gated dirt road.

The Five Brooks Trailhead is most popular with equestrians, but don't think that its trails are only suited for the hoofed and four-footed set. This tree-filled loop on Stewart and Greenpicker Trails provides a moderate climb to a small meadow at the top of a ridge, followed by a somewhat steeper descent on a narrow trail through the forest. It's the kind of trip that is well suited for a foggy day when you want to hike, but you don't want to feel like you're missing out on vistas. Here, the beauty is all close-up.

The loop begins from the gated dirt road at Five Brooks parking lot. Hike on the wide road past a pond and follow the signs to a right turn on to Stewart Trail. You'll stay on the wide dirt road. The trail enters the trees only a quarter mile from the parking lot and remains in the woods for the majority of the trip. The forest is a mix of Douglas fir, bay, and tanoak, with a large amount and variety of ferns growing along the banks of the road.

The Stewart Trail has a pleasant, moderate grade, is always shaded, and is wide enough so that if any equestrians or mountain bikers are sharing the trail with you, there is plenty of room for everybody. Follow Stewart Trail for three miles through many curves and turns until you reach a major junction of two wide roads. Turn right (toward Glen Camp) to reach Firtop in eight tenths of a mile.

Firtop is a small meadow at 1,324 feet in elevation, completely surrounded by Douglas firs. If the sun is out, you'll be amazed at the

Stewart Trail near Firtop

brightness of this tiny patch of open ground, compared to the dim light of the forest you've been hiking in. A right turn at Firtop puts you on the Greenpicker Trail, which heads downhill somewhat more steeply through a young forest of Douglas firs. (Much of the original forest was logged before the creation of the national seashore; the Douglas firs have grown up in the last 40 years.) It's two miles downhill to rejoin the Stewart Trail, under the fir canopy all the way. A left turn on Stewart Trail puts you back at the trailhead in just under a mile.

Note that if you're interested in other hikes leading from Five Brooks Trailhead, two interesting paths are the Olema Valley Trail to the south and Rift Zone Trail to the north. Both trails are nearly level; both can be hiked out-and-back from Five Brooks. They also make excellent shuttle hikes for hikers traveling with two cars. For Rift Zone Trail, you'd leave one car at Bear Valley Visitor Center, a 4.5-mile hike away. For Olema Valley Trail, you'd leave one car along Highway 1 near Dogtown, four miles south of Five Brooks, a 5.5-mile hike away.

20. BASS LAKE, DOUBLE POINT, & ALAMERE FALLS

Bolinas area, Point Reyes National Seashore
Lakes, ocean views, and a waterfall streaming to the sea

DISTANCE: 8.4 miles round-trip; 4 hours

ELEVATION: Start at 280 feet; total change 550 feet

BEST SEASON: February to May

LEVEL: Moderate

CROWDS: Moderate

RATING: ★ ★ ★ ★

DIRECTIONS: Follow the directions on page 128 to the town of Olema in western Marin County. At Olema, turn left (south) on Highway 1. Drive 8.9 miles on Highway 1 to Bolinas Road, which is often not signed. Turn right and drive 2.1 miles to Mesa Road. Turn right and drive 5.8 miles to the Palomarin Trailhead.

Quick—which California waterfall leaps off high coastal bluffs and cascades gracefully down to the sand and surf below? Most people think of famous McWay Falls in Big Sur, one of the most frequently visited and photographed waterfalls in the state. But don't forget the other coastal cataract that makes the same dramatic plunge from earth to sea, 150 miles up the coast in western Marin County. That's Alamere Falls in Point Reyes, which is less celebrated but no less dramatic than McWay Falls.

There may be no finer way to spend a spring day than walking to Alamere Falls. If you time your trip for a clear, sunny day, when the lupine and Douglas iris are in full bloom and the waterfall is running hard, the trailside beauty will knock your socks off.

Start hiking on the Coast Trail from the Palomarin Trailhead in Point Reyes, the southernmost trailhead in the national seashore. Despite its off-the-beaten-track location outside the town of Bolinas, the trailhead parking area is often full of cars. The occupants of many of those cars are backpacking the 15-mile Coast Trail, a spectacular two-day trip. You'll follow a portion of that route.

Alamere Falls

From the Palomarin Trailhead, the Coast Trail is a wide dirt road that begins in stands of eucalyptus. The first mile is nearly level and offers many lovely ocean views. Then the Coast Trail turns inland, climbing slightly to a junction with the Lake Ranch Trail at 2.1 miles. Stay on the Coast Trail as it veers left and passes a couple of seasonal ponds, which are often covered with paddling water birds. At 2.6 miles, you'll skirt the north edge of Bass Lake. Picnicking and swimming spots abound here; just follow the unsigned spur trail on the left, amid the Douglas firs. (The spur is about 100 yards beyond where you first glimpse the lake.)

Reach another trail junction where the Crystal Lake Trail heads right to small Crystal and Mud lakes. Continue straight on the Coast Trail, now heading toward the ocean. Three quarters of a mile beyond Bass Lake, prepare yourself for a stunning view of Pelican Lake, which is perched on a coastal bluff to your left. The Pacific Ocean forms its backdrop. After curving past the lake, reach an unmarked left spur trail that leads to the northern edge of Double Point. (If you take the spur, you'll reach a rocky overlook with views of the ocean and Stormy Stack, a big offshore rock outcrop. This is an excellent spot for whale watching.) Just beyond the Double Point spur, a sign points straight ahead for Wildcat Camp, and a second unmarked spur leads left, heading for the coastal bluffs and Alamere Falls. Follow this quarter-mile spur trail, which is narrow and frequently overgrown with poison oak and coastal scrub, until it meets up with Alamere Creek near the cliff edge. Although you are now practically on top of the fall, you can see little of its watery theatrics.

To see more, you must proceed with caution. Scramble downstream, then cross the stream wherever you safely can, so that you wind up on the north side of Alamere Creek. At the edge of the bluffs and alongside the fall's lip, you'll find a well-worn route leading down to the beach. A rope is usually tied in place to help you down the most vertical spots. Be wary of the loose sandstone and shale as you make your way down the cliffs.

Only when you touch down on the beach does the full drama of Alamere Falls unfold. Although the pristine coastline would be stunning even without the waterfall, it's made even more impressive by the sight of Alamere Creek dropping in a wide, effusive block over its cliff, then streaming across the sand and into the sea. The fall is 50 feet high, and although its width varies greatly according to how much water is flowing through the creek, it's always beautiful.

MUIR WOODS NATIONAL MONUMENT

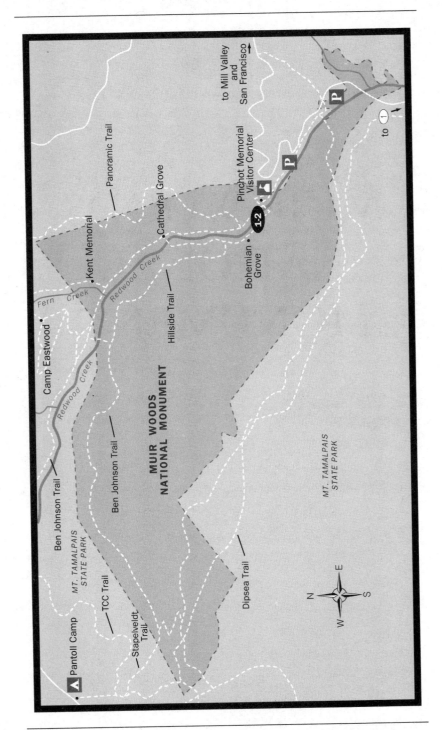

MUIR WOODS NATIONAL MONUMENT

to Mill Valley and San Francisco

to 1

P

P

Pinchot Memorial Visitor Center

1-2

Cathedral Grove

Bohemian Grove

Panoramic Trail

Kent Memorial

Fern Creek

Redwood Creek

Camp Eastwood

Hillside Trail

Redwood Creek

Ben Johnson Trail

MUIR WOODS NATIONAL MONUMENT

MT. TAMALPAIS STATE PARK

MT. TAMALPAIS STATE PARK

Ben Johnson Trail

TCC Trail

Stapelveldt Trail

Dipsea Trail

Pantoll Camp

N
W E
S

MUIR WOODS NATIONAL MONUMENT
TRAILS AT A GLANCE

Map Number/Trail Name	Page	Mileage	Difficulty
1. Panoramic, Lost Trail, & Fern Creek Loop	171	3.4	Easy/moderate
2. Bootjack, TCC, Ben Johnson, & Hillside Trail Loop	174	6.4	Moderate

ABOUT THE PARK

Muir Woods National Monument is home to a stand of virgin, old-growth coast redwoods. The tallest tree is 252 feet, and the broadest tree is more than 13 feet across. The redwoods are between 500 and 1,000 years old. The monument is small—less than 300 acres—but its land and trails adjoin with neighboring Mount Tamalpais State Park.

ADDRESS, PHONE, & WEBSITE

Muir Woods National Monument, Mill Valley, CA 94941; (415) 388-2595.
Website: www.nps.gov/muwo

VISITOR CENTER

The monument's visitor center is located by the main parking lot.

HOW TO GET THERE

• By air: The closest major airport is in San Francisco.

• By car: The park is located 15 miles north of San Francisco's Golden Gate Bridge in the town of Mill Valley. Cross the Golden Gate Bridge and drive north on U.S. 101 for four miles. Take the Mill Valley/Stinson Beach/Highway 1 exit and continue straight for one mile to a stoplight at Shoreline Highway (Highway 1). Turn left on Shoreline Highway and drive 2.5 miles, then turn right on Panoramic Highway. Drive nine-tenths of a mile and turn left on Muir Woods Road. Drive 1.5 miles to the Muir Woods parking area.

DRIVE TIME

• Drive time from Los Angeles: approximately 7 hours.

• Drive time from San Francisco: approximately 45 minutes.

ENTRANCE FEES

There is a $2 entrance fee per adult (ages 17 and older) at Muir Woods National Monument. Children ages 16 and under enter free. A Muir

Woods annual pass is available for $15. A Golden Eagle Passport, an annual pass for all 375 national park units, is available for $50. A Golden Age Passport, a lifetime pass for all 375 national park units, is available to U.S. citizens and residents aged 62 and over for a one-time $10 fee. You can purchase these passes at the park entrance station.

WHEN TO GO

Muir Woods National Monument is open year-round for hiking. The winter season is the least crowded, and it is also the best time to see Redwood Creek running full and deep.

WEATHER CONDITIONS

The weather in the monument is often cool and damp, even in summer. An extra layer of clothing is advisable; rain gear is often necessary in the winter months. Year-round temperatures usually range between 50 and 70 degrees.

WHERE TO STAY

Muir Woods is located in Marin County, near the towns of Mill Valley, Corte Madera, and San Rafael. Various motels and lodgings are available in these towns. Muir Woods is also 45 minutes away from San Francisco's lodgings, motels, and hotels. Camping is available at Mount Tamalpais State Park, which is adjacent to Muir Woods. You can hike to Muir Woods from Pantoll Campground at Mount Tamalpais State Park. Phone (415) 388-2070 for more information.

FOOD & SUPPLIES

A snack shop is located within the monument, next to the visitor center. Restaurants and supplies are available in the nearby town of Mill Valley.

SUGGESTED MAPS

Park maps are available at the monument's visitor center. An excellent map of Muir Woods, Mount Tamalpais, and surrounding parklands is available from Olmsted & Brothers Map Company. Phone (510) 658-6534.

1. PANORAMIC, LOST TRAIL, & FERN CREEK LOOP

Muir Woods National Monument
Big redwoods and a Douglas fir forest

DISTANCE: 3.4 miles round-trip; 1.5 hours
ELEVATION: Start at 150 feet; total gain 800 feet
BEST SEASON: December to May

LEVEL: Easy/moderate
CROWDS: Moderate
RATING: ★ ★ ★

DIRECTIONS: From San Francisco, cross the Golden Gate Bridge and drive north on U.S. 101 for four miles. Take the Mill Valley/Stinson Beach/Highway 1 exit, and continue straight for one mile to a stoplight at Shoreline Highway (Highway 1). Turn left on Shoreline Highway and drive 2.5 miles, then turn right on Panoramic Highway. Drive nine-tenths of a mile and turn left on Muir Woods Road. Drive 1.5 miles to the Muir Woods parking area.

The redwoods at Muir Woods National Monument are beauties. The foliage in the understory of the big redwoods—bays, tanoak, thimbleberry, sword ferns, and sorrel—is lush, green, and pretty year-round. Redwood Creek, which cuts through the center of the park, is a pristine, coursing stream.

Muir Woods is good—no doubt about it. The only problem with Muir Woods is its location: it's situated a bit too close to a major urban area. That means this little tiny national monument, not much larger than a few city blocks, gets visited by more than one million people each year.

How do you hike in the park and see its lovely redwoods without getting run over by the crowds? It's not easy. Summer is the busiest time, of course, so it's best to avoid May to September all together. Weekends tend to be more crowded than weekdays, but weekdays bring school groups. (Thirty sixth-graders on a field trip can be pretty boisterous.) The best choice? Try to show up early in the morning, as in 8 A.M. when the park gates open. During the week, the first school buses and tour buses don't usually arrive till 9 or 10 A.M. On the weekends, most visitors don't show up till mid-morning. An 8 A.M. start any day of the week should give you at least a two-hour window of peace among the redwoods. Winter and early spring are the least crowded and also the loveliest seasons, when Redwood Creek runs full and high.

And don't worry about visiting on a rainy day; just pack along your rain gear. A redwood forest is the best place to hike in the rain. You'll be partially protected by the big trees, and the drops of water on every fern, branch, and leaf only accentuate the beauty.

Muir Woods National Monument—map page 168   171

Redwood sorrel

Start your trip from the entrance gate to Muir Woods, near the small visitor center. The only trail choice is the wide, paved path that runs along the bottom of the canyon, passing the most impressive redwoods. You'll walk the entire length of this trail on your return; for now, bear right and in about 100 yards you'll reach a fork with Panoramic Trail. Panoramic Trail (once named the Ocean View Trail, although it has no ocean views) ascends up the hillside to the right. Take it and leave the pavement behind.

The path is completely forested, but the redwood trees are younger and smaller here, and interspersed with many Douglas firs. The climb is very moderately graded, and curves around the canyon until it reaches a junction with Lost Trail at 1.5 miles. Note this junction; then continue straight past it for another 200 yards until Panoramic Trail exits the forest just below Panoramic Highway, a busy road. A large boulder rests on the hillside between the trail and the road; this is the only place along the trail where you can get a long-distance view. On a sunny day, it's a nice spot, looking down over the forests of Muir Woods below.

When you've had your fill of sunshine, return to the shady woods and the previously noted junction. Turn right on Lost Trail, now heading downhill. Lost Trail is very similar to Panoramic Trail in that it cuts through a young redwood, Douglas fir, and bay forest. Soon it descends more steeply on railroad-tie stairsteps, and in seven-tenths of a mile it connects with Fern Creek Trail. Fern Creek is a narrower offshoot of Redwood Creek, the main stream that flows through Muir Woods' canyon. The path follows Fern Creek's delightful course for nearly a half mile, crossing it on two footbridges.

Near the end of the Fern Creek Trail you pass a sign marking the border of Muir Woods National Monument. In a few more steps, you're standing at the base of the Kent Memorial, a very large Douglas fir tree dedicated to the man who was responsible for the creation of Muir Woods National Monument.

There's a wonderful story about Congressman William Kent: he and his wife, Elizabeth, purchased this land and then granted it to the federal government in 1905, under the condition that it be named for naturalist John Muir. When President Theodore Roosevelt suggested that the forest be named "Kent Woods", Kent wrote back and said he couldn't accept, because naming the forest after himself was an implication that immortality could be bought, not earned. "So many millions of better people have died forgotten.... I have five good, husky boys that I am trying to bring up to a knowledge of democracy. If these boys cannot keep the name of Kent alive, I am willing it should be forgotten."

Interpretive signs on Muir Woods' main trail

Roosevelt wrote back: "By George, you are right... Good for you, and for the five boys who are to keep the name of Kent alive. I have four who I hope will do the same thing by the name of Roosevelt." Roosevelt officially created Muir Woods National Monument in 1908.

The loop trail ends with a three-quarter mile walk from the Kent Memorial back up the main trail to your starting point. For more information on Muir Woods' main trail, see the following story.

2. BOOTJACK, TCC, BEN JOHNSON, & HILLSIDE TRAIL LOOP

Muir Woods National Monument
Big redwoods, a sunny meadow, and solitude

DISTANCE: 6.4 miles round-trip; 3 hours   **LEVEL:** Moderate
ELEVATION: Start at 150 feet; total gain 1,100 feet   **CROWDS:** Moderate
BEST SEASON: December to May   **RATING:** ★ ★ ★

DIRECTIONS: From San Francisco, cross the Golden Gate Bridge and drive north on U.S. 101 for four miles. Take the Mill Valley/Stinson Beach/Highway 1 exit, and continue straight for one mile to a stoplight at Shoreline Highway (Highway 1). Turn left on Shoreline Highway and drive 2.5 miles, then turn right on Panoramic Highway. Drive nine-tenths of a mile and turn left on Muir Woods Road. Drive 1.5 miles to the Muir Woods parking area.

Muir Woods National Monument is filled with gems, like its virgin grove of coast redwoods and pristine Redwood Creek, which flows through the monument. But Muir Woods is small. If you want to take a hike of any distance, you have to leave the monument's borders and explore the adjoining lands of Mount Tamalpais State Park. This loop trail starts and ends in the monument and explores the best of it, then makes a brief tour of the equally fine redwood forest beyond its boundary.

The loop begins on the main trail in Muir Woods, a wide, paved path through the big trees that is often crawling with people. (For tips on how to avoid the crowds at Muir Woods, see the previous story.) Follow the trail as it parallels Redwood Creek, and rest assured that you will soon leave the majority of visitors behind. (You know you're in a heavily visited urban park when you see signs stating, "Help keep the creek clean. Do not throw coins in the water.")

If you've visited the coast redwood forests in Redwood National Park and its neighboring state parks, you may be surprised to find that the redwoods in Muir Woods are not as big. Whereas the trees around Redwood National Park grow to 20 feet in diameter, the broadest tree in Muir Woods in only 13.5 feet in diameter. What the redwoods lack in girth, however, they make up for in setting: they thrive in a steep, lush, stream-filled canyon that can appear almost mystical on a foggy or rainy day. The monument's highlights are the Cathedral Grove and the Bohemian Grove—dense stands of ancient redwoods. The Bohemian Grove has some of the tallest trees in the park at 250 feet.

You may notice a new section of the main trail about a quarter

"Population" sign at Van Wyck Meadow

mile in, where the park service has removed a substantial length of pavement and installed a boardwalk made of recycled redwood. This helps to protect the redwoods' fragile roots. The trail has also been moved a few yards away from Redwood Creek; this was done for the benefit of the fish who return to it each year to spawn. If you visit in winter, you may be lucky enough to spot some of the native wild population of steelhead trout or coho salmon that are born in Redwood Creek, live out their adult lives in the Pacific Ocean, then return here to breed and die.

Continue down the main trail, passing the Fern Creek Trail turnoff, then the Camp Alice Eastwood Trail turnoff, and in a few more yards you arrive at the end of the pavement at a junction with Bootjack Trail, which continues on a smooth dirt path along the stream to the right. You are now one mile from Muir Woods' entrance.

Bootjack Trail makes an easy to moderate ascent along the stream, passing a cornucopia of splashing cascades in winter. The trail stays close to the water's edge, making this a perfect rainy season hike for whitewater lovers. The forest is a dense blend of big-leaf maples, bays, and redwoods. The path steepens a bit, then travels up wooden stairsteps made out of old park signs, until at 1.3 miles from Muir Woods it tops out at Van Wyck Meadow. The postage stamp-sized meadow has a big boulder to sunbathe on and a brown sign stating "Van Wyck Meadow, population 3 stellar jays."

Enjoy this peaceful spot and its sunshine, then turn left on TCC Trail to head back into the woods. (The path is signed as TCC Trail to Stapelveldt Trail.) TCC Trail meanders on a nearly level course through young, slender Douglas firs for 1.4 miles. Most noticeable is the silence—for the first time on this hike, you're nowhere near a creek. At the end of this quiet, forested stretch, you reach two junctions immediately following one another. Bear left at both; you'll wind up on Stapelveldt Trail heading for Ben Johnson Trail in a half-mile.

Now you're back in a wetter forest again, with lots of mossy bay trees. By the time you junction with Ben Johnson Trail, you've returned to the redwoods. Many of these trees rival the size and beauty of the ones on the main trail in the monument.

In the last mile of the trip, you have a choice: turn right to walk the paved canyon trail back to the park entrance, or turn left to walk the Hillside Trail above the canyon. The Hillside Trail deposits you at Bridge #2 on the paved trail, where you turn right and walk the last few yards back to your car.

PINNACLES NATIONAL MONUMENT

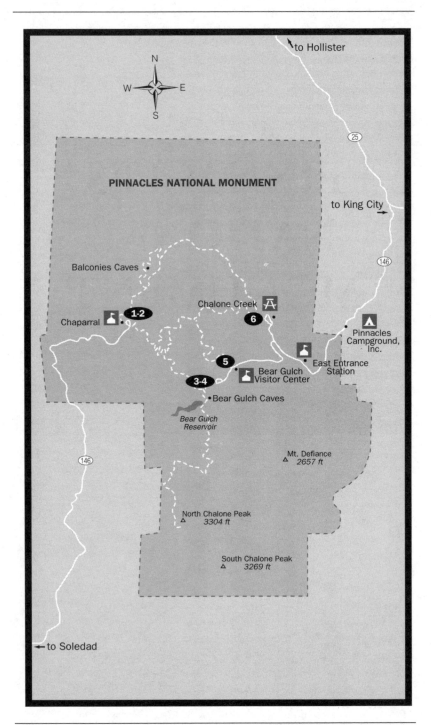

N
W E
S

PINNACLES NATIONAL MONUMENT

to Hollister

25

to King City

146

Balconies Caves

Chalone Creek

Chaparral

1-2

6

Pinnacles
Campground,
Inc.

5

Bear Gulch
Visitor Center

East Entrance
Station

3-4

Bear Gulch Caves

Bear Gulch
Reservoir

Mt. Defiance
△ 2657 ft

146

North Chalone Peak
△ 3304 ft

South Chalone Peak
△ 3269 ft

to Soledad

PINNACLES NATIONAL MONUMENT
TRAILS AT A GLANCE

Map Number/Trail Name	Page	Mileage	Difficulty
1. Juniper Canyon, High Peaks, & Old Pinnacles Loop	182	8.4	Moderate
2. Balconies Caves	184	2.4	Easy
3. Bear Gulch Caves	186	2.0	Easy
4. North Chalone Peak	188	8.4	Strenuous
5. Condor Gulch & High Peaks Loop	190	5.0	Moderate
6. Old Pinnacles Trail & Balconies Caves	192	5.6	Easy

THE TOP 3, DON'T-MISS DAY HIKES:

Map Number/Trail Name	Page	Features
1. Juniper Canyon, High Peaks, & Old Pinnacles Loop	182	tour of park highlights
4. North Chalone Peak	188	fire lookout, views
5. Condor Gulch & High Peaks Loop	190	climb rock pinnacles

TRAIL SUGGESTIONS FOR IF YOU ONLY HAVE ONE DAY:

Map Number/Trail Name	Page	Features
2. Balconies Caves	184	cave explorations
3. Bear Gulch Caves	186	cave explorations
5. Condor Gulch & High Peaks Loop	190	climb rock pinnacles

PINNACLES NATIONAL MONUMENT

ABOUT THE PARK

The striking cliffs, crags, and rock formations of Pinnacles National Monument were formed by an ancient volcano that erupted 200 miles to the southeast. Movement along the San Andreas Fault carried these formations to their current location amid the rolling grasslands and low hills of the Salinas Valley. Highlights of the monument include its caves (Balconies and Bear Gulch), its many rock climbing sites, and its well built trails over and around the rocky pinnacles.

ADDRESS, PHONE, & WEBSITE

Pinnacles National Monument, 5000 Highway 146, Paicines, CA 95043; (831) 389-4485.
Website: www.nps.gov/pinn

VISITOR CENTERS

The monument's main visitor center is located on the east side of the monument at Bear Gulch. There is a smaller ranger station/visitor center on the west side of the monument at Chaparral.

HOW TO GET THERE

• By air: The closest major airport is in San Jose, California.
• By car: No roads connect the east and west sides of the park. You can hike from one side to the other, but you can't drive through. When planning your trip, consider which side of the park you want to have vehicle access to, then follow the directions accordingly.

West/Chaparral Entrance—From Salinas, drive south on U.S. 101 for 22 miles to Soledad and take the Soledad/Highway 146 exit. Drive east on Highway 146 for 12 miles. (The road is signed for West Pinnacles.) Highway 146 dead-ends at the Chaparral Ranger Station and trailhead.

East/Bear Gulch Entrance—From King City on U.S. 101, take the First Street exit and head east. First Street turns into Highway G13/Bitterwater Road. Follow it for 15 miles to Highway 25, then turn left (north). Follow Highway 25 for 14 miles to Highway 146. Turn left on Highway 146 and drive 4.8 miles to the park visitor center.

If you are coming from the north, drive south on U.S. 101 for two miles and take the Highway 25 exit. Drive south on Highway 25 for 43 miles to Highway 146. Continue south on Highway 146 for 4.8 miles to the park visitor center.

DRIVE TIME

• Drive time from Los Angeles: approximately 5.5 hours.

• Drive time from San Francisco: approximately 2.5 hours.

ENTRANCE FEES

There is a $5 entrance fee per vehicle at Pinnacles National Monument, good for seven days. A Pinnacles annual pass is available for $15. A Golden Eagle Passport, an annual pass for all 375 national park units, is available for $50. A Golden Age Passport, a lifetime pass for all 375 national park units, is available to U.S. citizens and residents aged 62 and over for a one-time $10 fee. You can purchase these passes at the park entrance stations or visitor center.

WHEN TO GO

The best season in Pinnacles National Monument is from October to late April. Summer is too hot for comfortable hiking. The winter months are less crowded than spring or fall, but they also bring a chance of rain. Spring wildflowers are superb.

WEATHER CONDITIONS

Pinnacles National Monument has a semi-arid climate. May through September days can have temperatures higher than 100 degrees; other months of the year are cooler and mild. Expect possible rain from November to March. The general rule for hiking in the park: Wear or carry a variety of layers. Expect extreme heat in the summer.

WHERE TO STAY

Pinnacles National Monument closed its main campground in 1998. The only camping presently available is at a private campground just outside the monument, called Pinnacles Campground Inc. Campsites may be reserved in advance; phone (831) 389-4462. There is no lodging within the park; the nearest motels are in Soledad or Hollister.

FOOD & SUPPLIES

No services are available within the monument. A small store is located at Pinnacles Campground Inc. Restaurants and supplies can be found in Soledad on the monument's west side (12 miles away), or in Paicines on the northeast side (23 miles away).

SUGGESTED MAPS

Park maps are available at the ranger stations or by contacting Pinnacles National Monument at the address on page 180.

Pinnacles National Monument—map page 178   181

1. JUNIPER CANYON, HIGH PEAKS, & OLD PINNACLES LOOP

Chaparral (west) side, Pinnacles National Monument
A grand loop through the monument

DISTANCE: 8.4 miles round-trip; 4 hours   **LEVEL:** Moderate

ELEVATION: Start at 1,400 feet; total change 1,200 feet   **CROWDS:** Moderate

BEST SEASON: October to May   **RATING:** ★ ★ ★ ★

DIRECTIONS: From Salinas, drive south on U.S. 101 for 22 miles to Soledad and take the Soledad/Highway 146 exit. Drive east on Highway 146 for 12 miles. (The road is signed for West Pinnacles.) Highway 146 dead-ends at the Chaparral Ranger Station and trailhead parking lot.

Pinnacles National Monument is a hiker's park. You can tell right away because there are no roads going through the place, although you can hike from one side to the other. It's a perfect setup, ideal for people who like their national parks to seem, well, natural. The park's first-rate trail system makes it possible to string together a loop tour of the park on the Juniper Canyon Trail, High Peaks Trail, Old Pinnacles Trail, and Balconies Trail that shows off many of the park's best features. If you follow the trails in this order, you get almost all your climbing done in the first half of the trip, then have a fairly easy home stretch.

(If you don't have time for the whole 8.4-mile loop, you can also make an excellent 4.3-mile semi-loop by hiking up Juniper Canyon Trail, turning left on the High Peaks Trail, turning left again on the Tunnel Trail, and returning on the Juniper Canyon Trail.)

Begin hiking from the right side of the large parking lot near the Chaparral Ranger Station, following the Juniper Canyon Trail from grasslands into the rocky hills. The trail gets steeper as you go, but it's well built and has many strategically placed switchbacks in its second half. Ignore the left turnoff for the Tunnel Trail at 1.2 miles, and instead, continue another six-tenths of a mile to the junction with the High Peaks Trail. Here, at a saddle, you'll find a rest room, a bench, and fine views to the west and east.

From the saddle, the High Peaks Trail travels both north and southeast. Turn north (left) and climb higher along the shoulder of Hawkins Peak. Then descend a bit to reach the most exciting part of this trail—where it climbs up, around, and over the High Peaks. This is a narrow and precipitous trail segment leading through a maze of cliffs and spires. Clearly constructed by highly creative trail builders, the route features handholds and footholds carved into the rock, stairsteps blasted out of the rock, and metal railings to help keep you *on* the rock. (Although it isn't actually dangerous in any way, the High Peaks Trail is not recommended for people who are terrified of heights.)

The High Peaks escapades continue for about a half mile; then the trail reaches a junction with the northern end of the Tunnel Trail. Hikers opting for a shorter, 4.3-mile semi-loop can turn left here and

Ascending the High Peaks Trail

follow the Tunnel Trail back to Juniper Canyon Trail. This, too, is an interesting piece of trail building. You'll walk through a 106-foot tunnel bored in the rock below the High Peaks.

Hikers taking the full tour should continue on the High Peaks Trail, heading northeast and soon starting to descend. Bear left to stay on High Peaks Trail at a junction with the Condor Gulch Trail, then hike two miles downhill to Chalone Creek Picnic Area. There you can fill up your water bottles, rest a while, and then head northwest on the Old Pinnacles Trail. This is a pleasant, level route that meanders along the West Fork of Chalone Creek. (In winter, the creek has a substantial flow of water, and in spring, wildflowers are tremendous.)

At 2.3 miles from Chalone Creek Picnic Area, you'll reach a fork for the Balconies Trail. If you've never been to Balconies Caves, and you remembered to bring along a flashlight, take the left fork that leads through the caves. (For more information on the Balconies Caves, see the following story.) The right fork climbs above the caves for some excellent views of the Balconies Cliffs—a good option for those without flashlights.

After ducking your head and bending your knees as you wander through the rocky caves, you'll come out to an easy and flat section of the Balconies Trail. In less than a mile, this takes you right back to the Chaparral parking lot, and the completion of your hike.

2. BALCONIES CAVES

Chaparral (west) side, Pinnacles National Monument
A cave exploration for non-spelunkers

DISTANCE: 2.4 miles round-trip; 1.5 hours   **LEVEL:** Easy
ELEVATION: Start at 1,400 feet; total change 300 feet   **CROWDS:** Moderate
BEST SEASON: October to May   **RATING:** ★ ★ ★ ★

DIRECTIONS: From Salinas, drive south on U.S. 101 for 22 miles to Soledad and take the Soledad/Highway 146 exit. Drive east on Highway 146 for 12 miles. (The road is signed for West Pinnacles.) Highway 146 dead-ends at the Chaparral Ranger Station and trailhead parking lot.

If you're coming from U.S. 101 and the western edge of California, the west side of Pinnacles National Monument is a heck of a lot easier to get to than the east side. But if you're disappointed to learn that the Pinnacles' famous Bear Gulch Caves can only be accessed from the east side of the park, don't despair. The west side has its own caves—the Balconies Caves—and like the Bear Gulch Caves, they are a barrel of fun. Got your flashlights? Good, then you're ready. No spelunking experience is necessary.

From the trailhead near Chaparral Ranger Station, set off on the Balconies Trail, following the often dry West Fork of Chalone Creek to the northeast toward the soaring cliffs of Machete Ridge. The sound of the wind in the gray pines and the scurrying of squirrels will keep you company. A mere six-tenths of a mile of level hiking brings you to some huge, colorful, lichen-covered volcanic rocks—a preview of the caves to come.

At the fork with the Balconies Cliffs Trail, go right to enter the caves. Turn on your flashlights and prepare for some good clean fun and adventure—squeezing through clefts in the rock, ducking your head under ledges, and climbing down rocky staircases. What comment does almost every single hiker make inside the Balconies Caves? "Wow, it's dark in here." No kidding.

As you proceed through the pitch black maze of rocky tunnels, you'll reach a few interesting spots where it's unclear which way to proceed. If you look carefully with your flashlight you'll find tiny arrows painted on the walls, pointing the way. Make sure you stop for a few moments inside the cave to listen to the drip-drip of water on the rock walls, and to feel the cool air on your skin.

Ducking out of Balconies Caves

The caves at this park—Balconies Caves and Bear Gulch Caves— are not limestone caverns like many of California's caves, or lava tubes like the caves at Lava Beds National Monument. Instead, Pinnacles' caves were formed by rhyolitic rocks that were altered by water erosion. Over millions of years, running water slowly eroded deep, narrow canyons amid the giant volcanic outcrops of the Pinnacles. Simultaneously, huge boulder-like chunks of these outcrops fragmented, broke off, and fell into the canyons. In many cases, the boulders were too large to fit inside the canyons, so they laid on top, forming a "roof" and creating the tunnels of the caves.

At Balconies Caves, there are two separate cave sections to explore. In between them you come out into the daylight, then traverse a short stretch in which you must duck underneath boulders that are stuck in a crevice between two cliffs.

When you exit the second set of caves, turn left and loop back on the Balconies Cliffs Trail. Hiking above the caves on this path, you'll gain many lovely views of the park's rocky landscape. Birdwatchers take note: Prairie falcons and golden eagles have been spotted in the high cliffs of the Balconies.

3. BEAR GULCH CAVES

Bear Gulch (east) side, Pinnacles National Monument
The monument's main attraction

DISTANCE: 2.0 miles round-trip; 1 hour   **LEVEL:** Easy
ELEVATION: Start at 1,300 feet; total change 250 feet   **CROWDS:** Heavy
BEST SEASON: October to May   **RATING:** ★ ★ ★ ★

DIRECTIONS: From the south: From King City on U.S. 101, take the First Street exit and head east. First Street turns into Highway G13/Bitterwater Road. Follow it for 15 miles to Highway 25, where you turn left (north). Follow Highway 25 for 14 miles to Highway 146. Go left on Highway 146 and drive 4.8 miles to the park visitor center, then continue beyond it to the parking lot at the end of the road. If this lot is full, park by the visitor center and walk down the road to the trailhead.

From the north: From Gilroy, drive south on U.S. 101 for two miles and take the Highway 25 exit. Drive south on Highway 25 for 43 miles to Highway 146. Continue south on Highway 146 for 4.8 miles to the park visitor center. Follow directions as above.

NOTE: An interpretive brochure for the Moses Spring Trail is available at the trailhead or the visitor center.

Bear Gulch Caves are the main event at Pinnacles National Monument. Sure, the park has terrific hiking trails, hundreds of first-class rock climbing sites, abundant spring wildflowers, and fascinating geological features. But what most visitors at Pinnacles want to do is explore Bear Gulch Caves.

If you are planning a trip to Pinnacles specifically to see the caves, phone ahead to be sure that they are open. Bear Gulch Caves are frequently closed during the rainy season due to flooding, and also during certain periods of the year when endangered bats nest inside. (If Bear Gulch Caves are closed, you can usually visit Balconies Caves instead, located on the west side of the park. See the previous story.)

Got your flashlights? Good, you'll need them on this walk. From just beyond the park's Bear Gulch Visitor Center, start hiking on the Moses Spring Trail, also signed for Bear

Tunnel on the trail near Bear Gulch Caves

Gulch Caves. Pick up an interpretive brochure at the visitor center or the trailhead, and you'll learn to identify the flora of the Pinnacles. The first quarter-mile is nothing out of the ordinary, just a pleasant walk through oaks, gray pines, and buckeye trees. In spring, the buckeye flowers are so sweet smelling, they can make you giddy.

Shortly you'll enter and exit a rock tunnel that was built by an ambitious trail crew in the 1930s. Just beyond it, at a fork, take leave of the Moses Spring Trail, which goes up and over the Bear Gulch Caves instead of through them. Bear left for Bear Gulch Caves and turn on your flashlights. Now the fun begins: You'll squeeze through clefts in the rock, duck your head under ledges, and climb down rocky staircases. You'll walk into water-sculpted volcanic caverns where only occasional beams of sunlight flash through the ceiling. You'll twist and turn through narrow passageways in which the only sound is the dripping of water on the walls. If you don't have a good light with you, you may bump into a few boulders or tree roots, or get lost momentarily. But no worries—small painted arrows on the cave walls keep you going in the right direction. Every moment of this spelunking expedition feels like a great adventure, even though it's easy enough for a six-year-old to accomplish. Adults love it just as much as kids do. You'll probably find yourself giggling a few times, even if you're the type who is prone to claustrophobia. These caves are just plain fun.

In case you're wondering what made these intriguing caves and the surrounding rocky spires and crags of Pinnacles National Monument, they are the result of an ancient volcano which erupted some 200 miles to the southeast, in the general area of the northern San Fernando Valley. Movement along the San Andreas Fault carried these rock formations many miles from the rest of the volcano's remains, and deposited them in the smooth, grassy hills of this inland valley. This is part of what makes a visit to the Pinnacles seem so enchanting—the park's formations look strikingly unlike the land that surrounds them.

Water erosion over many thousands of years did a final job on the Pinnacles' mighty rock formations, creating deep, tunnel-like canyons covered by and partially filled with huge boulders. These tunnels form the Bear Gulch Caves, and the Balconies Caves on the park's west side.

The darkest stretch of Bear Gulch Caves ends abruptly when you step out into broad daylight. Then you head back into a tunnel-like area of filtered light, and finally exit the caves altogether. If you care to hike a little farther, continue beyond the caves, taking the stairs uphill to Bear Gulch Reservoir. Sorry, no swimming is allowed, but it's fun to watch the rock climbers along the reservoir's shores.

4. NORTH CHALONE PEAK

Bear Gulch (east) side, Pinnacles National Monument
A fire lookout tower with a view

DISTANCE: 8.4 miles round-trip; 4 hours   **LEVEL:** Strenuous
ELEVATION: Start at 1,300 feet; total change 2,000 feet   **CROWDS:** Minimal
BEST SEASON: October to May   **RATING:** ★ ★ ★ ★

DIRECTIONS: From the south: From King City on U.S. 101, take the First Street exit and head east. First Street turns into Highway G13/Bitterwater Road. Follow it for 15 miles to Highway 25, where you turn left (north). Follow Highway 25 for 14 miles to Highway 146. Go left on Highway 146 and drive 4.8 miles to the park visitor center, then continue beyond it to the parking lot at the end of the road. If this lot is full, park by the visitor center and walk down the road to the trailhead.

From the north: From Gilroy, drive south on U.S. 101 for two miles and take the Highway 25 exit. Drive south on Highway 25 for 43 miles to Highway 146. Continue south on Highway 146 for 4.8 miles to the park.

Sure, the High Peaks at Pinnacles National Monument are high—about 2,700 feet. But if you want to get up a little higher and get a better look around, take this hike to North Chalone Peak. The peak is located far down in the southern area of the park at 3,304 feet in elevation, right next door to South Chalone Peak. North Chalone Peak has a closed fire lookout tower on its summit, and it's a great place to take in the view and listen to the quiet.

The trail begins at the busy parking lot by Bear Gulch Visitor Center. You'll have to make your way past rock climbers heading to their climbing sites and hikers setting out on the park's more popular trails, but soon you will leave everyone behind. The North Chalone Peak route follows the Moses Spring Trail from the parking lot and connects to the Bear Gulch Caves Trail. If you haven't visited the caves, do so while you're here (see the previous story). If the caves are closed for any reason, take the bypass trail around them. Either way, you'll soon be climbing the rocky stairsteps up to Bear Gulch Reservoir, then skirting around its east side. (Turn left on the signed trail for North Chalone Peak.) Rock climbers are often seen plying their trade along the small reservoir's shores.

Once you pass the reservoir, you're only one mile from the trail-head but you've just left 99 percent of the people behind. You have slightly more than three miles of trail ahead of you, and you'll spend it wandering in sunny grasslands among fascinating volcanic rock formations. The next stretch is pleasant hiking with very mild elevation gain, and plenty of opportunities to admire the spring wildflowers blooming in the grasses. Besides the flowers, trailside foliage includes live oaks, holly-leaf cherry, buckbrush, chamise, and manzanita. Views of the park's many pinnacles, peaks, and boulder formations are excellent.

North Chalone Peak's fire lookout tower

At 2.6 miles out, you'll reach a ridge crest from which you can see blue Bear Gulch Reservoir far below. In spring, the trail from this point on is bordered by masses of purple Parry's delphinium. When you reach

a gate at 3.5 miles, go through it, follow the single-track trail uphill, then pass through a second gate and join the fire road to the summit.

The next three quarters of a mile on the fire road are the steepest stretch of the whole trip, but you're rewarded with views of the Salinas Valley to the west. When you reach the fire lookout tower on top, your views expand to 360 degrees. The tower is boarded up, but you can walk around its base and check out the scenery. An interpretive sign next to the hiker's rest room states that visibility from this peak on a poor day is 40 miles, but on an excellent day is 218 miles. So what can you see? The Salinas River curving through its valley, the mountains of the Santa Lucia Range, all of Pinnacles National Monument, and sometimes (only very rarely) the Pacific Ocean.

5. CONDOR GULCH & HIGH PEAKS LOOP

Bear Gulch (east) side, Pinnacles National Monument
An adventure-filled loop around the High Peaks

DISTANCE: 5.0 miles round-trip; 2.5 hours   **LEVEL:** Moderate
ELEVATION: Start at 1,260 feet; total change 1,350 feet   **CROWDS:** Heavy
BEST SEASON: October to May   **RATING:** ★ ★ ★ ★

DIRECTIONS: From the south: From King City on U.S. 101, take the First Street exit and head east. First Street turns into Highway G13/Bitterwater Road. Follow it for 15 miles to Highway 25, where you turn left (north). Follow Highway 25 for 14 miles to Highway 146. Turn left on Highway 146 and drive 4.8 miles to the park visitor center. The trailhead for the Condor Gulch Trail is across the road from the visitor center.

From the north: From Gilroy, drive south on U.S. 101 for two miles and take the Highway 25 exit. Drive south on Highway 25 for 43 miles to Highway 146. Continue south on Highway 146 for 4.8 miles to the park visitor center. The trailhead for the Condor Gulch Trail is across the road from the visitor center.

The Condor Gulch and High Peaks Loop is the most popular hike in Pinnacles National Monument, after the short walk to Bear Gulch Caves. The five-mile loop distance is just right for most people, and the route through the High Peaks' cliffs, pinnacles, and spires is famous for providing more adventure than your average day-hiking trail.

The Condor Gulch Trail begins across the road from the Bear Gulch Visitor Center. It starts with a solid 30-minute climb on a smooth, switchbacked trail to an overlook of the High Peaks. In spring, look for an abundance of white mariposa lilies along the trail, with their delicate brown and red markings on white, tulip-shaped flowers. The scent of wild sage and rosemary is enticingly aromatic along the route. Your eyes will be continually drawn to the colorful lichen growing on equally colorful rocks. The High Peaks overlook is just a piped railing on a ledge above a huge boulder, but it's a good spot to get your bearings and look out over the trail you just climbed.

This is just the start of the fun. Continue uphill for less than a half-mile to a junction with the High Peaks Trail at 1.7 miles. Turn left. (An alternate trail to the High Peaks comes in from Chalone Creek Picnic Area on your right.) In just over a half mile, you'll reach a junction with the Tunnel Trail. Anyone who is seriously afraid of heights should consider taking the Tunnel Trail downhill. They can then turn left on the Juniper Canyon Trail to meet up with their fellow hikers at the junction of Juniper Canyon Trail and High Peaks Trail, where there is a high overlook with a bench and a rest room. Those desiring some adventure should continue on the High Peaks Trail through a maze-like series of narrow passageways, climbing over, under, and in between huge rock formations. In many places the trail has been blasted into the rock, and the steep dropoffs can be dizzying for some people. Make sure you use the hand-holds and guard rails. (For more information on the High Peaks Trail, read the story on page 182).

The High Peaks frolicking continues for seven-tenths of a mile

Rock staircase on the High Peaks Trail

until you reach an intersection with the Juniper Canyon Trail at a saddle and overlook area. Here is where you can reunite with anyone in your group who opted for the Tunnel Trail instead of High Peaks Trail. Enjoy the view west of the Salinas Valley and Santa Lucia Mountains, then turn left to stay on the High Peaks Trail and head back to Bear Gulch. You'll have to walk up the Moses Spring Trail or the park road a short distance to get back to your car.

6. OLD PINNACLES TRAIL & BALCONIES CAVES

Bear Gulch (east) side, Pinnacles National Monument
Spring wildflowers along a stream and a visit to Balconies Caves

DISTANCE: 5.6 miles round-trip; 2.5 hours   **LEVEL:** Easy
ELEVATION: Start at 1,000 feet; total change 400 feet   **CROWDS:** Minimal
BEST SEASON: February to May   **RATING:** ★ ★ ★

DIRECTIONS: From the south: From King City on U.S. 101, take the First Street exit and head east. First Street turns into Highway G13/Bitterwater Road. Follow it for 15 miles to Highway 25, where you turn left (north). Follow Highway 25 for 14 miles to Highway 146. Go left on Highway 146 and drive four miles to the Chalone Creek Picnic Area (stay straight where the road to Bear Gulch Visitor Center turns left).

From the north: From Gilroy, drive south on U.S. 101 for two miles and take the Highway 25 exit. Drive south on Highway 25 for 43 miles to Highway 146. Continue south on Highway 146 for four miles to the Chalone Creek Picnic Area.

Check your calendar. If it's springtime, and you feel like stopping to smell the flowers, it's a good time to hike the Old Pinnacles Trail. Unlike most of the trails at Pinnacles, the Old Pinnacles Trail is mostly level and doesn't ascend the heights of massive volcanic outcrops. Instead, it closely follows the West Fork of Chalone Creek and makes a wide curve from the east to the west side of the park. Due to the proximity of the creek, the trail is rife with wildflowers, and it's partially shaded by willows, live oaks, buckeyes, and gray pines. It's a perfect path for a warm spring day.

Check with the park before you go, however. You need to make sure the creek is low enough to make the necessary crossings to complete the trail. No matter how dry and hot Pinnacles National Monument gets in summer, it can rain like the dickens in winter, turning the park's creeks into roaring torrents. The Old Pinnacles Trail requires multiple crossings of Chalone Creek, and only two of these are bridged.

Mariposa lilies on the Old Pinnacles Trail

The trail begins at Chalone Creek Picnic Area on the east side of the park. Start by crossing the footbridge to the west side of Chalone Creek, then turn right and hike alongside the stream. The trail is nearly level, with a very slight uphill grade, although its surface can become badly eroded from winter rains. Just wander along the edge of the creekbed, pausing when you wish to examine the many flowers. We noted a profusion of California poppies and mariposa lilies, plus elegant clarkia, owl's clover, yellow sticky monkeyflower, morning glories, woolly blue curls, and purple Chinese houses.

You may see bunnies hopping about, and quail scurrying through the brush. You will most likely see at least one of the seven kinds of lizards that live at Pinnacles: alligator lizard, desert night lizard, coast horned lizard, western fence lizard, Gilbert's skink, and western whip-tail lizard. We were lucky enough to catch sight of a gopher snake who was hunting a Gilbert's skink. Just in the nick of time, the skink got away.

At 2.3 miles from the trailhead, the Old Pinnacles Trail ends and meets up with the Balconies Trail coming in from the west side of the park. You're right at the entrance to Balconies Caves, and at a trail junction, you have a choice of going into them (left) or up and over them (right). (Read the story on pages 184 to 186 for information on

Balconies Caves.) If you choose to enter them, make sure you're carrying a flashlight, or you'll have a hard time getting back out without a headache or twisted ankle.

Most people explore inside the caves (or hike up and over the caves, staying in the light), then turn around and retrace their steps on the Old Pinnacles Trail. This makes a fine 5.6-mile round-trip. Hikers who are prepared for a more strenuous day can continue another half-mile west to the Chaparral parking lot, then pick up the Juniper Canyon Trail and hike 1.8 miles up to the High Peaks Trail. The High Peaks Trail leads 3.3 miles back to your starting point at Chalone Creek Picnic Area. Total mileage for this loop is 8.4 miles, and it involves a 1,300-foot elevation gain to the top of the High Peaks. For more information on the Juniper Canyon and High Peaks trails, see the story on page 182.

YOSEMITE NATIONAL PARK

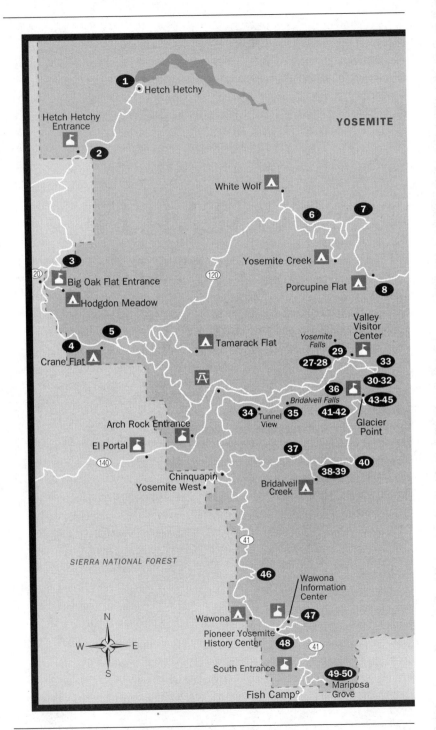

YOSEMITE

Hetch Hetchy

Hetch Hetchy Entrance

White Wolf

Yosemite Creek

Porcupine Flat

Big Oak Flat Entrance

Hodgdon Meadow

Valley Visitor Center

Tamarack Flat

Yosemite Falls

Crane Flat

Arch Rock Entrance

El Portal

Bridalveil Falls

Tunnel View

Glacier Point

Chinquapin
Yosemite West

Bridalveil Creek

SIERRA NATIONAL FOREST

Wawona Information Center

Wawona

Pioneer Yosemite History Center

South Entrance

Mariposa Grove

Fish Camp

N
W E
S

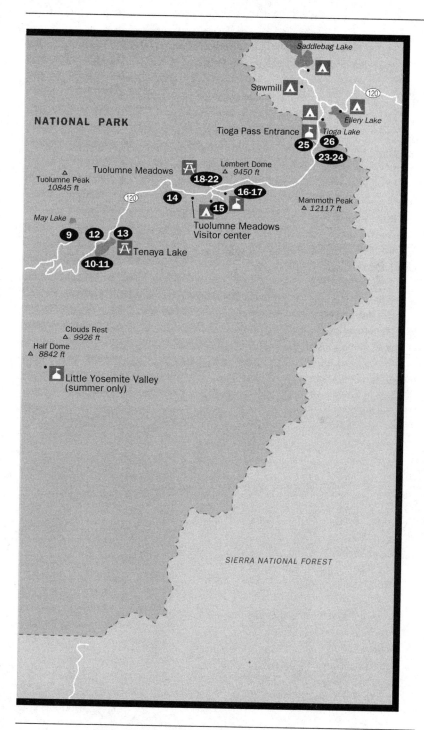

Saddlebag Lake

Sawmill

NATIONAL PARK

(120)

Ellery Lake

Tioga Pass Entrance

Tioga Lake

25 **26**

23-24

Tuolumne Meadows

Lembert Dome
△ 9450 ft

△
Tuolumne Peak
10845 ft

18-22

16-17

Mammoth Peak
△ 12117 ft

(120)

14

15

Tuolumne Meadows
Visitor center

May Lake

9 **12** **13**

10-11

Tenaya Lake

Clouds Rest
△ 9926 ft

Half Dome
△ 8842 ft

Little Yosemite Valley
(summer only)

SIERRA NATIONAL FOREST

YOSEMITE NATIONAL PARK
TRAILS AT A GLANCE

Map Number/Trail Name	Page	Mileage	Difficulty
1. Hetch Hetchy Reservoir	203	13.0	Moderate
2. Lookout Point	206	2.6	Easy
3. Carlon Falls	207	4.5	Easy
4. Merced Grove	209	3.0	Easy
5. Tuolumne Grove	211	2.5	Easy
6. Lukens Lake	213	1.8	Easy
7. Ten Lakes & Grant Lakes	214	12.8	Strenuous
8. North Dome	216	9.0	Moderate
9. May Lake	218	2.4	Easy
10. Clouds Rest	219	14.0	Strenuous
11. Sunrise Lakes	222	7.0	Moderate
12. Polly Dome Lakes	223	6.0	Easy/moderate
13. Tenaya Lake	225	2.0	Easy
14. Cathedral Lakes	226	7.4	Moderate
15. Elizabeth Lake	228	4.6	Easy/moderate
16. Lower Gaylor Lake	229	8.4	Moderate
17. Lyell Canyon	231	5.0	Easy
18. Young Lakes Loop	232	13.8	Strenuous
19. Glen Aulin & Tuolumne Falls	235	9.4	Moderate
20. Waterwheel Falls	237	16.0	Very strenuous
21. Lembert Dome	239	2.6	Easy/moderate
22. Dog Lake	241	2.8	Easy/moderate
23. Mono Pass	243	8.4	Easy/moderate
24. Spillway Lake	244	7.2	Easy/moderate
25. Middle & Upper Gaylor Lakes	246	4.0	Moderate
26. Mount Dana	248	5.8	Very strenuous
27. Upper Yosemite Fall & Yosemite Point	249	7.2	Strenuous
28. Eagle Peak	252	13.4	Very strenuous
29. Lower Yosemite Fall	253	0.5	Easy
30. Mist Trail to Vernal Fall	255	2.8	Easy/moderate
31. Mist & John Muir Loop to Nevada Fall	257	6.8	Moderate
32. Half Dome	259	16.8	Very strenuous
33. Mirror Lake & Tenaya Canyon Loop	261	4.6	Easy
34. Inspiration & Stanford Points	262	7.6	Strenuous
35. Bridalveil Fall	264	0.5	Easy
36. Four-Mile Trail	266	9.6	Strenuous
37. McGurk Meadow	268	2.0	Easy
38. Bridalveil Creek	269	3.0	Easy
39. Ostrander Lake	271	12.6	Moderate

THE TOP 15, DON'T-MISS DAY HIKES:

TRAIL SUGGESTIONS FOR IF YOU ONLY HAVE ONE DAY:

YOSEMITE NATIONAL PARK

ABOUT THE PARK

Yosemite National Park is undoubtedly California's most famous national park. It is one of the most heavily visited parks in the United States, due to its unique Sierra Nevada beauty—towering granite walls and domes, sparkling lakes, pristine meadows and rivers, and spectacular waterfalls.

ADDRESS, PHONE, & WEBSITE

Yosemite National Park Public Information Office, P.O. Box 577, Yosemite National Park, CA 95389; (209) 372-0200.
Website: www.nps.gov/yose

VISITOR CENTERS

Yosemite's main visitor center is in Yosemite Valley. Tuolumne Meadows has a smaller visitor center. Big Oak Flat and Wawona have small information stations.

HOW TO GET THERE

• By air: The closest major airport is in Fresno, California.

• By car: There are four different entrances to the park:

Big Oak Flat Entrance near Groveland—From Manteca, take Highway 120 east for 90 miles.

Arch Rock Entrance near Mariposa—From Merced, take Highway 140 east for 75 miles.

Tioga Pass Entrance in the eastern Sierra—From U.S. 395 at Lee Vining, take Highway 120 west for 13 miles.

South Entrance near Wawona—From Fresno, take Highway 41 north for 65 miles.

DRIVE TIME

• Drive time from Los Angeles: approximately 6 hours.

• Drive time from San Francisco: approximately 4 hours.

ENTRANCE FEES

There is a $20 entrance fee per vehicle at Yosemite National Park, good for seven days. A Yosemite annual pass is available for $40. A Golden Eagle Passport, an annual pass for all 375 national park units, is available for $50. A Golden Age Passport, a lifetime pass for all 375 national park units, is available to U.S. citizens and residents aged 62 and over for a one-time $10 fee. You can purchase these passes at the park entrance stations.

WHEN TO GO

Glacier Point Road and Tioga Road (Highway 120) are closed by snow each winter, usually by late October. Both roads usually re-open in June. The Hetch Hetchy Road, Big Oak Flat Road, and Mariposa Grove Road are also occasionally closed for snow. Chains may be required on park roads at any time.

A few areas of Yosemite are open year-round for hiking and/or cross-country skiing, specifically Yosemite Valley, the park's three Sequoia groves, and the Wawona region. Day-hikers should plan on most trails being clear on Glacier Point Road and Tioga Road (Highway 120) from July to October. As the timing of snowfall and snowmelt vary greatly from year to year, always phone the park for a road and trail update before planning your trip.

WEATHER CONDITIONS

The majority of Yosemite National Park is blessed with typical Sierra summer weather: warm, clear days with temperatures in the 70s and low 80s, and cool nights with temperatures in the 40s and 50s. However, portions of Yosemite are at lower elevations and are substantially hotter in the summer; these include Yosemite Valley (4,000 feet in elevation) and the Hetch Hetchy region (3,800 feet in elevation).

The general rule for summer in the park: Bring warm clothes for evenings (especially if you're camping) and a variety of layers for daytime hiking. Beware of afternoon thunderstorms in late summer; carry rain gear and stay off mountain peaks if a storm is threatening.

WHERE TO STAY

Yosemite has six campgrounds that are available on a first-come, first-served basis: Sunnyside Walk-In, Bridalveil Creek, Tamarack Flat, White Wolf, Yosemite Creek, and Porcupine Flat. Seven more campgrounds are available by advance reservation: North Pines, Upper Pines, Lower Pines, Wawona, Hodgdon Meadow, Crane Flat, and Tuolumne Meadows. Phone (800) 436-7275 to reserve. The following camps are open year-round: Upper Pines, Sunnyside Walk-In, Wawona, and Hodgdon Meadow. Only Upper Pines Campground can be reserved in advance in the off-season; the other year-round camps are first-come, first-served from October to April.

Neighboring national forests also have campgrounds available. For more information, contact Stanislaus National Forest at (209) 962-7825, Sierra National Forest at (209) 683-4665, or Inyo National Forest at (760) 647-3044.

Several types of lodging exist within the park and are available by reservation; phone Yosemite Concession Services at (209) 252-4848. Lodging choices inside Yosemite Valley include Yosemite Lodge, The Ahwahnee, Curry Village, and Housekeeping Camp. Lodging choices outside of the Valley include Wawona Hotel, White Wolf Lodge, and Tuolumne Meadows Lodge.

Just outside the park borders are lodgings of varying styles and prices:

On Highway 120 near the Big Oak Flat Entrance:
> Evergreen Lodge, (209) 379-2606
> Yosemite Riverside Inn, (800) 626-7408
> Yosemite Westgate Motel, (800) 253-9673
> Groveland Hotel, (800) 273-3314

On Highway 140 near the Arch Rock Entrance:
> Cedar Lodge, (209) 379-2612 or (800) 321-5261
> Yosemite View Lodge, (209) 379-2681 or (800) 321-5261

On Highway 41 near the Wawona/South Entrance:
> Yosemite West, (209) 642-2211
> Narrow Gauge Inn, (209) 683-7720
> Tenaya Lodge, (800) 635-5807
> Apple Tree Inn, (209) 683-5111

On Highway 120 near the Tioga Pass Entrance:
> Tioga Pass Resort, (209) 372-4471
> Best Western Lakeview Lodge, (760) 647-6543

FOOD & SUPPLIES

Yosemite Valley has several restaurants and snack shops, plus a large market. Food service is also available at Tuolumne Meadows, White Wolf, and Wawona. Limited supplies are available at Crane Flat, Tuolumne Meadows, and Wawona. Food and supplies can be found outside the park at El Portal, Groveland, Fish Camp, and Lee Vining.

SUGGESTED MAPS

Park maps are available at park entrance stations or by contacting Yosemite National Park at the address on page 200. A detailed map is available for a fee from Tom Harrison Cartography at (415) 456-7940.

1. HETCH HETCHY RESERVOIR

Hetch Hetchy area, Yosemite National Park
Waterfalls, granite, and a deep blue reservoir

DISTANCE: 13.0 miles round-trip; 7 hours   **LEVEL:** Moderate
ELEVATION: Start at 3,800 feet; total change 1,400 feet   **CROWDS:** Minimal
BEST SEASON: March to June   **RATING:** ★ ★ ★ ★

DIRECTIONS: From Groveland, drive east on Highway 120 for 22.5 miles to the Evergreen Road turnoff on the left, signed for Hetch Hetchy Reservoir (it's one mile west of the Big Oak Flat entrance to Yosemite). Drive north on Evergreen Road for 7.4 miles, then turn right on Hetch Hetchy Road. Drive 16 miles to the dam and trailhead.

When people see pictures of what Hetch Hetchy valley looked like before it was dammed and flooded in 1914 to provide water for San Francisco, they're always struck by how much it resembles today's Yosemite Valley (minus the parking lots and pavement, of course). Photos show the stark, pristine granite of Kolana Rock and Hetch Hetchy Dome jutting upward from the Hetch Hetchy valley floor, waterfalls dropping thousands of feet from hanging valleys like rivers falling from the sky, and lush, flower-filled meadows lining the edge of the meandering Tuolumne River.

You gotta wonder, what in the hell were those politicians thinking?

But here's the redemption: Despite man's best efforts to destroy it, Hetch Hetchy remains beautiful. Of course, the reservoir is not as spectacular as the river valley would have been, had it been left undammed, but when you hike along the shoreline of Hetch Hetchy Reservoir, observing the higher sections of granite and waterfalls that are visible above the water line, you get the sense that Mother Nature has ceased crying over Hetch Hetchy. Instead, she has done what she does best—heal, beautify, and make the most of what exists.

Certainly wildflower lovers and waterfall lovers still find plenty to treasure at Hetch Hetchy. For the best display of both, the key is to visit early in the year, no later than June. By mid-July, the summer heat and low elevation at Hetch Hetchy—3,800 feet—has taken its toll. It can also take a toll on hikers. The valley is notoriously hot in the summer months—as much as 15 degrees hotter than Yosemite Valley.

Your trip to Hetch Hetchy can be customized according to your hiking abilities and desires. Those looking for an easy, nearly level walk can hike to Wapama Falls for a 4.8-mile round trip. Those looking for a more strenuous, full-day hike can hike the entire length of the reservoir, a 13-mile round-trip. If you plan to hike the whole trail, get an early start and carry plenty of water, or carry a purification system.

From the parking lot by O'Shaughnessy Dam, begin by crossing over the dam, then enter the long tunnel on the dam's far side and walk through. You exit into a leafy oak and bay forest and hear the pleasant sound of water lapping along the reservoir's shore. After the first mile of trail, you reach a junction and bear right, continuing along the reservoir's edge for the entire length of your trip.

Hetch Hetchy supports a surprising amount and variety of foliage. Springtime gives rise to plentiful wildflowers, including Indian paintbrush, mariposa lilies, purple brodiaea, yampah, and blue penstemon, in addition to the omnipresent bear clover and plenty of poison oak. Shade-giving trees include oaks, bays, ponderosa pines, and incense cedars.

Tueeulala is the first waterfall you reach at 1.5 miles out. It's tall and wispy, and it becomes increasingly frail as the season wears on. If you arrive in July, it may have already disappeared, and you may wonder why the trail-makers built all those bridges over a pile of dry rocks. Tueeulala Falls drops about 1,000 feet before it hits the lake's edge, so it must have been about 1,400 feet tall before the great flood.

The star waterfall of the trip is Wapama, which you reach at 2.4 miles out. Wapama Falls on Falls Creek has such a wide, forceful flow that you can see it quite easily from O'Shaughnessy Dam and Hetch

On the shoreline of Hetch Hetchy Reservoir

Hetchy Road, even in mid- to late summer. Like at Tueeulala, you cross over Wapama's flow on a series of sturdy wood and steel bridges. In spring, you can get soaked standing on these bridges from the tremendous amount of spray and mist. Bring your raingear if it's a cool day.

Those looking for a short, easy day hike should turn around here, for a round-trip that's just shy of five miles long. For those who continue along the trail, the bad news is that it now starts to climb, and it's less shaded than before. The good news is that the trail is well-graded, with lots of gentle switchbacks.

You'll hike on granite and cast admiring glances at fine scenery. Kolana Rock rises grandly from Hetch Hetchy's southern shore. Because the trail ascends, your wide-angle views of the reservoir improve. The water is so deep—400 feet—and so dramatically edged by granite, sand, and pines, that sections of it are reminiscent of Lake Tahoe. Its depth causes the water to be a similar rich sapphire color. In the afternoon the sunlight creates a twinkling show on the reservoir's surface.

If you decide to stop for a rest or a picnic anywhere along the trail, keep in mind that the rules are strict at Hetch Hetchy: No swimming, no boating, and no water contact, although fishing is permitted. A park ranger told us it's OK to wade into the creeks to cool off, and we saw several hikers do this. Still, because the creeks empty into the reservoir, the logic of the regulations seems strange.

You reach Rancheria Creek at 5.7 miles out. Look for an unsigned fork a quarter-mile beyond where you first spot the creek, at a noticeable clearing along the right side of the trail. This spur trail passes a backpackers' camp that is currently being restored, then it leads to a section of stream 100 yards below 30-foot Rancheria Falls. This is the best viewing spot.

Here at creekside, under the shade of Jeffrey pines and black oaks, is a choice site for a picnic and a rest. Watch out for bears—a small one tried to steal our lunch when we turned our backs for 20 seconds to look at the falls. This was accompanied by a lot of yelling and general commotion as we realized the full catastrophic potential of losing our tuna sandwiches. Luckily, our bellowing was an effective ruse, and our lunch was saved. But be forewarned: The bears at Hetch Hetchy are known to be some of the biggest thieves in Yosemite.

For another look at Rancheria Falls, continue on the main trail for a half-mile beyond the spur trail. At a trail junction, head straight for Pleasant Valley. One-tenth mile farther is a bridge above Rancheria Creek, where in high water you can glimpse the downstream falls. It's a scenic spot to end your explorations, before you turn around and hike back down along the reservoir.

One final caveat: Occasionally the Hetch Hetchy trail is closed in spring when Wapama Falls becomes too effusive and its high water and heavy spray completely cover the trail. Call the park to check on conditions before you make the trip.

2. LOOKOUT POINT

Hetch Hetchy area, Yosemite National Park
An overlook of Hetch Hetchy Reservoir

DISTANCE: 2.6 miles round-trip; 1.5 hours   **LEVEL:** Easy
ELEVATION: Start at 4,700 feet; total change 600 feet   **CROWDS:** Minimal
BEST SEASON: March to June   **RATING:** ★ ★

DIRECTIONS: From Groveland, drive east on Highway 120 for 22.5 miles to the Evergreen Road turnoff on the left, signed for Hetch Hetchy Reservoir (it's one mile west of the Big Oak Flat entrance to Yosemite). Drive north on Evergreen Road for 7.4 miles, then turn right on Hetch Hetchy Road. Drive 1.7 miles to the entrance kiosk by the Mather ranger station; the trail begins 100 yards past the entrance kiosk, just beyond the ranger station on the right.

Check your calendar. Is it springtime? Are most of the trails in Yosemite National Park still snowed in? Then it's time to take the easy jaunt to Lookout Point, where you can admire Hetch Hetchy Reservoir and its waterfalls from an unusual perspective, and count the plentiful wildflowers along the trail as you walk.

The Lookout Point Trail begins by the Mather Ranger Station on Hetch Hetchy Road. Begin to hike at the trail sign for Cottonwood and Smith meadows and Hetch Hetchy (it's not signed for Lookout Point). Turn left at the first junction, then follow the trail as it roughly parallels Hetch Hetchy Road for a half-mile. You'll be walking in a grassy oak and pine woodland on an undulating, curving path.

The trail turns away from the road with a brief climb up a gully, then enters a level, forested area that was severely burned in the 1996 Hetch Hetchy wildfire. The standing trees are blackened, but at their bases, wildflowers bloom in profusion in springtime. Among the grasses at your feet, you'll find mariposa lilies and lupine.

Look for a trail junction at one mile out, then bear left for Lookout Point, three-tenths of a mile away. Walk past a tiny seasonal pond, and in short order you'll leave the ponderosa pines and incense cedars behind and start to hike on granite. The path gets rather faint in places,

View from Lookout Point

but trail cairns mark the way. Head for the highest point around, a granite knoll dotted with a few Jeffrey pines. When you're on top of Lookout Point, you'll know it, because you can see the west end of Hetch Hetchy Reservoir, including its immense dam, and two of Hetch Hetchy's beautiful waterfalls: Wapama and Tueeulala. (If you hike to Inspiration Point much later than May or June, you may see only Wapama Falls, which is the most robust of Hetch Hetchy's waterfalls. Tueeulala dries up early in the year.)

Although the vista is not perfect from Lookout Point—it would be better if the rocky point was a few hundred feet higher, or perhaps farther away from fast-growing ponderosa pines—this is still a fine spot to spread out a picnic.

3. CARLON FALLS

Big Oak Flat area, Yosemite National Park
Year-round waterfall on the South Fork Tuolumne River

DISTANCE: 4.5 miles round-trip; 2 hours   **LEVEL:** Easy
ELEVATION: Start at 4,500 feet; total change 150 feet   **CROWDS:** Minimal
BEST SEASON: March to October   **RATING:** ★ ★ ★

DIRECTIONS: From Groveland, drive east on Highway 120 for 22.5 miles to the Evergreen Road turnoff signed for Hetch Hetchy Reservoir (one mile west of the Big Oak Flat entrance to Yosemite). Follow Evergreen Road north for one mile to the far side of the bridge, just past Carlon Day-Use Area. Park on the right at the closed-off road on the north side of the bridge. (There is room for about five cars.) Begin hiking on the closed road, heading upstream. The road turns to single-track after about 100 yards.

In the minds of most park visitors, the words "Yosemite" and "waterfalls" go together like peanut butter and jelly. Except in autumn. That's when people show up in Yosemite Valley, look at all the dark, dried-up water stains on the granite walls, and have to squint real hard and visualize.

If you prefer your October waterfalls to be real and not imagined, autumn is a perfect time to make the trip to Carlon Falls, on the South Fork Tuolumne River in the northwest section of Yosemite. Spring and summer are also good seasons for lovers of wildflowers and swimming holes. The trip begins on Stanislaus National Forest land, then enters the Yosemite Wilderness, so a bonus is that you can visit Carlon Falls any time you want, without having to deal with the crowds and the day-use fees in Yosemite.

It's an easy hike, suitable for everyone. The key is to make sure you walk on the north side of the river and not on the south side, where the picnic area is located. The north side has an excellent trail with an easy grade; the south side has an unmaintained fisherman's route.

Carlon Falls

Head upstream and pass a Yosemite Wilderness sign a few hundred yards in, then walk by the foundation of an old house. The trail stays close to the creek for the first mile, then moves away from it as it climbs gently in its second mile. You're in a lovely mixed forest during the entire walk, with plentiful wildflowers in spring and autumn leaf color in the fall. An incredible amount of plant speciation surrounds the river, a result of the low elevation. In addition to a variety of oaks, there are incense cedars and pines, many of them covered with thick moss. Tons of ferns and reeds grow near the water. The Indian rhubarb clumped around the falls has some of the largest foliage I've seen anywhere. Together with the ferns, it turns a dazzling yellow color in fall.

It's just over two miles to Carlon Falls, which means you'll be there in about an hour. The 35-foot fall drops over a granite ledge in a wide stream, with more flow than you might expect from the size of the river. (It's additionally fueled by a feeder creek just upstream of the falls.) About 100 yards downstream of the main fall, there's a long, lacelike cascade, with water streaming over and around potholes in the granite.

This area is open for hiking almost year-round, because it receives little snow. In spring, the river and the falls run with incredible velocity and power, and the wildflowers put on a show. In summer, the air temperature is warm for hiking, but there are plenty of swimming holes for cooling off, including a wide one at the waterfall's base. In autumn—my favorite season here—the dogwoods and black oaks turn gold and red, the bear clover is aromatic in the crisp air, and miraculously, the waterfall still flows.

4. MERCED GROVE

Big Oak Flat area, Yosemite National Park
A secluded Sequoia grove

DISTANCE: 3.0 miles round-trip; 1.5 hours   **LEVEL:** Easy
ELEVATION: Start at 5,900 feet; total change 350 feet   **CROWDS:** Minimal
BEST SEASON: Year-round   **RATING:** ★ ★ ★

DIRECTIONS: From the Arch Rock entrance station at Yosemite National Park, drive east into the park for 4.5 miles to the turnoff for Tioga Road/Highway 120, which is Big Oak Flat Road. Turn left and drive 13.5 miles (past the Tioga Road/Highway 120 turnoff) to the Merced Grove parking area on the left.

Alternatively, from the Big Oak Flat entrance station on Highway 120, drive south into the park on Big Oak Flat Road for 4.3 miles to reach the Merced Grove on your right.

There are three giant Sequoia groves in Yosemite National Park— Merced, Tuolumne, and Mariposa. Because the Merced Grove is tucked into a western corner of the park and is the smallest of the groves, it is the least visited. Generally the Merced Grove only gets traffic from people who enter Yosemite at the Big Oak Flat entrance station, then drive by it on their way to Yosemite Valley. It's a fine place to go for some solitude and a walk through a lovely mixed forest, and of course, to be awed by the big Sequoias. Think of this as a simple, beautiful nature walk, perfect on any day, in any season.

The hiking trail is a closed-off dirt road that was Yosemite's first carriage road. It makes for good cross-country skiing in winter. The trail is level for the first half-mile until it reaches a junction. Take the left fork and head downhill through a lovely mixed forest of white firs, incense cedars, ponderosa pines, and sugar pines. Azaleas bloom in early summer beneath their branches.

You reach the small Sequoia grove at 1.5 miles. First you see a group of six, right along the trail to your right. They're not mammoth trees, but they're certainly large. Walk a few more feet down the trail and you spot two more big trees on the left and one on the right—they're getting bigger as you go. A total of only 20 trees are found in this grove, but because they grow extremely close together, they make a stately impression.

The Sequoias in this grove were "discovered" in 1833 by the Walker party, a group of explorers headed by Joseph Walker, who were looking for the best route through the Sierra Nevada. Most likely, local Indian tribes had long known about the location of the big trees.

Log cabin in the Merced Grove

The largest, granddaddy Sequoias of the grove are found directly across the road from a handsome old cabin. The cabin was originally built as a retreat for the park superintendent, but it is no longer in use. Beyond the cabin, the trail continues but becomes more overgrown and obstacle-ridden with fallen trees. Retrace your steps from the cabin, hiking uphill for your return.

5. TUOLUMNE GROVE

Big Oak Flat area, Yosemite National Park
Popular Sequoia grove featuring the Dead Giant

DISTANCE: 2.5 miles round-trip; 1.5 hours   **LEVEL:** Easy
ELEVATION: Start at 6,200 feet; total change 500 feet   **CROWDS:** Heavy
BEST SEASON: Year-round   **RATING:** ★ ★ ★

DIRECTIONS: From the Arch Rock entrance station at Yosemite National Park, drive east into the park for 4.5 miles to the turnoff for Tioga Road/Highway 120, which is Big Oak Flat Road. Turn left and drive 9.3 miles to Crane Flat, then turn right on Tioga Road/Highway 120 and drive a half-mile to the Tuolumne Grove parking lot on the left.

What's nice about the Tuolumne Grove of Giant Sequoias in Yosemite National Park is that you have to walk a mile to access it, unlike the old days before 1993 when motorists were allowed to drive right in.

What's not so nice is that its trailhead parking lot is always packed with cars, so your only chance at solitude among the big Sequoias is to arrive early in the morning in summer or to save your trip for the off-season. Consider this as an option: The grove is especially beautiful in early spring, when you can take a snowshoe walk or cross-country ski trek through the Sequoias. Of all the sights to be seen in Yosemite, there's nothing quite like the vision of those giant trees crowned with snow. Autumn hikes among the big trees are also lovely.

The large Tuolumne Grove is located on the old Big Oak Flat Road, a paved, six-mile historic road/trail that is open to cyclists and hikers. Leave your car at the parking lot near Crane Flat, then hike downhill for one mile into the big trees. You pass a sign that states "Entering the Tuolumne Grove" about 100 yards before you actually see any Sequoias. The first tree you come to, on your left, is the most impressive of the whole trip. It's worth the hike just to see this one mammoth giant. Across from it, the trail forks; take the right fork to see one of the grove's biggest attractions: the Dead Giant.

The tunneled Dead Giant in the Tuolumne Grove

The Dead Giant is one of the two remaining walk-through trees in Yosemite. It's a huge and wide shell of a tree (not quite a stump, not quite a full tree) that was tunneled in 1878 so wagons, and later automobiles, could drive through. A walk of about 200 feet from the fork leads you right to it. Go ahead, walk through it—everybody does.

Continue downhill from the Dead Giant and in another 100 yards, you'll reach a picnic area, with several tables and benches and a fine view of more large Sequoias. On the right side of the picnic area is a quarter-mile loop trail through the forest. This short loop is your only chance to walk on a "real" dirt trail, not a closed-off road. It's peaceful and pleasant.

Back at the picnic area, an odd-looking trail sign features a human hand, a big red "X," and a strange grouping of dots. At first, the sign puzzled us, until finally we realized that the dots were supposed to be a Sequoia cone, and the sign was expressing that we should not pick them up and carry them off. Too many souvenir-seekers would eventually destroy a Sequoia forest; without their cones, the trees cannot propagate.

The road continues downhill beyond the picnic area; you can hike farther if you like, although most people turn around here. Don't forget about the uphill return trip.

6. LUKENS LAKE

Tioga Road area, Yosemite National Park
Easy trail to a lake and meadow

DISTANCE: 1.8 miles round-trip; 1 hour   **LEVEL:** Easy
ELEVATION: Start at 8,150 feet; total change 300 feet   **CROWDS:** Moderate
BEST SEASON: July to October   **RATING:** ★ ★ ★

DIRECTIONS: From the Arch Rock entrance station at Yosemite National Park, drive east into the park for 4.5 miles to the turnoff for Tioga Road/Highway 120, which is Big Oak Flat Road. Turn left and drive 9.3 miles to Crane Flat, then turn right on Tioga Road/Highway 120 and drive 16.2 miles to the Lukens Lake Trailhead parking area on the south side of the road. The trail begins on the north side of the road.

The Lukens Lake Trail is the perfect introductory lake hike for families in Yosemite National Park. It has all the best features of a long backpacking trip to a remote alpine area, but without the long miles, steep climbs, and heavy weight to carry. A six-year-old could make the trip easily. A bonus is that the trailhead is on the western end of Tioga Road, so it can be quickly reached from points in Yosemite Valley.

After parking at the Lukens Lake Trailhead pullout, cross the road to reach the trailhead. The wide and easy trail climbs gently through a white pine and red fir forest for less than a half-mile until you reach a saddle. The red firs, with their red-brown, deeply ingrained bark look a little like ponderosa pines but are more red in color and have distinctive needles and cones. They grow to be very large (more than 150 feet tall) and cluster in thick stands, forming an impressive and lovely forest.

At the saddle, you've gained 200 feet, and now you descend gently to the lake, only a half-mile away. The trail cuts through a wet, corn lily-filled meadow, which is colorfully peppered with wildflowers. We saw shooting stars and mountain bluebells. If you visit early enough in the summer, the meadow can steal the show from the lake itself.

Lukens Lake is shallow and wide, and it is ringed by trees except for its southeastern meadow. Good picnicking spots are found on its far (north) side. Some optimistic anglers toss a line in the water and catch a rainbow or brook trout, but you shouldn't come with high expectations regarding size or quantity. Most hikers choose to swim. Because the lake is quite shallow, the water is surprisingly warm for this high elevation. Don't expect the smooth granite bottom that you find at many lakes in the high country—Lukens Lake is grassy and muddy underneath its blue waters.

7. TEN LAKES & GRANT LAKES

Tioga Road area, Yosemite National Park
A dozen alpine lakes and a spectacular overlook

DISTANCE: 12.8 miles round-trip; 7 hours   **LEVEL:** Strenuous
ELEVATION: Start at 7,500 feet; total change 2,800 feet   **CROWDS:** Moderate
BEST SEASON: July to October   **RATING:** ★ ★ ★ ★

DIRECTIONS: From the Arch Rock entrance station at Yosemite National Park, drive east into the park for 4.5 miles to the turnoff for Tioga Road/Highway 120, which is Big Oak Flat Road. Turn left and drive 9.3 miles to Crane Flat, then turn right on Tioga Road/Highway 120 and drive 19.4 miles to the Yosemite Creek and Ten Lakes Trailhead parking area on the south side of the road. The trail begins on the north side of the road.

The Ten Lakes and Grant Lakes area is tremendously popular with backpackers, and it's not hard to understand why: The trail into Ten Lakes' and Grant Lakes' basins features a dozen sparkling lakes, spectacular scenery, plentiful camping spots, and only one day of hiking time to reach the destination.

But there's no reason why day-hikers shouldn't get in on the fun. The round-trip mileage to either Grant Lakes or Ten Lakes is less than 13 miles. With an early morning start on the long days of summer, you can take a leisurely hike, visit as many lakes as you please, swim or fish, and still have plenty of daylight left for the walk home.

From the Ten Lakes Trailhead at Tioga Road, the path climbs steadily for the first four miles, mostly through lodgepole pine forest but with one sunny, exposed stretch over granite slabs. Count on two full hours of climbing, but with a moderate grade that is easily manageable. Conserve your energy, because the hard part comes between miles four and five, after a deceptively easy and pretty stroll around Half-Moon Meadow. (Look for the purple pinwheel flowers of penstemon lining its edge.) On the far side of the meadow, a series of tight, rocky switchbacks pull you through an 800-foot elevation gain to the top of a ridge. It's a butt-kicker of a climb, covering just under a mile.

At the top of the ridge, five miles out, you can pat yourself on the back: Your work is basically over. Here is the Ten Lakes/Grant Lakes junction, and you must decide: Grant Lakes or Ten Lakes, or one followed by the other?

The Ten Lakes are the most popular choice, mostly because of the larger number of lakes and because backpackers have a greater choice of campsites. Day hikers will find more solitude at the two Grant Lakes, possibly superior fishing prospects, and an easier climb back out on the way home. All of the lakes are sparkling, rockbound, and surrounded by thick forest cover. No matter which you choose, you can't go wrong.

To reach Grant Lakes, turn right and head gently downhill for a mile. You'll cavort over a beautiful, wildflower-laden hillside and then head into the trees. Deer are plentiful on the slopes, munching on the abundant flowers and grasses. The two Grant Lakes are only 150 yards apart, set at 9,500 feet in elevation, and surrounded by trees and rocks.

Fishing in Upper Grant Lake

To reach Ten Lakes, continue straight, heading slightly uphill for a half-mile and then very steeply downhill for another mile. The first of the Ten Lakes is set at 8,950 feet in elevation. (This is a 750-foot loss from the Ten Lakes/Grant Lakes junction, which you will have to gain back on your way out. Save some energy for it.)

If you choose to visit Grant Lakes instead of Ten Lakes, don't just head there directly. Instead, take a short side trip to the rocky overlook above the Ten Lakes basin. The overlook is only a half-mile from the Ten Lakes/Grant Lakes junction, and it's well worth the effort. Follow the Ten Lakes Trail, heading gently uphill on a lupine-covered ridge. Just before the trail drops steeply down to the Ten Lakes, take the unsigned use trail to the left, and head for the highest promontory. Four of the Ten Lakes are visible from this rocky point, as well as a section of the Grand Canyon of the Tuolumne River. For most day-hikers, this vista is the most spectacular part of the whole day, even better than the lakes themselves. A pair of lucky marmots make this promontory their home; you'll probably see them scampering among the rocks. What a fine back yard they have.

8. NORTH DOME

Tioga Road area, Yosemite National Park
The granite dome with the best view of Half Dome

DISTANCE: 9.0 miles round-trip; 5 hours   **LEVEL:** Moderate
ELEVATION: Start at 8,140 feet; total change 1,500 feet   **CROWDS:** Moderate
BEST SEASON: July to October   **RATING:** ★ ★ ★ ★ ★

DIRECTIONS: From the Arch Rock entrance station at Yosemite National Park, drive east into the park for 4.5 miles to the turnoff for Tioga Road/Highway 120, which is Big Oak Flat Road. Turn left and drive 9.3 miles to Crane Flat, then turn right on Tioga Road/Highway 120 and drive 24.5 miles to the Porcupine Creek Trailhead parking area on the right, a mile past Porcupine Flat Campground.

There are those who say that climbing Half Dome is a bit disappointing, and it's not just because of the crowds. The Half Dome Trail is excellent, and the infamous cable climb to the summit is pure heart-pounding excitement, but when you reach the top and check out the commanding view of Yosemite's granite monoliths, something's lacking. The panorama is not quite what you expected, but you can't quite put your finger on the missing element. Here's the problem: You can't see Half Dome, the quintessential landmark that characterizes the Yosemite landscape. You're standing on it.

If you seek an awe-inspiring view of Half Dome to complete your picture of Yosemite, the bald granite summit of North Dome is the place to get it. For day-hikers, North Dome is one of the must-do hikes in Yosemite, culminating in incredible vistas looking down into Tenaya Canyon and across at Half Dome and Clouds Rest. If you've climbed either Half Dome or Clouds Rest, you'll find that North Dome is easier to attain, and just as spectacular, if not more so.

The route begins at the Porcupine Creek Trailhead near Porcupine Flat Campground on Tioga Road. An old access road leads from the parking lot for a half-mile to a proper trail signed as Porcupine Creek. The trail undulates pleasantly through the forest, with no noticeable change in elevation in the first stretch. At 1.6 miles, you reach a trail junction and bear right, then almost immediately beyond it bear left, following the signs for Half Dome. The next mile brings the first noticeable climb, until at 2.8 miles, you arrive at an obvious saddle at 8,140 feet. This is the high point on the trail to North Dome; from here it's all downhill. Note the unsigned spur trail on the left at this saddle; you can follow it on your return for an interesting side trip.

Half Dome from North Dome

For now, continue onward, heading due south for North Dome. Your views begin to open up, providing good looks at North Dome and Half Dome and increasing your anticipation. At a junction at 4.1 miles, take the left spur for the final tromp to North Dome's summit. Surprise—it's a downhill grade to reach it.

Bring plenty of film with you. The vista from the top of North Dome is sublime. Most compelling is the heart-stopping view of Half Dome; the big hunk of granite appears close enough to touch, just across the canyon. Clouds Rest is an equally dramatic sight to the northeast. Also in view are Glacier Point, Liberty Cap, Sentinel Dome, and Illilouette Fall. To the southwest, you can see cars crawling along the Yosemite Valley floor. Be grateful that you're not in one of them as you pull out your picnic lunch.

On your return trip, take a short side trip to see Indian Rock, the only natural rock arch in Yosemite. It's accessible via the unsigned spur trail you passed at the saddle, 2.8 miles out. The spur leads a steep quarter-mile uphill to Indian Rock, a distinct rock formation with an arch at its crest. Many people just admire the rock from its base, but if you hike around to its back side, you can climb up the rock to the arch itself. At elevation 8,520 feet, Indian Rock is much higher than North Dome, and has its own fine views.

9. MAY LAKE

Tioga Road area, Yosemite National Park
A deep blue lake set below Mount Hoffman

DISTANCE: 2.4 miles round-trip; 1.5 hours
ELEVATION: Start at 8,850 feet; total change 500 feet
BEST SEASON: July to October

LEVEL: Easy
CROWDS: Heavy
RATING: ★ ★ ★ ★

DIRECTIONS: From the Arch Rock entrance station at Yosemite National Park, drive east into the park for 4.5 miles to the turnoff for Tioga Road/Highway 120, which is Big Oak Flat Road. Turn left and drive 9.3 miles to Crane Flat, then turn right on Tioga Road/Highway 120 and drive 26.6 miles to the May Lake Road turnoff on the left (near road marker T-21). Drive two miles to the trailhead parking lot.

Here's a hike that you can take the kids on. It's an easy 1.2 miles to rocky, gem-like May Lake, tucked in below 10,850-foot Mount Hoffman. The trail's total elevation gain is only 500 feet and its destination is top-notch, making it one of the most popular hikes on Tioga Road. If you don't like company, you should probably hike somewhere else, but May Lake is so pretty, go see it at least once.

May Lake and Mount Hoffman

The trail begins at the May Lake parking area two miles off Tioga Road, where the lot is almost always full of cars. Initially, the trail passes through a red fir and lodgepole pine forest, but soon most of the trees are left behind. The path ascends moderately, climbing over granite slabs and past large boulders, with good views to the east of Tenaya Canyon and the high Cathedral Range. In this open, rocky section, it's easy to spot the granite wall of May Lake's basin up ahead. You'll know exactly where you're headed.

The trail tops out in the forest near the lake's southern shore. A trail leads left to a backpackers' camp and the lakeshore and another leads right to the tent cabins of May Lake's High Sierra Camp. Head for the edge of the lake, then circle around it if you like. The only downer on the trip? No swimming is allowed in May Lake.

The High Sierra Camp is bound to have people nearby, sitting in camp chairs by the lake and enjoying the luxury of a backpacking trip without the effort. Each of Yosemite's High Sierra Camps are so popular that they must be reserved a year in advance, and even then, not everybody gets in.

The round, blue lake set at 9,329 feet would be pretty enough by itself, but towering Mount Hoffman behind it is the icing on the cake. Mount Hoffman is considered to be the exact geographical center of Yosemite National Park. Many people make the ascent to its summit, although there is no formal trail for doing so. From the edge of May Lake, it's a strenuous, two-mile climb to reach the top, with a 1,500-foot elevation gain. Mount Hoffman's summit view is considered to be one of the finest in the park, but it takes some serious work to see it.

10. CLOUDS REST

Tioga Road area, Yosemite National Park
A world-class summit view

DISTANCE: 14.0 miles round-trip; 8 hours　　**LEVEL:** Strenuous
ELEVATION: Start at 8,150 feet; total change 2,300 feet　**CROWDS:** Moderate
BEST SEASON: July to October　　**RATING:** ★ ★ ★ ★

DIRECTIONS: From the Arch Rock entrance station at Yosemite National Park, drive east into the park for 4.5 miles to the turnoff for Tioga Road/Highway 120, which is Big Oak Flat Road. Turn left and drive 9.3 miles to Crane Flat, then turn right on Tioga Road/Highway 120 and drive 30.3 miles to the Sunrise Lakes Trailhead on the south side of Tioga Road, just west of Tenaya Lake.

Hiking to Clouds Rest is a Yosemite high-country trip that's as classic as climbing Half Dome, but with fewer people to elbow you along the way. With 14 trail miles to cover and 2,300 feet of elevation gain, it's not for those who are out of shape. Still, the route is easier than climbing to the top of Half Dome, and most hikers who get an early morning start will have no problem reaching Clouds Rest by noon. That leaves an hour or so for a picnic lunch on the summit, and all afternoon to hike back down.

The trail begins on the paved, gated road leading from the parking lot. In about 75 yards, turn on to the dirt trail signed for Sunrise High Sierra Camp (HSC). You'll have several junctions to negotiate; just keep following the signs for Sunrise HSC for the first 2.8 miles. The grade starts out mellow as it winds through the thickly forested area west of Tenaya Lake. Watch for signs of a recent avalanche about one mile out—the devastation is obvious. Soon the trail starts to climb, and the grade increases substantially as you ascend along the eastern edge of Tenaya Canyon. When you start to lose your breath, turn around and take a look at the stellar views of Mount Hoffman, Tuolumne Peak, and other granite peaks and ridges to the north. You can even make out little tiny cars on Tioga Road.

The climb tops out at 2.8 miles, where you reach a junction for Sunrise High Sierra Camp to the left and Clouds Rest straight ahead. The good news is that much of your work is over; you've already gained 1,000 feet. Leave the Sunrise HSC signs behind here and continue straight. Descend steeply for a half-mile on a rocky, flower-filled slope and pass by Sunrise Mountain. Its stacked granite slabs make it look a bit like a miniature Clouds Rest.

The trail heads back into the forest, then starts to climb again, more moderately now. In short order, the forest thins and granite slabs start to appear. As the landscape becomes more bald and barren, you catch occasional glimpses of Clouds Rest, peeking up over the ridge ahead.

For those afraid of heights, the final ascent up Clouds Rest's ridge might seem treacherous, as it requires a stair-step walk on stacked granite slabs, with near vertical dropoffs on both sides. The most terrifying dropoff is on your right as you ascend—it's thousands of feet down to the bottom of granite-lined Tenaya Canyon. But as on many other Yosemite summits, if you simply watch your footing on the granite, you'll be fine.

The view from the top of Clouds Rest—of Tenaya Canyon, North Dome, Yosemite Valley, Tenaya Lake to the northeast, the Clark Range to the south, and various peaks and ridges—will knock your socks off. Not surprisingly, many hikers consider Clouds Rest to have the best view of any summit in the park. The most frequently heard comment on top of Clouds Rest (other than "Wow!") is "Where's Half Dome?" It's right where it's supposed to be, at the head of Yosemite Valley, but hikers have a hard time recognizing it from this angle. You aren't facing its infamous, vertical, cut-in-half side from here; instead you see the dome's strange profile.

Note that if this long hike has made you hot and sweaty, you can stop at the Sunrise Lakes for a swim on the way back. The first lake is only a quarter-mile from the Clouds Rest/Sunrise trail junction.

Clouds Rest's granite slabs

11. SUNRISE LAKES

Tioga Road area, Yosemite National Park
Three swimming and sunbathing lakes

DISTANCE: 7.0 miles round-trip; 4 hours   **LEVEL:** Moderate
ELEVATION: Start at 8,150 feet; total change 1,000 feet   **CROWDS:** Heavy
BEST SEASON: July to October   **RATING:** ★ ★ ★

DIRECTIONS: From the Arch Rock entrance station at Yosemite National Park, drive east into the park for 4.5 miles to the turnoff for Tioga Road/Highway 120, which is Big Oak Flat Road. Turn left and drive 9.3 miles to Crane Flat, then turn right on Tioga Road/Highway 120 and drive 30.3 miles to the Sunrise Lakes trailhead on the south side of the road, just west of Tenaya Lake.

Take all the people hiking to Clouds Rest, add in all the people hiking to the Sunrise Lakes, and the Sunrise Trailhead can look like a mall parking lot on a Saturday. But don't be scared off. The hike to Sunrise Lakes is an excellent trip, especially during the week or off-season, with only a 1,000-foot elevation gain and plenty of stellar scenery.

The trail begins on the paved, gated road leading from the parking lot. In about 75 yards, turn on to the dirt trail signed for Sunrise High Sierra Camp (HSC). There are several junctions to negotiate; just keep following the signs for Sunrise HSC. The grade starts out easy as it

Lower Sunrise Lake

winds through the lodgepole pine forest west of Tenaya Lake. You cross a few narrow creeks and pass meadowy areas filled with lupine and corn lilies in early summer. Watch for signs of a recent avalanche about one mile out—toppled lodgepole pines look like fallen pick-up sticks. Soon the trail starts to climb, and the grade increases substantially as you ascend along the eastern edge of Tenaya Canyon. When you start gasping for air, turn around and take a look at the stellar views of Mount Hoffman, Tuolumne Peak, and other granite peaks and ridges to the north.

The climb tops out at 2.8 miles, where you reach the junction for Sunrise High Sierra Camp to the left and Clouds Rest straight ahead. Turn left, and in about 10 minutes of easy, level walking, Lower Sunrise Lake shows up on the right, backed by a granite cliff and rocky talus slope. It has a nice rocky point for swimming. The middle and upper lakes are shortly beyond it, on the left. The middle lake is visible from the trail, but about 150 yards off of it. Small in size and crowned with a tree-lined island, it is the least visited of the Sunrise Lakes. The upper lake is the largest of the three and by far the most popular; lots of folks like to swim and picnic here on warm summer days. Unlike the lower and middle lakes, the upper lake requires a short but steep climb to reach it. It's worth it.

Hikers who aren't up for the marathon trek to Clouds Rest (see the previous story) get a bonus on the Sunrise Lakes Trail. On your return trip from the lakes, you have great views of Clouds Rest as you backtrack from the lakes to the Sunrise junction.

12. POLLY DOME LAKES

Tioga Road area, Yosemite National Park
A remote, easy-to-reach lake

DISTANCE: 6.0 miles round-trip; 3 hours   **LEVEL:** Easy/moderate
ELEVATION: Start at 8,150 feet; total change 150 feet   **CROWDS:** Moderate
BEST SEASON: July to October   **RATING:** ★ ★ ★

DIRECTIONS: From the Arch Rock entrance station at Yosemite National Park, drive east into the park for 4.5 miles to the turnoff for Tioga Road/Highway 120, which is Big Oak Flat Road. Turn left and drive 9.3 miles to Crane Flat, then turn right on Tioga Road/Highway 120 and drive 31.0 miles to the Murphy Creek Trailhead on the north side of Tioga Road, near Tenaya Lake.

The Polly Dome Lakes are just a bit off the trail, offering day hikers a chance to take a short cross-country walk and get away from

Glacial erratics along the Murphy Creek Trail to Polly Dome Lakes

the crowds at Tioga Road's more popular lakes, such as May Lake and Sunrise Lakes. Hikers who don't like off-trail travel will be happy to know that a maintained trail leads most of the way to the Polly Dome Lakes; only in the last half-mile must you find your own way. A bonus is that there is very little elevation gain on the trip; hikers fond of level trails will find this one to their liking.

The trip begins on the Murphy Creek Trail, with the trailhead located right across from huge Tenaya Lake. Unlike so many trails on the eastern end of Tioga Road, this one is not beaten down to a sandy pulp by horses' hooves or the feet of many hikers. Instead, it is a smooth dirt trail through the forest, well-graded and easy to follow.

The first stretch is completely shaded, offering a cool walk through the firs and pines as you follow the path of Murphy Creek. At 1.5 miles, you leave the trees and cross over a series of granite slabs, which are peppered with the smooth, randomly placed granite boulders called glacial erratics. Trail cairns keep you on the correct path as you traverse the slabs.

As you head back into the trees, start to pay attention to the landmarks on the right side of the trail. At 2.7 miles, you see a small, marshy pond. Look for a use trail just before you reach it (south of it). The use trail leads generally southeast. (If you're still on the main trail at the point where it leaves the edge of Murphy Creek and climbs uphill, you've missed the turnoff. You'll realize it before long, though, because the Murphy Creek Trail junctions with trails leading to May Lake and Glen Aulin in a half-mile. Just turn around and head back, looking for that marshy pond.)

Follow the use trail as it skirts several more marshy ponds. Try to stay on the south side of them, roughly following Murphy Creek as it leads to the north side of the largest Polly Dome Lake. If you can climb up high and get a look at the obvious chunk of granite known as Polly Dome, you'll know exactly which way to travel; the lake lies at its base.

Polly Dome Lake is popular with backpackers because it is so easy to reach, and it has good campsites. Day-hikers will be pleased with its swimming prospects—the lake has shallow, warm water.

13. TENAYA LAKE

Tioga Road area, Yosemite National Park
An immense, granite-lined glacial lake

DISTANCE: 2.0 miles round-trip; 1 hour
ELEVATION: Start at 8,150 feet; total change 60 feet
BEST SEASON: July to October

LEVEL: Easy
CROWDS: Moderate
RATING: ★ ★ ★

DIRECTIONS: From the Arch Rock entrance station at Yosemite National Park, drive east into the park for 4.5 miles to the turnoff for Tioga Road/Highway 120, which is Big Oak Flat Road. Turn left and drive 9.3 miles to Crane Flat, then turn right on Tioga Road/Highway 120 and drive 31.7 miles to the eastern Tenaya Lake picnic area (there is another Tenaya Lake picnic area a half-mile west of this one). The trail leads from the parking lot.

Lots of people drive east down Tioga Road in a big rush to get to Tuolumne Meadows, but when they see giant Tenaya Lake right along the road, it stops them in their tire tracks. Luckily the 150-acre, sapphire-blue lake has a parking lot and picnic area at its east end, where you can leave your car and take a stroll down to the lake's edge.

Whereas most people stop at the white-sand beach and picnic tables to swim, sunbathe, or watch the rock climbers on nearby Polly Dome (across the highway), you can leave the crowds behind and take a hike around the lake. From the parking lot, follow the trail west to the lake, then turn left and walk to the south side of the beach. Pick up the trail there that leads along the forested back side of Tenaya Lake, far from the road on the north side. You'll have to rock-hop across a small, shallow stream to access the trail, which comes in from the east (it travels all the way to Tuolumne Meadows).

The mostly level path meanders alongside the lake, then continues beyond it to Olmsted Point. You can hike as far as you like and then turn around. The best parts of the trail are in the first mile from the beach, before you connect with the busier trails on the southwest side of the lake. The lakeside forest is very lush in summer, with plenty of wildflowers growing in the understory of Douglas firs, spruce, hemlocks, and pines. The trees make the trail remarkably private, despite the proximity of Tioga Road and Tenaya Lake's beach and picnic area. Swimming is best on the lake's southwest side; although there is no sandy beach like on the east side, the shoreline is protected from the wind and fairly private.

For all its spectacular beauty, the lake has a grim history. In 1852, the United States government sent soldiers to round up the Yosemite Indians and "resettle" them on reservations. Members of the Ahwahneeche tribe, who were native to Yosemite Valley, fled to this remote lake to escape the round-up. The Ahwahneeches and their chief, Teneiya, were captured and resettled on the Fresno River. Even there, angry whites continued to persecute them, seeking vigilante justice for alleged Indian crimes. Chief Teneiya died in 1853, and Lake Tenaya was named for him, with a slight change in spelling.

The Ahwahneeches had their own name for Lake Tenaya— "Pywiack," or Lake of Shining Rocks. It's a name well-earned by the wall of polished granite framing the water.

14. CATHEDRAL LAKES

Tioga Road area, Yosemite National Park
Two sparkling lakes at the base of Cathedral Peak

DISTANCE: 7.4 miles round-trip; 4 hours   **LEVEL:** Moderate
ELEVATION: Start at 8,550 feet; total change 1,000 feet   **CROWDS:** Heavy
BEST SEASON: July to October   **RATING:** ★ ★ ★ ★

DIRECTIONS: From the Arch Rock entrance station at Yosemite National Park, drive east into the park for 4.5 miles to the turnoff for Tioga Road/Highway 120, which is Big Oak Flat Road. Turn left and drive 9.3 miles to Crane Flat, then turn right on Tioga Road/Highway 120 and drive 37.4 miles to the Cathedral Lakes Trailhead on the right, across from Tuolumne Meadows. (If you reach the visitor center turnoff, you've gone a half-mile too far east.) Park your car in the pullouts on either side of Tioga Road near the trailhead; there is no formal parking lot.

If an alien abducted me and demanded to be shown what the Yosemite high country was all about, I'd take her (or him) to Cathedral Lakes. On few other Yosemite trails do you get so much for so little: Two spectacular glacial lakes with good fishing and swimming prospects, lovely trailside forests and meadows, and amazing perspectives on one of the finest pieces of granite in Yosemite—Cathedral Peak.

If my alien and I went on a day hike to Cathedral Lakes instead of a backpacking trip, we'd be doing the world a favor. The Cathedral Lakes are surprisingly easy to reach, and hence, heavily visited, especially by overnighters. Day-hikers can enjoy all the splendor of the Cathedral Lakes while making a much smaller impact on its fragile, high alpine environment. Those who get an early start will also enjoy the trail without the crowds, at least on the way up to the lakes.

From the trail's start at Tioga Road, it's a 3.2-mile hike on the John Muir Trail to reach the Cathedral Lakes junction. By late summer, the sandy trail is heavily beaten down by foot traffic. The initial climb is a bit of a butt-kicker; you gain 600 feet in the first mile from the trailhead. The path is rocky and steep. Fortunately, much of the trail is shaded by lodgepole pines, which makes the work a little easier.

Cathedral Lake and Cathedral Peak

When the steepest part of the climb is over, the path breaks out of the trees, and views of 10,940-foot Cathedral Peak will leave you oohing and ahhing. With every few steps you take, your perspective on "The Great Cathedral" (as John Muir liked to call it) changes. If you've admired Cathedral Peak's towering spires from the Tuolumne Meadows area, you'll be amazed at how different the formation looks from close up.

At 2.5 miles, the trail starts to descend. At 3.2 miles, you'll reach a fork with a trail signed for Sunrise High Sierra Camp. Turn right on the Cathedral Lake spur to reach the lower, larger lake in a half-mile. You'll follow the lake's inlet stream through a gorgeous meadow to the water's edge, then start to snap photographs like crazy. The lake and its setting—a classic glacial cirque—is as scenic a spot as you'll find anywhere in Yosemite. You are surrounded by granite: Tresidder Peak, Echo Peaks, and the twin towers of Cathedral Peak. Swimming is excellent but cold, of course.

To reach the upper lake, retrace your steps back to the junction with the trail signed for Sunrise High Sierra Camp, and follow that fork for a half-mile. Fishing is usually better in the upper lake, swimming is just as good, and the scenery is almost, but not quite, as sublime.

15. ELIZABETH LAKE

Tioga Road area, Yosemite National Park
A meadow-lined lake below Unicorn Peak

DISTANCE: 4.6 miles round-trip; 2.5 hours   **LEVEL:** Easy/moderate
ELEVATION: Start at 8,600 feet; total change 850 feet   **CROWDS:** Heavy
BEST SEASON: July to October   **RATING:** ★ ★ ★ ★

DIRECTIONS: From the Arch Rock entrance station at Yosemite National Park, drive east into the park for 4.5 miles to the turnoff for Tioga Road/Highway 120, which is Big Oak Flat Road. Turn left and drive 9.3 miles to Crane Flat, then turn right on Tioga Road/Highway 120 and drive 39 miles to the Tuolumne Meadows Campground on the right. Turn right and follow the signs through the main camp to the group camp. The trail begins across from the group camp rest rooms, near group site number B49.

You can't expect that Elizabeth Lake won't be crowded with Yosemite day-hikers. The trail and its lake destination have three major things going for them: A short and fairly easy hike, a trailhead located in a busy campground, and classic high Sierra scenery.

The only thing against the Elizabeth Lake Trail is that almost nobody can find the trailhead, unless they stumble upon it by accident. It's tucked into the back of Tuolumne Meadows Campground, across from the group camp rest rooms. If you aren't staying at the campground, get directions from the rangers at the camp entrance kiosk on your drive in. This will save you some time negotiating your way through the campground maze.

Once you're at the trailhead, be prepared to climb steeply for the first mile, then breathe easier when the trail levels out. Luckily the route is mostly shaded by lodgepole pines. When you begin to hear the sound of Unicorn Creek at 1.5 miles, your climb is almost over and your destination is at hand. Leave the trees behind and emerge at a green meadow, where a right spur trail leads to Elizabeth Lake's edge, at elevation 9,487 feet. (If you miss this right spur, you can take a second right spur, 100 yards farther.)

Elizabeth Lake is set in a gorgeous glacier-carved basin at the foot of white granite Unicorn Peak. The lake is horseshoe-shaped, with some marshy, grassy edges. Use trails, mostly traveled by anglers, lead around its edges. Take a stroll around and find the perfect place to spread out a picnic. Views of Unicorn Peak are best from the lake's northeast side. The brave will want to swim; the water is relatively warm in late summer, although the lake bottom is marshy and muddy. Some daring folks try to climb the spire of Unicorn Peak (10,900 feet), but most are happy to sit around and admire the views of it and its neighboring peaks in the Cathedral Range.

16. LOWER GAYLOR LAKE

Tioga Road area, Yosemite National Park
A high elevation lake surrounded by meadows

DISTANCE: 8.4 miles round-trip; 4.5 hours
LEVEL: Moderate
ELEVATION: Start at 8,700 feet; total change 1,300 feet
CROWDS: Minimal
BEST SEASON: July to October
RATING: ★ ★ ★

DIRECTIONS: From the Arch Rock entrance station at Yosemite National Park, drive east into the park for 4.5 miles to the turnoff for Tioga Road/Highway 120, which is Big Oak Flat Road. Turn left and drive 9.3 miles to Crane Flat, then turn right on Tioga Road/Highway 120 and drive 39.5 miles to the Tuolumne Lodge and Wilderness Permits turnoff on the right. Turn right and drive four-tenths of a mile toward Tuolumne Lodge, then park in the lot on the left signed for Dog Lake and John Muir Trail. The trail begins across the road from the parking lot. (Additional parking is available in the Wilderness Permit parking lot, at the turnoff from Tioga Road.)

The trail to Lower Gaylor Lake is surprisingly different from the trail to Middle and Upper Gaylor Lakes (see the story on page 246). It begins at a different trailhead, it meanders more miles to reach its lake destination, and it features a much easier grade. But the main reason to hike this trail to Lower Gaylor Lake is that it sees far less foot traffic than the shorter, more publicized route to the middle and upper lakes. Then, from Lower Gaylor Lake, you can make an easy cross-country side trip to the Granite Lakes if you wish.

The trail to Lower Gaylor Lake begins on the John Muir Trail near Tuolumne Lodge. From the trailhead parking lot a quarter-mile west of the lodge, cross the access road and follow the wide trail to the left. You'll reach a bridge crossing the Dana Fork Tuolumne River less than a quarter-mile away. After you cross, you soon leave the John Muir Trail behind. The trail to Lower Gaylor Lake turns left and heads eastward along the south side of the Dana Fork. This is a pleasant, flat stretch covering nearly two miles, with plenty of opportunities for fishing and swimming. The Dana Fork does not get the hordes of hikers, backpackers, and horses that convene on the nearby Lyell Fork of the Tuolumne River.

At 1.9 miles, the trail crosses the river and soon afterward, Tioga Road. Across the highway, the trail follows the outlet stream of Lower Gaylor Lake and the Granite Lakes, heading uphill. You'll ascend very gently, although at this high elevation, you may notice even the slightest climb. At 4.2 miles, the trail reaches Lower Gaylor Lake, elevation 10,049 feet. The lake is a deep turquoise color and surrounded by high-alpine meadows. From its edge you get wide vistas of the peaks in the Tuolumne Meadows area.

Crossing of the Dana Fork of the Tuolumne River

If you want to get to the Upper and Middle Gaylor Lakes from the lower lake, you have to go cross-country (to the northeast). Although this is fairly easily accomplished, most people opt to drive to the Tioga Pass Trailhead and hike to the Upper and Middle Gaylor Lakes from there. The middle lake is only one steep mile from the trailhead (see page 246). A more interesting option from Lower Gaylor Lake is to head cross-country to the north to see the less visited Granite Lakes. To do so, walk to the far (north) side of Lower Gaylor Lake. Follow the lake's inlet stream uphill through lovely meadows for one mile. A 300-foot elevation gain will bring you to long and slender Lower Granite Lake; the upper lake is just above it. Both lakes are deep blue and hemmed in by stately granite cliffs. Brave day-hikers will throw off their clothes and dive in for an icy swim.

17. LYELL CANYON

Tioga Road area, Yosemite National Park
An easy riverside ramble

DISTANCE: 5.0 miles round-trip; 2.5 hours **LEVEL:** Easy
ELEVATION: Start at 8,700 feet; total change 200 feet **CROWDS:** Moderate
BEST SEASON: July to October **RATING:** ★ ★ ★ ★

DIRECTIONS: From the Arch Rock entrance station at Yosemite National Park, drive east into the park for 4.5 miles to the turnoff for Tioga Road/Highway 120, which is Big Oak Flat Road. Turn left and drive 9.3 miles to Crane Flat, then turn right on Tioga Road/Highway 120 and drive 39.5 miles to the Tuolumne Lodge and Wilderness Permits turnoff on the right. Turn right and drive four-tenths of a mile toward Tuolumne Lodge, then park in the lot on the left signed for Dog Lake and John Muir Trail. The trail begins across the road from the parking lot. (Additional parking is available in the Wilderness Permit parking lot, at the turnoff from Tioga Road.)

The trail into Lyell Canyon is one of the easiest in the Yosemite high country. Since it is virtually flat, and it starts out beautiful and stays that way for its entirety, you can hike it for as long as you like.

The trip follows the combined Pacific Crest Trail/John Muir Trail, which parallels the Lyell Fork of the Tuolumne River. I suggest a five-mile round-trip hike, but how far you go is up to you. What matters is that you come equipped with one or more of the following: Your camera, your fishing rod, your lunch, and your loved ones.

To reach the Lyell Fork, you must first cross the Dana Fork on a sturdy footbridge less than a quarter-mile from the parking lot. Simply cross the access road, pick up the well signed John Muir Trail and go left, heading toward Vogelsang High Sierra Camp (HSC). After crossing the Dana Fork, continue south for a quarter-mile to a second footbridge—this one crossing the Lyell Fork. Pay close attention at these junctions; there are many use trails along the river and they can be confusing. All of the "true" junctions are marked; don't turn onto a trail unless it is signed for the John Muir Trail/Pacific Crest Trail or Vogelsang HSC.

From the Lyell Fork footbridge, continue due south for 150 feet until you reach a junction with a trail coming in from the right from Tuolumne Meadows Campground. Turn left here and hike along the river's south side. A half-mile farther, a third bridge takes you across Rafferty Creek and into Lyell Canyon. This is the first time you will veer away from the Vogelsang HSC Trail, although you are still on the combined John Muir Trail/Pacific Crest Trail.

You've just crossed three footbridges in your first 1.2 miles and negotiated your way through an awful lot of junctions. Now your concerns are over; there's nothing left to do but meander along the river and hunt for catchable trout or suitable swimming holes. There's no elevation change to concern yourself with and no more trail forks...just occasional forest, wide meadows, plentiful wildflowers, and a musical river. Every now and then, you'll have a fine view of Mammoth Peak and the Kuna Crest to the east, looming above the trees. It won't be easy, but try to remember to come back before sunset.

18. YOUNG LAKES LOOP

Tioga Road area, Yosemite National Park
Three glacial lakes set below craggy Ragged Peak

DISTANCE: 13.8 miles round-trip; 8 hours   **LEVEL:** Strenuous
ELEVATION: Start at 8,600 feet; total change 1,900 feet   **CROWDS:** Moderate
BEST SEASON: July to October   **RATING:** ★ ★ ★ ★

DIRECTIONS: From the Arch Rock entrance station at Yosemite National Park, drive east into the park for 4.5 miles to the turnoff for Tioga Road/Highway 120, which is Big Oak Flat Road. Turn left and drive 9.3 miles to Crane Flat, then turn right on Tioga Road/Highway 120 and drive 39 miles to the Lembert Dome/Soda Springs/Dog Lake/Glen Aulin Trailhead parking on the left. Begin hiking on the western edge of the parking lot, where there is a gated dirt road signed "Soda Springs, 0.5 mile."

Upper Young Lake and Ragged Peak

The Young Lakes Loop is a classic Yosemite trip that works equally well as a long day hike or short backpacking trip. Hardy day-hikers who get an early start will have plenty of time to explore all three of the Young Lakes and return to the trailhead with daylight to spare. Plus, they'll enjoy the fact that their main trail companions will be backpackers, not hordes of other day-hikers. The route is simply too long and strenuous for hikers in anything less than good shape, so the field of trail travelers is naturally limited.

Your destination is the Young Lakes, a series of three lakes that are set in a deep and wide glacial cirque. This is the kind of awesome, high alpine scenery that sticks in your mind months later when you're sitting at a desk somewhere staring at your computer screen. A bonus on the trip is that without adding any extra mileage, you can make a loop on your return, tacking on even more spectacular scenery and a side trip to Dog Lake or Lembert Dome.

The trip begins on the west side of the Lembert Dome parking lot, following the wide dirt road that leads a half-mile to Soda Spring. At Soda Spring, veer to the right and pick up the trail near Parsons Lodge that is signed for Glen Aulin. Follow the trail through a sparse lodgepole pine forest for 1.5 miles. The first part of the trip is likely to be crowded and rather unremarkable except for lovely views to the south of Unicorn and Cathedral peaks. At a junction with the Young Lakes

Trail at two miles out, say good-bye to the masses traveling the busy trail to Glen Aulin, and look forward to a more peaceful jaunt to Young Lakes.

The Young Lakes Trail proceeds for three miles, first crossing fantastic looking slabs of polished granite, then re-entering the pine forest, but always climbing moderately and steadily. A short descent and an easy level stretch are a pleasant diversion between miles four and five. At five miles from the trailhead, you spot a junction, where the return leg of your loop leads off to the right (signed for Dog Lake). For now, continue straight for another 1.5 miles, with another short climb, to Lower Young Lake at elevation 9,850 feet. The lake features a stunning view of craggy Ragged Peak. (The peak looks exactly like what its name implies.)

But don't stop there—two more lakes are accessible within a mile to the east. Cross the lower lake's outlet creek and follow a use trail a quarter-mile to the second, smaller lake. It's an easy walk to reach it. If you have the energy, don't pass up a visit to the third, upper lake, the most visually stunning of them all. Accessing it is more difficult: Walk to the far side of the second lake and pick up a use trail that leads toward a small waterfall—the third lake's outlet. Then, climb up and above the waterfall (this requires some minor scrambling on a steep and muddy slope), and hike across a glorious high meadow filled with lupine and other wildflowers.

You won't be sorry you made the extra effort. The best seat in the house is anywhere along the water's edge. Upper Young Lake is nestled at the base of Ragged Peak, and edged by rocks and wildflowers. It's beyond spectacular. Most backpackers stay at the first or second lake, so you'll have more privacy at this lake.

When you're ready to head home, retrace your steps to the trail junction and take the eastern (left) fork, returning via Dog Lake and Lembert Dome. Be forewarned: If you loop back this way, you won't be adding any mileage, but you'll have an additional 400-foot elevation gain, mostly in the first half-mile from the junction. Still, the meadow scenery and far-off mountain vistas between the top of this climb and the junction for Dog Lake are as awe-inspiring as the scenery at Upper Young Lake, so it would be a pity to miss them. If you like far-reaching views and high alpine meadows dotted with granite boulders, be sure to take the loop. If you're completely exhausted from your adventures at the lakes, skip the loop and return the way you came—it's downhill all the way.

19. GLEN AULIN & TUOLUMNE FALLS

Tioga Road area, Yosemite National Park
A sparkling cataract on the Tuolumne River

DISTANCE: 9.4 miles round-trip; 5 hours   **LEVEL:** Moderate
ELEVATION: Start at 8,600 feet; total change 400 feet   **CROWDS:** Heavy
BEST SEASON: June to August   **RATING:** ★ ★ ★ ★ ★

DIRECTIONS: From the Arch Rock entrance station at Yosemite National Park, drive east into the park for 4.5 miles to the turnoff for Tioga Road/Highway 120, which is Big Oak Flat Road. Turn left and drive 9.3 miles to Crane Flat, then turn right on Tioga Road/Highway 120 and drive 39 miles to the Lembert Dome/Soda Springs/Dog Lake/Glen Aulin Trailhead parking on the left. Begin hiking on the western edge of the parking lot, where there is a gated dirt road signed "Soda Springs, 0.5 mile."

Those who aren't up for the Epic Waterfall Trip to Waterwheel Falls described in the following story can take this trip to Tuolumne Falls instead. It offers all of the same Tuolumne River whitewater scenery, but in a shorter, easier version that is of manageable difficulty for most park visitors. The trail is 9.4 miles round-trip, but with only a 400-foot elevation change (down on the way in, and up on the homeward stretch).

A nice bonus is the chance to sneak in a good meal at the Glen Aulin High Sierra Camp, which is located right next door to Tuolumne Falls. To stay in the camp, you must reserve a space a year in advance, but you can often purchase a hot meal just by showing up. If you prefer to picnic on your own, there are plenty of spots alongside the clear pools of the river or at the base of the falls.

Start your trip at the trailhead parking area for Dog Lake, Lembert Dome, and Soda Springs. Begin hiking on the gated dirt road that is signed "Soda Springs 0.5 mile." Follow the road until you near Parsons Memorial Lodge and see the sign for Glen Aulin Trail. Veer right and head for Glen Aulin.

The first couple miles of trail are quite flat, only faintly downhill, but the descent increases as you near Glen Aulin and waterfall country. The scenery is spectacular all the way. After leaving the forest in the first mile, the trail veers closer to the Tuolumne River and moves from trees to granite. The result is wide-open views of Cathedral and Unicorn peaks and Fairview Dome to the south. The trail meanders through a mix of meadows, granite, and woodland, where deer and marmots abound.

Upper cascade of Tuolumne Falls

When the path reaches its first bridge over the Tuolumne River, a sign states that Glen Aulin is only 1.7 miles away. In fifteen minutes of walking, you reach the very top section of Tuolumne Falls, a stunning 100-foot drop. But this is merely a preview of good things to come. Now you begin a steep descent to the base of the falls and another bridge, which takes you across the river to Glen Aulin High Sierra Camp. When you cross the bridge to the Glen Aulin side, be sure to descend to the small, pebbly beach at the water's edge. This beach is a great spot for viewing and taking pictures of the lower drop of Tuolumne Falls. From the bridge itself, your view is slightly obstructed by trees, but from this beach, you have a clear shot. Some people call this lower waterfall Glen Aulin Falls or White Cascade, but most consider it to be a section of Tuolumne Falls.

A second bridge to your right heads into the High Sierra Camp and your chance for a hot meal. Follow it if you wish, or continue to hike for another quarter-mile to a granite promontory. Head straight downstream, then at a junction take the left fork to stay along the river. As you climb up on granite, turn around for a fine view of some of the upper cascades of Tuolumne Falls. Choose your picnic spot and revel in the scenery.

Note that although you have a 400-foot elevation gain on the return trip, most of it is completed in the first half-mile—getting up and around Tuolumne Falls. After that, the grade is fairly tame.

20. WATERWHEEL FALLS

Tioga Road area, Yosemite National Park
Yosemite's most unusual waterfall

DISTANCE: 16.0 miles round-trip; 10 hours   **LEVEL:** Very strenuous
ELEVATION: Start at 8,600 feet; total change 1,900 feet   **CROWDS:** Moderate
BEST SEASON: June to August   **RATING:** ★ ★ ★ ★

DIRECTIONS: From the Arch Rock entrance station at Yosemite National Park, drive east into the park for 4.5 miles to the turnoff for Tioga Road/Highway 120, which is Big Oak Flat Road. Turn left and drive 9.3 miles to Crane Flat, then turn right on Tioga Road/Highway 120 and drive 39 miles to the Lembert Dome/Soda Springs/Dog Lake/Glen Aulin Trailhead parking on the left. Begin hiking on the western edge of the parking lot, where there is a gated dirt road signed "Soda Springs, 0.5 mile."

This hike is the Epic Waterfall Trip. If you hike the entire route, you're guaranteed to see so many waterfalls and so much water that you'll have enough memories to get you through a 10-year drought.

Before you start, it's important to know what you're in for. The round-trip mileage from the Lembert Dome parking lot all the way to Waterwheel Falls is a whopping 16 miles. Most people do not attempt this as a day hike; it is far more common to backpack in to Glen Aulin, then hike to Waterwheel Falls as a day hike from camp. Still, with an early morning start, Waterwheel Falls is a manageable day-hiking destination for those in excellent physical condition. The trip has the same mileage as climbing Half Dome, but with much less elevation gain. Unfortunately, all the gain is on your return trip home, when you're already tired. Bring plenty of food and water with you, or better yet, bring a purification system and canteen, so you can filter all the river water you want instead of carrying it.

Those looking for a shorter trip should opt for traveling only part of this route to Tuolumne Falls, which is a 9.4-mile round-trip and nearly flat. (See the previous story.)

Start to hike on the gated dirt road at the west end of the Lembert Dome parking lot. Follow the trail instructions in the previous story for 4.7 miles to Tuolumne Falls and Glen Aulin High Sierra Camp. At this point, you've lost only 400 feet in elevation; you'll lose another 1,500 feet from here to Waterwheel Falls. Give your knees fair warning.

From Glen Aulin, the trail drops down to a level section in a beautiful meadow, where backpackers make their camps near the river. Here the lupine grows waist high, the river is placid, and ferns and aspens thrive. You may never want to leave this tranquil, flowery spot, but if you do, you'll find that another stretch of granite leads you to another level, flower-filled meadow. Throughout this stretch, the river is so quiet that it's hard to believe it could produce a waterfall.

But soon enough you hear a roaring sound up ahead, and you pass by boisterous California Falls at 6.4 miles out. The waterfall is just off the trail by a few hundred feet. A spur trail on your left leads to the huge, block-shaped cataract, which has some great swimming holes near its base.

(Note: Downstream of Tuolumne Falls, make sure you follow each and every spur trail leading to your left. The spur trails access the falls; none of them except Tuolumne Falls can be seen from the main trail.)

The path, which has been a fairly even grade up to California Falls, now drops steeply downhill on rock stair-steps for what seems like eternity. LeConte Falls shows up one mile beyond California Falls, just after a large, placid, green pool. At the edge of the pool it seems that the world drops off and disappears, but you're just at the top of LeConte Falls' main cascade.

Beyond LeConte Falls, watch for a trail sign for Pate Valley and Tuolumne Meadows. Near it, there's another spur trail on your left. This one takes you to your final destination, Waterwheel Falls, which is often billed as Yosemite's most unusual waterfall. Shortly, you discern why; the spur trail brings you to the center of the giant Waterwheel

Waterwheel Falls

cascade. You are directly across from some of the lower "waterwheels." These are sections of churning water that dip into deep holes in the granite, then shoot out with such velocity that they seem to double back on themselves, appearing to circle around like waterwheels. As soon as you see them, you understand the cascade's moniker. Six different waterwheels spin in the middle section, and a few more circle up above. Find a spot on the granite alongside them, pull out your lunch and your camera, and linger a while. But be sure to leave enough time before dark for the long haul back to the trailhead.

21. LEMBERT DOME

Tioga Road area, Yosemite National Park
A scramble to the top of a granite dome

DISTANCE: 2.6 miles round-trip; 1.5 hours   **LEVEL:** Easy/moderate
ELEVATION: Start at 8,600 feet; total change 850 feet   **CROWDS:** Moderate
BEST SEASON: July to October   **RATING:** ★ ★ ★ ★

DIRECTIONS: From the Arch Rock entrance station at Yosemite National Park, drive east into the park for 4.5 miles to the turnoff for Tioga Road/Highway 120, which is Big Oak Flat Road. Turn left and drive 9.3 miles to Crane Flat, then turn right on Tioga Road/Highway 120 and drive 39 miles to the Lembert Dome/Soda Springs/Dog Lake/Glen Aulin Trailhead parking on the left. Begin hiking on the trail near the rest rooms.

When you see 800-foot-high Lembert Dome from the trailhead and parking area, you'll never think you can make it to the top. It just seems too big and imposing to be scaled without ropes and carabiners. But the secret of Lembert Dome is that although the west side is an intimidating sheer face—the playground of technical climbers—the northeast side is nicely sloped.

Granite domes, a common geological feature in the Sierra, are essentially large rounded rocks, formed by the creation of slowly expanding granite. As the granite expands, cracks form, creating individual layers of rock near the surface. Over time, a process called exfoliation occurs, in which these outer layers of rock break apart and fall off, removing all sharp corners and angles from the rock and leaving a smooth round dome. Lembert Dome is a special kind of granite dome called a *roche moutonée*. This is a French geologic term that designates a dome with one sheer side and one sloping side. It roughly means "rock sheep."

To hike to Lembert Dome, take the trail by the rest rooms that is signed for both Dog Lake and Lembert Dome. In less than a quarter mile, the trail splits off from the path to Dog Lake. You'll take the right fork for Lembert Dome and begin to climb more steeply through a lodgepole pine forest. The sandy, rocky, well-worn trail can make somewhat tricky footing, which is even trickier on the way back down. As you pass underneath Lembert Dome's west side, you'll see rock climbers dangling from the granite high above you, and hear their commanding shouts to their companions.

The trail curves around the back (north) side of the dome and becomes rather faint, then disappears completely once you're on hard granite. Pick your own route to Lembert Dome's exposed summit. You'll see other hikers going every which way—some making a beeline for the top, others switchbacking and lateraling their way to it.

Hikers on Lembert Dome

Any way you get there, the effort is completely worthwhile. The views from the top of Lembert Dome (elevation 9,450 feet) are outstanding, taking in all of Tuolumne Meadows and its surrounding peaks. The steepness of the dome combined with its high vista can be downright dizzying, so if you're afraid of heights, hold on to your hiking partner. The wind often howls on top, adding to the excitement.

For your return from Lembert Dome, make sure you follow the trail signs for "Lembert Dome Parking." Otherwise, you could wind up back at the horse stables or Tuolumne Lodge instead of at your car; several other trails connect with the Lembert Dome Trail.

22. DOG LAKE

Tioga Road area, Yosemite National Park
An easy-to-reach lake for swimming and fishing

DISTANCE: 2.8 miles round-trip; 1.5 hours   **LEVEL:** Easy/moderate
ELEVATION: Start at 8,600 feet; total change 650 feet   **CROWDS:** Heavy
BEST SEASON: July to October   **RATING:** ★ ★ ★

DIRECTIONS: From the Arch Rock entrance station at Yosemite National Park, drive east into the park for 4.5 miles to the turnoff for Tioga Road/Highway 120, which is Big Oak Flat Road. Turn left and drive 9.3 miles to Crane Flat, then turn right on Tioga Road/Highway 120 and drive 39 miles to the Lembert Dome/Soda Springs/Dog Lake/Glen Aulin Trailhead parking on the left. Begin hiking on the trail near the rest rooms.

Dog Lake is an easy-to-reach destination from Tuolumne Meadows, and a perfect place for families to spend an afternoon picnicking or swimming at a lovely alpine lake. Keep in mind that although this is a relatively easy hike, the air is very thin at this elevation and even a moderate climb can feel difficult, especially if you're not acclimated.

The trail begins by the rest rooms at the Lembert Dome parking lot. Initially, you'll walk through a pretty meadow, with views of snowy Cathedral Peak and Unicorn Peak in the distance. (Guess which is which—their names tell you all you need to know.) Notice how the trail is dug a few inches into the ground to keep hikers on a single, definitive route and protect the fragile meadow. In spring, colorful wildflowers add contrast to the emerald green grasses.

Immediately after you cross the meadow, you reach a huge horizontal slab of granite, marked by rock trail cairns to show you the way. Next comes a trail split—Dog Lake to the left and Lembert Dome to the right; you should head left.

Now your climb begins in earnest, heading up a sandy, rocky trail to the top of a ridge behind Lembert Dome. The dome is behind your right shoulder as you mount the ridge; you have plenty of opportunity during the 500-foot climb to stop and admire it as you catch your breath. The forest surrounding you is primarily lodgepole pines and firs. If you hike this trail early in summer, a stream accompanies you on your left for much of the climb. By late summer, it goes dry.

After a half-mile of huffing and puffing, you'll cross the streambed and top the ridge. The trail flattens out, but you're not done climbing yet. A more moderate grade takes you to a junction with the Young Lakes Trail to your left. Bear right here and you'll reach Dog Lake in less than a quarter mile.

After the climb, Dog Lake is a joy to see. Set at 9,240 feet in elevation, the lake is wide, shallow, and deeply blue. The colorful red peaks to the east are Mount Dana and Mount Gibbs. Although the lake's edges are grassy and partially forested, you can still hike around its perimeter. If you head to your right from the main trail, you'll reach a pretty meadow and sandy swimming area on the lake's far side. Getting there requires a stream crossing, but it's very shallow and narrow by summer.

Some people toss a line in the water. We've witnessed plenty of fishing taking place at Dog Lake, but not much catching. Nobody seems to mind.

If you have the energy, you can make a one-mile side trip to Lembert Dome on your return from Dog Lake. Leaving the lake, you'll pass the junction with the Young Lakes Trail. Stay left and continue downhill a third of a mile farther, to where a trail sign for Lembert Dome and Tuolumne Lodge points left. Take it; you'll pass a small pond on your left, then see an unmarked spur trail on your right that leads to the base of the dome. Pick any route up the granite slabs to the summit. (See the previous story on Lembert Dome.)

For your return trip from either Dog Lake or Lembert Dome, make sure you follow the trail signs for "Lembert Dome Parking." Otherwise, you could wind up back at the horse stables or Tuolumne Lodge instead of at your car; several other trails connect with this trail.

Note that a separate hiking trail leads to Dog Lake from near Tuolumne Lodge. This trail is about the same length and grade as the trail from the Lembert Dome parking lot, but it begins on the south side of Tioga Road. The trail crosses the highway and then proceeds up the eastern flank of Lembert Dome to the lake. This trail is not quite as scenic, although it is usually less crowded.

23. MONO PASS

Tioga Road area, Yosemite National Park
19th century mining cabins and a high vista

DISTANCE: 8.4 miles round-trip; 4 hours　　**LEVEL:** Easy/moderate
ELEVATION: Start at 9,700 feet; total change 900 feet　　**CROWDS:** Moderate
BEST SEASON: July to October　　**RATING:** ★ ★ ★ ★ ★

DIRECTIONS: From the Arch Rock entrance station at Yosemite National Park, drive east into the park for 4.5 miles to the turnoff for Tioga Road/Highway 120, which is Big Oak Flat Road. Turn left and drive 9.3 miles to Crane Flat, then turn right on Tioga Road/Highway 120 and drive 44.5 miles to the Mono Pass Trailhead parking on the south side of the road (near road marker T-37, 1.5 miles west of Tioga Pass).

The trail to Mono Pass is so fine and so easy that it attracts many day-hikers and backpackers in the short season when the high country is accessible. The path takes hikers to a terrific viewpoint of Mono Lake from just beyond 10,600-foot Mono Pass, and provides an opportunity to visit several restored mining cabins from the 19th century.

With an elevation gain of only 900 feet spread out over four miles, you'll hardly even notice that you're climbing. The first two miles are almost completely level, with even a few mild downhill stretches. The trail crosses the Dana Fork of the Tuolumne River in its first half-mile

Viewpoint just beyond Mono Pass

(an easy boulder-hop), then passes through an alternating series of high-elevation lodgepole pine forests and meadows. We were amazed at the variety of wildflowers we found along the trail—wild onions, lupine, fireweed, dog-tooth violets, corn lilies, columbine, and more. The hike also provides great views of the Kuna Crest.

You pass an extremely dilapidated cabin right along the trail at 1.5 miles; the ones ahead near the pass have been restored and are in far better shape. At a trail fork at two miles out, bear left for Mono Pass (the right fork leads to Spillway Lake; see the following story). Only at this point do you start to ascend with any seriousness. The trail still alternates between forest and meadows, but now with better views of Mammoth Peak, on your right as you climb. (The peak is a standout at 12,117 feet.) You'll pass another dilapidated old cabin at 2.9 miles.

Just before you reach the Mono Pass marker, 3.7 miles from the trailhead, take the unsigned spur trail on the right to see the 19th century log cabins. The spur leads gently uphill for a quarter-mile to a mining camp with a group of four cabins, sitting side-by-side. To the east of these cabins, about 50 yards away, you'll find some ore tailings, a slag pond, a mine shaft, and other remains. Hardy miners searched for silver here in the late 1870s. Little was found, and in this austere environment, the miners' mere existence was difficult.

After you've visited the cabins, return to the Mono Pass sign, then continue on the main trail for another half-mile beyond the pass. The trail is mostly level as it leaves the national park boundary and enters Inyo National Forest, passing a small pond along the way. Beyond the boundary sign, look for a group of high boulders off to the right of the trail, with a small lake hidden just below them. These boulders make a perfect picnicking spot, with an excellent vista looking down Bloody Canyon at Mono Lake, its neighboring volcanic craters, and the surrounding desert.

24. SPILLWAY LAKE

Tioga Road area, Yosemite National Park
High elevation lake and meadows

DISTANCE: 7.2 miles round-trip; 3.5 hours   **LEVEL:** Easy/moderate
ELEVATION: Start at 9,700 feet; total change 750 feet   **CROWDS:** Minimal
BEST SEASON: July to October   **RATING:** ★ ★ ★ ★

DIRECTIONS: From the Arch Rock entrance station at Yosemite National Park, drive east into the park for 4.5 miles to the turnoff for Tioga Road/Highway 120, which is Big Oak Flat Road. Turn left and drive 9.3 miles to Crane Flat, then turn right on Tioga Road/Highway 120 and drive 44.5 miles to the Mono Pass Trailhead parking on the south side of the road (near road marker T-37, 1.5 miles west of Tioga Pass).

The trail to Spillway Lake offers a more solitary hike than the neighboring trail to Mono Pass, plus some spectacular high-country scenery of its own. The two trails share the same pathway for the first two miles; read the description in the previous story for details. But at the two-mile point, where most hikers bear left for Mono Pass and its 1870s mining ruins, you bear right for Spillway Lake. (If you choose to hike both trail forks and visit both Mono Pass and Spillway Lake, you'll have a round-trip of 11 miles.)

From the junction, it's another 1.6 miles to Spillway Lake, with only 400 feet of elevation gain. The trail climbs gently alongside meadows, roughly following boisterous Parker Pass Creek. This stretch is very sunny, with only occasional lodgepole pines providing shade. (Wear a hat and plenty of sunscreen at this high elevation.)

The trail moves in close to the stream a mile from the junction, and enters a small stand of willows. Then it leads back out in the open again and climbs some more beneath the towering Kuna Crest's mammoth peaks. At 3.6 miles from the trailhead, you reach Spillway Lake, elevation 10,450 feet. It's hard to decide which is best—the rocky lake itself or the fragile, flowery, high-alpine meadow that surrounds it.

Deer in the meadows near Spillway Lake

Backpackers are not permitted to camp at Spillway Lake, so you'll probably have little company except perhaps other day-hikers. Take a swim, have a picnic, shoot some photographs, or lie down on a rock and take a nap. The good news is that the fun doesn't end when you leave—views of surrounding peaks are excellent all the way back down the trail.

25. MIDDLE & UPPER GAYLOR LAKES

Tioga Road area, Yosemite National Park
Two 10,000-foot-high lakes

DISTANCE: 4.0 miles round-trip; 2 hours **LEVEL:** Moderate
ELEVATION: Start at 9,960 feet; total change 1,100 feet **CROWDS:** Heavy
BEST SEASON: July to October **RATING:** ★ ★ ★ ★

DIRECTIONS: From the Arch Rock entrance station at Yosemite National Park, drive east into the park for 4.5 miles to the turnoff for Tioga Road/Highway 120, which is Big Oak Flat Road. Turn left and drive 9.3 miles to Crane Flat, then turn right on Tioga Road/Highway 120 and drive 46 miles to the parking lot just west of the Tioga Pass Entrance Station, on the north side of Tioga Road.

The trail to Middle and Upper Gaylor Lakes is incredibly popular, but that's simply because it is short in length and offers world-class scenery that wows visitors. Don't let the crowds stop you from making this hike; just get an early start and beat everybody to it.

Beginning near Tioga Pass at just shy of 10,000 feet in elevation, the trail makes a butt-kicking, high-altitude climb in its first three quarters of a mile. There's no opportunity for a warm-up; you just have to go for it, then pause as many times as necessary to catch your breath, slow down your racing heart, and beg for mercy. Luckily, views to the east of austere-looking Mount Dana hold your interest. Every steep step will soon prove worth the effort.

The great surprise of this hike is that after your difficult grunt up the ridge, you gain the top and see that Middle Gaylor Lake is not located there, it's far below you on the other side. Views of the lake are excellent and will encourage you to descend the 200 feet to reach it. The middle lake is set at 10,330 feet, and it's deep blue and remarkably large—the length of a few football fields. Anglers often try their luck from its shores. Lower Gaylor Lake, accessible by a cross-country ramble or by following the trail outlined on pages 229 to 231, can be seen to the west.

Middle and Upper Gaylor Lakes and Gaylor Peak from above

For now, head for Upper Gaylor Lake. From where the trail deposits you at the edge of the middle lake, hike to your right and then follow its inlet creek gently uphill to the east. A mile of rambling through pretty meadows will bring you to smaller Upper Gaylor Lake, elevation 10,500 feet. The lake is backed by singular, conical-shaped Gaylor Peak. Just to assure you that you're really in the high country, you'll probably see a marmot or pika peeking up from the rocks.

As scenic as this upper lake is, there's still more to see. Take the trail around the left (north) side of the lake and then hike steeply uphill for a few hundred yards. This will bring you to the site of the Great Sierra Mine and the remains of an old stone cabin, a souvenir of mining days in the early 1880s. The cabin itself is remarkable, built by layering rocks one on top of another, with walls as thick as two feet. It is in excellent condition. Even more remarkable is the view of Upper Gaylor Lake and Gaylor Peak from the high point where the cabin is located. It's a stunner. If you hike a few yards farther on the trail beyond the cabin, you'll find several mine shafts and other mine ruins.

The Great Sierra Mine, like most mines in this area, turned out to be not so great. No silver ore was ever refined and the mine was eventually abandoned. The town of Dana, which was built here in expectation of a huge influx of money and settlers, quickly became a ghost town. The hauntingly beautiful glacial scenery is what remains.

26. MOUNT DANA

Tioga Road area, Yosemite National Park
Yosemite's second highest peak

DISTANCE: 5.8 miles round-trip; 3 hours   **LEVEL:** Very strenuous
ELEVATION: Start at 9,960 feet; total change 3,100 feet **CROWDS:** Moderate
BEST SEASON: August to October   **RATING:** ★ ★ ★ ★ ★

DIRECTIONS: From the Arch Rock entrance station at Yosemite National Park, drive east into the park for 4.5 miles to the turnoff for Tioga Road/Highway 120, which is Big Oak Flat Road. Turn left and drive 9.3 miles to Crane Flat, then turn right on Tioga Road/Highway 120 and drive 46 miles to the parking lot just west of the Tioga Pass Entrance Station, on the north side of Tioga Road. This is the trailhead for Gaylor Lakes. For Mount Dana, cross Tioga Road and begin to hike on the unsigned trail for the summit. (Look for it just a few yards east of the entrance kiosk, leading from a parking pullout.)

Let's be honest: Mount Dana is a grueling hike. The 3,100-foot elevation change listed above is no typographical error, and what's worse, it's condensed into three miles of hiking. To make things more difficult, there's no maintained trail to the summit, just a huge variety of use trails created by the many Yosemite visitors who have made this epic climb.

But Mount Dana is worth the effort. If you're in good shape, if you have good hiking boots, and if you can withstand a tough uphill climb at high elevation, reaching the summit of Mount Dana is a thrill worth experiencing. Just follow these four rules: Get an early start (it is absolutely critical to beat any possible afternoon thunderstorms), carry plenty of water, wear good sunglasses and sun protection, and pace yourself in the thin air.

Located on the eastern border of Yosemite near the Tioga Pass entrance station, Mount Dana is Yosemite National Park's second highest peak at 13,057 feet. (Mount Lyell is the highest, but it's only 61 feet higher.) Because of its elevation, Mount Dana is covered with snow long after other Tioga Road destinations are snow-free. Wait until August or later to climb the peak, unless you have a lot of experience with snow climbing.

From the Gaylor Lakes Trailhead by the Tioga Pass entrance kiosk, cross Tioga Road and begin to hike on the unsigned but obvious trail to Mount Dana. The hike begins as a pleasant ramble through Dana Meadows, heading due east and gently uphill, then enters a thick lodgepole pine forest.

In a half-mile the grade becomes far more intense as you head into a series of rocky switchbacks that traverse a rocky slope. The plentiful and varied wildflowers will distract you as you climb, but watch for trail markers to keep you on the path. Feeling out of breath? No wonder; you're already above 11,000 feet. You get no relief until you reach the 11,600-foot mark, where a huge, high trail cairn marks a large plateau. Views are excellent from this spot, including the summit of Mount Dana, which up till now was hidden from view.

If you're feeling OK with the altitude, continue onward and upward. You still have 1,450 feet of elevation gain ahead, and a mile of hiking. The good trail you've been following basically ends, and a huge variety of use trails lead uphill from the plateau. Pick the one that seems the most well-used. As long as you're going up, you're going the right way. The continually expanding views will spur you on.

Somehow, with what may seem like your last breath, you finally reach the summit. Once there, you know why you came: You are witness to one of the finest views in all of the Sierra. Your field of vision encompasses 360 degrees: Mono Lake to the northeast is a standout, with its neighboring Mono Craters. Closer in, Ellery Lake sparkles deep blue alongside the highway to the north. Saddlebag Lake is farther north and slightly west. Tuolumne Meadows glows bright green to the west, marked by Lembert Dome on its eastern border. Visible high peaks are almost too numerous to mention, but some of the highlights are Mount Conness, Tuolumne Peak, Mount Hoffman, Cathedral Peak, Unicorn Peak, Mount Gibbs, and Mount Lyell. Bring a map and identify what you can, or forget the map and just take in the majesty of it all. The names of the landmarks mean little; the grandeur of the landscape says everything.

27. UPPER YOSEMITE FALL & YOSEMITE POINT

Yosemite Valley, Yosemite National Park
The brink of North America's highest waterfall

DISTANCE: 7.2 miles round-trip; 4 hours   **LEVEL:** Strenuous
ELEVATION: Start at 3,990 feet; total change 2,700 feet   **CROWDS:** Heavy
BEST SEASON: March to July   **RATING:** ★ ★ ★ ★ ★

DIRECTIONS: From the Arch Rock entrance station at Yosemite National Park, drive east into the valley for 10.5 miles. Just beyond the Yosemite Chapel, bear left at a fork signed for Yosemite Village and Visitor Center, then turn left and drive west on Northside Drive for three-quarters of a mile to the Yosemite Lodge parking lot. Turn left and park in the lot, then walk to the

Upper Yosemite Fall Trailhead, which is across the road and a quarter-mile to the west, between the parking lot for Sunnyside Walk-In Campground and the camp itself. You may not park in the Sunnyside lot unless you camp there. (If you are riding the free Yosemite Valley shuttle bus, take stop number 8 and walk to the trailhead.)

At a combined height of 2,425 feet—almost a half-mile— Yosemite Fall is ranked as the fifth highest free-falling waterfall in the world and the highest in North America. It is also probably the most visited and most famous waterfall in the world. Upper Yosemite Fall alone is a whopping 1,430 feet of plunging water. It leaps off the canyon rim, reaches a less-vertical chunk of rock and cascades for 675 feet, then hits a ledge and forms Lower Yosemite Fall, which plunges for another 320 feet.

Nearly 100 percent of all visitors to Yosemite Valley take the short and easy walk to the base of Lower Yosemite Fall. Far fewer, although still a huge number, decide to look at the falls from the top down, by climbing to the high lip of Upper Yosemite Fall.

Despite how tempting it seems, the hike to Upper Yosemite Fall is not for everybody. It's a grunt of a trip, climbing 2,700 feet over 3.6 miles one-way, with more than 100 switchbacks. Then on the return, you must jar your knees and ankles for another 3.6 miles heading downhill. The work is not in vain, however: The trail offers one heck of a view, and if you're in good shape, you shouldn't miss it.

In order to keep the crowds on the trail from trying your patience, start hiking as early in the morning as possible, and pick a weekday, preferably not during peak vacation season. (Summer is too hot on this trail, anyway, and by July the waterfall usually drops to a meager flow.)

From the trailhead near Sunnyside Campground, the route begins to climb immediately, switchbacking upward through oaks and manzanita. At 1.2 miles and 1,000 feet up, you reach Columbia Rock (5,031 feet), an extraordinary viewpoint that looks down over the valley floor and east toward Half Dome. Many people tire of the climb and are satisfied with the view from here, but if you push on, you get a sudden, surprising look at Upper Yosemite Fall at 1.4 miles, after a brief tromp downhill. For the next stretch of trail, you get a front seat perspective on the towering plume of water. You are eye to eye with the waterfall, close enough to feel its tremendous energy.

More ascent lies ahead, as the trail switchbacks above the trees and into a rocky area that is the recipient of frequent slides. In 1980, a rockfall covered about a mile of the trail here. The area is completely exposed and can be very warm, especially since your legs are pushing through a steady climb. Luckily, your view keeps getting more and more expansive and it will distract you from the hard work.

At 3.4 miles, you complete your ascent, and the trail levels out and heads east, reaching a trail junction. The left fork heads to Eagle Peak (see the following story). Go right toward Yosemite Point, then take the short right spur trail signed as "Overlook," which leads downhill on a treacherous set of granite stair-steps to near the edge of roaring Yosemite Creek—practically on top

Upper Yosemite Fall from the trail

of Upper Yosemite Fall. Check out the stunning view of the valley from this vantage point, but stay safely behind the metal railing.

Still haven't had enough? Go back to the main trail and continue another three-quarters of a mile, crossing a bridge above the falls, to Yosemite Point (6,936 feet). There you get an even better view of the south rim of the canyon, as well as Half Dome and North Dome, and a look at the top of Lost Arrow Spire, a single shaft of granite jutting into the sky.

If there is any downer to Yosemite Fall, it's that it doesn't run year-round. Plenty of first-time visitors show up in August or September, or any time during serious drought years, and wonder why the park rangers turned off the waterfall. Yosemite Fall drains a watershed that is composed of smooth, bare granite and little vegetation. Runoff from snowmelt and rainfall is rapid—the all-or-nothing effect of water on a hard, impenetrable surface. Once the rain and snow have drained, the waterfall show is over for the year. For the fullest flow of water, visit between March and June.

28. EAGLE PEAK

Yosemite Valley, Yosemite National Park
The highest rock of the Three Brothers formation

DISTANCE: 13.4 miles round-trip; 8 hours   **LEVEL:** Very strenuous
ELEVATION: Start at 3,990 feet; total change 3,800 feet   **CROWDS:** Moderate
BEST SEASON: May to October   **RATING:** ★ ★ ★ ★ ★

DIRECTIONS: From the Arch Rock entrance station at Yosemite National Park, drive east into the valley for 10.5 miles. Just beyond the Yosemite Chapel, bear left at a fork signed for Yosemite Village and Visitor Center, then turn left and drive west on Northside Drive for three-quarters of a mile to the Yosemite Lodge parking lot. Turn left and park in the lot, then walk to the Upper Yosemite Fall Trailhead, which is across the road and a quarter-mile to the west, between the parking lot for Sunnyside Walk-In Campground and the camp itself. You may not park in the Sunnyside lot unless you camp there. (If you are riding the free Yosemite Valley shuttle bus, take stop number 8 and walk to the trailhead.)

If you seek more of a challenge than the day hike to Upper Yosemite Fall, the trail to Eagle Peak gives you all of the stunning destinations of that trip—Columbia Point, Upper Yosemite Fall, Yosemite Point—plus an additional three miles one way to a lookout atop of the highest rock of the Three Brothers formation, Eagle Peak.

The Three Brothers, a distinct set of triple jagged pinnacles, can be viewed from almost anywhere in Yosemite Valley. From on top of Eagle Peak, you see not just the whole of Yosemite Valley, but also all the way to the mountains and foothills of the Coast Range to the west, and the tall, barren peaks of the Eastern Sierra to the east. Just make sure you pick a clear day to make your trip.

The mileage to Eagle Peak is long, so pack along plenty of snacks and water. To lighten your load, you can bring along a purification system and filter water out of Yosemite Creek. Although the distance involved makes this trip quite strenuous, keep in mind that by the time you've reached Upper Yosemite Fall, most of your work is over. This trail gains only 1,000 feet more between the waterfall and Eagle Point.

Follow the trail directions for Upper Yosemite Fall, detailed in the previous story. After taking the spur trail to the fall's brink, backtrack a quarter-mile to the trail junction for the Eagle Peak Trail. Follow the Eagle Peak Trail to the north for three quarters of a mile, enjoying the pleasant shade of firs and pines. You'll roughly parallel Yosemite Creek, traveling upstream until you reach a junction where the Yosemite Creek Trail continues north, and the Eagle Peak Trail curves west. Turn left.

Prepare for a short but steep climb. The ascent tops out at 7,000 feet when it reaches an area of hard granite littered with boulders. The path curves to the south, and a gentler climb continues for another mile to Eagle Peak Meadows. Beyond the meadow, the trail crosses Eagle Peak Creek and soon reaches a junction with El Capitan Trail. Bear left for the final three-quarter-mile ascent to your destination—the summit of Eagle Peak, elevation 7,779 feet. In short order, you'll find yourself sitting on top of the highest "brother" of the Three Brothers formation.

There is little surface area on the summit, and the wind can howl, but the view is awesome—particularly of the other two "brothers" and of Yosemite Valley, 4,000 feet below. It's difficult to believe that down *there* is where you began your hike and where you must return.

If the summit register is in place on Eagle Peak, be sure to peruse the comments of other hikers and add a few pithy words of your own. After completing this trip, you'll never view the Three Brothers the same way again.

29. LOWER YOSEMITE FALL

Yosemite Valley, Yosemite National Park
One of Yosemite's star attractions

DISTANCE: 0.5 mile round-trip; 20 minutes **LEVEL:** Easy
ELEVATION: Start at 3,990 feet; total change 50 feet **CROWDS:** Heavy
BEST SEASON: March to July **RATING:** ★ ★ ★ ★

DIRECTIONS: From the Arch Rock entrance station at Yosemite National Park, drive east into the valley for 10.5 miles. Just beyond the Yosemite Chapel, bear left at a fork signed for Yosemite Village and Visitor Center, then turn left and drive west on Northside Drive for three-quarters of a mile to the Lower Yosemite Fall parking lot on your right. (If you are riding the free Yosemite Valley shuttle bus, take stop number 7.)

Probably the most stunning sight from a walking path in Yosemite Valley is the straight-line view of Upper and Lower Yosemite Fall piggybacked one on top of the other, which awes visitors as they walk up the short trail to Lower Yosemite Fall. The great mountain tramp John Muir said, "Yosemite Fall comes to us as an endless revelation," and for once, he wasn't exaggerating.

No visit to Yosemite Valley would be complete without a stroll up the quarter-mile path from the Lower Yosemite Fall parking lot to the bridge below the falls. It's so short you can hardly call it a hike, and the route is paved and crawling with people, but, nonetheless, Lower Yosemite Fall is an absolute must-do walk for Yosemite visitors. One thing is for sure: You won't need a map for this trip.

From the Lower Yosemite Fall parking lot, head up the trail to the footbridge below the falls. Because the path is paved, wheelchairs and baby strollers can negotiate the trail. The route has only a slight uphill grade.

The viewing area for Lower Yosemite Fall is huge, sporting several benches and a wide footbridge across Yosemite Creek. It's inviting to have a seat and stay a while unless the falls are flowing like crazy, in which case you need to wear your rain gear if you want to hang around. In the spring, while standing at the footbridge below the falls, you can get soaked by mist so heavy it falls like rain.

Remember that from this viewpoint you are seeing only the lower portion of Yosemite Fall—a mere 320 feet of its total 2,425-foot height. Yosemite Fall in its entirety (upper, lower, and middle cascades) is the tallest waterfall in North America.

A special time to view Lower Yosemite Fall is on full moon nights in April and May, when lucky visitors get the chance to see pale-colored

Upper and Lower Yosemite Falls

"moon-bows" dancing in the waterfall's spray. It's an incredibly romantic treat. And speaking of romantic, check out Yosemite Fall in winter, when a giant ice cone forms at the base of the upper fall. Composed of frozen spray and fallen chunks of ice, the ice cone can sometimes grow to a height of 300 feet.

The only downer to Lower Yosemite Fall is that by late summer, it and its big brother, Upper Yosemite Fall, often dry up completely. If you like water in your waterfalls, plan your trip for sometime between March and July. And to avoid the masses, try to see the falls very early in the morning, when most park visitors are still in their beds or having breakfast.

If visiting Lower Yosemite Fall gives you a hankering to hike to Upper Yosemite Fall, be aware that you can't get there from here (even though you can see the upper fall on the first part of this walk). The only way to hike to the upper fall is from the trailhead near Sunnyside Campground. See the Upper Yosemite Fall story on page 249.

30. MIST TRAIL to VERNAL FALL

Yosemite Valley, Yosemite National Park
500 stairsteps to the brink of the fall

DISTANCE: 2.8 miles round-trip; 1.5 hours   **LEVEL:** Easy/moderate
ELEVATION: Start at 4,020 feet; total change 1,050 feet **CROWDS:** Heavy
BEST SEASON: March to July   **RATING:** ★ ★ ★ ★

DIRECTIONS: From the Arch Rock entrance station at Yosemite National Park, drive east into the valley for 11.6 miles to the day-use parking lot at Curry Village. From there, ride the free Yosemite Valley shuttle bus to Happy Isles, stop number 16. In winter, when the shuttle does not run, you must hike from the day-use parking lot in Curry Village, adding two miles to your round-trip. (Trails may be closed in winter; call to check on weather conditions.)

Vernal Fall on the Merced River is best described with a long line of superlatives punctuated by commas: awesome, majestic, breathtaking, magnificent, and so on. Or perhaps it is best described not with words at all, but by the millions of photographs, famous and not-so-famous, that have been taken of it over the years.

Like the trails to Lower Yosemite Fall and Bridalveil Fall, the Mist Trail to Vernal Fall is almost a prerequisite path for visitors to Yosemite Valley. Those traveling with very small children or those preferring not to climb can call it quits at the footbridge below Vernal Fall. This is a round-trip of only 1.5 miles and manageable by almost anyone.

But most park visitors grunt it out to the top of Vernal Fall, even if this is the only hike they take all year. What this means is that your field of trail companions is not just limited to people who call themselves hikers; those on the trail could be just about anyone who drives into Yosemite Valley. This being the case, you must follow the cardinal rules for hiking to Yosemite's celebrated sights: Be mentally prepared for hordes of people, and start as early in the morning as possible to get ahead of them.

Visiting Vernal Fall before summer vacation begins is also wise

Mist Trail to Vernal Fall

(weekdays are preferred). This will cut down on foot traffic and also allow you to see the waterfall's most prolific flow.

Happy Isles is your trailhead, reached via free shuttle bus from Curry Village or other points in the valley. Many people will remember Happy Isles as the site of the incredible rockslide of the summer of 1996, when a huge chunk of Glacier Point broke off and dropped 3,000 feet to the valley floor, devastating the area and killing one bystander. Today you must look hard to see evidence of the slide, since the granite rubble quickly becomes a normal-looking part of the ever-changing glacial landscape.

Walk three-quarters of a mile on the paved, moderately graded trail to the Vernal Fall footbridge. From there you get a good view of the beautiful 317-foot fall, a voluminous block of water that forms where the Merced River drops over vertically jointed rock. At peak flow, the fall can be as wide as 80 feet.

Some visitors shoot off a roll of film and turn back here, but if you don't mind some stair-climbing, continue to the top of the waterfall, a half-mile farther up the trail. This infamous route is called the Mist Trail, and it's as good as all the guidebooks say. At a trail fork shortly beyond the bridge, take the left fork that stays close to the water's edge. (The right fork is the John Muir Trail, which bypasses Vernal Fall.) The trail climbs up a steep granite staircase consisting of more than 500 steps, and curves tightly around the fall's right side. Sections of the trail are completely covered by the fall's billowing mist and spray. Raincoats are often a necessity in spring.

One note of caution: If you are traveling the Mist Trail with kids, keep a hand-hold on them. The wet stairs, combined with hundreds of people coming at you from ahead and behind, can be hazardous.

If you can look up from the sight of your feet clinging to the granite stairs, you'll notice a tremendous amount of moss and deep green foliage growing alongside the fall. This lush vegetation thrives even on granite because of Vernal Fall's nonstop misting action. When you reach the top of the fall and its overlook, you're in barren, exposed granite country again. Peer over the railing and look down into the swirling mist of Vernal Fall. The effect is stark, dramatic, and awe-inspiring. No doubt about it—this is a hike you must take at least once in your life.

If you're interested in hiking farther, note that you can continue to the top of Nevada Fall from this overlook. See the following story.

31. MIST & JOHN MUIR LOOP to NEVADA FALL

Yosemite Valley, Yosemite National Park
The grandeur of Vernal and Nevada falls on a loop hike

DISTANCE: 6.8 miles round-trip; 3.5 hours **LEVEL:** Moderate
ELEVATION: Start at 4,020 feet; total change 2,000 feet **CROWDS:** Heavy
BEST SEASON: March to July **RATING:** ★ ★ ★ ★ ★

DIRECTIONS: From the Arch Rock entrance station at Yosemite National Park, drive east into the valley for 11.6 miles to the day-use parking lot at Curry Village. From there, ride the free Yosemite Valley shuttle bus to Happy Isles, stop number 16. In winter, when the shuttle does not run, you must hike from the day-use parking lot in Curry Village, adding two miles to your round-trip. (Trails may be closed in winter; call to check on weather conditions.)

If you've made it to the top of Vernal Fall, chances are good that you'll feel so exhilarated that you'll want to keep hiking. Conveniently, Nevada Fall is located 1.5 miles up the trail from the top of Vernal Fall, requiring another 1,000 feet of elevation gain but with enough spectacular scenery to make it well worth your while.

Technically, you can hike either the John Muir Trail or the Mist Trail to reach Yosemite's classic Nevada Fall, but the best choice is to make a loop trip by hiking up on the Mist Trail, then back down on the John Muir Trail. The Mist Trail gives you the opportunity to hike alongside the Merced River and visit Vernal Fall on the way to Nevada Fall. (The John Muir Trail bypasses Vernal Fall and is routed farther from the river's edge.) Both trails join at two different points, above and below Nevada Fall, so you have some options.

Begin your trip at Happy Isles, following the trail to the footbridge across the Merced River below Vernal Fall. Turn left on the Mist

Nevada Fall and Liberty Cap

Trail and hike up to the overlook on top of Vernal Fall (see the previous story for details). From the top of Vernal Fall, continue uphill along the river's edge, still following the Mist Trail. In a half-mile, the path crosses the river, then climbs for another mile. The ascent is hard work, but your heart will pound more from the stunning views than from the cardiovascular workout. You'll ascend the left flank of Nevada Fall; views of it are spectacular from every angle.

Named after *nevada,* the Spanish word for snow-covered, Nevada Fall drops 594 feet like a liquid avalanche—a seemingly endless cataract of white, churning water. Whereas Vernal Fall is a square, block-shaped waterfall, Nevada has a more unusual shape, something like a horsetail or an inverted V.

From the fall's summit and overlook area, you have a less compelling vista than you had on your climb up. Still, if you lean over the piped railing (hold on tightly), you can look deep into the swirling mist at the bottom of the waterfall, which appears like a giant block of dry ice, clouded and mysterious.

For your return trip, cross the footbridge above Nevada Fall, then follow the John Muir Trail downhill. As you travel, keep looking over your shoulder for tremendous vistas of Nevada Fall framed by Liberty Cap and Half Dome. The best perspective is had as you lateral away from the fall along a rocky ledge, but you must turn around to see it.

You have a choice on your way back down: You can walk the entire route to the valley floor on the John Muir Trail, which is the less steep option. If you'd prefer to see Vernal Fall again and hike at least a portion of the stair-stepped Mist Trail again, you can transfer over to the Mist Trail at Clark Point, just above Vernal Fall.

32. HALF DOME

Yosemite Valley, Yosemite National Park
An epic hike and a cable climb

DISTANCE: 16.8 miles round-trip; 10 hours   **LEVEL:** Very strenuous
ELEVATION: Start at 4,020 feet; total change 4,800 feet   **CROWDS:** Heavy
BEST SEASON: June to October   **RATING:** ★ ★ ★ ★ ★

DIRECTIONS: From the Arch Rock entrance station at Yosemite National Park, drive east into the valley for 11.6 miles to the day-use parking lot at Curry Village. From there, ride the free Yosemite Valley shuttle bus to Happy Isles, stop number 16.

There's no argument about it: Half Dome is one of those once-in-your-life-you-gotta-do-it hikes. Just be sure you know what you're in for before you set out on this epic trail: You're looking at 16.8 miles round-trip, a 4,800-foot elevation gain, a cable climb that is not suitable for those afraid of heights, and an incredible amount of company. During the summer, about 500 people a day make this trip. Although you can backpack to Half Dome, by spending the night at Little Yosemite Valley, the majority of people make the journey as a day hike.

To do so, make sure you are prepared. Be in good physical condition. Wear sturdy boots. Bring a load of water and food with you; you'll be handing it out to others on the trail who are not so well prepared, as well as gulping it down yourself. It doesn't hurt to bring along some blister-repair first aid equipment and an extra pair of socks. (Your socks will be pretty grungy by the time you make it to the top.) Also pack rain gear, especially if it's early in the season and Vernal and Nevada falls are spraying water all over the trail. Lastly, get an early start (such as 7 A.M.) to beat the afternoon thunderstorms. Aim to reach the summit, and get off of it, as early as possible. Most people take about 10 hours to hike the entire round-trip, some take longer.

The adventure begins at Happy Isles. You can follow either the John Muir Trail or the Mist Trail up the Merced River to the top of Nevada Fall, but the obvious choice is the Mist Trail. It is the shorter, steeper trail, and it is also the more scenic trail, leading you directly alongside the river and passing both Vernal and Nevada falls. (See the previous story on Nevada Fall.) Most people stop for a rest break on top of Nevada Fall; this is 3.4 miles from Happy Isles and 2,000 feet up—almost halfway to Half Dome.

From the top of Nevada Fall, the Half Dome route continues uphill on the John Muir Trail on the north side of the Merced River.

It enters Little Yosemite Valley in another mile. The trail goes flat for a brief stretch; a right fork leads to the crowded backpackers' camp, 4.6 miles from the trailhead. Continue on the John Muir Trail for just shy of two miles to a junction where the John Muir Trail splits off from the Half Dome Trail. You head left for Half Dome. The next 1.5 miles continue to climb, but the trail is nicely shaded by a forest of incense cedars, firs, and pines.

When you leave the trees behind, you have only three-quarters of a mile remaining to reach the summit of Half Dome. The serious ascent begins here, with a series of granite stair-steps that lead to the top of a smaller dome alongside Half Dome. Walk across this dome, then descend slightly to reach the start of the infamous Half Dome cable climb.

For most hikers, everything usually goes smoothly up to this point. Here, anyone who has ever been afraid of heights should do some serious soul-searching before they begin the cable climb up Half Dome's eastern face. Turning around is not much of an option once you're halfway up. Even those who feel relatively comfortable with the extreme exposure, slippery granite surface, and 45-degree slope may find themselves 1) praying a lot; or 2) wishing there weren't so many other hikers sharing the 200-yard long cables, heading in the opposite direction. There is little or no room for error, either on your part or anyone else's. Muster your courage and your upper body strength before you start to climb. A pile of work gloves are usually available; put on a pair to protect your hands from the steel cables and improve your grip.

When you reach Half Dome's 8,842-foot summit, you'll be so thrilled that you made it that you'll forget all about your tired arms and feet. If there are no thunderstorms threatening as far as your eyes can see, you can stay on top for a while, savoring your accomplishment. From the summit, all of Yosemite Valley is in view, plus Clouds Rest, the Quarter Domes, Tenaya Canyon, the rounded dome of Mount Starr King, and distinctive Cathedral Peak.

Half Dome's bald granite summit is immense, so even if a crowd has assembled on top, there is plenty of room for everybody. Gatherings of more than 100 people on the summit are not uncommon on summer weekends. Over the years, many strangers have become friends on top of Half Dome. Explore around its broad surface all you wish, but make sure you stay safely away from the edges. And be sure to muster your courage again, and your caution, before you descend on the cables.

33. MIRROR LAKE & TENAYA CANYON LOOP

Yosemite Valley, Yosemite National Park
A scenic walk through Yosemite Valley history

DISTANCE: 4.6 miles round-trip; 2.5 hours   **LEVEL:** Easy
ELEVATION: Start at 4,020 feet; total change 80 feet   **CROWDS:** Heavy
BEST SEASON: March to July   **RATING:** ★ ★

DIRECTIONS: From the Arch Rock entrance station at Yosemite National Park, drive east into the valley for 11.6 miles to the day-use parking lot at Curry Village. From there, ride the free Yosemite Valley shuttle bus to Mirror Lake Junction, stop number 17. In winter, when the shuttle does not run, you must hike from the day-use parking lot in Curry Village, adding 1.5 miles to your round-trip.

In the late nineteenth century, visitors swarmed to Yosemite Valley to see the spectacular sights they'd heard and read about. Along with viewing the waterfalls and granite walls of this magnificent valley, tourists of the late 1800s wanted to see Mirror Lake, which was well known for its magnificent mirror-like reflections of surrounding peaks. Visitors came from miles around to travel the toll road to Mirror Lake and see the reflection of Half Dome in the lake's glassy surface. After a visit to the lake in 1880, Professor F.V. Hayden wrote in *The Great West:* "You are face to face with the perpendicular side of Half Dome. You are dazzled. You close your eyes for the moment. You pay 50 cents' toll and go home."

Mirror Lake is no less an attraction for Yosemite visitors today. The major difference, besides the increase in the size of the crowds and the disappearance of the 50-cent toll road, is that nowadays there's less lake than there used to be. Mirror Lake was never a true lake; it was, and is, a large, shallow pool in Tenaya Creek, which varies in size from season to season. Over the years, it has undergone the process of sedimentation—it has filled with sand and gravel from Tenaya Creek. Today, even in spring the lake is quite shallow.

Still, the reflections in Mirror Lake's surface are worth a look, and a hike beyond the lake into Tenaya Canyon is an opportunity to get away from Yosemite Valley's masses.

Start your trip from Mirror Lake Junction (take the free valley shuttle bus to stop number 17). Walk a half-mile on pavement to Mirror Lake, and do your best to enjoy the mass of humanity sharing the road with you. Your first stop is a lower pool, separated from Mirror Lake by a rock rubble dam. To make the reflection better in

Mirror Lake

Mirror Lake, early entrepreneurs built up the natural dam that was there by adding rocks.

By the lower pool and the roadside rest rooms, you can get off the pavement and on to a dirt trail. Take the right fork just beyond the lower pool and walk a few more yards to the edge of Mirror Lake. When Tenaya Creek is full of water, Mirror Lake is a sight to see. The view of Half Dome's 4,700-foot perpendicular face, seen from its base, is as awe inspiring today as it must have been 100 years ago. Directly in front of Half Dome is Ahwiyah Point; Mount Watkins is the prominent rounded peak on the left. The smooth trail at the lake's edge is bordered by a split-rail fence, and interpretive signs describe the history of Yosemite Valley and Mirror Lake.

After you've taken in the view, follow the foot trail beyond Mirror Lake up Tenaya Creek for 1.6 miles. The route is forested all the way, and offers continual looks at lovely Tenaya Creek and towering Half Dome. At a junction where the Snow Creek Trail veers left and heads uphill, continue straight, then cross Tenaya Creek on a footbridge. The trail then circles back on the south side of the stream. From this perspective, you have great views of both Half Dome (on your side of the creek) and Basket Dome (on the north side).

34. INSPIRATION & STANFORD POINTS

Yosemite Valley, Yosemite National Park
A climb with a view

DISTANCE: 7.6 miles round-trip; 4 hours   **LEVEL:** Strenuous
ELEVATION: Start at 4,400 feet; total change 2,250 feet   **CROWDS:** Moderate
BEST SEASON: June to October   **RATING:** ★ ★ ★

DIRECTIONS: From the Arch Rock entrance station at Yosemite National Park, drive east into the valley for 6.3 miles to the right fork for Highway

41/Wawona/Fresno. Bear right and drive 1.5 miles to the parking lots on both sides of the road just before you enter the Wawona Tunnel. The trailhead is at the parking lot on the left (south) side of the road.

You need a little inspiration? You came to the right place. The view from the Wawona Tunnel Trailhead should be enough to inspire you (check out the panorama of Yosemite Valley, El Capitan, Half Dome, and Bridalveil Fall), but if all the tour buses and the video camera-toting crowds get on your nerves, take this hike to Inspiration Point and Stanford Point beyond.

Be prepared to climb. The trail is uphill all the way but well graded. The first mile has numerous switchbacks, with fine views every time you face eastward toward Yosemite Valley and Half Dome. The trail climbs 1,000 feet over this stretch; your heart and lungs will notice. Three-quarters of a mile up the trail, you cross an old road. If you followed it to the left, you would end up at the Bridalveil Fall parking lot. This road was the original stage road into Yosemite Valley, built in 1875. It was replaced in the 1930s with the current Wawona Road, which you parked your car alongside.

Cross the road and continue climbing. At 1.3 miles you see evidence of the old road again and your path reaches Inspiration Point. Once considered one of Yosemite's scenic highlights, the view from Inspiration Point today is largely obscured by trees. No matter; keep

View from the trail to Inspiration Point

heading upward, marching through another 1,000-foot climb. This ascent is spread out over 2.5 miles, so after a half-dozen initial switchbacks, the grade is much easier. Most of the trail is in the trees, offering a cool climb. Eventually you cross Meadow Brook and reach your destination.

Perched on the valley's rim at Stanford Point, elevation 6,659 feet, you're 3.8 miles from the trailhead and you've climbed 2,250 feet. Your reward is an eagle-eye view of the valley floor 3,000 feet below, and a vista to the east of Half Dome and all its granite neighbors. To the west, you can observe Silver Strand Fall's 1,170-foot drop, formed where Meadow Brook takes a dive off Yosemite's south canyon wall. The fall is only a quarter-mile away, to your left as you face Yosemite Valley. If you hike late in the summer, you have less chance of seeing Silver Strand Fall take the plunge. (On the other hand, if it's too early in the summer, crossing Meadow Brook can be a dangerous undertaking. Snow can exist along this high, shady stretch of trail until late in June, and heavy snowmelt can make the stream impassable.)

Stanford Point makes an excellent lunch spot and turnaround point for a 7.6-mile day. But if you're still loaded with energy at this overlook, you can continue another three quarters of a mile to Crocker Point, elevation 7,090 feet, for an even better panorama. From Crocker Point, you can see Bridalveil Fall, as well as Half Dome and all of Yosemite Valley. Six-tenths of a mile farther is Dewey Point, by far the most stellar of these four overlooks, at elevation 7,485 feet. (For more information on Dewey Point, see the Pohono Trail story on page 278.) If you hike all the way from the Wawona Tunnel Trailhead to Dewey Point and back, you'll have made a 10-mile round-trip with a 3,000-foot elevation gain. Wow, what a day!

---

35. BRIDALVEIL FALL

Yosemite Valley, Yosemite National Park
The valley's most reliable waterfall

DISTANCE: 0.5 mile round-trip; 20 minutes **LEVEL:** Easy
ELEVATION: Start at 3,980 feet; total change 50 feet **CROWDS:** Heavy
BEST SEASON: April to July **RATING:** ★ ★ ★ ★ ★

DIRECTIONS: From the Arch Rock entrance station at Yosemite National Park, drive east into the valley for 6.3 miles to the right fork for Highway 41/Wawona/Fresno. Bear right at the fork, then turn left almost immediately into the Bridalveil Fall parking lot. The trail begins by the parking lot.

There's a story about a guy who visits Yosemite National Park for the first time and says to a park ranger, "I only have one day to spend in Yosemite. What should I do with my time?" And the park ranger says, "If I only had one day to spend in Yosemite, I'd just sit down and have myself a good cry."

Well, if you have only one day in Yosemite, stop your cryin' and make a beeline for Bridalveil Fall, which drops 620 feet over the south wall of Yosemite's canyon in a spectacular display of spray and mist. In spring, the water can flow with such force that seasoned waterfall-goers know to wear rain gear when visiting the fall's overlook. Otherwise, you just get wet.

Probably the best thing about Bridalveil Fall, besides its incredible beauty, is its reliability. Whereas other falls in Yosemite Valley can dry up completely by late summer, Bridalveil Fall has a dependable flow year-round. That's because Bridalveil Creek drains a large area, including a lush upper valley with plenty of vegetation and deep, rich soil, which acts as a sponge, releasing water slowly and steadily. In most months of the year, Bridalveil Fall is a continually replenished, swaying plume of white water.

Bridalveil Fall from the overlook

It's less than a quarter mile walk to the fall's overlook on a paved trail that is suitable for wheelchairs and baby strollers. Follow the trail from the parking lot, then take the right cutoff that is signed "Vista Point." The path also continues straight to Southside Drive, for folks who choose to walk to the falls from other points in the valley.

The small overlook area is about 70 yards from the falls. You can look straight up and see Bridalveil Creek plunging 620 feet off the canyon wall. In high wind, the fall billows and sways, and if you are lucky, you might see rainbows dancing in its mist. This is a guaranteed crowd-pleaser.

The trees within a quarter-mile of Bridalveil suffer from wind-pruning, the result of constant exposure to the downdrafts and spray of the fall. They look as if they've been tended by a mad gardener, who pruned only one side of each tree. The sound of the waterfall in spring and early summer is often as loud and staccato as gunshots, with the water dropping in great sheets and then billowing out in layers of mist.

As with the other famous sights of Yosemite Valley, a good plan is to visit Bridalveil Fall before 8 A.M., when nobody is around, but the morning light is perfect.

36. FOUR-MILE TRAIL

Yosemite Valley, Yosemite National Park
A hiker's route to Glacier Point

DISTANCE: 9.6 miles round-trip; 5 hours   **LEVEL:** Strenuous
ELEVATION: Start at 4,000 feet; total change 3,200 feet   **CROWDS:** Moderate
BEST SEASON: June to October   **RATING:** ★ ★ ★ ★

DIRECTIONS: From the Arch Rock entrance station at Yosemite National Park, drive east into the valley for 9.5 miles. The Four-Mile Trailhead is located next to mile marker V18, on the right side of the road. Park in the pullouts along the road.

Many, many years ago, I hiked the Four-Mile Trail on my first-ever visit to Yosemite. Everything went smoothly and I was having a terrific time until I reached the trail's high point and found a giant parking lot and refreshment stand located there. I was shocked and dismayed, then greatly amused. What, you mean I could have driven to Glacier Point?

If I had read the park map before I started, I would have known. But even now, although I certainly know that I can drive there, I still like to hike the Four-Mile Trail to Glacier Point at least once a year. It's partly out of nostalgia for that first wonderful Yosemite trip, but also because the Four-Mile Trail is a fine pathway, with a terrific destination. Somehow, your arrival at dramatic, view-filled Glacier Point is made all the more meaningful if you get there the hard way, by hiking uphill from the valley floor, gaining 3,200 feet in 4.8 miles. (The trail is not four miles, as the name implies.)

The Four-Mile Trail is partially shaded, and it makes a terrific day hike with an early morning start. You can have a leisurely brunch or lunch from your bird's-eye perch on Glacier Point. You don't even have to pack a picnic; just bring a few greenbacks and you can buy your lunch from the point's refreshment stand.

The first mile of trail is a bit pedestrian; the route starts out on pavement and the road noise from the valley floor can be annoying. The grade is initially quite moderate as the trail ascends through an oak and manzanita forest. It's not until 1.5 miles out, where the trail crosses a small stream, that the climb begins in earnest. The path carves a turn around the base of Sentinel Rock, heading first northeast and then southeast.

Most of the work gets done between 1.5 miles and 3.8 miles; plan on at least an hour of hiking time for that middle stretch, plus maybe a few rest breaks. (The top and bottom sections of the trail, in contrast, are much easier.)

While you climb, you are compensated for your efforts by increasingly fine views, which are only occasionally obstructed by trees. The oak forest now has white firs and other conifers mixed in. About halfway up, you'll have excellent views of Yosemite Fall; hopefully you've chosen to hike this trail early in the summer, when the falls are running hard. Don't be so distracted that you forget to watch your footing on the rocky trail. In several areas, there are steep dropoffs.

The switchbacks seem to go on and on, but now Sentinel Rock, El Capitan, and the Three Brothers are in view, and sooner than you'd expect—just shy of four miles from the trailhead—you'll leave the last switchback behind. The final mile of trail is a breeze, comparatively. The Yosemite Valley views are now simply awesome: You can see Upper and Lower Yosemite Fall and the Middle Cascades, Half Dome, North Dome, Basket Dome, Mount Watkins, Mirror Lake, Tenaya Canyon, and Clouds Rest.

It seems like it couldn't get any better, but then you reach the top. From Glacier Point's promontory, you get unobstructed views of just about everything that's good to see. Not only is Yosemite Valley in view, 3,200 feet below you, but there's also a complete panorama of Yosemite's major peaks and canyons. Vernal and Nevada falls can be seen and heard thundering in the Merced River Canyon. Half Dome is a granite monolith, too large in size to comprehend. And so on.

Buy yourself some lunch and explore the point. A quarter-mile paved trail leads around it; check out the new amphitheater (constructed in 1998) and the old Geology Hut. Most of all, savor the drama of the view. Now aren't you glad you hiked up here instead of driving?

37. McGURK MEADOW

Glacier Point Road, Yosemite National Park
A wildflower-filled meadow and an old pioneer cabin

DISTANCE: 2.0 miles round-trip; 1 hour **LEVEL:** Easy
ELEVATION: Start at 7,100 feet; total change 250 feet **CROWDS:** Minimal
BEST SEASON: June to October **RATING:** ★ ★ ★ ★

DIRECTIONS: From the Arch Rock entrance station at Yosemite National Park, drive east into the valley for 6.3 miles to the right fork for Highway 41/Wawona/Fresno. Bear right at the fork, then drive 9.2 miles to the Glacier Point Road turnoff. Turn left and drive 7.5 miles to the McGurk Meadow Trailhead on the left. Park in the pullout about 75 yards farther up the road.

The McGurk Meadow Trail is an often-overlooked path that leads through a lovely fir and pine forest to a pristine, mile-long meadow with a stream meandering through its center. It's easily as beautiful (although not nearly as large) as Tuolumne Meadows, but without all the people. The trail also travels right past an old pioneer cabin still standing in half-decent repair, a remnant of bygone days when sheep and cattle ranchers grazed their stock in Yosemite.

After parking at the pullout, walk west along the road for about 70 yards to the McGurk Meadow trailhead sign. Fifteen minutes of downhill hiking on a forested trail will bring you to the pioneer cabin, only eight-tenths of a mile from the trailhead. Built with logs and nails, the cabin must have been used only in the summer, as its front door is so low that it would be covered by snow in the winter.

After you pass the old cabin, a few more footsteps take you to the edge of McGurk Meadow, where a trail sign points you to Dewey Point in three miles and Glacier Point in seven. No need to hike that far, though, since this meadow is a perfect destination in and of itself. A footbridge carries you over a small stream, which cuts long, narrow "S" marks end over end through the tall grass.

For a too-brief period, usually in July and August, McGurk Meadow abounds with wildflowers. If you time your trip carefully, you can see a stunning display of purple alpine shooting stars with tiny rings of white and yellow, their stigma tips pointing to the ground like bowed heads. Hundreds of corn lilies may also flower, along with patches of penstemon, Indian paintbrush, gentian, lupine, and yampah.

Cross the footbridge and walk to McGurk Meadow's far side, where the trail turns right and skirts the meadow's edge as it abuts with the forest. You'll add another quarter-mile to your trip by walking the

Shooting stars in McGurk Meadow

path along the length of the pristine meadow. When the trail heads away from the meadow and deeper into the forest, turn around and retrace your steps.

Note that some hikers use McGurk Meadow as a starting point for the trip to Dewey Point, a spectacular overlook on the south wall of Yosemite Valley. This eight-mile round-trip from Glacier Point Road (with an amazingly easy 300-foot elevation gain) is highly recommended, especially for those who do not wish to hike the entire Pohono Trail, which also travels to Dewey Point. See the Pohono Trail story on page 278 for more information on Dewey Point.

38. BRIDALVEIL CREEK

Glacier Point Road, Yosemite National Park
An easy ramble through meadows and wildflowers

DISTANCE: 3.0 miles round-trip; 1.5 hours   **LEVEL:** Easy
ELEVATION: Start at 7,000 feet; total change 70 feet   **CROWDS:** Minimal
BEST SEASON: June to October   **RATING:** ★ ★

DIRECTIONS: From the Arch Rock entrance station at Yosemite National Park, drive east into the valley for 6.3 miles to the right fork for Highway 41/Wawona/Fresno. Bear right at the fork, then drive 9.2 miles to the Glacier Point Road turnoff. Turn left and drive 9.0 miles to the Ostrander Lake Trailhead on the right.

Maybe the best time to hike to Bridalveil Creek from Glacier Point Road is immediately after visiting Bridalveil Fall. In contrast to its massive, 620-foot waterfall, the upstream area of Bridalveil Creek is a babbling brook that seems far too tame to be able to produce the downstream spectacle.

The trail to Bridalveil Creek is the same as the Ostrander Lake Trail for the first 1.4 miles. Start walking from the trailhead on Glacier Point Road, taking an incredibly easy stroll on level terrain. A quarter mile in, you'll cross a sturdy footbridge over a stream. The landscape is a mix of meadows and a regenerating forest, recovering from a fire. The blaze occurred in 1987, and already a huge amount of new growth can be seen, including small trees. If it wasn't for the still standing, charred trunks of lodgepole pines, it would be difficult to tell that a forest fire had raged through here.

The path is framed by colorful bunches of lupine and larkspur. On the trunks of taller trees, yellow markers are nailed up high to alert cross-country skiers of the general direction of the snow-covered trail. In wintertime, Ostrander Lake is a popular cross-country skiing destination. A ski hut is located along its shores.

Bridalveil Creek

When the trail splits at 1.4 miles, take the right fork toward Bridalveil Creek. You reach it in less than a quarter mile. The stream is so tame here that there is no bridge crossing it—it's an easy rock-hop by midsummer. By September, the water is only a few inches deep. Pick a spot along its banks, then spend some time counting the wildflowers or watching the small, darting trout. (If you take this hike early in the summer, the little stream will be more like a raging river—difficult or even deadly to cross.)

It would be wise to pack along a wildflower

identification book. From late June to August, you'll see columbine, brodiaea, bluebells, groundsel, and paintbrush, as well as the more common lupine and larkspur.

The mileage noted above suggests a turnaround at Bridalveil Creek, but if you like, you can cross it and continue hiking for 1.8 miles all the way to Bridalveil Campground. The trail remains similarly level, and the wildflowers continue. A popular option for hikers who stay in the campground is to have a companion drop them off at the Ostrander Lake Trailhead. Then they can make an easy, one-way hike of 3.3 miles back to the campground.

39. OSTRANDER LAKE

Glacier Point Road, Yosemite National Park
A not-too-steep hike to an alpine lake

DISTANCE: 12.6 miles round-trip; 7 hours   **LEVEL:** Moderate
ELEVATION: Start at 7,000 feet; total change 1,600 feet   **CROWDS:** Moderate
BEST SEASON: June to October   **RATING:** ★ ★ ★ ★

DIRECTIONS: From the Arch Rock entrance station at Yosemite National Park, drive east into the valley for 6.3 miles to the right fork for Highway 41/Wawona/Fresno. Bear right at the fork, then drive 9.2 miles to the Glacier Point Road turnoff. Turn left and drive 9.0 miles to the Ostrander Lake Trailhead on the right.

Getting to Ostrander Lake is easy, maybe even too easy. The trail mileage is long enough to sound like a solid day hike—12.6 miles— but the elevation gain is a mere 1,600 feet. By Yosemite standards, that's not much. In fact, the trail to the lake is so moderately graded that in winter, it is a popular cross-country skiing route.

Your hiking companions will most likely be weekend backpackers who have obtained wilderness permits to camp near the lake's shores. Because the trailhead is located far out on Glacier Point Road, and because the trail mileage is so long, most day-hikers don't consider making the trip. Nonetheless, Ostrander Lake is a great day hike destination. Although the fishing is lousy, the swimming is fine. Wildflower lovers will find plenty to enjoy along the meadowy walk to the lake.

The first half of the trail—three miles' worth—is nearly flat. The first section traverses a series of meadows and a regenerating lodgepole pine forest, which was badly burned in a 1987 wildfire. Wildflowers are excellent along this stretch. At 1.4 miles, you reach a junction, where the right trail leads to Bridalveil Creek. Bear left and stroll onward, crossing a small stream, to reach another junction at 2.5 miles. Bear left again. A few hundred yards later, your climb begins, as you switchback up Horizon Ridge on an old road. Since you've only climbed about 100 feet thus far on the trail, you still have 1,500 feet of elevation gain ahead. (The work has to start some time.)

The first part of the ascent is shaded by firs and pines, but soon the trail enters a more exposed granite area. Then it's back into the forest again. Upward you climb. Nearing six miles out, you reach the highest point on this trail, a saddle on top of 8,700-foot Horizon Ridge. Views of Half Dome, North Dome, Basket Dome, Liberty Cap, and Mount Starr King will make you stop to catch your breath and gaze in admiration.

Less than a half-mile farther, you reach Ostrander Lake, after a short downhill stretch. The wide, blue lake is set at 8,580 feet. The stone building you see on the right is the Ostrander Ski Hut, which is reserved by the Yosemite Association for early spring ski trips. (The yellow markers posted high up on trees along the trail are the skiers' trail signs.) The lake is bounded by the rocky, talus slope of Horse Ridge and a thick fir and pine forest. It's similar in size to the Cathedral Lakes or May Lake on Tioga Road but has more trees and less granite. A few sandy, bouldery beach areas make good swimming, sunbathing, and picnicking spots.

40. MONO MEADOW & MOUNT STARR KING VIEW

Glacier Point Road, Yosemite National Park
A granite picnic spot with a view

DISTANCE: 3.6 miles round-trip; 2 hours
ELEVATION: Start at 7,000 feet; total change 400 feet
BEST SEASON: June to October
LEVEL: Easy/moderate
CROWDS: Minimal
RATING: ★ ★

DIRECTIONS: From the Arch Rock entrance station at Yosemite National Park, drive east into the valley for 6.3 miles to the right fork for Highway 41/Wawona/Fresno. Bear right at the fork, then drive 9.2 miles to the Glacier Point Road turnoff. Turn left and drive 10.1 miles to the Mono Meadow Trailhead on the right. The trail begins on the left side of the parking area.

If you've driven to Glacier Point and reveled in the view but felt discouraged by the crowds, here's your chance to get away from them. Just a few miles west of the point is the trailhead for Mono Meadow,

Mount Starr King from the overlook

one of the least-used starting points along Glacier Point Road. The trail's primary travelers are not day hikers; they're backpackers heading off on multiday trips to far-off lakes. As a result, you have a better chance at solitude here than anywhere else around Glacier Point. The trail leads to a wide meadow filled with wildflowers in early summer, followed by a granite knoll with a view of Mount Starr King, Half Dome, and Clouds Rest.

Got your picnic supplies packed? Good. Begin your hike with a half-mile downhill tromp on the Mono Meadow Trail. Have no fear; the 250 feet of elevation that you're losing is easily gained back on your return. The trail bottoms out at Mono Meadow, a series of wet meadows interspersed with lodgepole pines. The pines are doing their best to infiltrate the meadow and eventually turn it into a forest; in another few hundred years, they probably will succeed. The meadows are perpetually marshy; you may get your boots wet as you cross them. Water-loving purple shooting stars bloom profusely here.

Beyond the meadows, the trail re-enters the trees. This is a remarkably dense forest of red and white firs, with a huge amount of branch litter and fallen trees. It has been a long time, perhaps too long, since the occurrence of a forest fire, which would clear away the debris and make way for new growth.

You reach a view-less clearing off to the left, then cross a tributary to Illilouette Creek. (You have to boulder-hop or ford carefully; there's no bridge.) The trail starts to climb on the far side of the big creek, then tops out a few minutes later at your destination. Look for a clearing to the left of the trail, where a granite knoll has only a few trees growing on it. Leave the trail and head for the knoll, then wander around it to locate the best viewing spot (you have to get up high and peer around the trees, which partially block the view). The big, rounded dome you see is Mount Starr King, elevation 9,092 feet—the most prominent dome in this area. Also in view are Half Dome, only 250 feet lower (to the left of Starr King, across the giant chasm of the Merced River canyon) and Clouds Rest, 850 feet higher than Starr King, but farther away. Directly east is Mount Clark, Gray Peak, and the Clark Range.

OK, so the view is not quite as good as at Glacier Point. But then again, there are no parking lots and no tour buses anywhere nearby. Time to pull out your picnic supplies and cherish the peace and quiet.

41. SENTINEL DOME

Glacier Point Road, Yosemite National Park
A granite dome with a world-class view of Yosemite Valley

DISTANCE: 2.4 miles round-trip; 1 hour   **LEVEL:** Easy
ELEVATION: Start at 7,700 feet; total change 400 feet   **CROWDS:** Moderate
BEST SEASON: June to October   **RATING:** ★ ★ ★ ★ ★

DIRECTIONS: From the Arch Rock entrance station at Yosemite National Park, drive east into the valley for 6.3 miles to the right fork for Highway 41/Wawona/Fresno. Bear right at the fork, then drive 9.2 miles to the Glacier Point Road turnoff. Turn left and drive 13.2 miles to the Taft Point/Sentinel Dome Trailhead parking lot, on the left side of the road.

It's hard to believe you can get so much for so little, but on the Sentinel Dome Trail, you can. The granite dome is located about a mile west of Glacier Point, and its elevation is 1,000 feet higher than the point's. That means stellar views are yours for the asking. The Sentinel Dome Trail gives you a complete understanding of the word "panorama."

You'd expect a view like this to come with a price, but since the trailhead is conveniently located at 7,700 feet in elevation, reaching the top of Sentinel Dome at 8,122 feet requires only a brief ascent. Even very small children can make it to the top.

A nearly flat one-mile walk leads you to the base of Sentinel

Dome. From the Taft Point/Sentinel Dome trailhead, take the path to the right. Hike very gently uphill on the easy-to-follow trail. The terrain is mostly exposed granite except for some Jeffrey pines and white firs. In summer, tiny purple and white mountain wildflowers bring a splash of color to the ground. As you near the dome, the Yosemite Valley views grow more spectacular. You'll enter a grove of old-growth fir trees and then approach Sentinel Dome from the southeast side. Your trail meets up with an old, once-paved road, which leads around the right side of the dome to its northern flank. (Stay left at two junctions.)

You're deposited right at the base of Sentinel Dome. Leave the trail to climb up the granite slope. The route is obvious, and you'll probably see others ahead of you. In a matter of a few minutes, you're on top.

The view is simply amazing. You can see both Lower and Upper Yosemite Fall and the Middle Cascades. Other landmarks include El Capitan, Half Dome, Basket Dome, North Dome, Quarter Dome, Tenaya Canyon, Liberty Cap, and Nevada Fall. If you hike this trail early enough in the year, you can see as many as five waterfalls in one peek (and on one peak), including some that are rarely seen, such as

Little hiker on top of Sentinel Dome

Pywiack Cascade and Bunnell Cascade. Bring your camera for this trip, because few places in the park offer such spectacular views. In all of Yosemite Valley, only Half Dome is a higher summit, and reaching it is a heck of a lot more work.

Expect the wind to be fierce on top of Sentinel Dome. Although there's almost no soil structure at all, a few plants manage to dig their roots into the hard granite and survive. Among them are a couple of manzanita bushes, as well as wildflowers tucked into creases in the rock.

To make a longer day out of your trip to Sentinel Dome, you can easily combine this hike with the following trail to Taft Point and The Fissures. That trail begins at the same trailhead but heads in the opposite direction. It is also possible to make a loop hike from Sentinel Dome to Taft Point, by connecting with the Pohono Trail (north of the dome) and following it to the west for 1.5 miles until it junctions with the Taft Point Trail.

42. TAFT POINT & THE FISSURES

Glacier Point Road, Yosemite National Park
A breathtaking overlook of Yosemite Valley

DISTANCE: 2.2 miles round-trip; 1 hour   **LEVEL:** Easy
ELEVATION: Start at 7,700 feet; total change 250 feet   **CROWDS:** Moderate
BEST SEASON: June to October   **RATING:** ★ ★ ★ ★

DIRECTIONS: From the Arch Rock entrance station at Yosemite National Park, drive east into the valley for 6.3 miles to the right fork for Highway 41/Wawona/Fresno. Bear right at the fork, then drive 9.2 miles to the Glacier Point Road turnoff. Turn left and drive 13.2 miles to the Taft Point/Sentinel Dome Trailhead parking lot, on the left side of the road.

It's not so much the sweeping vista from Taft Point that you remember, although certainly the point's views of Yosemite Valley and its north rim are stunning. Instead, what sticks in your mind is the incredible sense of awe that you felt, perhaps mixed with a little fear and a lot of respect, as you peeked over the edge of Taft Point's 3,000-foot cliff, or looked down into The Fissures in Taft Point's granite—huge cracks in the rock that plunge hundreds of feet down toward the valley.

The Taft Point Trail starts off innocently enough from the same trailhead as the Sentinel Dome Trail (see the previous story). Take the path to the left through a dense forest of Jeffrey pine, lodgepole pine, and white fir. In the first quarter-mile, you pass by a large pile of white quartz on your right, its orange and grey veins visible upon closer inspection.

Continue through the forest and cross a couple of small creeks, including one that is surrounded by dense corn lilies and grasses. At nearly one mile out, the trees disappear and you begin to descend along a rocky slope. The trail more or less vanishes on the granite; just head toward Yosemite Valley. In a few hundred feet, you reach the edge of the cliff you're standing on. You expect to be able to see some distance down, but nothing can prepare you for how far down it is.

If you can stop your knees from knocking, walk a few hundred feet farther, contouring along the edge of the cliff. Head for the metal railing you see at the high point on top of Profile Cliff. On the way, you'll pass a few of The Fissures, remarkably skinny clefts in the cliff that drop straight down to the valley below. One of The Fissures has a couple of large granite boulders captured in its jaws; they're stuck there waiting for the next big earthquake or Ice Age to set them free. Then they'll make a half-mile, one-way journey to the valley floor.

The high overlook on Profile Cliff caps off the trip. Its railing, a meager piece of metal, performs an important psychological job. Although it's only a hand rail, it takes away some of the fear of peering 3,000 feet straight down, because you can clutch it tightly while you gawk at the view. If you have kids with you, be sure to keep a firm hand-hold on them.

Taft Point and Profile Cliff

At 7,503 feet in elevation, Profile Cliff is approximately the same height as 7,569-foot El Capitan, which means you get the same kind of unnerving view as those daring rock climbers on El Cap. Squint carefully, or pull out your binoculars, and you can see those El Capitan climbers almost directly across from you.

Also in view are Upper Yosemite Fall across the valley, the Merced River cutting down in front of El Capitan, and tiny cars parked near the meadow by its side. From this height you can't see Lower Yosemite Fall, which is obscured in the canyon, but you get a rare look at the stream that feeds the upper falls.

Walk another hundred yards to the west to reach Taft Point proper, which has even better views of El Capitan. There is no railing here, but the clifftop is broad enough so that you can locate a safe, and view-filled, picnic spot.

To make a longer day out of your trip to Taft Point, you can easily combine this hike with the previous trail to Sentinel Dome. The best option is to hike back on the Taft Point Trail for a half-mile, then bear left at a trail junction. Follow the Pohono Trail for 1.5 miles to the Sentinel Dome cutoff, then turn right and follow the trail uphill to the dome. To finish out your loop, you can circle back to the parking lot on the Sentinel Dome Trail.

43. POHONO TRAIL

Glacier Point Road, Yosemite National Park
A one-way hike along Yosemite's south rim

DISTANCE: 13.0 miles one-way*; 7 hours
ELEVATION: Start at 7,200 feet; end at 4,400 feet*
BEST SEASON: June to October

LEVEL: Strenuous
CROWDS: Moderate
RATING: ★ ★ ★ ★

DIRECTIONS: From the Arch Rock entrance station at Yosemite National Park, drive east into the valley for 6.3 miles to the right fork for Highway 41/Wawona/Fresno. Bear right at the fork, then drive 9.2 miles to the Glacier Point Road turnoff. Turn left and drive 15.7 miles to Glacier Point. Park and walk toward the main viewing area, across from the cafe and gift shop. Look for the Pohono Trail sign about 150 feet southeast of the cafe building.

*****NOTE:** This is a one-way hike requiring a car shuttle. The elevation listings reflect the elevations at the start and finish of the trail. The majority of the hike is downhill, but the trail also climbs about 1,500 feet.

If you can arrange a shuttle trip, the Pohono Trail from its start at Glacier Point to its end at Wawona Tunnel has some incredible offerings. For starters, the two ends of the trail have the best drive-to viewpoints in all of Yosemite. In between, you are treated to dozens of other scenic spots, including Sentinel Dome at 1.5 miles, Taft Point at 3.8 miles, as well as four bird's-eye lookouts over the valley floor: Dewey, Crocker, Stanford, and Inspiration points. It makes for a day of hiking that you'll long remember.

First, understand that you have some options for customizing your trip. Starting at Glacier Point and ending at Wawona Tunnel, the Pohono Trail covers a 2,800-foot descent, but there are some considerable "ups" along the way, too. The first uphill is from Glacier Point to Sentinel Dome, right at the start of the trail. This is why many people start hiking at the Sentinel Dome/Taft Point trailhead instead of Glacier Point. They take a more level path to Sentinel Dome, then continue downhill on the Pohono Trail.

Some hikers (who presumably have visited Sentinel Dome on another trip) begin at the Sentinel Dome/Taft Point trailhead and head directly west to Taft Point, skipping the first two miles of the Pohono Trail altogether. A final option, for those who want to avoid climbing as much as possible, is to start hiking at the McGurk Meadow Trailhead farther west on Glacier Point Road. An easy trail of 2.5 miles leads you through lovely McGurk Meadow to connect with the Pohono Trail. Turn left (west) and enjoy a gentle 2.5-mile climb to Dewey Point, followed by a downhill hike of five miles to the Wawona Tunnel, passing Dewey, Crocker, Stanford, and Inspiration Points. (You'll miss out on Taft Point and Sentinel Dome, but you can always make a separate day hike to them. See the stories on pages 274 and 276.)

Leaving those shorter (but still excellent) options up to you, I'll give you a synopsis of the entire Pohono Trail. The trail begins at Glacier Point at a sign for the Panorama Trail and Pohono Trail. Take the Pohono Trail to the right, crossing Glacier Point Road and heading uphill through fir forest. You gain 800 feet in the first 1.5 miles, which is why many hikers choose to forego it.

At a junction with the spur trail to Sentinel Dome, leave the Pohono Trail, turn left and follow the spur uphill to the base of the 8,122-foot dome. Scramble up its north side for one of the best 360-degree views in all of Yosemite, including an unusual look at Yosemite Fall. (For details on Sentinel Dome, see the story on page 274.)

With this fine side trip completed, retrace your steps down Sentinel Dome and back to the Pohono Trail, then continue west, heading downhill through the forest. You'll cross Sentinel Creek, which may or may not be dry, then climb back uphill to a junction with the Taft Point Trail (1.5 miles from Sentinel Dome).

Continue west for a half-mile, then veer right on to granite slabs, heading a few hundred feet off the trail to visit Taft Point, Profile Cliff, and The Fissures, elevation 7,503 feet. The view of El Capitan from Taft Point will knock your socks off. So will the tremendous dropoff from Profile Cliff. (See the Taft Point story on page 276.)

From Taft Point, rejoin the Pohono Trail from where you left it and continue west again. The trail makes a 680-foot descent, curving south and away from the spectacular valley rim. There's a long, view-less stretch in the trees before you return to the rim. After crossing Bridalveil Creek on a footbridge, 2.5 miles from Taft Point, bear right at a trail fork and prepare for a serious climb ahead. Remember all that elevation you just lost? Now you have to gain it back. Your destination is spectacular Dewey Point, a 680-foot climb over two miles.

Dewey Point at 7,485 feet in elevation is at least as spectacular as Taft Point, perhaps more so. Whereas Taft Point's view of Yosemite Valley is more direct, Dewey Point gives you a perspective looking deep into Tenaya Canyon and the east end of Yosemite Valley. Standout granite landmarks are Half Dome, Clouds Rest, Sentinel Dome, Cathedral Rocks, and Cathedral Spires. Imagine standing on top of Clouds Rest (perhaps you have in real life); this is the opposite view of what you see from its summit. Directly across from Dewey Point is the obvious granite stain of a dry waterfall—that's Ribbon Fall, which drops 1,612 feet for a very short season in spring and early summer.

When you can tear yourself away, return to the Pohono Trail. You still have 3,000 feet of elevation loss ahead of you, and it will occur in the next five miles.

Dewey Point on the Pohono Trail

Luckily, there are many stops along the way. The first is only six-tenths of a mile from Dewey Point. It's Crocker Point, elevation 7,090 feet. Here your perspective on Yosemite is different again. You get your first look at Bridalveil Fall, off to the right (you see its profile, not a front view). Also in view are Cathedral Rocks, the Three Brothers, Clouds Rest, El Capitan, and far-off Mount Hoffman. (High praise for the Creator is in order.) Hike another seven-tenths of a mile and reach Stanford Point, elevation 6,659 feet. Here, the trail and the valley rim have curved more to the north, so your perspective on Half Dome changes considerably. You see more of its sharp, flat, vertical face. Your view of Yosemite Valley is a more western perspective.

Although Dewey, Crocker, and Stanford points are quite close together, the Pohono Trail now makes another long, forested descent away from the valley rim. It's 2.5 miles farther to Inspiration Point, and the downhill gets serious here, even moving into some switchbacks. Compared to the other overlooks, Inspiration Point is a disappointment—the trees have obscured the view. But keep hiking downhill, and you'll soon get more vistas, each time the trail switches back to face east. A half-mile below Inspiration Point, you cross an old dirt road; pick up the Pohono Trail on the other side and keep descending. Enjoy the final valley views as you drop down to the Wawona Tunnel parking area, where (hopefully!) your car shuttle will be waiting for you.

One piece of advice: Remember to bring along a good map on this trip. Some of the best destinations are just off the main Pohono Trail. If you don't take the short spur routes to reach them, you'll miss out on some spectacular scenery.

44. ILLILOUETTE FALL

Glacier Point Road, Yosemite National Park
An early season Yosemite waterfall

DISTANCE: 4.0 miles round-trip; 2 hours   **LEVEL:** Moderate
ELEVATION: Start at 7,200 feet; total change 1,200 feet   **CROWDS:** Moderate
BEST SEASON: June to August   **RATING:** ★ ★ ★ ★

DIRECTIONS: From the Arch Rock entrance station at Yosemite National Park, drive east into the valley for 6.3 miles to the right fork for Highway 41/Wawona/Fresno. Bear right at the fork, then drive 9.2 miles to the Glacier Point Road turnoff. Turn left and drive 15.7 miles to Glacier Point. Park and walk toward the main viewing area, across from the cafe and gift shop. Look for the Panorama Trail sign about 150 feet southeast of the cafe building, on your right.

Of all the ways to see Yosemite's sights, a short walk on the Panorama Trail is one of the best. The trailhead is located just steps away from the huge, busy parking lots at Glacier Point, but most people who visit that scenic drive-to overlook never set foot on it. Not only does the Panorama Trail give you the same vistas you get at Glacier Point minus the crowds, but a two-mile walk on the trail will bring you to the brink of spectacular Illilouette Fall.

To see the waterfall at its best, time your trip for early in summer, as close as possible to Glacier Point Road's opening.

The Panorama Trail starts at 7,200 feet in elevation at Glacier Point, just to the right of the main viewing area. Both the Pohono and Panorama trails share this trailhead, but you'll take the Panorama Trail, heading north. A trail sign states that Illilouette Fall is two miles away, but you quickly forget about the destination as the journey provides eyeful upon eyeful of grandeur. In your first footsteps, your view encompasses Half Dome, Basket Dome, North Dome, Liberty Cap, Vernal and Nevada falls, and many peaks and ridges beyond. The scenery changes with every footstep; a different perspective on the panorama is offered with each passing moment.

Illilouette Fall

The Panorama Trail slowly switchbacks downhill, curving through a fire-scarred area. Chaparral growth proliferates, as is typical after a fire, including ceanothus, bear clover, and deerbrush, plus young dogwood trees. Deer adore the leafy foliage found on the slopes. On several trips here, I've had a few does or a buck for companions along the trail.

After a series of switchbacks, the Panorama Trail junctions with a trail leading to Mono Meadow, but continue left for Illilouette Fall. In a few minutes more you reach an overlook directly across from the waterfall. You may be surprised to find that you've approached the fall sideways, rather than from behind or in front. That's because Illilouette doesn't pour from the back of a canyon; it rushes over its side cliff, where the creek drops 370 feet over a granite lip. The canyon is pencil-thin with vertical rock walls, so the only vantage point is from the side. It's a spectacular sight.

"Illilouette" sounds like a French name, but it's not; it's actually an awkward English translation of a Yosemite Indian word, which was originally something like "Tooloolaweack." To the Indians, the word was the name for the place where they gathered to hunt for deer.

After you've admired the waterfall, follow the trail as it descends and then crosses a bridge over Illilouette Creek, just above the falls. Posted signs warn hikers not to swim here, because the bridge is only about 50 yards above the drop. Enjoy the granite and whitewater scenery by the bridge and rest up: You have a 1,200-foot climb back to Glacier Point.

If this trip whets your appetite for a longer exploration of the Panorama Trail, consider hiking the entire 8.5-mile trail one-way from Glacier Point to Happy Isles. See the following story.

45. PANORAMA TRAIL

Glacier Point Road, Yosemite National Park
The grandest views in the West

DISTANCE: 8.5 miles one-way*; 5 hours   **LEVEL:** Moderate
ELEVATION: Start at 7,200 feet; end at 4,020 feet*   **CROWDS:** Moderate
BEST SEASON: June to October   **RATING:** ★ ★ ★ ★ ★

DIRECTIONS: From the Arch Rock entrance station at Yosemite National Park, drive east into the valley for 6.3 miles to the right fork for Highway 41/Wawona/Fresno. Bear right at the fork, then drive 9.2 miles to the Glacier Point Road turnoff. Turn left and drive 15.7 miles to Glacier Point. Park and walk toward the main viewing area, across from the cafe and gift shop. Look for the Panorama Trail sign about 150 feet southeast of the cafe building, on your right.

*__NOTE:__ This is a one-way hike requiring a car shuttle. The elevation listings reflect the elevations at the start and finish of the trail. The majority of the hike is downhill, but the trail also climbs about 750 feet.

A walk from Glacier Point to Yosemite Valley along the Panorama Trail is a hike-of-a-lifetime. I'm talking about the kind of trip where your hiking partner takes your photograph at some scenic spot along the trail, and you hang that picture above your desk so you can look at it every day and remember.

Memories like this are made on the Panorama Trail, an 8.5-mile route that begins at Glacier Point and descends 3,200 feet to Happy Isles. The trail offers bird's-eye views of Vernal and Nevada falls, Half Dome, Basket Dome, Liberty Cap, and plenty more of the valley's stunning geological features.

The one-way hike takes about five hours and requires a car shuttle, or else it's one heck of a long climb back up. A great option is to take the Yosemite Hiker's Bus for one leg of the trip (phone 209/372-1240 for rates and pickup times), rather than driving two cars. Adding in transportation to and from the trail's end points, the five-hour hike usually winds up filling a whole day. Note that just because the hike is mostly downhill, that doesn't make it easy. The 3,200-foot elevation loss can play havoc on your knees.

The Panorama Trail begins at Glacier Point, elevation 7,214 feet. You switchback down from the point, accompanied by ever-changing perspectives on Half Dome, Basket Dome, North Dome, Liberty Cap, and far-off Vernal and Nevada falls. You will gape a lot. For details on the first two miles of the Panorama Trail, see the previous story on Illilouette Fall.

From the Illilouette Creek footbridge, the trail climbs uphill for the first time, gaining 750 feet over 1.2 miles en route to the high southeast canyon wall. From there, you can see all the way across Yosemite Valley to Upper Yosemite Fall, and after a few more minutes of walking, you can see Lower Yosemite Fall as well. North Dome and Basket Dome make an appearance, as well as the Royal Arches and Washington Column. Keep walking; in a few more minutes you will see Nevada Fall.

Your one-and-only ascent of the day is over; start to switchback downhill again, bearing left at a junction for Nevada Fall. At 4.8 miles from the trailhead, you reach a right spur trail for 594-foot Nevada Fall, now only two-tenths of a mile away. After the peace and quiet of the trip thus far, you might want to prepare yourself for the hordes of people you will soon face. Hundreds of people daily make the hike uphill from Happy Isles to Nevada and Vernal falls.

The spur trail takes you to a bridge just above the big drop, where the Merced River gathers steam to form the fall's tremendous flow. You can cross the bridge to an overlook area on the fall's north side, although you can't see much when you're at its brink. Still, it's exciting. From here, you have two choices for your descent: You can take the John Muir Trail (on the south side of the falls) or the Mist Trail (on the north). The Mist Trail is more well-known, and perhaps more dramatic, but both trails offer great views. If your knees or ankles are bothering you from the five-plus miles of downhill hiking you've done, give yourself a break and take the John Muir Trail, which is less steep. But understand that the John Muir Trail does not go directly to Vernal Fall; you must cut over to the Mist Trail at Clark Point in order to visit Vernal Fall.

However you get there, make sure you wind up on the Mist Trail near the well-named Emerald Pool above

Granite and waterfalls from the Panorama Trail

317-foot Vernal Fall, so you can take the spur that leads to the overlook above the falls. Vernal, like Nevada, has a railed overlook area at the brink of its drop.

From the top of Vernal Fall, take the Mist Trail's stunning granite staircase down-canyon. If you're hiking in early summer, this is the time to don your raingear. The waterfall's spray can be a downpour. Use caution on the staircase, especially if the rocks are wet with spray. Go slow and enjoy the scenery.

After you cross the footbridge below Vernal Fall (take a last look), you have only seven-tenths of a mile left to reach Happy Isles. It's an easy stroll back to the trail's end, although the path is sure to be jammed with people. Check out the last-minute, bonus view of Illilouette Fall in the final stretch of trail after you cross the Vernal Fall footbridge. This time you see it from the bottom looking up.

The hike ends at Happy Isles, where you take the free valley shuttle bus to the pickup point for the Yosemite Hiker's Bus, or to your shuttle car parked somewhere in the valley. Then go get those pictures developed, so you can hang them above your desk at work.

46. ALDER CREEK FALLS

Wawona area, Yosemite National Park
A waterfall hidden in the wilderness

DISTANCE: 8.2 miles round-trip; 4 hours   **LEVEL:** Moderate
ELEVATION: Start at 4,800 feet; total change 1,000 feet   **CROWDS:** Minimal
BEST SEASON: April to July   **RATING:** ★ ★ ★

DIRECTIONS: From the Wawona/southern entrance station at Yosemite National Park, drive north on Highway 41 for 7.5 miles to Wawona. Set your odometer. From Wawona, continue north on Highway 41 for another 4.2 miles. The trailhead is at a hairpin turn on the east side of the Wawona Road. There is no trail marker except for a mostly hidden Yosemite Wilderness sign. Park in the large dirt pullout on the west side of the road.

The best thing about Alder Creek Falls is that with all the world-famous waterfalls in Yosemite, this one just gets overlooked. Or maybe the best thing about the waterfall is the adventure of finding it and the work required to access it.

The adventure begins with a search for the unmarked trailhead along Wawona Road. This is no small feat. (Follow the directions exactly.) Then you must hike straight uphill into the Yosemite Wilderness, with nary a switchback, for just shy of a mile. Luckily, you're in a dense pine and cedar forest, so the steep trail is shaded.

After the initial beeline climb, things start to get easier. Catch your breath, then make a left turn at a signed junction, which indicates that Alder Creek is 3.2 miles away (the trail on the right goes to Wawona in 2.9 miles). The path continues to climb through dense ponderosa pines and incense cedars, although the grade is now a bit tamer.

After a total of three miles of climbing through the forest—just trees, trees, and more trees—the trail suddenly levels out. Now you walk on an old railroad grade, and if you look carefully, you'll spot occasional wooden railroad ties embedded in the dirt. It was on this section of trail that we surprised a big black bear lumbering along in front of us, making his morning rounds. He turned around and stared at us with a shocked expression on his face, then darted off into the woods.

You may be as surprised as he was when suddenly you hear pounding water through the silence of the trees. In a few moments your view opens up to Alder Creek and its 250-foot waterfall, pouring grandly over a granite lip. The railroad grade laterals alongside it, heads upstream, and brings you near the brink of the falls. The best overlook of the entire drop is right along the trail, about 100 yards before you reach the falls.

Beyond the waterfall, the trail continues along Alder Creek, paralleling it for 3.5 miles all the way to Deer Camp and Empire Meadow. But there's no need for day-hikers to go that far. Instead, hike a quarter mile beyond the falls, where you'll find a tiny feeder stream watering some lovely wildflowers, including mariposa lilies, Douglas iris, blue lupine, and purple vetch. Check out the interesting rock formation with trees growing on top. Any number of places around the creek make good stopping points, where you can un-shoulder your day pack and have lunch.

47. CHILNUALNA FALLS

Wawona area, Yosemite National Park
An early season waterfall

DISTANCE: 8.2 miles round-trip; 4.5 hours   **LEVEL:** Strenuous
ELEVATION: Start at 4,200 feet; total change 2,200 feet   **CROWDS:** Moderate
BEST SEASON: March to July   **RATING:** ★ ★ ★ ★

DIRECTIONS: From the Arch Rock entrance station at Yosemite National Park, drive east into the valley for 6.3 miles to the right fork for Highway 41/Wawona/Fresno. Bear right at the fork, then drive 25 miles to Wawona. Turn left on Chilnualna Falls Road. Drive 1.7 miles east and park in the lot on the right side of the road. Walk back to Chilnualna Falls Road and pick up the single-track trail across the pavement.

Alternatively, from the Wawona/southern entrance station on Highway 41, drive north on Highway 41 for 7.5 miles to Wawona. Turn right on Chilnualna Falls Road and follow the directions as above.

Most people don't pay much attention to the southern section of Yosemite National Park near Wawona. Sure, everyone visits the Mariposa Grove to see the giant Sequoias, but other than that, the Wawona area doesn't take up too much of the average visitor's itinerary. So while everyone else is crowding Yosemite Valley, Glacier Point, or Tuolumne Meadows, you can sneak off to the southern part of the park, take a rigorous hike, and be rewarded with some solitude and a terrific waterfall, Chilnualna Falls.

An early morning start is a good idea. You hike at a low elevation—4,200 feet—and you must gain 2,200 feet over four miles to reach the falls. It's a steady, nonstop climb through only partial shade.

Bring plenty of water for your two-hour uphill aerobics session, plus the long downhill return.

From the Chilnualna Falls parking lot, cross the road and hike uphill on the single-track trail. In a few minutes you're at a tremendous cascade on Chilnualna Creek, where the stream rushes furiously over room-sized boulders. It looks like someone took Stonehenge apart, piled up all the rocks, and started a downpour over them. It's extremely noisy here in spring and early summer.

As nice as this spot is, you must say good-bye to the creek. You won't see it again for a few miles. Heading upward on the trail, you reach a Yosemite Wilderness sign and begin to switchback your way up, up, and up through oaks, manzanita, mountain misery, and bear clover. In spring, the aroma of all this flowering brush is intoxicating—it's easy to understand why bears and deer munch on it.

After nearly an hour of climbing (about two miles), you reach a granite plateau with a terrific view of the tree-filled canyon below and Wawona Dome (6,897 feet) across from you. Stop here to stretch your hamstrings, eat a snack, and make comments like, "Boy, this waterfall better be good." You're halfway there, and yes, it is good.

Chilnualna Falls

The nearby roar of Chilnualna Creek, heard but not yet seen, assures you that you're on the right track. At 2.5 miles out, look for glimpses of Chilnualna Falls on the far back wall of the canyon, way up high. What you can see is only a small section of the fall, and as you switchback uphill your view of it will change to include more and more length. It provides an incentive to spur you on.

At three miles, you reach a small, cascading stream crossing the trail. Since you've gained so much elevation, the forest is now dense with shady pines and incense cedars.

Finally, you come to what seems like the canyon rim, and start to lateral toward the waterfall. This is the most exciting vantage point: From here you see a giant free-falling plume of water at the bottom of Chilnualna Falls. Even the trail is dramatic: It's a ledge trail that has been blasted out of granite.

You curve around to the brink of the free-falling waterfall, then ascend above it. Chilnualna Falls is a series of cascades totalling hundreds of feet, separated by more level stretches where the stream glides over granite slabs. Keep climbing, following the trail along the stream, to reach the falls' upper tiers. You'll walk up and over granite stair-steps, passing one cascade after another. A half mile from the lowest section of the waterfall is a trail sign; the path leads off to Turner Meadows, Grouse Lake, and Chilnualna Lakes. This is where the major cascades end. On your right is the upper Chilnualna cascade, our favorite of the trip—a series of six rounded granite pools connected by a continually descending flow of water. Leave the trail and walk 100 yards to the right to the creek's edge. Here, on the bare outcrop of granite surrounding the waterfall, is the perfect place to savor the beauty.

48. WAWONA MEADOW LOOP

Wawona area, Yosemite National Park
An easy wildflower walk

DISTANCE: 3.0 miles round-trip; 1.5 hours   **LEVEL:** Easy
ELEVATION: Start at 4,200 feet; total change 20 feet   **CROWDS:** Minimal
BEST SEASON: April to July   **RATING:** ★ ★

DIRECTIONS: From the Arch Rock entrance station at Yosemite National Park, drive east into the valley for 6.3 miles to the right fork for Highway 41/Wawona/Fresno. Bear right at the fork, then drive 27 miles to the trailhead, which is just south of the golf course and across the road from the Wawona Hotel.

Alternatively, from the Wawona/southern entrance station on Highway 41, drive north on Highway 41 for seven miles to the Wawona Hotel. The trail begins across the road.

Hey, sometimes you just want to take a stroll in the park, and the Wawona Meadow Loop is just that. On several trips to Yosemite, we ignored this trail because of its proximity to the Wawona Golf Course, the presence of which insulted our hiking sensibilities. But finally we gave the Wawona Meadow Loop a try, and to our surprise we liked it.

The Wawona Meadow Loop has three major things going for it: It's a flat and easy trail, it has wildflowers galore, and it's located just across the road from the Wawona Hotel. If you're staying at the hotel, or at the Wawona Campground a few miles north, the hike around the meadow is a perfect after-dinner stroll or early morning jog. There's only one negative, and that's the proximity of the Wawona Road (Highway 41). But when you're on the far side of the meadow, you won't even notice it.

On the trail, you're more likely to see deer than people. You'll enjoy the good company of butterflies, and see and smell a huge variety of meadow wildflowers, most notably lupine, larkspur, yampah, and sneezeweed. The deer are usually busy trying to munch down all the blooms, but they don't make much of a dent.

From the signed trailhead across the road from the Wawona Hotel, hike to your left on the dirt and gravel road, following the split rail fence, then circle around the meadow. You're even allowed to bring your dog or ride your bike, both of which are rarely permitted on trails in Yosemite.

If you're staying at the Wawona Hotel, you can hike right from the front door, by crossing the Wawona Road and walking along the gravel road at the edge of the golf course for 50 yards to the start of the trail. The trail finishes up around the back of the hotel.

49. MARIPOSA GROVE SHORT TOUR

Wawona area, Yosemite National Park
The largest Sequoia grove in Yosemite

DISTANCE: 2.0 miles round-trip; 1 hour   **LEVEL:** Easy
ELEVATION: Start at 5,600 feet; total change 400 feet   **CROWDS:** Heavy
BEST SEASON: Year-round   **RATING:** ★ ★

DIRECTIONS: From the Wawona/southern entrance station at Yosemite National Park, drive north on Highway 41 for 100 feet. Turn right on the Mariposa Grove access road and drive two miles to the Mariposa Grove parking lot. (This access road may be closed in winter.)

Alternatively, from the Arch Rock entrance station at Yosemite National Park, drive east into the valley for 6.3 miles to the right fork for Highway 41/Wawona/Fresno. Bear right at the fork, then drive 32 miles to the Mariposa Grove turnoff on the left, by Yosemite's southern entrance station. Turn left and drive two miles to the Mariposa Grove parking lot.

NOTE: An interpretive brochure/trail map is available at the trailhead.

Giant Sequoias are the largest living things on earth in terms of volume. That, quite simply, is the single most important reason that hundreds of people each day tour the Mariposa Grove in Yosemite National Park. Sure, the trees are also old—as much as 3,000 years—but they're not the oldest living things on earth. They're the biggest.

The Mariposa Grove is the largest of Yosemite's three Sequoia groves, and it's the most developed. There's a big parking lot, rest rooms, and a museum. Motorized trams run through the grove, so visitors can alternate riding and walking without getting too tired to see the forest for the trees, or the trees for the forest. But you don't have to ride the trams; day-hikers can choose between a short trail in the lower grove (two miles) or a longer trail covering the entire grove (6.5 miles). For the longer hike, see the following story. For the short trail, read on.

Begin to hike at the trailhead by the parking lot, and head immediately for the Fallen Monarch, a big Sequoia that fell more than 300 years ago. It was made famous by an 1899 photograph of the U.S. Cavalry and their horses standing on top of it. Even though it has been on the ground all these centuries, its root ball and trunk are still huge and intact, a testament to how long it takes for Sequoias to decay. That's because of a surfeit of tannic acid in the Sequoia's wood.

The Mariposa Grove's giant Sequoias

Continue to hike gently uphill on the obvious trail through the forest. The Sequoias are mixed in with lots of other trees, especially white firs, sugar pines, and incense cedars; the giants appear sporadically, like treasures in a treasure hunt. Your next "find" is the Bachelor and Three Graces (an odd reference to one big tree with three smaller trees at its side). Then turn right and start a steeper uphill climb to the Grizzly Giant. This is the largest tree in the

Mariposa Grove, with a circumference of more than 100 feet. The tree has one particularly impressive branch that is almost seven feet in diameter. It's also one of the oldest giant Sequoias in this grove, at approximately 2,700 years old. Thinking about this gives you a little perspective on your short time on Earth.

Now start to descend to the California Tunnel Tree, which was tunneled in 1895 so stagecoaches could drive through it. Just beyond the California Tree, you'll see a trail marker that points you to the Upper Grove and Museum. This marker is the turnaround point for the short tour of the grove, so turn left to circle back to the parking area. For your return, you can take the fork that leads past the Bachelor and Three Graces and the Fallen Monarch again, or you can stay straight at the next junction and make a slightly wider loop back to the parking lot.

Note that to get the most out of your trip, you must visit the Mariposa Grove either very early in the morning or late in the day, when the crowds have lessened and the forest is quiet. The grove is so popular that at times the rangers close off the parking lot during mid-day, when visitation is highest. The best time to visit the big trees is in the early and late hours, when you have the chance to see more playful ground squirrels than tourists with video cameras.

50. MARIPOSA GROVE LONG TOUR

Wawona area, Yosemite National Park
Giant Sequoias and an overlook at Wawona Point

DISTANCE: 6.5 miles round-trip; 3 hours   **LEVEL:** Moderate
ELEVATION: Start at 5,600 feet; total change 1,200 feet   **CROWDS:** Heavy
BEST SEASON: Year-round   **RATING:** ★ ★ ★

DIRECTIONS: From the Wawona/southern entrance station at Yosemite National Park, drive north on Highway 41 for 100 feet. Turn right on the Mariposa Grove access road and drive two miles to the Mariposa Grove parking lot. (This access road may be closed in winter.)

Alternatively, from the Arch Rock entrance station at Yosemite National Park, drive east into the valley for 6.3 miles to the right fork for Highway 41/Wawona/Fresno. Bear right at the fork, then drive 32 miles to the Mariposa Grove turnoff on the left, by Yosemite's southern entrance station. Turn left and drive two miles to the Mariposa Grove parking lot.

NOTE: An interpretive brochure/trail map is available at the trailhead.

The Mariposa Grove is the largest of the three groves of giant Sequoias in Yosemite National Park. That's why on summer weekends, the parking lot fills up and people wait in line in their cars to see the 250 or so big trees here. Day-hikers should remember the two best tricks in the hiking world for avoiding the crowds: Get an early start (avoid the 9 A.M. to 5 P.M. window), and head uphill.

If you want to see only the most famous trees in the grove—the Grizzly Giant, California Tunnel Tree, and the Bachelor and Three Graces—you can take the well-signed two-mile hike through the lower grove, then turn around when you see the signs pointing to the upper grove. (This short tour is described in the previous story). If you want to see more Sequoias and less people, plan on a longer round-trip of 6.5 miles (although you can cut this a bit shorter if you skip a few side trips). In general, you'll find that the upper grove is a prettier forest with more big trees than the lower grove, so it's probably worth your time and energy to see it.

Begin to hike at the trailhead right by the parking lot. You'll pass the Fallen Monarch, the Bachelor and Three Graces, and the Grizzly Giant as you head gently uphill (see the previous story for details about this first mile of trail). After descending slightly to reach the California Tunnel Tree, a trail sign points uphill to the Upper Grove.

Now the climb becomes a bit more serious, as you head up a dry slope covered with white firs, sugar pines, and incense cedars, but no Sequoias. At last, you meet a junction with the Upper Grove Loop Trail, near the paved tram road. (The Upper Grove Loop parallels the upper tram road. To follow this route as described, keep the tram road on your left.) Turn right on the Upper Grove Loop, and continue climbing through more Sequoias. You pass the Telescope Tree, a fire-hollowed tree that still lives. You can stick your head in it and look up to the sky, gaining the strange view that gives the tree its nickname.

At the top of the climb, you pass some of the best looking Sequoias of the whole trip—unnamed giants that tower majestically over passers-by. Where the trail levels off, take the left spur trail that leads downhill to the Wawona Tunnel Tree. Like the California Tunnel Tree in the lower grove, the Wawona Tunnel Tree was tunneled in 1881 so that stagecoaches could drive through it. But the Wawona Tunnel Tree is no longer standing; it was crushed by the weight of a record snowpack in 1969. The tree died approximately 1,000 years prematurely, enfeebled by the tunnel cut into its base.

Retrace your steps uphill to the main trail, then hike to your left to reach the Galen Clark Tree, named for the man who served as the

Standing inside a split in a giant Sequoia

guardian for these big trees. (His cabin is the present-day museum building.) From the Clark Tree, continue uphill for a quarter mile on an old road to Wawona Point, elevation 6,810 feet. There are no Sequoias here, but there is a terrific view of the Merced River canyon, Wawona Dome, and the Wawona Meadow.

After you enjoy the vista, return to the Galen Clark Tree and turn right (west) to skirt the north end of the upper grove. At the next junction, take your pick: Right will take you on the Outer Loop Trail downhill and back to the parking lot; left will take you to the upper grove's museum. From the museum, you can head back downhill the same way you came up. The Outer Loop Trail is better for solitude lovers; the museum route is better for history lovers.

DEVILS POSTPILE NATIONAL MONUMENT

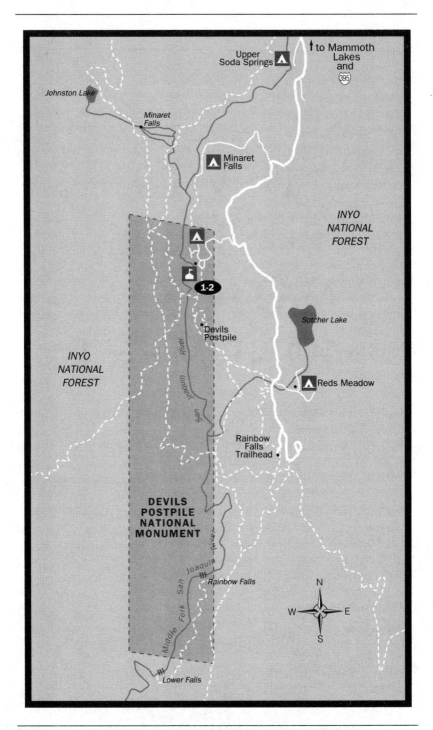

DEVILS POSTPILE NATIONAL MONUMENT
TRAILS AT A GLANCE

Map Number/Trail Name	Page	Mileage	Difficulty
1. Devils Postpile & Rainbow Falls	299	5.0	Easy
2. Devils Postpile Grand Tour	301	8.0	Moderate

ABOUT THE PARK

Devils Postpile National Monument was established to preserve two unique geological features: Devils Postpile, one of the world's finest examples of columnar-jointed basalt; and Rainbow Falls, a 101-foot waterfall on the Middle Fork San Joaquin River. The monument's spectacular scenery includes forests, meadows, and cascading streams.

VISITOR CENTER

The monument visitor center is located at the Devils Postpile Ranger Station by the main parking lot.

ADDRESS, PHONE, & WEBSITE

Devils Postpile National Monument, P.O. Box 501, Mammoth Lakes, CA 93546; (760) 934-2289. (Or contact the Mammoth Lakes Ranger District at 760-924-5500.) Website: www.nps.gov/depo

HOW TO GET THERE

- By air: The closest major airport is in Reno, Nevada.
- By car: From the town of Mammoth Lakes near U.S. 395, take Highway 203 west for four miles, then turn right on Minaret Road (which is still Highway 203) and drive 4.5 miles to the Devils Postpile entrance kiosk, across from Mammoth Mountain Ski Area. If you arrive between the hours of 7:30 A.M. and 5:30 P.M., you must park your car and take the shuttle bus ($8) into the monument. Disembark at the Devils Postpile Ranger Station. If you arrive before 7:30 A.M. or after 5:30 P.M., you may drive your own car into the monument. To do so, from the entrance kiosk continue straight for 7.8 miles, then turn right for Devils Postpile. Drive a quarter mile and park in the lot next to the ranger station.

DRIVE TIME

- Drive time from Los Angeles: approximately 6 hours.
- Drive time from San Francisco: approximately 7 hours.

ENTRANCE FEES

There is no entrance fee at Devils Postpile National Monument, but if you arrive between the hours of 7:30 A.M. and 5:30 P.M., you will have to pay $8 to ride the shuttle bus into the monument.

WHEN TO GO

Devils Postpile National Monument is usually open from mid-June until late October, depending on snowfall and snowmelt.

WEATHER CONDITIONS

Devils Postpile is blessed with typical Sierra summer weather: warm, clear days with temperatures in the 70s and low 80s, and cool nights with temperatures in the 40s and 50s. The general rule for visiting the monument: Bring warm clothes for evenings (especially if you're camping) and a variety of layers for hiking.

WHERE TO STAY

A 21-site campground is available in the monument. Sites are available on a first-come, first-served basis. Numerous other campgrounds are available in surrounding Inyo National Forest land. The nearest camps are Minaret Falls, Agnew Meadows, Reds Meadow, Pumice Flat, and Upper Soda Springs. For more information, contact Inyo National Forest, Mammoth Lakes Ranger District at (760) 924-5500.

Numerous motels and lodgings are available in the town of Mammoth Lakes, 10 miles away. Contact the Mammoth Lakes Chamber of Commerce at (760) 934-2712.

FOOD & SUPPLIES

A small camp store is located at Reds Meadow Resort. Restaurants and larger stores can be found in nearby Mammoth Lakes.

SUGGESTED MAPS

Park maps are available at the entrance station and also at the monument's ranger station. An excellent map of trails surrounding Devils Postpile is available for a fee from the Mammoth Ranger District of Inyo National Forest. Phone (760) 924-5500 and ask for the "Mammoth Trails" map.

1. DEVILS POSTPILE & RAINBOW FALLS

Devils Postpile National Monument
The monument's main attractions

DISTANCE: 5.0 miles round-trip; 2.5 hours   **LEVEL:** Easy
ELEVATION: Start at 7,600 feet; total change 200 feet   **CROWDS:** Heavy
BEST SEASON: June to September   **RATING:** ★ ★ ★ ★ ★

DIRECTIONS: From the town of Mammoth Lakes, take Highway 203 west for four miles, then turn right on Minaret Road (which is still Highway 203) and drive 4.5 miles to the Devils Postpile entrance kiosk, across from Mammoth Mountain Ski Area. If it is between the hours of 7:30 A.M. and 5:30 P.M., you will have to park your car and take the shuttle bus ($8) into the monument. Disembark at the Devils Postpile Ranger Station. If you arrive before 7:30 A.M. or after 5:30 P.M., you may drive your own car into the monument. From the kiosk, continue straight 7.8 miles to a junction; turn right for Devils Postpile. Drive a quarter mile and park in the lot next to the ranger station. The trail begins from the left (south) side of the parking area, just beyond the ranger station.

What the heck is the Devils Postpile? People ask themselves this question time and time again as they read the road signs while driving up U.S. 395 on their way to Mammoth Lakes for skiing or fishing vacations. Getting the answer requires only a short walk in Devils Postpile National Monument—three-quarters of a mile round-trip—but if you add in a few more miles, you'll see spectacular Rainbow Falls as well.

There's one catch, though. The road into the park is narrow, steep, and winding, and because of that, the park closes the road from 7:30 A.M. until 5:30 P.M. each day. During these hours, visitors must pony up eight bucks to ride a shuttle bus in and out. You have a choice: you can get up early or stay out late and drive your own car into the park, or you can take the shuttle bus.

Note that solitude lovers should seriously consider the pre-7:30 A.M. option, and visit on a weekday besides. The trail to Devils Postpile and Rainbow Falls is incredibly popular; summer weekends bring a continual parade of hikers.

Once you're in the park, go straight to the Devils Postpile parking area and set out on the trail by the ranger station. The footpath begins in a pretty meadow alongside the headwaters of the San Joaquin River. If you time your trip right, you will be wowed by the meadow wildflowers, especially the masses of shooting stars and Indian paintbrush. In a mere four-tenths of a mile on a level, easy trail, your curiosity will

---

Devils Postpile National Monument—map page 296   299

be sated as you reach the base of the Devils Postpile. What is it? It's a pile of volcanic rock posts or columns made from lava that was forced up from the earth's core. At the base of the standing columns is a huge pile of rubble—the crumbled remains of columns that collapsed. Notice the shapes of the various lava columns; some are almost perfectly straight, while others curve like tall candles that have been left out in the sun.

The Mammoth Lakes area is volcano country. Less than 100,000 years ago, lava filled this river valley more than 400 feet deep. As the lava began to cool from the air flow on top, it simultaneously cooled from the hard granite bedrock below. This caused the lava to harden and crack into tall, narrow pieces, forming nearly perfect columns or posts. The Devils Postpile is considered to be the finest example of lava columns in the world.

After examining the base of the Postpile, take the trail on either side of it up to its top. You can stand on the columns and marvel at the fact that they are all nearly the same height. Under your feet, the tops of the columns look like honeycomb, or tiles that have been laid side by side. A bonus is that the view of the San Joaquin River from the top of the Postpile is quite lovely.

The Devils Postpile

When you're ready, return to the base of the Postpile and continue past it on the well-marked trail to Rainbow Falls. You'll skirt in and out of the monument boundary and Inyo National Forest as the trail descends gently through lodgepole pines. The forest fire damage you'll notice was caused by a wildfire in 1992. The sound of the San Joaquin River is always apparent, although you won't see the stream again until you get close to the waterfall.

At a trail junction directing you straight to Rainbow Falls or left to Reds Meadow, continue straight. (From this junction onward, the trail gets even more crowded with hikers coming in from a short access trail near Reds Meadow Resort.) After a stream crossing on a two-log bridge, the path begins its final descent to Rainbow Falls.

The anticipation mounts as you walk closer to a big channel in the river gorge. The gorge is cut very steeply, with almost no foliage on its walls—just stark, vertical rock. The roar of Rainbow Falls can be heard before you see it; the trail brings you in above the falls. If you're hiking in the late morning or at midday, you'll see Rainbow Falls' namesake— two big, beautiful rainbows arcing over the falls' mist. The angle of the midday sun on the water droplets creates the perfect recipe for a rainbow.

Keep walking past the lip of the falls. You'll see that Rainbow Falls' drop makes a grand statement, plunging 101 feet over hard rock. The trail has two viewing areas for the falls, about 30 yards apart. A path from the second viewpoint descends steep granite steps to the base of the falls. Ferns and moss grow on the rock at the cliff bottom; they benefit from the waterfall's constant mist.

2. DEVILS POSTPILE GRAND TOUR

Devils Postpile National Monument
Three waterfalls and the Devils Postpile

DISTANCE: 8.0 miles round-trip; 4 hours   **LEVEL:** Moderate
ELEVATION: Start at 7,600 feet; total change 400 feet   **CROWDS:** Moderate
BEST SEASON: June to September   **RATING:** ★ ★ ★ ★

DIRECTIONS: From the town of Mammoth Lakes, take Highway 203 west for four miles, then turn right on Minaret Road (which is still Highway 203) and drive 4.5 miles to the Devils Postpile entrance kiosk, across from Mammoth Mountain Ski Area. If it is between the hours of 7:30 A.M. and 5:30 P.M., you will have to park your car and take the shuttle bus ($8) into the monument. Disembark at the Devils Postpile Ranger Station. If you arrive before 7:30 A.M. or after 5:30 P.M., you may drive your own car into the monument. From the kiosk, continue straight 7.8 miles to a junction; turn right for Devils Postpile. Drive a quarter mile and park in the lot next to the ranger station. The trail begins from the left (south) side of the parking area, just beyond the ranger station.

Rainbow Falls is one of the prized geologic possessions of Devils Postpile National Monument. The Devils Postpile, of course, is another. Add in Minaret Falls and Lower Falls, which can be seen along with Rainbow Falls and the Devils Postpile in a half-day, moderate hiking tour, and we're talking about a trip filled with natural wonders. That's three stunning waterfalls and one intriguing volcanic formation in an eight-mile round-trip hike, which I call the "Devils Postpile Grand Tour."

Start your trip at the Devils Postpile parking lot, near the ranger station. Hike south, following the sign for Devils Postpile in four-tenths of a mile. In your first footsteps you'll be wowed by a pristine meadow filled with purple shooting stars and views of the meandering river. Hang on to your hat; this is just the beginning.

Next you'll reach the Postpile, a formation of towering "posts" composed of columnar basalt left from a lava flow nearly 100,000 years ago. Be sure to take either of the trails on the sides of the Postpile that climb to its crest, where you can see that the top of the formation looks like a slightly off-kilter parquet floor. (See the previous story for more information on the Devils Postpile.)

Continue hiking south past the Postpile. Notice how the thriving pine forest changes to a severely burned area, the result of a 1992 wildfire. The undergrowth has already returned in full force, although some blackened trees still stand.

Rainbow Falls

Keep heading gently downhill until you reach the two viewing areas for Rainbow Falls, which plummets 101 feet over a volcanic cliff. If you arrive at midday, when direct light rays are passing through water droplets, you'll see light being refracted and separated into its component colors. Translation? That means the falls' namesake rainbows are dancing through the mist.

Although Rainbow Falls drops over volcanic rock, it's different volcanic rock from the basalt of Devils Postpile. It's rhyodacite, and it has two extremely hard horizontal rock layers at the top of its cliff, much like Niagara Falls. That keeps the San Joaquin River from eroding the waterfall and eventually beveling it off.

When you've seen enough, leave the crowds behind at Rainbow Falls and head downstream for a half-mile to often-snubbed Lower Falls. Poor Lower Falls; if Rainbow Falls gets 100 visitors an hour on a peak summer day, Lower Falls gets one or two. Rainbow Falls gets the limelight; Lower Falls doesn't even get an imaginative name.

Beautiful in its own right, Lower Falls is a nearly vertical drop of about 40 feet. Because its cliff is not as wide as Rainbow Falls', Lower Falls' flow is channeled, which increases its volume as the river funnels through its narrow chute. Almost no plant life grows on the fall's cliff, except for a few fire-scarred trees standing near the top.

After visiting Lower Falls, retrace your steps. Head back uphill on the busy trail past Rainbow Falls and the Devils Postpile again. After passing the Devils Postpile, watch for a trail fork on your left where a scenic footbridge crosses the San Joaquin River. This is your route to the third waterfall in the park, Minaret Falls. Again you'll have the pleasure of leaving the crowds behind as you cross this footbridge.

Turn right on the far side of the bridge and walk upstream. Watch for a fork a half-mile from the bridge, where you bear right on the Pacific Crest Trail. The route is basically level, with just a slight ascent as you approach the falls.

The Pacific Crest Trail brings you close to the base of the Minaret Falls, where you'll be surprised at both its noise and size. Whereas Rainbow and Lower falls are classic river falls— imposingly wide but not immense in height— Minaret Falls drops on Minaret Creek, in a streaming cascade that's 300 feet long and as much as 100

Lower Falls

feet wide. The waterfall doesn't have the dramatic impact that Rainbow and Lower falls have; nonetheless, it's an impressive cascade.

Leave the Pacific Crest Trail and make a short cross-country scramble over rocks and fallen trees to choose your viewing spot. Even in July, the fall is so loud that conversation is nearly impossible. Shout a few words to your hiking partner, take some photographs, then retrace your steps back to the bridge, turning left to return to the Devils Postpile parking lot.

OTHER OPTIONS IN & AROUND DEVILS POSTPILE:

• If you want to see Rainbow and/or Lower Falls via a shorter walk, you can start from the trailhead at Reds Meadow for a two-mile round-trip, plus an extra half-mile round-trip to Lower Falls. To reach Reds Meadow, take the shuttle bus (or drive your own car) past the Devils Postpile turnoff for another 1.5 miles to the Rainbow Falls Trailhead, located on a spur road just before Reds Meadow Resort.

• For an all-day, 15-mile marathon loop hike that begins and ends in Devils Postpile but travels mostly in Ansel Adams Wilderness, begin hiking at the Devils Postpile ranger station. Cross the river bridge and access the John Muir Trail heading north (right). Follow the John Muir Trail past a series of lakes: Johnston Lake, Trinity Lakes, Gladys Lake, Rosalie Lake, and Shadow Lake. (The lakes get larger and prettier as you go; Rosalie and Shadow lakes are the best of the lot.) Then leave the John Muir Trail and loop back around the edge of Shadow Lake. You'll make a steep descent down to the Middle Fork San Joaquin River and follow the River Trail back to Agnew Meadows Campground. Walk to the end of the camp access road; you can take the Devils Postpile shuttle bus back to the ranger station and your car. Wow, what a day.

SEQUOIA &
KINGS CANYON
NATIONAL
PARKS

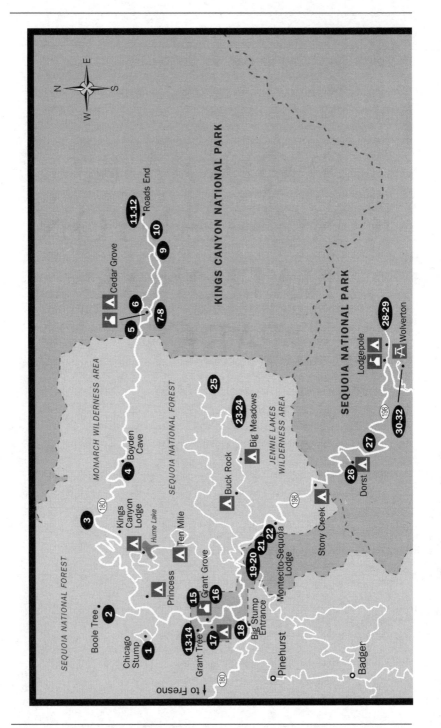

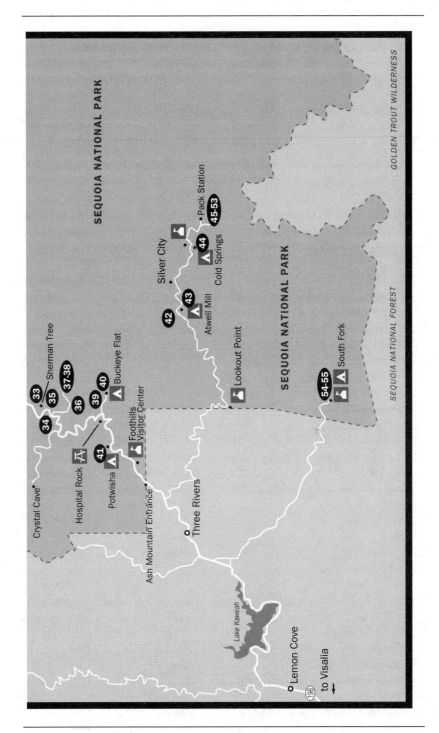

SEQUOIA NATIONAL PARK

GOLDEN TROUT WILDERNESS

Pack Station

45-53

Silver City

44

Cold Springs

Atwell Mill

43

42

SEQUOIA NATIONAL PARK

Lookout Point

South Fork

54-55

SEQUOIA NATIONAL FOREST

Sherman Tree

33

35

37-38

34

36

39

40

Buckeye Flat

Crystal Cave

Hospital Rock

Potwisha

41

Foothills
Visitor Center

Ash Mountain Entrance

Three Rivers

Lake Kaweah

Lemon Cove

to Visalia

198

SEQUOIA/KINGS CANYON NATIONAL PARKS
TRAILS AT A GLANCE

Map Number/Trail Name	Page	Mileage	Difficulty
1. Chicago Stump Trail	313	0.4	Easy
2. Boole Tree Loop	314	2.5	Easy/moderate
3. Yucca Point	316	4.0	Moderate
4. Windy Cliffs	317	3.0	Easy/moderate
5. Lewis Creek Trail	318	8.6-11.6	Strenuous
6. Hotel Creek Trail to Cedar Grove Overlook	319	5.0-7.0	Moderate
7. Don Cecil Trail to Sheep Creek	321	2.0	Easy/moderate
8. Don Cecil Trail to Lookout Peak	322	11.6	Very strenuous
9. Roaring River Falls	323	0.4	Easy
10. Zumwalt Meadow Loop	325	1.5	Easy
11. Mist Falls	326	8.2	Moderate
12. Copper Creek Trail to Lower Tent Meadow	328	7.4	Strenuous
13. General Grant Tree	329	0.6	Easy
14. North Grove & Dead Giant Loop	331	3.0	Easy/moderate
15. Panoramic Point & Park Ridge Lookout	332	4.7	Easy/moderate
16. Manzanita & Azalea Loop	333	3.3	Easy/moderate
17. Sunset Trail	334	5.5	Moderate
18. Big Stump Trail	336	1.0	Easy
19. Redwood Canyon	338	4.0	Easy/moderate
20. Redwood Mountain Loop	339	10.0	Moderate
21. Buena Vista Peak	341	2.0	Easy/moderate
22. Big Baldy	342	4.6	Easy/moderate
23. Weaver Lake	344	4.2	Moderate
24. Jennie Lake	345	10.0	Strenuous
25. Mitchell Peak	347	5.2	Strenuous
26. Muir Grove	348	4.0	Easy
27. Little Baldy	349	3.5	Easy/moderate
28. Tokopah Falls	350	3.4	Easy
29. Twin Lakes	353	13.6	Strenuous
30. Lakes Trail & The Watchtower	354	8.4-10.8	Strenuous
31. Alta Peak	356	13.2	Very strenuous
32. Panther Gap Loop	358	6.0	Moderate
33. General Sherman Tree & Congress Trail	360	2.1	Easy
34. Sunset Rock	362	2.0	Easy
35. Hazelwood & Huckleberry Loop	363	4.5	Easy/moderate
36. Moro Rock	365	0.6	Easy/moderate
37. Crescent Meadow & Tharp's Log	367	2.2	Easy

Map Number/Trail Name	Page	Mileage	Difficulty
38. High Sierra Trail to Eagle View	368	1.5	Easy
39. Middle Fork Trail to Panther Creek	370	6.0	Moderate
40. Paradise Creek Trail	371	2.6	Easy/moderate
41. Marble Falls	373	7.0	Moderate
42. Paradise Ridge	374	3.2	Moderate
43. Hockett Trail to East Fork Grove	375	4.0	Easy/moderate
44. Cold Springs Nature Trail	377	2.4	Easy
45. Farewell Gap Trail to Aspen Flat	378	2.0	Easy
46. Mosquito Lakes	380	8.4	Strenuous
47. Eagle Lake	382	6.8	Strenuous
48. Franklin Lake	383	10.8	Strenuous
49. White Chief Mine	385	5.8	Moderate
50. Timber Gap	387	4.0	Moderate
51. Monarch Lakes	388	8.4	Strenuous
52. Crystal Lake	390	9.8	Very strenuous
53. Black Wolf Falls	392	0.5	Easy
54. Ladybug Trail to Cedar Creek	393	6.4	Moderate
55. Garfield-Hockett Trail	395	5.8	Strenuous

THE TOP 10, DON'T-MISS DAY HIKES:

Map Number/Trail Name	Page	Features
10. Zumwalt Meadow Loop	325	meadow, Kings River
11. Mist Falls	326	waterfall, Kings River
20. Redwood Mountain Loop	339	giant Sequoias
28. Tokopah Falls	350	1,200-foot waterfall
30. Lakes Trail & The Watchtower	354	lakes and granite
31. Alta Peak	356	11,204-foot summit
36. Moro Rock	365	vistas from granite dome
47. Eagle Lake	382	lakes, granite, vistas
49. White Chief Mine	385	meadows, mine ruins
51. Monarch Lakes	388	lakes, granite, vistas

TRAIL SUGGESTIONS FOR IF YOU ONLY HAVE ONE DAY:

Map Number/Trail Name	Page	Features
10. Zumwalt Meadow Loop	325	meadow, Kings River
19. Redwood Canyon	338	giant Sequoias
27. Little Baldy	349	views of High Sierra
28. Tokopah Falls	350	1,200-foot waterfall
33. General Sherman Tree & Congress Trail	360	largest living thing
36. Moro Rock	365	vistas from granite dome
37. Crescent Meadow & Tharp's Log	367	meadows, history

SEQUOIA & KINGS CANYON NATIONAL PARKS

ABOUT THE PARKS

Sequoia National Park was established in 1890. It was California's first national park, and the United States' second national park (after Yellowstone). Kings Canyon National Park was established in 1940. These two side-by-side parks are located on the western slope of the Sierra Nevada Mountains, and are jointly managed by the National Park Service. Both are famous for their giant Sequoia groves, tall mountains, deep canyons, and spectacular hiking trails with views of the jagged peaks of the Great Western Divide.

ADDRESS, PHONE, & WEBSITE

Sequoia and Kings Canyon National Parks, Three Rivers, CA 93271-9700; (209) 565-3341, (209) 565-3134, or (209) 335-2856. Website: www.nps.gov/seki

A few trails in this chapter lie outside the boundary of the national parks in national forest land. For more information on these trails, contact Sequoia National Forest, Hume Lake Ranger District, 35860 East Kings Canyon Road, Dunlap, CA 93621; (209) 338-2251.

VISITOR CENTERS

There are three major visitor centers in the park: Grant Grove, Lodgepole, and Foothills. The Grant Grove visitor center is located near the Big Stump Entrance, the Lodgepole visitor center is located at Lodgepole Campground in the central part of Sequoia National Park, and the Foothills visitor center is located near the Ash Mountain Entrance.

HOW TO GET THERE

• By air: The closest major airport is in Fresno, California.
• By car: The parks are located 55 miles east of Fresno via Highway 180, or 36 miles east of Visalia via Highway 198. There are four different entrances. One main road (the Generals Highway) connects the main western stretch of Kings Canyon and Sequoia. It runs north to south from the Big Stump Entrance to the Ash Mountain Entrance. The South Fork and Mineral King areas of Sequoia National Park are only accessible by the South Fork and Mineral King entrances; both require long out-and-back drives.

Big Stump Entrance near Grant Grove—Take Highway 99 to Fresno. From Fresno, take Highway 180 east for 55 miles to the park entrance station.

Ash Mountain Entrance in the Foothills—Take Highway 99 to Visalia. From Visalia, take Highway 198 east for 36 miles to the park entrance station. Note: Due to the steep, winding nature of the Generals Highway in southern Sequoia National Park, vehicles longer than 22 feet are advised to use the Big Stump Entrance on Highway 180.

Mineral King Entrance—Take Highway 99 to Visalia. From Visalia, take Highway 198 east for 35 miles to the town of Three Rivers. Turn right on Mineral King Road and drive 11 miles to the park entrance station, then another 10 miles into Mineral King Valley. Note: Allow 90 minutes for the circuitous drive.

South Fork Entrance—Take Highway 99 to Visalia. From Visalia, take Highway 198 east for 33 miles to one mile west of the town of Three Rivers. Turn right on South Fork Road and drive 13 miles to South Fork Campground.

DRIVE TIME
• Drive time from Los Angeles: approximately 5 hours.
• Drive time from San Francisco: approximately 5 hours.

ENTRANCE FEES
There is a $10 entrance fee per vehicle at Sequoia and Kings Canyon National Parks, good for seven days. A Sequoia and Kings Canyon annual pass is available for $20. See the "entrance fees" section on page 200 for information on purchasing an annual pass to all national parks.

WHEN TO GO
The roads into Kings Canyon and Mineral King are closed by snow each winter, usually by late October. The Kings Canyon Road often re-opens by April; the Mineral King Road usually re-opens in May or June. The Generals Highway, which runs between Grant Grove in Kings Canyon and southern Sequoia National Park, is also sometimes closed for snow. Chains may be required on park roads at any time.

Only a few areas of Sequoia and Kings Canyon are open year-round for hiking, specifically those in the Foothills region near the Ash Mountain entrance. Day-hikers should plan on most trails being clear of snow in the lower elevations from April to October and in the higher elevations from June to October. As the timing of snowfall and snowmelt vary greatly from year to year, always phone the park for a road and trail update before planning your trip.

WEATHER CONDITIONS

The majority of Kings Canyon and Sequoia National Parks is blessed with typical Sierra summer weather: warm, clear days with temperatures in the 70s and low 80s, and cool nights with temperatures in the 40s and 50s. However, portions of Kings Canyon and Sequoia are at lower elevations and are substantially hotter in the summer; these include the Cedar Grove area of Kings Canyon (4,600 feet in elevation) and the Foothills region of Sequoia (1,500 to 3,500 feet in elevation).

The general rule for summer in the parks: Bring warm clothes for evenings (especially if you're camping) and a variety of layers for hiking. Beware of afternoon thunderstorms in late summer; carry rain gear and stay off mountain peaks if a storm is threatening.

WHERE TO STAY

The parks have 12 campgrounds that are available on a first-come, first-served basis. Two more campgrounds are available by advance reservation: Lodgepole and Dorst in Sequoia National Park. Phone (800) 365-2267 to reserve.

Neighboring Sequoia National Forest also has nine campgrounds available; some sites can be reserved by phoning (800) 280-2267. For more information on Sequoia National Forest, phone the Hume Lake Ranger District at (209) 338-2251.

Several types of lodging exist within the park. One call to a general reservations line (209-335-5500) can reserve you a space at Wuksachi Lodge near Giant Forest, Grant Grove Lodge in Grant Grove, Cedar Grove Lodge in Cedar Grove, or Stony Creek Lodge between Grant Grove and Lodgepole. Three other lodgings exist within the park: Silver City Resort in Mineral King: (209) 561-3223; Kings Canyon Lodge between Grant Grove and Cedar Grove: (209) 335-2405; and Montecito-Sequoia Lodge between Grant Grove and Lodgepole: (800) 227-9900 or (209) 565-3388.

FOOD & SUPPLIES

Restaurants and small stores are located at Grant Grove, Cedar Grove, Lodgepole, Stony Creek, Mineral King, and Wuksachi Village.

SUGGESTED MAPS

Park maps are available at park entrance stations or by contacting Sequoia and Kings Canyon National Parks at the address on page 310. A more detailed map is available for a fee from Tom Harrison Cartography at (415) 456-7940 or Trails Illustrated at (800) 962-1643.

1. CHICAGO STUMP TRAIL

near Grant Grove, Sequoia National Forest
Peaceful stroll in a second-growth forest

DISTANCE: 0.4 mile round-trip; 20 minutes   **LEVEL:** Easy
ELEVATION: Start at 6,600 feet; total change 0 feet   **CROWDS:** Minimal
BEST SEASON: June to October   **RATING:** ★ ★

DIRECTIONS: From the Big Stump Entrance Station at Kings Canyon National Park, drive north for 1.5 miles and turn left for Grant Grove. Drive approximately 4.5 miles, passing Grant Grove Village, then turn left at the sign for Forest Service Road 13S03. Drive two miles, then turn right on Road 13S65 and continue one-tenth of a mile to the Chicago Stump Trailhead.

Some might argue that this trail is too short to be considered a hike, but if you're looking for a chance to get away from the crowds in the Grant Grove Village area, or maybe take an after-dinner walk on a summer evening, this easy walk is for you. The Chicago Stump Trail is actually in Sequoia National Forest, not Kings Canyon National Park. The national park's highway goes right through Sequoia National Forest; it's the only road available to get from one section of Kings Canyon to the next. A two-mile drive off the highway brings you to the trailhead for the Chicago Stump.

The Chicago Stump Trail traverses a small part of the Converse Basin, which was once one of the largest and finest groves of giant Sequoias in the world. Then, at the turn of the century, a couple of lumber companies got the bright idea to chop down all the trees. In 1877, after hearing word of the massive logging operations, conservationist John Muir hiked to Converse Basin, only to find the damage already done. This served as part of his impetus to fight for the preservation of other Sequoia groves in what is now national park land. The battle wasn't won, however, until 13 years later when Sequoia National Park was created in 1890.

Today, where the giants once stood, second-growth Sequoias have taken hold, as well as many other mixed conifers and hardwoods. As you walk, you'll see that this is a young and pretty forest, although its scenery certainly doesn't compare to the glory days when the giant Sequoias reigned.

A 10-minute walk on a flat, dirt trail brings you to the Chicago Stump—a massive stump that belonged to the General Noble Tree, which was one of the largest trees in the world. The fire-blackened, centuries-old stump is 20 feet high and 70 feet around its perimeter.

The tree was cut down in 1893, and the lower portion of the tree was exhibited at the Chicago World's Exposition in 1895. It took an incredible feat of engineering, remarkable even by today's standards: The tree was cut about 20 feet from its base, and six-inch thick, 14-foot long sections of it were removed with the bark still attached. Each section was carefully labeled and marked for reassembly, then shipped to Chicago, where the pieces were painstakingly put back together.

What seems like a terrible tragedy today was called "education" then; the exhibition of the great tree pieces was the only way to show the public (and have them actually believe) the true size of the Sequoias of California.

2. BOOLE TREE LOOP

near Grant Grove, Sequoia National Forest
Kings Canyon vistas and one of the largest trees in the world

DISTANCE: 2.5 miles round-trip; 1.2 hours   **LEVEL:** Easy/moderate
ELEVATION: Start at 6,200 feet; total change 600 feet   **CROWDS:** Minimal
BEST SEASON: June to October   **RATING:** ★ ★ ★ ★

DIRECTIONS: From the Big Stump Entrance Station at Kings Canyon National Park, drive north for 1.5 miles and turn left for Grant Grove. Drive approximately six miles, passing Grant Grove Village, then turn left at the sign for Forest Service Road 13S55, Boole Tree, Converse Basin, and Stump Meadow. Drive 2.6 miles and park in the wide parking pullout.

The drive in to the Boole Tree trailhead is worth the trip by itself—you pass through Stump Meadow, a beautiful, ghostly meadow filled with more than 60 giant Sequoia stumps. It is believed that this meadow held a nearly pure stand of Sequoias (with few or no other trees among them) before it was logged. The clusters of huge stumps create an eerie impression that will stay ingrained in your memory for a long time.

Like the Chicago Stump Trail (see the previous story), the Boole Tree Trail is in Sequoia National Forest, not Kings Canyon National Park, but it's easily accessible off the Kings Canyon highway. But unlike the Chicago Stump Trail, this hike has some distance to it, and enough elevation change to make you feel like you got some exercise. Although the prime attraction is the Boole Tree, the largest tree in any of our national forests (not our national parks), the route also offers some fine views of the high peaks of Kings Canyon.

The Boole Tree hike is a loop, and it's a good idea to take the right side of the loop first, making the ascent more gradual. You climb 500 feet to the top of a ridge via some railroad-tie stair-steps at the start. The trail is well-built, with a smooth surface, and leads through a thick, mixed forest. At the top of the ridge, the trail descends down the other side, reaching the Boole Tree at one mile from the trailhead. (It's just off the main loop, accessible via a short, obvious spur on your right.)

At 269 feet tall and with a diameter of 35 feet, the Boole Tree qualifies as one of the largest trees in the world. It is estimated to be more than 2,000 years old. Unfortunately, it is one of only a few older Sequoias left standing in the Converse Basin grove. The rest were clear-cut at the turn of the century. Here's the weirdest part: The giant tree was named after Frank Boole, the superintendent at the Converse Basin Mill. Apparently, he was the guy who decided to spare this tree, even as he ordered his men to saw down all the rest.

Although some people go see the Boole Tree and then turn around for a two-mile hike, it's better to finish out the loop. For an extra half mile of hiking, you're rewarded with a stellar overlook of Spanish Mountain and the Kings River Canyon. This makes an excellent spot for lunch.

View of Spanish Mountain from the Boole Tree Loop

3. YUCCA POINT

near Cedar Grove, Sequoia National Forest
Fishing and swimming in the Kings River

DISTANCE: 4.0 miles round-trip; 2 hours   **LEVEL:** Moderate
ELEVATION: Start at 3,400 feet; total change 1,200 feet   **CROWDS:** Minimal
BEST SEASON: May to October   **RATING:** ★ ★ ★

DIRECTIONS: From the Big Stump Entrance Station at Kings Canyon National Park, drive north for 1.5 miles and turn left for Grant Grove. Continue 16 miles on Highway 180, past Kings Canyon Lodge, to the Yucca Point Trailhead on the left. Park in the pullouts alongside Highway 180.

The Yucca Point Trail is an upside-down hike, the kind where you go down on the way in (so easy) and up on the way back (not so easy). The path descends from Highway 180 to the Kings River, dropping 1,200 feet along the way. We looked at it from the top and assumed it would be brutal on the way back, but as long as you don't climb uphill at high noon, it's not as bad as it looks.

The path is primarily used by anglers heading down to the wild trout section of the Kings River, but hikers like the excellent views it provides and the access to the river's cool, sandy, emerald-green pools. Would-be swimmers, use extreme caution: The Kings River is one of the most powerful rivers in California, and some years, it runs with a fury even into mid-summer. Entering the water should only be attempted late in the summer, after the river level has dropped substantially and the current has dissipated.

Note that wearing long pants and long sleeves may be a good idea on this trail, not just because of the scratchy chaparral plants, but also because of possible poison oak and ticks.

The trail is well graded with many switchbacks. Views are excellent, especially in the first mile of trail. Huge Spanish Mountain soars to the north at 10,051 feet, and far below you is the confluence of the South and Middle Forks of the Kings River. If you hike early enough in the year when the buckeye trees are blooming along the lower portion of the trail, you'll be treated to many flitting butterflies and an intoxicatingly sweet smell from the tree's prolific white flowers.

In a fast two miles, the trail deposits you near the confluence of the South and Middle Forks. If the flow is low enough, you can wander up and down along the river, looking for the best fishing or swimming holes. If the water is high or fast, don't take any chances. Just sit down on a rock and watch the spectacle of a wild, free-running stream.

4. WINDY CLIFFS

near Cedar Grove, Sequoia National Forest
A view-filled trail by Boyden Cave

DISTANCE: 3.0 miles round-trip; 1.5 hours   **LEVEL:** Easy/moderate

ELEVATION: Start at 3,050 feet; total change 400 feet   **CROWDS:** Minimal

BEST SEASON: May to October   **RATING:** ★ ★ ★

DIRECTIONS: From the Big Stump Entrance Station at Kings Canyon National Park, drive north for 1.5 miles and turn left for Grant Grove. Continue 22 miles on Highway 180 to the parking area for Boyden Cave, on the right side of the road.

The Windy Cliffs Trail begins near the entrance to Boyden Cave, one of many limestone caverns in the vicinity of Kings Canyon and Sequoia National Parks. The cave was discovered in 1906 by J.P. Boyden, a cook at a nearby logging camp who was fishing in the Kings River on his day off. Today the cave is one of Kings Canyon's most popular attractions; the parking lot is always busy with busloads and carloads full of people waiting to take a guided tour. Boyden Cave has electric lights; you won't need your headlamp to see its stalactites and stalagmites.

The cave tour is worthwhile, but it will cost you a few bucks. While you're waiting for your tour to start, or even if you don't take the tour at all, you can take this stellar hike on the Windy Cliffs Trail and get million-dollar views of Kings Canyon for free.

From the gift shop, walk up the paved path and take the left fork near the entrance to the cave. (You may want to tell the people in charge that you're going to hike the Windy Cliffs Trail; otherwise they may think you're trying to sneak into the cave for free.) The trail is signed as "not maintained," but never fear, it's well used. The cliffs have some steep dropoffs, however, so use caution and common sense. If you have young children with you, this trail may not be a good idea.

Right from the start you have views of the Windy Cliffs—2,000-foot-high marble cliffs that are bluish in color. You'll see some of this blue marble close-up as you pass Windy Gulch. This is the carbonate rock that, combined with the eroding power of water and high acidity levels, caused Boyden Cave's formation.

In no time, you'll climb a little higher and attain a sweeping panorama of the fast-flowing Kings River and Highway 180 below. In one mile of hiking, you'll spy Boulder Creek cascading down the hillside. The trail curves away from the Kings River and Highway 180 and turns into Boulder Creek's canyon. The hike is over when the trail reaches creekside at 1.5 miles; at one time the trail continued across a bridge here, but it washed out and was never replaced. Find a good spot to sit by the creek and listen to its music before you head back.

5. LEWIS CREEK TRAIL

near Cedar Grove, Kings Canyon National Park
A challenging climb to a large, lush meadow

DISTANCE: 8.6 or 11.6 miles round-trip; 5 or 7 hours
ELEVATION: Start at 4,600 feet; total change 1,900 feet or 3,200 feet
LEVEL: Strenuous   **CROWDS:** Minimal
BEST SEASON: May to July   **RATING:** ★ ★ ★

DIRECTIONS: From the Big Stump Entrance Station at Kings Canyon National Park, drive north for 1.5 miles and turn left for Grant Grove. Continue 31 miles on Highway 180 to the Lewis Creek Trail parking area on the north side of the road (1.3 miles before you reach Cedar Grove Village).

Up, up, and up. If you're willing to climb 3,200 feet over the course of 5.8 miles, your reward is pristine Frypan Meadow at 7,800 feet in elevation. If you make it, there's an excellent chance that you'll be the only day-hiker around for miles. Any other humans you'll meet will be backpackers making camp near the meadow, and they'll be surprised to see you.

In early summer, the circular meadow is green and littered with wildflowers, a glorious sight after the hot, sunny climb. But there's no way to see it without first putting in some effort on the Lewis Creek Trail. The good news is that if the first mile or so proves to be too demanding (or too hot if you don't start first thing in the morning), you can always take the right fork at 1.6 miles and head back downhill on the Hotel Creek Trail, making a seven-mile loop out of the trip. Alternatively, the crossing of Lewis Creek at 4.3 miles out also makes a fine day-hiking destination.

The first couple miles of trail are a bit monotonous, as you climb relentlessly upward along the Lewis Creek drainage. If you're lucky enough to be hiking when the trailside ceanothus is blooming bright white and sweetly scented, your trip will be much more pleasant. The ceanothus has grown with a fury since a wildfire here in 1980. At your feet you'll see bright red Indian paintbrush and blue lupine.

Pass the junction with the Hotel Creek Trail at 1.6 miles, enjoying an easier grade for the next couple of miles as well as blessed shade. At 3.2 miles, you'll cross Comb Creek in a thick stand of pines and cedars. You may want to take a dip in the shallow pools here before continuing your ascent.

At 4.3 miles and 6,500 feet in elevation, you'll finally meet up with Lewis Creek, which you've been paralleling all day. The trail crosses the creek to its west side. Many day-hikers make this crossing their destination for the day; there are fine pools for swimming and flat spots for picnicking. If you decide to press onward, be forewarned: The climb is

Lewis Creek Trail

not over. If you grunt it out, in a mile and a half you'll find yourself at the edge of Frypan Meadow, elevation 7,800 feet, counting the leopard lilies and shooting stars. What a day.

6. HOTEL CREEK TRAIL to CEDAR GROVE OVERLOOK

near Cedar Grove, Kings Canyon National Park
Loop trail with a spectacular viewpoint

DISTANCE: 5.0 or 7.0 miles round-trip; 3 or 4 hours   **LEVEL:** Moderate
ELEVATION: Start at 4,650 feet; total change 1,200 feet   **CROWDS:** Minimal
BEST SEASON: May to October   **RATING:** ★ ★ ★ ★

DIRECTIONS: From the Big Stump Entrance Station at Kings Canyon National Park, drive north for 1.5 miles and turn left for Grant Grove. Continue 31.5 miles on Highway 180 to Cedar Grove Village. Turn left at the sign for the visitor center and Cedar Grove Lodge. Continue on the main road past the lodge for a quarter-mile, then turn right. The Hotel Creek Trailhead is on the left in a few hundred feet.

The destination on this trip is a stunning overlook of Kings Canyon, one of the deepest canyons in the United States. In fact, the canyon vistas are continual for most of the hike, so even if you don't make it to the overlook, you'll still get an eyeful of the Kings River and its tall granite surroundings: Lookout Peak, Avalanche Peak, Buck Peak, and Sentinel Dome.

The Hotel Creek Trail consists of dozens of switchbacks over open, sunny slopes, climbing 1,200 feet over two miles. Although in your first few feet of trail you'll encounter some oaks and pines, don't be misled: This is not a forested hike. Within a half-mile, the trees vanish, and you'll be left with nothing but brush and chaparral for companions. Your best bet is to start this hike early in the morning, before the day heats up.

At two miles, the climb ends when you reach a trail junction with the Overlook Trail. Turn left to head to the overlook, at the far point on the ridgeline nearly a half-mile away. It's an easy saunter to the overlook, which peers down on Cedar Grove and the length of Kings Canyon. Some people call this the Kings Canyon Overlook; others call it the Cedar Grove Overlook. Arguably, the best views aren't of either Cedar Grove or Kings Canyon; they're to the north, of the high peaks of the Monarch Divide. Hope you came with picnic supplies. If you're hot and tired of the sunshine, you can find a little shade from one

Hotel Creek Trail above the Cedar Grove Overlook

lonely pine tree growing out of the rock.

For a five-mile round-trip, retrace your steps back to Cedar Grove. But if you want to walk farther, you can continue north from the overlook junction for another 1.5 miles, then turn left and hike downhill on the Lewis Creek Trail, making a seven-mile loop out of the trip. This loop is highly recommended because of the lovely conifer forest just north of the overlook junction, and the ease of the trail. You've climbed high enough already to be out of the chaparral; it is replaced by a yellow pine forest that suffered substantial fire damage in 1980 but is recovering nicely. It's noticeably cooler and shadier up here, and the trail is mostly level. Through the tall, straight pines, you get continual views of the Monarch Wilderness peaks. Early in summer, the mountains are often still crowned with snow.

The loop trail will make only one more short rise as it curves around to the neighboring canyon to meet up with the Lewis Creek Trail. Turn left on this trail and prepare for a long downhill stretch, paralleling Lewis Creek. The path is lined with sweet-smelling ceanothus, but it offers no shade.

At the Lewis Creek Trailhead in Kings Canyon, you must turn left to return to your car on either the park road or the trail, which parallels the road. The road is flatter and easier. These final 1.2 miles of the loop are a bit dull, but the rest of the hike is so good, you won't complain.

7. DON CECIL TRAIL to SHEEP CREEK

near Cedar Grove, Kings Canyon National Park
A deep gorge with pretty cascades

DISTANCE: 2.0 miles round-trip; 1 hour   **LEVEL:** Easy/moderate
ELEVATION: Start at 4,650 feet; total change 600 feet   **CROWDS:** Minimal
BEST SEASON: May to October   **RATING:** ★ ★ ★

DIRECTIONS: From the Big Stump Entrance Station at Kings Canyon National Park, drive north for 1.5 miles and turn left for Grant Grove. Continue 31.5 miles on Highway 180 and take the right fork for Cedar Grove. The Don Cecil Trailhead is on the right side of the road, a quarter-mile east of the turnoff for Cedar Grove Village and the visitor center. (If you reach Canyon View and Moraine campgrounds, you've gone too far.)

Here's the good news: The Don Cecil Trail has the gentlest grade and coolest shade of any of the trails that ascend Cedar Grove's towering canyon walls. Hallelujah! Here's the bad news: Even so, the trail still climbs with a vengeance, and by mid-day, the trail is hot.

Still, the path is smooth and lined with needles, not rocky or dusty. Unlike many trails in Kings Canyon, equestrians do not frequent this trail, so you don't have horse droppings to contend with. Shade is provided by an array of healthy trees: Incense cedars, sugar pines, white firs, and black oaks. The sweet scent of mountain misery is ubiquitous.

Start walking from the trailhead, and in a third of a mile, you'll cross a dirt service road, then continue uphill on the path. At three-quarters of a mile, after climbing about 600 feet, you'll reach an overlook with views of the high peaks of the Monarch Divide to the north.

From here, the trail drops into Sheep Creek's deep gorge. A bridge over the chasm provides views both up- and downstream of boisterous cascades sliding over granite ledges. The only disappointment is that you are prohibited from swimming here; Sheep Creek is the domestic water supply for Cedar Grove.

If you're wondering about the stream's name, Sheep Creek was christened by early sheepherders in Kings Canyon. Accordingly, the trail's namesake was Don Cecil, a sheepherder.

8. DON CECIL TRAIL to LOOKOUT PEAK
near Cedar Grove, Kings Canyon National Park
Grueling hike to a stellar summit

DISTANCE: 11.6 miles round-trip; 6 hours   **LEVEL:** Very strenuous
ELEVATION: Start at 4,650 feet; total change 3,900 feet   **CROWDS:** Minimal
BEST SEASON: May to October   **RATING:** ★ ★ ★ ★

DIRECTIONS: From the Big Stump Entrance Station at Kings Canyon National Park, drive north for 1.5 miles and turn left for Grant Grove. Continue 31.5 miles on Highway 180 and take the right fork for Cedar Grove. The Don Cecil Trailhead is on the right side of the road, a quarter-mile east of the turnoff for Cedar Grove Village and the visitor center. (If you reach Canyon View and Moraine campgrounds, you've gone too far.)

Lookout Peak at 8,531 feet in elevation is a summit worth ascending, even though it's an all-day trip with a 3,900-foot elevation gain. Of course, that's assuming you hike it in the manner of the "true mountaineer," meaning the hard way, from Cedar Grove. However, some people prefer to access Lookout Peak in a far different manner: They drive most of the way, via roads from the south in Sequoia National Forest through Horse Corral Meadow and Summit Meadow. With the long drive completed, they are left with a half mile hike to the summit of Lookout Peak, and only a 500-foot elevation gain.

Choose your route. Despite the huge difference in mileage and difficulty, I'd choose the long Cedar Grove path, because when you reach the top of Lookout Peak, you know you've earned it. A climb like this makes a summit feel like it should feel. The key for your trip is to carry plenty of water and plan on an early-morning start to beat the heat. (You can filter water from Sheep Creek at one mile in and again at four miles in.)

The trail that gets you to the peak is the Don Cecil Trail, the first mile of which is detailed in the previous story. You're blessed with a surprising amount of shade from pines, cedars, and firs, a rarity in Cedar Grove. Enjoy the pleasant first stretch and the scenic crossing of Sheep Creek at one mile out. From there, the switchbacks begin in earnest, and it's not until 3.5 miles that you get your first glimpse of Lookout Peak, as well as views across the canyon to the Monarch Divide. Mount Clarence King is the major peak to the northeast.

At 4.0 miles, you'll cross Sheep Creek again (now it's the west fork of the creek), amid a stretch of trail bearing prolific wildflowers. You'll leave the stream and climb to a ridge for the final mile and a half to the summit trail turnoff. The turnoff is at an obvious saddle south of the peak, where the trail meets the Big Meadows/Horse Corral Meadow Road. (Here you'll be joined by "peak hikers" who drove most of the way to the summit.) Take the half-mile summit trail from the saddle; the path peters out near the top, so just pick your way over the granite. The peak is littered with some microwave equipment, but just ignore it and focus on the fabulous surroundings.

From the 8,531-foot summit, you get an unforgettable Sierra view, with Kings Canyon far below you and peaks and ridges all around. The sight of the Sierra Crest to the east and the Monarch Divide to the north is truly awe-inspiring. Chances are good that the wind will be blowing hard; hopefully you stuffed a jacket into your daypack. Now this is how a summit should feel.

9. ROARING RIVER FALLS

near Cedar Grove, Kings Canyon National Park
An easy stroll to a river waterfall

DISTANCE: 0.4 mile round-trip; 20 minutes   **LEVEL:** Easy
ELEVATION: Start at 4,850 feet; total change 20 feet   **CROWDS:** Moderate
BEST SEASON: May to July   **RATING:** ★ ★ ★

DIRECTIONS: From the Big Stump Entrance Station at Kings Canyon National Park, drive north for 1.5 miles and turn left for Grant Grove. Continue 35 miles on Highway 180 to the sign for Roaring River Falls and the River Trail, three miles past Cedar Grove Village. The trailhead is on the right.

You might think that Roaring River Falls is the name of a waterfall that makes a lot of noise, but no; Roaring River Falls is a waterfall that falls on the Roaring River.

A great feature of Roaring River Falls is that it's the only waterfall in Kings Canyon and Sequoia National Parks that is accessible via wheelchair. The trail is paved, wide, and only four-tenths of a mile round-trip. If hikers on foot want a longer hike, they can continue upstream on the River Trail to Zumwalt Meadow in 1.6 miles or Road's End in 2.7 miles.

Getting to the falls is a breeze. After leaving your car in the Roaring River Falls parking lot, just follow the paved trail through the forest and you'll arrive in about five minutes. At the trail's end, you have a perfect view of the falls, nicely framed by a big Jeffrey pine on the right and two red firs on the left. The river funnels down through a narrow rock gorge, forming two water chutes—one is 40 feet tall; the one behind it is 20 feet tall. Your viewpoint is directly across from the waterfall, on the north side of the dark, gray, rocky bowl into which the water pounds.

Roaring River Falls

Roaring River Falls' pool is so large—probably 50 feet wide—and the cliffs surrounding it are so tall and sheer, that the falls are somewhat dwarfed. Keep in mind, however, that you are seeing only their final drop. The cascades continue for hundreds of feet upstream, hidden from view and inaccessible.

A good extension of this trip is to hike eastward on the River Trail to Zumwalt Meadow, follow the Zumwalt Meadow Loop, and then return on the River Trail to your parked car at the Roaring River Falls Trailhead. This is a nearly level, five mile round-trip. For details on the Zumwalt Meadow Loop, see the following story.

10. ZUMWALT MEADOW LOOP

near Cedar Grove, Kings Canyon National Park
Beautiful meadow along the South Fork Kings River

DISTANCE: 1.5 miles round-trip; 45 minutes   **LEVEL:** Easy
ELEVATION: Start at 4,950 feet; total change 50 feet   **CROWDS:** Moderate
BEST SEASON: May to October   **RATING:** ★ ★ ★ ★

DIRECTIONS: From the Big Stump Entrance Station at Kings Canyon National Park, drive north for 1.5 miles and turn left for Grant Grove. Continue 36 miles on Highway 180 to the parking area for Zumwalt Meadow, on the right side of the road.

What's the prettiest easy hike in Kings Canyon National Park? The Zumwalt Meadow Loop Trail wins hands down. It's a scenic, 1.5-mile hike along the South Fork Kings River that's suitable for hikers of all abilities, with surprises at every curve and turn of the trail.

Many people bring their fishing rods on this trail and try their luck in the river, but for most, the hiking is better than the fishing. The best part of angling in the South Fork Kings River is that it extends the time you spend on the Zumwalt Meadow Loop.

From the parking area, walk downstream along the river to a picturesque suspension footbridge, then cross it and walk back up-stream. The loop begins at an obvious fork, and you can hike it in either direction. We hiked the south side first, by bearing right at the fork. The path traverses a boulder field of jumbled rocks, evidence of a powerful rockslide. The trail is cut right through the rubble, which tumbled down from the Grand Sentinel, elevation 8,504 feet (on your right).

As you walk among the rocks, you have lovely views across the meadow and river of the cliffs on the north side of the canyon. Vistas of 8,717-foot North Dome are as awe-inspiring as the views of the Grand Sentinel on your side of the canyon.

As you start to loop back on the north side of the trail, you come out at the edge of a meadow in a thick, waist-high fern forest. We were surprised by a deer who was standing up to her neck in the ferns, nearly hidden from view. Walk downstream alongside the river, with the

Suspension bridge by Zumwalt Meadow

meadow on your left. When the trail reaches a marshy area, it leads up and over a wooden walkway, and sadly, you've finished out the loop. Take the short connector trail back to the suspension bridge and your starting point.

If you aren't in any hurry to leave, you can keep meandering on the River Trail, which heads downstream from the suspension bridge for 1.6 miles to Roaring River Falls (see the previous story).

11. MIST FALLS

near Cedar Grove, Kings Canyon National Park
A mist-spraying waterfall on the South Fork Kings River

DISTANCE: 8.2 miles round-trip; 4 hours   **LEVEL:** Moderate
ELEVATION: Start at 5,035 feet; total change 650 feet   **CROWDS:** Heavy
BEST SEASON: May to July   **RATING:** ★ ★ ★ ★ ★

DIRECTIONS: From the Big Stump Entrance Station at Kings Canyon National Park, drive north for 1.5 miles and turn left for Grant Grove. Continue 38 miles on Highway 180 to Road's End, six miles past Cedar Grove Village. The trailhead is at the east end of the parking lot, near the wilderness ranger station.

The Mist Falls Trail is easily the busiest hiking trail in the Cedar Grove area of Kings Canyon National Park. Although it's an eight mile round-trip to Mist Falls, they're easy miles, with a well-marked trail and only 650 feet of elevation gain. The route is equally shared by day-hikers heading to the river waterfall and backpackers heading to Paradise Valley and beyond, so if you want to have any solitude on your walk, you simply must start early in the morning.

The trail begins level and stays that way for the first two miles. That's convenient, because the scenery is so spectacular that you won't want to think about anything else. You find yourself craning your neck a lot, always looking up at the imposing canyon walls on both sides of the trail.

The oak, pine, and cedar forest is sparse, sandy, and dry at first, then becomes increasingly dense. Giant boulders are scattered around the trail, having dropped from the cliffs above sometime in the last 100,000 years. The roar of the South Fork Kings River is a pleasant accompaniment.

After a lovely shaded stretch where the forest closes in and ferns grow squeezed in between big boulders, you'll reach a junction at two miles out. Bear left and climb slightly, rising above the river. As you leave the forest and enter granite country, your views get increasingly spectacular. At three miles out, make sure you turn around and check out the vista of the Kings River canyon behind you, framed by 9,000-foot mountains on both sides. The epitome of classic Sierra drama is the silhouette of The Sphinx (an odd-shaped granite peak that looks remotely like the Egyptian Sphinx) with Avalanche Peak alongside.

At exactly four miles from the trailhead, after a few switchbacks on exposed granite and some heavy breathing, you're at a signed

Downstream of Mist Falls

overlook of Mist Falls at the Kings River's edge. If you don't like the view from here, veer right on the use trails that drop to the base of the falls, but use caution. Although the fall is not high, only about 45 feet, it exhibits tremendous flair as it fans out over a wide granite ledge and then crashes into a boulder-lined pool. Mist Falls is famous for the mist and spray it exudes, but it's perhaps more impressive for the amount of noise it makes. In spring and early summer, you have to shout at your hiking companions to be heard.

If the crowds get too heavy for you on the Mist Falls Trail, there's a less-used alternate route for the homeward trip: When you return to the trail junction at the halfway point, turn left and cross Bailey Bridge. Walk an eighth of a mile, passing by the Bubbs Creek Trail junction, then turn right, heading back on the River Trail on the south side of the Kings River. In addition to leaving most of the crowds behind, this trail has great views. You'll need to walk slightly downstream of the trailhead to reach a bridge where you can cross the river and head back to your car.

12. COPPER CREEK TRAIL to LOWER TENT MEADOW

near Cedar Grove, Kings Canyon National Park
An ascent to a high meadow

DISTANCE: 7.4 miles round-trip; 4 hours   **LEVEL:** Strenuous
ELEVATION: Start at 5,050 feet; total change 2,800 feet   **CROWDS:** Minimal
BEST SEASON: May to October   **RATING:** ★ ★ ★

DIRECTIONS: From the Big Stump Entrance Station at Kings Canyon National Park, drive north for 1.5 miles and turn left for Grant Grove. Continue 38 miles on Highway 180 to Road's End, six miles past Cedar Grove Village. The trail begins at the long-term parking area on the north side of the loop at Road's End.

The Copper Creek Trailhead is at 5,050 feet, and Lower Tent Meadow is at 7,850 feet, so it's not hard to do the math. If you're up for a day hike with a 2,800-foot elevation gain over less than four miles, the Copper Creek Trail is your ticket to happiness. But keep in mind that the route is often hot and dry as it switchbacks up manzanita-covered slopes. An early morning start is a must. This trail is considered one of the most strenuous in the Cedar Grove area, but since you won't travel very far on it, you'll be fine as long as you carry plenty of water.

If you've hiked the Hotel Creek Trail just down the road in Kings Canyon, this trail will feel remarkably familiar at its start. It climbs the steep north wall of the canyon on a sandy trail, beginning in a stand of conifers but quickly leaving them for chaparral country. The trail is well graded and well built, with extensive rock work. Views are even better than on the Hotel Creek Trail. The most prominent landmark is the Grand Sentinel, elevation 8,504 feet, directly across the canyon.

After the first mile and about a dozen switchbacks, the trail starts to veer into the Copper Creek Canyon, and you lose some of your views of Kings Canyon.

Luckily, you re-enter the forest, and by two miles out your elevation is high enough so that you're shaded by a mix of beautiful conifers: cedars, pines, and white firs. The hardest work of this trip is over; the trail runs a straighter uphill course with almost no switchbacks.

Slightly more than three miles out, you'll reach a stand of aspens, their leaves swaying in the breeze. Only a half-mile farther is the edge of Lower Tent Meadow, a series of small grassy spots near a tributary of Copper Creek. You'll most likely see backpackers making camp here; they are resting up for the long trek into the Granite Lake Basin, below the peaks of the Monarch Divide.

13. GENERAL GRANT TREE

near Grant Grove, Kings Canyon National Park
A visit to the third largest tree in the world

DISTANCE: 0.6 mile round-trip; 20 minutes   **LEVEL:** Easy
ELEVATION: Start at 6,350 feet; total change 50 feet   **CROWDS:** Heavy
BEST SEASON: Year-round   **RATING:** ★ ★ ★

DIRECTIONS: From the Big Stump Entrance Station at Kings Canyon National Park, drive north for 1.5 miles and turn left for Grant Grove. Drive two miles, passing Grant Grove Village, to the left turnoff for General Grant Tree. Turn left and follow the access road for one mile to the parking lot.

NOTE: An interpretive brochure is available at the trailhead.

No visit to the Grant Grove area of Kings Canyon National Park is complete without a stop to see the General Grant Tree, the third largest tree in the world. The problem, of course, is that everyone else in the park is stopping to see the General Grant Tree, making the parking lot and paved hiking trail look something like Times Square on New Year's Eve. To make your trip more pleasant, visit either very early in the

Giant Sequoia near the General Grant Tree

morning (before 9 A.M. is best) or in the last hours of daylight, when most people are having dinner.

The best asset of this paved loop through the giant Sequoia grove is that it allows both wheelchair users and hikers to have a look at the General Grant Tree and numerous other big trees. Many of them have patriotic names, like the Robert E. Lee Tree and the Lincoln Tree, while others are named after 29 of our country's 50 states. Although the tree-naming seems a little silly, the big trees are truly impressive. Because visitation in this grove is so heavy, almost all of the trees are protected by split-rail fences. It's a bit unnerving—kind of like watching wild animals in the zoo—but the fences protect the trees' fragile roots.

The star of the trail, of course, is the General Grant Tree. Estimated at 1,800 to 2,000 years old, the General Grant is 267 feet tall and 107 feet in circumference at its base. Although it is only the third largest tree in the world, it has the widest base diameter of any tree, at more than 40 feet. If those numbers are hard for you to visualize, consider this modern-day analogy: If the General Grant Tree was transplanted to the middle of a freeway, its immense girth would block more than three lanes of traffic. If you tried to move it out of the freeway, you would find that it weighs more than 700 large cars.

President Calvin Coolidge proclaimed the tree to be "the nation's Christmas tree." Every year since 1926, the park has held a Christmas celebration around its base.

Two other highlights on the trail are the Fallen Monarch (a hollow, downed tree that is so wide, it was once used as a stable for the U.S. Cavalry, and as a park employee camp), and the Gamlin Cabin. The cabin was built in 1872 by Canadians Thomas and Israel Gamlin, who attempted to establish squatter's rights on these 160 acres of giant Sequoias. Although the cabin has been rebuilt and altered to make it more decay-resistant, it gives visitors some idea of what life was like for the Gamlin brothers and other early lumbermen.

14. NORTH GROVE & DEAD GIANT LOOP

near Grant Grove, Kings Canyon National Park
A longer hike near the General Grant Tree

DISTANCE: 3.0 miles round-trip; 1.5 hours   **LEVEL:** Easy/moderate
ELEVATION: Start at 6,350 feet; total change 400 feet   **CROWDS:** Moderate
BEST SEASON: Year-round   **RATING:** ★ ★

DIRECTIONS: From the Big Stump Entrance Station at Kings Canyon National Park, drive north for 1.5 miles and turn left for Grant Grove. Drive two miles, passing Grant Grove Village, to the left turnoff for General Grant Tree. Turn left and follow the access road for one mile to the parking lot. The North Grove Loop starts from the far end of the lower parking lot.

For people who want a little more hiking and a little less company than the General Grant Tree Trail provides (see the previous story), the combined North Grove and Dead Giant loop trails are the answer. The walk begins on an old dirt road, which leads downhill through a mixed forest of Sequoia, sugar pine, white fir, and dogwood. Don't expect to see dense groves of Sequoias here; the big trees are few and far between. But the forest is pleasant, quiet, and shady.

Stay to the right at the first junction to follow the North Grove Loop. At the bottom of the hill, you'll pass an obscure junction with an old wagon road that was used to take logged Sequoias to Millwood, an 1890s mill town. Stay on the main road and climb back uphill to a more obvious junction at one mile out. Here, hikers who want a shorter trip can turn left and walk back to the trailhead for a 1.5-mile round-trip. Everyone else should turn sharply right and walk a quarter mile downhill to Lion Meadow. Turn right on a single-track trail and circle around the meadow, heading for the Dead Giant. This Sequoia, like some others in the park, is a nearly hollow, long dead tree that miraculously keeps standing. It appears that humans caused this tree's death: If you look closely, you can see axe marks in its side.

From the Dead Giant it's a short tromp to the Sequoia Lake Overlook, a tranquil high point where you can have a snack and enjoy the view of a large, private lake in Sequoia National Forest. The lake was formed in 1889, when the Sanger Lumber Company dammed what was previously a meadow to make a mill pond. The lumber company then built a flume which traveled 54 miles from their mill to the railroads in the San Joaquin Valley. The flume, filled with water supplied from the mill pond, was capable of carrying 250,000 board feet of lumber in one day.

From the overlook, backtrack a few yards, then turn right to finish out the loop. When you reach the wide dirt road, turn left and head back uphill to your starting point. You'll have a 400-foot gain on the return trip.

15. PANORAMIC POINT & PARK RIDGE LOOKOUT

near Grant Grove, Kings Canyon National Park
Long-distance views from a fire lookout tower

DISTANCE: 4.7 miles round-trip; 2.5 hours   **LEVEL:** Easy/moderate
ELEVATION: Start at 7,150 feet; total change 500 feet   **CROWDS:** Minimal
BEST SEASON: June to October   **RATING:** ★ ★ ★

DIRECTIONS: From the Big Stump Entrance Station at Kings Canyon National Park, drive north for 1.5 miles and turn left for Grant Grove. Drive 1.5 miles to Grant Grove Village and turn right by the visitor center and store. Follow the road past the cabins, and take the right fork for Panoramic Point. It's 2.3 miles from the visitor center to Panoramic Point.

This view-filled hike begins with a warm-up: A 300-yard paved walk uphill to Panoramic Point, elevation 7,250 feet. The point delivers what its name implies—a stunning panoramic vista. An interpretive display names the many peaks and valleys you can see across the national parks, including the big pointy one, Mount Goddard at 13,560 feet. On clear days, this is a highly memorable introduction to Kings Canyon.

From Panoramic Point, take the dirt trail that leads to the right along the ridge. The trail starts out flat and then switchbacks uphill for a couple turns, following the ridgeline. There are plenty of boulders on which you can sit and enjoy the view, as well as blooming wildflowers along the forested route.

At a junction with a dirt road, follow the road to the left for about 50 yards, then pick up the trail again (on your left). If you want to cut some distance off your trip, you can stay on the dirt road and follow it all the way to the Park Ridge Fire Lookout. The road and trail run roughly parallel, but the road is more direct. The trail, however, has much finer views.

If you stay on the trail, you'll meet the dirt road again about 100 yards below the fire lookout. Turn left and take the final uphill walk. When you reach the lookout tower, check out the nifty outdoor shower at its base. If someone is stationed in the tower and they give you permission to come upstairs, do so. Meet the friendly lookout person, and sign the visitor register. (The lookout person rarely gets visitors on cloudy days, but he or she gets plenty of them when it's sunny and the vista extends for miles.)

Because the trail and/or road you hiked made a consistent curve to the south, the fire lookout tower has surprisingly different views than those at Panoramic Point. Your field of vision includes the postcard-like Sierra Crest to the east, but you can also look down on the town of Pinehurst and the San Joaquin Valley to the west. The lookout person told us that on a clear day, you can see all the way to the Coast Range, 100 miles westward. The lookout is staffed only during the fire season, which is usually May to October.

For your return trip, you have two choices: Walk back down the dirt road and then take the trail back to Panoramic Point, or follow the dirt road all the way downhill to the parking lot.

16. MANZANITA & AZALEA LOOP

near Grant Grove, Kings Canyon National Park
A forested hike featuring blooming azaleas

DISTANCE: 3.3 miles round-trip; 1.5 hours **LEVEL:** Easy/moderate
ELEVATION: Start at 6,600; total change 800 feet **CROWDS:** Minimal
BEST SEASON: June to October **RATING:** ★ ★

DIRECTIONS: From the Big Stump Entrance Station at Kings Canyon National Park, drive north for 1.5 miles and turn left for Grant Grove. Drive 1.5 miles to Grant Grove Village and park in the large parking lot near the visitor center. Walk on the service road behind the village buildings (and near the tent cabins) to reach the start of the Manzanita Trail.

This hike is a good exercise route for vacationers staying in the cabins at Grant Grove Village or in the nearby campgrounds. It climbs 800 feet, which gives your heart and lungs a workout, and it's pretty every step of the way. Unlike the "glamour" trails in the area, like the General Grant Tree Trail, this one is free of crowds at almost any time of the day.

In part, that's because the trailhead may be the most well hidden of any in the park. Here are some clues for finding it: Walk on the paved road behind the village market and restaurant. Look for an adjoining road that leads due east, signed as "Residential Area." Follow that road for a quarter-mile until you see a signed, narrow trail branching off to the right. Take it; this is the Manzanita Trail, which climbs a dry slope to Park Ridge.

Fortunately, as you ascend, you'll have plenty of cool shade from firs and pines. You'll bear the brunt of the work in the first mile; after that the grade gets much easier. Stay right at two junctions with adjoining trails, and prepare for your views to the west to start opening up. You'll see miles of forest, and the San Joaquin Valley far beyond.

True to this trail's name, the primary flora you'll find (aside from the conifers) is manzanita, the shrubby "little apple" bush. It is named for its sour, dry, red berries. Near the top of your climb, you'll parallel the dirt road that leads to the Park Ridge Fire Lookout. Then at 1.5 miles, Manzanita Trail meets up with the fire road and also the Azalea Trail. Turn right on the Azalea Trail and descend on a much shadier, wetter slope, still in thick forest. The trail's namesake azaleas bloom bright white in June and July; one of the best places to see them is along the moist, fern-covered banks of Sequoia Creek, about a half-mile from the fire road. (Don't wait till late in the summer to hike this trail, or the upper reaches of Sequoia Creek may be dry.)

Keep descending, staying close to the pretty stream, and you'll soon near the boundary of Wilsonia, a private community within the national park. At the paved road to Wilsonia, take your pick: Either follow the Wilsonia road back to the Grant Grove area (turn right), or cross the road to stay on the Azalea Trail back to Grant Grove. The last three-quarters of a mile on the Azalea Trail are a dull stretch; the trail parallels Highway 180 and then crosses to the south side. You'll have to cross the highway again to get back to your car.

---

17. SUNSET TRAIL

near Grant Grove, Kings Canyon National Park
Small waterfalls, giant Sequoias, and dense firs

DISTANCE: 5.5 miles round-trip; 3 hours   **LEVEL:** Moderate
ELEVATION: Start at 6,590 feet; total change 1,200 feet   **CROWDS:** Moderate
BEST SEASON: June to October   **RATING:** ★ ★ ★ ★

DIRECTIONS: From the Big Stump Entrance Station at Kings Canyon National Park, drive north for 1.5 miles and turn left for Grant Grove. Drive 1.5 miles to

Grant Grove Village and park in the large parking lot near the visitor center. Cross the road and walk on the paved trail toward Sunset Campground's amphitheater. Continue heading left through the camp to site #179, where the trail begins.

The Sunset Trail starts at Sunset Campground, right across the road from Grant Grove Village. It features a beautiful forest of pines and firs, stands of ceanothus and western azalea, two small waterfalls, and numerous stream crossings with sturdy wooden footbridges. With all this going for it, you might expect the Sunset Trail to be extremely popular, but usually it's not crowded.

The scenery is so pretty that you can easily become distracted, so keep this in mind: The trail is downhill all the way, with a total 1,200-foot elevation loss that you must gain back on the return trip. Luckily, the grade is moderate, and the return climb is easier than you think it's going to be.

Head gently downhill through an open forest filled with immense sugar pines, tall firs, and blooming azaleas in early summer. At 1.5 miles, you'll find a junction with the South Boundary Trail. If you like, take a short side trip to the left to Viola Falls, which isn't much of a waterfall but is a memorably scenic spot on granite-sculpted Sequoia Creek. The best thing about tiny Viola Falls is the huge Sequoia tree

Sunset Trail

that grows just upstream of it. The Sequoia has chunks of granite permanently fused in its above-ground roots. The big old tree grew right around the rocks, imprisoning them in its grasp.

If you continue farther on Sunset Trail, you'll reach Ella Falls at 2.25 miles, which also drops on Sequoia Creek. It's a 50-foot-tall narrow cascade that shimmers bright white among the gray rocks and dense green foliage along the stream. The granite streambed is an exquisite piece of rock art, having been continually rounded, sculpted, and eroded by the coursing stream. Alders and willows border the stream's edge. Look for tall cow parsnips and colorful leopard lilies growing along the banks.

If you'd like to continue hiking before making the uphill return trip to Sunset Campground, you can follow Sunset Trail for another half-mile to the YMCA camp on Sequoia Lake. Although Sequoia is a privately owned lake and not part of the park, you're allowed to stroll along the water's edge, but you must stay out of the private camp area. Swimming and fishing are not allowed, but picnic tables are situated near the lake's edge.

18. BIG STUMP TRAIL

near Grant Grove, Kings Canyon National Park
Cultural and natural history of men and big trees

DISTANCE: 1.0 mile round-trip; 30 minutes   **LEVEL:** Easy
ELEVATION: Start at 6,250 feet; total change 200 feet   **CROWDS:** Moderate
BEST SEASON: June to October   **RATING:** ★ ★

DIRECTIONS: From the Big Stump Entrance Station at Kings Canyon National Park, drive north for a half-mile and turn left into the Big Stump Picnic Area.

NOTE: An interpretive brochure is available at the trailhead.

If you're approaching Sequoia and Kings Canyon National Parks from the Fresno area, the first trailhead you'll reach in the parks is the Big Stump Trail, a mere half-mile from the park entrance station. Here is an excellent place to get out of the car, stretch your legs, and take an easy walk that reveals a fascinating history.

Be sure to pick up an interpretive brochure at the trailhead for the Big Stump Trail. The history lesson is well worth the 50 cents it will cost you. The brochure is an entertaining read; it is cleverly written in the voice of a late 1800s logger.

The Big Stump Trail leads gently downhill from the parking lot, then makes a short loop around a meadow. For the first few feet, the trail is paved, but it quickly changes to hard-packed dirt. Although many trails in Sequoia and Kings Canyon National Parks tell the stories of living Sequoia trees, this trail tells the story of logged Sequoias and the men who did the logging. Most of the big trees in this area were cut for timber in the 1880s.

A few giant Sequoias still thrive along the route, including one in the first 50 feet from the parking lot. The path's highlights include the Burnt Monarch (a shell of a Sequoia that

A big stump on the Big Stump Trail

has been ravaged by fire, but somehow still stands) and the Mark Twain Stump. The latter belonged to a 26-foot-wide tree that took two men 13 days to cut down. It was approximately 1,700 years old when it was felled in 1891. The tree wasn't used by the loggers; instead, a piece of it was sent to the American Museum of Natural History in New York to be placed on exhibition.

The trail leads right across the Sutter Giant, a huge fallen Sequoia. Just off the loop is the Sawed Tree, a still living Sequoia that exhibits the gash of the lumberjack's saw. Look for pink, fresh-looking sawdust piles in place along the trail. The piles have been sitting here for a century; the tannin in the Sequoia wood makes its sawdust slow to decay.

Perhaps the biggest irony (and tragedy) of the era of Sequoia logging was that the trees made terrible lumber. When the big Sequoias fell, their wood shattered and split. The loggers dug "featherbeds," or huge trenches lined with soft branches, to help cushion the fall of the giant trees, but still the brittle wood shattered. At least half of every logged Sequoia was wasted, and the parts that were used went for relative nonessentials like pencils, grape stakes, and shingles.

19. REDWOOD CANYON

near Grant Grove, Kings Canyon National Park
Spectacular Sequoia grove along Redwood Creek

DISTANCE: 4.0 miles round-trip; 2 hours   **LEVEL:** Easy/moderate
ELEVATION: Start at 6,200 feet; total change 700 feet   **CROWDS:** Minimal
BEST SEASON: May to October   **RATING:** ★ ★ ★ ★ ★

DIRECTIONS: From the Big Stump Entrance Station at Kings Canyon National Park, drive north for 1.5 miles and turn right on the Generals Highway, heading for Sequoia National Park. Drive approximately three miles on the Generals Highway to Quail Flat (signed for Hume Lake to the left) and turn right on the dirt road to Redwood Saddle. Drive 1.5 miles and park in the parking lot. Take the trail signed for the Hart Tree and Redwood Canyon.

———————

You visited the General Sherman Tree, the Washington Tree, and the General Grant Tree in Sequoia and Kings Canyon National Parks—the three largest trees on earth. You were impressed, of course. But now you'd like to see some giant Sequoias that don't have asphalt and fences around them, thriving in the same unaltered woodland that they've lived in for a couple thousand years.

Get in your car and drive to Redwood Canyon in Kings Canyon National Park, a short drive from Grant Grove. Several loop trips are possible in this Sequoia-laden area, but one of the prettiest and simplest hikes is just an out-and-back walk on the Redwood Canyon Trail, paralleling Redwood Creek. The beauty begins before you even start walking. On the last mile of the drive to the trailhead, the road winds through giant Sequoias that are so close, you can reach out your car window and touch them.

The Redwood Canyon Trail (also signed as Redwood Creek Trail) leads downhill from the parking area. In a third of a mile you reach a junction and follow the path to the right, through the big trees. Because the grove is situated along Redwood Creek, the Sequoias grow amid a dense background of dogwoods, firs, ceanothus, and mountain misery. The canyon is reminiscent of the damp, lush coastal redwood forests of northwestern California, rather than the typically dry mountain slopes that are home to Sierra redwoods.

Although the standing Sequoias in Redwood Canyon are impressive, some of the fallen ones along the trail are really amazing, because you get a close-up look at their immense girth and thick bark. You can see how the trees shattered under their own weight when they hit the ground.

As you walk, keep on the lookout for wildflowers. We spotted orange paintbrush, an unusual yellow-colored paintbrush, pink wild rose, and unusually deep purple lupine. And ponder this: the first Sequoias started growing about 130 million years ago. For many thousands of years, the trees ranged widely all over the Sierra, but climate changes slowly reduced their habitat to only 70 small groves, containing less than 60,000 mature trees. Each Sequoia you see here in Redwood Canyon is one in a population of fewer than 60,000 trees.

Be sure to hike the full two miles to the stream crossing of Redwood Creek. Some of the best tree specimens are by the crossing; others are near a junction with the Sugar Bowl Loop Trail. (Look for the turnoff for the Sugar Bowl Loop on your right. Immediately following it is a cluster of about 10 giant Sequoias, grouped together like ancient, close friends.)

When you reach Redwood Creek, munch a snack from your daypack, watch and listen to the water flowing by, and then turn around and retrace your steps. The return trip is all uphill, but it's easier than you'd expect, and what the heck—you get to see those marvelous trees all over again.

20. REDWOOD MOUNTAIN LOOP

near Grant Grove, Kings Canyon National Park
A long day hike among plentiful giant Sequoias

DISTANCE: 10.0 miles round-trip; 5 hours   **LEVEL:** Moderate
ELEVATION: Start at 6,200 feet; total change 1,500 feet   **CROWDS:** Minimal
BEST SEASON: May to October   **RATING:** ★ ★ ★ ★ ★

DIRECTIONS: From the Big Stump Entrance Station at Kings Canyon National Park, drive north for 1.5 miles and turn right on the Generals Highway, heading for Sequoia National Park. Drive approximately three miles on the Generals Highway to Quail Flat (signed for Hume Lake to the left) and turn right on the dirt road to Redwood Saddle. Drive 1.5 miles and park in the parking lot. Take the trail signed as Burnt Grove/Sugar Bowl Loop.

If you've got a whole day to hike in the Redwood Mountain area of Kings Canyon National Park, you're in luck. The Redwood Mountain Loop combines all the best highlights of the area into one long trail, on which you'll wander in near solitude among the giant Sequoias. If the paved, people-laden trails to the General Grant Tree and General Sherman Tree turn you off, this trail will turn you on.

Start by hiking on the signed Burnt Grove/Sugar Bowl Loop Trail,

Giant Sequoias in Redwood Canyon

which leads uphill from the parking lot. It's one mile to Burnt Grove and 2.5 miles to Sugar Bowl Grove, both very dense stands of Sequoias. The climb is steep at first, but only for a short stretch. Then the grade mellows and you can start appreciating the rejuvenated mixed forest you're hiking in, which shows old evidence of a 1970s fire. As you travel, you'll have superb views of the granite block of Big Baldy, the San Joaquin Valley to the west, and Redwood Canyon below.

At two miles out, you'll start to descend into the Sugar Bowl Grove. Enjoy this impressive stand of big trees; you won't see any more Sequoias for a half-hour or so. The next two miles are a long descent on a dry slope as the trail curves its way down to Redwood Creek.

At the Sugar Bowl Trail's intersection with the Redwood Canyon Trail, you'll be awestruck by a dense grove of almost a dozen extra-large Sequoias. They grow to their immense size here because of the proximity of water, and the richness of the canyon soil. Turn right, head downhill and cross Redwood Creek (there is no bridge; you'll have to ford or rockhop in the early summer).

Proceed a third of a mile to the Fallen Goliath, a mammoth fallen tree that has been hollowed and scarred by fire. Climb for a mile and you'll reach a short right spur to the Hart Tree, the tallest tree in this area. It's worth the 100-yard side trip to see it. Another mile of gentle uphill travel brings you to the Tunnel Log, a hollowed Sequoia that you walk through. Don't forget to duck. Very shortly after, you reach the edge of the Buena Vista Grove, which has still more immense, beautiful trees. (At this point in the loop trail, my hiking partner commented that between the two of us, we had said, "Wow, look at that tree!" about 1,000 times.)

The trail's high point is at pretty Hart Meadow. From there, it's all downhill to the parking area, now less than two miles away. Still, there are a few more treats along the trail: Redwood Log Cabin, a fire-scarred Sequoia log that was converted into a summer home, probably by turn-of-the-century loggers. The hollowed log is tall enough to stand up in, and has a rock fireplace. You'll also pass the site of an old logging camp.

Note that if you tire out halfway through this loop, you can always turn left where the Sugar Bowl Trail meets Redwood Canyon Trail, and follow the Redwood Canyon Trail uphill back to the start. This will cut three miles off your round-trip.

21. BUENA VISTA PEAK

near Grant Grove, Kings Canyon National Park
An easily accessed granite dome with a view

DISTANCE: 2.0 miles round-trip; 1 hour
ELEVATION: Start at 7,150 feet; total change 550 feet
BEST SEASON: May to October

LEVEL: Easy/moderate
CROWDS: Minimal
RATING: ★ ★ ★

DIRECTIONS: From the Big Stump Entrance Station at Kings Canyon National Park, drive north for 1.5 miles and turn right on the Generals Highway, heading for Sequoia National Park. Drive approximately five miles on the Generals Highway to the Buena Vista Peak Trailhead on the right, just across the road and slightly beyond the large pullout for the Kings Canyon Overlook on the left.

Almost everybody stops at the drive-up Kings Canyon Overlook, where they get out of their cars (or just roll down the windows) and admire the roadside vista of "the second largest roadless landscape in the lower 48 states." That's what the sign says, and indeed, it's an awesome view, although the fast-growing trees are starting to hide some of it. Most of the roadless landscape is made up of the John Muir and Monarch wildernesses. Some of the highlights include Spanish Mountain at 10,051 feet, Mount McGee at 12,969 feet, Mount Goddard at 13,568 feet, Kettle Dome at 9,446 feet, and Finger Peak at 12,404 feet. When crowned in snow, these peaks are a sight to behold.

But with all the cars stopping at the Kings Canyon Overlook, surprisingly few people bother to hike the short, easy trail to Buena Vista Peak located just across the road. On the Buena Vista Peak Trail, you get the same views as at the roadside overlook and more, plus a chance at a private picnic spot on a wide slab of granite with a view.

Buena Vista Peak is really a rocky dome, peaking at 7,603 feet. The summit offers 360-degree views: You can see a million conifers at your feet and the hazy, sometimes smoggy foothills and valley to the southwest. But the best vistas are to the east—of the snow-capped peaks of the Silliman Crest and the Great Western Divide. Pick your vista; once on top of the dome, you can situate yourself so you are looking in any direction.

It's an easy half-hour walk up the gently sloped back side of the dome, passing through a pine and fir forest, manzanita, ceanothus, and lupine. The most interesting feature along the trail, aside from its first-class destination, is the odd piles of granite scattered here and there. Check out the giant boulder sculpture in the first quarter-mile of trail—it's a big, flat rock with three round rocks balanced side-by-side on top, looking as if they were placed there on display. The trail's only negative aspect is some road noise from the park highway; you'll get away from this as you hike.

When you reach the top of the dome, walk around on its wide summit, taking in all possible perspectives. Then pick your spot for picnicking, sunbathing, or philosophizing, all of which are good activities on Buena Vista Peak.

22. BIG BALDY

near Grant Grove, Kings Canyon National Park
Wide views to the west from a granite dome

DISTANCE: 4.6 miles round-trip; 2.5 hours **LEVEL:** Easy/moderate
ELEVATION: Start at 7,600 feet; total change 600 feet **CROWDS:** Minimal
BEST SEASON: May to October **RATING:** ★ ★ ★

DIRECTIONS: From the Big Stump Entrance Station at Kings Canyon National Park, drive north for 1.5 miles and turn right on the Generals Highway, heading for Sequoia National Park. Drive approximately 6.5 miles on the Generals Highway to the Big Baldy Trailhead on the right, shortly before the turnoff for Big Meadows on the left. Park alongside the road.

The trip to Big Baldy comes with a million views and a little workout. Views? We're talking Redwood Canyon, Redwood Mountain, Buena Vista Peak, Little Baldy, Buck Rock, and the Great Western Divide. A little workout? You have to climb 600 feet, but it's nicely spread out over 2.3 miles. Most of the time, you don't even realize you're climbing. Pick a clear day, early morning is usually best, and get ready for an easy and beautiful walk.

The trail begins in thick forest cover, but quickly exits the trees and winds along the granite rim of five-mile-long Redwood Canyon. The big chunk of granite to your right is Buena Vista Peak (see the

On top of Big Baldy

previous story). The path alternates between Christmas-scented fir forest and rocky stretches with open views. It also alternates between Kings Canyon National Park and Sequoia National Forest; every few hundred yards, you'll see the national park boundary signs. You'll also notice cross-country skiing markers on the trees; this path is so level that it makes an excellent snowshoeing or cross-country skiing trail in winter.

Birdwatchers take note: In the forested trail stretches, we were amazed at how many birds were singing in the tall firs and cedars. We couldn't see them without binoculars, but we could hear them loud and clear. We did spy a blue grouse on the trail, as well as several deer foraging for food.

The trail's initial vistas are to the west, but they just keep changing and getting more interesting. Even in the wooded sections, you get occasional glimpses above the trees to the east of the Silliman Crest. But nothing compares to the view from Big Baldy's 8,209-foot summit, where your panorama opens up to 360 degrees. Here you get your first wide-open views to the east, of the High Sierra peaks and the Great Western Divide, plus more of the western views you've had all along.

This trail is so fun and rewarding, with so little suffering involved, you may feel like you're getting away with something. A bonus: Because the trail's first mile faces to the west, this is a great path for watching the sun set.

23. WEAVER LAKE

near Big Meadows, Sequoia National Forest
A granite-bound lake in the Jennie Lakes Wilderness

DISTANCE: 4.2 miles round-trip; 2 hours   **LEVEL:** Moderate
ELEVATION: Start at 7,900 feet; total change 800 feet   **CROWDS:** Moderate
BEST SEASON: June to October   **RATING:** ★ ★ ★ ★

DIRECTIONS: From the Big Stump Entrance Station at Kings Canyon National Park, drive north for 1.5 miles and turn right on the Generals Highway, heading for Sequoia National Park. Drive seven miles and turn left on Forest Service Road 14S11, at the sign for Big Meadows and Horse Corral. Drive four miles, passing Big Meadows Trailhead and Big Meadows Campground, then turn right on the dirt road a half-mile beyond the camp (it's just past the bridge over Big Meadows Creek). Drive a half-mile to a fork, turn left, then turn right immediately afterward. Drive one more mile and park at the road's end at the Fox Meadow trailhead. (Total mileage from Big Meadows Road is 1.5 miles.)

Tucked into a corner just outside the border of Kings Canyon and Sequoia National Parks, the Jennie Lakes Wilderness is a 10,500-acre wilderness area that is often overlooked by park visitors. It offers much of the same scenery as the parks—beautiful lakes, meadows, forests, and streams—but without all the fanfare. Weaver Lake is the easiest-to-reach destination in the Jennie Lakes Wilderness, and it makes a perfect family backpacking trip or an equally nice day hike.

You have two choices on how to make the trip. Most people choose the easier option, which is a two-mile hike from Fox Meadow, located a few miles beyond the Forest Service campground at Big Meadows. If you're not in a hurry to get to the lake and would rather take a longer hike (or if you don't want to drive your car on a bumpy dirt road), you can leave your car at the trailhead just west of Big Meadows and hike in 3.5 miles to the lake. Take your pick.

Starting from the Fox Meadow Trailhead, the path is well signed all the way, and passes through a mix of red fir forests and meadows. Almost immediately, you'll cross Fox Creek. In the spring, you'll see plenty of wildflowers in bloom near its banks. Soon after crossing, you'll note the longer, alternate trail from the Big Meadows Trailhead coming in from the right to join your trail. You'll climb through the red firs above small Fox Meadow, then reach a second trail junction at seven-tenths of a mile. The right fork leads to Jennie Lake (see the following story). Take the left fork for Weaver Lake, climbing uphill on an open slope to the lake's basin. You'll spy the shelf-like granite slabs of

Shell Mountain peeking out above the trees.

At 1.8 miles, you'll reach a third junction; left heads to Rowell Meadow and right goes to Weaver Lake. Bear right and in less than a quarter mile, you'll reach shallow but pretty Weaver Lake at 8,700 feet, set at the base of Shell Mountain's high, rounded ridge. You can try your luck fishing, or just find a lakeside seat and gaze at the view. On warm days, the brave go swimming. Late in the summer, the lake gets even shallower and the water temperature warms up.

Note that the road to Big Meadows and Fox Meadow is usually one of the last roads to open after snowmelt. During the summer of 1998, the road didn't open until July 4, and even then, Weaver Lake was still iced over. If you're planning an early season trip, call to check on road and trail conditions.

24. JENNIE LAKE

near Big Meadows, Sequoia National Forest
A remote, granite-lined wilderness lake

DISTANCE: 10.0 miles round-trip; 5 hours   **LEVEL:** Strenuous
ELEVATION: Start at 7,900 feet; total change 1,600 feet   **CROWDS:** Minimal
BEST SEASON: June to October   **RATING:** ★ ★ ★ ★

DIRECTIONS: From the Big Stump Entrance Station at Kings Canyon National Park, drive north for 1.5 miles and turn right on the Generals Highway, heading for Sequoia National Park. Drive seven miles and turn left on Forest Service Road 14S11, at the sign for Big Meadows and Horse Corral. Drive four miles, passing Big Meadows Trailhead and Big Meadows Campground, then turn right on the dirt road a half-mile beyond the camp (it's just past the bridge over Big Meadows Creek). Drive a half-mile to a fork, turn left, then turn right immediately afterward. Drive one more mile and park at the road's end at the Fox Meadow trailhead. (Total mileage from Big Meadows Road is 1.5 miles.)

This trail into the Jennie Lakes Wilderness offers more of a challenge than the route to Weaver Lake (see the previous story), as it climbs 1,600 feet over five miles with some short, steep pitches. But the rewards are greater, too, because Jennie Lake is a beauty, and it receives less visitors than Weaver Lake.

The trail is the same as the Weaver Lake Trail for seven-tenths of a mile. (Read the trail description in the previous story for details.) At the junction, bear right for Jennie Lake. You'll ascend a bit, then pass a sign for the Jennie Lakes Wilderness. The trail climbs and dips through fir and pine forest and manzanita. At 1.4 miles out, you'll stroll past

Weaver Lake and snow-covered Shell Mountain in the Jennie Lakes Wilderness

Poison Meadow. As your elevation increases, you'll gain far-reaching views of Big Baldy and the San Joaquin Valley to the west. The trail continues to climb moderately as you contour around the southwest side of Shell Mountain. Soon you leave the forest behind and hike on granite slabs.

At 2.5 miles, the trail descends for a quarter-mile, then climbs again, passing a side trail coming in from Stony Creek Campground. Well-named Poop Out Pass is reached at 3.5 miles and 9,150 feet in elevation, but unfortunately, it offers no views through the trees. Even more unfortunately, after all the climbing you've done, the next half-mile is a steep, rocky downhill stretch into the Boulder Creek drainage. Bear with it, then climb more gently for the final stretch of the trip.

At 4.8 miles you reach an unsigned junction with the trail to Jennie Lake, near the lake's outlet stream. Leave the main trail to follow the lake spur, and shortly you come to the lake itself, set at 9,012 feet.

With a white granite backdrop on one side and a red fir forest on the other, Jennie Lake's shoreline has something to please everybody. Catching a rainbow or brook trout is a fair possibility; Jennie Lake gets less fishing pressure than nearby Weaver Lake.

The emerald green lake is also larger in size and deeper than Weaver Lake. If fishing doesn't interest you, swimming might, but be forewarned that the waters of Jennie Lake are icy cold.

25. MITCHELL PEAK

near Big Meadows, Sequoia National Forest
Highest point in the Jennie Lakes Wilderness

DISTANCE: 5.2 miles round-trip; 2.5 hours   **LEVEL:** Strenuous
ELEVATION: Start at 8,400 feet; total change 2,000 feet   **CROWDS:** Minimal
BEST SEASON: June to October   **RATING:** ★ ★ ★ ★ ★

DIRECTIONS: From the Big Stump Entrance Station at Kings Canyon National Park, drive north for 1.5 miles and turn right on the Generals Highway, heading for Sequoia National Park. Drive seven miles and turn left on Forest Service Road 14S11, at the sign for Big Meadows and Horse Corral. Drive four miles to Big Meadows Campground, then continue 6.7 more miles to Horse Corral Meadow. Turn right (south) on Forest Service Road 13S12 and drive 3.5 miles to the Marvin Pass Trailhead.

If you have the legs for a 2,000-foot climb over 2.6 miles, you can stand atop the summit of Mitchell Peak, the highest point in the Jennie Lakes Wilderness, at 10,365 feet in elevation. The peak used to have a fire lookout on its summit, but the Forest Service stopped using it and burned it down. What remains is the fabulous view—one of the best in this area.

It's a one-mile climb from the Marvin Pass Trailhead to Marvin Pass and the boundary of the Jennie Lakes Wilderness. The ascent is mostly shaded by red firs and lodgepole pines, but you'll be huffing and puffing as you quickly gain 600 feet. Bear left (east) at a junction with the trail to Rowell Meadow, then continue to climb just as steadily.

At 1.6 miles you reach a second junction, which may or may not be signed for Mitchell Peak. (I've see it both ways.) Turn left (north) and climb one more mile, curving around to the north side of the peak. The first stretch is fairly brutal; then the grade mellows considerably. As you near Mitchell Peak's summit, notice the border signs for Kings Canyon National Park; the peak straddles the boundary between the national forest and national park.

When the trail vanishes a tenth of a mile below the summit, just make your own way uphill. At the top, you are rewarded with a spectacular view of the Great Western Divide and the Silliman Crest. Right below you is Williams Meadow, bordered by lodgepole pines; tiny Comanche Meadow lies just south of it.

The summit is broad enough for a picnic, although with the probable howling wind, you might not want to stay that long. You're sure to notice the concrete foundation remains of Mitchell Peak's fire lookout. Many hikers were irritated and disappointed when the Forest Service destroyed the unused tower building, because the summit view was even better when you could climb up on the tower's landing and look around. Of course, even without the tower, Mitchell Peak is still a fine spot to catch your breath.

26. MUIR GROVE

near Dorst Campground, Sequoia National Park
Secluded Sequoia grove in a field of lupine

DISTANCE: 4.0 miles round-trip; 2 hours   **LEVEL:** Easy
ELEVATION: Start at 6,750 feet; total change 150 feet   **CROWDS:** Minimal
BEST SEASON: May to October   **RATING:** ★ ★ ★ ★

DIRECTIONS: From the Big Stump Entrance Station at Kings Canyon National Park, drive north for 1.5 miles and turn right on the Generals Highway, heading for Sequoia National Park. Drive approximately 17 miles on the Generals Highway to the right turnoff for Dorst Campground. Turn right and drive through the campground to the amphitheater parking lot. Park there; the trail begins at a footbridge between the amphitheater parking lot and the group campground.

Few people hike the Muir Grove Trail unless they happen to be staying at Dorst Campground, so you have a lot better chance of seeing big Sequoias in solitude in the Muir Grove than at many places in Sequoia National Park. Granted, the grove of big trees is only a small grouping, but the path to reach it is gorgeous, nearly level, and loaded with early season wildflowers. The trail is easy enough for children and will be enjoyable for them because there is so much to examine and marvel at.

After crossing a wooden footbridge at its start, the trail enters a mixed forest of red fir, white fir, sugar pines, and incense cedars. The prolific ferns at your feet make up their own miniature forest; this may be the most fern-filled trail in the entire national park, especially after a wet winter. Where you cross tiny streams, the wildflowers explode into bloom: Columbine, cow parsnip, leopard lilies, lupine, and Indian paintbrush. The trail undulates along, never climbing or dropping much, making this an easy and pleasant stroll.

The route heads west, then curves around a deeply carved canyon at one mile out. (Just off the trail to your right is a bare granite slab with an inspiring westward view. A few Jeffrey pines miraculously grow out of the rock.) At 1.9 miles you enter the Muir Grove, a small, pristine stand of huge Sequoias. The first one you come to, on your left, is a doozy. More show up on your right, a few feet farther. The trail gradually diminishes among the trees; just have a seat at the base of one of the giants and sit for a while. Muir Grove is made even more enchanting by the thick undergrowth of blue and purple lupine blooming amid the trees. You may suddenly find yourself whispering, and not know why. It's that kind of place.

Lupine bushes among the Muir Grove Sequoias

27. LITTLE BALDY

near Dorst Campground, Sequoia National Park
World-class panorama of high peaks

DISTANCE: 3.5 miles round-trip; 2 hours
ELEVATION: Start at 7,400 feet; total change 650 feet
BEST SEASON: June to October
LEVEL: Easy/moderate
CROWDS: Moderate
RATING: ★ ★ ★ ★

DIRECTIONS: From the Big Stump Entrance Station at Kings Canyon National Park, drive north for 1.5 miles and turn right on the Generals Highway, heading for Sequoia National Park. Drive approximately 18 miles on the Generals Highway to the Little Baldy Trailhead on the left, a mile beyond the turnoff for Dorst Campground.

Little Baldy, Big Baldy, Buena Vista Peak... Along this stretch of the Generals Highway, there are so many big pieces of granite that you can hike on, it's hard to know where to begin. The Little Baldy Trail is an excellent starting point. It's a little more challenging than the Buena Vista Peak Trail or the Big Baldy Trail, but it's still easy enough for most people to accomplish. And on a clear day, its views are stupendous.

In fact, some claim that Little Baldy's view of the Silliman Crest, the Great Western Divide, Castle Rocks, Moro Rock, the Kaweah River canyon, and the San Joaquin foothills is the best panorama in the park accessible by day-hiking. An added bonus is that you can also view Big Baldy to the northeast from this trail, an interesting perspective that you don't get from anywhere else.

Like other peaks in the area, Little Baldy is a granite dome, with a smooth rounded shape that makes it easy to hike. The summit is at 8,044 feet, and the trail's long moderate switchbacks make the 650-foot gain from the trailhead quite manageable.

Start your trip at Little Baldy Saddle, right along the highway. The only disappointment on the trail is that you hear some road noise, which doesn't leave you for almost a half-hour of hiking. You're compensated with a fine view of Big Baldy about a quarter-mile up the trail (look over your left shoulder), and by the lovely wildflowers and ferns that grow enthusiastically alongside the path.

As you climb, the trail gets rockier and more exposed, and you start to see harbingers of the high country—Jeffrey pines. Although at the start of the trail you hiked to the north, the switchbacks you've tackled deposit you south of your starting point. Vistas open up wider, giving you a look at far-off snowy peaks.

Before you know it, you're on top of Little Baldy's summit, with a front-seat view of the high mountains of the national parks. Look for the jagged spires of Castle Rocks to the southeast. In addition, there's an excellent view to the east of the massive Silliman Crest and Great Western Divide. Tokopah Valley is slightly southeast, and far to the south is Mineral King Valley and distinctive Sawtooth Peak.

28. TOKOPAH FALLS

Lodgepole/Wolverton area, Sequoia National Park
Best waterfall in Sequoia and Kings Canyon

DISTANCE: 3.4 miles round-trip; 2 hours   **LEVEL:** Easy
ELEVATION: Start at 6,780 feet; total change 500 feet   **CROWDS:** Heavy
BEST SEASON: April to July   **RATING:** ★ ★ ★ ★ ★

DIRECTIONS: From the Big Stump Entrance Station at Kings Canyon National Park, drive north for 1.5 miles and turn right on the Generals Highway, heading for Sequoia National Park. Drive approximately 25 miles on the Generals Highway to the Lodgepole Campground turnoff, then drive three-quarters of a mile to the Log Bridge area of Lodgepole Camp. Park in the large lot just before the bridge over the Marble Fork Kaweah River, and walk 150 yards to the trailhead, which is just after you cross the bridge.

Alternatively, from the Ash Mountain Entrance Station at Sequoia National Park, drive north on the Generals Highway for 21 miles to the Lodgepole turnoff.

Tokopah Falls is hands-down the best waterfall in Sequoia and Kings Canyon National Parks. Accept no substitutes or imitations; if you want to have the best possible waterfall experience in the two parks, head to Lodgepole Campground and the Tokopah Falls trailhead. For the best viewing, take this hike in late spring or early summer when the waterfall is a showering spectacle.

Sure the trail's crowded—why wouldn't it be? The walk to the falls is only 1.7 miles of flat trail through gorgeous High Sierra scenery, culminating at the base of 1,200-foot-high Tokopah Falls. But if you follow the cardinal rule for popular outdoor destinations and start hiking early in the morning, the crowds will still be sleeping in their tents. You can be out to the falls and back before most people have finished brushing their teeth.

The trail is almost as awesome as the falls. Although it climbs a bit at the start, it becomes more level as you go. In a little more than a mile and a half, you get awesome views of the Watchtower, a 1,600-foot-tall glacially carved cliff on the south side of Tokopah Valley. Your perspective on the Watchtower changes with every few steps you take, and it's breathtaking from every angle. Then there's Tokopah Valley itself, with Tokopah Falls pouring down the smooth back curve of its U-shape. Tokopah Valley is similar in geological type and appearance to Yosemite Valley. Like Yosemite, it was formed partially by the river flowing in its center but mostly by slow-moving glaciers.

Tokopah Falls

Marmot on the Tokopah Falls Trail

The Tokopah Falls Trail also provides a near guarantee of seeing yellow-bellied marmots, the largest and most charming member of the squirrel family. In a completely nonscientific survey, I determined that this area has more marmots per square acre than anywhere in the Sierra. Their great abundance is due in part to the proximity of the campground and the marmots' great love of food. (Don't give them any handouts.) You'll have dozens of chances to photograph the cute little guys or just to admire their beautiful blonde coats, as they sun themselves on boulders or stand on their back legs to whistle at you.

The trail is a mix of conifers and granite, always following close to the Marble Fork of the Kaweah River. It leads gently uphill all the way to the falls. If the route seems rather rocky at the start, don't fret; its surface changes. Sometimes the trail travels on a soft forest floor of conifer needles, other times over bridges that cross tiny feeder creeks, and still other times in meadow areas overflowing with ferns, orange columbine, yellow violets, and purple nightshade.

The final quarter-mile of the path, which traverses rocky slopes, gives you wide-open views of Tokopah Falls' impressive 1,200-foot height. The trail has been dynamited into granite; in one section you must wedge in between rocks and duck your head under a granite ledge. You can hike right to the edge of the waterfall, which drops over fractured granite. Choose a rock to sit on and marvel at the cacophony of cascading water, but don't get too close—Tokopah flows fast, and it can be dangerous in springtime.

29. TWIN LAKES

Lodgepole/Wolverton area, Sequoia National Park
Long day hike to two high alpine lakes

DISTANCE: 13.6 miles round-trip; 8 hours   **LEVEL:** Strenuous
ELEVATION: Start at 6,780 feet; total change 2,800 feet   **CROWDS:** Moderate
BEST SEASON: June to October   **RATING:** ★ ★ ★ ★

DIRECTIONS: From the Big Stump Entrance Station at Kings Canyon National Park, drive north for 1.5 miles and turn right on the Generals Highway, heading for Sequoia National Park. Drive approximately 25 miles on the Generals Highway to the Lodgepole Campground turnoff, then drive three-quarters of a mile to the Log Bridge area of Lodgepole Camp. Park in the large lot just before the bridge over the Marble Fork Kaweah River. Walk across the bridge and past the Tokopah Falls Trailhead. Shortly beyond it is the Twin Lakes Trailhead.

Alternatively, from the Ash Mountain Entrance Station at Sequoia National Park, drive north on the Generals Highway for 21 miles to the Lodgepole turnoff.

The trail to Twin Lakes is a very long day hike, and it shouldn't be attempted by anyone except the hardy and determined. If you make it all the way to the lakes, you are likely to be the only day-hiker there. Your lightweight day-pack will be the envy of all the heavily burdened backpackers you pass along the trail.

Less ambitious hikers looking for an easier trip can still take the Twin Lakes Trail, but they will only want to go as far as Cahoon Meadow at 2.5 miles out.

The trail begins by skirting around the edge of one of Lodgepole's popular campgrounds. It then climbs steeply for three quarters of a mile through a forest of firs, lodgepole pines, and ponderosa pines. After this initial effort, a reprieve is in sight: You climb again, but almost imperceptibly, up to the edge of Silliman Creek at two miles out. Cross the creek any way you can; early in the year, the fast flow can be dangerous. Use caution and good judgment.

After another quarter-mile of ascent, you reach the edge of Cahoon Meadow; a stream makes lazy S-turns down its center. The trail edges the meadow's east side. You may see backpackers making camp here. If the hiking gods have granted you perfect timing, you'll visit Cahoon Meadow when the shooting stars are blooming but the mosquitoes have already hatched and vanished.

Another 1.7 miles of relentless climbing through fir forest brings

---

you to Cahoon Gap at 4.2 miles and 8,700 feet in elevation. The forested gap provides no views to speak of, but at least you've gained the ridge and now can descend pleasantly down its other side. You lose 250 feet in elevation over the next three quarters of a mile to Clover Creek. More backpackers will be found here, camping under the trees and fishing for supper in the creek. If you didn't stop for a rest and a snack at Cahoon Meadow, do it here. You still have another hour of hiking and 1,000 feet of elevation gain to reach your destination.

Note the J.O. Pass Trail crossing Clover Creek and heading north. Bear right instead, following Clover Creek upstream, then cross a fork of it. This is the Twin Lakes' outlet stream, which you will parallel for the final 1.3-mile climb to Twin Lakes. The ascent is fairly steep, but just grunt it out. The trail leads you directly to the north shore of the larger Twin Lake at 9,500 feet; the smaller lake can be accessed by following a spur to the left.

Don't expect a stark, granite basin like that of the lakes along the Lakes Trail to the south (see the following story). The Twin Lakes are shallow and partially surrounded by meadow and forest. The larger lake is the most dramatic, with trees edging its southern side and a plethora of granite cliffs and boulders. The Twin Peaks and Silliman Crest form the backdrop for both lakes.

30. LAKES TRAIL & THE WATCHTOWER

Lodgepole/Wolverton area, Sequoia National Park
Gem-like lakes and a rocky promontory above Tokopah Valley

DISTANCE: 8.4 to 10.8 miles round-trip; 5 to 6 hours **LEVEL:** Strenuous
ELEVATION: Start at 7,250 feet; total change 2,250 feet **CROWDS:** Heavy
BEST SEASON: June to October **RATING:** ★ ★ ★ ★

DIRECTIONS: From the Big Stump Entrance Station at Kings Canyon National Park, drive north for 1.5 miles and turn right on the Generals Highway, heading for Sequoia National Park. Drive approximately 27 miles on the Generals Highway, past the Lodgepole Village turnoff, to the Wolverton turnoff on the left (east) side of the road. Turn left and drive 1.5 miles to the parking area and trailhead on the left.

Alternatively, from the Ash Mountain Entrance Station at Sequoia National Park, drive north on the Generals Highway for 19.5 miles to the Wolverton turnoff.

The Wolverton trailhead is at 7,250 feet in elevation, which gives you a boost at the start for this trip into the high country. The Lakes

Trail is the most popular backpacking trip in Sequoia National Park, and it's equally popular with day-hikers. It's easy to see why: Wide-open views, dramatic granite cliffs, beautiful fir forest, and gem-like lakes are standard fare.

Part of the Lakes Trail is on a loop, with the north side of the loop accessing the Watchtower, a breathtaking 1,600-foot-tall granite promontory. This is the preferred way to hike the Lakes Trail, but in early summer, the Watchtower leg may be closed to hikers due to lingering snow and ice. When it's closed, hikers must take the alternate Hump Trail, the south side of the loop. The Hump Trail is shorter, steeper, and nowhere near as scenic. If you plan to hike the Lakes Trail, check with the visitor center to be sure the Watchtower is open.

The trail begins in a shady red fir forest. Ignore two trail junctions in the first quarter-mile of trail, and continue uphill through the big trees. Climb moderately but steadily to a junction at 1.8 miles. Bear left at this junction, then keep climbing—still surrounded by big, moss-covered trees. In a quarter-mile, you reach the fork for the Watchtower and Hump trails. Bear left for the Watchtower, enjoying a more gradual climb to the top of this remarkably steep granite cliff. From on top, the view of Tokopah Valley is tremendous. If you're experienced and sure-footed, you can leave the main trail and climb around on the Watchtower's cliffs, but use extreme caution. It's a better idea to

Hiking on the Watchtower's ledge trail

keep hiking; the next half-mile of trail has even better views than the Watchtower itself.

Beyond the Watchtower, the route becomes a ledge trail, blasted into hard granite, which creeps along the high rim of Tokopah Valley. Your view is straight down, 1,500 feet below. You can even see little tiny people walking on the path to Tokopah Falls (see the story on pages 350 to 352). From your high perch, you have a clear view of the tip-top of Tokopah Falls' 1,200-foot-high cascade, which cannot be seen from the valley floor.

In another half-mile, the route rejoins with the Hump leg of the loop, and in a few hundred yards farther you're at Heather Lake, 4.2 miles from the trailhead. The lake is designated for day-use only, so it has no campsites. It has a steep granite backdrop and a few rocky ledges to sunbathe on. After a rest and perhaps a swim, you can opt to take the easy walk to more scenic Aster and Emerald lakes, only 1.2 miles farther. There is very little elevation gain to reach these lakes, and most likely, you'll find fewer people there. You see Aster Lake first, off the main trail to the left. Emerald Lake is only a few hundred feet away (on the main trail), hidden from view in the rocky basin up ahead.

There's one more lake on the Lakes Trail: Pear Lake is another mile beyond Emerald Lake and 400 feet higher; this is the preferred lake for backpackers. Hardy day-hikers can visit Pear Lake too, but they will most likely find enough pleasure in the rocky basin at Aster and Emerald lakes.

31. ALTA PEAK

Lodgepole/Wolverton area, Sequoia National Park
A hard-to-reach summit with views of the Great Western Divide

DISTANCE: 13.2 miles round-trip; 7 hours   **LEVEL:** Very strenuous
ELEVATION: Start at 7,250 feet; total change 4,000 feet   **CROWDS:** Minimal
BEST SEASON: July to September   **RATING:** ★ ★ ★ ★

DIRECTIONS: From the Big Stump Entrance Station at Kings Canyon National Park, drive north for 1.5 miles and turn right on the Generals Highway, heading for Sequoia National Park. Drive approximately 27 miles on the Generals Highway, past the Lodgepole Village turnoff, to the Wolverton turnoff on the left (east) side of the road. Turn left and drive 1.5 miles to the parking area and trailhead on the left.

Alternatively, from the Ash Mountain Entrance Station at Sequoia National Park, drive north on the Generals Highway for 19.5 miles to the Wolverton turnoff.

You say you like heights? You like vistas? You like a challenge? Here's your trail, a 4,000-foot climb to the top of Alta Peak, an 11,204-foot summit in the Alta Country. Here's something to consider: Alta Peak and Mount Whitney are the only major summits in Sequoia National Park that have established trails for hikers. But both are still butt-kickers to reach. If you're in good physical condition, both are worth the effort.

To "bag" the summit of Alta Peak, an early morning start is an absolute prerequisite. This will allow you enough time for the long round-trip, and it will increase your chances of reaching the summit before any afternoon clouds show up.

The trail to Alta Peak and Alta Meadow begins on the Lakes Trail from the Wolverton parking area. At a junction at 1.8 miles, the peak route heads south (right) on the Panther Gap Trail. (For details, see the following story.) After climbing steeply through the forest to Panther Gap at 2.6 miles and 8,450 feet, you get your first set of eye-popping views—of the Middle Fork Kaweah River canyon, Castle Rocks, and the Great Western Divide. Consider this your warm-up for the summit vista.

Continue to the east (left), now on the Alta Trail on a sunny, exposed slope with only occasional bouts of shade from Jeffrey pines. Enjoy more views of the Great Western Divide along your way to Mehrten Meadow at 3.9 miles. You'll most likely find backpackers near Mehrten Creek, alongside the meadow. (This is the "easy" way to see Alta Peak—split it into two days!)

Enjoy a stretch of level walking, then reach a junction six-tenths of a mile beyond the meadow where you can go left to Alta Peak or right to Alta Meadow. Although Alta Meadow is spectacular, you may not

On the Alta Trail near Mehrten Meadow

have enough energy or daylight to take both forks in the trail, so bear left now for the peak. You can always visit Alta Meadow on the way back downhill.

Now for the bad news: Alta Peak is two miles away, with a 1,900-foot climb. These two miles are considered to be one of the toughest stretches of trail in all of Sequoia National Park, due to the brutal grade and the 10,000-plus foot elevation above treeline. It may seem like the longest two miles of your life. (Plan on at least an hour and a half to the summit.) The trail ascends steep slopes below Tharps Rock's granite dome, climbing with a vengeance. Now you have good views to the west; enjoy them while you tackle the climb to get above Tharps Rock. Say good-bye to the last of the few hardy foxtail pines, and make a final push to reach Alta Peak's summit at 11,204 feet.

Not surprisingly, the summit provides a complete panorama of vistas. To the east, the Great Western Divide looks close enough to touch. Castle Rocks and Triple Divide Peak are most prominent. Look carefully beyond the divide and see if you can pick out 14,495-foot Mount Whitney. Alta Peak is one of the few points on the western side of Sequoia National Park from which Mount Whitney can be seen, because you're high enough so that the Great Western Divide isn't blocking it. Turn to the west, and see if you can make out the Coast Range, about 100 miles away. Closer in, look to the north, where the lakes of the Lakes Trail—Emerald, Aster, and Pear—shine like blue sapphires. Large Moose Lake lies beyond them.

On your return trip, if by some miracle you still have energy and plenty of daylight left, take the left turnoff to Alta Meadow. It's a gentle 1.1-mile walk to the extensive meadow, with only a 250-foot elevation gain. The gorgeous meadow shows off a condensed version of Alta Peak's summit views: the Great Western Divide is directly to the east. It's looks like something out of the opening scenes of *The Sound of Music*. Only it's better, because it's real.

32. PANTHER GAP LOOP

Lodgepole/Wolverton area, Sequoia National Park
Vista of Castle Rocks and the Great Western Divide

DISTANCE: 6.0 miles round-trip; 3 hours   **LEVEL:** Moderate
ELEVATION: Start at 7,250 feet; total change 1,200 feet   **CROWDS:** Moderate
BEST SEASON: June to October   **RATING:** ★ ★ ★ ★

DIRECTIONS: From the Big Stump Entrance Station at Kings Canyon National Park, drive north for 1.5 miles and turn right on the Generals Highway, heading for Sequoia National Park. Drive approximately 27 miles on the Generals Highway, past the Lodgepole Village turnoff, to the Wolverton turnoff on the left (east) side of the road. Turn left and drive 1.5 miles to the parking area and trailhead on the left.

Alternatively, from the Ash Mountain Entrance Station at Sequoia National Park, drive north on the Generals Highway for 19.5 miles to the Wolverton turnoff.

If you're not up for the marathon trip to Alta Peak detailed in the previous story (and certainly not everybody is), you can still get a taste of the high country on the Panther Gap Loop. Because you begin to hike at 7,250 feet at the Wolverton trailhead, your car has already done much of the climbing for you. You still have a good ascent ahead to reach Panther Gap at 8,450 feet, but you will be well rewarded with views of the jagged, snowy peaks of the Great Western Divide.

Start to hike on the Lakes Trail from the north side of the Wolverton parking lot, heading uphill through a dense red fir forest. Ignore two trail junctions in the first quarter-mile of trail, and continue uphill through the big trees. At 1.8 miles, bear right at the sign for Panther Gap, staying roughly parallel to Wolverton Creek. The fir forest gradually becomes more open as the trail curves around the creek canyon. In eight tenths of a mile, you reach Panther Gap. Here, at an obvious

Panther Gap Loop

saddle at 8,450 feet, your climb is over. You have an inspiring vista of the deep Middle Fork Kaweah River canyon 4,000 feet below you. To the east is the massive, jagged bulk of the Great Western Divide. Check out 9,081-foot Castle Rocks, an obvious landmark because of its craggy spires. If it's a clear, calm day, a picnic is probably in order.

From the gap, turn right (west) and follow the Alta Trail to lovely Panther Meadow on the right, then equally lovely Red Fir Meadow on the left. Whereas on the first part of the loop you had mostly trees for companions, now you have meadows and abundant wildflowers. At a junction two miles from Panther Gap, bear right and complete the loop by descending steeply to Long Meadow, then edging along its east side to return to the parking lot. This last stretch of trail is very sandy and carved up from horses' hooves.

By the way, don't get any smart ideas about hiking this loop in the opposite direction. We did, and found out that it's a much steeper climb.

33. GENERAL SHERMAN TREE & CONGRESS TRAIL

Giant Forest, Sequoia National Park
The largest trees in the world

DISTANCE: 2.1 miles round-trip; 1 hour **LEVEL:** Easy
ELEVATION: Start at 6,800 feet; total change 200 feet **CROWDS:** Heavy
BEST SEASON: Year-round **RATING:** ★ ★ ★ ★ ★

DIRECTIONS: From the Big Stump Entrance Station at Kings Canyon National Park, drive north for 1.5 miles and turn right on the Generals Highway, heading for Sequoia National Park. Drive approximately 28 miles on the Generals Highway, past Lodgepole and Wolverton, to the signed turnoff on the left for the General Sherman Tree.

Alternatively, from the Ash Mountain Entrance Station at Sequoia National Park, drive north on the Generals Highway for 19 miles to the Sherman Tree turnoff on the right.

NOTE: An interpretive brochure is available at the trailhead.

John Muir is probably the most often quoted naturalist in American history, and his words about the giant Sequoia trees demonstrate why: "Walk the Sequoia woods at any time of the year and you will say they are the most beautiful and majestic on earth." You just can't argue with him.

The Congress Trail, a two-mile loop that starts (or ends) at the General Sherman Tree, is a much-traveled route through the Giant Forest's prize grove of Sequoias—trees loved by John Muir and many others before and since.

The General Sherman Tree gets the most visitors, of course, because it is recognized as the largest living thing in the world (not by height, but by volume). It is taller than a 27-story building and has a circumference of 102.6 feet. Scientists estimate that it is about 2,500 years old. Pay homage to the great tree, then leave the throngs of visitors behind and walk the quieter Congress Trail. After you leave General Sherman's side, the crowds lessen substantially.

The McKinley Tree on the Congress Trail

On the Congress Trail, you pass by many huge trees with very patriotic names, like the House and Senate clusters, the General Lee Tree, the McKinley Tree, the Lincoln Tree, and.... you get the idea. Every single giant tree is worth stopping to gape at. The dense groupings of trees, like the Founders, House, and Senate clusters, are so surreal that they seem to belong to the forests of a dream world, not the real world.

Perhaps the most intriguing Sequoia is an unnamed, fallen tree that crosses the trail a half-mile before the end of the loop. A sign states that this tree suddenly fell on a still and clear evening in June, 1965. Rangers who were working two miles away heard a tremendous noise, and "knew that a giant had fallen."

Despite the lack of solitude, we rate the Congress Trail as the best flat, easy trail for Sequoia viewing in the park. Anybody can hike it, and the big trees are worth seeing again and again. Of course, the farther you walk from the parking lot and the General Sherman Tree, the more peace and quiet you get.

34. SUNSET ROCK

Giant Forest, Sequoia National Park
A granite dome with a western vista

DISTANCE: 2.0 miles round-trip; 1 hour   **LEVEL:** Easy
ELEVATION: Start at 6,400 feet; total change 50 feet   **CROWDS:** Minimal
BEST SEASON: May to October   **RATING:** ★ ★ ★

DIRECTIONS: From the Big Stump Entrance Station at Kings Canyon National Park, drive north for 1.5 miles and turn right on the Generals Highway, heading for Sequoia National Park. Drive approximately 30 miles on the Generals Highway, past Lodgepole and Wolverton, to the Giant Forest area of Sequoia National Park. Park near the market/museum (see the note below).

Alternatively, from the Ash Mountain Entrance Station at Sequoia National Park, drive north on the Generals Highway for 17 miles to Giant Forest.

NOTE: As of February 1999, Giant Forest Village is in the final stages of a complete renovation. The lodge, cabins, restaurants, and market are being moved to the new visitor service center at Wuksachi Village, north of Giant Forest. The historic market building will be transformed into a Sequoia museum during the summer of 1999. The road to Crescent Meadow is planned for closure to auto traffic in 1999 or 2000; visitors will have to hike in to Crescent Meadow or ride a shuttle bus. Eventually, the road to Moro Rock may also be closed. The following trails numbered 34 through 38 have been written according to road and trail status as of February 1999. Please call for updated parking and hiking information.

The trail to Sunset Rock is a first-rate easy hike, perfect at sunset or any time. It's a pleasant walk through forest to a huge, flat slab on top of a granite dome, exhibiting fine views to the west and north. A bonus is that this trail is much less traveled than many others in the Giant Forest area, since it does not lead to any world-famous Sequoia trees.

To hike to Sunset Rock, leave your car in the parking lot by Giant Forest's market/museum, then use the crosswalk on the northeast side of the lot to cross the General Highway and pick up the signed Sunset Rock Trail.

The path is lined with worn pavement, and it's almost completely flat. It leads through a pretty mixed forest of white firs, Sequoias, and cedars, crossing Little Deer Creek on a footbridge only 100 yards from the road. Slightly less than a half-mile in, you pass the tiny meadow called Eli's Paradise on your right, which shows off a few Sequoia trees near its edges.

Your views to the west begin to open up as you near the edge of the Marble Fork Kaweah River Canyon. In a few more minutes of walking, you reach a fork for Sunset Rock, where you bear left. The rock is an immense granite dome with a flat top about the size of a football field. It is set at 6,365 feet in elevation. Standing on top of it, you have a terrific overlook of Little Baldy to the north, and a sea of conifers in the Marble Fork Kaweah River Canyon below. The summer haze and smog from the San Joaquin Valley to the west often creates riotous sunset colors. Best of all, you hear the sound of silence, or perhaps the wind in the trees and nothing else.

If you've come to Sunset Rock to watch the sunset, don't forget to bring a flashlight for the trip home. The trail is easy to follow, but a little light in the darkness will make it a lot easier.

35. HAZELWOOD & HUCKLEBERRY LOOP

Giant Forest, Sequoia National Park
An 1880s cabin and the second largest tree in the world

DISTANCE: 4.5 miles round-trip; 2 hours   **LEVEL:** Easy/moderate
ELEVATION: Start at 6,400 feet; total change 600 feet   **CROWDS:** Minimal
BEST SEASON: May to October   **RATING:** ★ ★ ★ ★

DIRECTIONS: From the Big Stump Entrance Station at Kings Canyon National Park, drive north for 1.5 miles and turn right on the Generals Highway, heading for Sequoia National Park. Drive approximately 30 miles on the Generals Highway, past Lodgepole and Wolverton, to the Giant Forest area of Sequoia National Park. The Hazelwood Trailhead is on the south side of the highway, a quarter-mile before you reach the Giant Forest market/museum (see the note on page 362). Park in the small pullout area.

Alternatively, from the Ash Mountain Entrance Station at Sequoia National Park, drive north on the Generals Highway for 17 miles to Giant Forest.

This hike combines two loop trails in the Giant Forest area for an easy but excellent day hike, passing by many giant Sequoias and grassy meadows, plus an old log cabin and the giant Washington Tree. A bonus: These trails are generally less crowded than the other day hikes in the Giant Forest area.

From the Generals Highway, pick up the Hazelwood Nature Trail and take the right side of the loop to join up with the Alta Trail and the Huckleberry Meadow Trail Loop. The Hazelwood Nature Trail is an easy interpretive trail bearing signs that describe the human history of Sequoia National Park, especially as it relates to the giant Sequoias.

After a half-mile, leave the Hazelwood loop and join the Alta Trail.

Follow it uphill for a quarter-mile, then bear right on the Huckleberry Meadow Trail. In the next mile, climb up and over a forested ridge to the site of Squatter's Cabin. This partially restored log cabin is one of the oldest structures in Sequoia National Park, dating back to the 1880s. It was built by a member of a San Francisco-based utopian community called the Kaweah Colony. The utopians intended to support themselves by constructing a mill and logging the huge Sequoias of Giant Forest. When Giant Forest became a part of Sequoia National Park in 1890, the colony's plans fell apart, and the group eventually split up.

To stay on the loop, turn left by the cabin (don't take the trail signed for the Dead Giant). The trail skirts the edge of Huckleberry Meadow and heads north to Circle Meadow, where giant Sequoia trees line the meadow's edges. There are several possible junctions, but just stay on the Huckleberry Meadow Trail. A half-mile farther is a short spur trail on the left for the Washington Tree. Take this spur to see the second largest tree in the world (second only to the General Sherman Tree). It is 30 feet in diameter and 246 feet tall.

The trip finishes out on the Alta Trail, on which you return to the Hazelwood Nature Trail and walk the opposite side of its short loop, back to the Generals Highway.

Squatter's Cabin on the Huckleberry Meadow Trail

36. MORO ROCK

Giant Forest, Sequoia National Park
Sequoia National Park's most famous vista point

DISTANCE: 0.6 mile round-trip; 20 minutes
ELEVATION: Start at 6,400 feet; total change 325 feet
BEST SEASON: May to October

LEVEL: Easy/moderate
CROWDS: Heavy
RATING: ★ ★ ★ ★ ★

DIRECTIONS: From the Big Stump Entrance Station at Kings Canyon National Park, drive north for 1.5 miles and turn right on the Generals Highway, heading for Sequoia National Park. Drive approximately 30 miles on the Generals Highway, past Lodgepole and Wolverton, to the Giant Forest area of Sequoia National Park. Just beyond the market/museum, turn left on Crescent Meadow Road, drive 1.5 miles, and take the right fork to the Moro Rock parking area (see the note on page 362).

Alternatively, from the Ash Mountain Entrance Station at Sequoia National Park, drive north on the Generals Highway for 17 miles to Giant Forest.

Almost everybody has heard of Moro Rock, the prominent, pointy granite dome in Sequoia National Park with the top-of-the-world sunset vistas. Certainly everybody has seen the T-shirts that proclaim "I climbed Moro Rock!"

If you're visiting the Giant Forest area of Sequoia National Park, you should climb Moro Rock, too. When you ascend the 380 stairs to the dome's summit and check out the view, you realize that unlike many famous attractions, Moro Rock is not overrated. It's as great as everybody says, maybe even better.

If you start your trip from the Moro Rock parking area, it's only three-tenths of a mile to the top, climbing switchbacks, ramps, and granite stairs the whole way. Railings line the rock-blasted trail; they're intended to stop you from dropping off the 6,725-foot granite dome. The path is steep enough to get you panting, but it's the vistas that will really take your breath away.

So what's the view like? Well, on a clear day, you can see all the way to the Coast Range, 100 miles away. In closer focus is the Middle Fork of the Kaweah River 4,000 feet below you, the winding Generals Highway snaking its way down to the foothills to the south, the massive Great Western Divide to the east, Castle Rocks at 9,180 feet, Triple Divide Peak at 12,634 feet, Mount Stewart at 12,205 feet... and on and on. In a word, it's awesome. And even better, you don't get this panorama just from the top of Moro Rock—you get it all the way up, at every turn in the trail.

On top of Moro Rock

But here's the catch: To get the best view, you must climb Moro Rock when the air is crystal clear. On most warm summer days, the San Joaquin Valley smog and haze obscures much of the vista from Moro Rock by early in the afternoon. Start your trip early in the morning in summer, or visit Moro Rock at any time in spring or fall, when the temperatures are cooler and the inversion layer is nonexistent. (This has the added bonus of minimizing the crowds at this popular spot.) Our favorite tip: Check out the view from Moro Rock at sunset. Even if the smog has obscured some of the view, the sky's colors will be incredible. Also, the vista from Moro Rock during a full moon is magnificent.

Make sure you read the interpretive sign by the parking lot and base of Moro Rock that describes the building of this complex granite trail in 1931. Imagine what it was like to climb Moro Rock in the 1920s, when there were no granite stair-steps, just rickety wooden ones. The sign also gives credit to the first woman to climb Moro Rock, settler Hale Tharp's daughter. She climbed it before the turn of the century, when there was no trail at all. (See the following story on Tharp's Log for more information on Hale Tharp.)

If you want a longer hike, you can walk to Moro Rock from the Giant Forest market/museum on the Moro Rock, Bear Hill, or Soldiers trails, adding about three miles to your round-trip. Each of these is a pleasant stroll through the forest and will spare you the usual midday parking fiasco at Moro Rock. The National Park Service hopes to eventually close the road to Moro Rock; then visitors will have to hike in or take a shuttle bus.

37. CRESCENT MEADOW & THARP'S LOG

Giant Forest, Sequoia National Park
A Sequoia log cabin and two giant meadows ringed with big trees

DISTANCE: 2.2 miles round-trip; 1 hour   **LEVEL:** Easy
ELEVATION: Start at 6,700 feet; total change 150 feet   **CROWDS:** Heavy
BEST SEASON: May to October   **RATING:** ★ ★ ★ ★

DIRECTIONS: From the Big Stump Entrance Station at Kings Canyon National Park, drive north for 1.5 miles and turn right on the Generals Highway, heading for Sequoia National Park. Drive approximately 30 miles on the Generals Highway, past Lodgepole and Wolverton, to the Giant Forest area of Sequoia National Park. Just beyond the market/museum, turn left on Crescent Meadow Road and drive 3.5 miles to the Crescent Meadow parking area (see the note on page 362). Park and begin hiking by the rest rooms.

Alternatively, from the Ash Mountain Entrance Station at Sequoia National Park, drive north on the Generals Highway for 17 miles to Giant Forest.

John Muir called Crescent Meadow "the gem of the Sierras." I don't know how he would feel about the pavement that surrounds some of this precious meadow today, but I hope that Muir would like this loop hike anyhow.

What makes Crescent Meadow a gem? It's more than a mile long, it's filled with blooming wildflowers and surrounded by giant Sequoias, and it sits nearly side by side with Log Meadow, which is equally as large and beautiful.

From the southeastern edge of the parking area, follow the paved trail, crossing Crescent Creek on a footbridge. In a few hundred feet you're skirting the southern edge of Crescent Meadow. Take the right fork and head for Log Meadow, saving Crescent Meadow for later. In 150 feet, bear right again, heading around the back (west) side of Log Meadow. Big ferns line the path, and the massive Sequoias look particularly magnificent standing guard at the meadow's edges. Cross Log Meadow's tiny stream on a footbridge and look closely at the water—you may see small trout swimming.

At Log Meadow's far end, you'll find Tharp's Log. A big downed Sequoia log was the homestead of Hale Tharp, supposedly the first white man to enter this forest. Tharp came here in 1858, accompanied by two Yokut Indians. Unlike most white settlers and homesteaders, Tharp liked and respected the Yokuts, and he befriended them. Tharp grazed cattle and horses in the meadows and built his modest summer home inside this fire-hollowed Sequoia. Peering inside Tharp's Log, hikers can see his bed, fireplace chimney, dining room table, and the door and windows he fashioned. Tharp lived in his log during almost 30 summers, from 1861 to 1890. He was visited by the great mountain tramp John Muir, who called Tharp's log home a "noble den."

From Tharp's Log, continue your loop back to Crescent Meadow and around its west side. The trail drops you off on the northeast side of the parking lot, near the picnic area and just a few yards from where you left your car.

38. HIGH SIERRA TRAIL to EAGLE VIEW

Giant Forest, Sequoia National Park
World-class views from the rim of the Kaweah River Canyon

DISTANCE: 1.5 miles round-trip; 45 minutes   **LEVEL:** Easy
ELEVATION: Start at 6,700 feet; total change 100 feet   **CROWDS:** Moderate
BEST SEASON: May to October   **RATING:** ★ ★ ★ ★

DIRECTIONS: From the Big Stump Entrance Station at Kings Canyon National Park, drive north for 1.5 miles and turn right on the Generals Highway, heading for Sequoia National Park. Drive approximately 30 miles on the Generals Highway, past Lodgepole and Wolverton, to the Giant Forest area of Sequoia National Park. Just beyond the market/museum, turn left on Crescent Meadow Road and drive 3.5 miles to the Crescent Meadow parking area (see the note on page 362). Park and begin hiking by the rest rooms.

Alternatively, from the Ash Mountain Entrance Station at Sequoia National Park, drive north on the Generals Highway for 17 miles to Giant Forest.

The High Sierra Trail is a popular trans-Sierra route that eventually leads to Mount Whitney, the highest peak in the contiguous United States at 14,495 feet in elevation. From the Crescent Meadow Trailhead, the mammoth mountain is 70 miles to the east. You won't go quite that far on this trip, but you'll still get a taste of the visual delights of the scenic High Sierra Trail. In less than a half-mile from the trailhead, you'll be walking on the edge of the Middle Fork Kaweah River Canyon, witnessing wondrous, edge-of-the-world views.

Are you ready to be wowed? From the lower parking lot at Crescent Meadow, follow the trail that leads to the southern edge of the meadow. Cross two footbridges, and in about 200 feet, take the right fork that leads off the pavement and up the ridge on the High Sierra Trail. From where the trail tops out, continue walking to the east, toward Eagle View.

Numerous wildflowers line the sunny path, which contours along the edge of the Middle Fork Kaweah River Canyon. At eight-tenths of a mile from the trailhead, you reach Eagle View, an unsigned but obvious lookout from which you get a fascinating perspective on Moro Rock to your right, craggy Castle Rocks straight ahead, and the dozens of peaks and ridges of the Great Western Divide far across the canyon. The vistas are so fine, and the trail is so good, that you might just decide to walk all the way to Mount Whitney someday.

If you want to continue farther on this trail, the views are almost nonstop. The first true "destination" beyond Eagle View is not until Bearpaw Meadow, 10 miles to the east, so just walk as far as you please and then turn around and head back. Another option is to retrace your steps on the High Sierra Trail back down to about 50 feet before Crescent Meadow. There, you'll see a fork leading west (left) signed for Bobcat Point. Follow this fork for another half-mile to yet another viewpoint of the Middle Fork Kaweah River Canyon and its awe-inspiring granite peaks. You can loop back to the parking lot from Bobcat Point, by connecting with Sugar Pine Trail and turning right.

View of Moro Rock from the High Sierra Trail

39. MIDDLE FORK TRAIL to PANTHER CREEK

Foothills region, Sequoia National Park
Granite views and Panther Creek swimming holes

DISTANCE: 6.0 miles round-trip; 3 hours   **LEVEL:** Moderate
ELEVATION: Start at 3,300 feet; total change 600 feet   **CROWDS:** Minimal
BEST SEASON: February to June   **RATING:** ★ ★ ★

DIRECTIONS: From the Ash Mountain entrance station to Sequoia National Park, drive northeast on Highway 198/Generals Highway for 6.3 miles to the turnoff on the right for Buckeye Flat Campground, across from Hospital Rock. Turn right and drive a half mile to a left fork just before the campground. Bear left on the dirt road and drive 1.3 miles to the trailhead and parking area. In the winter, you must park at Hospital Rock and walk in to the trailhead, adding 3.6 miles to your round-trip.

You want to be alone? You don't want to see anybody else on the trail? Okay, just sign up for this trip any time between June and September. We hiked the Middle Fork Trail on Labor Day Weekend, when every campground in the national park was jammed and every trail was a veritable parade of hikers, and ours was the only car at the trailhead. Of course, the price for solitude is the summer heat, but if you start early enough in the morning, you can beat it.

Don't let the name mislead you. The Middle Fork Trail does indeed parallel the Middle Fork of the Kaweah River, but this is no streamside ramble. You are high above the river for the entire length of your trip, traversing steep canyon slopes. The trail is mostly level to Panther Creek, but there is almost no shade and very little water available. Because the route is so high and open, it often catches a breeze blowing through the canyon, making the exposed slopes somewhat more hospitable for hiking.

After leaving the trailhead, you'll cross over Moro Creek, a pretty cascading stream just two minutes down the trail. Enjoy the shade around its banks, then say goodbye and put on your sun hat. You'll hike through chamise, manzanita, yuccas, and scrub oaks—nothing tall enough to provide any shade, or obscure the fine views in all directions. The first two miles of trail provide sweeping vistas of the Upper Middle Fork canyon area, Moro Rock, the Great Western Divide, and Castle Rocks. With all the peaks and ridges in your scope, there's enough stunning geology to keep anyone enthused, even on a hot day.

At three miles, the Middle Fork Trail brings you right on top of the waterfall on Panther Creek, which drops into the Middle Fork

Kaweah River. Now is the time to warn everyone in sight to be darn careful if they go near the edge to get a better view. The sight of the Middle Fork Kaweah River below is awesome, with its many green pools and small falls, and Panther Creek's 150-foot freefall drop is stunning, but the granite you're standing on is very slippery. Exercise extreme caution.

The safer upstream areas of Panther Creek warrant exploration. If you want to cool off, head upstream and off-trail for a few hundred feet, where there are several cascades and cold, clear pools to wade into.

If you'd prefer to hike this trail in winter, when the air is cool and the foothills are moist and green, you'll have to earn it. The road to Buckeye Flat Campground is closed during winter months, so you must park at Hospital Rock and walk an extra 1.8 miles one-way to the trailhead.

40. PARADISE CREEK TRAIL

Foothills region, Sequoia National Park
Spring wildflower heaven

DISTANCE: 2.6 miles round-trip; 1.5 hours   **LEVEL:** Easy/moderate
ELEVATION: Start at 2,700 feet; total change 400 feet   **CROWDS:** Moderate
BEST SEASON: February to June   **RATING:** ★ ★ ★

DIRECTIONS: From the Ash Mountain entrance station to Sequoia National Park, drive northeast on Highway 198/Generals Highway for 6.3 miles to the turnoff on the right for Buckeye Flat Campground, across from Hospital Rock. Turn right and drive six-tenths of a mile to the campground. Park in any of the dirt pullouts outside of the camp entrance; no day-use parking is allowed in the camp. (You can also park at Hospital Rock and walk to the campground.) The trailhead is near campsite number 28.

Wildflower lovers, rejoice. You've just found a lovely trail in the foothills for kicking up your heels among the blooms. Even after the petals have dropped, this trail along Paradise Creek still has much to offer—like rocky pools, splashing cascades, swimming holes, shady trees, and an unusual perspective on Moro Rock.

Campers at Buckeye Flat Campground have easy access to the Paradise Creek Trail; they simply saunter over to site #28, where the trail begins. Day-hikers, on the other hand, have to park alongside the road outside the camp, or a half-mile farther back at Hospital Rock, then walk into the camp and pick up the trail.

From the Paradise Creek Trailhead, you hike only a few hundred

Buckeye blossoms along the Paradise Creek Trail

feet under the shade of blue oaks, buckeyes, and ponderosa pines before reaching a picturesque, 40-foot-long bridge over the Middle Fork Kaweah River. There's a huge swimming hole on its downstream side that looks nearly Olympic-size. Teenagers sometimes dive off the bridge into the river here.

Save the pool for later; for now, take the signed Paradise Creek Trail to the left at the far side of the bridge. You'll briefly visit the pretty creek with its huge, rocky pools, then leave its side, climbing uphill into oaks and giant-sized manzanita. In a couple of switchbacks, you get some high views of Moro Rock and Hanging Rock as the trail levels out. Moro Rock looks narrow, not rounded, from this vantage point.

The trail now parallels Paradise Creek, and the next third of a mile offers plentiful swimming spots under the shade of ponderosa pines, buckeye trees, blue oaks, and black oaks. Each time you near the water, look for flowers. You're most likely to see purple Chinese houses, bleeding hearts, and Indian pink. The sweet smell in the spring air comes not from the flowers but from the buckeye trees, with their long, cone-shaped bouquets of white blossoms.

At just shy of one mile out, you'll cross the creek under the shade of alders. (In the spring, you have to ford; use caution if the stream flow is high.) Switchback upward, then a quarter mile later, cross the stream once more. The trail then leaves the creek, heading uphill. You'll

Only when the giant trees are lying down can you really grasp their immense girth.

At the half-mile point, the grade becomes easier as it moves into long, curving switchbacks instead of a straight beeline uphill. At your feet are low-growing mountain misery and manzanita in the drier areas, and tons of ferns in the wetter areas. As you climb, the views through the trees keep improving, of the East Fork Kaweah River Canyon across from you and far below, and the sawtoothed peaks of the Great Western Divide.

At 1.6 miles, you reach another stand of Sequoias, the last on this trail. You can hike all the way to the top of the ridge if you like—it's another 1.5 miles—but the views aren't much better than they are on the way up. Most people just cruise uphill on this trail for a mile or two, then turn around when they've had their senses sated by the giant Sequoias. In addition to the big trees and the big views, on our trip we were delighted to see more bears than people.

43. HOCKETT TRAIL to EAST FORK GROVE

Mineral King, Sequoia National Park
Big conifers and a river waterfall

DISTANCE: 4.0 miles round-trip; 2 hours   **LEVEL:** Easy/moderate
ELEVATION: Start at 6,500 feet; total change 800 feet   **CROWDS:** Minimal
BEST SEASON: June to October   **RATING:** ★ ★ ★ ★

DIRECTIONS: From Visalia, drive east on Highway 198 for 38 miles to Mineral King Road, 2.5 miles east of Three Rivers. (If you reach the Ash Mountain entrance station, you've gone too far.) Turn right on Mineral King Road and drive 19 miles to the Hockett Trail parking area on the right, a quarter-mile past Atwell Mill Camp. Park there and walk into the campground to site 16, where the trail begins.

The Hockett Trail makes a fine day-hiking path in Mineral King, suitable for all kinds of hikers. This short trip on the Hockett Trail is one of the few hikes in the Mineral King area of Sequoia National Park that is suitable for families, or people who don't want a long and arduous hike to reach a pretty destination. Hikers with small children can cut this trip short by just walking a mile downhill to the footbridge over the East Fork Kaweah River, then returning. People who want a longer trip can continue another mile to the East Fork Grove of Sequoias and Deer Creek, making a four-mile round-trip.

The trail begins between sites 16 and 17 at Atwell Mill Camp;

Footbridge over the East Fork Kaweah River

take the fork that is signed for Hockett Meadow. You pass by many huge Sequoia stumps that are 12 to 15 feet wide. They're left from the days when people thought it was a good idea to cut down the mammoth trees for cheap lumber. In a small meadow, you'll see the remains of an 1880s sawmill, with which the Sequoias were transformed into fenceposts, pencils, and shingles.

Be prepared for olfactory bliss, because the scent of mountain misery is pervasive on the downhill route to the river. Listen for the tap-tap-tap of woodpeckers as you walk, and look for the large pileated variety with their bright red heads. We saw two. We also saw a black bear, who scampered away from us.

The trail descends through a forest of big conifers, including young Sequoias, pines, cedars, and firs—many with velvety mosses growing on their bark. At a half-mile, you can hear the rumble of the East Fork Kaweah River. Cross a small stream, and in just a few minutes you come to a picture-perfect log footbridge over the river. A 20-foot waterfall descends into an aquamarine pool just upstream of the bridge. What perfects the scene are the big Sequoias that grow along the river banks; apparently these were just far enough from the lumber mill to escape its giant saw.

Some hikers set up a picnic right here by the bridge, or just take a few photographs and head back uphill. If you choose to continue, the trail climbs uphill and away from the river, traveling through a burned area on its way to the East Fork Grove of Sequoias. The grove is small: Only about a dozen trees can be seen from the trail, but they are huge specimens. The path continues uphill, crosses a tiny stream, then reaches Deer Creek. Instead of fording the creek, sit by its banks, listen to the water flow, and count the wildflowers.

44. COLD SPRINGS NATURE TRAIL

Mineral King, Sequoia National Park
A riverside walk with views of Sawtooth Peak

DISTANCE: 2.4 miles round-trip; 1.5 hours

ELEVATION: Start at 7,800; total change 300 feet

BEST SEASON: June to October

LEVEL: Easy

CROWDS: Minimal

RATING: ★ ★ ★ ★

DIRECTIONS: From Visalia, drive east on Highway 198 for 38 miles to Mineral King Road, 2.5 miles east of Three Rivers. (If you reach the Ash Mountain entrance station, you've gone too far.) Turn right on Mineral King Road and drive 23 miles to Cold Springs Campground on the right. The trail begins near site 6. If you aren't staying in the camp, you can park by the Mineral King Ranger Station and walk into the campground.

Mineral King: It's a glacial-cut valley, surrounded by 12,000-foot granite and shale peaks, and home to the headwaters of the East Fork Kaweah River. Many people say that the valley's beauty is comparable to that of Yosemite Valley, but without all the pavement. That's a bit like comparing apples to oranges, but regardless—Mineral King is drop-dead gorgeous.

You might not expect much from a campground nature trail, but because this is Mineral King, the Cold Springs Nature Trail will far exceed your expectations. Not only is it lined with wildflowers along the East Fork Kaweah River, but the views of the high peaks of the Sawtooth Ridge are divine. The nature trail is less than a half-mile long, but from the far end of it, a path continues along the East Fork Kaweah River, traveling another mile into the heart of Mineral King Valley.

If you are camping at Cold Springs Campground, just start hiking by campsite number 6. If you're not, you'll have to park your car by the ranger station across the road, then walk in to the campground. Along the interpretive section of the trail, informative signposts teach you to identify junipers, cottonwoods, and aspens. You'll learn about corn lilies, native gooseberries or currants, how to identify red and white firs by their cones, and that the junipers along the trail are as old as 1,000 years. You'll also see the remains of some mining activity that was begun and then abandoned.

When you reach the trail's last interpretive sign, instead of looping back, continue to hike eastward. This will bring you closer to the riverbank, and provide views of dramatic Sawtooth Peak. Wildflowers are excellent near the river, including purple wandering daisies and black-eyed Susans. There are many lovely pools and cascades to admire when the water flow is high; they are accented by colorful rocks shimmering just beneath the surface. You can walk all the way into Mineral King Valley if you wish, and you might as well. The scenery just keeps getting prettier as you go. (The trail enters the valley by connecting with a residential road; it's OK to walk on this private road.)

Here's the best Mineral King tip we know: Hike this trail right before sunset, when the valley's surrounding mountain peaks turn every imaginable shade of pink, orange, and coral, reflecting the sun setting in the west. The vistas are so beautiful, you may never want to leave.

45. FAREWELL GAP TRAIL to ASPEN FLAT

Mineral King, Sequoia National Park
Vivid scenery and wildlife on a riverside stroll

DISTANCE: 2.0 miles round-trip; 1 hour
ELEVATION: Start at 7,800 feet; total change 20 feet
BEST SEASON: June to October

LEVEL: Easy
CROWDS: Moderate
RATING: ★ ★ ★ ★

DIRECTIONS: From Visalia, drive east on Highway 198 for 38 miles to Mineral King Road, 2.5 miles east of Three Rivers. (If you reach the Ash Mountain entrance station, you've gone too far.) Turn right on Mineral King Road and drive 25 miles to the end of the road and the Eagle/Mosquito Trailhead. (Take the right fork at the end of the road to reach the parking area.) Walk back out of the parking lot and follow the road to the pack station; the Farewell Gap Trail begins just beyond it.

This short walk on the Farewell Gap Trail is perfect for families, or for non-hikers who want to see some scenery. The path offers many opportunities to wander off-trail, examine the wildflowers, picnic at the river's edge, and maybe even do a little fishing. Small children will be thrilled to see mule deer and marmots; adults will be awed at the soaring granite cliffs that surround glacial-cut Mineral King Valley.

The Farewell Gap Trail begins in the valley, then traces a long route from the valley floor up and over Farewell Gap and into the wild backcountry beyond. The first mile of this extensive trail is an easy stroll along Mineral King's canyon floor, leading past waterfalls and alongside the headwaters of the East Fork Kaweah River.

You'll have to park your car a short distance from the actual trailhead, which is located by the Mineral King pack station. Leave your car at the Eagle/Mosquito parking area, but don't take the Eagle Lake Trail that leads from there. Instead, walk back down the road and cross the bridge over the East Fork Kaweah River. Turn right on the dirt road to the pack station and walk past the corral. Just beyond the corral, you'll see the sign for Farewell Gap Trail.

The path begins as a wide dirt road, heading straight into the heart of the beautiful canyon, with the headwaters of the East Fork Kaweah River flowing by on your right. You may see anglers working the river, mostly flyfishing.

It's almost guaranteed that you'll see deer munching the foliage along the riverbanks, or grazing on the mountain slopes. Mineral King Valley is filled with deer, as well as the

Mineral King Valley

ferns and wildflowers they like to eat. You may also see yellow-bellied marmots sunning themselves on rocks, or a sage grouse strutting in the shrubbery. The grouse is a large, bold bird, and it's likely to just stare at you curiously instead of flying away.

Everywhere you look, you see 12,000-foot peaks, their shale and granite surfaces colored rust, red, white, and black. The Farewell Gap Trail stays level as it travels up the canyon floor. At one mile from the trailhead, Crystal Creek pours down the mountainside on your left. Your destination is close at hand; shortly after crossing Crystal Creek, take the right fork off the main trail. (It may have branches or logs across it; this is to warn long-distance hikers that the right fork is not the main trail. Go around the logs.)

This fork brings you closer to the river, where you follow a narrow use trail to Aspen Flat, a lovely grove of quaking aspens, and to Soda Springs, situated right along the river's edge. At Soda Springs, if you look closely, you'll see mineral springs bubbling up from the ground, turning the earth around them a bright orange color.

Find a comfortable seat in the verdant grasses, either in the shade of the aspens or in the sun by Soda Springs. Then count the wildflowers, try to discern every hue of color in the peaks, and listen to the music of the river.

46. MOSQUITO LAKES

Mineral King, Sequoia National Park
Fir forest, granite, and a deep blue lake

DISTANCE: 8.4 miles round-trip; 4 hours
ELEVATION: Start at 7,800 feet; total change 2,350 feet
BEST SEASON: June to October

LEVEL: Strenuous
CROWDS: Moderate
RATING: ★ ★ ★

DIRECTIONS: From Visalia, drive east on Highway 198 for 38 miles to Mineral King Road, 2.5 miles east of Three Rivers. (If you reach the Ash Mountain entrance station, you've gone too far.) Turn right on Mineral King Road and drive 25 miles to the end of the road and the Eagle/Mosquito Trailhead. (Take the right fork at the end of the road to reach the parking area.) The trail begins at the far end of the parking lot.

There are five Mosquito Lakes in Mineral King, all connected by rushing Mosquito Creek and situated in the high country near 10,000 feet. Only one of them is anything less than stunning; unfortunately, it's the first one. This hike takes you past the first Mosquito Lake to Mosquito Lake #2, making a perfect 8.4-mile round-trip for a Sierra summer day.

The Eagle/Mosquito Trailhead is at 7,800 feet in elevation, and you set out from the parking lot near one of Mineral King's adorable cabins, remaining from early in the 20th century and privately owned. Feel jealous? Keep walking; you'll get over it. In minutes you cross a footbridge over Spring Creek's cascade, called Tufa Falls because of the calcium carbonate in Spring Creek's water. Don't expect to see much of a waterfall—most of it is hidden by brush. At one mile, reach the junction for Eagle Lake, the Mosquito Lakes, and White Chief, and take the right fork, climbing steadily. At two miles, you'll reach the Mosquito Lakes junction shortly beyond the Eagle Sink Holes and go right, leaving the Eagle Lake Trail for another day (see the following story). The worst of the climb is over.

You traverse a level, fir-shaded section, then make a gentle, forested ascent over Miner's Ridge at 9,300 feet. Next—surprise—you have a steep descent down the other side, with several switchbacks. You drop 260 feet in the final half-mile to the first Mosquito Lake, reached at 3.6 miles from the trailhead.

This first lake is considered to be the easiest lake to reach in Mineral King, having only a 1,500-foot gain on the way in, a 260-foot gain on the way out, and a mostly shaded trail. But despite its easy access, the lake's appearance is disappointing. It's small, shallow, and greenish in color, with too many snags in the water for good swimming. Anglers will notice plenty of trout surfacing, however.

Keep hiking to Mosquito Lake #2, only six-tenths of a mile away. Although the next stretch is quite steep and has no maintained trail, it is completely worth the effort. If you follow the faint use trail by Mosquito Creek, the going is easier. Circle to your right around the first lake. The use trail begins on the west side of the creek, navigates around a boulder field behind the lake, then crosses

Mosquito Lake #2

the stream above it. Hike through a level, granite stretch, then climb upward again over a second rocky ridge, now on the east side of the creek. Watch for trail ducks marking the way.

The climb to the second lake has a 600-foot elevation gain in just over a half mile, so take your time. Mosquito Lake #2 is a prime destination for day-hikers; it's a deep, clear, granite-bound beauty set at 9,600 feet. Granite cliffs ringing the lake's edges and a couple of rocky islands perfect the scene. The scenery is classic High Sierra. Swimming is first-rate, although cold.

Hikers with excess energy to burn can continue on to the next three Mosquito Lakes, all found within one more mile. The third and fourth lakes are smaller and less appealing than the second lake, but the fifth lake is a winner. It's larger than all the others, and it's also more stark and exposed, with fewer trees. Hengst Peak, which looks imposing from the second Mosquito Lake, is superbly dramatic from the fifth lake.

47. EAGLE LAKE

Mineral King, Sequoia National Park
The most photographed lake in Mineral King

DISTANCE: 6.8 miles round-trip; 4 hours
ELEVATION: Start at 7,800 feet; total change 2,200 feet
BEST SEASON: June to October

LEVEL: Strenuous
CROWDS: Moderate
RATING: ★ ★ ★ ★ ★

DIRECTIONS: From Visalia, drive east on Highway 198 for 38 miles to Mineral King Road, 2.5 miles east of Three Rivers. (If you reach the Ash Mountain entrance station, you've gone too far.) Turn right on Mineral King Road and drive 25 miles to the end of the road and the Eagle/Mosquito Trailhead. (Take the right fork at the end of the road to reach the parking area.) The trail begins at the far end of the parking lot.

Eagle Lake is the glamour destination in Mineral King, the trail to hike if you can hike only one trail in the area. Why? The blue-green lake is drop-dead gorgeous, and its trail is challenging but manageable for most day hikers. Total elevation gain to the lake is 2,200 feet, but it's well spread out over the 3.4-mile journey.

The Eagle Lake Trail follows the same route as the Mosquito Lake Trail (see the previous story) up until the two-mile point near the Eagle Sink Holes. Visible to the left of the trail, the sink holes are two small

Eagle Lake

craters where Eagle Creek suddenly disappears underground. At the trail junction shortly beyond the sink holes, go left for Eagle Lake. Enjoy the brief level stretch here, because shortly, you'll gain another 1,000 feet over 1.4 miles. Much of the climb is in an exposed, rocky area—a tremendous boulder field that gets baked by the sun on warm days. Well-graded switchbacks and beautiful scenery make the climb easier. Down canyon, you can see Sawtooth Peak and Mineral Peak far to the northeast.

(If you've hiked to the neighboring Mosquito Lakes, you'll notice that this trail to Eagle Lake seems more difficult. It's simply because this trail maintains a relentless "up," while the Mosquito Lakes Trail meanders through ups and downs. The Eagle Lake Trail is also much sunnier; make sure you wear a hat and sunglasses.)

Soon you arrive at Eagle Lake's dam at 10,000 feet. Like many lakes in Mineral King, Eagle Lake was enlarged in the early 1900s by the building of this dam. Southern California Edison still utilizes the water today. The big lake with its rocky islands is surrounded by glacially carved rock wearing coats of many colors. The trail continues along the lake's west side to many good picnicking spots and photo opportunities. Campsites are found near the shore; backpackers may be seen setting up camp here.

Anglers, take note: Brook trout swim in Eagle Lake's clear waters. If you can stop staring at the scenery, you might be able to catch a fish or two.

48. FRANKLIN LAKE

Mineral King, Sequoia National Park
Largest lake in Mineral King accessible by day-hiking

DISTANCE: 10.8 miles round-trip; 6 hours   **LEVEL:** Strenuous
ELEVATION: Start at 7,800 feet; total change 2,500 feet   **CROWDS:** Minimal
BEST SEASON: June to October   **RATING:** ★ ★ ★ ★

DIRECTIONS: From Visalia, drive east on Highway 198 for 38 miles to Mineral King Road, 2.5 miles east of Three Rivers. (If you reach the Ash Mountain entrance station, you've gone too far.) Turn right on Mineral King Road and drive 25 miles to the end of the road and the Eagle/Mosquito Trailhead. (Take the right fork at the end of the road to reach the parking area.) Walk back out of the parking lot and follow the road to the pack station; the Farewell Gap Trail begins just beyond it.

Franklin Lake is huge—about double the size of Eagle Lake and four times the size of Mosquito Lake in Mineral King. In fact, it's the largest lake accessible by day-hiking in the Mineral King area, unless you count Columbine Lake, which requires a grueling 12-mile round-trip that is best saved for a backpacking excursion.

Still, surprisingly few people day hike to Franklin Lake. Perhaps it's the mileage that scares them off—it's almost 11 miles round-trip to Franklin Lake compared with about eight miles round-trip to Eagle and Mosquito lakes. But here's the secret: Those 11 miles feel about the same on your legs and lungs as the shorter hikes to the other lakes do, because the Franklin Lakes Trail is so well graded. You must cover a 2,500-foot elevation gain, but it's spread out smoothly over 5.4 miles.

In fact, between the excellent trail, the waterfalls and cascades, the prolific wildflowers, the granite-bound lake, and the spectacular views over Mineral King Valley, we rate this trail to be about as close to hiking perfection as we've found. Only one cautionary note is in order: The trail is sunny and exposed. Get an early morning start, and make sure you wear sun protection.

The first two miles are nearly flat, as the route winds along the bottom of Mineral King's canyon, following the Farewell Gap Trail alongside the East Fork Kaweah River. Pass Tufa Falls across the canyon at a quarter-mile, then Crystal Creek's cascades on your side of the

Hiking back from Franklin Lake

canyon at one mile. The trail then leaves the valley floor and starts to climb moderately, reaching the bottom of Franklin Creek's cascades at 1.7 miles. After crossing Franklin Creek, continue south along Farewell Canyon, negotiating a snake-like series of long, sweeping switchbacks to gain elevation. The wildflower show is extravagant, featuring paintbrush, gentian, lupine, wandering daisies, black-eyed Susans, shooting stars, and wild onions near the streams. The views get better and better as you head toward Farewell Gap.

One mile after crossing Franklin Creek, the Franklin Lakes Trail forks left off the Farewell Gap Trail and starts to climb in earnest up the Franklin Creek canyon. Now you've left the wildflower-covered, verdant slopes for a rocky, talus-lined canyon—the visual equivalent of leaving the earth for the moon.

At nearly 10,000 feet, the trail crosses Franklin Creek again, then parallels the creek for another mile to the largest Franklin Lake. When you see the lake's dam straight ahead, and an obvious campsite with a bear box about 150 yards below it (to the right of the trail), cut off the main trail. Walk to the camp, then follow its use trail to the dam and the lake. (The main trail switchbacks up and above the lake to Franklin Pass, and doesn't go directly to its shoreline.)

Franklin Lake is a dramatic sight, set in a granite bowl at 10,300 feet in elevation. It is surrounded by steep, snow-covered slopes and a few foxtail pines and junipers. To the northeast is Rainbow Mountain at 12,000 feet; to the southwest is Tulare Peak at 11,500 feet.

49. WHITE CHIEF MINE

Mineral King, Sequoia National Park
Alpine meadows and an old mine tunnel

DISTANCE: 5.8 miles round-trip; 3 hours **LEVEL:** Moderate
ELEVATION: Start at 7,800 feet; total change 1,600 feet **CROWDS:** Minimal
BEST SEASON: June to October **RATING:** ★ ★ ★ ★

DIRECTIONS: From Visalia, drive east on Highway 198 for 38 miles to Mineral King Road, 2.5 miles east of Three Rivers. (If you reach the Ash Mountain entrance station, you've gone too far.) Turn right on Mineral King Road and drive 25 miles to the end of the road and the Eagle/Mosquito Trailhead. (Take the right fork at the end of the road to reach the parking area.) The trail begins from the far end of the parking lot.

If you're one of those liberated hikers who doesn't need to have an alpine lake in your itinerary to be happy, the trail to White Chief Bowl

Below White Chief Peak

is a scenic route with much to offer, including an exploration of the White Chief Mine tunnel. For years, the mine was private property within the national park and off-limits to hikers until the Park Service purchased it in 1998. Today it adds an interesting historical element to a trail already overflowing with visual delights.

The first mile of the trail is the same as the route to Eagle and Mosquito lakes, but you'll leave almost everyone behind when you continue straight at the one-mile junction, while they bear right for the lakes (see pages 380 to 383). The White Chief Trail continues with a hefty grade—this second mile is the toughest part of the whole trip. Take your time in the thin, high-elevation air, and know that the third mile of the trip will compensate you for the second. Colorful views across the Mineral King canyon spur you on.

Just after you cross a seasonal stream at two miles out (this is often a dry ravine by late summer), look for the ruins of Crabtree Cabin to the right of the trail. The ruins are what is left of the oldest remaining structure in Mineral King. It was built by John Crabtree, the discoverer of the White Chief Mine, in the 1870s. You'll find a few scraps of rusted pipes and metal and some notched logs.

You've reached the edge of White Chief Meadow in the Lower White Chief Bowl, and now you have the pleasure of walking through it. The dream-like meadow is surrounded by high granite walls and filled with summer wildflowers. The meadow is also filled with dozens of downed trees, the evidence of harsh winter avalanches, giving it an almost surreal appearance.

Beyond the meadow, the trail ascends slightly until it nears a waterfall on White Chief Creek. Shortly before the falls, the trail crosses the creek and heads uphill on a flower-filled slope toward White Chief Peak. Look for the opening to White Chief Mine in a jumble of gleaming white rock just above the trail. Scramble off the trail a few yards to reach it.

The mine tunnel is about seven feet high and horizontal. If you walk into it, you'll find that it dead-ends in about 150 feet. Even without a flashlight, you'll have just enough daylight to see that initials and names are scratched into the tunnel walls, many of them dating back to the early 1900s.

The White Chief Mine, like most of the mines in Mineral King, was completely unproductive. Although much money was invested in developing the mine, not one scrap of silver or gold was ever extracted.

50. TIMBER GAP

Mineral King, Sequoia National Park
A high vista point and Mineral King mining history

DISTANCE: 4.0 miles round-trip; 2 hours   **LEVEL:** Moderate
ELEVATION: Start at 7,800 feet; total change 1,650 feet   **CROWDS:** Minimal
BEST SEASON: June to October   **RATING:** ★ ★ ★

DIRECTIONS: From Visalia, drive east on Highway 198 for 38 miles to Mineral King Road, 2.5 miles east of Three Rivers. (If you reach the Ash Mountain entrance station, you've gone too far.) Turn right on Mineral King Road and drive 24.5 miles to the Sawtooth parking area, a half-mile before the end of the road.

The first thing you need to know: If you don't like horses, you'd better find another trail to hike in Mineral King, because the Timber Gap Trail is popular with the folks at the pack station. In addition to horses, expect to see many mule deer on this trail; the Mineral King Valley is full of them and they love to eat the young foliage along the hillsides.

If you're OK with having some hoofed companions, the Timber Gap Trail is an excellent and interesting route, on which you gain a glimpse into Mineral King's mining history. The trail climbs steeply from the Sawtooth Trailhead on an old mining path along Monarch

Creek, then forks in a quarter-mile. Take the left fork for Timber Gap, which climbs more gently over short switchbacks through a dense fir forest.

One mile out, the trail leaves the trees and the switchbacks behind and makes a long sweep to the north. The path traverses a wide and treeless slope—the result of continual winter avalanches. This exposed, sunny slope is home to many mountain wildflowers. Although the climb is barely noticeable for much of this stretch, the sun can be hot.

At two miles, you re-enter the trees and reach Timber Gap, elevation 9,450 feet. The forested pass is well named; the trees barely make room for the view of the Middle Fork Kaweah River Canyon to the north. (Look for Alta Peak on the far side of that canyon, the tallest mountain around at 11,204 feet.) To the south, you can clearly see Farewell Gap. The stumps you see among the red firs at the gap remain from miners who cut the trees to fuel their fires and support their mining tunnels. The Empire Mine was located only a mile to the east of Timber Gap; a wagon road was built to cart lumber from the gap to the mining camp. A stamp mill was set up closer to Mineral King Valley to process the silver ore; it was located just northwest of the trailhead where you began hiking. The Empire Mine produced a small amount of silver in 1880. It was more profitable than most Mineral King mines, but it still never made anybody rich.

51. MONARCH LAKES

Mineral King, Sequoia National Park
Stark, high alpine scenery and two lakes

DISTANCE: 8.4 miles round-trip; 4 hours   **LEVEL:** Strenuous
ELEVATION: Start at 7,800 feet; total change 2,800 feet   **CROWDS:** Moderate
BEST SEASON: June to October   **RATING:** ★ ★ ★ ★ ★

DIRECTIONS: From Visalia, drive east on Highway 198 for 38 miles to Mineral King Road, 2.5 miles east of Three Rivers. (If you reach the Ash Mountain entrance station, you've gone too far.) Turn right on Mineral King Road and drive 24.5 miles to the Sawtooth parking area, a half-mile before the end of the road.

The Monarch Lakes Trail leads from the Sawtooth Trailhead at 7,800 feet in elevation and climbs 2,500 feet to rocky, gem-like Monarch Lake. This first lake is scenic, but a second, higher Monarch Lake 300 feet above it is simply awesome. For lake lovers who are willing to make some effort, this is a first-class day hike. Along every step of the trail, the scenery is unforgettable.

Start at the Sawtooth parking area, and make the initial steep climb to the trail fork a quarter-mile out. Bear right for Monarch and Crystal lakes. After one steep mile, you'll reach Groundhog Meadow, named for the adorable yellow-bellied marmots that make Mineral King their home. Look for wildflowers among the meadow grasses.

Cross Monarch Creek with a jump, then start switchbacking seriously in and out of red fir forest, making a gut-thumping climb to the Crystal Lake trail junction. If you're breathing harder than you might expect, it's because you're now at 10,000 feet. The trail forks sharply right for Crystal Lake (see the following story), but bear left for one more mile—a relatively smooth mile with the easiest grade of the whole route—to Lower Monarch Lake, elevation 10,400 feet. This final trail stretch laterals across an incredible talus slope, the result of centuries of rock slides. Only a few hardy, windblown foxtail pines can grow here.

Snow is often found near the small lower lake even in late summer. Its setting is dramatic, with Sawtooth Peak dominating the skyline to the east. Backpackers are often seen camping near the shores of this lake, preparing to head onward to Sawtooth Pass.

Day-hikers shouldn't stop here. While the main trail continues

Looking down on Lower Monarch Lake

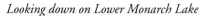

north to the pass, a faint use trail leads southeast from the lower lake for a half-mile to Upper Monarch Lake. The basic route is to head directly up the cliff that forms the back wall of the lower lake.

It's worth the steep, short climb. The upper lake at 10,650 feet is double the size of the lower lake. It's wide, deep blue, and dramatic, set at the base of barren, pointy Mineral Peak. The view from the upper lake's basin, looking back down at the lower lake and the granite walls of Monarch Canyon, is breathtaking. A big surprise is that the upper lake has been dammed, like many of the high lakes in Mineral King, and it is operated by Southern California Edison. But this is no way detracts from its beauty. Nothing possibly could.

52. CRYSTAL LAKE

Mineral King, Sequoia National Park
A hard-to-reach, granite-lined lake

DISTANCE: 9.8 miles round-trip; 6 hours   **LEVEL:** Very strenuous
ELEVATION: Start at 7,800 feet; total change 3,000 feet   **CROWDS:** Minimal
BEST SEASON: June to October   **RATING:** ★ ★ ★ ★

DIRECTIONS: From Visalia, drive east on Highway 198 for 38 miles to Mineral King Road, 2.5 miles east of Three Rivers. (If you reach the Ash Mountain entrance station, you've gone too far.) Turn right on Mineral King Road and drive 24.5 miles to the Sawtooth parking area, a half-mile before the end of the road.

Crystal Lake is one of the less visited lakes in Mineral King, and it has absolutely nothing to do with its scenic beauty. The lake is at least as lovely as all the others in the area, but the path to reach it is longer and more difficult. For those who prefer a day-hiking challenge, this is an excellent trip. For those who prefer to visit an alpine lake in solitude, you'll have a better chance of achieving that here than at neighboring (and easier to reach) Monarch Lake.

The path to Crystal Lake follows the same route as the trail to Monarch Lakes for the first 3.2 miles (see the previous story for details). There, at 10,000 feet, a sharp right-hand turn puts you on the trail to Crystal Lake, heading south. Day-hikers heading to the Monarch Lakes know that at this junction, most of their work is over, but it's not so for those bound for Crystal Lake. The lake is still 1.7 miles and 800 feet of elevation gain away, half of which must be achieved in the last half-mile.

Shortly, you enter Chihuahua Bowl, then climb past the ruins of the Chihuahua Mine on the right, one of Mineral King's last hopes for silver riches. Like the other mines in the area, it never produced ore to equal the miners' dreams. You'll be able to see ore tailings and some building foundations where the mine once stood.

The trail climbs abruptly to a ridge lined with reddish foxtail pines, where your vista opens wide. Far off to the south are the Farewell Gap peaks, and to the east is Upper Crystal Creek, pouring down from Crystal Lake to the Mineral King Valley and the East Fork Kaweah River. Shortly beyond, the trail drops suddenly for 150 yards, passing a junction on the right with a trail to the small Cobalt Lakes. Stay left.

The trail continues on a level stretch for a quarter-mile, then heads into short, steep switchbacks. You have only a half-mile of rocky, talus-lined trail left till you reach upper Crystal Creek and large Crystal Lake at 10,800 feet. Just sweat it out. The trail tops out at the lake's dam, which was built in 1903. Off to the left (north), Mineral Peak stands out at 11,550 feet, and to the right (south), Rainbow Mountain shows off its colorful rock. Granite is visible in every direction; there are no trees growing in the lake's stark basin. If you scramble a quarter-mile off-trail toward Mineral Peak, you reach tiny Upper Crystal Lake, a worthy side-trip.

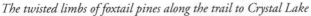

The twisted limbs of foxtail pines along the trail to Crystal Lake

53. BLACK WOLF FALLS

Mineral King, Sequoia National Park
Short stroll to a waterfall

DISTANCE: 0.5 mile round-trip; 20 minutes

ELEVATION: Start at 7,800 feet; total change 20 feet

BEST SEASON: June to October

LEVEL: Easy

CROWDS: Minimal

RATING: ★ ★ ★

DIRECTIONS: From Visalia, drive east on Highway 198 for 38 miles to Mineral King Road, 2.5 miles east of Three Rivers. (If you reach the Ash Mountain entrance station, you've gone too far.) Turn right on Mineral King Road and drive 24.5 miles to the Sawtooth parking area, a half-mile before the end of the road. Walk up the road about 150 feet toward Black Wolf Falls, which drops just east of the road, on your left. Look for a use trail across the road from the "No Parking Any Time" sign, just beyond where Monarch Creek flows under the road.

This hike is really just a stroll, and the destination is readily apparent from the Sawtooth Trailhead: Black Wolf Falls, tumbling down the canyon wall in Mineral King Valley. But aside from the chance to get close to a pretty waterfall, the hike is interesting because of its historical significance. Black Wolf's name is actually an alteration of its original moniker, which was Black Wall Falls, named for the Black Wall copper mine that was located at the waterfall's base. Back in the 1870s, when miners believed that Mineral King was rich in more than just scenery, they mined the base of Monarch Creek with a modicum of success. Today you can walk right up to the falls and see the mine tunnel on its right side. It looks like a cave, but don't go inside; it's walls and ceiling are dangerously unstable.

Although the route to Black Wolf Falls isn't an

Black Wolf Falls

official trail, the path is well used and clearly visible. After you find its beginning across the road from the "No Parking Any Time" sign, the rest of the hike is easy. Just follow the use trail through the sagebrush to the creek's edge near the waterfall.

In summer, rangers lead group hikes to this waterfall and discuss Mineral King's mining history. Check at the Mineral King ranger station to see when one of these interpretive walks is being held; they often occur on Saturdays.

54. LADYBUG TRAIL to CEDAR CREEK

South Fork region, Sequoia National Park
Conifers, a waterfall, and creekside picnicking

DISTANCE: 6.4 miles round-trip; 3 hours   **LEVEL:** Moderate
ELEVATION: Start at 3,600 feet; total change 1,400 feet   **CROWDS:** Minimal
BEST SEASON: February to October   **RATING:** ★ ★ ★

DIRECTIONS: From Visalia, drive east on Highway 198 for 35 miles to one mile west of Three Rivers. Turn right on South Fork Drive and drive 12.8 miles to South Fork Campground. (At nine miles, the road turns to dirt.) Day-use parking is available just inside the camp entrance. The trailhead is at the far end of the campground loop.

It was Labor Day Weekend in the foothills section of Sequoia National Park and we braced ourselves for the worst. We expected swarms of people, no room at the campgrounds, and boiling daytime heat. What could be worse than a national park on a holiday weekend? Combine it with low elevation and a hot day.

Well, we drove out to South Fork Campground and the Ladybug Trailhead, and discovered we were wrong on all counts. The camp still had open campsites—the only available sites in the whole park. Plus, not a single soul was hiking on the Ladybug Trail. And since we started our trip early in the morning, we actually got chilled from swimming in the river pools along the trail, and found ourselves enjoying the low-elevation warmth.

The Ladybug Trail starts from the far end of the South Fork Campground, where a sign states that Ladybug Camp is 1.7 miles, Cedar Creek is 3.2 miles, and so on. A few hundred feet from the camp, the route crosses the South Fork Kaweah River on the Clough Cave Footbridge.

The hike leads through dry foothill country, but with a surprising amount of shade from canyon oaks and bay trees. The route is only

Ladybug Falls on the South Fork Kaweah River

slightly uphill, so the 1.7 miles to Ladybug Camp can be easily covered in less than an hour. You travel parallel to the river for the entire trip, with occasional views of tree-covered ridges to the south, and increasingly wider views of the entire canyon as you climb.

No signs alert you to when you've reached Ladybug Camp at 1.7 miles; you'll simply notice a few primitive campsites between the trail and the river in a flat clearing beneath big incense cedars. The camp makes a fine destination not just because it's a lovely, shaded spot along the clear pools of the South Fork Kaweah, but also because it's home to a secret waterfall. You won't see it from the trail—that's what makes it secret. To see the falls, you must scramble downstream along the river on a steep use trail. It's only about 30 yards from the camp to the falls, but you may have to do some hands-and-feet scrambling. The waterfall is tucked into a rocky grotto; the only way to see it is to position yourself at its base. It's a perfect 25-foot freefall, shooting over rocks and ferns.

So why the name Ladybug for the camp and the trail? Because the little brick-red beetles predominate here. Thousands of ladybugs come to this riverbank to nest every winter. You can find at least a few hundred near the camp at any time of the year. We didn't see any until we sat down by the swimming holes near the camp; then we noticed they were all around us, on every rock and blade of grass. I even found a rare yellow one.

Be sure to head upstream of Ladybug Camp, beyond where the trail switchbacks away from the river. There's a marvelous stretch of stream with pristine pools, rounded boulders, and ferns growing in huge clumps, making little rock-and-waterfall gardens.

Hikers who wish to continue onward can follow the trail past

Ladybug Camp, then switchback uphill and away from the river. Now the trail returns to sunny, grassy slopes. You'll ascend moderately until you have a good view of the distinctive granite dome called Homers Nose. In another mile, you'll enter a grove of black oaks and incense cedars as you approach Cedar Creek, 3.2 miles from the trailhead. A few Sequoia trees grow here by the creek. This makes an excellent spot for a rest and then a turnaround.

55. GARFIELD-HOCKETT TRAIL

South Fork region, Sequoia National Park
A challenging hike to an immense Sequoia grove

DISTANCE: 5.8 miles round-trip; 3 hours   **LEVEL:** Strenuous
ELEVATION: Start at 3,600 feet; total change 2,100 feet   **CROWDS:** Minimal
BEST SEASON: Year-round   **RATING:** ★ ★ ★

DIRECTIONS: From Visalia, drive east on Highway 198 for 35 miles to one mile west of Three Rivers. Turn right on South Fork Drive and drive 12.8 miles to South Fork Campground. (At nine miles, the road turns to dirt.) Day-use parking is available just inside the camp entrance. The trailhead is on the right side of the campground, about 100 yards from the entrance.

The trip to the magnificent Garfield Grove is only 2.9 miles from South Fork Campground, and if you don't mind a steep climb and possibly sharing the trail with horse packers, you should be sure to take this hike.

Remember that I said a *steep* climb. The trail ascends immediately and keeps ascending, but fortunately it is shaded by black oaks and bays most of the way. This trail is not as dry or as warm as you might expect from the South Fork region of the park; instead it features many moist ravines that are deeply shaded with leafy trees like maples and alder. Ferns and wildflowers grace the ground in these cool spots.

The trail continues its relentless climb, heading up the slopes of Dennison Ridge. Your elevation gain rewards you with a view of distant Homers Nose, a granite landmark that, although prominent, looks little like anybody's nose.

In just under three miles of nonstop climbing, you reach the first of many Sequoias in the Garfield Grove. The grove was named for the 20th president of the United States, James A. Garfield. This grove is reported to be one of the largest groves in the national parks, mostly because it lies adjacent to another grove on the other side of Dennison

Gazing up at a giant Sequoia

Ridge. With the two Sequoia groves side by side, you can walk through a mixed forest of Sequoias and other trees for a few miles.

From the point where you see the first Sequoia, the trail's grade slacks off somewhat, giving you a much needed break. Considering you've just gained 2,100 feet in elevation, you deserve the rest. Keep following the trail through the Sequoia grove as far as you desire, or just pick a big tree to lean against and pull out your lunch.

DEATH VALLEY NATIONAL PARK

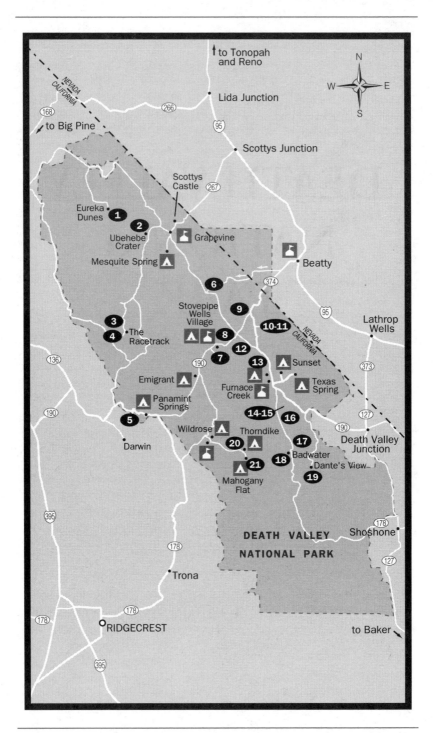

DEATH VALLEY NATIONAL PARK
TRAILS AT A GLANCE

Map Number/Trail Name	Page	Mileage	Difficulty
1. Eureka Dunes	402	2.0	Moderate
2. Ubehebe & Little Hebe Craters	404	1.5	Easy
3. Ubehebe Peak	406	6.0	Strenuous
4. The Racetrack's Sliding Rocks	409	2.0	Easy
5. Darwin Falls	411	1.8	Easy
6. Fall Canyon	412	6.6	Moderate
7. Mosaic Canyon	414	1.0-3.0	Easy
8. Mesquite Flat Sand Dunes	416	1.5	Easy
9. Death Valley Buttes	418	3.6	Moderate
10. Keane Wonder Mine	419	3.2	Strenuous
11. Keane Wonder Springs	421	2.0	Easy
12. Salt Creek Interpretive Trail	422	1.0	Easy
13. Harmony Borax Works & Borax Flats	424	1.0	Easy
14. Golden Canyon to Red Cathedral	425	2.5	Easy
15. Gower Gulch Loop & Zabriskie Point	427	6.4	Moderate
16. Desolation Canyon	429	2.4	Moderate
17. Natural Bridge Canyon	430	1.2	Moderate
18. Badwater Salt Flats	432	1.0	Easy
19. Dante's Ridge	433	2.0	Easy
20. Wildrose Peak	435	8.4	Strenuous
21. Telescope Peak	437	14.0	Very strenuous

THE TOP 5, DON'T-MISS DAY HIKES:

Map Number/Trail Name	Page	Features
1. Eureka Dunes	402	700-foot sand dunes
3. Ubehebe Peak	406	summit views, Racetrack
7. Mosaic Canyon	414	colorful narrows
10. Keane Wonder Mine	419	mining history, views
21. Telescope Peak	437	highest park summit

TRAIL SUGGESTIONS FOR IF YOU ONLY HAVE ONE DAY:

Map Number/Trail Name	Page	Features
7. Mosaic Canyon	414	colorful narrows
8. Mesquite Flat Sand Dunes	416	silky, graceful dunes
10. Keane Wonder Mine	419	mining history, views
14. Golden Canyon to Red Cathedral	425	soaring golden cliffs

DEATH VALLEY NATIONAL PARK

ABOUT THE PARK

Death Valley is the largest U.S. national park outside of Alaska. Although its name is foreboding, the park comprises a vast landscape of desert beauty, from soaring dunes and mountain ranges to below-sea-level salt flats. In summer, the park is the hottest place in North America, but in the winter months, it's cool and mild for hiking.

ADDRESS, PHONE, & WEBSITE

Death Valley National Park, Death Valley, CA 92328; (760) 786-2331 or (760) 786-3244. Website: www.nps.gov/deva

VISITOR CENTERS

The main park visitor center is located in Furnace Creek on Highway 190. A ranger station and information center is located at Stovepipe Wells on Highway 190.

HOW TO GET THERE

• By air: The closest major airport is in Las Vegas, Nevada.

• By car: Many roads access the park:

From the west, via U.S. 395: From Lone Pine, take Highway 190 (or Highway 136 to Highway 190) west for 45 miles to the western border of the park.

From the southwest, via Highway 178: From Ridgecrest, drive north on Highway 178 for 90 miles to the park.

From the southeast, via Interstate 15: From Baker, drive north on Highway 127 for 80 miles, then turn west on Highway 190 to enter the park.

From the east, via U.S. 95 in Nevada: From U.S. 95, take highways 267 or 374 east for 25 miles to the park.

DRIVE TIME

• Drive time from Los Angeles: approximately 5 hours.

• Drive time from San Francisco: approximately 9 hours.

ENTRANCE FEES

There is a $10 entrance fee per vehicle at Death Valley National Park, good for seven days. A Death Valley annual pass is available for $20. A Golden Eagle Passport, an annual pass for all 375 national park units, is available for $50. A Golden Age Passport, a lifetime pass for all

375 national park units, is available to U.S. citizens and residents aged 62 and over for a one-time $10 fee. You can purchase these passes at the park visitor center in Furnace Creek.

WHEN TO GO
For hikers, the time to visit Death Valley is from November to March. During the rest of the year, it's just too darn hot, except for in the higher regions of the park. If you wind up in Death Valley in the summer, however, two excellent hikes are located in the cool mountains: Wildrose Peak and Telescope Peak (see pages 435 to 438).

WEATHER CONDITIONS
Death Valley has a well earned reputation for being hot. And so it is, every year from April to October, when daytime temperatures are often between 90 and 120 degrees. November to March brings comfortable daytime temperatures ranging in the 60s and 70s. Winter nights often drop down to the 40s. It rains less than two inches per year in Death Valley, but the mountains surrounding the valley may be snow-covered from November to April. Roads and trails in the mountains may be impassible in winter.

WHERE TO STAY
Death Valley has nine campgrounds with more that 1,500 sites. Eight of the camps are available on a first-come, first-served basis: Texas Spring, Sunset, Stovepipe Wells, Emigrant, Mesquite Spring, Wildrose, Thorndike, and Mahogany Flat. Furnace Creek Ranch Campground is available by advance reservation; phone (800) 365-2267 to reserve. Most campgrounds are open year-round.

There are four lodging possibilities within the park: Furnace Creek Inn and Furnace Creek Ranch at (760) 786-2361, Stovepipe Wells Village Motel at (760) 786-2387, and Panamint Springs Resort at (702) 482-7680. A list of motels outside of the park is available by mail; phone the park at (760) 786-2331.

FOOD & SUPPLIES
Restaurants and services are available within the park at Stovepipe Wells and Furnace Creek.

SUGGESTED MAPS
Park maps are available at ranger stations or by contacting Death Valley National Park at the address on page 400. A more detailed map is available for a fee from Tom Harrison Cartography at (415) 456-7940.

1. EUREKA DUNES

Scotty's Castle area, Death Valley National Park
Tallest sand dunes in California

DISTANCE: 2.0 miles round-trip; 1 hour   **LEVEL:** Moderate
ELEVATION: Start at 2,800 feet; total change 680 feet   **CROWDS:** Minimal
BEST SEASON: October to April   **RATING:** ★ ★ ★ ★ ★

DIRECTIONS: From the Furnace Creek Visitor Center, drive north on Highway 190 for 17 miles, then bear right on Scotty's Castle Road. In 32 miles, you will reach the Grapevine entrance station. A quarter-mile beyond it, bear left at the fork with Scotty's Castle Road. Continue northwest for three miles to the dirt road on the right signed for Eureka Dunes (Big Pine Road). (If you reach Ubehebe Crater, you've missed the turnoff.) Turn right and drive 34 miles to the South Eureka Valley Road turnoff. Turn left and drive 10 miles to the Eureka Dunes parking area. A high-clearance vehicle may be required.

Let's talk sand dunes, those great icons of the desert. Here in California we are blessed with several sets of them—Kelso Dunes in Mojave National Preserve, Mesquite Flat Sand Dunes near Stovepipe Wells, and Saline Valley Dunes on the far west side of Death Valley. But the king of them all is Eureka Dunes, once the featured attraction of Eureka Dunes National Natural Landmark, and now one of the shining stars of Death Valley National Park.

The Eureka Dunes are the tallest sand dunes in California. Arguably, they're also the tallest in North America. They rise nearly 700 feet from their base, and they are home to several rare and endangered plants, including Eureka dune grass, Eureka evening primrose, and shining locoweed.

For photographers, Eureka Dunes are a "must-see" in Death Valley. If you can keep the sand out of your camera, you'll go home with many weird and wonderful photographs of wind patterns on sand and your hiking partner traveling along swirling dune ridgetops. Yet the dunes' most alluring feature has little to do with their immense size or immeasurable beauty, but rather with their musical talent. When sand tumbles down the steep face of the dune, usually provoked by the clumsy weight of some hiker's footsteps, it sometimes emits a deep bass tone, like the drone of a distant engine. Some compare it to the meditators' mystical sound of "om." Unfortunately, the dune music doesn't occur all the time. The sand must be completely dry to create enough friction between the sliding grains; only then can the magical sound can be heard.

What you do after you reach the top of Eureka Dunes

Eureka Dunes were only recently tacked on to the rest of Death Valley National Park. You'll see when you drive to the trailhead that the dunes are really far out there, even by Death Valley driving standards. Do not attempt this trip unless you have a high-clearance vehicle; although plenty of people have made it to the dunes in small passenger cars, it's not a good idea. As with anywhere in Death Valley, be absolutely certain that you have plenty of water with you, both in your car and in your day-pack when you hike.

The best way to make the long trip to Eureka Dunes is to combine it with a tour of Scotty's Castle, and/or a visit to Ubehebe Crater (see the following story). Either of these destinations will break up the long drive to the dunes, which is about 90 miles one-way if you start from Furnace Creek or Stovepipe Wells. A whopping 44 of those 90 miles are on dirt road. It's slow going.

When you finally reach the trailhead, just walk any which way you please, heading for the nearby dunes. There isn't any marked trail, of course, because of the continually shifting desert sands, so just make a beeline to any point that interests you. It's best to climb to the top of the tallest dune you see, and then trace a narrow ridgeline path from dune to dune. It's like being on the narrowest backbone trail you can imagine, with steep slopes dropping away from you on both sides. The difference is that this trail conforms to your footsteps, and the sand cushions you and supports your weight as you walk. There's no way to fall off the narrow ridge, and even if you did, the sand is silky soft.

The only difficult hiking is where you head steeply uphill. On some ascents, you do the old, familiar dance: Two steps forward, one step back. Just take your time and enjoy the uniqueness of the experience. We stopped to rest for a moment and noticed the tiny tracks of a kangaroo rat in the dunes. If we hadn't paused to catch our breath, we surely would have missed this delicate sight.

2. UBEHEBE & LITTLE HEBE CRATERS

Scotty's Castle area, Death Valley National Park
A trip around the rim of a giant volcano

DISTANCE: 1.5 miles round-trip; 1 hour   **LEVEL:** Easy
ELEVATION: Start at 2,600 feet; total change 250 feet   **CROWDS:** Moderate
BEST SEASON: October to April   **RATING:** ★ ★ ★

DIRECTIONS: From the Furnace Creek Visitor Center, drive north on Highway 190 for 17 miles, then bear right on Scotty's Castle Road. In 32 miles, you will reach the Grapevine entrance station. A quarter-mile beyond it, bear left at the fork with Scotty's Castle Road. Continue northwest for six miles to the end of the pavement at the parking area for Ubehebe Crater.

It's not beautiful. It's not scenic. It's not even easy to photograph. But when you stand on its cinder and gravel rim, you shake your head in wonder, and memories of its yawning abyss stay with you for a long, long time.

That's the appeal of Ubehebe Crater, the reason that hundreds of Death Valley visitors drive to its gravel edge every day. It's a volcanic fossil, a giant scar on the earth left from vulcanism that occurred about 2,000 years ago. The crater was born when molten magma rising from deep beneath the earth's crust came in contact with groundwater. Like a cup of water poured on hot rocks in a sauna, the groundwater turned instantly to steam, which exploded from the earth. The energy from this super-heating process was many times stronger than that of a nuclear blast.

The resultant Ubehebe Crater is 500 feet deep and one half mile from rim to rim. Considering that it is surrounded by absolutely nothing—only in Death Valley is the true definition of nothingness understood—it's an awesome sight. There are no trees or foliage around its edges; nothing mars your view of the giant, gravelly abyss, except the trail sign at the parking lot. The crater is mostly black and ash-colored inside, but its eroded walls reveal a colorful blend of orange and rust from the minerals in the rock.

Many visitors make a beeline for the bottom of the crater, 500 feet down, and then find themselves a bit dismayed at the uphill return trip. Fewer people hike the trail from Ubehebe's rim to the edge of Little Hebe Crater, one of Ubehebe's smaller (and younger) siblings, then make a loop return around the far side of Ubehebe. This is the more interesting hike. Although the trail is covered in fine volcanic gravel, which has the annoying habit of finding its way into your hiking boots, it is relatively easy to walk, with only a few short and steep sections. (The gravel is some of the debris left from the volcanic explosion. The force of the blast is believed to have caused 100 mile-per-hour winds, which in turn scattered ash and fine gravel over an area of six square miles.)

From the parking area at the edge of Ubehebe Crater, head to your right along the trail, which leads uphill. Walk along Ubehebe Crater's southwest rim, then veer right off the main trail toward Little Hebe Crater. (A sign points the way.) The trail curves and winds for a quarter-mile around the strange, arid landscape. Your shoes will sink into the gravel somewhat, and you may face a head-wind, so the going can be slower than you expect.

When you arrive, you see that Little Hebe Crater looks a lot like

Ubehebe Crater

Ubehebe Crater, only it's much smaller. It was formed by the same chain of events that formed the larger crater, but with a less powerful explosion. Scientists guess that Little Hebe is even younger in age than Ubehebe, perhaps only 400 years old. Several other small craters can be seen along the trail, although none are as impressive as these two.

For your return, hike back to the junction bearing the Little Hebe trail sign, and continue on the main trail to the north. This leads you back uphill to the rim of Ubehebe Crater, which you can circumnavigate. If you take your eyes off the huge crater's interior, you have nice views of the far-off Last Chance Range from Ubehebe's high rim.

So what does Ubehebe mean? Nobody's quite sure. The popular misinterpretation is that Ubehebe means "big basket" in the Shoshone Indian language, but that isn't true. The Shoshone Indians called Ubehebe Crater "Tempin-ttaa Wo'sah," which translates to "basket in the rock." The word Ubehebe was first applied to a mountain peak 20 miles away, and no one knows why the crater came to share the name.

---

3. UBEHEBE PEAK

Scotty's Castle area, Death Valley National Park
A Last Chance Range summit with otherworldly views

DISTANCE: 6.0 miles round-trip; 3 hours   **LEVEL:** Strenuous
ELEVATION: Start at 3,700 feet; total change 2,100 feet   **CROWDS:** Minimal
BEST SEASON: October to May   **RATING:** ★ ★ ★ ★

DIRECTIONS: From the Furnace Creek Visitor Center, drive north on Highway 190 for 17 miles, then bear right on Scotty's Castle Road. In 32 miles, you will reach the Grapevine entrance station. A quarter-mile beyond it, bear left at the fork with Scotty's Castle Road. Continue northwest for 5.8 miles. A quarter-mile before you reach the parking area for Ubehebe Crater, turn right on the dirt road signed for the Racetrack. Drive 20 miles on Racetrack Road, then bear right at Teakettle Junction. Drive 5.9 miles farther to a pullout on the right side of the road, across from a large rock formation known as the Grandstand. (A high-clearance vehicle may be required.)

Are you prepared for a long drive and then a strenuous hike? If so, you're in luck, because the rewards on this trip are great. The ascent of Ubehebe Peak has many things going for it: An excellent trail for most of the climb, terrific views of the Grandstand, the Racetrack playa, and the Saline Valley, an interesting side trip to some mining ruins, and an exciting, trail-less scramble to Ubehebe's summit, suitable for experienced hikers. Those who prefer to live less dangerously can be satisfied

The Grandstand and the Racetrack playa from the Ubehebe Peak Trail

with the high views from just below the summit.

The climb to Ubehebe Peak would be strenuous enough if you just accounted for the steep grade, but add in the fact that this is Death Valley and the hike becomes a butt-kicker. Make sure you've picked a cool day in fall, winter, or spring to take this hike, and carry plenty of water. The trail is a narrow miners' route that switchbacks up and up and up, and you can be darn sure that you won't come across any shade on the way.

From the small parking pullout across from the Grandstand rock formation, start hiking on the well-maintained trail. You'll head west through an alluvial fan dotted with creosote bushes, then curve northwest. The trail ascends very gently at first but soon moves into steep switchbacks. The first two miles of the hike offer increasingly fascinating views of the vast mud flats of the Racetrack playa, and of the Grandstand, a dark-colored outcrop of rock that looks like an island in the midst of the Racetrack's sea. The higher you climb above the playa, the more island-like the Grandstand appears. The Grandstand is actually a mountain peak that stood in this valley thousands of years ago, before nearly 1,000 feet of material slowly washed down from the surrounding mountains and filled in this basin, burying all but the peak's summit. The Grandstand's rock is composed of quartz monzonite and limestone.

At just shy of two miles, the trail tops out at a saddle on the crest of the Last Chance Range. You get your first views down the other side of the divide, into the strange looking Saline Valley, 3,500 feet below you, backed by the tall Inyo Mountains. (The Saline Valley is 2,700 feet lower than the Racetrack Valley.) You have to convince yourself that what you see is not water; the Saline Valley looks like one huge lake when in fact it is only salt flats.

From the saddle, an obvious trail continues uphill to the south. A lesser used trail leads a quarter-mile southwest to the site of an old copper mine; this makes an interesting diversion and provides more fine views of the Saline Valley. You can't see much of the copper mine, except for a few loose boards and a large mine shaft on a distant hillside. (You may have noticed luminous, bright blue-green rocks on the climb up to the divide. These are malachite—the same rocks that inspired early miners to dig shafts in this area and hunt for copper ore.)

Take the side trip if you like, then return to this junction and continue uphill. You'll be heading directly toward an obvious peak, but this isn't Ubehebe; it's Ubehebe's unnamed neighbor to the north. Hike up its western shoulder on a much steeper, narrower trail than the one you've been following.

Looking down on Saline Valley from the divide

Finally you see another saddle ahead of you—between the two peaks—that you must descend to reach. Now it's decision time: You can stop here, and scramble up to the top of the peak you're standing on, or you can drop to the saddle, then scramble up to the top of Ubehebe Peak. Consider carefully. If you're experienced with trail-less, hands-and-feet scrambling on a rocky, loose surface, you might want to go to Ubehebe's summit. Be forewarned that it has a dauntingly steep slope, and a misstep could be fatal. If you feel satisfied with the view from where you are, if you've never done any class 2 to 3 climbing, or if you only feel comfortable on a real trail, forget about Ubehebe's summit. As an alternative, an easier few feet of scrambling will take you to the top of the unnamed peak's summit, where you are only 200 feet lower than Ubehebe's summit at 5,678 feet in elevation.

Whichever summit you choose, you're rewarded with tremendous views of the snowy Sierra Nevada, the Inyo Mountains, the Cottonwood Mountains, the Last Chance Range (on which you stand), and Racetrack and Saline valleys.

Before or after your trip, be sure to explore around the Racetrack. Many hikers enjoy climbing on the Grandstand formation, but you can also drive farther down the road to an area where you can readily see Death Valley's famous Sliding Rocks—the long tracks of rocks that have slid along the surface of the Racetrack playa, pushed by strong winds. For more details on this area, see the following story.

4. THE RACETRACK'S SLIDING ROCKS

Scotty's Castle area, Death Valley National Park
Rocks pushed across the mudflats by an unseen hand

DISTANCE: 2.0 miles round-trip; 1 hour   **LEVEL:** Easy
ELEVATION: Start at 3,700 feet; total change 0 feet   **CROWDS:** Minimal
BEST SEASON: October to April   **RATING:** ★ ★ ★ ★

DIRECTIONS: From the Furnace Creek Visitor Center, drive north on Highway 190 for 17 miles, then bear right on Scotty's Castle Road. In 32 miles, you will reach the Grapevine entrance station. A quarter-mile beyond it, bear left at the fork with Scotty's Castle Road. Continue northwest for 5.8 miles. A quarter-mile before you reach the parking area for Ubehebe Crater, turn right on the dirt road signed for the Racetrack. Drive 20 miles on Racetrack Road, then bear right at Teakettle Junction. Drive eight more miles to an interpretive signboard on the left side of the road, two miles past the large rock formation on the left known as the Grandstand. (A high-clearance vehicle may be required.)

Maybe you've seen pictures of them: Small boulders as well as large and small rocks that have carved tracks in the smooth mudflats of Death Valley. The rocks travel like race cars across the wind-blown surface called the Racetrack, then roll to a stop at the command of some unseen referee.

The moving rocks at the Racetrack may be Death Valley's greatest mystery. Countless studies have been performed at the Racetrack,

The Racetrack's sliding rocks

trying to assess what makes the rocks move, why they move in seemingly random patterns, and why they suddenly stop. It is generally agreed that extreme winds—as strong as 70 miles per hour—combined with occasional light rainfall on the mud and salt flats is the magic combination that makes the rocks move. But no one is quite sure why the rocks sometimes travel in straight lines, sometimes in curved lines, sometimes side-by-side with other rocks, and sometimes even in complete circles. And strangest of all is that no one has ever seen a rock move; they've only seen the rocks' locations change and the tracks that were left behind. Go figure.

To see the rock tracks for yourself, drive out to Racetrack Valley and follow the dirt road past the Grandstand (a fascinating rock formation in the middle of the Racetrack playa). Exactly two miles beyond it, you see a signpost on the left. Park your car, read the sign's information about the sliding rocks, and then start to hike.

You could head in any direction and eventually come across the rock tracks, but the fastest and surest way is to walk straight across the playa from the sign, heading due east. At first, you see nothing. Don't be discouraged; keep walking. About a half-mile from your car, you start to see the tracks, and as you keep walking, they're all around you. Most of the tracks are about five inches wide, although it depends on the size of the rock that made them. The rocks leaving the tracks can be large or small; most of them seem to be somewhere between the size of an orange and a basketball. Many are too heavy for a human to lift.

The rocks can travel in any direction, and their tracks can be as long as 660 feet. Most of them head northeast, although in 1997 a park naturalist discovered a rock that made a circular track 50 feet in diameter. The rock circled around and stopped about four feet from where it started.

The closer you get to the mountains on the far side of the playa, the more rocks and rock tracks you'll find. (These mountains are the main source of the sliding rocks, although the Grandstand also contributes.) The playa is completely flat, and its surface is easy to walk on. So just wander around as much as you like, shake your head in wonder, and then meander back to your car.

5. DARWIN FALLS

Panamint Springs area, Death Valley National Park
A rare waterfall in the desert

DISTANCE: 1.8 miles round-trip; 1 hour **LEVEL:** Easy
ELEVATION: Start at 2,500 feet; total change 120 feet **CROWDS:** Minimal
BEST SEASON: October to April **RATING:** ★ ★ ★

DIRECTIONS: From Stovepipe Wells, drive west on Highway 190 for 28 miles to Panamint Springs Resort. Continue past the resort for one mile to the left (south) turnoff for Darwin Falls. Turn left and drive 2.5 miles on the dirt road to a fork, then bear right and drive three-tenths of a mile to the parking area.

Alternatively, from Lone Pine on U.S. 395, drive east on Highway 136 for 18 miles, then continue straight on Highway 190 for 30 miles. The right (south) turnoff for Darwin Falls is exactly one mile before you reach Panamint Springs Resort.

Darwin Falls is a must-do desert hike. A waterfall in the desert is a rare and precious thing, a miracle of life in a harsh world. Hiking into a narrow desert canyon, you follow the trail of a tiny trickle of water as it slowly expands into a full-flowing stream. You trace the stream's path, and at the back of the canyon you discover that it drops over a 30-foot-high cliff to form Darwin Falls. The slender waterfall is perfectly showcased in a rock gallery.

The hike to the falls is just under one mile each way, and except on hot summer days, it is well suited for families. Just be sure to carry plenty of water with you.

The path is not a well-defined trail; it's more like a well-used route following an old jeep road and some water pipes, then turning into single-track. At several points you must cross the stream to follow the trail, but rocks are conveniently placed for easy rock-hopping. Route-finding is simple because you just walk up-canyon, following the stream. Canyon walls on both sides keep you channeled in the correct direction.

The stream flow increases as you approach the waterfall, and the canyon walls narrow, requiring some minor rock scrambling. It feels like a real desert adventure. The amount of vegetation also increases as you near the fall; notice the proliferation of willows, cattails, and reeds jockeying for position next to the running water. If it's spring, you may have some winged companions on your hike. More than 80 species of resident and migrating birds have been sighted in this canyon.

You pass a small stream-gauging station right before you reach Darwin Falls, then round a corner and enter a box canyon. The rocks surrounding you have turned more and more colorful as you've progressed; now you are completely surrounded by shades of yellow, coral, orange, and crimson. Darwin Falls drops over a rock cliff, with a large cottonwood tree growing at its lip. The water pours down in two separate streams, one on either side of the tree, giving life to ferns and colorful mosses growing on the rock face.

Stay for a while and savor the miracle of this desert oasis.

6. FALL CANYON
Stovepipe Wells area, Death Valley National Park
A colorful high-walled canyon

DISTANCE: 6.6 miles round-trip; 3.5 hours **LEVEL:** Moderate
ELEVATION: Start at 1,000 feet; total change 1,200 feet **CROWDS:** Moderate
BEST SEASON: October to April **RATING:** ★ ★ ★ ★

DIRECTIONS: From the Furnace Creek Visitor Center, drive north on Highway 190 for 17 miles, then bear right on Scotty's Castle Road. In 14 miles, turn right at the sign for Titus Canyon. Drive 2.7 miles to the parking area just before Titus Canyon Road becomes a one-way road. Begin hiking to the left of Titus Canyon, on a narrow, unsigned trail leading north.

Many park visitors take the one-way drive through Titus Canyon to experience a desert canyon with giant alluvial fans and towering rock walls. Some hikers even dare to walk through the narrows of Titus Canyon, but they usually find that their trip is made unpleasant by the continual passing of cars and the roar of approaching engines. Titus Canyon is worth seeing, but as long as it's open to cars, you might as well drive through it, and save your walking for somewhere more peaceful.

One such place is located right next door to Titus Canyon. It is

Fall Canyon, and it is accessed from the trailhead at the mouth of Titus Canyon. Like many of the canyons in Death Valley, your hike in Fall Canyon is not on a real trail, but instead on a gravel alluvial fan bordered by soaring rock walls. Having no trail doesn't mean you'll get lost—the canyon walls keep you funneled in the right direction—but it does mean that the walking is more tiring than you'd expect. Hiking on the fine gravel surface is a little like walking at the beach—your ankles get a workout.

Still, Fall Canyon is worth seeing, and it provides a true Death Valley experience without any of the crowds you may find at Mosaic Canyon or Golden Canyon. The incredible silence of Death Valley is best heard in one of its canyons, and Fall Canyon offers plenty of it. Hikers find themselves equally awed by the lack of sound and by the desert beauty.

First, you must find your way into the canyon. From the parking area at Titus Canyon, hike to your left (north) on the unsigned trail. A half-mile of walking on an undulating trail leads you to a wash, where you turn right and walk up the wash into Fall Canyon. The canyon's mouth is at least 50 yards wide, but it soon narrows. Its soft walls, dramatically sculpted by flash floods, tower above you. As you walk past them, look for tiny arch formations, miniature caves, alcoves, and sculpted shapes of all kinds, some high up off the ground. The canyon narrows and then widens, then repeats the sequence again and again. Desert colors are a wide array of cream, gold, pink, and yellow, with the colors changing and deepening as the day wears on.

Fall Canyon

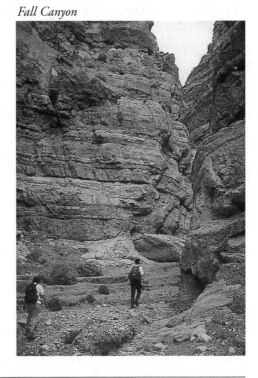

At 2.8 miles, you are faced with a 20-foot dry fall. Most hikers turn around here for a 5.6-mile round-trip, but if you're an experienced rock scrambler,

you can negotiate around the fall. (Don't try this if you're inexperienced.) To do it, backtrack for about 75 yards and look for a use trail leading up the canyon's south side (on your right as you face the fall). If you can scramble up the use trail, you'll bypass the fall and enter the polished narrows of Fall Canyon. This nearly half-mile stretch of deep, winding passages is the best part of the whole trip. The polished narrows are similar to those at the start of Mosaic Canyon (see the following story), but they seem even more magical because you will most likely experience them in solitude. Some people consider Fall Canyon to have the most beautiful narrows in Death Valley.

Where the narrows end and the canyon opens up again is an excellent turnaround point. If you make it this far, you'll have a 6.6-mile round-trip.

7. MOSAIC CANYON

Stovepipe Wells area, Death Valley National Park
Gem-like marble canyon walls

DISTANCE: 1.0 to 3.0 miles round-trip; 1 to 2 hours   **LEVEL:** Easy
ELEVATION: Start at 950 feet; total change 450 feet   **CROWDS:** Moderate
BEST SEASON: October to April   **RATING:** ★ ★ ★ ★ ★

DIRECTIONS: From Stovepipe Wells, drive west on Highway 190 for less than a quarter-mile to the Mosaic Canyon turnoff on the south (left) side of the road. Turn left and drive 2.2 miles to the trailhead parking lot.

Mosaic Canyon is one of the crown jewels of Death Valley, accessible to all kinds of hikers. Its gem-like marble walls are considered to be a "geologic outdoor museum." The trail through the colorful, smooth-walled canyon is easy to follow, and the hiking is relatively easy. As such, the canyon should be on every hiker's itinerary.

The trailhead is located just two miles from Stovepipe Wells and 25 miles from Furnace Creek. Unlike so many trails in Death Valley, which require a long, arduous drive to their trailheads, Mosaic Canyon is an easy-to-reach destination, perfect for an after-dinner or early morning stroll. Once you're on the trail, you can walk as little or as much as you like, heading gently uphill through the gorgeous marble-lined canyon.

If you've hiked in Golden Canyon in Death Valley (see the story on page 425), don't make the mistake of bypassing this trail because you think you've already seen similar sights. The pastel-colored rock in

Mosaic Canyon is far different from that of other desert canyons. The trail shows off smooth, water-polished marble from ancient lakebeds as it winds its way up the narrow, high-walled canyon, which was formed by a fault zone. Particularly unique are the "mosaics" on the canyon walls: Multicolored rock fragments that appear to be cemented together are visible in several areas, especially in the first quarter mile of trail. This is a rock formation known as "mosaic breccia." It's a gorgeous mix of red, white, black, and gray stone.

Mosaic Canyon

Occasionally, you must do a little easy scrambling over foot-high boulders and small dry waterfalls—the kind of scrambling that makes the trip seem like a real adventure, but in fact it's quite easy and safe. Kids have a ball on this trail.

From the trailhead, the route enters the canyon almost immediately, so the fun begins right away. In some places, Mosaic Canyon's smooth marble walls close in around you, then the fissure you're walking through suddenly opens wider into "rooms" lined with marble walls. At various points the canyon walls are as little as 10 feet apart, and there are good spots for safe rock scrambling. If you choose to stay on the ground, the trail surface is gravel—ground-up bits of the canyon walls—and easy to walk on.

If you're wondering exactly what kind of rock this is, most of the canyon is a limestone called noonday dolomite. It was formed hundreds of millions of years ago when the desert was undersea. After being buried by other types of rocks and subjected to pressures and temperature swings, the limestone slowly metamorphosed into marble. Eventually, erosion and running water channeling through the layers of rock and soil carved out and re-exposed the limestone, creating the canyon we see today.

After a third of a mile, the canyon opens out to a wide alluvial fan, which is not quite as fascinating as the narrows. Many people just turn around and head back through the narrows again, but if you wish, you can continue hiking for another mile or two. Mosaic Canyon tapers once more, and with some easy to moderate scrambling you can reach a second narrows area, 1.2 miles from the trailhead, which shows off more stream-polished marble. Eventually the canyon becomes impassible at a dry waterfall, too high to be scaled.

8. MESQUITE FLAT SAND DUNES

Stovepipe Wells area, Death Valley National Park
Easy-to-access sand dunes; a photographer's delight

DISTANCE: 1.5 miles round-trip; 1 hour **LEVEL:** Easy
ELEVATION: Start at 0 feet; total change 100 feet **CROWDS:** Moderate
BEST SEASON: October to April **RATING:** ★ ★ ★ ★

DIRECTIONS: From Stovepipe Wells, drive east on Highway 190 for 2.2 miles to the pullouts alongside the highway, directly across from the dunes. Begin to hike right from the road, heading directly for the dunes.

Alternatively, from Stovepipe Wells, drive east on Highway 190 for 7.5 miles to the junction with Scotty's Castle Road. Turn left (north) on Scotty's Castle Road, drive three miles, then turn left at the signed turnoff for Sand Dunes Picnic Area. Follow the dirt road to its end at the picnic area and trailhead.

Next door to Stovepipe Wells is the start of a fun and easy cross-country walk to 100-foot-tall sand dunes. No, these aren't the giant sand dunes that Death Valley is famous for; those are the Eureka Dunes way out in Eureka Valley (see page 402). But the Mesquite Flat Sand Dunes are situated two miles from Stovepipe Wells, and they are a heck of a lot easier to reach than the Eureka Dunes. Hiking them, photographing them, rolling around on them—all of these are part of the quintessential Death Valley experience. If you've just arrived at the park, this trip will convince your senses that you're really in Death Valley, a place unlike any other.

There are two ways to access the dunes, which are plainly visible from the highway. Most people drive to the narrow pullouts alongside Highway 190, two miles east of Stovepipe Wells, where numerous cars are often parked. This puts you as close as possible to the tallest and most scenic of the dunes. Other people drive to the Sand Dunes Picnic Area instead, which is just around the corner on Scotty's Castle Road.

This puts you within only a few yards of smaller dunes, which are great for families with small children who just want to play in the sand. Hikers and photographers generally prefer the Highway 190 trailhead.

One small point of confusion: Although the dunes are officially called the Mesquite Flat Sand Dunes, some people call them the Death Valley Sand Dunes or just The Sand Dunes. If you say "the dunes next to Stovepipe Wells," everybody knows what you're talking about.

There's no marked trail to the dunes, of course, because of the continually shifting desert sands. Just make a straight beeline path (or a curvy, circuitous path—it's up to you) from your parked car to the dunes. How far you wander is your decision. If you hike from Highway 190 straight to the tallest dune, the distance is about 1.5 miles round-trip. To reach it, you'll have to go up and down a repeating series of smaller dunes, which rise and fall in a wavelike fashion. It's fun hiking, but it's harder than you'd expect. The sand is very soft, so your feet sink in deeply, especially when you go uphill. At the crest of a steep dune, you can push with your feet and make cascading sand avalanches.

The graceful dunes are punctuated by foliage—mesquite trees, saltbrush, and creosote. The plants help to stabilize the dunes and provide shelter for dune animals like the kangaroo rat. Desert winds blow sand into mounds around the larger plants; the piles are called sand shadows. Sometimes sand will completely cover a part of the plant, causing that part to die.

Mesquite Flat sand dunes by Stovepipe Wells

The best times of day to visit the dunes are early in the morning or right about sunset, because of the incredible show of color, shadow, and light. Early mornings are excellent times to look for tiny animal footprints in the sand. If you think there is little wildlife in Death Valley, you'll be amazed at the number and variety of tracks. The footprints of coyotes, kangaroo rats, and birds are the most common, but lucky visitors may find those of a kit fox or lizard.

Full moon nights are also popular times to visit the dunes, and it's easy to imagine why. They'll have you dreaming of Arabian nights.

9. DEATH VALLEY BUTTES

Stovepipe Wells area, Death Valley National Park
A trail-less scramble to high vistas

DISTANCE: 3.6 miles round-trip; 2 hours   **LEVEL:** Moderate
ELEVATION: Start at 2,200 feet; total change 1,100 feet   **CROWDS:** Minimal
BEST SEASON: October to April   **RATING:** ★ ★ ★

DIRECTIONS: From Stovepipe Wells, drive east on Highway 190 for 7.5 miles to the left turnoff for Scotty's Castle Road. Turn left, then in a half-mile, turn right at the sign for Mud Canyon and Daylight Pass. Drive seven miles on Daylight Pass Road to the Hell's Gate parking area on the left side of the road.

Alternatively, from the Furnace Creek Visitor Center, drive 10 miles north on Highway 190 to the Beatty Cutoff Road. Turn right (north) on Beatty Cutoff Road and drive 10 miles to where it intersects with Daylight Pass Road. The Hell's Gate parking area is across Daylight Pass Road.

If you're the kind of hiker who likes to make your own trail, you'll love this cross-country ascent to the top of the Death Valley Buttes. The two stark buttes are located at the foot of the Grapevine Mountains near Hell's Gate, just a few miles before Daylight Pass takes travelers to and from Nevada. From the top of the buttes, you get a fine view of Death Valley, including Stovepipe Wells and its sand dunes, and the Funeral, Grapevine, and Panamint Mountains.

Although there's no clearly marked route to the top of the Buttes and you must choose your own path, it's easy enough to see where you're going. From the trailhead parking area, the Buttes are clearly visible to the southwest. Hike straight toward them across an alluvial fan. After a half-mile of level walking among scattered creosote bushes, you reach the base of the easternmost butte. This is the easiest one to climb; just start making your way up its rocky ridge. You'll see evidence that others have gone before you, in the form of a faint use trail.

The first summit is at 2,725 feet, and from it you get the promised view. The most distinctive tall landmark is Corkscrew Peak to the north, at elevation 5,804 feet. It is shaped like its name and draped in a fine coat of layered colors, as if it were painted in stripes. Thimble Peak sits on its left side, and is 500 feet higher. All of central Death Valley is spread out before you; only the western vista is partially obscured by the second, higher butte.

Most hikers turn around here, making a two-mile round-trip, but "peak baggers" will want to continue to the second butte. To do so, descend down the west side of the ridge, dropping about 300 feet to a saddle. Be extremely wary of the steep dropoffs and loose rock, especially when going downhill. When you reach the saddle, simply climb up the next stretch of ridgeline to the second, higher butte. You gain about 600 feet in a half-mile on an extremely steep grade. The route is very narrow and exposed. When you reach the top, at elevation 3,017 feet, you get a surprise—the view is basically the same as from the first butte, only now it's with no obstructions. Pat yourself on the back for being such a fine mountaineer.

10. KEANE WONDER MINE

Furnace Creek area, Death Valley National Park
An old gold mine and tramway with high views

DISTANCE: 3.2 miles round-trip; 2 hours   **LEVEL:** Strenuous
ELEVATION: Start at 1,300 feet; total change 1,600 feet   **CROWDS:** Minimal
BEST SEASON: October to April   **RATING:** ★ ★ ★

DIRECTIONS: From the Furnace Creek Visitor Center, drive 10 miles north on Highway 190 to the Beatty Cutoff Road. Turn right (north) on Beatty Cutoff Road and drive 5.7 miles to the right turnoff for Keane Wonder Mine. Turn right and drive 2.8 miles (on a rough dirt road) to the parking area.

Alternatively, from Stovepipe Wells, drive 14 miles east on Highway 190 (bear right at the fork for Scotty's Castle) to the left turnoff for Beatty Cutoff Road. Follow the directions as above.

You wouldn't think a three-mile round-trip trail could be this hard. But then again, most people don't usually climb 1,600 feet in a little over mile and a half, and especially not this close to sea level in the desert.

The million-dollar vistas on the Keane Wonder Mine Trail are worth the trek, though. They may not pay off as well as the Keane gold

Looking down from the upper tramway station at Keane Wonder Mine

and silver mine did in the early 1900s, but for Death Valley views, they're priceless.

The trail begins 100 feet from the Keane Wonder Mill, which processed gold and silver ore from the mine up the hill. The Keane Wonder Mine was one of the few big success stories of Death Valley's mining days. In 1903, prospector Jack Keane discovered gold in this area of the Funeral Mountains. Even before his claim was developed, its ore appeared to be so promising and of such high quality that the mine was sold for $150,000 before one single hole was dug. The mine's most productive years were from 1909 to 1911, when it produced 74,000 tons of gold, silver, and lead ore, worth about $700,000. The vein ran dry in 1915.

Although many park visitors poke around at the stamp mill by the trailhead, far fewer hike steeply uphill to view the remains of the mine and its mile-long aerial tramway, which was built to carry loads of rock down the mountainside to the mill—a 1,500-foot elevation change. The tramway consisted of 11 wooden towers, strong cables that ran between them, and large ore buckets. The buckets moved by gravity down the tramway, which also provided mechanical power to operate an ore crusher up at the mine. As you hike, you'll be able to spot a few of the ore buckets (still attached to their cables and the remaining towers) dangling over the mountain canyon.

The trail is very rocky and steep; you definitely will need your hiking boots. After only a half-mile of climbing, your views of Death Valley and the Panamint Mountains open wide; meanwhile the path steepens as it continues up the mountain. As you climb, take advantage of all the spur trails you see; they lead short distances to mine shafts or overlooks. These spurs will give you a chance to catch your breath, as well as provide an interesting diversion from the relentless "up." As you pass mine shafts along the trail, remember to stay out of them—they can be very dangerous. The vistas, on the other hand, are perfectly safe and yours for the taking.

When you reach the top of the tramway, wander around a bit to get a good look at the mine shafts, old stone cabin ruins, rail tracks, wire cables, and of course, the upper tramway station. The latter is remarkably well preserved.

11. KEANE WONDER SPRINGS

Furnace Creek area, Death Valley National Park
A travertine-edged spring and an old miner's cabin

DISTANCE: 2.0 miles round-trip; 1 hour   **LEVEL:** Easy
ELEVATION: Start at 1,300 feet; total change 80 feet   **CROWDS:** Moderate
BEST SEASON: October to April   **RATING:** ★ ★

DIRECTIONS: From the Furnace Creek Visitor Center, drive 10 miles north on Highway 190 to the Beatty Cutoff Road. Turn right (north) on Beatty Cutoff Road and drive 5.7 miles to the right turnoff for Keane Wonder Mine. Turn right and drive 2.8 miles (on a rough dirt road) to the parking area.

Alternatively, from Stovepipe Wells, drive 14 miles east on Highway 190 (bear right at the fork for Scotty's Castle) to the left turnoff for Beatty Cutoff Road. Follow the directions as above.

If you aren't up for the hot and steep climb to the top of the tramway at Keane Wonder Mine (see the previous story), this easy trail to Keane Wonder Springs provides a more level alternative. Make sure you visit the Keane Wonder Mill near the trailhead before taking this hike; you'll want to learn about the history of the mill and Keane Mine to understand why water piped from Keane Springs was so critical to its operation.

At the trailhead, you'll see extensive mining debris littering the canyon to your left. Hike up the hill for 100 feet to visit the Keane Wonder Mill, then return to the parking area and walk toward the largest rusting metal tank among the mining ruins. The trail to the springs is on the left (downhill) side of it.

The trail's condition improves as you walk; within a quarter-mile you'll be on firm footing on a clearly marked path, which is carefully bordered by rocks. The trail roughly parallels an old, rusting pipeline along the base of the mountains—the same pipe that carried water from Keane Springs to the mill.

Cross a wash and pass occasional mine shafts and more ruins. Pay attention to the rocks at your feet, and notice them becoming lighter in color as you near the three-quarter-mile mark, close to where the spring is located. Soon you see wet slabs of cream-colored travertine (a marble-like rock formed by the sulfur-rich spring water), colorful algae growth, and white salt formations at the edge of a trickling seep. If you leave the trail and follow the wet slabs uphill, you'll find a more substantial stream. Reeds and grasses grow in bunches along the water's edge.

Another 100 feet uphill is the spring itself and an old well shaft. The spot is marked with a sign about the dangers of this shaft: Because it taps right into the spring, the smell of hydrogen sulfide is fierce. (If you've ever visited Lassen Volcanic National Park, you will be very familiar with this odor. But here it is far more concentrated in the tight confines of the shaft.) You can hear, and barely see, water rushing through the bottom of the well. Although the water appearing above ground near the spring is minimal, the water below ground is plentiful. The water is noxious to humans, but birds and animals make heavy use of this spring.

Most people visit Keane Springs and then return to the trailhead, but a more interesting option is to follow the trail another quarter mile, across and beyond the spring's stream, to the remains of an old miner's cabin, stamp mill, and mine shaft. The small wooden cabin is in surprisingly good condition.

12. SALT CREEK INTERPRETIVE TRAIL

Furnace Creek area, Death Valley National Park
Streamside walk to see the rare Salt Creek pupfish

DISTANCE: 1.0 mile round-trip; 30 minutes   **LEVEL:** Easy
ELEVATION: Start at -180 feet; total change 0 feet   **CROWDS:** Moderate
BEST SEASON: February to April   **RATING:** ★ ★ ★

DIRECTIONS: From the Furnace Creek Visitor Center, drive 12 miles north on Highway 190 to the left turnoff for Salt Creek. Turn left and drive one mile to the Salt Creek parking area.

Alternatively, from Stovepipe Wells, drive 11.6 miles east on Highway 190 (bear right at the fork for Scotty's Castle) to the right turnoff for Salt Creek.

NOTE: Interpretive brochures are available at the trailhead.

The Salt Creek Trail is well worth the short time it takes to hike it. It offers a chance to see wildlife, it features excellent views of Death Valley and the Black Mountains, and it provides a great education on adaptability to desert life. In short, it's like nothing else in Death Valley.

Salt Creek is exactly what its name implies, a stream of saline water. It is home to the Salt Creek pupfish, which lives nowhere else in the world. This fish underwent an incredible evolutionary change in order to live in the saline creek, which was once a part of a much larger freshwater lake. Over time, the pupfish evolved with the ability to filter saltwater and remove the excess salt through its gills. The biological alteration the fish had to undergo would be roughly equivalent to humans deciding to drink gasoline instead of water.

If you time your trip properly, you can walk the streamside trail, look down into Salt Creek, and easily spot the minnow-sized pupfish darting about in the deeper pools. Of course there is never any guarantee of spotting them, but late winter and spring—February through April—are the best times for pupfish viewing. At the right time, the two-foot wide stream can seem to overflow with schools of pupfish.

Salt Creek Interpretive Trail

The rest of the year, the inch-long fish hibernate in the creek mud to lay their eggs and wait for the stream level to rise from occasional winter rains. Still, Salt Creek is worth hiking at any time, because for hikers, it is a refreshing change from the dryness of Death Valley.

The trail is on a wooden boardwalk, so it is accessible to all hikers, including wheelchair users. The boardwalk parallels the stream and occasionally crosses over it, providing many strategic spots to look for pupfish. Interpretive signs along the trail describe the plants and wildlife that can be seen in the area. The plants are those typically found in California coastal wetlands—salt grass and pickleweed. Birds may be seen congregating by the stream, including resident great blue herons and others flying through on their migration paths.

13. HARMONY BORAX WORKS & BORAX FLATS

Furnace Creek area, Death Valley National Park
The story of borax in Death Valley

DISTANCE: 1.0 mile round-trip; 30 minutes   **LEVEL:** Easy
ELEVATION: Start at -100 feet; total change 40 feet   **CROWDS:** Moderate
BEST SEASON: October to April   **RATING:** ★ ★

DIRECTIONS: From the Furnace Creek Visitor Center, drive north on Highway 190 for 1.3 miles to the left turnoff for Harmony Borax Works and Mustard Canyon. Turn left, then stay to the left to reach the trailhead parking area.

A stroll on the Harmony Borax Works Interpretive Trail combined with a longer excursion on neighboring Borax Flats makes an easy and interesting walk through Death Valley's borax history.

Although most people equate borax with detergent, it is also used in many other products, including metals, paints, porcelain, ceramics, and fiberglass. Borax was first found in California in 1836; it was discovered in Death Valley in 1881. The discoverer, Aaron Winters, sold his claim to William Coleman of San Francisco, and Coleman built the Harmony Borax Works in 1882. Because the nearest railroad in Mojave was 165 miles away over fierce, rugged terrain, transportation was the biggest problem the borax mine faced. The problem was eventually solved: Specially designed wagons were built that could carry huge, extra heavy loads, pulled by teams of 20 mules.

To begin your history lesson, hike the paved loop trail by taking the left fork first. This brings you to the remains of some machinery and large tanks, which were used to dissolve the "cottonball" borate (borax ore) that Chinese laborers culled from the nearby borax flats. The borax was then processed and loaded on the wagons for transportation to the railroad in Mojave.

Examples of the 20-mule team wagons are on display along the trail. The huge empty wagons weighed 7,800 pounds. Loaded to full capacity with borax, one of the 20-mule team wagons weighed 31,800 pounds. Two wagons, plus the weight of the full water tank needed to sustain the mules and the teamsters, made a total load of 73,000 pounds or 36.5 tons. Twenty mules pulled it all.

After walking the short, paved loop trail, follow the unpaved trail that leads from the west end of the loop out to the site where Chinese laborers gathered cottonball borax from the salt flats. The flats are easy to walk on; the crusty, hard surface is completely level. The salt flats are the result of the evaporation of ancient Lake Manly, which once filled this basin. Salt layers extend downward to a depth of 1,000 feet.

The trail dissipates in the mud in a half-mile or so. When your curiosity is satisfied, just turn around and head back.

14. GOLDEN CANYON to RED CATHEDRAL

Furnace Creek area, Death Valley National Park
A narrow canyon of colorful sediments

DISTANCE: 2.5 miles round-trip; 1.5 hours **LEVEL:** Easy
ELEVATION: Start at –150 feet; total change 400 feet **CROWDS:** Moderate
BEST SEASON: October to April **RATING:** ★ ★ ★ ★

DIRECTIONS: From the Furnace Creek Visitor Center, drive southeast on Highway 190 for 1.3 miles to the right fork for Badwater. Bear right and drive south for two miles to the Golden Canyon parking area on the east (left) side of the road.

NOTE: Interpretive trail brochures are available at the trailhead.

Many hikers say that there are too many roads and too few trails in Death Valley National Park. The Golden Canyon Trail is Mother Nature's revenge on this state of affairs, because the trail exists where a paved road was destroyed by a flash flood in 1976.

As the saying goes, Mother Nature always bats last. Where park visitors in cars once drove up Golden Canyon to park near the base of Red Cathedral and view its majesty, today hikers get to walk the distance. No one's complaining; it's much better this way.

The interpretive trail is a perfect path for first-timers in Death Valley National Park. Be sure to purchase an interpretive brochure at the trailhead or park visitor center so that you understand what you see as you hike. The trail leads up a flat alluvial fan that displays a colorful array of volcanic rocks, sand, and gravel. Golden Canyon's cliffs exhibit every shade of gold you can think of—from yellow to orange to apricot. In fact, you see almost nothing but yellow and gold rock as you hike, except for scarlet Red Cathedral looming in the background.

Golden Canyon and Red Cathedral

As you walk, notice the occasional evidence of an old paved road that once traveled up this canyon. It seems inconceivable that cars could have fit through some of the narrower sections—they must have just squeezed by.

Travel slowly and admire the colorful rock walls. These are actually the layers of ancient lakebeds, tilted upward on their sides by earthquakes and fault activity. The beautiful colors are caused by minerals in the ancient lakebed soils mixing with minerals in the volcanic ash that settled over this area. All of this is ancient history, of course—Golden Canyon has looked as it does today for a few thousand years.

At one mile out, you'll reach the last numbered marker of the interpretive trail (number 10). Continue beyond it, bearing left for Red Cathedral. You'll pass numerous side canyons, but just continue straight ahead for a quarter-mile to the huge, red-colored cliff. Its lovely hue is caused by the weathering of its rocks, which contain large quantities of iron compounds.

If you want to see Golden Canyon at its best, visit either first thing in the morning or right around sunset. Not only will the national park crowds be some place else, but the colors are more vivid at the edges of the day. The golds and yellows are more saturated; everything seems to glow.

15. GOWER GULCH LOOP & ZABRISKIE POINT

Furnace Creek area, Death Valley National Park
Colorful badlands and classic desert vistas

DISTANCE: 6.4 miles round-trip; 3 hours   **LEVEL:** Moderate
ELEVATION: Start at –150 feet; total change 900 feet   **CROWDS:** Moderate
BEST SEASON: October to April   **RATING:** ★ ★ ★ ★

DIRECTIONS: From the Furnace Creek Visitor Center, drive southeast on Highway 190 for 1.3 miles to the right fork for Badwater. Bear right and drive south for two miles to the Golden Canyon parking area on the east (left) side of the road.

This hike is a longer version of the Golden Canyon Interpretive Trail for slightly more experienced hikers. Read the trail notes for the previous story, and begin your hike by exploring Golden Canyon. When you reach the last interpretive trail marker (number 10), take the right fork for Zabriskie Point instead of heading farther back in the canyon to Red Cathedral.

The path is signed with small "hiker" symbols; watch for them as you continue your uphill trek into the colorful badlands—deeply creased, eroded, and barren hillsides. The trail leads across the shoulder of Manly Beacon (a yellow sandstone hill with lovely views), then descends back into the badlands. At the base of Manly Beacon's south slope, you reach a junction. The right fork is the return of your loop through Gower Gulch; for now, take the left fork to the east to Zabriskie Point, another mile away. (Keep following the posted directional signs.) The trail climbs for the whole stretch, then deposits you at the point's parking lot. Turn right and walk uphill for 100 feet to access Zabriskie Point's spectacular vistas of the surrounding badlands and the Panamint Mountains. You're likely to have plenty of company; this is a popular stop for those touring by car. Be proud of yourself for walking to Zabriskie Point instead of driving like everybody else.

Return to the previous junction with the trail into Gower Gulch; now bear left to finish out your loop through the gulch. There are no trail signs for this part of the hike; make sure you stay in the main wash and head downhill. The path leads through a wide, gravelly wash to

The view from Zabriskie Point

barren, gray-colored Gower Gulch, which has been permanently altered due to man-made construction designed to protect Furnace Creek from flooding. The gulch is much wider than Golden Canyon due to premature erosion.

As you walk, notice the white outcrops in the rock, the *raison d'être* for the old borax mines that are still found in the area. Also look for mine shafts; several of them are bored into the canyon walls.

Eventually the canyon narrows and some rock scrambling is required. When you reach an abrupt, 40-foot dry fall, take the use trail on the right to bypass it. The final mile of trail leads north, paralleling the highway, back to the mouth of Golden Canyon and its parking area.

One thing to keep in mind: Be sure to carry enough water for the few hours you'll be out on the trail. The total elevation gain on the loop is only 900 feet, but it's completely without shade. Plus, walking on the rough surface of the canyon floor is more tiring than following a "real" trail.

A shorter, easier version of this trip is possible if you can arrange a car shuttle: Begin to hike on the signed trail at the parking lot at Zabriskie Point, then walk downhill for three miles, passing by Manly Beacon and through Golden Canyon. You'll need a friend to pick you up at the mouth of Golden Canyon. If you've already done the Golden Canyon hike from the other end, start at Zabriskie Point and hike downhill through Gower Gulch.

16. DESOLATION CANYON

Furnace Creek area, Death Valley National Park
Silence, solitude, and soaring canyon walls

DISTANCE: 2.4 miles round-trip; 1 hour

LEVEL: Moderate

ELEVATION: Start at 80 feet; total change 500 feet

CROWDS: Minimal

BEST SEASON: October to April

RATING: ★ ★

DIRECTIONS: From the Furnace Creek Visitor Center, drive southeast on Highway 190 for 1.3 miles to the right fork for Badwater. Bear right and drive south for 3.7 miles to the Desolation Canyon turnoff on the east (left) side of the road. Turn left and drive a half-mile; where the road forks, bear left. Park near the road's end, then walk back down the road to access the wash to the northeast.

If you've taken your car through Artist's Drive south of Furnace Creek, or if you've hiked in Golden Canyon, you know the myriad colors of gold, yellow, and coral that are possible in Death Valley. If you'd like to see more of them, a hike through Desolation Canyon is a feast for the eyes, and it will give you a better chance to feast in solitude.

Like Golden Canyon, Desolation Canyon is a series of yellowed hills and cliffs composed of mud and silt. It was formed from the deposits of ancient sedimentary lakebeds, which were folded and up-lifted by erosion. Its cliffs are soft and crumbly to the touch, requiring that you take care to soften your impact in the canyon.

First you have to figure out how to access it. Where the dirt road ends, park your car, then walk back down the road for 150 yards. Look for a good place to enter the wash that's located to the northeast of the road (on your left as you drive in) without having to hike across dozens of small badlands-type hills. Some people just drive back down the road and park their car where the wash begins. If you see any cars parked a short distance before the end of the road, that's where you should start to hike.

If the wash entrance looks a little bleak, have faith and keep going. A quarter-mile in, Desolation Canyon narrows, and it doesn't widen again. Its clay-like rock walls soar more than 100 feet above you, colored in soft pastels. Stay to the right each time the canyon forks; this will keep you in the main passageway. Stop occasionally to appreciate the incredible silence of the place. You won't hear a sound—no birds, no footsteps, no cars, no wind. It seems lifeless and a bit eerie, but it's beautiful nonetheless.

To continue farther into the canyon, you must do a little scrambling over short dry falls, most under six feet high. Most people can negotiate them and travel back as far as 1.2 miles in the canyon. There, a 20-foot fall blocks farther progress. Make this your turnaround point, then have an easy down-canyon ramble back to your car.

17. NATURAL BRIDGE CANYON

Furnace Creek area, Death Valley National Park
A 40-foot-high rock bridge

DISTANCE: 1.2 miles round-trip; 30 minutes   **LEVEL:** Moderate
ELEVATION: Start at 500 feet; total change 450 feet   **CROWDS:** Moderate
BEST SEASON: October to April   **RATING:** ★ ★ ★

DIRECTIONS: From the Furnace Creek Visitor Center, drive southeast on Highway 190 for 1.3 miles to the right fork for Badwater. Bear right and drive south for 13.2 miles to the left turnoff for Natural Bridge Canyon. Turn left and drive 1.7 miles to the trailhead.

This 1.2-mile hike in Natural Bridge Canyon is not as easy as you might think. The canyon has an abrupt slope, and its loose, gravel surface makes walking a workout. But no matter—hikers of all abilities can make it to the Natural Bridge, the main highlight of this trip. It's only a third of a mile from where you park your car.

You climb right away, heading uphill through the gravel wash that empties out of the mouth of the canyon. The canyon walls are about 30 feet apart, rising tall and majestic. The formation of Natural Bridge Canyon, and of the rest of Death Valley, began about three million years ago. It was borne of large fractures or faults in the earth's crust. Many faults of various sizes are exposed within the walls of the canyon; a geologist could "read" the walls and learn the history of the canyon's formation. Small faults are visible at the mouth of the canyon on the south wall.

Only a third of a mile in, or about 10 to 15 minutes from your car, you'll see the bridge that Natural Bridge Canyon is famous for. It is about 40 feet high and 25 feet wide. Walk underneath it and to its far side; then sit on the canyon floor and watch other people hike up the canyon and under the bridge's imposing overhang. The bridge was formed by repeated flash flooding over thousands of years. When water rushed through this canyon, it encountered a hard, erosion-resistant type of rock, which wouldn't give way to the water. The water diverted itself around the rock and cut through its softer underlayer. In this way, the main span of the bridge was carved.

The bridge isn't the only interesting feature to see in the canyon. About 200 feet uphill from it, on the right side, there's a smoothly rounded vertical chute in the wall, which is obviously a dry waterfall. It's very easy to picture water plunging down it. Several more dry falls can be seen in the canyon.

Another feature near the bridge is an array of "wax drippings." As water drips down the canyon walls, it mixes with sediments in the rock and forms a type of mud, then quickly evaporates. This causes what is called "wax drippings," which look like wax dripped from a mud-colored candle.

You leave many of your fellow hikers behind at the bridge (it's a popular turnaround spot), but you can continue up the canyon for another third of a mile. The canyon walls get narrower as you walk, slowly closing in on you. You have to climb over and around a few boulders, but this just makes things more adventurous. At six-tenths of a mile, the walls come together at a dry fall, about 15 feet high. Without climbing equipment and experience there's no way to get over it, so make this your turnaround point.

Natural Bridge Canyon

Because you've gained a few hundred feet, you have nice views going back down canyon, especially of the Badwater basin, which looks strikingly like a huge lake. Make sure you drive down the road to pay a visit to Badwater and hike on its salt flats.

18. BADWATER SALT FLATS

Furnace Creek area, Death Valley National Park
A walk near the lowest point in the western hemisphere

DISTANCE: 1.0 mile round-trip; 30 minutes   **LEVEL:** Easy

ELEVATION: Start at -280 feet; total change 0 feet   **CROWDS:** Moderate

BEST SEASON: October to April   **RATING:** ★ ★ ★

DIRECTIONS: From the Furnace Creek Visitor Center, drive southeast on Highway 190 for 1.3 miles to the right fork for Badwater. Bear right and drive south for 16.8 miles to the Badwater parking area on the west side of the road.

Almost everybody knows that Badwater has the lowest elevation of any point in the western hemisphere. If they don't know it already, they'll know it as soon as they set foot in Death Valley and realize what an immense tourist attraction Badwater is. But there's more to do at Badwater than just get out of your car and take a picture of your spouse at 280 feet below sea level. Your best bet is to set out on an easy, flat walk across the Badwater salt flats.

Badwater is a white bed of almost pure salt. Its salt pan is a thick crust as much as six feet deep. On its surface, sharp salt crystals form intricate patterns and crunchy miniature mountain ranges. If you visit soon after a period of rainfall, the surface may feel spongy; the hard salt pan sits on top of layers of mud soaking in briny salt water. Sometimes it rains enough so that the surface becomes slippery and muddy, or a small, temporary lake may form. The salt pan is one of the strangest surfaces you'll ever walk on. It's otherworldly.

From the parking lot, walk out to the salt flats on the short trail, but then continue beyond its end, heading away from the crowds and the highway. Check out the sign on the cliff to the east that indicates where sea level is, high above you. Look up at Dante's View at elevation 5,475 feet, and Telescope Peak to the west at 11,048 feet. This is the best way to get perspective on how low you are. Dante's View is usually 25 degrees Fahrenheit cooler than Badwater, and the summit of Telescope Peak is often 60 degrees cooler than Badwater.

Consider this: Badwater may be the lowest spot in the western hemisphere, but it's not the lowest spot in the world. The surface of the Dead Sea holds that honor: it's at 1,300 feet below sea level.

One more note about Badwater: Don't even consider hiking here in the heat of summer. Because of its low elevation, this is the hottest spot in the entire park. The ground temperature is searing; it's usually 40 percent higher than the air temperature, which is likely to be 120 degrees on a July afternoon. If you must visit in summer, consider a nighttime walk under a full moon. Like many places in Death Valley, Badwater is enchanting in the moonlight.

19. DANTE'S RIDGE

Furnace Creek area, Death Valley National Park
Dante's View vistas without the crowds

DISTANCE: 2.0 miles round-trip; 1 hour   **LEVEL:** Easy
ELEVATION: Start at 5,475 feet; total change 250 feet   **CROWDS:** Moderate
BEST SEASON: October to April   **RATING:** ★ ★ ★

DIRECTIONS: From the Furnace Creek Visitor Center, drive southeast on Highway 190 for 1.3 miles to the major fork by the Furnace Creek Inn. Bear left to stay on Highway 190 and drive 10.9 miles to the right fork for Dante's View. Turn right and drive 13.5 miles to the end of the road at Dante's View.

Many hikers think that Dante's View is just a drive-to destination for park visitors in their RVs, so they pass it by and miss out on this great hike with some of the best views in Death Valley. Here's the news: Dante's View is not just an overlook point; it's the start of a terrific two-mile hike along Dante's Ridge. On the trail, you are rewarded with the world-class vistas that Dante's View is famous for, but you have the

View from Dante's Ridge

privilege of enjoying them in solitude.

The highest point along Dante's Ridge is Dante Peak at 5,704 feet, which is just north of the Dante's View parking lot (on your right as you face Badwater). No matter how many people are crowding the lot at Dante's View, all you have to do is walk uphill to your right and you leave 99 percent of them behind. It's a steep but short hike to the summit of Dante Peak, but the half-mile trail is in excellent shape. Walk 200 feet along the road from the parking lot to access it.

There's plenty of cactus and sagebrush along the path; the elevation is much higher here than in most of Death Valley, so vegetation thrives. Several good perches near the summit provide places to sit and admire the stunning view of Badwater and the Panamint mountains beyond. Badwater is more than one mile below you, straight down. That's a little deeper than the bottom of the Grand Canyon from the south rim.

From Dante Peak, retrace your steps to the parking lot, then follow the ridgeline in the opposite direction. You've just traveled a half-mile out and back to the north; now you will do the same to the south. The trail leads from the southern end of the parking lot, clinging to the edge of the cliff on which Dante's View sits. The scenery is more of the same splendid panorama—Badwater, the Panamint Range, the Sierra Nevada, and the Cottonwood Mountains. You'd expect to have to hike 10 miles and climb a few thousand feet to get a view this good.

An interesting interpretive sign a quarter-mile south on the ridgeline describes the geography of the Great Basin Range, which one 1880s geologist described as "an army of caterpillars crawling toward Mexico." Basically, the mountain ranges run north to south, paralleling each other. They are separated by low basins. Between the Sierra Nevada and the Great Salt Lake, from west to east, the mountain-to-basin-to-mountain series goes like this: Sierra Nevada Mountains, Owens Valley, Inyo Mountains, Saline Valley, Argus Range, Panamint Valley, Panamint Range, Death Valley, Funeral and Black Mountains, Greenwater Range. I don't know about you, but I certainly never thought about it that way before.

If you're interested in obtaining even more views, a nearby summit offers fascinating vistas to the east, into the mountains and valleys of Nevada. The peak is Coffin Peak; it's accessible via a moderate trail-less hike from the rest room area a half mile below the Dante's View parking lot. Locate the faint use trail near the rest room and follow it uphill, then mostly south and east along the ridgeline. You'll climb up and over two smaller peaks on your way to Coffin Peak.

20. WILDROSE PEAK

Wildrose area, Death Valley National Park
Summertime peak hike at high elevation

DISTANCE: 8.4 miles round-trip; 4 hours

ELEVATION: Start at 6,900 feet; total change 2,160 feet

BEST SEASON: May to October

LEVEL: Strenuous

CROWDS: Minimal

RATING: ★ ★ ★ ★

DIRECTIONS: From Stovepipe Wells, drive west on Highway 190 for eight miles to Emigrant Canyon Road, then turn left (south). Drive 21 miles to the junction with Wildrose Canyon Road. Turn left (east) and drive seven miles to the small parking area across from the Charcoal Kilns. The Wildrose Peak Trailhead is on the northwest side of the kilns.

If it's boiling in Death Valley, you can always make the long drive out to Wildrose Canyon and hike to the summit of Wildrose Peak. What, climb a mountain in July in Death Valley, when you can barely take the heat standing still? Sure, because the trailhead for this hike is set at 6,900 feet. Get this—they even have trees here. By the time you reach the windy summit of 9,064-foot Wildrose Peak, you'll probably have to put on your jacket, even though it may be well over 120 degrees in Death Valley.

The hike begins alongside a set of huge stone kilns that were constructed in the 1870s to make charcoal for the local mines. Pinyon pine wood from nearby slopes was burned in the 10 kilns to produce charcoal, a process which took about two weeks. The charcoal was then transported to the Modock Mine smelter, 30 miles away, where it was used to extract lead and silver out of the rich ore from Modock's mines.

Take a minute to explore the kilns, which look strangely like bee hives. They are 25 feet high, 30 feet wide, and remarkably symmetrical. Although they were built by Chinese laborers, they were designed by Swiss engineers.

Walk to the northwest end of the kilns to find the signed Wildrose Peak Trail, and start to climb through scattered pinyon pines and junipers. Only a quarter-mile in, you get your first good set of views— of Wildrose Canyon below and the far-off snowy peaks of the Sierra Nevada. After that, you've got a long, gut-thumping, view-less climb up a ridge, but you're shaded most of the time by the pinyon pines, the same tree that the miners burned in their kilns. (You may see some stumps in the early part of the trail.)

An excellent trail surface and well-built trail make the steep ridge climb manageable. At two miles out, you reach a saddle on the crest of the Panamints and get to take a breather. Here your views really open up—you have your first looks down into Death Valley to the east. The vast, barren desert floor is hard to comprehend from this forested ridgetop.

Enjoy an easier grade for the next mile as you hike northward along the crest of the ridge to a second saddle. With the grade lessened, you have the chance to examine the beautifully colored slate rocks found all along the trail. Enjoy this trail stretch, and the desert views from the second saddle, because the next and final mile to the summit is the steepest. You gain 800 feet in that distance, in what seems like far too many switchbacks. But with every short, steep curve in the trail, there is ample opportunity to look to the east at the increasingly spectacular views of Death Valley.

When at last you attain the broad, grassy summit, your eastern desert views are complemented by a larger panorama: Telescope Peak is the nearby, looming summit directly south; Rogers Peak with its microwave tower lies in between Telescope and Wildrose; the Panamint Range extends to the north. To the west, of course, is the jagged, snow-covered bulk of the Sierra Nevada. If the wind isn't ferocious, you'll want to stay up here for a long while. (Unfortunately, it's rare that the wind isn't ferocious.)

No matter how long your summit stay lasts, Wildrose Peak is definitely worth the climb. And who knows, after you've tackled

Descending from Wildrose Peak

Wildrose, you may get inspired to hike to the top of Telescope Peak another day (see the following story). But when planning a trip to either mountain, keep this in mind: Their trails can be snowed in at any time between November and May. If you don't visit in summer or early fall, check with the park before making the long drive.

21. TELESCOPE PEAK

Wildrose area, Death Valley National Park
Spectacular vistas from the highest summit in Death Valley

DISTANCE: 14.0 miles round-trip; 8 hours   **LEVEL:** Very strenuous
ELEVATION: Start at 8,130 feet; total change 2,900 feet   **CROWDS:** Minimal
BEST SEASON: May to October   **RATING:** ★ ★ ★ ★ ★

DIRECTIONS: From Stovepipe Wells, drive west on Highway 190 for eight miles to Emigrant Canyon Road, then turn left (south). Drive 21 miles to the junction with Wildrose Canyon Road. Turn left (east) and drive 8.8 miles to the end of the road at Mahogany Flat Campground. The dirt road gets rough and steep in the last 1.8 miles beyond the Charcoal Kilns; a high-clearance or four-wheel-drive vehicle may be required.

The big selling point for making the long hike to the summit of Telescope Peak is this: When you get there, you can pivot yourself around and in one long, sweeping glance take in Mount Whitney to the west and Badwater to the east. For the uninitiated, that means you see the highest point in the contiguous United States and the lowest point in the Western Hemisphere from the same spot. (One is ahead of you and one is to your back.)

The hike's other big selling point is that the trailhead is at 8,130 feet, so you don't have to worry about it being too hot in the summertime, when the rest of Death Valley is baking. In fact, this hike should be taken in the summer, because from November to May, the peak is usually snow-covered.

Telescope Peak is the highest mountain in Death Valley National Park at 11,049 feet, and mercifully, the trail to reach it is well graded and well maintained. Nonetheless, the 3,000-foot climb and the long mileage takes its toll, so don't try it unless you're in good shape. Some people choose to turn this trip into a backpacking excursion, but plenty of others get an early morning start and have a spectacular day hike. Make sure you're well equipped with plenty of water and snacks, and carry a jacket for the summit, which will almost certainly be windy.

The trail begins with a moderate ascent through pinyon pines and junipers, circling the east side of Rogers Peak. (You see a dirt road heading to the microwave towers on Rogers Peak right next to the Telescope Peak trailhead.) The first two miles are a continual climb and mostly in the trees, until at 2.5 miles you reach a 9,600-foot saddle at Arcane Meadows. This is where some backpackers make camp. You have your first views to the west—a preview of what is to come.

The next two miles are surprisingly level, as the trail hugs the ridge crest and serves up alternating views to the east and the west. Death Valley and Panamint Valley appear remarkably wide, long, and barren, compared to the high, cool ridge from which you see them. At 4.3 miles out, you reach an unsigned fork with a spur trail to Eagle Spring (no water is available at the spring). Stay left and continue to head for the peak on a moderate uphill grade. The higher you go, the thinner the forest becomes, until at last the pinyon pines and junipers disappear. What replaces them are scattered limber pines and ancient bristlecone pines. The snag-like trees seen here are the same as the ones found in the Ancient Bristlecone Pine Forest in the White Mountains to the north. Ancient bristlecone pines are the oldest living things on earth; although the ones found near Telescope Peak are only 3,000 years old, others in the White Mountains are as old as 4,600 years.

The ancient bristlecone pines appear only in the last 1.3 miles of trail, when you are above 10,000 feet and the air is noticeably thinner than it was down below. Unfortunately, this is also the steepest part of the trip, with many switchbacks. But you're almost at the top, so just march onward. When at last you reach Telescope's summit, you are amply rewarded: The promised views of Mount Whitney and Badwater are delivered, and you also witness the rest of Death Valley and Panamint Valley, and the White Mountains to the north. On clear days, you can pick out Las Vegas. The vertical drop from Telescope's summit to Badwater, almost directly below, is more than 11,000 feet. This kind of extreme elevation change can be witnessed from only a few high summits in the United States, including Mount Rainier and Mount McKinley. It's beyond spectacular.

If you plan a trip, remember that the best time for hiking to the summit of Telescope Peak is between May and October. Although some mountaineers make the trip in the winter when the peak is covered in snow, it is not advised for hikers who aren't carrying (and experienced with) climbing equipment such as ice axes, crampons, and ropes. The clearest visibility days usually occur in May, June, and October, when the valley is not too hot and there is less chance of haze obscuring the view.

CHANNEL ISLANDS NATIONAL PARK

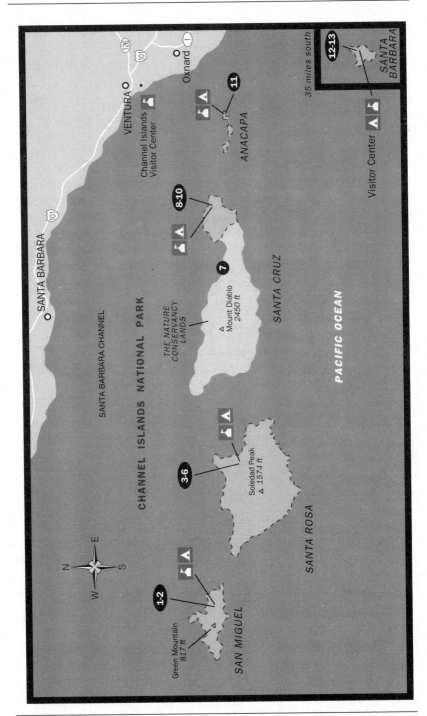

CHANNEL ISLANDS NATIONAL PARK
TRAILS AT A GLANCE

Map Number/Trail Name	Page	Mileage	Difficulty
1. Caliche Forest	444	6.6	Easy/moderate
2. Point Bennett	446	14.0	Moderate
3. Torrey Pines Trail	448	5.0	Easy/moderate
4. Water Canyon Beach	449	1.0-5.0	Easy
5. Lobos Canyon	451	3.0-15.0	Strenuous
6. Black Mountain	453	7.0	Moderate
7. Pelican Bay to Prisoners Harbor	455	2.0	Easy/moderate
8. Potato Harbor	457	4.6	Easy/moderate
9. Smuggler's Cove	458	7.0	Moderate
10. Cavern Point	460	1.2	Easy
11. East Anacapa Island Trail	462	2.0	Easy
12. Signal Peak Loop	465	3.8	Easy/moderate
13. Elephant Seal Cove	467	3.2	Easy/moderate

THE TOP 3, DON'T-MISS DAY HIKES:

Map Number/Trail Name	Page	Features
2. Point Bennett	446	caliche forest, pinnipeds
7. Pelican Bay to Prisoners Harbor	455	native flora
11. East Anacapa Island Trail	462	easy island adventure

TRAIL SUGGESTIONS FOR IF YOU ONLY HAVE ONE DAY:

Map Number/Trail Name	Page	Features
7. Pelican Bay to Prisoners Harbor	455	native flora
11. East Anacapa Island Trail	462	easy island adventure

CHANNEL ISLANDS NATIONAL PARK

ABOUT THE PARK

The five Channel Islands of Channel Islands National Park lie off the coast of Southern California, mostly in the vicinity of Santa Barbara and Ventura. (One of the five, Santa Barbara Island, is located much farther south, off the coast of San Pedro.) The islands are often called the "Galapagos of California" because of the amount and diversity of endemic animals and plant life. The only way to reach the islands is by boat or plane; see below for information.

ADDRESS, PHONE, & WEBSITE

Channel Islands National Park, 1901 Spinnaker Drive, Ventura, CA 93001; (805) 658-5730.
Website: www.nps.gov/chis

VISITOR CENTERS

The main Channel Islands Visitor Center is at the address above in Ventura. Anacapa and Santa Barbara islands also have small visitor centers.

HOW TO GET THERE

- By air: The closest major airports are in Santa Barbara or Los Angeles; you will need to connect with boat transportation in Santa Barbara or Ventura. Santa Rosa Island is directly accessible by air from Camarillo Airport; phone Channel Islands Aviation at (805) 987-1301 for information.
- By sea: Two boat concessionaires are authorized by the National Park Service to take passengers to the Channel Islands: Island Packers of Ventura and Truth Aquatics at Sea Landing of Santa Barbara. For information and reservations phone Island Packers at (805) 642-7688 or (805) 642-1393, or phone Truth Aquatics at (805) 963-3564. If you plan to travel to the Channel Islands in your own boat, check with the visitor center in Ventura for current regulations.

BOAT PASSAGE DURATION

- To Anacapa Island: approximately 1.25 hours one-way
- To Santa Cruz Island: approximately 1.5 hours one-way
- To Santa Rosa Island: approximately 4.0 hours one-way
- To San Miguel Island: approximately 5.0 hours one-way
- To Santa Barbara Island: approximately 5.0 hours one-way

ENTRANCE FEES

There is no entrance fee at Channel Islands National Park, although you will have to pay for your boat transportation from Ventura or Santa Barbara to the islands. Current rates are $37 to $48 for Anacapa Island, $42 to $54 for Santa Cruz Island, $49 to $75 for Santa Barbara Island, $62 to $80 for Santa Rosa Island, and $75 to $90 for San Miguel Island. (All rates are round-trip, per person. The higher fee is for campers staying overnight; day visitors pay the lesser fee.) The cost to fly to Santa Rosa Island from Camarillo Airport is $85 for a day-trip or $150 for a camping trip.

WHEN TO GO

You can visit the Channel Islands year-round, but boat service is limited in the winter months when the seas are high. The concessionaires' schedule the most trips to the islands between April and October.

WEATHER CONDITIONS

The Channel Islands have typical Southern California weather, but in a more intense and dramatic version. The climate is basically mild, but harsh coastal wind and dense fog are common, especially on the outer islands of Santa Rosa and San Miguel. (Campers in particular need to plan for strong island winds.) The early autumn months (between August and October) usually have the clearest days and least wind. Generally, rain falls only between November and April. Temperatures are usually in the 60s or 70s during the day, and drop into the 50s at night. Hikers should carry many layers of clothing, and come with a good hat and sunscreen, just in case the sun shines. There is very little shade on any of the islands.

WHERE TO STAY

There are no lodgings on any of the national park islands, but each island has its own campground. A camping permit is required; it can be obtained by phoning (800) 365-2267. Of the five island campgrounds, only one has water (Santa Rosa Island's Water Canyon Camp), and one allows wood fires (Santa Cruz Island's Scorpion Canyon Camp). At the other camps, you must bring bottled water and a backpacking stove for cooking. All of the camps require a walk of at least a half-mile from where the boat or plane drops you off.

FOOD & SUPPLIES

No food or supplies of any kind are available on the islands; you must bring everything with you.

1. CALICHE FOREST

San Miguel Island, Channel Islands National Park
A ghost forest of calcified trees

DISTANCE: 6.6 miles round-trip; 3.5 hours

ELEVATION: Start at 0 feet; total change 850 feet

BEST SEASON: April to October

LEVEL: Easy/moderate

CROWDS: Minimal

RATING: ★ ★ ★ ★

DIRECTIONS: Island Packers provides boat transportation to San Miguel Island from Ventura Harbor. Truth Aquatics at Sea Landing provides boat transportation to San Miguel Island from Santa Barbara Harbor. Advance reservations are required. Phone Island Packers at (805) 642-7688 or (805) 642-1393, or phone Truth Aquatics at Sea Landing at (805) 963-3564.

When some people find out there's an easy way and a hard way to do something, they immediately choose the hard way. If you're in that camp, you'll choose San Miguel Island as the Channel Island you want to visit, instead of Anacapa, Santa Cruz, or any of the other islands. San Miguel is the furthest island from the mainland, requiring a much dreaded five-hour boat ride from Ventura, or a slightly shorter four-hour boat ride from Santa Barbara. Boat trips are not scheduled very often, and even when they are, they are prone to cancellation due to bad weather or too few passengers. The most promising season for trips to San Miguel is from April to October.

As if the boat ride wasn't hardship enough, you also have to contend with San Miguel's weather, which is usually extreme wind and fog but might also be baking, hot sun. You must plan accordingly: Bring clothes for every possible kind of weather. The most probable element you'll encounter is constant, strong wind.

If you're stalwart, you should make this spectacular trip. Although most visitors go to San Miguel Island to camp for a few days (see the following story), one-day trips are occasionally available. To make the long voyage in one day, you leave the mainland the night before, sleep on the boat, then arrive at the island around 7 A.M. You have five to six hours on the island before the boat departs again at 1 P.M. and shuttles you back to the mainland in time for dinner.

This allows day-trippers just enough time to take a guided hike to the Caliche Forest with a ranger or naturalist. (Outside of the harbor and ranger station area on San Miguel, you can hike only in the company of a ranger. This is to help protect the island's fragile resources.) On this 6.6-mile guided hike, you'll follow the island's main trail, which bisects San Miguel from east to west. Your destination is the

Caliche Forest, an eerie forest of ancient tree trunks encased in calcium carbonate, located about halfway across the island.

From the stunning white beach at Cuyler Harbor where the boat drops you off, hike eastward along the sand, then follow the path a half-mile up Nidever Canyon. It's a steep stretch on sketchy trail with a 500-foot elevation gain, but you'll be so happy to be off the boat and on dry land, you'll probably shout for joy.

When you reach the ridge at the top, you can visit the stone monument to Juan Rodriguez Cabrillo, who claimed this island for the Spaniards in 1542. Cabrillo may or may not be buried on this island—nobody's sure. He died from a case of gangrene after he broke either an arm or a leg in a scuffle with the native Chumash Indians. The Chumash were not aggressive toward Cabrillo or his men; apparently the conflict arose because the party-loving Chumash wanted to keep dancing and celebrating with the Spaniards, but the Spaniards were tired and wanted to go back to their camp to sleep.

The trail continues to the ranger station and campground, then heads south to the remains of the Lester Ranch. In 1930, Herbert Lester was hired to manage the sheep that grazed on the island. He and his wife lived on San Miguel Island for 12 years, raising two children. Lester proclaimed himself "The King of San Miguel." He collected all kinds of memorabilia that washed up from shipwrecks and the sea and proudly displayed them in his yard. But in June of 1942, Herbert Lester walked to a scenic viewpoint on the island and killed himself. Apparently, he was in despair over his ailing health. All that is left of the Lester ranch today is the brick rubble of the walls and foundation. (A side note: Lester's wife went back to Santa Barbara and lived for another 40 years. She died in 1981 and was buried next to her husband near Harris Point on San Miguel.)

From the Lester Ranch, the trail continues another 2.5 miles to the Caliche Forest. Along the way, you climb to the summit of San Miguel Hill, the highest point on the island at 831 feet, and then drop back down the other side. You'll have many opportunities to see the island's unique vegetation. Plant life and wildflowers may be better on San Miguel than on any of the other Channel Islands. Despite a history of human abuse—including nearly a century of sheep grazing and 20 years of Navy bombing—native plants have persisted on San Miguel, fighting to maintain their hold in the island's nonstop wind. Unlike Anacapa or Santa Cruz islands, which often roast in the summer sun, San Miguel is usually fogged in, creating a more hospitable environment for vegetation. Seaside daisies, San Miguel Island buckwheat, lupine, bromegrass, and creamy dudleya are profuse. Giant coreopsis erupt into bright yellow blooms between March and May. Other wildflowers may continue to bloom as late as July and August, due to the often present, moisture-giving fog.

At nearly three miles from Cuyler Harbor, you'll reach a right spur to the Caliche Forest. Turn right and walk the last few hundred feet to the edge of the phantom forest, which is made up of calcium carbonate sandcastings of dead tree roots and trunks. They were formed when the ancient trees' organic acid mixed with calcium carbonate.

The caliche stand like frozen statues, looking much like the tufa spires at Mono Lake. Some are as tall as five feet; others are only a few inches. The near-constant northwesterly winds on San Miguel Island continually reveal new sandcastings while simultaneously burying others. Caliche (pronounced "ka-LEE-che") is found on other Channel Islands, but this is the best and most extensive example.

2. POINT BENNETT

San Miguel Island, Channel Islands National Park
A massive congregation of seals and sea lions

DISTANCE: 14.0 miles round-trip; 7 hours **LEVEL:** Moderate
ELEVATION: Start at 0 feet; total change 1,200 feet **CROWDS:** Minimal
BEST SEASON: April to October **RATING:** ★ ★ ★ ★

DIRECTIONS: Island Packers provides boat transportation to San Miguel Island from Ventura Harbor. Truth Aquatics at Sea Landing provides boat transportation to San Miguel Island from Santa Barbara Harbor. Advance reservations are required. Phone Island Packers at (805) 642-7688 or (805) 642-1393, or phone Truth Aquatics at Sea Landing at (805) 963-3564.

Before even considering a trip to San Miguel Island, read the previous story on the Caliche Forest so you see what you're getting yourself into. Although visiting any of the Channel Islands involves far more effort and planning than just driving to other California national parks, getting to San Miguel Island requires the most effort of all.

The best way to make the trip is to spend a couple of days camping at the island's campground. Because of San Miguel Island's dicey weather, large land area, and the long boat ride required to reach it, a camping trip provides hikers with an insurance policy. If you camp, you'll have an extra day or two in case you have bad weather. Plus, you'll have enough time to take the best hike on the island, an all-day, 14-mile excursion to Point Bennett.

As with many challenging situations in the outdoors, the payoff for the effort required to see San Miguel Island is great. On the ranger-guided hike from the campground to Point Bennett, campers will get to sample all of the island's best features: rolling dunes, native vegetation, ocean views, the famous Caliche Forest (see the previous story), and Point Bennett on the island's western tip, one of the greatest wildlife viewing spots in all of California.

Caliche Forest sandcastings

Point Bennett's main inhabitants are pinnipeds, or seals and sea lions. At certain times of the year, you can see more than 30,000 individuals from as many as six different species, including California sea lions, northern fur seals, northern elephant seals, harbor seals, and less frequently, Guadalupe fur seals and stellar sea lions. Grouped on the sandy beaches in immense numbers, the animals create a cacophonous symphony of bellows and roars. This is guaranteed to be a sound—and a sight—you'll never forget.

The best time to see the pinnipeds is during breeding season. Point Bennett is considered to be one of the world's largest breeding rookeries for California sea lions; a full one-third of all the sea lions in California are born there. Thousands of sea lions show up annually to give birth at Point Bennett; the peak months are May and June. At any time of the year, large numbers of seals and sea lions are present on the point's huge, protected beach—hauling out on the sand, mating, barking, fighting, or playing in the surf.

If you tire of watching the masses of seals and sea lions, you can always pull out your binoculars and look for birds. Sea birds are ubiquitous: Some 60 percent of the birds nesting in the Channel Islands do so on San Miguel, or on its tiny neighboring Prince Island, near Cuyler Harbor. Primary nesting species include Cassin's auklets and three species of cormorants. In addition, there are myriad Western gulls and California brown pelicans. On your hike across the interior of the island, you are likely to spot colorful western meadowlarks, rock wrens, and an endemic species of song sparrow.

Note that hiking on San Miguel Island is on more level terrain than on either Santa Rosa or Santa Cruz islands. Much of your walking will be on or around dunes or gentle hills. But what San Miguel lacks in difficult ascents, it makes up for in wind. Fierce wind and fog are nearly constant on the island, so you must plan accordingly for both hiking and camping.

---

3. TORREY PINES TRAIL

Santa Rosa Island, Channel Islands National Park
A rare stand of native Torrey pines

DISTANCE: 5.0 miles round-trip; 2.5 hours   **LEVEL:** Easy/moderate
ELEVATION: Start at 100 feet; total change 600 feet   **CROWDS:** Minimal
BEST SEASON: April to October   **RATING:** ★ ★ ★

DIRECTIONS: Island Packers provides boat transportation to Santa Rosa Island from Ventura Harbor. Advance reservations are required. Phone Island Packers at (805) 642-7688 or (805) 642-1393 for information and reservations. Truth Aquatics at Sea Landing provides boat transportation to Santa Rosa Island from Santa Barbara Harbor. Phone Truth Aquatics at (805) 963-3564. Channel Islands Aviation provides air transportation to Santa Rosa Island from Camarillo Airport. Phone Channel Islands Aviation at (805) 987-1301.

One of the many charms of Santa Rosa Island is that you can fly there in about 20 minutes in a small plane, instead of taking the four-hour boat ride from Ventura or Santa Barbara. The National Park Service has allowed one airplane concessionaire to take passengers to the park's islands (in addition to the two boat concessionaires), and Santa Rosa Island just happens to have an airstrip. For people prone to seasickness, this makes Santa Rosa Island the Channel Island of choice.

The flight is breathtaking. Departing from Camarillo Airport, you soar for a few minutes over land, followed by a few more minutes over open ocean. In no time at all you glimpse the Channel Islands: First you see Anacapa with its three distinct islets, then you fly right over the interior of giant Santa Cruz, then Santa Rosa appears in front of you. Depending on which route the pilot takes, you may get a glimpse of smaller San Miguel Island as well, farther to the west.

The plane lands on Santa Rosa on a dirt airstrip that parallels the beach. Campers must carry their gear a half-mile uphill to the camp-ground at Water Canyon. Day visitors can start hiking right from the airstrip.

Within a mile's walk is another of the island's charms—a stand of native Torrey pines. These are the same species of conifer that you see at Torrey Pines State Reserve in San Diego. Only in these two places in the world do the slow-growing, windswept Torrey pines exist.

To see them, from either the landing strip or the boat pier, follow the dirt coastal road to the southeast, paralleling the shore. Near the far end of the landing strip, on the inland side, you'll see a gate and a trail that leads uphill to Water Canyon Campground. Pass by this trail and continue on the coastal road to the next "Y" junction. The upper road follows a ridge above the Torrey pines; the lower road skirts below them. Take your pick. The lower road stays close to the coast and is mostly level; the upper road involves some climbing but provides out-standing coastal views. If you like, you can loop around the Torrey pines on the two dirt roads; they intersect again. The loop hike is a five mile round-trip. (Bring a map with you. There are many dirt roads on this island, and almost none are signed.)

If you're in the mood for a longer hike, keep following the main coastal road southeast beyond the Torrey pines grove. The road travels another four miles to East Point and more of Santa Rosa's beautiful beaches. But check with the ranger on trail closures before you go: Some of the beaches on the east end of the island are closed in spring and summer to protect nesting snowy plovers.

4. WATER CANYON BEACH

Santa Rosa Island, Channel Islands National Park
Three-mile long beach with sand dunes

DISTANCE: 1.0 to 5.0 miles round-trip; 1 to 3 hours   **LEVEL:** Easy
ELEVATION: Start at 100 feet; total change 100 feet   **CROWDS:** Minimal
BEST SEASON: April to October   **RATING:** ★ ★ ★ ★

DIRECTIONS: Island Packers provides boat transportation to Santa Rosa Island from Ventura Harbor. Advance reservations are required. Phone Island Packers at (805) 642-7688 or (805) 642-1393 for information and reservations. Truth Aquatics at Sea Landing provides boat transportation to Santa Rosa Island from Santa Barbara Harbor. Phone Truth Aquatics at (805) 963-3564. Channel Islands Aviation provides air transportation to Santa Rosa Island from Camarillo Airport. Phone Channel Islands Aviation at (805) 987-1301.

There are no formal hiking trails on Santa Rosa Island, but there are plenty of dirt ranch roads and animal trails. Unfortunately, the ranch roads and animal trails are mostly steep, rocky, and completely lacking in signage, which makes them suitable only for intrepid hikers. Visitors looking for an easier trek can hike the ranch road to the island's stand of Torrey pines (see the previous story), but they may find other island trails to be too strenuous.

There's a simple solution for those desiring easy hiking on Santa Rosa Island: Water Canyon Beach, the fabulous three-mile stretch of coastline that runs along the edge of Bechers Bay. It's a huge expanse of gleaming white sand, complete with windswept dunes, tide pools, sandstone bluffs, and no people. Quite simply, it is a beach lover's dream.

Access is easy from the airplane landing strip or the island's campground: Simply start from the southeast end of the landing strip or from the entrance to the camp and follow the dirt road steeply downhill to the beach. (It's less than a quarter-mile.) If you're hiking from the ranger station or boat pier, just follow the main coastal road southeast until you reach the far end of the landing strip, then turn left on the steep dirt road, heading downhill to the ocean.

From this long, uninterrupted beach, you have a direct view of Santa Cruz Island, and on clear days, the mainland beyond. Because

Sandstone formations on Water Canyon Beach, Santa Rosa Island

you are facing east, you are in a perfect spot for viewing sunrises. If you hike to your left (north), you'll come across a lovely group of sand dunes, some as high as 50 feet, which are continually refreshed by the near-constant island winds. The dunes back up against sandstone and mudstone marine terraces.

Hiking past the dunes, you'll head into a rockier area, teeming with tidepool life. We found a giant spider crab washed up on the beach; each of his legs was at least a foot long. Mussels seem to be attached to every possible rock surface. The rocks on the inland side of the beach are conglomerates, showing signs of early volcanic activity mixed in with the erosion of marine terraces. A generous amount of sandstone caves are carved into the bluffs along the beach, and beautifully sculpted and rounded sandstone rocks are perched along the shoreline.

If you've brought your fishing gear, you're in luck: You're allowed to fish right off the beaches on Santa Rosa Island. You don't necessarily need surf casting gear to do it, although it helps. Watch out for clever sea lions, who will gather around, act really cute, and then steal your bait. The most frequent catch at the beach is surf perch, which is reportedly quite tasty. I don't know for sure.... a sea lion stole my bait.

Hike along the pristine sand for as long as you like. It's a 1.5-mile jaunt to the north to the huge pier jutting out into the ocean; you can continue past it if you wish. You can also hike southward on Water Canyon Beach, although at high tide, you may get stopped by rock outcrops.

5. LOBOS CANYON

Santa Rosa Island, Channel Islands National Park
Native island flora and ancient Chumash sites

DISTANCE: 3.0 or 15.0 miles round-trip; 2 or 8 hours   **LEVEL:** Strenuous
ELEVATION: Start at 100 feet; total change 300 feet   **CROWDS:** Minimal
BEST SEASON: April to October   **RATING:** ★ ★ ★ ★

DIRECTIONS: Island Packers provides boat transportation to Santa Rosa Island from Ventura Harbor. Advance reservations are required. Phone Island Packers at (805) 642-7688 or (805) 642-1393 for information and reservations. Truth Aquatics at Sea Landing provides boat transportation to Santa Rosa Island from Santa Barbara Harbor. Phone Truth Aquatics at (805) 963-3564. Channel Islands Aviation provides air transportation to Santa Rosa Island from Camarillo Airport. Phone Channel Islands Aviation at (805) 987-1301.

Native flora, Santa Rosa Island

The best hike on Santa Rosa Island is in Lobos Canyon on the island's north side. Lobos Canyon is the only place on 84-square-mile Santa Rosa Island where the terrain has remained mostly untouched and large quantities of native vegetation can be seen. During the island's long ranching history, stock animals were unable to access the steep, narrow canyon, so the native plants survived.

Unfortunately, Lobos Canyon is too far away from the campground and visitor drop-off area to be a reasonable day hike for most people. The hardy can make the 15-mile round-trip from the camp, but only if they start early and take the whole day to do it. (If you attempt it, make sure you carry a map with you; there are no signs. Also, get updated trail information from a ranger before you set out. The basic instructions are: Follow the coastal road north to the ranch buildings, then take the dirt Smith Highway inland to where it crosses Lobos Creek. Exit the road and hike down the canyon.)

Anyone unwilling to do a 15-mile round-trip has to rely on the good graces of the park ranger on duty. The ranger will frequently drive visitors to this remote canyon, then lead a three-mile hike through its beautifully carved sandstone walls and along its year-round stream.

To visit Lobos Canyon is to understand the intrinsic value of these islands as a national park, beyond their natural beauty and diversity. Although many visitors come to Santa Rosa Island for its beaches and fishing opportunities, or to see its rare stand of Torrey pines, Santa Rosa's greatest resource may be its archaeological heritage. Chumash Indians inhabited this island as many as 11,000 years ago. Their descendants remained on the island until the early 1800s, when the Europeans began showing up. Some researchers consider Santa Rosa Island to be one giant archaeological site. It abounds with Chumash middens, or "kitchen garbage dumps," containing items such as fish bones, pieces of discarded tools, mussel and limpet shells, chert, and red abalone shells that date back as much as 6,000 years. Several of these middens and a Chumash village site can be seen in Lobos Canyon. The village was built at the mouth of the canyon, close to the ocean but still protected from the strong coastal winds.

In addition to its ancient human history, Lobos Canyon also abounds with natural history. Thriving native flora include island monkey flower, coreopsis, and dudleya or live-forever. At one time, all of Santa Rosa Island looked much like Lobos Canyon, before the grazing livestock chewed up all the native plants and the ranchers sowed non-native grasses. Hopefully, in time, all of Santa Rosa Island will return to its native state.

After exploring Lobos Canyon, the ranger will often lead visitors over the hill into neighboring Cow Canyon. Where the canyon meets the sea is an excellent tidepooling area, overflowing with mussels, starfish, crabs, limpets, and sea anemones.

6. BLACK MOUNTAIN

Santa Rosa Island, Channel Islands National Park
A high summit on Santa Rosa Island

DISTANCE: 7.0 miles round-trip; 3.5 hours   **LEVEL:** Moderate
ELEVATION: Start at 100 feet; total change 1,200 feet   **CROWDS:** Minimal
BEST SEASON: April to October   **RATING:** ★ ★ ★

DIRECTIONS: Island Packers provides boat transportation to Santa Rosa Island from Ventura Harbor. Advance reservations are required. Phone Island Packers at (805) 642-7688 or (805) 642-1393 for information and reservations. Truth Aquatics at Sea Landing provides boat transportation to Santa Rosa Island from Santa Barbara Harbor. Phone Truth Aquatics at (805) 963-3564. Channel Islands Aviation provides air transportation to Santa Rosa Island from Camarillo Airport. Phone Channel Islands Aviation at (805) 987-1301.

Black Mountain at 1,298 feet may be only the second highest mountain on Santa Rosa Island, but its summit views are rewarding enough. Sure, Soledad Peak at 1,574 feet is taller, but it's too far from the campground, the landing strip, and the boat pier for a reasonable day trip. Getting to the summit of Black Mountain provides enough of a challenge for most day-hikers, and it is often made more challenging by Santa Rosa's fierce, blustery winds.

There are several ways to reach the summit, but the best route is to start at the ranger station, then take the ranch road alongside it (called Soledad Road) that leads into the island's interior. At a fork in the road a half mile out, stay left (the right fork dead-ends at a windmill site). The trail winds its way up deeply eroded Cherry Canyon, passing some of the island's groves of lovely, gnarled oak trees. The going can get steep in places on the rocky dirt road. Take every opportunity to turn around and notice the views you are gaining as you climb, of the island's interior, a wide expanse of Bechers Bay and the Pacific Ocean, and San Miguel Island to the west.

The summit of 1,298-foot Black Mountain is reached at 3.5 miles from the ranger station. It has a weather station on top, and a grove of oak trees just below. If the wind isn't fierce, stay on top of the peak for a picnic with a view. Within your sight is much of Santa Rosa Island, plus San Miguel, Santa Cruz, and the mainland. If the wind is fierce, do what we did: Seek shelter in the oaks.

Note that if you are camping, you can hike to Black Mountain

Hiking down from Black Mountain; Santa Cruz Island in the distance

Channel Islands National Park—map page 440

directly from Water Canyon Campground, by hiking up Water Canyon on livestock trails until you meet up with another dirt road to the peak. Although this route is much shorter, I wouldn't recommend it unless you are comfortable with route-finding and steep, rocky terrain.

7. PELICAN BAY to PRISONERS HARBOR

West Santa Cruz Island, Channel Islands National Park
A guided nature walk on The Nature Conservancy's land

DISTANCE: 2.0 miles round-trip; 1.5 hours   **LEVEL:** Easy/moderate
ELEVATION: Start at 0 feet; total change 400 feet   **CROWDS:** Minimal
BEST SEASON: April to October   **RATING:** ★ ★ ★ ★

DIRECTIONS: Island Packers provides boat transportation to Santa Cruz Island from Ventura Harbor. Advance reservations are required. Phone Island Packers at (805) 642-7688 or (805) 642-1393 for information and reservations. Truth Aquatics at Sea Landing provides boat transportation to Santa Cruz Island from Santa Barbara Harbor. Phone Truth Aquatics at (805) 963-3564.

Santa Cruz Island is the largest of all the Channel Islands. It's 96 miles square, or almost 100 times larger than its neighbor Anacapa. But 90 percent of Santa Cruz Island's land area—all except for the very eastern tip—is owned by the nonprofit organization The Nature Conservancy, not the National Park Service. The NPS co-manages the island with The Nature Conservancy, but because the land is privately held, this huge chunk of Santa Cruz Island is not open for visitation in the same manner as the rest of Channel Islands National Park.

Nonetheless, I've included this hike on The Nature Conservancy land on western Santa Cruz Island for two reasons: One, the boat concessionaires authorized by the National Park Service run frequent trips to this part of the island; and two, The Nature Conservancy's land is a fine example of what the rest of Santa Cruz Island should look like in another few decades.

That's because western Santa Cruz Island has been protected from overuse much longer than the eastern side, which came under the wing of the national parks in 1997. The Nature Conservancy has managed its part of the island since 1978. Perhaps its most important strategy was to end decades of overgrazing by removing all the livestock from the land, which has given the native vegetation a chance to grow back. Eventually, the same will occur on the east side of Santa Cruz Island.

The best trip for day-hikers to west Santa Cruz Island is a guided hike from Pelican Bay to Prisoners Harbor. This trip is offered several times a year through the boat concessionaires listed above. (Hikers are not permitted to explore The Nature Conservancy land without a guide.) Here's how it works: The boat concessionaire drops you and your fellow hikers off at Pelican Bay. You hike with a naturalist guide for two miles one-way to Prisoners Harbor, trekking along the scenic north shore of the island. The boat picks you up at Prisoners Harbor and takes you back to the mainland.

At Pelican Bay, where the trip begins, you climb up the seaside cliffs on a sketchy trail to a picnic spot overlooking the bay. The building foundations and ornamental plantings you see are all that remain of Pelican Bay Camp, a camping resort that was popular with movie and film companies, wealthy vacationers, and outdoor adventurers in the early part of the 20th century. A fascinating memoir about Pelican Bay Camp was written by Margaret Holden Eaton, who ran the camp with her husband Ira from 1910 to 1937. If you're heading to Pelican Bay, pick up a copy of *Diary of a Sea Captain's Wife: Tales of Santa Cruz Island.*

From Pelican Bay, the hike heads eastward along the ocean bluffs to Prisoners Harbor. Each guide customizes the trip to his or her area of expertise, but most likely you will be shown two of Santa Cruz Island's best examples of its botanical diversity: A stand of Santa Cruz Island ironwood trees, which are actually members of the rose family and are found only on this island and Santa Rosa Island; and a grove of Santa Cruz Island pines, which are a type of bishop pine that remains from the Pleistocene epoch. Lucky hikers might spot an island fox, which is smaller than a mainland fox—about the size of a house cat. Birdwatching is also excellent. The hike is moderate in intensity; although the trail is rough and steep in places, you travel quite slowly in your group.

The trip ends at Prisoners Harbor, which was used as a penal colony for a brief time in 1830. The Mexican government had sent a shipload of convicts out to sea with livestock and farming supplies, figuring they would find somewhere else to land and live. The captain of the ship tried to take the prisoners to San Diego and Santa Barbara, but not surprisingly, they were denied permission to land. The captain decided to off-load the prisoners on Santa Cruz Island, since there was no government to refuse them there. According to legend, a fire burned all the prisoners' supplies a few months after their arrival, and many of them built rafts and floated to the mainland.

This will not be your fate. The boat concessionaire will be waiting to pick you up at Prisoners Harbor and will shuttle you back to Ventura in time for dinner.

8. POTATO HARBOR

East Santa Cruz Island, Channel Islands National Park
Ocean vistas and a potato-shaped cove

DISTANCE: 4.6 miles round-trip; 2.5 hours
ELEVATION: Start at 0 feet; total change 350 feet
BEST SEASON: Year-round

LEVEL: Easy/moderate
CROWDS: Minimal
RATING: ★ ★ ★

DIRECTIONS: Island Packers provides boat transportation to Santa Cruz Island from Ventura Harbor. Advance reservations are required. Phone Island Packers at (805) 642-7688 or (805) 642-1393 for information and reservations. Truth Aquatics at Sea Landing provides boat transportation to Santa Cruz Island from Santa Barbara Harbor. Phone Truth Aquatics at (805) 963-3564.

Only the very eastern tip of huge Santa Cruz Island belongs to the National Park Service; the other 90% of the island is owned by The Nature Conservancy. Although it's possible to visit The Nature Conservancy side of the island (see the previous story), you may only hike with a guide on their land. Those who prefer to wander on their own should visit the eastern, national park side of Santa Cruz Island.

The boat ride is short enough to make visiting eastern Santa Cruz possible as a day trip—it's less than two hours each way. But if you prefer to stay longer, the park service runs a campground in Scorpion Canyon. It is the only campground on the Channel Islands that has shade (from eucalyptus trees) and that allows wood fires. That makes it the most popular of the five islands' campgrounds.

Potato Harbor

Whether you're staying overnight or just visiting for the day, you'll have ample time to hike the easy trail to Potato Harbor. The trail starts in the campground, which is located a half mile beyond Scorpion

Anchorage, where the boat drops you off. Head back into the upper end of the campground (passing the ranch buildings and the first grouping of campsites) until you see a dirt road veering off to the right, climbing out of the canyon. Like almost all of the trails on eastern Santa Cruz Island, this trail is a wide dirt road. It is best hiked before the end of summer, when it can get excessively dry and dusty. The road climbs steeply for a half-mile, then levels. It leads nearly due west along the blufftops, paralleling the mainland coast. Far in the distance, you can see a long series of hills and canyons that eventually fade out of view in the haze, and it's easy to assume that this land is one of the neighboring Channel Islands. Not so. It's more of the immense bulk of Santa Cruz Island, the largest in the chain at 96 miles square.

At two miles out, the trail curves to the southwest, following the line of a fence at the bluff's edge. Look for a spur trail that leads toward the ocean, and follow it to the obvious overlook of Potato Harbor. The harbor is well named—it's a potato-shaped cove, lined with rugged cliffs and filled with deep, clear water. If the wind is not blowing too hard, you'll want to linger at this viewpoint. Pelicans dive into the waves, and seals swim in the brown kelp forests. With binoculars, you'll have the best seat in the house to watch the show.

9. SMUGGLER'S COVE

East Santa Cruz Island, Channel Islands National Park
A secluded beach and a shady picnic area

DISTANCE: 7.0 miles round-trip; 4 hours
ELEVATION: Start at 0 feet; total change 700 feet
BEST SEASON: Year-round

LEVEL: Moderate
CROWDS: Minimal
RATING: ★ ★ ★ ★

DIRECTIONS: Island Packers provides boat transportation to Santa Cruz Island from Ventura Harbor. Advance reservations are required. Phone Island Packers at (805) 642-7688 or (805) 642-1393 for information and reservations. Truth Aquatics at Sea Landing provides boat transportation to Santa Cruz Island from Santa Barbara Harbor. Phone Truth Aquatics at (805) 963-3564.

If you're camping on East Santa Cruz Island and have more time than the day-trippers, make sure you take the seven-mile round-trip hike to Smuggler's Cove, where you'll find a lovely, accessible beach. Two great side trips are also possible from Smuggler's Cove: A jaunt to Yellowbanks Anchorage, adding 2.5 miles to your round-trip, or a trek to San Pedro Point, adding 3.5 miles to your round-trip.

The trail begins at the junction of roads by the old ranch buildings, a few hundred yards from the boat drop-off point at Scorpion Anchorage. Turn left on the road signed for Smuggler's Cove, 3.5 miles away, and start to climb out of Scorpion Canyon. The wide dirt road curves east, then west, leading past a large grove of cypress trees on your left and numerous outcroppings of volcanic rock. The Channel Islands were formed by a variety of forces: First volcanic activity millions of years ago, then plate tectonics and the succeeding rise and fall of the sea level.

At a junction of roads, stay left (the right fork would take you a half-mile out of your way, then bring you back to this main road). The dirt road is more level now, and rolls along the ridgetop. Stay left at another junction at 1.5 miles out, and a half-mile farther look for a faint trail leading to the left across the bluffs. This is the spur trail to San Pedro Point, which you might want to visit on your return.

Start to descend rapidly now, dropping toward an eastern valley which is edged by a large airstrip. As you draw closer to the airstrip, you'll find various pieces of abandoned and rusted machinery, a strange contrast to the natural beauty of the nearby sea. Curve past the air strip and you have only three quarters of a mile remaining to reach Smuggler's Cove.

The road drops steeply down to the beach, where you find a stand of non-native eucalyptus trees that provide shade to a few picnic tables

The rocky, driftwood-covered beach at Smuggler's Cove

by the sand. The overgrown rows of olive trees you see on the hillsides above the beach and along the road are also non-native; they were planted in the 1880s by Justinian Caire, a rancher who owned this part of the island. The adobe ranch building just a few hundred feet from the beach also belonged to Caire.

At the rocky beach at Smuggler's Cove, you'll find all kinds of treasures and trash deposited by the nonstop waves. Beachcombing is highly recommended. Be careful if you go swimming; the water looks lovely, but the large, rounded rocks pummeled our ankles with every incoming wave.

Santa Cruz Island's most famous inhabitant is probably the endemic Santa Cruz Island scrub jay, a blue jay that is as loud and squawky as its mainland counterpart but about 30 percent larger and a brighter blue. The bird is found nowhere else in the world but on this island. Although rangers recommend that you hike in Scorpion Canyon for the best chance at seeing the scrub jay, we saw a pair of them making a ruckus in the eucalyptus trees at Smuggler's Cove.

Hikers who want to continue on to Yellowbanks Anchorage should follow the ranch road inland, past the ranch house. The road climbs above the ranch, heading steeply west toward the interior of the island for about a mile, then curves around and heads east again. Where the road vanishes near the edge of the ocean bluffs, follow use trails down the canyon to the beach at Yellowbanks. Make sure you carry a map with you.

10. CAVERN POINT

East Santa Cruz Island, Channel Islands National Park
A vista point rich in Chumash history

DISTANCE: 1.2 miles round-trip; 45 minutes   **LEVEL:** Easy
ELEVATION: Start at 0 feet; total change 300 feet   **CROWDS:** Minimal
BEST SEASON: Year-round   **RATING:** ★ ★

DIRECTIONS: Island Packers provides boat transportation to Santa Cruz Island from Ventura Harbor. Advance reservations are required. Phone Island Packers at (805) 642-7688 or (805) 642-1393 for information and reservations. Truth Aquatics at Sea Landing provides boat transportation to Santa Cruz Island from Santa Barbara Harbor. Phone Truth Aquatics at (805) 963-3564.

Santa Cruz Island is the largest, the tallest, and the most varied of all the Channel Islands. Its massive land area covers 62,000 acres, its highest peak is at 2,400 feet in elevation, and its terrain is a rich mix of stark bluffs, deep-cut canyons, and grassy hills.

With an island this large, with this much diversity, it's hard to know where to begin to explore. A good starting place is on the short Cavern Point Trail on the northeastern tip of Santa Cruz Island. The trail is brief and easy enough so that even the most casual day visitors can make the trip. A bonus is that from December to February, Cavern Point is an excellent spot to scan the sea for migrating grey whales.

From Scorpion Anchorage, where the boat drops you off, hike past the ranch buildings to a four-way junction of dirt roads. (The main ranch building will soon become the island's visitor center. This section of Santa Cruz Island only came into the hands of the National Park Service in 1997, so expect many changes over the next several years.) The road on the left is signed for Smuggler's Cove; straight ahead is Scorpion Canyon and the campground. Turn right instead and hike northward on the dirt road, heading uphill above the ranch area. The rock outcrops you see are volcanic in origin. The Channel Islands were originally formed by volcanic activity some 14 million years ago. Various periods of glacial activity since then have radically changed their shapes and forms; wind and waves continue to alter them.

A climb of less than a mile brings you to Cavern Point, with its straight-down drop to the sea and excellent shoreline and channel views. Look for tiny fragments of shells at your feet; these are the

Returning from grassy Cavern Point and gaining views of Anacapa Island

remains of a Chumash Indian shellmound. The Chumash lived on this island for thousands of years. They used pieces of abalone as bead money or shell money; it was the widely accepted currency until the Europeans came on the scene in the early 1800s. Pieces of chert can also be found in this shellmound; the chert is a quartz that was used as a tool for drilling holes in the abalone, so the shell money could be strung together.

On the way back downhill from Cavern Point, don't miss the fine views of Anacapa Island to the east.

11. EAST ANACAPA ISLAND TRAIL

Anacapa Island, Channel Islands National Park
An easy island adventure showcasing the giant coreopsis

DISTANCE: 2.0 miles round-trip; 1 hour   **LEVEL:** Easy
ELEVATION: Start at 0 feet; total change 200 feet   **CROWDS:** Minimal
BEST SEASON: March to May; good year-round   **RATING:** ★ ★ ★ ★ ★

DIRECTIONS: Island Packers provides boat transportation to Anacapa Island from Ventura Harbor and Oxnard (Channel Island Harbor). Advance reservations are required. Phone Island Packers at (805) 642-7688 or (805) 642-1393 for information and reservations. Truth Aquatics at Sea Landing occasionally provides boat transportation to Anacapa Island from Santa Barbara Harbor, although the boat trip is shorter from Ventura. Phone Truth Aquatics at Sea Landing at (805) 963-3564.

NOTE: An interpretive brochure is available at the Anacapa visitor center.

Of all the Channel Islands to choose from, why do more people go to Anacapa Island than any other? Because it's easy. At only 12 miles from Port Hueneme, it's the closest island to the mainland, which means that the boat ride doesn't take forever—only about an hour and a half. When you get to the island, its one hiking trail is short and easy, manageable for almost all hikers.

The adventure starts when you leave the mainland. As your boat cruises out into the Santa Barbara Channel, you're likely to be entertained by common dolphins and sea lions, and sometimes even flying fish. The dolphins and sea lions usually appear in large, boisterous groups, but the flying fish tend to show up one at a time. To see one, you have to pay close attention: The "winged" fish will often sail right over the bow of the boat, then dive into the water 150 yards away. But they move with incredible speed; the show is over in a few seconds.

View of west and middle Anacapa islets from Inspiration Point

Whales frequently make an appearance, especially gray whales and occasionally blue whales. Of the 67 kinds of whales in the world, 29 have been spotted in the Santa Barbara Channel.

Anacapa Island is actually three tiny islets, and the boat drops you off on the easternmost one. If you're feeling the slightest bit seasick, you'll quickly get over it when the boat pulls away and your first task is to climb up the 154 metal stair-steps that cling to the island's cliffs. You'll get plenty of fresh air as you make your way to the island's visitor center, where you can pick up some interpretive information.

Because Anacapa is only one mile square, it has only one trail, which makes a semi-loop around the island. It's short, sweet, and easy to follow. There are no trees or tall shrubs on the island, so you are surrounded by continual panoramic views—just ocean and neighboring islands. The open exposure is a plus, but it can also be a minus: Because of the lack of trees, Anacapa is prone to hot sun during the summer. Make sure you wear a hat and carry plenty of water.

A few red-roofed buildings are located near the visitor center. The one that looks like a church holds two huge water tanks; the others are ranger residences. Anacapa's lighthouse is perched on the eastern tip of the island; you'll hear its mournful horn. The lighthouse was constructed in 1912 in order to steer ships away from these treacherous shores. Anacapa's hiking trail goes near the lighthouse, but not too near: You are required to keep your distance from the structure because of possible hearing damage.

The trail's main highlights are two overlooks at Inspiration Point and Cathedral Cove, where you can look down on seals and sea lions on the rocks below. From Inspiration Point on the western edge of East Anacapa Island, you can gaze at the smaller West and Middle Anacapa islets, and huge Santa Cruz Island beyond them, five miles away. A few benches are in place at Inspiration Point. Where you can see over the edge of the rocky cliffs, you'll spot some of the island's 130 sea caves, which provide top-notch kayaking adventures.

Bring your binoculars: There are millions of opportunities for birdwatching, especially for brown pelicans, sea gulls, and cormorants. West Anacapa Island is closed to the public because it is a major breeding ground for gulls and pelicans. Over 3,000 pairs of western gulls nest on Anacapa each spring. (Alfred Hitchcock filmed some of the most bird-filled scenes of *The Birds* on Anacapa, even though most of the movie was made in Bodega Bay in Northern California.)

The brown pelican nesting colony on West Anacapa is the largest in the western United States: About 5,000 pelicans nest on West Anacapa for nine months of the year. On your boat trip in, the captain will usually cruise past West Anacapa so you can see the pint-size juvenile pelicans learning how to fly.

Despite the proliferation of bird life, Anacapa's chief attraction is its springtime flora. The ultimate Anacapa Island experience is to visit on a spring day when the wildflowers are in full bloom, including the spectacular giant coreopsis or "tree sunflower," which reportedly blooms so brightly that it can be seen from the mainland. The coreopsis can reach as high as six feet. The flower is common to all five islands of the national park and is also found on the mainland near Point Mugu, but it is most prolific on Anacapa.

If you don't see the coreopsis during its brief blooming period, which occurs sometime between March and May, you will most likely see it during its nine months of dormancy. When dormant, this huge flashy flower looks like a two-foot-high, lifeless tree trunk, with a bushy bird's nest on its crown.

Note that beaches on East Anacapa are not accessible, because the sea cliffs are hundreds of feet high. But on calm summer days you can swim at the landing cove. Bring your bathing suit and snorkeling gear so you can look eye-to-eye with the garibaldis and giant sea kelp.

Yes, it's true that 90 percent of all visitors to the Channel Islands choose Anacapa as the island to visit—that's approximately 25,000 people a year. But if you're concerned that the island might be too crowded; consider this: That figure is about half the number of people who visit Yosemite on any single summer day. Even though East Anacapa Island is small and its one hiking trail is short, it rates as one of the greatest day trips possible in the state of California. Don't miss it.

12. SIGNAL PEAK LOOP

Santa Barbara Island, Channel Islands National Park
The highest peak on Santa Barbara Island

DISTANCE: 3.8 miles round-trip; 2 hours   **LEVEL:** Easy/moderate
ELEVATION: Start at 0 feet; total change 650 feet   **CROWDS:** Minimal
BEST SEASON: April to October   **RATING:** ★ ★ ★ ★

DIRECTIONS: Island Packers provides boat transportation to Santa Barbara Island from Ventura Harbor. Advance reservations are required. Phone Island Packers at (805) 642-7688 or (805) 642-1393 for information and reservations.

Santa Barbara Island is the loneliest island in Channel Islands National Park. It's a speck of rock in the midst of a giant ocean, with a total land area of only one square mile. Its terrain is frequently described as "desolate," with no natural shade, no fresh water, winds too strong for anyone but the birds, and soil that is as hard as rock.

As the southernmost island in the national park, Santa Barbara Island is also geographically isolated from the other four islands that comprise the park. It is closest in latitude to San Pedro, California, whereas the other islands of the national park line up off the coast of Ventura and Santa Barbara. Santa Barbara Island's closest neighbor is developed Catalina Island, but Santa Barbara Island is 24 miles to the west of it, in the middle of the sea.

Getting to Santa Barbara Island requires a four-hour boat ride from Ventura, and the boat concessionaire runs only about a dozen trips to the island each year—much less frequently than to the other islands. Both day trips and camping trips are available. Trips are sometimes cancelled because of bad weather, strong swells, or high winds.

Similar to Anacapa Island in both its small size and barren-looking landscape, Santa Barbara Island has 5.5 miles of hiking trails, all of which are worth exploring. One of the best is the Signal Peak Trail, which makes a loop around much of the southern half of the island. The trail travels from the landing cove to Signal Peak, the highest point on the island at 634 feet. A great feature of this trail is its fine views of

Hiker on Santa Barbara Island

Sutil Island, an even smaller island that lies a quarter-mile southwest of Santa Barbara Island.

The path begins by heading inland from the landing cove. At the ranger station, you might want to take the quarter mile loop walk on the Canyon View Nature Trail to familiarize yourself with Santa Barbara Island's geology and vegetation. Then continue on the westward trail beyond the ranger station, taking the left fork to head southwest. A half-mile farther, bear left again for the start of your loop. The trail crosses through the eroded, rocky hills in the middle of the island, then turns sharply east to visit a sea lion rookery and parallel the island's southern coastline. At 1.4 miles, the trail descends to the edge of a steep canyon and turns inland briefly to curve around it. The path then climbs again for almost a mile, reaching the summit of Signal Peak at 2.5 miles. The view from the summit takes in many of the southern Channel Islands, including ones outside of the national park, like Catalina and San Clemente.

From the peak, you'll loop back through the center of the island over gently rolling grasslands. At a four-way junction, bear right, heading downhill. At the next junction, continue straight for the final half mile back to the ranger station.

Birders, take note: Santa Barbara Island is a major sea bird rookery. In addition to prolific western gulls, which have been known to pester hikers during the nesting season, two other species use this island as their nesting site: the rare Xantus' murrelet and the black storm petrel. Tiny Sutil Island, just off Santa Barbara Island's coast, belongs exclusively to the birds. Land birds are also plentiful, including warblers, finches, horned larks, owls, and hummingbirds.

If you're wondering which season is best to visit Santa Barbara Island, keep this in mind: As on Anacapa Island, the tree-like giant coreopsis blooms its bright yellow flowers here sometime between March and May. In the same season, barren-looking Santa Barbara

Island is made remarkable by its colorful display of tidy tips, goldfields, and poppies.

And don't forget your bathing suit and snorkeling gear. As on Anacapa Island, most of the beaches at Santa Barbara Island are inaccessible because of precipitous cliffs, but swimming in the landing cove is a popular activity. Your companions may include bright orange garibaldi (California's state saltwater fish), sea urchins, giant kelp, and starfish.

13. ELEPHANT SEAL COVE

Santa Barbara Island, Channel Islands National Park
Elephant seals and sea lions basking on the beach

DISTANCE: 3.2 miles round-trip; 1.5 hours   **LEVEL:** Easy/moderate
ELEVATION: Start at 0 feet; total change 450 feet   **CROWDS:** Minimal
BEST SEASON: April to October   **RATING:** ★ ★ ★ ★

DIRECTIONS: Island Packers provides boat transportation to Santa Barbara Island from Ventura Harbor. Advance reservations are required. Phone Island Packers at (805) 642-7688 or (805) 642-1393 for information and reservations.

NOTE: See the previous story for general information on Santa Barbara Island.

If you're going to hike to Elephant Seal Cove, you better study up on northern elephant seals and California sea lions before you go. Although the cove is named for the former, both types of pinnipeds are present.

First, understand the difference between sea lions and seals: Sea lions have visible ear flaps, uniform tan, gray, or brown coats, loud, barking calls, and the ability to walk on their flippers. Seals have no ear flaps, mottled grey or tan coats, and are usually seen swimming in kelp. They are more solitary creatures than sea lions.

Elephant seals are the kings of the seal family: Their gigantic size makes them impossible to mistake. The males can grow longer than 18 feet and weigh more than two tons; the females reach as long as 12 feet and weigh more than one ton. Aside from their immense size, their most elephantine characteristic is their snout. Particularly on the male elephant seal, the snout resembles a shorter version of an elephant's trunk. It is used for vocalization—to amplify their strange roars.

The California sea lion, in contrast, is a smaller pinniped. The males can be as long as nine feet and weigh 700 pounds; the females can be as long as six feet and weigh 300 pounds. They breed and pup

Elephant seals on Santa Barbara Island

their young between May and July, whereas the elephant seals breed and pup their young in December and January.

Don't forget your binoculars for this hike. Although the animals are plentiful at Elephant Seal Cove, you'll look down at them from cliffs 250 feet above. If you want a close-up look at their strangely human-like antics, you'll need your field glasses.

From the ranger station on Santa Barbara Island, head southwest through the island's interior. At a junction a half-mile out, bear right and climb gradually to a four-way junction. Go straight at this junction, heading downhill and due west to the coastal bluffs, then follow the trail as it curves northward along the bluffs. The path cuts across the peninsula of land at Webster Point, then descends steeply to the overlook at Elephant Seal Cove. You'll hear the raucous roar of the pinnipeds long before you see them. The rocky, protected beach below is the seals' and sea lions' temporary home while they haul out of the ocean to rest and breed. If you spy on the creatures for a while, you'll find that they spend their time barking, biting each other on the neck, sleeping, swimming in the surf, fighting over the best positions on the beach, and sunbathing.

Seeing the elephant seals in such great numbers in this cove is a testament to the healing power of nature. By the year 1900, less than 100 elephant seals were left in the world; the rest had been killed for their fur. Today, the animals number in the tens of thousands.

MOJAVE NATIONAL PRESERVE

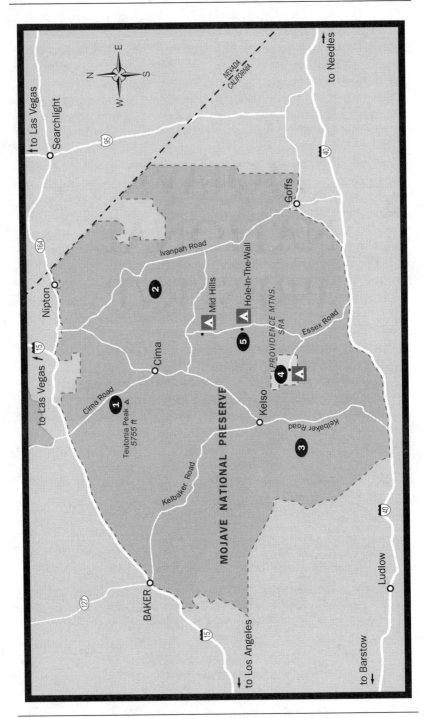

MOJAVE NATIONAL PRESERVE
TRAILS AT A GLANCE

Map Number/Trail Name	Page	Mileage	Difficulty
1. Teutonia Peak	474	4.0	Moderate
2. Caruthers Canyon	475	3.0	Easy/moderate
3. Kelso Dunes	477	3.0	Easy/moderate
4. Crystal Springs Trail	479	2.0	Moderate
5. Rings Climb & Hole-in-the-Wall to Mid Hills Trail	481	2.0-16.0	Moderate

THE TOP 3, DON'T-MISS DAY HIKES:

Map Number/Trail Name	Page	Features
1. Teutonia Peak	474	high summit views
3. Kelso Dunes	477	swirling sand dunes
5. Rings Climb & Hole-in-the-Wall to Mid Hills Trail	481	a rocky adventure

TRAIL SUGGESTIONS FOR IF YOU ONLY HAVE ONE DAY:

Map Number/Trail Name	Page	Features
3. Kelso Dunes	477	swirling sand dunes
5. Rings Climb & Hole-in-the-Wall to Mid Hills Trail	481	a rocky adventure

MOJAVE NATIONAL PRESERVE

ABOUT THE PARK

Mojave National Preserve is located where the Mojave, Great Basin, and Sonoran deserts join. As a result, it contains a wide diversity of plant and animal life, as well as interesting geological features. These include Cima Dome, a batholith which is covered with a dense forest of Joshua trees, and the volcanic rock cliffs of Hole-in-the-Wall. The soaring Kelso Dunes are another of the preserve's attractions. Because Mojave is a national preserve, not a national park, hunting and grazing are permitted within its boundaries.

ADDRESS, PHONE, & WEBSITE

Mojave National Preserve, 222 East Main Street, Suite 202, Barstow, CA 92311; (760) 255-8801.
Website: www.nps.gov/moja

VISITOR CENTERS

The main park visitor center is located at Hole-in-the-Wall Campground in the central part of the preserve. It is only open as staffing allows; phone (760) 928-2572. The Mojave National Preserve Baker Information Center is located at 72157 Baker Boulevard in Baker; it is open daily. Phone (760) 733-4040.

HOW TO GET THERE

• By air: The closest major airports are in Ontario or Las Vegas.
• By car: The preserve is located near the town of Baker, 40 miles west of Needles and 80 miles east of Barstow. It is bounded by Interstate 40 to the south and Interstate 15 to the north. From Interstate 15, the major access roads into the park are Kelbaker Road and Cima Road. From Interstate 40, the major access roads are Kelbaker Road, Essex Road, and Ivanpah Road.

DRIVE TIME

• Drive time from Los Angeles: approximately 3 hours.
• Drive time from San Francisco: approximately 10 hours.

ENTRANCE FEES

There is no entrance fee at Mojave National Preserve.

WHEN TO GO
October through May is the best season for comfortable hiking temperatures. February through May is the wildflower season, but the exact timing of the bloom varies from year to year. Call the park for an update.

WEATHER CONDITIONS
The Mojave National Preserve is located mostly in the high desert, with elevations ranging from 2,000 feet to 5,000 feet. In most of the park, daytime temperatures range from 40 to 75 degrees from October to May, and from 75 to 115 degrees from June to September. Nighttime temperatures in winter can drop below freezing. December to February is frequently windy and cold; higher elevations of the park are sometimes dusted in snow.

WHERE TO STAY
Mojave has two developed campgrounds that are available on a first-come, first-served basis: Hole-in-the-Wall and Mid-Hills. Providence Mountains State Recreation Area, located within the borders of Mojave National Preserve, also has a campground. Phone (760) 928-2586 for more information. Primitive roadside camping is permitted in Mojave National Preserve at established roadside camping areas.

There are no lodgings within the park. However, there are numerous motels in the nearby towns of Baker and Needles. The town of Barstow, 80 miles from the preserve, has a wider selection of accommodations. For something different from an average motel, try the Hotel Nipton in the small hamlet of Nipton on Interstate 15 north of the preserve. The Hotel Nipton is loaded with desert charm but has only four rooms; phone (760) 856-2335 to reserve.

FOOD & SUPPLIES
No supplies are available within the park. The closest stores and restaurants are in Baker on Interstate 15, at the park's northern border. Barstow, 80 miles west of the preserve, offers a wider selection.

SUGGESTED MAPS
Park maps are available at the Hole-in-the-Wall Visitor Center or by contacting Mojave National Preserve at the address on page 472. A more detailed map is available for a fee from Tom Harrison Cartography at (415) 456-7940.

1. TEUTONIA PEAK

Mojave National Preserve
A high-desert high summit

DISTANCE: 4.0 miles round-trip; 2 hours   **LEVEL:** Moderate
ELEVATION: Start at 5,018 feet; total change 750 feet   **CROWDS:** Minimal
BEST SEASON: November to May   **RATING:** ★ ★ ★ ★

DIRECTIONS: From Baker, drive east on Interstate 15 for 25 miles to the Cima Road exit. Turn right (south) on Cima Road and drive 11 miles to the sign for the Teutonia Peak trailhead, on the right side of the road.

Cima Dome is a summit for geometry and geology enthusiasts. The granite dome's big claim to fame is that it's the most symmetrical dome of its type in the country. And what type is that? Glad you asked. It's a batholith—a molten mass of igneous rock that stopped in its rising far below the surface of the earth, then cooled and hardened. Millions of years of erosion eventually exposed the batholith.

The dome sits 1,500 feet above the surrounding landscape, and it's almost 70 miles square. It's so big that when you're on it, it's almost impossible to understand that you're on it. It looks like you're standing on a broad, flat plain—the same as much of the desert.

In contrast, the summit of Cima Dome is Teutonia Peak, at elevation 5,767 feet. When you're on top of narrow, pointed Teutonia Peak, you know it for sure—the wind blows hard and the desert vistas are head-swiveling.

You can hike to Teutonia Peak via a four-mile round-trip trail, one of the best and most interesting hikes in Mojave National Preserve. The first mile of walking is level and pleasant, leading through pinyon pines, cholla cactus, and grazing lands. (Because Mojave is a national preserve, not a national park, grazing is permitted within its borders.) As you hike on the broad, flat surface of the dome, you clearly see your destination, Teutonia Peak, as well as the rugged-looking New York Mountains and Ivanpah Mountains in the distance. Although the dome was once covered with volcanic debris, it is now covered with Joshua trees, some as tall as 25 feet and as old as 400 years. (They're a different variety of Joshua tree from the kind found in Joshua Tree National Park.) There is so much vegetation on Cima Dome that it feels vastly unlike the western side of Mojave National Preserve. At times, it's hard to believe this is still the same park.

The Joshua forest is inviting to animals and birds, too. The yellow bird you may see is the Scott's oriole, which makes its nest in the

Joshua's foliage. Ladder-backed woodpeckers can also be spotted, usually boring holes in dead pinyon pines and Joshua trees.

After passing through a couple of cattle gates (watch out for cow patties), the trail gets progressively steeper, but it's only in the last half-mile that you really do some climbing. At 1.9 miles, you reach a saddle just shy of Teutonia's summit, where you have panoramic desert views. The wind can blow hard up here, so you may want to take shelter among the many rock outcroppings.

If you choose, you can scramble the last short

Summit view from Teutonia Peak

stretch to the boulder-covered summit, or just stay at the saddle and enjoy the vistas. For the geology-minded, the rocks all around you are quartz monzonite—the same type as many of the rocks in Joshua Tree National Park.

As you gaze around at the surrounding flatlands, try to keep it straight: You're overlooking massive Cima Dome. But because it's so large and you never see its edges, you'd just never know it.

2. CARUTHERS CANYON

Mojave National Preserve
An old gold mine in a pinyon pine woodland

DISTANCE: 3.0 miles round-trip; 1.5 hours   **LEVEL:** Easy/moderate
ELEVATION: Start at 5,600 feet; total change 400 feet   **CROWDS:** Moderate
BEST SEASON: November to May   **RATING:** ★ ★ ★

DIRECTIONS: From Barstow, take Interstate 40 east for approximately 100 miles to the Mountain Springs Road exit. (It's about 13 miles east of the exit for Essex and Providence Mountains State Recreation Area, and 25 miles west of Needles.) Drive north on Mountain Springs Road for six miles to the small town of Goffs. Turn left at the junction with Goffs Road, then turn right immediately onto Lanfair Road. Continue north on Lanfair Road for about 24 miles; it will change names to Ivanpah Road. When you reach the OX Ranch, turn left on New York Mountains Road. Drive 5.8 miles on New York Mountains Road, then turn right on an unsigned road leading north into Caruthers Canyon. Continue straight for about 1.8 miles, then where the road becomes impassable, park your car and start walking into the wash, passing several campsites.

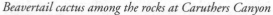

Has the eastern Mojave gotten too hot for you? Are you yearning for greener pastures, maybe even a flowing stream? Take a drive out to Caruthers Canyon in the New York Mountains, where a pinyon pine and juniper woodland awaits the desert-weary hiker, and fascinating rock formations and an old gold mine will fire the imagination.

The trail into Caruthers Canyon is the continuation of the road you drove in on, leading past some makeshift campsites. As you hike, stay on the main road and avoid all the spurs that lead to various camping areas. At a major fork at two-tenths of a mile, bear left—just keep heading into the canyon.

The farther you go, the more rocky the scenery gets. Think Joshua Tree National Park. Think boulders and rock formations in strange shapes, piled one on top of another. Think rounded pinnacles, spires, and odd-looking outcrops. That's what you'll see in Caruthers Canyon,

Beavertail cactus among the rocks at Caruthers Canyon

mixed in with small oak trees, pinyon pines, manzanita, ceanothus, and yerba santa. Many of these plants are members of the coastal scrub family; you would expect to see them in San Diego or Santa Barbara. Caruthers Canyon is an unusual place, an isolated community of vegetation in stark contrast to the drier, more barren desert around it. The rocky canyon has a high enough elevation, and just enough water running through it, to allow this lush vegetation to thrive.

At three-quarters of a mile, you'll cross a wash that flows with water almost every winter and spring. If you are fortunate enough to visit then, you'll have a good chance at seeing many kinds of birds (western tanagers, red-tailed hawks, gray-headed juncos, or humming-birds), and also possibly some wildlife.

The trail undulates in and out of the wash, crossing and recrossing it and meandering around odd-shaped boulders until it ends high in the canyon at the remains of the Giant Ledge Mine. The mine ruins aren't much to look at. Where prospectors once searched for gold, you'll find a rickety wooden ore chute, a few mine shafts, and piles of ore tailings. Don't be tempted to explore inside the shafts; the list of possible dangers is long. The mine operated from the 1860s to the 1920s with a modicum of success. The beauty of this canyon, on the other hand, has had a much longer and more successful run.

3. KELSO DUNES

Mojave National Preserve
A scramble to the top of 500-foot sand dunes

DISTANCE: 3.0 miles round-trip; 1.5 hours   **LEVEL:** Easy/moderate
ELEVATION: Start at 2,500 feet; total change 500 feet   **CROWDS:** Moderate
BEST SEASON: November to May   **RATING:** ★ ★ ★ ★

DIRECTIONS: From Interstate 15 at Baker, turn south on Kelbaker Road and drive 42 miles, past Kelso, to the signed road on the right for Kelso Dunes. Turn right (west) and drive three miles to the dunes parking area. (Coming from the south on Interstate 40, take the Kelso/Amboy exit and drive 14 miles north on Kelbaker Road to the signed road on the left for Kelso Dunes.)

What's the most popular place in Mojave National Preserve to watch the sun set? Unquestionably, it's Kelso Dunes.

Kelso Dunes are the second highest sand dunes in California, and probably the most frequently visited of the tall desert dunes. (Eureka Dunes in Death Valley National Park are the tallest dunes, but they require an arduous drive; see the story on page 402.) The entire Kelso

Dunes complex is 50 miles square, and the dunes reach a height of 500 feet.

When you park your car at the Kelso Dunes trailhead, you'll see the dunes clearly before you. But before you start hiking to them, read the posted interpretive signs. You'll learn all about these wind-shaped land forms and how they were created from the sands of the Mojave River. Start hiking on the old jeep road that leads a short distance from the parking area toward the dunes. When it diminishes, just set out any which way toward the closest dune. (Constantly shifting sand makes a formal trail impossible.)

Kelso Dunes exhibit a wide variety of plant life. More than 100 different plants live here, including grasses, shrubs, and wildflowers. In a wet spring, desert wildflowers paint the dunes with color. Sand verbenas and desert primrose are the major springtime bloomers. You'll see creosote bush, dune grass, burrowbush, sand mat, and galleta grass year-round.

The dunes themselves are gold in color, which you can plainly see from the parking area. From close up, you see they also show traces of pink and black, and they appear more pink by the glow of the setting sun. The sand grains that cause the dunes' colors include rose quartz, feldspar, and black magnetite.

If you climb high enough in the dunes, you are rewarded with views of surrounding desert peaks, including the Granite and Providence mountains. You're also rewarded with the thrill of running, tumbling, or leaping back downhill through the soft sand. (Plan on one hour to reach the top of the highest dune, and 10 minutes to come back down.)

Most people don't bother to go all the way to the top of the highest dune, though. They just plop themselves down somewhere in the endless waves of sand and make sand angels, or roll around on the dunes' silky surface. Another popular activity is causing miniature sand avalanches with your feet, which will sometimes result in a harmonic booming sound. Most geologists agree that the strange dune sound is caused by the extreme dryness of the East Mojave air, combined with the movement of the wind-polished, ultra-smooth sand grains.

Similar to the dune complexes in Death Valley, Kelso Dunes is best visited early in the morning or close to sunset, because of the incredible show of color and light at the edges of the day. If you hike on the dunes in the early morning, you'll have a good chance of seeing tiny animal tracks in the dunes. The most commonly spotted tracks are those of kangaroo rats and kit foxes.

4. CRYSTAL SPRINGS TRAIL

Providence Mountains State Recreation Area
A mountain spring and sweeping vistas

DISTANCE: 2.0 miles round-trip; 1 hour

ELEVATION: Start at 4,300 feet; total change 600 feet

BEST SEASON: November to May

LEVEL: Moderate

CROWDS: Minimal

RATING: ★ ★ ★

DIRECTIONS: From Barstow, take Interstate 40 east for approximately 90 miles to the exit for Essex Road, Mitchell Caverns, and Providence Mountains State Recreation Area (near the town of Essex). Turn north on Essex Road and drive 15.5 miles to the Providence Mountains visitor center.

NOTE: A $5 state park day-use fee is charged per vehicle. A park map is available for $1 at the visitor center. For more information about touring Mitchell Caverns, contact Providence Mountains State Recreation Area, P.O. Box 1, Essex, CA 92332; (760) 928-2586 or (805) 942-0662. (An additional fee is charged for the cavern tour.)

It doesn't matter how big you are, it's what's inside that counts. That was the moral of our walking tour of Mitchell Caverns in Providence Mountains State Recreation Area.

Mitchell Caverns is the feature attraction at Providence Mountains, a state-run subdivision of Mojave National Preserve. The limestone cavern is one of the smallest in the United States that is open to the public on a commercial basis. For its size, it boasts an extra large helping of rare and unique cavern features.

We didn't know anything about caverns before we visited, but after a few minutes on the walking tour we were identifying stalagmites, stalactites, helictites, draperies, cavern coral, and flowstone, or at least admiring them when our guide pointed them out. In every chamber of Mitchell Caverns, our park ranger tour guide was telling us something like: "Such-and-such a formation is so rare, and so unique, that it's one of only two such formations in all of the United States' 10,000 limestone caverns." (Cavern people take their statistics seriously, we learned.)

If you've made the long drive all the way out to Providence Mountains State Recreation Area—a major haul from almost everywhere—you should plan to spend the day, or camp overnight in the campground, and do more than just tour spectacular Mitchell Caverns. The tour itself involves a 1.5-mile walk, but the park also has an excellent two-mile trail to Crystal Springs, which can easily fill the time before or after your allotted cavern tour.

Entering Mitchell Caverns

It's a short uphill trek on the Crystal Springs Trail, which leads from the park visitor center to a spectacular rocky overlook in the Providence Mountains. Along the way, you'll see a wide variety of high desert flora, including more types of cactus than you can shake a stick at. Remember, this is the high desert at 4,300 feet in elevation, so the climate is not as inhospitable to plant and animal life as it is in Death Valley or other low-desert areas. The terrain seems almost lush; we were amazed at the wide variety of plants, including barrel cactus, chollas, mormon tea, creosote, cliff rose, catclaw, and blue sage.

The hike is surprisingly steep and feels unusually remote for a state park trail. Rocky outcrops shoot up from both sides of the pathway. You walk among pinyon pines, junipers, and trailside cacti that may attempt to reach out and grab you. Just watch where you put your hands and feet, and you'll be fine. Better yet, wear pants instead of shorts on this hike.

The trail leads up Crystal Canyon, where bighorn sheep are sometimes seen by lucky hikers. Every once in a blue moon, someone spots a wild burro high up on the canyon walls, but they are even more elusive than the bighorns.

The trail ends without fanfare near Crystal Springs, but we scrambled off-trail a few feet to a jumble of boulders where we could sit in the sun and admire the lovely view of the Marble Mountains and Clipper Valley. On a clear day, you can see all the way to Arizona.

5. RINGS CLIMB &
HOLE-IN-THE-WALL to MID HILLS TRAIL

Mojave National Preserve
A vertical descent into Banshee Canyon

DISTANCE: 2.0 to 16.0 miles round-trip; 1 to 8 hours **LEVEL:** Moderate
ELEVATION: Start at 4,260 feet; total change 200 feet **CROWDS:** Moderate
BEST SEASON: November to May **RATING:** ★ ★ ★ ★

DIRECTIONS: From Barstow, take Interstate 40 east for approximately 90 miles to the exit for Essex Road, Mitchell Caverns, and Providence Mountains State Recreation Area (near the town of Essex). Turn north on Essex Road and drive about 10 miles to the fork in the road for Providence Mountains. Bear right at the fork (now on Black Canyon Road) and drive eight miles north to the Hole-in-the-Wall Campground turnoff. Turn left at the sign for the visitor center and follow the dirt road past the visitor center to the picnic area.

The start of this hike is just plain fun, and what follows is pretty good, too. The adventure begins at Hole-in-the-Wall Campground, one of the two developed campgrounds in Mojave National Preserve. Head over to the adjoining picnic area, where the trailhead is located. When you see the hole-pocked maze of cliffs there, you'll understand where the camp got its name.

The story of the fascinating rock cliffs at Hole-in-the-Wall is a tale of volcanism. About 15 million years ago, volcanic eruptions coated this area with lava, ash, and rocky debris. Gases captured during the eruption were trapped in the rock, and as they cooled unevenly, they created holes. The action of wind and rain over millions of years enlarged these holes in the rock, creating the formations and caverns that exist today. The extraordinary color of the formations (a mix of red and maroon on grey) is the result of iron compounds slowly rusting.

Your mission on this trip is to explore Hole-in-the-Wall's odd-shaped rock formations, then hike beyond them on the trail that runs between Hole-in-the-Wall and Mid Hills campgrounds. How far you go on that trail is up to you. The entire distance is eight miles, which would make a marathon 16-mile round-trip. Some hikers arrange a car shuttle between the two ends of the trail—a fine solution if you can manage it. Otherwise, just hike out and back for a few miles.

At the picnic area, locate the trail sign for the Rings Climb and Overlook. The overlook is to the left; go there first and peer down into the rocky abyss into which you'll descend. Then backtrack and follow the signed Rings Trail for a few hundred feet to the Rings Climb.

The cliffs at Hole in the Wall

You can leave your ropes and carabiners at home for the Rings Climb. Although it may be too difficult for very inflexible or overweight hikers, most people pass easily through the vertical rock chute. Here's how it works: At a particularly narrow rock passage, the park service has drilled large iron hooks connected to circular rings into the cliff face. You put your hands and feet through the rings, one at a time, and make your way up or down the rock. Most people find that the upward direction is easier, because you can clearly see where you're going. Your first passage will be downward, however, as you descend into Banshee Canyon, 200 feet below.

At the bottom of the Rings Climb, the fun continues. Now you wander through a cathedral-like wonderland of hole-pocked rock cliffs. If you're into photography, this place will slow you down, because you'll be spinning around and shooting everything in sight.

After completing your exploration of Hole-in-the-Wall, the next part of the trip is a "real" hike. A footpath leaves the rocky cliffs and connects to the trail between Hole-in-the-Wall and Mid Hills campgrounds. This eight-mile-long trail is open to hikers and equestrians. It's a highly scenic route through classic Mojave Desert scenery, passing by volcanic formations, tabletop mesas, and dense fields of sagebrush. Desert varnish polishes the boulders and cliffs. Occasional pinyon pines and yucca make an appearance. You'll spot Mormon tea, cliff rose, blue sage, and desert primrose; in springtime, you may see them in bloom.

The trail provides ample desert beauty, but no shade or water, so make sure you carry plenty of it. The path eventually starts to climb, gaining a total of 1,400 feet by the time it reaches Mid Hills Campground, eight miles distant. (Hikers who arrange a car shuttle so they can hike the trail one-way often start at Mid Hills and end at Hole-in-the-Wall, resulting in a downhill trip.)

JOSHUA TREE NATIONAL PARK

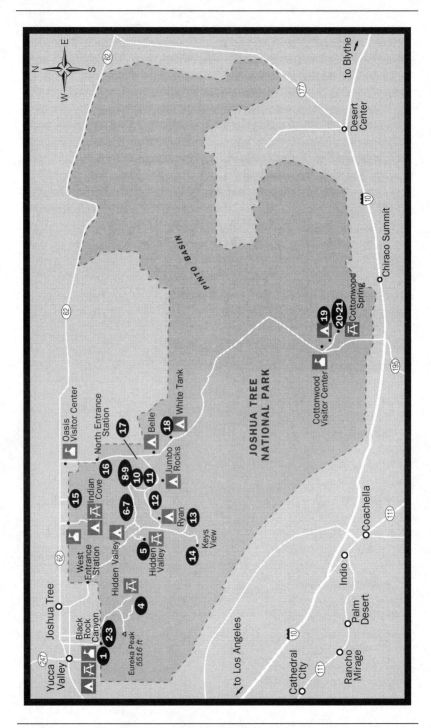

JOSHUA TREE NATIONAL PARK
TRAILS AT A GLANCE

Map Number/Trail Name	Page	Mileage	Difficulty
1. High View Nature Trail	488	1.3	Easy
2. Warren Peak	489	5.6	Moderate
3. Eureka Peak	490	10.5	Moderate
4. Tallest Joshua Tree	492	0.4	Easy
5. Hidden Valley	494	1.0	Easy
6. Barker Dam Loop	495	1.2	Easy
7. Wall Street Mill	497	1.5	Easy
8. Desert Queen Mine	498	1.2	Easy
9. Pine City	500	3.0	Easy
10. Lucky Boy Vista	501	2.5	Easy
11. Skull Rock Nature Trail	502	1.7	Easy
12. Ryan Mountain	504	3.0	Easy/moderate
13. Lost Horse Mine	505	4.0	Easy/moderate
14. Keys View & Inspiration Peak	507	1.5	Easy/moderate
15. Fortynine Palms Oasis	509	3.0	Easy
16. Contact Mine	511	3.4	Moderate
17. Pinto Wye Arrastra	512	1.5	Moderate
18. Arch Rock Nature Trail	514	0.3	Easy
19. Cottonwood Spring Nature Trail	516	1.0	Easy
20. Mastodon Peak	517	2.8	Easy
21. Lost Palms Oasis	519	7.4	Moderate

THE TOP 5, DON'T-MISS DAY HIKES:

Map Number/Trail Name	Page	Features
3. Eureka Peak	490	summit views
7. Wall Street Mill	497	mining history
12. Ryan Mountain	504	summit views
20. Mastodon Peak	517	summit, mining history
21. Lost Palms Oasis	519	largest palm oasis

TRAIL SUGGESTIONS FOR IF YOU ONLY HAVE ONE DAY:

Map Number/Trail Name	Page	Features
5. Hidden Valley	494	rocky hideout
7. Wall Street Mill	497	mining history
12. Ryan Mountain	504	summit views
14. Keys View & Inspiration Peak	507	summit views

JOSHUA TREE NATIONAL PARK

ABOUT THE PARK

Rugged mountains, wide desert plains covered with strange looking Joshua trees, amazing rock formations and boulder piles, the ruins of gold mining sites—all of these can be found at Joshua Tree National Park. The park is situated where the high Mojave Desert meets the low Colorado Desert, producing a wide variety of desert flora and fascinating geological features.

ADDRESS, PHONE, & WEBSITE

Joshua Tree National Park, 74485 National Park Drive, Twentynine Palms, CA 92277; (760) 367-5500.
Website: www.nps.gov/jotr

VISITOR CENTERS

The main information center in the park is the Oasis Visitor Center, located on National Park Drive, just off Highway 62 in the town of Twentynine Palms. It's on the way to the North Entrance Station. A much smaller visitor center is located at Cottonwood Spring in the south part of the park.

HOW TO GET THERE

- By air: The closest major airports are in Ontario, Palm Springs, or San Diego.
- By car: The park is located 150 miles east of Los Angeles via Interstate 10. Exit off Interstate 10 near Palm Springs on to Highway 62 East. Drive east on Highway 62 for 30 miles to the town of Joshua Tree and the west entrance to the park, or for 40 miles to the town of Twentynine Palms and the north entrance to the park. To reach the park's south entrance at Cottonwood Spring, take Interstate 10 for 25 miles east of Indio.

DRIVE TIME

- Drive time from Los Angeles: approximately 2.5 hours.
- Drive time from San Francisco: approximately 9 hours.

ENTRANCE FEES

There is a $10 entrance fee per vehicle at Joshua Tree National Park, good for seven days. A Joshua Tree annual pass is available for $25. A Golden Eagle Passport, an annual pass for all 375 national park units, is available for $50. A Golden Age Passport, a lifetime pass for all 375 national park units, is available to U.S. citizens and residents aged 62 and over for a one-time $10 fee. You can purchase these passes at the park entrance stations.

WHEN TO GO

October through May is the best season for comfortable hiking temperatures. February through May is the wildflower season, but the exact timing of the bloom varies from year to year. Call the park for an update.

WEATHER CONDITIONS

Much of Joshua Tree is located in the high desert, with elevations ranging from 3,200 feet to 4,500 feet. Daytime temperatures range from 50 to 85 degrees from October to May. Summer daytime temperatures are frequently well above 100 degrees. On winter nights, temperatures can drop below freezing. Occasionally it snows at higher elevations in the park.

WHERE TO STAY

Joshua Tree has a total of nine campgrounds, eight for families and one for large groups. Six campgrounds are available on a first-come, first-served basis: Belle, Cottonwood, Hidden Valley, Jumbo Rocks, Ryan, and White Tank. Three campgrounds are available by advance reservation: Black Rock, Indian Cove, and Sheep Pass Group Camp. Phone (800) 365-2267 to reserve. Campgrounds are open year-round.

There are no lodgings within the park, but there are numerous motels in the nearby towns of Twentynine Palms, Yucca Valley, and Joshua Tree. For accommodation information, contact these towns' chambers of commerce: Twentynine Palms at (760) 367-3445, Yucca Valley at (760) 365-6323, and Joshua Tree at (760) 366-3723.

FOOD & SUPPLIES

Restaurants and stores are plentiful in the towns just north of the park: Joshua Tree, Yucca Valley, and Twentynine Palms.

SUGGESTED MAPS

Park maps are available at park entrance stations or by contacting Joshua Tree National Park at the address on page 486. A more detailed map is available for a fee from Tom Harrison Cartography at (415) 456-7940 or Trails Illustrated at (800) 962-1643.

1. HIGH VIEW NATURE TRAIL

Black Rock Canyon area, Joshua Tree National Park
Easy loop trail with desert and mountain views

DISTANCE: 1.3 miles round-trip; 1 hour   **LEVEL:** Easy
ELEVATION: Start at 4,100 feet; total change 350 feet   **CROWDS:** Minimal
BEST SEASON: October to April   **RATING:** ★ ★ ★

DIRECTIONS: From Highway 62 in Yucca Valley, turn south on Joshua Lane (signed for Black Rock Canyon) and drive five miles to the entrance to Black Rock Canyon Campground. Just before the camp entrance, turn right on a dirt road signed for South Park Parking Area, and follow it for three-quarters of a mile to its end at the trailhead. The parking area is just outside of the national park boundary, but the trail is inside the park. If you are camping at Black Rock Canyon, the trail can also be accessed from the campground, via a half-mile spur trail that begins just west of the ranger station.

NOTE: An interpretive brochure is available from the Black Rock Canyon ranger station.

You're unlikely to have much company on the High View Nature Trail, which, along with its fine vistas and easy grade, is one of its best selling points. The trail is a loop that begins and ends from the South Park parking area near Black Rock Canyon Campground. If you pick up an interpretive brochure at the Black Rock Canyon Ranger Station (you'll pass it as you drive in), you can get a brief education on desert plants and animals as you walk.

The trail undulates, climbing a total of only 350 feet, over a hillside dotted with yuccas, Joshua trees, pinyon pines. If you tire out, a few benches are placed at intervals the trail. You'll notice outcrops of a distinctive rock; it's striped or banded Pinto gneiss, the oldest exposed rock in the park. It was formed 1.5 billion years ago.

The trail tops out at a high point on the hill with a lovely view of Mount San Gorgonio, Southern California's tallest mountain at 11,499 feet. In winter, San Gorgonio and its immediate neighbors in the San Bernardino Mountains often glisten with bright white snow, in stark contrast to the deep blue desert sky. You also have a less inspiring view to the north of the sprawling desert towns of Yucca Valley and Joshua Tree. Because of its easily accessible views, this trail is perfect for a clear winter morning's hike. A bench marks the trail's high point, and there is a register where you can record your comments.

The side of the loop heading back downhill is longer and flatter than the way up. It drops down the hillside, then travels through a

Coyote near Black Rock Campground

sandy wash back to the trailhead. From the parking lot, you have the option of adding on a short loop hike to South Park Peak, which is located just outside of the national park. The South Park Peak Trail begins on the opposite side of the parking lot. It is less than a mile on an easy, dirt trail with only a 250-foot elevation gain to the summit of South Park Peak. The peak offers an even better view than the High View Nature Trail.

2. WARREN PEAK

Black Rock Canyon area, Joshua Tree National Park
Seldom-visited peak in the northwest corner of the park

DISTANCE: 5.6 miles round-trip; 3 hours   **LEVEL:** Moderate
ELEVATION: Start at 4,000 feet; total change 1,100 feet   **CROWDS:** Minimal
BEST SEASON: October to April   **RATING:** ★ ★ ★ ★

DIRECTIONS: From Highway 62 in Yucca Valley, turn south on Joshua Lane (signed for Black Rock Canyon) and drive five miles to the Black Rock Ranger Station. Park at the ranger station, then walk uphill to the Black Rock Canyon trailhead at the upper end of the campground.

If you seek a less tame adventure than what you get on many short trails in Joshua Tree National Park, the trip to Warren Peak might suit you well. Located in the far northwest corner of the park, the trail and its 5,103-foot summit destination feel surprisingly remote. The peak provides a terrific view of Southern California's tallest mountains, which are usually crowned with a mantle of snow in winter and early spring, plus the Coachella and Morongo desert valleys.

Make sure you begin hiking on the Black Rock Canyon Trail from the upper end of Black Rock Canyon Campground, not on the nearby California Riding and Hiking Trail. The Black Rock Canyon Trail leads past a water tank, then travels through a desert wash with plenty of Joshua trees, pinyon pines, and cholla cactus to keep you company. The sandy floor makes the travel a little slow.

Keep your eyes on the trail signs (they are marked as "WP" for Warren Peak), which will funnel you into the correct forks in the wash. (There are two critical forks, one slightly before the two-mile point and one a half-mile farther. At both forks, bear right.) The sandy wash narrows to a walled canyon, then broadens again. As you climb gently but steadily, you see junipers, oaks, and pinyon pines replacing some of the lower desert flora.

At 2.5 miles from the trailhead, you spy Warren Peak's pointy summit rock ahead and to the right. The trail gets a bit hard to discern in places as the wash disappears, but watch for trail ducks and keep your eye on Warren Peak. The last quarter-mile is steep and requires some rock scrambling, but it can be accomplished easily enough. The best route is to head up the peak's right (northeast) side.

If it's not too windy, you'll want to linger on the tiny surface area of Warren Peak for a while, and not just so you can read the summit register. Unobstructed views of Mount San Gorgonio, Mount San Jacinto, San Gorgonio Pass, and the Mojave Desert will make your heart pound. To the southwest are Palm Springs and the Morongo and Coachella valleys. Far to the southeast is the giant Salton Sea, shining like a mirror in the desert sunlight.

3. EUREKA PEAK

Black Rock Canyon area, Joshua Tree National Park
Highest western summit in Joshua Tree

DISTANCE: 10.5 miles round-trip; 5 hours **LEVEL:** Moderate
ELEVATION: Start at 4,000 feet; total change 1,500 feet **CROWDS:** Minimal
BEST SEASON: October to April **RATING:** ★ ★ ★ ★

DIRECTIONS: From Highway 62 in Yucca Valley, turn south on Joshua Lane (signed for Black Rock Canyon) and drive five miles to the Black Rock Ranger Station. Park at the ranger station, then walk uphill to the California Riding and Hiking Trail trailhead on the east (left) side of the campground entrance.

The total elevation gain to reach the summit of Eureka Peak is only 1,500 feet, but it feels like more. The problem is sand and rocks—lots of them—and the fact that the trail is a bit tricky to discern in places. However, if you're willing to put in some effort, your reward is a commanding view of the western edge of Joshua Tree National Park and the Coachella Valley, plus the towering peaks of Mount San Jacinto and Mount San Gorgonio.

Begin to hike from Black Rock Canyon Campground on the California Riding and Hiking Trail, which you'll follow for two miles through a Joshua tree forest. This is a good section of trail and easy to follow; just watch for the brown posts marked as "CRH." At the two-mile point, the trail enters a major wash. The wash forks and so does the trail: The California Riding and Hiking Trail goes left (east); you head right (south). This is where you must start paying attention; look for trail markers signed as "EP" (for Eureka Peak) to keep you on track. The signs are intermittent but strategically placed.

Travel up the second wash and in a third of a mile, take the right fork. (Basically, you follow the main wash.) Hike through this wash for 1.7 miles to its end, four miles from the trailhead. A trail marker directs you up a ridge. Climb a narrow path up a ravine for nearly a mile to the crest of Eureka Peak's summit ridge. You have one more junction: Turn left and walk the last 100 yards to the summit.

Eureka Peak at 5,518 feet in elevation offers the commanding view you'd expect from its dramatic perch above the desert floor. The

Eureka Peak's summit view

vista is similar to what you get at nearby Keys View, but with a more northerly perspective: Mount San Gorgonio appears closer and larger, Palm Springs and its neighboring windmills are right below you, and the Salton Sea is a distant shimmer far to the southeast. Mount San Jacinto, slightly to the south, appears like a monolith in comparison to the low desert of the Coachella Valley and Palm Springs.

What's the only downer on this trip? That last junction you passed connected with a short trail to the Eureka Peak parking area. You guessed it; some people drove to this peak instead of hiking to it. (To find out how, see the following story on the park's tallest Joshua tree.)

Of course, you may not consider the road to be a negative: On the one hand, it gives you an option for a five-mile one-way shuttle hike, if you and your hiking partner have two cars or if someone is willing to pick you up. It also gives you an option for a loop hike, instead of an out-and-back trip. Just follow the road from the parking area downhill for a half mile until it intersects with the California Riding and Hiking Trail. Turn left and follow the California Riding and Hiking Trail all the way back to Black Rock Canyon Campground. Making this loop adds less than a mile to your round-trip distance.

---

4. TALLEST JOSHUA TREE

Covington Flat area, Joshua Tree National Park
A giant among Joshuas

DISTANCE: 0.4 mile round-trip; 20 minutes   **LEVEL:** Easy
ELEVATION: Start at 4,600 feet; total change 0 feet   **CROWDS:** Moderate
BEST SEASON: October to April   **RATING:** ★ ★ ★

DIRECTIONS: From Highway 62 in Yucca Valley, turn south on La Contenta Road and drive one mile to where the pavement ends at an intersection with Yucca Trail. Cross Yucca Trail and continue straight ahead on a dirt road. At 1.7 miles on the dirt road, turn left. Continue 5.9 miles, passing the park boundary sign, to a junction. Turn right here, drive 1.8 miles, then turn left. Drive 1.8 miles farther to the backcountry trailhead at Upper Covington Flat. Take the trail on the right, which heads south.

If you want to see the tallest Joshua tree in Joshua Tree National Park, you have to take a long drive on dirt roads from Yucca Valley. This area of the park is not connected to other park roads; it's a long-way-in, long-way-out kind of deal. But a bonus is that you can lump together this trip with a drive to the nearby summit of Eureka Peak, where you get all the pleasures of mountaintop views without actually hiking a mountain. Together with the promise of seeing a 40-foot-tall Joshua tree, this should be enough to inspire you to visit.

Start your trip at the trailhead at Upper Covington Flat. Take the California Riding and Hiking Trail to the south (another section of the trail leads north from the same parking lot). Right away, you'll notice that the Joshua trees in this area are unusually large in size. You may wonder how you will pick out the largest of them. Here's how: About 250 yards from the parking lot (two-tenths of a mile), you'll reach a small backcountry signboard with rules and regulations for backpackers. Just a few feet farther, on the right, is the granddaddy Joshua tree, which is estimated to be more than 900 years old. It's only a few feet off the trail, but notice the use trail that leads through the sandy soil to its base. So many people have walked over to examine the tree and have their picture taken with it, that a path has been beaten down.

Continue to hike, if you like, and enjoy the immense desert plain of proportionately immense Joshua trees. Or turn around here and head back to your car for the second part of this excursion: A trip to Eureka Peak's summit.

Drive back over the last 1.8-mile stretch to Upper Covington Flat. When you reach a junction, turn left (right would take you back to Highway 62 in Yucca Valley.) Drive 1.1 miles to where the road ends near Eureka Peak, then get out of your car and walk the last few hundred yards to the summit. Halfway there, you'll see a trail coming in on your left; this is the trail that hikers use to reach Eureka Peak from Black Rock Campground (see the previous story).

A lonely Joshua tree marks the 5,518-foot summit of Eureka Peak. The view on a clear winter day is remarkable: Snow-capped Mount San Gorgonio and Mount San Jacinto soar to

The tallest Joshua tree in the national park

the west, the spinning windmills of Palm Springs' wind farm are directly below you, and the Salton Sea shines like a desert mirage far to the south.

5. HIDDEN VALLEY

Park Boulevard area, Joshua Tree National Park
The secret rocky hideout of cattle rustlers

DISTANCE: 1.0 mile round-trip; 30 minutes   **LEVEL:** Easy
ELEVATION: Start at 4,200 feet; total change 50 feet   **CROWDS:** Moderate
BEST SEASON: October to April   **RATING:** ★ ★ ★

DIRECTIONS: From Highway 62 in the town of Joshua Tree, turn south on Park Boulevard. Drive 14.1 miles to the right turnoff for the Hidden Valley Nature Trail and Picnic Area, located just before Hidden Valley Campground. Turn right and drive a quarter-mile to the trailhead parking area.

Now here's a trail that will spark the imagination of eight-year-olds and 80-year-olds alike: the Hidden Valley Trail, an easy one-mile loop right off Park Boulevard.

According to legend, Hidden Valley was the home of 1880s cattle rustlers who stole cattle and horses from New Mexico and Arizona, pastured them for a few months among Hidden Valley's fortress-like rocks, then re-branded them and sold them as their own. At the turn of the century, this area received more than 10 inches of rain per year, making it more hospitable for grazing than it would be today. When you walk the trail and see the corral-like structure of rock-enclosed Hidden Valley, the cattle rustling legend seems entirely plausible.

Hidden Valley's most famous occupants were Bill and Jim McHaney, two brothers who made their living first in cattle and horses and later in gold prospecting. By 1894 the brothers had made quite a reputation for themselves as cattle ranchers (and perhaps rustlers), but they tired of the business and turned to gold mining. They were even more successful in that endeavor: Their Desert Queen Mine produced upwards of two million dollars of gold.

Even though the cattle rustling story may be more legend than truth, Hidden Valley's boulders and rocks ignite your imagination. As you walk, you can't help but notice that one formation looks like a barking sea lion, another looks like an elf with a hat on, and so on. The number of possible hiding places for men or cattle among the labyrinthine rocks would be infinite.

You may see rock climbers with ropes and harnesses scaling the taller formations, but many of the smaller boulders are easily accessible with just hands and feet. People hiking with young children will find this trail takes forever to hike, because every rock will require a stop to scramble and explore.

The trail is an easy loop, with very little elevation gain except for a short uphill stretch on the return. Watch carefully to stay on the main path; a spider web of trails interweaves with the main trail, leading to various bouldering and climbing sites. Excellent examples of desert flora can be seen along the trail, including junipers, Joshua trees, beavertail cactus, cholla cactus, and turbinella oak. Interpretive signs explain the history of the valley—first the Native American history, then the white settlers' history. The latter consisted of the infamous cattlemen and gold miners, and later, sightseers and visitors with the first Model T automobiles looking for desert adventure.

6. BARKER DAM LOOP

Park Boulevard area, Joshua Tree National Park
A surprising lake in the desert

DISTANCE: 1.2 miles round-trip; 30 minutes   **LEVEL:** Easy
ELEVATION: Start at 4,240 feet; total change 80 feet   **CROWDS:** Moderate
BEST SEASON: October to April   **RATING:** ★ ★ ★

DIRECTIONS: From Highway 62 in the town of Joshua Tree, turn south on Park Boulevard. Drive 14.2 miles to the left turnoff for Hidden Valley Campground. Turn left and then bear right immediately on the signed dirt road. Drive 1.6 miles, past the campground, to the signed trailhead for Barker Dam.

There's a lake in the desert in Joshua Tree National Park, and it's hidden in a magical place called the Wonderland of Rocks. You can't waterski or fish there, but you can birdwatch and photograph the reflections of odd-shaped boulders in the water's surface.

The lake is formed by Barker Dam, which was built at the turn of the century to improve upon a natural boulder dam. The original dam captured rain runoff and contained it in a large, rock-lined basin, to the delight of desert animals and birds. When rancher C.O. Barker of the Barker and Shay Cattle Company traveled through the area and found the natural dam and its tiny lake, he thought he might be able to turn this part of the desert into viable ranch land. After all, it had the magic ingredients for survival—water, and a way to store it.

Barker Dam

Barker built a bigger, stronger dam, then brought his cattle in to graze. After several years, Barker moved on, and a decade later the dam was enlarged by William Keys, owner of the nearby Desert Queen Ranch. With Keys' development in the 1950s, the lake attained its largest size— about 20 acres.

Eventually, this desert site became a part of Joshua Tree National Park, and today, Barker Dam's lake is once again a watering hole for native animals, such as bighorn sheep and coyotes. It is also visited by resident and migratory birds; lucky visitors may spot American coots, grebes, ducks, and even an occasional shorebird. Every now and then a green-backed heron, great blue heron, or night heron will show up, as it takes a break during its long migration.

From the Barker Dam parking area, head straight on the trail. (The path that forks to the left will be the return of your loop.) This is fun hiking—you get to walk over and around various rocks and boulders as you proceed along the sandy trail. You'll reach the lake in a half-mile, and although it can appear rather stagnant, it is larger than you might expect. Willows, cattails, and saltbrush grow near its edges.

The trail loops back past some petroglyphs (take the short signed spur trail) and Indian grinding holes. If the petroglyphs seem remarkably visible and clear to you, it's because years ago a movie crew painted over them to make them more visible to the camera. For this tragic reason, the park calls these paintings the "Disney petroglyphs." Still, they are worth seeing, and you can muse over their intended meanings.

7. WALL STREET MILL

Park Boulevard area, Joshua Tree National Park
Abundant mining and homesteading ruins

DISTANCE: 1.5 miles round-trip; 1 hour   **LEVEL:** Easy
ELEVATION: Start at 4,300 feet; total change 50 feet   **CROWDS:** Minimal
BEST SEASON: October to April   **RATING:** ★ ★ ★ ★

DIRECTIONS: From Highway 62 in the town of Joshua Tree, turn south on Park Boulevard. Drive 14.2 miles to the left turnoff for Hidden Valley Campground. Turn left and then bear right immediately on the signed dirt road. Drive 1.6 miles, past the campground, following the signs for Barker Dam. Continue past the left turnoff for Barker Dam and turn left on the next (unsigned) dirt road. Drive a quarter-mile to the parking area.

Joshua Tree National Park has an abundance of three things: Monolithic rock formations, Joshua trees, and mining ruins. The most abundant examples of the latter are found on the trail to the Wall Street Mill, where an odd assortment of structures—an old house foundation, a windmill, a few rusting trucks, and a stamp mill—still stand as testimony to the gold mining days.

The trail begins just outside of Hidden Valley Campground, in the Wonderland of Rocks. You follow a sandy road from the parking area and veer left in 75 yards when you spot the ruins of a farmhouse. Sections of its pink walls still stand, glowing in the desert sunlight, as well as its foundation and fireplace. This was the home of William Keys and his wife, who ran a nearly self-sustaining ranch here.

Explore around the farmhouse grounds, then backtrack to the old road and follow it as it turns sharply northeast and cuts across the desert plain. Look for a rusting old truck off the trail to the left in a few hundred yards, followed by a tall windmill on the right, with a water pump at its base and a rusted tank by its side.

The trail now curves around to the north and starts to narrow. In a few hundred yards you spot another vestige of the old days—a granite marker on the left side of the trail, which states: "Here is where Worth Bagley bit the dust at the hand of W.F. Keys, May 11, 1943." (Oddly, the lettering on the marker has been painted over with obviously new paint, perhaps to make it easier to read.) Keys shot Bagley in an argument over the use of this road, which passed over Bagley's land on its way to Keys' ore processing mill. Keys served five years in San Quentin prison, but he was eventually freed when it was ruled that he shot in self-defense. Keys was fortunate to have friends in high political places.

Ranch house remains on the trail to Wall Street Mill

A few more minutes of walking brings you to the end of the trail and more ruins—the large two-stamp mill structure that Keys used to process gold ore from 1930 to 1966, and a few more rusting old trucks, circa 1935. One of them, on the right side of the trail, still has some semblance of tires, and its original gear shift, parking brake, headlights, and steering wheel. (How well the desert air preserves!) Walk around the mill site and you'll find large cyanide tanks manufactured by the Demmitt Company in Los Angeles. They bear this catchy slogan: "Why pay more?"

8. DESERT QUEEN MINE

Park Boulevard area, Joshua Tree National Park
Rich gold mine remains and rich human history

DISTANCE: 1.2 miles round-trip; 30 minutes   **LEVEL:** Easy
ELEVATION: Start at 4,400 feet; total change 200 feet   **CROWDS:** Minimal
BEST SEASON: October to April   **RATING:** ★ ★ ★

DIRECTIONS: From Highway 62 in the town of Joshua Tree, turn south on Park Boulevard and drive 15.8 miles to Cap Rock Junction (signed for Keys View). Turn left, then drive six miles to the Geology Tour Road turnoff. Don't turn right on the Geology Tour Road; instead turn left on the dirt road opposite it. Drive 1.4 miles to the backcountry trailhead. Take the trail on the right (east side of the parking area) to Desert Queen Mine.

The Desert Queen Mine was one of the richest gold mines in the area of Joshua Tree National Park, producing almost 4,000 ounces of gold over its lifetime. It also had one of the richest histories of the area's mines—a past filled with tales of murder, intrigue, robbery, payment for back wages, and bank foreclosure.

The mine operated sporadically from 1895 to 1961, an unusually long period for the gold mines in this area. Frank James first discovered gold here in 1894, but James was shot and killed by one of Jim and Bill McHaney's cowboys. (If you hike to Lost Horse Mine or read the story on page 505, you'll learn that the McHaney brothers had a bad habit of sending their cowboys around to harass local gold prospectors.) The McHaneys took over the mine, and rumor has it that they made over two million dollars from the Desert Queen. But like so many stories of the desert, this one has been contradicted: Other estimates place the number at $100,000 or less.

Whatever their profit was, the McHaney brothers wasted it, and the bank that had loaned them money to develop the mine foreclosed on the loan. The Desert Queen Mine was purchased by another investor in 1910, who hired local rancher and prospector Bill Keys to be its caretaker. Eventually the mine and neighboring ranch were deeded to Keys in lieu of back wages.

Massive tailings pile and a fenced-off shaft

What remains of the Desert Queen Mine is an immense pile of ore tailings, two cyanide tanks, the foundations of a cabin, miscellaneous parts of mining machinery, and some fenced-off mine shafts. To see them, head down the trail, and, after 200 yards, bear left to walk to an overlook of the mine. The brief path ends at an interpretive sign, from which you can observe the entire mining camp area. Take a look, then backtrack to the fork and take the other trail, which leads to an old stone cabin foundation with remarkably low doorways. Continue past the cabin on a steep and rocky downhill stretch, then curve around the canyon to reach the mine remains that you saw from the overlook. Be sure to climb above the ore tailings pile to see the numerous fenced-off mine shafts.

9. PINE CITY

Park Boulevard area, Joshua Tree National Park
A hidden, rocky valley filled with pinyon pines

DISTANCE: 3.0 miles round-trip; 1.5 hours   **LEVEL:** Easy
ELEVATION: Start at 4,400 feet; total change 150 feet   **CROWDS:** Minimal
BEST SEASON: October to April   **RATING:** ★ ★ ★

DIRECTIONS: From Highway 62 in the town of Joshua Tree, turn south on Park Boulevard and drive 15.8 miles to Cap Rock Junction (signed for Keys View). Turn left, then drive six miles to the Geology Tour Road turnoff. Don't turn right on the Geology Tour Road; instead turn left on the dirt road opposite it. Drive 1.4 miles to the backcountry trailhead. Take the trail on the north side of the parking area to Pine City.

Pine City is a place that's just plain different from the rest of Joshua Tree National Park. Yes, it has its own weird and wonderful rock formations, and yes, it has plenty of Joshua trees, yucca, and bright red barrel cactus. But it also has pinyon pine trees—lots of them—as well as turbinella oaks and junipers, producing frequent splashes of dark green foliage that are rarely seen in the desert.

Pine City was a small mining camp at the turn of the century. No structures remain, but a few closed-off mine shafts can be seen alongside the trail, which is an old road that was built for travel to the mines. The dirt road is wide, smooth, and easy to follow, which makes it ideal for hikers of all abilities. Simply follow the road until at 1.5 miles, you reach the rim of a valley that extends on both sides of you. It is formed by rock cliffs and precipices, somewhat like Hidden Valley to the west.

Although the distance to Pine City is short, make sure you allow plenty of extra time to explore. You'll want to wander around the valley's rocky jumbles, boulder piles, buttresses, and pinnacles to see what's hidden there. You could easily spend a few hours investigating the nooks and crannies of the thousands of rock formations. Just off the trail we found an overhanging, tunnel-like rock; its "roof" was hollowed out like an umbrella. We could stand underneath the rock and put out heads inside it.

"Lush" desert foliage of Pine City

Pay close attention to how the pinyon pines have managed to survive in the bouldery landscape. You will see them wrapped around small boulders for support or digging their roots into granite surfaces. For the Native Americans who once dwelled in this area, the pinyon pines were an important source of food—pinyon nuts could be ground and used as flour or meal.

10. LUCKY BOY VISTA

Park Boulevard area, Joshua Tree National Park
An old road leading to an overlook of the Split Rock jumbles

DISTANCE: 2.5 miles round-trip; 1.2 hours   **LEVEL:** Easy
ELEVATION: Start at 4,400 feet; total change 100 feet   **CROWDS:** Minimal
BEST SEASON: October to April   **RATING:** ★ ★

DIRECTIONS: From Highway 62 in the town of Joshua Tree, turn south on Park Boulevard and drive 15.8 miles to Cap Rock Junction (signed for Keys View). Turn left, then drive six miles to the Geology Tour Road turnoff. Don't turn right on the Geology Tour Road; instead turn left on the dirt road opposite it. Drive nine-tenths of a mile to the backcountry trailhead on the right.

An easy walk to a great view is provided on the Lucky Boy Vista Trail. The path, and its viewpoint, are perfectly oriented to the east for sunrise or moon rise views, but even if you can't time your trip for these occasions, you should take this hike.

At the turn of the century, the Elton Mine was situated at the end of this sandy road/trail. But you won't find much in the way of mining remains here, just a few fenced-off shafts. Instead you get a wide overlook of the Eagle Cliff Hills, and down into the bouldery jumbles of Split Rock.

Because the trail is located near the Pine City area (see the previous story), you'll see some pinyon pines growing out of and around boulders along the route. The other desert flora is typical of the Joshua Tree high desert: Joshua trees, yuccas, beavertail cactus, and a few bright pink and red barrel cactus that add color to the landscape.

The trail is an old road that led to the mine. It's easy to follow and nearly level. You'll notice a couple of forks leading off the trail, but stay on the main route until you reach an overlook at the edge of a high plateau. Only at the farthest point does the vista becomes apparent. Once you see it, you may decide to stay for a picnic, or at least a long, protracted discussion.

When you've had enough, turn around and head back. The return trip offers fine views of Mount San Gorgonio and Mount San Jacinto to the west.

11. SKULL ROCK NATURE TRAIL

Park Boulevard area, Joshua Tree National Park
A close-up look at Joshua Tree's weird rock formations

DISTANCE: 1.7 miles round-trip; 45 minutes   **LEVEL:** Easy
ELEVATION: Start at 4,400 feet; total change 50 feet   **CROWDS:** Moderate
BEST SEASON: October to April   **RATING:** ★ ★

DIRECTIONS: From Highway 62 in Twentynine Palms, turn south on Utah Trail Road and drive 8.5 miles to a Y junction. Bear right and continue four miles to the trailhead parking area alongside the road, shortly before the entrance to Jumbo Rocks Campground. Begin hiking on the right (northwest) side of the road. (Campers can begin hiking from the campground by Loop E.)

Joshua Tree National Park is probably as famous for rock formations as it is for Joshua trees. If you've been admiring the park's weird and wonderful hunks of quartz monzogranite from your car window, a walk on the Skull Rock Nature Trail will bring you in for a closer look.

The trail begins right along the road near Jumbo Rocks Campground. If you're not staying in the camp, park your car along the road and start hiking on the northwest side at the signed trailhead. This way,

On the Skull Rock Nature Trail

you'll head counterclockwise and save Skull Rock and its many odd-shaped companions for last.

The Skull Rock Trail is highly recommended not just for its fine examples of Joshua Tree National Park geology, but also for its excellent interpretation of desert flora. Signs along the pathway point out paper-bag bush, which has many inflated seed pods that look like white paper bags; dwarf-sized turbinella oak or Mojave desert oak, which has tiny oak-like leaves; and teddy bear cholla cactus, which has sharp, barbed spines that look as soft as teddy bear fur. You get a complete high-desert botany lesson along the Skull Rock Trail. Soon you can quiz your hiking partner on the identifying characteristics of peachthorn, creosote, buckwheat, and cat's claw acacia. The most interesting fact we learned was that the park's plentiful Joshua trees got their name from the Mormons, who said that the Joshua's uplifted branches reminded them of the Biblical Joshua in prayerful supplication.

The trail winds among sculpted and weathered rock formations, then reaches the park road, crosses it, and heads into Jumbo Rocks Campground. You might expect that this would result in a boring stretch of trail, but at the camp, there's just more to see, including some wind-sculpted rock caves and campsites that are made perfectly private by nature's positioning of the boulders.

Just beyond the entrance to the camp's Loop E, pick up the trail again, heading for Skull Rock, which looks eerily like the top half of a skull. When you near it, the path deteriorates into a spider web …s, with footprints leading in all directions. This is where every-…y sets out on their own, climbing around on Skull Rock and the many interesting rock formations surrounding it. If you get confused about which way to go, just scramble to the top of any high rock, and you'll spot the nearby road, where you parked your car.

---

12. RYAN MOUNTAIN

Park Boulevard area, Joshua Tree National Park
An excellent trail to a top-notch summit view

DISTANCE: 3.0 miles round-trip; 1.5 hours   **LEVEL:** Easy/moderate
ELEVATION: Start at 4,450 feet; total change 1,000 feet   **CROWDS:** Minimal
BEST SEASON: October to April   **RATING:** ★ ★ ★ ★

DIRECTIONS: From Highway 62 in the town of Joshua Tree, turn south on Park Boulevard and drive 15.8 miles to Cap Rock Junction (signed for Keys View). Turn left, then drive 2.5 miles to the trailhead on the right.

The view from Ryan Mountain's summit is one of the finest in all of Joshua Tree National Park. Not only that, but the trail to reach it is one of the best maintained, and easiest to follow, of all the park's trails. This hike should be on everybody's itinerary.

Our first visit to Ryan Mountain was on a cool day in December, when the wind was blowing hard. By the time we reached the 5,460-foot summit, we could barely keep our balance in the howling gale. Still, the panorama was so transfixing that we stayed on the peak for as long as we could. The summit vista includes Queen Valley, the Wonderland of Rocks, Pinto Basin, Lost Horse Valley, and Pleasant Valley, as well as the high peaks of far-off Mount San Gorgonio and Mount San Jacinto. (In winter, these two peaks are usually covered in snow, so they are easy to identify.)

The weather isn't always cold and blustery on Ryan Mountain. In summer it can be hot, still, and extremely uncomfortable for making the short climb to the mountaintop. If your trip is between May and September, make sure you get an early morning start to beat the heat.

The Ryan Mountain Trail begins at a roadside parking area, then travels through boulders and Joshua trees—no surprises here—on an easy-to-follow trail. The ascent may seem a bit steep, even though it's only a 1,000-foot elevation gain, but it's over with quickly. Just sweat it out. You'll want to stop every few minutes to look around at the

---

increasingly widening desert views, which you gain as you climb.

When you reach the summit, have a seat on one of the rocks of Ryan Mountain and enjoy the show. The peak's boulders are estimated to be several hundred million years old, which is much older than most of the rocks in Joshua Tree National Park. If you pace around a few yards on the peak's surface, you get a full 360-degree panorama: Mountains on one horizon, miles of desert on the other.

You may find a summit register at the top of Ryan Mountain; it's usually buried in a pile of rocks.

On the blustery summit of Ryan Mountain

The register may be a coffee can filled with tiny notebooks, scraps of paper, and the like, or it may be something more formal—it just depends on who has been on the summit recently. If you find the register, spend a few minutes perusing the comments of other hikers, then add a few acute observations of your own.

13. LOST HORSE MINE

Keys View area, Joshua Tree National Park
A well-preserved stamp mill and gold mine shafts

DISTANCE: 4.0 miles round-trip; 2 hours
ELEVATION: Start at 4,600 feet; total change 500 feet
BEST SEASON: October to April

LEVEL: Easy/moderate
CROWDS: Moderate
RATING: ★ ★ ★ ★

DIRECTIONS: From Highway 62 in the town of Joshua Tree, turn south on Park Boulevard and drive 15.8 miles to Cap Rock junction (signed for Keys View). Bear right and drive 2.4 miles to the graded dirt road on the left that is signed for Lost Horse Mine. Turn left and drive 1.1 miles to the trailhead parking area.

You get the full "desert experience" on the Lost Horse Mine Trail, including mountain and valley vistas, high desert flora, an intriguing story, and a visit to an old gold mine and its well preserved stamp mill.

At the trailhead, take the left fork to go directly to the mine. The rocky trail (really an old mine road) leads gently uphill for 1.9 miles to Lost Horse Mine. It climbs, then dips, then climbs again, offering views of Pleasant Valley and the Hexie Mountains to the east whenever it tops a rise. Shortly beyond the one-mile point, you'll get your first look at the dark brown mine building perched on the hillside ahead. Follow the old road to the base of it, then climb uphill on any of the steep use trails to get a closer view.

This main building was the ten-stamp mill for the Lost Horse Mine. The stamp mill operated off and on between 1893 and 1936, crushing ore so that its gold could be extracted. Above and below the mill, you'll find several fenced-off mine shafts, cyanide tanks, and a winch that was used to lower men and machinery into the main shaft.

The Lost Horse Mine was a highly productive small-scale operation: The main mine shaft was 500 feet deep, and major tunnels were developed at the 100, 200, and 300-foot levels. A total of six working levels were dug into the hillside behind the stamp mill. The mine produced a profit of more than 9,000 ounces of gold for its owner, Johnny Lang, who had bought the mining claim from its discoverer, Frank Diebold, for a mere $1,000.

Lost Horse Mine stamp mill

Apparently Diebold had been unable to develop his claim because of threats on his life from neighboring cowboys who worked for Bill and Jim McHaney. The McHaneys worked at both gold prospecting and ranching, and they were frequently accused of being dishonest in their dealings. Apparently Johnny Lang met Diebold when he was looking for his lost horse, which most likely had been stolen by the same McHaney cowboys. This fortuitous event led to the naming of the mine. (For more information on the infamous McHaneys, see the story on the Desert Queen Mine on page 499.)

Three years passed before Lang was able to overcome interference by the McHaney boys and develop the mine with the help of two partners. When they finally got it up and running, the Lost Horse Mine became the most successful gold mining operation in what is now Joshua Tree National Park.

The mine is also considered to be one of the best preserved mines in the national park, but this comes with a price: Its stamp mill is surrounded by a tall chain link fence. The fence greatly detracts from the mill's appearance but helps to preserve it, while simultaneously protecting visitors from the unstable mine shafts.

If you'd like some fine vistas to top off your hike to Lost Horse Mine, you have two choices: Climb to the top of the hill directly behind the stamp mill, or continue another third of a mile on the old mining road and follow a use trail that leads uphill to the right, to the top of Lost Horse Mountain. Both routes provide you with high vistas of the Queen Valley, Lost Horse Valley, Pleasant Valley, and the eastern stretch of the national park.

It is possible to make a loop out of this hike by continuing on the mine road, then traveling through a wash. This makes an interesting eight-mile loop, but the route is extremely difficult to follow in places. If you don't have a good map and compass with you, return the way you came.

14. KEYS VIEW & INSPIRATION PEAK

Keys View area, Joshua Tree National Park
Two side-by-side overlooks with some of the best views in the park

DISTANCE: 1.5 miles round-trip; 45 minutes **LEVEL:** Easy/moderate
ELEVATION: Start at 5,150 feet; total change 400 feet **CROWDS:** Moderate
BEST SEASON: October to April **RATING:** ★ ★ ★ ★

DIRECTIONS: From Highway 62 in the town of Joshua Tree, turn south on Park Boulevard and drive 15.8 miles to Cap Rock junction (signed for Keys View). Bear right and drive 5.6 miles to the end of the road at Keys View.

Don't make the mistake of driving to the overlook at Keys View, taking the short, paved, 200-yard walk to admire the vista, and then driving off again. There's a longer trail to be hiked from the same parking area, and it delivers surprisingly better views than Keys View itself.

Begin your exploration with a walk to the brief overlook trail at Keys View, which begins on the left (south) side of the parking lot. Railings line the paved trail, and several interpretive signs discuss the effects of air pollution on Keys View and the desert in general. If you arrive on a clear day (best in the morning), you will be treated to a fabulous overlook of Mount San Jacinto at 10,804 feet and Mount San Gorgonio at 11,499 feet. San Gorgonio is on the far right; although it's the tallest mountain in Southern California, it looks smaller from here because it's farther away. In the foreground is Palm Springs and the Coachella Valley, the San Andreas Fault, the Colorado River Aqueduct, 1000 Palms Oasis, and Indio. To the southeast is the Salton Sea. Most astonishing is that on the best air quality days, Signal Mountain in Mexico can be seen. The mountain is at 2,262 feet in elevation and it's more than 90 miles from where you stand.

After getting a grip on your general position in the landscape, return to the parking lot and look for a hiker symbol marker on its right (north) side. Your destination is Inspiration Peak, the summit next to Keys View.

Looking south from Keys View

Start to climb steeply up the slope above Keys View. The grade is sharp here, but the trail is short, so just relax and take your time. In only a few minutes of hiking, you can see why you're heading for better vistas: You've already climbed substantially higher than Keys View. Don't stop at the first high point you reach; Inspiration Peak is broad and has two summits, and the second one is higher than the first.

The higher summit is

marked by a distinct pile of black and grey boulders. Climb on them to reach the optimal viewing spot. From the top of Inspiration Peak, you can admire the same expanse to the south and west that you enjoyed from Keys View, but now with a wider angle. To the north and east, you have an excellent view of a major chunk of the national park—the Wonderland of Rocks, Queen Valley, and Lost Horse Valley, with distinctive Malapai Hill directly east. Because Inspiration Peak is at 5,558 feet in elevation (higher than Eureka Peak, Ryan Mountain, or any of the park's other famous summits), its views are unsurpassed.

15. FORTYNINE PALMS OASIS
Twentynine Palms area, Joshua Tree National Park
One of five palm oases in Joshua Tree

DISTANCE: 3.0 miles round-trip; 1.5 hours | **LEVEL:** Easy
ELEVATION: Start at 2,700 feet; total change 350 feet | **CROWDS:** Minimal
BEST SEASON: October to April | **RATING:** ★ ★ ★

DIRECTIONS: From the town of Joshua Tree on Highway 62, drive east on Highway 62 for 10 miles to the western edge of Twentynine Palms. Turn south on Canyon Road (located by the High Desert Animal Hospital or 1.8 miles east of the park entrance at Indian Cove Road). Drive 1.7 miles on Canyon Road; bear left where the road forks. The pavement ends at the Fortynine Palms Oasis trailhead.

The biggest surprise on the Fortynine Palms Oasis Trail is not the large and lovely grove of fan palms at the trail's end. It's that there are no Joshua trees to be found anywhere along the trail. What? No Joshua trees? If you've spent a few days in Joshua Tree National Park, you get accustomed to seeing the tall yucca-like plants everywhere you look. When you don't see them, it seems odd.

But the Fortynine Palms Oasis Trail is located at the far northern edge of the park, where the elevation is low enough to be just outside of the Joshua trees' reign. Because the trailhead is located off the main park roads, this oasis is less visited than some of the others in the park.

The Fortynine Palms Oasis Trail is an old Indian pathway, and it's well maintained and easy to follow. It winds around, then undulates up and over a small ridge, so you're never sure exactly where you're heading. Your trailside companions include a multitude of round, reddish-colored barrel cactus; and brittlebush, a shrub with silvery green leaves and a yellow, daisy-like flower.

A strange contradiction on this seemingly remote trail is that you

Fortynine Palms Oasis

can still see and hear far-off Highway 62 and the town of Twentynine Palms. The road noise travels right up the canyon, and from the trail's high plateau, you can look out over the suburban desert sprawl.

This odd mix of the wild and the civilized ends when you reach the rocky palm grove. There, civilization is left behind, and you're cloistered in a small, hidden valley filled with fan palms. You see a group of 10 palm trees first, then a larger cluster about 50 yards away. Many have blackened trunks from occasional natural fires in the canyon. Fire is actually beneficial for mature palm trees, although it can kill young ones. Fire increases seed production and opens up space for the seeds to germinate.

You may hear water trickling among the palms, but rarely does much appear above ground, except for a few stagnant-looking pools. If you have kids or kids-at-heart with you, they'll want to clamber around on the granite boulders surrounding the palms. The large boulders are covered with beautifully colored lichens and make a fine spot for a picnic while you listen to the wind in the palms. Birdwatchers can sit and wait for the appearance of an oriole, finch, or hummingbird, all of which are commonly seen. Every once in a while a lucky hiker will spot a bighorn sheep on the rocky ridges above the oasis, warily awaiting his or her turn at the watering hole.

The only negative at the oasis is that many of the palm trees have been carved with people's initials. Take this opportunity to teach your children (or your hiking partner!) about the evils of this type of graffiti.

16. CONTACT MINE

Twentynine Palms area, Joshua Tree National Park
Mining ruins and views of the Pinto Mountains

DISTANCE: 3.4 miles round-trip; 1.5 hours
ELEVATION: Start at 2,900 feet; total change 700 feet
BEST SEASON: October to April

LEVEL: Moderate
CROWDS: Minimal
RATING: ★ ★ ★

DIRECTIONS: From Highway 62 in Twentynine Palms, turn south on Utah Trail Road and drive four miles to the park entrance kiosk. Continue beyond the kiosk for another half-mile to a covered sign board on the right (west) side of the road. Follow a use trail that angles from the signboard to the right (northwest). If this use trail isn't obvious, walk north on the road for 25 yards to a brown sign noting park rules. A faint dirt road leads west from the sign.

Here's the place for kids (and adults) to play "miner." The Contact Mine has enough ruins left from the mining days of the early 1900s to let imaginations run wild. There's an old mining road, rusted bits and pieces of an old homestead, four side-by-side mine shafts, plus a cable winch and two lines of track.

The trail to Contact Mine is long enough to feel like a hike, not a walk. It's rated as "moderate," but keep in mind that there is no formal trail for the first stretch of the hike, and the route is very sandy and rocky. Also, the path is sadly lacking in trail signs or markers, so pay close attention to rock cairns and the following description until you get on the old miner's road. Once you're on the road, the route is clear.

Follow the faint dirt road/trail from either the signboard or the park road. In a few hundred yards, cross over a low dirt dike. Fifty yards farther, you reach a second dike, which parallels a wash. Follow this wash southwest toward the rocky hills ahead. Keep watching for footprints in the sand to confirm your route.

When the wash forks at four-tenths of a mile, bear right, heading even closer to the rocky hills. In only a quarter-mile, bear right again to leave the wash and join the old mining road that runs through the hills. This is probably the least obvious junction, so watch for trail cairns. (We saw plenty of footprints in the sand going the wrong way at this junction—continuing up the wash instead of climbing out of it to the right.) At three-quarters of a mile from the trailhead, you should be on the old road, which is rocky and eroded at first, but soon becomes smoother and easy to follow. Although the first part of the hike was mostly level, the mine road climbs quickly, heading up into the hills to the Contact Mine.

Cable winch at the Contact Mine site

Your first sighting will be of ore tailings. When you reach the mine site, climb uphill to examine the cable winch, which is the highlight of the mine remains. This piece of machinery was used to lower men and equipment down into the mine shafts. A long stretch of cable still drops from its coil into a nearby shaft, making it easy to imagine what it was like for the miners heading below ground for a day's work.

Below the cable winch and the mine shafts, you can find broken bits and pieces of an old homestead, including rusted cans, sections of a furnace or water heater, and an old bed frame. All around the mine are beautiful shards of white quartz.

The return trip is much easier than the way up, now that you know the way. You are rewarded with lovely views of the Pinto Mountains as you descend.

---

17. PINTO WYE ARRASTRA

Twentynine Palms area, Joshua Tree National Park
A cross-country ramble to an unusual mining relic

DISTANCE: 1.5 miles round-trip; 45 minutes **LEVEL:** Moderate
ELEVATION: Start at 3,500 feet; total change 300 feet **CROWDS:** Minimal
BEST SEASON: October to April **RATING:** ★ ★

DIRECTIONS: From Highway 62 in Twentynine Palms, turn south on Utah Trail Road and drive four miles to the park entrance kiosk. Continue south for another four miles past the kiosk to a circular turnout on the left (east) side of the road. (This turnout is a half-mile before the road reaches Pinto Wye junction.) Begin to hike across the road from the turnout. There is no official trail or sign.

The Pinto Wye Arrastra is a nineteenth century mining relic, a primitive machine for crushing ore that was built by an unknown miner. If you've visited Cottonwood Spring Oasis in the southern part of Joshua Tree National Park, then you've seen the park's only other example of an arrastra—a circular mill that ground ore using stones attached to sweeps, like spokes on a wheel.

There is no trail to the Pinto Wye Arrastra, so be prepared for a rocky scramble and some easy route finding if you want to see this vestige of gold mining days in Joshua Tree. If you make the trip, wear long pants and long sleeves, because cat-claw acacia, creosote, and cholla are plentiful in this part of the park.

Here's how to find your route: From the parking pullout, walk across the road and look for the split between two hills. Head across the sandy plain directly toward this split, then pick your way up its rocky, dry ravine. You may find a use trail; if you don't, just follow the easiest path, climbing over rocks and avoiding the prickly desert plants. Ascend until you reach the divide at the top, between the two hills.

From this high point, start to angle down the far slope, heading

Pinto Wye arrastra

toward the canyon bottom and also to your right. After a few hundred feet of descending and angling right, you should spot a pile of gray-colored mine tailings. Fifty yards below it, you'll see the dark brown circle of the arrastra.

This arrastra is unusual because it was built using a large wagon wheel. It was powered by a gasoline engine, using a drive belt around the central wheel. Although no one knows who built this arrastra, it was probably used in the 1930s. Earlier arrastras were usually powered by animals, steam, or water.

An interpretive sign below the arrastra explains its workings: Gold ore, water, and mercury were placed on its round stone floor. Large stones were dragged around the floor by the arms or sweeps of the arrastra, powered by the gas engine. The stones crushed the ore and mixed it with water and mercury. Mercury combined with gold to form an amalgam. The amalgam was then heated, separating the mercury from the gold, and producing the final product.

18. ARCH ROCK NATURE TRAIL

Twentynine Palms area, Joshua Tree National Park
A geology lesson in a rock wonderland

DISTANCE: 0.3 mile round-trip; 15 minutes   **LEVEL:** Easy
ELEVATION: Start at 3,800 feet; total change 50 feet   **CROWDS:** Minimal
BEST SEASON: October to April   **RATING:** ★ ★ ★

DIRECTIONS: From Highway 62 in Twentynine Palms, turn south on Utah Trail Road and drive 8.5 miles to a Y junction. Bear left and drive 2.8 miles to White Tank Campground. Turn left into the camp; the trail begins by campsite number 9.

The Arch Rock Nature Trail provides an experience similar to the Skull Rock Nature Trail (see the story on page 502), but it's in a more condensed version. If you've been driving around Joshua Tree National Park admiring its prolific, wacky rock formations, this trail gives you a chance to get up close with some of the best of them, and learn about their ancient geological history.

Arch Rock—a natural granite arch—may be the star of this trail, but there are many other fascinating rock shapes to admire. The trail winds among giant, rounded boulders, which look a lot like sandstone but are actually White Tank granite. This granite is a type of igneous rock that was formed when molten rock or magma was pushed up from deep within the earth, forcing itself into the overlaying rock. It then cooled and hardened, and was eventually exposed when the overlaying rock wore away. It is estimated that White Tank granite came into existence 135 million years ago, when dinosaurs roamed the earth.

Under the arch of Arch Rock

Although they were originally larger, solid pieces, the White Tank granite boulder formations were segmented by joints or cracks. Eventually erosion, rain, and alternating cold and hot air went to work on these cracks, split-ting the rocks into smaller, odd shapes. Succeeding years of erosion rounded off their rough edges, similar to ice cubes being held under a faucet. The jumbled mounds of rocks that you see were piled up by flash floods.

The trail also shows off various examples of "sculpted rock"— granite that has been shaped by processes known as cavernous weather-ing and undercutting. These processes occur when moisture is trapped under a rock's surface long enough to dissolve away and decompose certain minerals. Considering this, imagine how long it must have taken to "sculpt" Arch Rock, which spans 35 feet and arches 15 feet above its underlying rock. It's virtually impossible to resist crawling around on the formation's concrete-like surfaces. Climb up and stand underneath the arch to get the full effect, then explore around the maze of rocks at the arch's base. You can't get lost; eventually the rocky tunnels of the labyrinth end, and you must turn back. Could there possibly be a better place for a game of hide-and-seek?

19. COTTONWOOD SPRING NATURE TRAIL

Cottonwood Spring area, Joshua Tree National Park
A shady oasis and a desert education

DISTANCE: 1.0 mile round-trip; 30 minutes   **LEVEL:** Easy
ELEVATION: Start at 3,000 feet; total change 50 feet   **CROWDS:** Minimal
BEST SEASON: October to April   **RATING:** ★ ★

DIRECTIONS: From Indio, drive east on Interstate 10 for approximately 25 miles. Turn north on Cottonwood Spring Road and drive eight miles to Cottonwood Spring Campground and the trailhead, located near site number 13 at the end of the camp. You can also begin hiking from the day-use area at Cottonwood Spring Oasis, 1.2 miles beyond the campground.

Some people say that there's nothing in the desert but sand, rocks, and Joshua trees, but a walk on the Cottonwood Spring Nature Trail will convince you otherwise and give you a little history lesson along the way. No interpretive brochures are necessary on this hike, because the park has placed informative signs in front of every item of interest.

The trail travels out-and-back between Cottonwood Spring Campground and Cottonwood Spring Oasis. Hikers can start at either place, and head in either direction. Cottonwood Spring Oasis is the highlight of the route—a little slice of watery paradise for birds and wildlife, surrounded by a few fan palms and cottonwoods. Today this natural spring produces a water supply of about 30 gallons an hour, although a century ago it may have been four or five times as much.

Long before white people set foot in the desert, the Cahuilla Indians knew of this year-round spring and of the useful properties of the desert flora surrounding it. Signs along the interpretive trail explain how the Cahuillas made use of desert plants for food, tools, and medicine. The Cahuillas lived fruitfully in this area and adapted well to their desert surroundings. Look for signs of Native American life in the form of bedrock mortars (grinding holes) in the granite. They're right along the trail by the oasis.

Long after the Cahuillas, in the 1880s and 1890s, prospectors and miners came to this oasis on their way to and from the desert gold mines. They improved upon the spring in order to make it a more reliable water source, and they planted palms and cottonwood trees for shade. Because water was an essential element not just for human consumption but also for gold processing, several ore processing mills were built near the oasis. The remains of a circular arrastra, a very primitive type of mill, can be found below the spring. It looks something like a decaying wheel made of wood and stone, but in its original state, it was used to process gold amalgam. (This is one of only two remaining arrastras in the park—the other is Pinto Wye Arrastra, detailed on pages 512 to 514.)

In addition to sighting numerous songbirds flitting about the oasis, lucky visitors may spot a roadrunner, desert cottontail rabbit, Gambel's quail, or coyote. For visitors, Cottonwood Spring is a pleasant and interesting diversion, but for wildlife, it is a life-giving necessity.

20. MASTODON PEAK

Cottonwood Spring area, Joshua Tree National Park
A strangely shaped rocky peak, plus an old gold mine

DISTANCE: 2.8 miles round-trip; 1.5 hours   **LEVEL:** Easy
ELEVATION: Start at 3,000 feet; total change 450 feet   **CROWDS:** Minimal
BEST SEASON: October to April   **RATING:** ★ ★ ★ ★

DIRECTIONS: From Indio, drive east on Interstate 10 for approximately 25 miles. Turn north on Cottonwood Spring Road and drive eight miles to Cottonwood Spring ranger station. Turn right and drive 1.2 miles, passing the campground entrance, to the day-use parking area at Cottonwood Spring Oasis. (Campers can begin hiking on the trail out of Cottonwood Spring Campground.)

The loop trail to Mastodon Peak is an excellent trip for families, combining elements of human and natural history on a pleasant excursion in the southern part of Joshua Tree National Park.

The trail begins at Cottonwood Spring Oasis, a trickling spring surrounded by fan palms and cottonwoods. The oasis has a fascinating history of its own (see the previous story for details). Continue past the oasis, following the trail signed for Lost Palms Oasis and Mastodon Peak. At a junction a half-mile farther, take the left fork for Mastodon Peak, one mile away.

The Mastodon Peak Trail is an easy walk, curving around tall ocotillo plants, yucca, and many smaller cacti. You pass a trail coming in on your left from Cottonwood Spring Campground; stay to the right and continue the short distance to the peak. When you reach the Mastodon's base, you see the reason for its name—it certainly does resemble that prehistoric animal. Take a look at the rocky summit, then make a decision: Scramble to the top, or be content with the views from where you are? If you choose the former, head to your right, toward the back (east) side of the peak, then scale the large boulders to

On the trail to Mastodon Peak

reach the summit. It's a short and exciting rock scramble, completely worth the effort required, but it may be too risky for small children or for those who are afraid of heights.

The Mastodon's summit views are excellent—you can see all the way to the Salton Sea, shimmering in the distance some 30 miles away, plus the Eagle Mountains to the east. The vista also includes Mount San Jacinto to the west, Monument Mountain to the northwest, and the Cottonwood Spring area immediately north.

After you take it all in, climb back down from the summit, then retrace your steps to the trail junction for Cottonwood Spring Campground. Turn right and head for the camp; you'll loop back past the Mastodon Gold Mine and the Winona Mill Site. The mine was worked from 1919 to 1932 with a modicum of success. You can still see its main shaft, which is now fenced off. The Winona Mill Site, one mile farther, is where a small town was built in the 1920s for local miners and ore-processing workers. Today, little is left of the town besides some non-native cottonwood and eucalyptus trees and a few concrete house foundations. The trees provide welcome shade for wildlife and tired hikers.

From the mill site, continue a short distance to a fork in the trail. The right fork continues to Cottonwood Spring Campground; the left fork will take you to your car at Cottonwood Spring Oasis.

21. LOST PALMS OASIS

Cottonwood Spring area, Joshua Tree National Park
One of the largest palm oases in the park

DISTANCE: 7.4 miles round-trip; 3.5 hours   **LEVEL:** Moderate
ELEVATION: Start at 3,000 feet; total change 550 feet   **CROWDS:** Minimal
BEST SEASON: October to April   **RATING:** ★ ★ ★ ★

DIRECTIONS: From Indio, drive east on Interstate 10 for approximately
25 miles. Turn north on Cottonwood Spring Road and drive eight miles to
Cottonwood Spring ranger station. Turn right and drive 1.2 miles, passing the
campground entrance, to the day-use parking area at Cottonwood Spring
Oasis. (Campers can begin hiking on the trail out of Cottonwood Spring
Campground.)

If the weather is cool and accommodating, and you're in the mood
for a longer hike in southern Joshua Tree National Park, the Lost Palms
Oasis Trail is an excellent choice. Many visitors consider Lost Palms
Oasis to be the best palm grove in Joshua Tree; certainly it is one of the
largest and most dense. Despite the long trail mileage, the hike to reach
the grove has little elevation change and is easily accomplished (as long
as the weather is cool).

The trail begins at Cottonwood Spring Oasis and follows the same
path as the Mastodon Peak Trail for the first half-mile (see the previous
story). Stay straight at the junction with the trail to Mastodon Peak,
then continue through a series of washes and low ridges covered with
low-elevation desert cacti. The route maintains a gently rolling series
of ups and downs, with no serious climbs or descents along the way.
Lucky visitors will hike here in February or March after a rainy winter;
then the ocotillo, cholla, and yuccas will put on their showy, but too
brief, flower display.

There is no indication of the huge palm oasis until you are almost
on top of it at 3.4 miles out. The main trail climbs gently to an overlook point above a hidden, rocky canyon filled with leafy fan palms.
A steep use trail descends a quarter-mile into the grove. Be sure to
make the rugged 200-foot descent to the canyon bottom. The remote-
ness of the area and the lush atmosphere of the palm grove are worth
experiencing close-up.

The Lost Palms Oasis grove contains more than 100 palms
(*Washingtonia filifera*) in its main canyon. The trickling water of a
stream will sound like music to your desert-dry ears, but little surface
water can be seen. The only other sounds you'll hear are the singing

Leafy palm fronds in Lost Palms Oasis

of birds and the rustling of wind in the palms. Pick a sandy spot or a boulder— there are hundreds of them—and have a seat while you enjoy the majesty of the palms. Consider this: There are only 158 desert fan palm oases in North America, and you're in the middle of one of the finest.

In the upper end of the canyon is a side canyon (to the north) with a spring and more palms. Adventurous hikers may want to seek them out; others will be satisfied with the leafy splendor in the main Lost Palms canyon.

CABRILLO NATIONAL MONUMENT

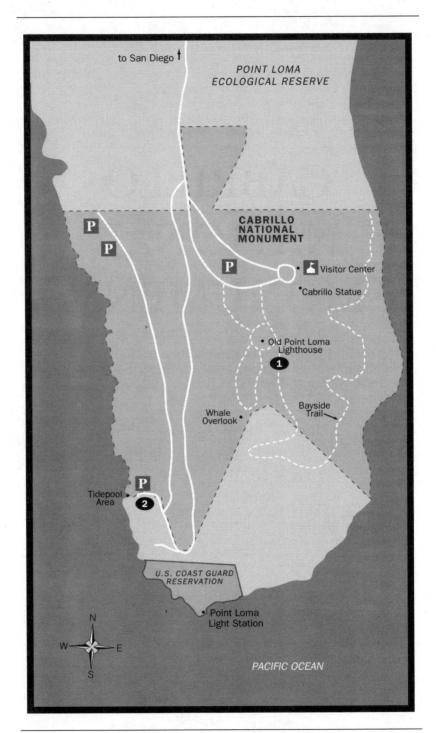

to San Diego ↑

*POINT LOMA
ECOLOGICAL RESERVE*

**CABRILLO
NATIONAL
MONUMENT**

P
P
P

Visitor Center

•Cabrillo Statue

• Old Point Loma
Lighthouse

❶

Whale
Overlook •

*Bayside
Trail*

P
❷

Tidepool
Area •

*U.S. COAST GUARD
RESERVATION*

• Point Loma
Light Station

N
W E
S

PACIFIC OCEAN

CABRILLO NATIONAL MONUMENT
TRAILS AT A GLANCE

Map Number/Trail Name	Page	Mileage	Difficulty
1. Bayside Trail	525	2.0	Easy
2. Cabrillo Tide Pools	527	1.0	Easy

ABOUT THE PARK

Cabrillo National Monument was established to honor explorer Juan Rodriguez Cabrillo, who landed in San Diego Bay in 1542. The park features a statue of Cabrillo, an 1850s lighthouse, several superb ocean and bay overlooks, one hiking trail, and an excellent tide pool area.

ADDRESS, PHONE, & WEBSITE

Cabrillo National Monument, 1800 Cabrillo Memorial Drive, San Diego, CA 92106; (619) 557-5450.
Website: www.nps.gov/cabr

VISITOR CENTER

The monument's visitor center is located at the main parking lot.

HOW TO GET THERE

- By air: The closest major airport is in San Diego, California.
- By car: From Interstate 5 in San Diego, take the Rosecrans Street exit (Highway 209) and drive south. Staying on Highway 209, turn right on Cañon Street, then left on Catalina Boulevard, and continue to the monument entrance.

DRIVE TIME

- Drive time from Los Angeles: approximately 2.5 hours.
- Drive time from San Francisco: approximately 10 hours.

ENTRANCE FEES

There is a $5 entrance fee per vehicle at Cabrillo National Monument, good for seven days. A Cabrillo annual pass is available for $15. A Golden Eagle Passport, an annual pass for all 375 national park units, is available for $50. A Golden Age Passport, a lifetime pass for all 375 national park units, is available to U.S. citizens and residents aged 62 and over for a one-time $10 fee. You can purchase these passes at the park entrance station or visitor center.

WHEN TO GO

Cabrillo National Monument is open year-round for hiking. The winter season is the least crowded, and it is also the best time for gray whale watching. Between December and the end of February, more than 20,000 whales cruise past Cabrillo National Monument on their way from their northern feeding grounds in the Arctic to their calving lagoons in Baja, Mexico.

The best time to visit Cabrillo National Monument's tide pools is during very low or minus tides in late fall, winter, and early spring.

WEATHER CONDITIONS

Cabrillo National Monument is blessed with San Diego's sunny skies and mild weather. Rain is a rare event, occurring only occasionally between November and April. Spring and summer are characterized by morning fog and sunny afternoons. Temperatures are typically in the 60s and 70s during the day. There is only minor variation between summer and winter temperatures.

WHERE TO STAY

San Diego is a major metropolitan area with myriad lodgings, motels, and hotels. Contact the San Diego hotel reservations line at (619) 581-6200. Your best bets for nearby camping are up the coast at two state beaches: South Carlsbad at (760) 438-3143 or San Elijo at (760) 753-5091. If you plan to camp in the summer, make reservations far in advance by phoning (800) 444-7275.

FOOD & SUPPLIES

There are no food or supplies available at the monument, but anything you might want can be purchased in the city of San Diego.

SUGGESTED MAPS

Park maps are available at the entrance station and also at the monument's visitor center.

1. BAYSIDE TRAIL

Cabrillo National Monument
Bay and ocean views plus a nature lesson

DISTANCE: 2.0 miles round-trip; 1 hour
LEVEL: Easy
ELEVATION: Start at 400 feet; total change 250 feet
CROWDS: Moderate
BEST SEASON: Year-round
RATING: ★ ★ ★

DIRECTIONS: From Interstate 5 in San Diego, take the Rosecrans Street exit (Highway 209) and drive south. Staying on Highway 209, you will turn right on Cañon Street, then left on Catalina Boulevard. The road ends at Cabrillo National Monument. The trail begins by the old lighthouse.

While everybody else at Cabrillo National Monument is visiting the old Point Loma lighthouse, or having their picture taken by the statue of Señor Cabrillo, or checking out the wonderful view of San Diego from the visitor center buildings, you can sneak off for a hike on the Bayside Trail and find a surprising amount of solitude.

As luck would have it, your solitude comes with plenty of gorgeous coastal vistas, as well as an interesting lesson in native coastal vegetation. But first, start your trip with a couple of side trips: Take the paved trail from the main parking lot to the Point Loma lighthouse, where you can climb up the narrow stairway and peer inside the rooms at the period furniture. Children like to try to imagine what life was like for the lighthouse keeper and his family who lived in these tiny rooms in the late 1800s; modern adults find it almost impossible to imagine.

Point Loma lighthouse first lit its beacon in 1855, and it served as the southernmost Pacific Coast lighthouse in the United States until 1891. Its light could be seen 20 miles out to sea. Originally the beacon was fueled by whale oil, later it was fueled by lard oil, and in its last years it was fueled by kerosene. The lighthouse sat idle for 40 years until it was restored in the 1930s as a part of the designated national monument.

After visiting the lighthouse, check out the great ocean views from the overlooks on its far side. (We favored these coastal vistas over the panorama of the city of San Diego and its harbor, which you see from the visitor center.) Because you are at 400 feet above sea level with a wide field of vision, you are perfectly situated for gray whale watching.

Having completed your side trips, get on with the main attraction. Pick up the paved road back on the east side of the lighthouse, signed as Bayside Trail. Take the left fork, which is gravel, and wind gently

Point Loma Lighthouse

downhill around Point Loma. On every step of the trail, the whole of San Diego Bay and the Pacific Ocean are yours to survey. You'll see huge Navy ships sailing out to sea, flocks of seagulls following the fishing boats back into harbor, sailboats, jet-skiers, and large offshore kelp beds.

Try to tear your eyes away from the goings-on in the bay so you can read the trail's interpretive signs. If you do, you'll learn about coastal sage scrub, including California sagebrush, black sage, chamise, cliff spurge, San Diego barrel cactus, and manzanita. All of these plants thrive in this seaside environment, despite the fact that Point Loma gets only about 10 inches of rain per year. Because the 640 acres of Point Loma are protected as a national monument, the natural environment is much the same here as when Cabrillo came ashore in 1542. Park rangers remove nonnative plants such as ice plant and acacia.

If you're hiking in winter, you may see local birds such as California quail, American kestrels, and morning doves. In spring, the migrating birds show up, including seven kinds of hummingbirds, warblers, bushtits, and wrentits. The birds are partial to the bluffs along this trail for one of the same reasons that people are—the bluffs are sheltered from the wind. The headlands on the east side of Point Loma protect San Diego Bay from the strong gale you probably experienced on the west side, by the lighthouse. In contrast, it's very still and peaceful on the bay side.

The trail ends directly below the statue of Cabrillo. The marble monument is about 300 feet above you on the bluffs; you can hear the voices of visitors having their pictures taken. A rather abrupt sign reads "Trail ends—Return by the same route." Darn. We had no interest in leaving.

2. CABRILLO TIDE POOLS

Cabrillo National Monument
Low tide explorations

DISTANCE: 1.0 mile round-trip; 30 minutes   **LEVEL:** Easy
ELEVATION: Start at 0 feet; total change 0 feet   **CROWDS:** Moderate
BEST SEASON: October to March, during low tides   **RATING:** ★ ★ ★ ★

DIRECTIONS: From Interstate 5 in San Diego, take the Rosecrans Street exit (Highway 209) and drive south. Staying on Highway 209, you will turn right on Cañon Street, then left on Catalina Boulevard, and continue to the monument entrance. After paying the entrance fee at the kiosk, take the right fork (immediately following the kiosk) that is signed as "Tide Pools Parking Area." Continue down the hill to the parking area.

NOTE: Interpretive brochures on the tidepool areas are available at the Cabrillo visitor center.

Everybody loves tidepools, and the ones at Cabrillo National Monument are some of the best in Southern California. There are only two things you must do to optimize your trip: First, check the tide chart in the newspaper so that you plan your visit during low tide, or even better, during a minus tide. Second, stop in at the Cabrillo National Monument visitor center to get their free handouts on how to explore the tidepools and identify the creatures that you find.

There are two low tides and two high tides each day, so do your homework and then show up at the tidepool area at the right time. With proper planning, you can walk the farthest and see the most sea critters. The tidepools are separate from the main part of Cabrillo National Monument—where the visitor center, lighthouse, and Bayside Trail are located—requiring a one-mile drive from the visitor center. It's often a bit more peaceful over in this section of the park.

From the parking lot, a fenced trail takes you along the tops of the sandstone bluffs for a few hundred feet, then you descend to the rocky beach and walk as far as you please. You'll get a peek at mussels, crabs, abalones, barnacles, starfish, anemones, snails, and limpets. If you're lucky, you might see an octopus or a sea urchin.

The park's brochures explain about the four central zones of a tidepool area. The first is the low intertidal zone, which is underwater 90 percent of the time, so you only get to see its inhabitants during the lowest tides of the year. This is where the most interesting creatures are: eels, octopus, purple sea urchins, sea hares, brittle stars, giant keyhole limpets, sculpins, and bat stars. The second area is the middle intertidal zone, which is underwater only 50 percent of the time, so it's in between the low and high tide line. This area has the creatures we usually associate with tide pools: sea stars, urchins, sea anemones, gooseneck barnacles, red algae, and mussels.

In the high intertidal zone (underwater only 10 percent of the time), you see the common acorn barnacles, shore crabs, black tegulas, and hermit crabs. These creatures can live out of water for long periods of time. The final area of a tidepool region is the splash zone, where you see rough limpets, snails, and periwinkles.

Armed with all this knowledge and your tidepool identification brochures, start wandering among the rocks and pools. If you have children with you, remember to tell them that they may look at and gently touch the sea creatures, but they may not pick them up or take them out of their environment. Because this is a national monument, every rock, plant, shell, and marine animal is protected by law.

Walking down to the Cabrillo tide pools

INDEX

WHEN TO HIKE WHERE

JANUARY
Cabrillo, Death Valley, Joshua Tree, Mojave, Muir Woods, Pinnacles, Point Reyes, Redwood

FEBRUARY
Cabrillo, Death Valley, Joshua Tree, Mojave, Muir Woods, Pinnacles, Point Reyes, Redwood

MARCH
Cabrillo, Channel Islands, Death Valley, Joshua Tree, Mojave, Muir Woods, Pinnacles, Point Reyes, Redwood, Sequoia (southern foothills area), Yosemite (Valley for waterfalls)

APRIL
Cabrillo, Channel Islands, Death Valley, Joshua Tree, Lava Beds, Mojave, Muir Woods, Pinnacles, Point Reyes, Redwood, Sequoia (southern foothills area), Yosemite (Valley for waterfalls)

MAY
Cabrillo, Channel Islands, Kings Canyon, Lava Beds, Muir Woods, Pinnacles, Point Reyes, Redwood, Sequoia (southern foothills area), Yosemite

JUNE
Cabrillo, Channel Islands, Devils Postpile, Kings Canyon, Lava Beds, Lassen, Point Reyes, Redwood, Sequoia, Yosemite

JULY
Cabrillo, Channel Islands, Devils Postpile, Kings Canyon, Lava Beds, Lassen, Point Reyes, Redwood, Sequoia, Yosemite

AUGUST
Cabrillo, Channel Islands, Devils Postpile, Kings Canyon, Lava Beds, Lassen, Point Reyes, Redwood, Sequoia, Yosemite

SEPTEMBER
Cabrillo, Channel Islands, Devils Postpile, Kings Canyon, Lava Beds, Lassen, Point Reyes, Redwood, Sequoia, Yosemite

OCTOBER
Cabrillo, Channel Islands, Devils Postpile, Kings Canyon, Lava Beds, Mojave, Pinnacles, Point Reyes, Redwood, Sequoia, Yosemite

NOVEMBER
Cabrillo, Death Valley, Joshua Tree, Mojave, Muir Woods, Pinnacles, Point Reyes, Redwood

DECEMBER
Cabrillo, Death Valley, Joshua Tree, Mojave, Muir Woods, Pinnacles, Point Reyes, Redwood

And don't forget winter activities like snowshoeing and cross-country skiing in Yosemite and Sequoia national parks!

FACTS ABOUT CALIFORNIA'S NATIONAL PARKS

Play *Trivial Pursuits* with all your national park-loving friends....

• The world's largest living thing is the General Sherman Tree, found in the Giant Forest area of Sequoia National Park. It is the largest living thing by volume. Other trees are taller (including numerous coast redwood trees) and other trees are wider, but none have the combined height and width of the General Sherman. Here are its statistics: The tree is 275 feet tall, with a circumference at the ground of 102.6 feet. It is approximately 2,500 years old. One large branch of the General Sherman Tree is larger than the majority of trees east of the Mississippi.

• The world's second largest living thing is the Washington Tree, also found in the Giant Forest area of Sequoia National Park.

• The world's third largest living thing is the General Grant Tree, found in Kings Canyon National Park. Although it is smaller in total volume than both the General Sherman Tree and the Washington Tree, it has the largest diameter at its base of any tree.

• Despite their immense size, the giant Sequoias are not the oldest living things on earth. The ancient bristlecone pine tree is older. It is found in a few high alpine areas of California, such as the White Mountains in the eastern Sierra and the Panamint Mountains in Death Valley.

• The coast redwood tree is a distant cousin of the giant Sequoia. The coast redwood has the distinction of being the world's tallest living thing. It has its beginnings in a tiny cone that is about one inch long.

• The world's tallest tree is found in the Tall Trees Grove in Redwood National Park. It is 367 feet high. The world's third and sixth tallest trees are found in the same grove.

• The destiny of the unique redwood forests did not come into the public's interest until about 1900, with the setting aside of Muir Woods National Monument in 1908 followed by the 1918 organization of the Save the Redwoods League.

• One of the most frequently asked questions in Sequoia, Kings Canyon, Yosemite, and Redwood national parks is "Where is the tree that I can drive my car through?" The answer is: Not in any of these places. There are three drive-through redwood trees off U.S. 101, on private lands near Redwood National Park. (A fee is charged to drive through.) Yosemite National Park used to have a drive-through tree in the Mariposa Grove, but the tree toppled over in 1969. In its heyday, Yosemite's Wawona Tunnel Tree was the most photographed tree in the world.

• However, Sequoia National Park has a *fallen* tree you can drive through, called the Tunnel Log, and another fallen tree you can drive *on,* called the Auto Log. Both of these are in Giant Forest.

• Also, standing "walk-through" trees exist in various places. The Tuolumne Grove in Yosemite has a standing walk-through tree that was tunneled in 1878. The Mariposa Grove in Yosemite has a standing walk-through tree that was tunneled in 1895. There exist several fallen walk-through trees, or walk-through logs, including the Tunnel Log in Redwood Canyon in Kings Canyon National Park.

• Yosemite Fall at 2,425 feet is the highest freefalling waterfall in the United States. In the list of the 10 highest freefalling waterfalls in the world, Yosemite Valley's waterfalls score two spots: #5 for Yosemite Fall and #8 for Sentinel Fall (at 2,000 feet).

• The highest point in the contiguous United States is found in Kings Canyon National Park. That's Mount Whitney at 14,495 feet. Most people don't access the peak from the national park side, however. They begin hiking from Whitney Portal off U.S. 395, on Inyo National Forest land. The trail is about 60 miles shorter this way.

• The lowest point in the western hemisphere is found in Death Valley National Park. That's Badwater at 282 feet below sea level.

• Perhaps most remarkable is that the highest point and the lowest point in the contiguous United States are so close together geographically. If you climb to the top of Telescope Peak in Death Valley National Park, you can see them both at once.

• Death Valley is California's largest national park, covering more than 3.3 million acres. It is the largest national park outside of Alaska.

• Yosemite National Park has the highest visitation of any national park in California. Since the mid-1990s, the park has seen more than four million people each year.

• California is home to three of the 20 most visited national parks in the United States. Yosemite is #3 (after Great Smoky Mountains and Grand Canyon), Death Valley is #18, and Joshua Tree is #19.

HOW CAN I HELP THE PARKS ?

• *Sequoia and Kings Canyon:* Join the Sequoia Natural History Association, HCR 89, Box 10, Three Rivers, CA 93271; (209) 565-3759.

• *Sequoia and Kings Canyon:* Contribute to the Sequoia and Kings Canyon National Parks Foundation, P.O. Box 3047, Visalia, CA 93278; (209) 739-1668.

• *Yosemite:* Join the Yosemite Association, P.O. Box 230, El Portal, CA 95318; (209) 379-2646.

• *Yosemite:* Contribute to the Yosemite Fund, P.O. Box 637, Yosemite National Park, CA 95389; (415) 434-1782. (Alternative address: 155 Montgomery Street, Suite 1104, San Francisco, CA 94104.)

• *Cabrillo:* Contact the Cabrillo Historical Association, 1800 Cabrillo Memorial Drive, San Diego, CA 92106; (619) 557-5450.

• *Muir Woods and Point Reyes:* Contact the Golden Gate National Park Association, Fort Mason, Building 201, San Francisco, CA 94123; (415) 657-2757.

• *Lava Beds:* Contact the Lava Beds Natural History Association, P.O. Box 867, Tulelake, CA 96134; (530) 667-2282.

• *Joshua Tree:* Join the Joshua Tree National Park Association, 74485 National Park Drive, Twentynine Palms, CA 92277; (760) 367-5525.

• *Redwood:* Join the Redwood Natural History Association, 1111 Second Street, Crescent City, CA 95531; (707) 464-9150.

• *Lassen:* Contribute to the Lassen Park Foundation, P.O. Box 3155, Chico, CA 95927-3155; (530) 898-9309.

• *Lassen:* Join the Lassen Loomis Museum Association, P.O. Box 100, Mineral, CA 96063; (530) 595-3399.

• *Death Valley:* Join the Death Valley Natural History Association, P.O. Box 188, Death Valley, CA 92328; (760) 786-3285.

ABOUT THE AUTHOR

Ann Marie Brown is an outdoors writer who lives in Marin County, California, near Muir Woods National Monument and Point Reyes National Seashore. She is the author of eight books with Foghorn Press:

California Waterfalls
California Hiking (with Tom Stienstra)
Day-Hiking California's National Parks
101 Great Hikes of the San Francisco Bay Area
Easy Hiking in Northern California
Easy Hiking in Southern California
Easy Biking in Northern California
Easy Camping in Southern California

FOGHORN ✔ OUTDOORS

Founded in 1985, Foghorn Press has quickly become one of the country's premier publishers of outdoor recreation guidebooks. Foghorn Press books are available throughout the United states in bookstores and some outdoor retailers. If you cannot find the title you are looking for, visit Foghorn's Web site at www.foghorn.com or call 1-800-FOGHORN.

The Complete Guide Series

- *California Hiking* (688 pp) $20.95—4th edition
- *California Fishing* (768 pp) $20.95—5th edition
- *California Camping* (776 pp) $20.95—11th edition
- *California Waterfalls* (408 pp) $17.95—1st edition
- *California Boating and Water Sports* (552 pp) $19.95—2nd edition
- *Tom Stienstra's Outdoor Getaway Guide for Northern California* (448 pp) $ 18.95—5th Edition
- *The Outdoor Getaway Guide for Southern California* (344 pp) $14.95—1st edition
- *California Beaches* (640 pp) $19.95—2nd edition
- *California Golf* (1056 pp) $24.95—8th edition
- *Pacific Northwest Camping* (656 pp)$20.95—6th edition
- *Pacific Northwest Hiking* (648 pp) $20.95—3rd edition
- *Washington Fishing* (480 pp) $20.95—2nd edition
- *Tahoe* (678 pp) $20.95—2nd edition
- *Utah and Nevada Camping* (384 pp) $18.95—1st edition
- *Arizona/New Mexico Camping* (500 pp) $17.95—3rd edition
- *Colorado Camping* (480 pp) $16.95—2nd edition
- *Baja Camping* (288 pp) $14.95—2nd edition
- *Alaska Fishing* (448 pp) $20.95—2nd edition
- *Florida Camping* (672 pp) $20.95—1st edition
- *Florida Beaches* (680 pp) $19.95—1st edition
- *New England Hiking* (402 pp) $18.95—2nd edition
- *New England Camping* (520 pp) $19.95—2nd edition

The National Outdoors Series

- *America's Secret Recreation Areas—Your Recreation Guide to the Bureau of Land Management's Wild Lands of the West* (640 pp) $17.95
- *America's Wilderness—The Complete Guide to More Than 600 National Wilderness Areas* (592 pp) $19.95
- *The Camper's Companion—The Pack-Along Guide for Better Outdoor Trips* (458 pp) $15.95
- *Wild Places: 20 Journeys Into the North American Outdoors* (320 pp) $15.95

A book's page count and availability are subject to change.
For more information, call 1-800-FOGHORN,
email: foghorn@well.com, or write to:
Foghorn Press
P.O. Box 2036
Santa Rosa, CA 95405-0036